MAKING SENSE OF WOMEN'S LIVES

An Introduction to Women's Studies

MICHÈLE PLOTT AND LAURI UMANSKY, EDITORS
Suffolk University

COLLEGIATE PRESS

Collegiate Press
San Diego, California

Executive editor: Christopher Stanford
Senior editor: Steven Barta
Senior developmental editor: Jackie Estrada
Design and production: Christopher Davis
Permissions editor: Carol Kushner
Photo research: Susan Holtz
Cover design: Christopher Davis
Cover art: Marisol, "Women and Dog," 1964. Whitney Museum of American Art, New York, NY. Photo © 1999 Whitney Museum of American Art, New York, NY. Copyright © Marisol/Licensed by VAGA, New York, NY.

Library of Congress Control Number: 00-131970

ISBN: 0-939693-53-4

Printed in the United States of America

10 9 8 7 6 5 4 3 2 1

For our daughters,
Lucy
&
Carenna and Wendy

ACKNOWLEDGMENTS

To the following people, whose support and assistance made this project possible, we wish to express our appreciation: Steve Barta, Krisanne Bursik, Mari Jo Buhle, Jackie Estrada, Carenna Ferguson, Kenneth Greenberg, Aviva Griffler, Amy Kesselman, Carol Kushner, Sharon Lenzie, Lisa Lieberman, Fred Marchant, Jim Mitchell, Lucy Mitchell, Sheila O'Brien, Peter Onek, Wendy Onek, John Paulsen, Gerald Peary, Susan Schroeder, Faye Small, Rickie Solinger, Alexandra Todd, and the staff of the Schlesinger Library at Radcliffe College.

CONTENTS

PREFACE IX

INTRODUCTION: WHY WOMEN'S STUDIES? 1

Jean Fox O'Barr, "The Necessity of Women's Studies in a Liberal Arts Education" 3
Catharine R. Stimpson, "Women's Studies: Issues and Approaches" 10
Lisa Marie Hogeland, "Fear of Feminism: Why Young Women Get the Willies" 17

PART I: THE LIFE CYCLE 23

Making Girls, Making Women 24
Curtis Sittenfeld, "Your Life as a Girl" 25
Karen Houppert, "The Curse" 31
Robin A. Robinson, "Bearing Witness to Teen Motherhood: The Politics of Violations of Girlhood" 40
Marisa Navarro, "Becoming *La Mujer*" 49
Veronica Chambers, "Dreading It" 54

"Girlfriends": Friends and Sisters 58
Carroll Smith-Rosenberg, "The Female World of Love and Ritual" 59
Martha Manning, "Betrayal" 84
Mona Simpson, "Sisters" 89
Sharon Olds, "The Elder Sister" 92
Maxine Kumin, "How It Is" 93

Mothers and Daughters 94
Nancy Chodorow, "Family Structure and Feminine Personality" 95
Gish Jen, "Who's Irish?" 116
Anna Quindlen, "Mothers" 123
Molly Ladd Taylor and Lauri Umansky, "'Bad' Mothers" 125
Betty Jean Lifton, "Bad/Good, Good/Bad: Birth Mothers and Adoptive Mothers" 142
Toi Derricotte, "Christmas Eve: My Mother Dressing" 148

Heart and Home: The Personal Is Political 150
Betty Friedan, "The Problem That Has No Name" 151
Patricia Mainardi, "The Politics of Housework" 163
Neil Miller, "A Time of Change" 179
Venny Villapando, "The Business of Selling Mail Order Brides" 178
Mary Helen Washington, "Working at Single Bliss" 185
Irena Klepfisz, "they're always curious" 192

Women Working 194
Germaine Greer, "Work" 195
Randy Albelda and Chris Tilly, "It's a Family Affair: Women, Poverty, and Welfare" 203
Carolyn J. Aman and Paula England, "Comparable Worth: When Do Two Jobs Deserve the
    Same Pay?" 208
Deborah Tannen, "Men and Women Talking on the Job" 218
Fanny Howe, "The Low Road" 222

Are There No Great Women Artists? 223
Virginia Woolf, "If Shakespeare Had a Sister" 224
Alice Walker, "In Search of Our Mothers' Gardens" 226
Mary Gordon, "Mary Cassatt" and "The Case of Berthe Morisot" 233
Judy Chicago, "My Struggle as a Woman Artist" 239
Audre Lorde, "Poetry is Not a Luxury" 248

In Sickness and in Health 251
Boston Women's Health Book Collective, "Women as Healers" 252
Audre Lorde, "The Cancer Journals" 259
Peg Byron, "HIV: The National Scandal" 276
Gloria Steinem, "Ruth's Song (Because She Could Not Sing It)" 287
Jane Kenyon, "Having It Out with Melancholy" 299

Getting Older 303
Alma Luz Villanueva, "Blood Ties" 304
Margaret Forster, "How Was It for You?" 311
Cynthia Rich, "Ageism and the Politics of Beauty" 317
Kay Boyle, "A Poem on Getting Up Early in the Morning (or Even Late in the Morning) When
    One Is Old" 322
Maude Meehan, "Gift for My Mother's 90th Birthday" 323

Bibliography/Filmography for Part I 324

PART II: FLASHPOINTS 331

Reproductive Rights 332
Rickie Solinger, "Pregnancy and Power Before *Roe v. Wade,* 1950–1970" 333
Childbearing Rights Information Project, "To Bear or Not to Bear" 351
Laura Hershey, "Choosing Disability" 355
Elaine Tyler May, "Non-Mothers as Bad Mothers" 363
Katha Pollitt, "Checkbook Maternity" 379
Gwendolyn Brooks, "The Mother" 385

The Politics of Inclusion 387
bell hooks, "Racism and Feminism: The Issue of Accountability" 388
Esther Ngan-Ling Chow, "The Feminist Movement: Where Are All the Asian American Women?" 412
Suzanne Pharr, "Homophobia: A Weapon of Sexism" 424
Barbara Macdonald, "Politics of Aging: I'm *Not* Your Mother" 438
Rita Dove, "The House Slave" 443
Lucille Clifton, "slave cabin, sotterly plantation, maryland, 1989" 444
Toi Derricotte, "The Weakness" 445

Violence Against Women 447
Susan Griffin, "Rape" 448
Paula Kamen, "Acquaintance Rape: Revolution and Reaction" 462
Dorothy Allison, "Two or Three Things I Know for Sure" 471
Debra Dickerson, "Too Sexy for My Shirt" 475
Ann Jones, "Battering: Who's Going to Stop It?" 479
Marie Howe, "How Many Times" 487
Belle Waring, "Children Must Have Manners" 488

Debating Sex 489
Deirdre English, "The Fear That Feminism Will Free Men First" 490
Sara Diamond, "Pornography: Image and Reality" 495
Gloria Steinem, "Erotica and Pornography: A Clear and Present Difference" 507
Helen E. Longino, "Pornography, Oppression, and Freedom: A Closer Look" 511
Sharon Olds, "First Sex" 522
Cherrie Moraga, "The Slow Dance" 523

Bibliography/Filmography for Part II 525

PART III: HOW THINGS SHOULD BE   529

Audre Lorde, "Uses of the Erotic: The Erotic as Power"   530
bell hooks, "Living to Love"   535
Molly Haskell, "Bearded Ladies: Women in Comedy"   545
Ellen Goodman, "What About the Boys?"   553
Amelia Richards, "Body Image: Third Wave Feminism's Issue?"   555

Bibliography for Part III   559

INDEX   560

PREFACE

Making Sense of Women's Lives presents a wide range of writings about women's lives in the United States. We have drawn on our experience as both students and professors to assemble the collection. Seeking to provide as full a sampling from a diverse and intellectually vibrant field as one volume permits, we have also chosen writing that we—and our students—enjoy reading. A few of the selections here represent the undisputed "classics" of the field. More of them constitute simply the works, drawn from academic and nonacademic sources alike, that have made a difference in our lives as we have sought to understand what it means to be female in America.

Making Sense of Women's Lives will be used as the primary text in many introductory Women's Studies courses. With that usage in mind, we have provided brief introductions to each article to help students understand the authors' perspectives. Thought and discussion questions follow each selection. The book contains, as well, numerous "Flash Exercises"—suggestions for class exercises and assignments. We have used these activities in our courses over the past decade, in conjunction with the readings in this volume, and have found that the full complement of materials coalesces into an intellectually and emotionally powerful introduction to Women's Studies.

The book's opening section introduces the history and scope of Women's Studies as an academic discipline. From its inception in the late 1960s, the field has grown astronomically.

Colleges and universities in the United States now offer over 30,000 Women's Studies courses. These courses draw their subject matter and their faculty from a variety of disciplines—history, psychology, sociology, anthropology, philosophy, literature, linguistics, political science, and others. If one common thread runs through the variegated enterprise that is Women's Studies, we believe it is this: the desire to change women's lives for the better. Women's Studies seeks not just to describe the conditions of women's lives, but to analyze those conditions; when analysis uncovers areas of subordination, it seeks change. Women's Studies, in other words, is linked to the feminisms that gave birth to it thirty years ago.

Perhaps one basic concept underlies all that follows in Women's Studies. That is the distinction between sex, a biological status, and gender, which is a social, cultural, learned status. While Women's Studies scholars do debate the genesis of gender differences, most—and we include ourselves here—consider the "social construction" of gender to be of crucial importance. Girls learn to be girls; women learn to be women. How they learn, what they learn, and why they learn particular messages depends on the institutions of culture and society. Families, schools, the economy, the political structure, the media, and other institutional structures help to define what it means to be a person in a female body.

Part I of this book applies a life cycle approach to what it means to be female in our culture and society. The readings trace the common stages, milestones, and struggles that girls and women encounter from childhood through old age. The essays raise a host of questions, such as: How crucial is gender to individual women's lives at various stages? How have women's life courses changed over the past two hundred years, and why? What are some of the crisis points in development? Why do girls seem to "drop off the map" in many ways in early adolescence? The life cycle structure is a loose one, for not only do individual differences preclude absolute generalization, but so too do differences of race, class, ethnicity, disability, sexual orientation, and more. Nonetheless, for each life phase, we endeavor to illuminate a wide range of women's experiences. In each case, we ask readers to look at the structures of power and culture that shape women's particular lives.

Part II of the book highlights areas of concentration—and, at times, dispute—within Women's Studies over the past thirty years. By focusing on specific "flashpoints," we follow the development of Women's Studies, and the wider feminist movements, in this country over time. This section of the book, in other words, offers an intellectual and an activist overview of selected areas of concern. Contrary to recent attacks on Women's Studies by critics within and outside the academy, the discipline and the social movements around it have never been monolithic. Debate abounds, as this section illustrates. Since the 1960s, in ever more complex terms, scholars have debated the question of whether women have a particular "nature," and if so, how and why that has come about. Is there any way to recognize, even to celebrate, differences between women and men without reducing women to their biology? Indeed, the right to determine the fate of one's own body has been at the core of feminist thinking from the start of the modern women's liberation movement. Yet reproductive self-determination means different things to dif-

ferent groups of women, feminists have learned. This realization of diversity among women, along with a recognition of deep lines of difference among even close feminist allies, has fueled vigorous discussion since the 1970s. If women cannot claim a universal sisterhood, if race, class, ethnicity, age, sexual orientation, disability, and other identity factors separate women, then on what basis other than their inhabitation of roughly similar bodies can women unite? For a time, particularly in the mid-to-late 1970s, it seemed as if women might be united de facto by their experiences as victims of male violence. Feminists brought out of silence a multitude of crimes against women: rape, incest, domestic violence, sexual harassment. But these matters, too, have proven less clearcut than they seemed on first exposure. Some women, who claim the mantle of feminism no less firmly than others, say that attention to the dangers of being female has exceeded its usefulness, that in fact such focus encourages stereotypes of women as helpless, childlike, in need of protection. This "flashpoint" in feminism has taken several forms, most notably the "sex debates" of the past two decades. By providing a range of readings on each of these debates within Women's Studies, we hope to deepen students' understanding of an academic discipline that has complicated resonance in all of our daily lives.

In the closing section of the book, we present several authors' visions for change. While their suggestions do not correlate directly to the problems raised in other essays, each of five writers ventures a set of changes that she believes will improve women's lives. From Audre Lorde's vision of lives infused with a healthy eroticism, to Ellen Goodman's support for the modest proposal to "bring our daughters to work" one day a year, these recommendations cover a broad spectrum of current feminist thought.

Our selection of readings reflects as much partisanship and idiosyncrasy as any. In contrast to many Women's Studies collections, this one emphasizes the humanities over the social sciences; it draws as often from popular literature as from scholarly; and it includes the writing of many young women and new writers as well as a smattering of the "classics." We have sought to present a fair and varied sampling of writings from the field. We certainly do not agree with all the viewpoints expressed by the authors in these pages. Nor, we hope, will our readers.

READING FEMINISM

When you read feminist writings, you can ask yourself certain questions to clarify the author's point of view:

- What state of affairs is this writer protesting against?
- What future plan of action does she plan or envision?
- Do the writer's ideas reveal that she sees women as inherently different from men— as more emotional, more peace-loving, or less sexual? Or is the writer arguing that men and women are the same in their natures?
- Is there more than one feminist viewpoint on the issue at hand? If so, how do these viewpoints differ in their conception of what women as a gender are, and what they need from the state and from society?
- Why does the author focus on this particular area? Is it one in which women are oppressed by the law, by social conventions, or in their individual relationships with men or their families?

READING/VIEWING POPULAR CULTURE

Mainstream movies, magazine articles, short stories or novels, and even advertisements can tell us a lot about women's place in our society. We can learn as much, and sometimes more, than from feminist texts about relations between men and women, and about what our society expects of women, by looking at these manifestations of mainstream culture. What do these works tell women and girls to be? Their messages are in their art—in their choice of perspective, the mood they create, the nature of their happy (or unhappy) endings—as well as in the information they convey, and they are all the more powerful for this reason.

Sometimes these messages are subtle, but they shape how women view themselves, and what we, as women and men, think about the choices we make in our own lives. We need to make these views explicit in order to understand how we respond when our lives do not conform to society's prescriptions for us. How do girls feel if they do better than boys in middle school? How do women feel about themselves if they have sex outside of marriage? How do women feel about themselves if they want to go to school or take a job when their parents want them to take care of a family member—particularly in an emergency? How do people feel if they decide they don't want to have children? What if a woman gets married and then finds that she makes more money than her husband—particularly if that makes him feel less of a man? What if a girl discovers that she loves women instead of men?

It is important to be able to see how the messages we get from the outside influence us, and how they shape our answers to these questions when we encounter them in our own lives. Being able to see what attitudes women are supposed to take can do two things. First, it can help free women and men from feeling forced to think about these questions in the way they think they should. You might decide that society's answer isn't necessarily the right answer—maybe a man is still a "real" man, even if his wife makes more money than he does. Second, understanding what society's answers to such questions are can point out places where you want society to change.

Ask yourself these questions:

- Is this movie or book prescriptive? That is, does it prescribe a certain kind of behavior for women—should they be better house-wives, or should they devote themselves to their children, or should they be incredibly sexy and attractive to men? If so, how does it get this message across to its audience? Is the message subtle, or is it direct and explicit?

- Does this story or film describe what life is like in a particular society? If so, what can we learn about women's roles and opportunities in that society? How are the female characters' lives different from the male characters' lives?

READING POEMS

Here are some questions to ask yourself when you are reading the poems in this book:

- What is happening in the poem? Is there a story being told? Can you retell that story in your own words?

- Who is the speaker in the poem? Is the voice in the poem a woman or a man? A child or an adult? How old is the speaker in the poem?

- What are the emotions you feel when you read the poem? What mood does it create? Is it intensely emotional? Does it draw you into the feelings in the poem? Or is the voice in the poem detached? Does it keep the emotion in the poem under control? Does it keep you, the reader, at arm's length, and, if so, why?

- Ask yourself why a woman might write this poem. Is she recording her life as a woman and examining its meaning? Is she protesting or challenging women's oppression by speaking out about it? Is she exploring daring ideas in a form that allows her to imagine more widely (as Audre Lorde suggests in her essay, "Poetry Is Not a Luxury")?

INTRODUCTION

WHY WOMEN'S STUDIES?

The Necessity of Women's Studies in a Liberal Arts Education

Jean Fox O'Barr

If the ultimate goal of a liberal arts education is to "establish the integral links between learning, knowing, and living," as Duke University's Jean Fox O'Barr states, then Women's Studies surely enriches that endeavor. This succinct recounting of Women's Studies' intellectual and institutional rise over the past thirty years enumerates the benefits the field has brought to students, to the curriculum, and to intellectual discourse in the widest sense. A "Women's Studies perspective," O'Barr explains, serves to complicate the questions we ask of the world around us.

I begin with a story about bulletin boards. As we all know, bulletin boards are the stuff of academic life. Students have small ones on their dormitory doors to let friends know of their comings and goings. Faculty members and departments rely on bulletin boards to announce events and information. Administrators use bulletin boards to comply with the requirements of the law and to advertise their activities. I'd venture to say that there is hardly an academic building on a U.S. college campus that does not have a bulletin board.

When Duke University built a new student center in the early 1980s, a series of bulletin boards was installed on the main walkway. These fancy bulletin boards—with lights, glass doors, and locks—were offered for sale to campus groups. Although I considered the price outrageous—$450—in my capacity as direc-

tor of Women's Studies I immediately sent in the form and enclosed the paperwork for payment. Several weeks later, I received the paperwork back, along with a note from a student union committee saying that my request had been turned down. No reason was given. Knowing how to network, I called a friend on the student union staff to ask what was up. My friend reported that they were having trouble selling the bulletin boards, but a student committee had to approve each request. He advised me to appeal the decision. I contacted the student in charge of the committee and arranged to come to the next meeting.

I took along a senior Women's Studies student known for her keen sense of humor as well as her leadership in student politics. The chair opened the meeting by saying that Dr. O'Barr and her student Colleen wanted to discuss the Women's Studies bulletin board request. He reminded the committee that the request had been turned down at the last meeting because the committee had never heard of Women's Studies. Before I could recover enough to say a word, Colleen spoke up: "Well, in that case, we are just the program that needs a bulletin board—to educate *you* as well as visitors to the student union." Silence, shock, and laughter followed in that order. I never did have to give my reasoned arguments. The committee simply agreed that the function of bulletin boards was to convey information about new ventures and we were on our way.

Getting the bulletin board was only the first step. I then had to decide how to use it, what to say—in short, to answer the question "What is Women's Studies?"

I would like now to talk with you about what I understand the women's studies enterprise to be. This is a necessary prelude to describing the contributions of women's studies to the liberal arts curriculum.

We usually date the offering of the first courses in women's studies from the late 1960s. Researchers now know that there were many courses on women and their social positions in colleges and universities from the early 1900s. Other investigators are documenting the history of women's writing about women's positions across centuries and continents. But that is another subject.

WHAT IS WOMEN'S STUDIES?

In the late 1960s most of the professional positions in U.S. higher education were, of course, held by men. But beginning in the mid-1960s larger numbers of women were earning Ph.D.'s and joining faculties. While women tended to be more interested than their male colleagues in researching questions relating to women, it is important to stress that very few people could answer the questions being asked. The few

feminists already in the academy, spurred by their involvement with the nascent women's movement, began to ask new questions of their own data.

I think of myself as typical. I entered graduate school in 1964 as a Woodrow Wilson fellow, bound for college teaching. I completed course work in three years and headed out for fieldwork in northeast Tanzania in the shadow of Mt. Kilimanjaro. My husband, an anthropologist, and I planned to stay for two years and study local communities. I was interested in how the then-new countries of Africa were becoming modern nation-states through setting up democratic political structures. I talked to local leaders. I hired men to help me interview people, and I went to every meeting of every local party and government unit and hung out with the male political leaders at party headquarters. It never once occurred to me to talk to women as women. Nor were there any women in decision-making positions. I never even noticed their absence, much less stopped to consider whether women's absence was important.

At one point in my investigations, I realized that in one of the two villages I was researching, 25 percent of the lowest-level party volunteers were female. Locals explained this by the "vacuum theory" of female political participation—this was an area of high male labor migration, and women had to fill in when men were absent. But it wasn't normal (read good), they said. I also learned that the women of this same area had led tax riots in the late 1940s that succeeded in pressuring the British colonial government to reverse its policies. But people assured me this wasn't usual either. I wrote up both these bits of information in my dissertation without making anything of them.

Some five years later, Ph.D. completed, first job landed, initial courses taught, I began to read the first few collections in women's studies. I read Millett's *Sexual Politics;* I raced through Robin Morgan's collections. I began to see that the small kernels of information I had observed could have led to a great deal more if I had asked some other questions. Had African women participated in politics before colonialism? Under what conditions did they become active politically? Was the political structure I studied the one that was determining outcomes, or had I failed to see other, equally influential processes at work? Why did people say having women in political decision-making roles wasn't normal?

I relay my own story, not because it is exceptional, but because I think it is typical. Literally hundreds of scholars were beginning to rethink what they did and taught once they had been confronted with a new set of questions, questions generated outside the academy.

HOW DID THE WOMEN'S STUDIES MOVEMENT GET STARTED?

Those who were beginning to research new questions, write about new issues, and teach new topics quickly began to engage in a series of common activities. There are now more than 525 programs in women's studies across this county, offering some 30,000 courses to well over one million students. Although they began in different contexts, at different times, and with different resources, they have common characteristics:

- Programs sponsor a core course, Introduction to Women's Studies, that surveys the field. Sometimes there is a senior seminar as well.
- Faculty members in departments from art to zoology teach courses on women in such fields as art, literature, history, religion, science, and many more.
- Course offerings are coordinated by a director who also sponsors public lectures and seminars, gives career advice to students concentrating in the field, works with the library and related student services

to bring women-centered perspectives to campus, encourages faculty in the women's studies program to do ever more, and urges faculty that look askance at women's studies to consider the possibilities.

In short, women's studies programs have been created in most major colleges and universities and are flourishing after two decades of operation. They simultaneously pursue two goals. One goal relates to the generation of new knowledge through research and teaching. Programs support individual *and* collective research. They pioneer the teaching of courses. They present new knowledge in whatever forums are available. They investigate alternate pedagogies.

The other goal relates to the incorporation of new knowledge. Program personnel try to get other parts of the university to incorporate the information being generated by feminist inquiry. They are interested in curriculum transformation, integration, mainstreaming, and gender-balancing. Sometimes this is done by giving stipends to faculty so that they can rework their courses, either by participating in a seminar or individually. Sometimes curriculum transformation occurs through the adoption of new standards, the requirement that all new courses contain the appropriate amount of the new scholarship on women. Sometimes it occurs through osmosis: Through simply being there, women's studies stimulates people to become curious and change their perspectives.

Every women's studies program realizes that it must pursue both goals simultaneously—both create new information and see to its widespread use. A successful women's studies program will not wither or die in five years—as critics often hope—because all the new ideas and information have been figured out. A successful one will not go off in the corner by itself rather than work with the rest of the college—hard as it may be—to accomplish change across the institution.

WHAT IS INVOLVED IN DEVELOPING A WOMEN'S STUDIES PERSPECTIVE?

Understanding the critical perspective that characterizes women's studies is a necessary piece in the story linking women's studies to the liberal arts curriculum. Those of us involved in setting up programs, teaching courses, and working with our colleagues often speak of a three-step process. We used to call it Correct, Add, Revise. If we are trying to be trendy these days, we say Deconstruct, Construct, Reconstruct.

Let me use three brief examples. Consider Betsy Ross. Let us pretend that we are playing Pictionary and we are to draw her. Close your eyes and imagine. Is she sitting or standing? Is she alone or with others? How is she dressed? Is there a cat and a geranium nearby? Most of us see Betsy Ross as a well-dressed, older, solitary figure, forever sewing a flag. Is our understanding of her historically accurate or does it require deconstruction? Betsy Ross was in fact an upholsterer, a Philadelphia businesswoman who won the flag contract on a competitive bid, working out of a home-based commercial enterprise. She certainly was not alone, neat, or at leisure. How did the Betsy Ross we know come to differ so markedly from her reality? Would it make a difference to you, to your understanding of women's economic roles in society, and to your belief in received wisdom if you knew the real Betsy Ross? Women's studies pushes us to correct old ideas and ask much more about what we think we know. Yes, male figures are also distorted by historical interpretation, but we have many of them; comparing their stories gives us varied ideas about male possibilities. In many cases Betsy Ross is our sole role model, our first foremother.

Consider a second case—quilts. Why are quilts not conventionally thought of as an art form? We in North Carolina have seen a great deal of recent attention given to quilts. But put that recent activity aside and ask yourself why Jansen, the most widespread art history textbook for decades, does not contain quilts. How would our understanding of what constitutes art be altered if quilts were included? What would we learn about the subject matter, the producers, the funders, and the consumers of art if we added quilts to portraits, landscapes, and still lifes? What would we learn if we insisted on considering multipatterned African American quilts alongside the symmetrical quilts familiar to most white Americans? How much farther would we have to go in understanding the relationship between women, culture, and art in order to do this? Women's studies asks us to add new information, especially information about diversity, and to struggle with the difference it makes to have to process all this when things no longer add up in the same way.

Consider sex and sexuality, a third case. History and the social sciences, as I remember them and as they are often still taught, focus on the public events of our lives. They tell us what governments did, what religious institutions said we should do, what social conventions we create and follow. They rarely tell us about our private lives; about intimacy and interpersonal behavior; about how public conventions set down the possibilities for private behavior and how private activities modify, indeed challenge, public conventions. How have the twin descriptions that for every woman there is a man and for every man there is a woman affected our ability to value same-sex relationships—mothers and daughters, sisters, friends, role models, lovers? Why do we think that the course of our lives and the nature of our culture are more determined by what a small group of leaders proclaims than by the daily choices of most people as they allocate their resources and energies? How would history and the other social sciences look if we included the historical, social, and developmental study of sexuality at their center along with the study of more public topics? Women's studies asks us to revise our thinking about what constitutes full and appropriate information and think critically about the consequences of those choices.

The questions I have just posed, about Betsy Ross, quilts, and sexuality, illustrate how women's studies researchers develop a critical perspective and ask questions to provide more complete information for the formulation of social policy and personal values. The number of examples could go on and on. But I want to shift my focus here. I want to move from considering what questions are at the center of women's studies for feminist scholars and think about how students benefit from all of this activity. Women's studies is, above all else, student-centered.

WHAT DOES WOMEN'S STUDIES DO FOR STUDENTS?

Florence Howe, an early women's studies scholar who currently heads the Feminist Press, wrote that women's studies is the perfect liberal art. She said it accomplishes five objectives:

- It is interdisciplinary and unifying.
- It teaches skills in critical analysis.
- It assumes a problem-solving stance.
- It clarifies the issue of value judgment in education.
- It promotes socially useful ends.

By naming issues central to women's lives and teaching about them, women's studies crosses disciplinary boundaries and brings new perspectives to bear on questions that were once unnamed. The issue of domestic violence comes immediately to mind. Not more than twenty years ago, the phrase "battered woman" was unknown. The practice, however, was not. But the idea that the family was not necessarily a safe, much less happy, place for all people

was unspeakable. To understand the issues of domestic violence, students cannot rely on the insights of only one discipline. Sociology might tell them this problem exists in every income bracket, but they need history to tell them how privileging men and male authority seems to encourage domestic violence. Anthropology might explain that other societies do not have domestic violence, but they need literature to understand how people have been prevented from speaking about it in this culture. Policy analysts might tell them about programs for correcting it, but students need psychologists to help them understand who perpetuates battering and why. Economics helps them understand the circumstances in which women believe that enduring is preferable to risking lack of support. Philosophers have an enormous contribution to make in helping students make sense of the issue of domestic violence, weighing the claims and unifying the insights from across a disciplinary landscape.

I think my comments so far tonight have demonstrated how women's studies teaches skills in critical analysis. Let me reiterate the point by saying that students are very aware both of what it means to take in information that challenges current values and of how painful it is to be forced to think anew on one's own. There is always a point in the spring semester in the introductory Women's Studies course, along about week 6, when students start saying, "Gosh, ignorance was bliss." They'll come up to me and exclaim, "You've no idea how much easier it was when I didn't notice all of this! It's hard to have to figure out where I stand and to convince my friends who aren't in the class that it matters." The arrival of the swimsuit issue of *Sports Illustrated* always comes around this time; it provides a concentrated version of sexism that plunges every Women's Studies student, male and female, into a critical analysis of where they stand and why.

I would add here a word about men in women's studies. Male enrollments are rarely as high as female. Yet for the men who do engage in the critical thinking skills offered in women's studies, the rewards are many. One ongoing task in the women's studies agenda involves incorporating men into our constituencies while continuing to focus on women in the male-centered environment of the academy.

The most exciting aspect of women's studies from a student's point of view is that women's studies assumes a problem-solving stance. This approach to knowledge is the hallmark of the liberally educated person. In women's studies students repeatedly find problems defined, solutions proposed, personal positions developed. Let's take a very simple example. It is a rare young woman who, by the time she has reached her senior year in college, has not noticed that classroom dynamics are different for her than for her male counterparts. She may not come up with the analysis herself, but she will tell you, when queried, that she does not speak in class as often as the men or that, when she does, she is put down as pushy; that while she doesn't really care and can do the math problems just as readily as everyone else, all the talk about baseball that surrounds working with batting averages doesn't really interest her; and that when talk turns to social problems arising from single parenthood, she alternates between rage at the lack of understanding dominant in the culture and her own positive experiences of being part of an extended female family. I could give you a hundred examples of the ways in which students express to me what Bernice Sandler and her colleagues at the Association of American Colleges call the chilly classroom climate. Sufffice it to say that once classroom dynamics have been identified as ways in which seemingly objective knowledge is processed and made personal, female students almost always identify their silence and begin working on it. Most women simply do not have the same classroom experience as men; until the ways knowledge is transmitted are

identified, the problem of why women and men develop different learning styles simply cannot be addressed.

Much that I have said this evening points to the fact that women's studies is in many ways an exercise in making things complicated. It desimplifies the world as we know it. This is particularly so for students. But in the act of making things complicated, women's studies clarifies the issue of value judgments in education. Women's studies is about the task of asking how we know what we know, who evaluates the knowledge, and what the consequences of such an evaluation scheme are. Nowhere is this clearer than in a college music curriculum. The basic introduction is often called the "masterworks" course, and it is just that—a review of the works of men. The composing and performing of women, contemporary as well as classical, is virtually unknown. Yet family records, the histories of academies and religious houses, and court accounts all suggest that women wrote, played, and sang. Why do we not now consider them worthy of study? How can we dismiss their importance to the cultural milieu? What values are at stake in dismissing the problems of shifting notions of "greatness"? What difference does it make in a student's education when the musical canon rarely includes women? What does it say about the concert agenda and recording-buying habits that this liberally educated person will pursue over a lifetime? And what does it say to the aspiring women composers, conductors, and performers about their chances?

I want to return to my own discipline of political science to discuss the last of Howe's points—that women's studies promotes socially useful ends. There has been a recent explosion of scholarship in feminist political theory about the question of what promotes citizenship and how the age-old ideas of citizenship preclude women. I would need another speech to explore this issue with you in any detail. Suffice it to say that rather than simply urging women to be more like men in their political activity, feminist scholars are now able to explain the ways in which political participation is grounded in rules and ideas that exclude women. It is not socially useful to simply urge women to do the self-defeating. It is socially useful to expose the gendered rules of the political game and begin working on their transformation.

T-SHIRTS

I began with bulletin boards. Let me end with T-shirts. If there is a bulletin board in every academic building in the United States, there are surely at least half a dozen T-shirts in the wardrobe of every college student in the country. They say everything, from advertising the name of the schools you visit to promoting the events in which you participate. Hanes Beefy-T's are considered the best, and extra large is the preferred size these days. Two weeks ago Duke University's Women's Studies Program sponsored a sesquicentennial celebration. For three days the campus was filled with alumnae visitors, distinguished speakers, and eager students attending lectures and participating in workshops. Prior to the weekend, the students who live in the Women's Studies Dormitory held a contest and selected a T-shirt design. They sold them throughout the weekend to one and all, building up their programming funds. The front side symbolizes the Women's Studies enterprise. A magnifying glass, scientific tool and educational symbol in all the liberal arts, is used to bring the words *Women's Studies* into focus. The slogan on the back is Carolyn Heilbrun's statement, "Today's shocks are tomorrow's conventions." The shock of twenty years ago, that the study of women and gender systems was a legitimate endeavor, has largely passed. But the challenges of feminist scholarship to traditional assumptions in the liberal arts curriculum are still going strong. It is the challenging of those assumptions that I hope will become convention for liberal arts students of the future. Women's studies is necessary to keep the liberal arts growing, to aid them in conveying a more accurate and complete picture of the human enterprise, and to enable students to establish the integral links between learning, knowing, and living.

Study/Discussion Questions

1. What are the goals of women's studies, in the author's view?
2. What is the "critical perspective" of women's studies?
3. Pick one of O'Barr's examples (Betsy Ross, quilts, sex and sexuality) and explain how our ideas about them can change through the perspective of women's studies.
4. How does women's studies "make things complicated"? While you are reading the articles in this book, notice where they challenge your assumptions about how things "really" are. Is O'Barr right? Does women's studies make things complicated?

Women's Studies:
Issues and Approaches

Catharine R. Stimpson

"Casual observers of women's studies may underestimate how large and refined it has become as an intellectual enterprise," writes Catharine Stimpson. If scholars began with the essentially compensatory project of putting women in where they had been left out, they moved quickly to more complex analyses of gender. From anthropologist Gayle Rubin's early distinction between sex and gender, to substantive debates over the universality of women's subordination, to later dialogue between those who minimalize and those who emphasize sexual difference, the field of Women's Studies has sizzled with cross-disciplinary intellectual energy from the start.

Casual observers of women's studies may underestimate how large and refined it has become as an intellectual enterprise. Investigating the subject of women within specific disciplines and across disciplinary boundaries, women's studies has generated several constellations of questions, theories, and facts. The first constellation grew out of the simple but challenging assumption that women as a group are a legitimate subject of scholarly study. Precisely how this would be carried out was problematic. Should women be treated as a class, a caste, or a biological category? No matter which mode of analysis was employed, women's studies quickly documented how much women's experience had differed from that of men. Such adventurous intellects as Gerda Lerner, Juliet Mitchell, and the late Joan

Kelly argued that the categories we all use to think about history required a radical revision in order to take women's lives and experience into account. Suppose, historian Joan Kelly suggested in her 1977 essay "Did Women Have a Renaissance?" that women's lives during the Renaissance did not enjoy a rebirth, but rather underwent a contraction. If so, to use the word "Renaissance" would be, at best, an ironic joke.

In codifying women's experience, scholars have developed two different, though not mutually exclusive, methods. Some scholars concentrated on women's separate histories, culture, work, and habits, while others were more intent on examining the structure or systemic arrangements in society that shaped men's and women's lives. An influential exposition of the latter method was published in 1975 by Gayle

Reprinted with permission from *Women's Studies in the United States,* a report to the Ford Foundation, by Catharine R. Stimpson with Nina Kressner Cobb.

Rubin, then a graduate student in anthropology at the University of Michigan. She argued that just as psychoanalysts have shown us how we organize our unconscious lives, economists our goods and services, anthropologists our kinship systems, so women's studies can illuminate the structures erected to organize our dimorphism—the social architecture of gender, of femininity and masculinity—that we have built on the biological grounds of the sexual division of the species into female and male. Rubin's work reflects what has become a cornerstone of women's studies, the distinction between gender and sex.[1]

Documentation of sexism in women's lives and in their education was another goal of women's studies scholarship. All women's studies scholars agree that relations between men and women involve questions of power. Comparatively, more men have wielded power over women than women over men. Sexism, sex discrimination, and sexual stratification are undeniable realities. According to feminist economist Barbara Bergmann,

> . . . employment discrimination [was] . . . not a personal foible of the individuals who make hiring decisions, but [derived] from a system of social organization in which woman's role is as a servant of men. The existence of this tradition influences the behavior of individuals, men and women, even as they carry on their economic business.[2]

The consensus about women's comparative powerlessness broke apart over the *universality* of their subordination. Some, influenced by Simone de Beauvoir's *The Second Sex,* espoused the view that women have always been subordinate. Others, using theories of Friedrich Engels or Mary Beard, argued that societies did exist, or had once existed, in which women shared a rough parity with men. The latter group raised profound questions about social change and changing gender roles. If women once had equality with men, when and why did it end? How do such large-scale social changes as urbanization or development affect men and women *qua* men and women? Must one sex gain at the expense of the other?

The study of sexism had a profound impact on students. In classes throughout the country, some students, female and male, found reports of discrimination exaggerated, melodramatic, and self-serving, while others saw the world in a new way. Still others became angry and depressed. Teachers throughout the country revised courses to show that an analysis of sexism need not lead to inertia or sorrowful stupor but to strategies for change. At Oregon State University, enrollment declined in the introductory women's studies course until 1978, when it was redesigned "to bring an analytical rigor" to women's issues and to specify the goals of the course "in a positive way."[3] At the University of Colorado/Colorado Springs, a faculty member concluded:

> We know from our classes in Women's Studies the importance of pushing our criticism past itself to the visions that the criticism suggests. Unless we do that, we offer no hope for directing the anger that is often generated by the critical awareness, and we are left with paralyzing fury or hopeless resignation. ("Is this another moan course?" a Women's Studies major asked on the first day of class.)[4]

These strategic shifts in curriculum in the 1970s paralleled changes in women's studies scholarship. Much of the early scholarship, particularly inquiries into the causes of women's oppression, treated women as victims—"sad sacks" of socialization, passive, without any past. During the 1970s, other important studies of women as victims continued to appear, including research on racism, rape, incest, and sexual harassment. However, as women gained a past, traditions, and a history of accomplishments, they began to appear more powerful and vibrant. In keeping with this new image, historians began to treat women as active agents, in charge of their destinies though sometimes subject to the tyranny and folly of others. In the mid-1970s Adrienne Germain urged institutions, organizations, and governments to plan for women's development and economic self-sufficiency, not for welfare services. She asked that programs have their root in a knowledge of the "*facts* of women's lives, not [in] . . . idealized role and status concepts. Recognize," she said, "women's *strengths,* not simply their 'problems.'"[5]

Through new research and greater awareness, women of color became an important model of strength for many women in the United States. The Center for Research on Women at Memphis State University has pioneered studies on the intersection of race, class, and gender—a compelling, but still unresolved issue. Collaboration between women's studies and minority studies has been facilitated by conferences such as the one held at the University of Massachusetts at Amherst, "Black Studies/Women's Studies: An Overdue Partnership," in 1983.

No matter which path their research took, women's studies scholars inevitably had to confront the issue of sexual difference. Are men and women different? How? How much is biological? Cultural? Until scholars began to ask these hard questions, sexual difference was viewed either as a joyous fact of life—"*Vive la différence*"—or as part of the order of things, too entrenched to be challenged. Traditional scholarship tended to accept these notions, buttressing bias with psychological measures of masculinity and femininity that equated *masculine* with health and normality, *feminine* with neurosis and abnormality.

Women's studies, on the other hand, began to analyze the psychological, social, and cultural manifestations of difference. Led by historians and anthropologists, scholars concep-

tualized reality as two separate spheres. Males inhabited a public sphere of productive activity, political power, and cultural authority. This was the domain of the father and of the son. Females lived in a privatized, domestic world of reproductive activity, political marginality, and discontinuous cultural authority. This was the domain of the mother and of the daughter. Each sphere had its own work, although there was some crossing over—for example, women working in offices, essentially part of the male world.

The study of male and female worlds followed many paths that frequently crossed. One path examined women's association with the domestic sphere to explain their subordinate status. A second studied a wide range of women's worlds that varied in scale, scope, and purpose. It looked at purdah, women's political movements, including feminism, women's clubs, lesbian subcultures, schools, and prisons. Scholars found that women's institutions—colleges, convents, and associations—enhanced women's self-esteem and strength. If women had some social space that they controlled, they were empowered—at least partially.[6] Such evidence was invaluable for the supporters of women's colleges who resisted the lemming-like rush to coeducation in the early 1970s.

A third path charted the motives, performance, difficulties, and success of women who entered the male world, especially as wage earners. Films like *Rosie the Riveter* popularized the dignity and deprivations of such a passage, and there have also been scholarly analyses of women in male worlds. Alice Kessler-Harris published an account of wage-earning women in the United States in 1982; Cynthia Fuchs Epstein a sociology of women lawyers in 1981; Judith Stiehm a narrative of women's admission to the Air Force Academy in 1981; Elaine Showalter a study of women novelists who entered the masculinized world of culture in 1977; and Jeane J. Kirkpatrick a picture of women in state legislatures in 1974.[7]

At the same time, women's studies stimulated a new interest in the subject of men. Though women's studies had earlier called the traditional fields of scholarship "men's studies" because they ignored women, the new "men's studies" now examined masculinity as a social construct that took its toll even while granting power and privilege.

Another approach was to study the family, the terrain on which men and women commingle so closely. This path took several directions. One aimed at a precise description of family roles: work (such as housework), power, and identity. In the studies of Nancy Chodorow, among others, the family emerged as the crucible of gender identity.[8]

Through historical or anthropological inquiry, others sought alternatives to the nuclear family. A variation on this theme was the effort to ascertain how and when the nuclear family appeared. Others analyzed problems of women in families today. Among these are child abuse and wife-battering, incest, and the double burden of house- and wage-work.

Women's studies has also examined how social policies, based on the assumption that women are primarily wives and mothers, have made women's lives more difficult—both outside and inside the home. Lenore J. Weitzman, a sociologist who had taught one of the earliest women's studies courses, examined the effects of the California no-fault divorce law. She found that, on the average, the husband's standard of living had risen 42 percent one year after a divorce, while the wife's had declined 73 percent. She then stated:

> The time has come for us to recognize that divorced women and their children need greater economic protection—and to fashion remedies to accomplish that goal.[9]

In the mid-1970s the inquiry into sexual differences turned into a debate between "minimalists" and "maximalists." The majority of women's studies scholars hold a minimalist position about sexual difference. They acknowledge difference—both biological and sociological—between men and women, but contend that such differences as work, life spans, moral capacities, speech, and aptitudes have been shaped by historical rather than by cosmic or hormonal forces. Sociologist Cynthia Fuchs Epstein sums up the current minimalist position:

> On the basis of current research, the biological differences between men and women have little or no relevance to their behavior and capacities apart from the sexual and reproductive roles; even the effects of early gender socialization may be reversed by adult experiences. A growing body of knowledge indicates that, under the same conditions, men and women show similar competence, talent, ambition, and desire in activities that range from running races to doing scientific research. That conditions vary so regularly and decisively for men and women has more to do with divisions of power in society than with innate sex difference.[10]

Given different historical circumstances and conditioning, sexual difference could become irrelevant or everyone could become "androgynous."

Maximalists sharply dispute the theory that social conditioning is the basis for gender difference. They argue that deep, transcultural forces cause many sex differences and that the connection between sex, a biological category, and gender, a social one—far from being trivial—is more profound than minimalists believe. Maximalists also contend that these differences, though deep-seated, are no basis for inequality and do not justify women's subservience within the family, community, and state.

The debate between minimalists and maximalists is significant—not only politically, but also intellectually. At the moment, there are at least four different maximalist approaches. The first is associated with the work of Carol Gilligan, and the second with Alice Rossi. Both urge caution in tampering with sex differences. Rossi argues that sex differences are essentially bioevolutionary—that is, the product of biological forces, rooted primarily in the endocrine system and in the need for species survival. She gives salience to the body as a lawgiver of social relations and urges scholars to look at parenting from a perspective that recognizes that women bear and rear children for evolutionary and physiological reasons. An egalitarian approach to parenting is both unrealistic—requiring "compensatory education" for men—and potentially harmful to mothers and children.[11] Gilligan, on the other hand, offers no explanation for gender differences, but argues that female characteristics should be preserved because they are good in and of themselves.

A third position, associated with certain French feminist theoreticians, celebrates female difference. They believe that difference is most profoundly revealed in language. They locate the causes of difference in the structures of the body, of mother-child and father-child relationships, of the unconscious, and of desire. A fourth school, "revisionary maximalism," views difference between men and women as biological, based on women's reproductive capacities. As the importance of that role diminishes in the modern world, however, the reasons for difference, and the difference itself, should fade away. Thus historian Mary Hartman says,

> What was truly remarkable about the "capitalist" era was not the labor, paid or unpaid, that women performed but instead the slow undoing of the links between their biological selves and the roles available for them to play in society. What had happened to men centuries before now happened to women, as the bonds which had always confined women's world within narrower limits than men's were loosened.[12]

The debate between these various points of view will be difficult to resolve. The relation between nature and nurture, biology and culture, is too complex, subtle, and dynamic to admit of any precise and final measurement. Even if one could be derived, it might be an inappropriate guide for policy. Moreover, similarities between men and women are greater than their differences. To emphasize difference over similarity polarizes human nature and reinforces sexual duality as a basis for society.

In addition, emphasis on sexual difference obscures the vital recognition of differences among women. In the United States, women of color demonstrated that ideas about white women do not always apply to them.[13] A serious study of the impact of racial oppression on women's lives could add an international dimension to women's studies, linking it to the study of South Africa, for example. Similarly, such lesbian scholars in the United States as Adrienne Rich condemned the heterosexual bias in women's studies that erased or miswrote lesbian experience.[14] Scholars outside the United States argued that American scholarship had to grasp the particularities of other nations and other regions, a view forcefully voiced in 1976 at a major conference on women and national development organized by the Wellesley Center for Research on Women. Among those particularities was the effect of colonial and neocolonial practices and structures on Third World countries. As a Kenyan scholar who attended the Wellesley conference wrote, the study of African women means understanding.

> . . . . economic and political relationships through which our peoples have found themselves increasingly involved with metropolitan Europe . . . and the United States of America.[15]

An important result of these demands for specificity was a decrease in naive global assertions of women's commonality.

NOTES

1. Gayle Rubin, "The Traffic in Women: Notes on the 'Political Economy' of Sex," in *Towards an Anthropology of Women,* ed. Rayna Rapp Reiter, New York: Monthly Review Press, 1975, pages 157–210.
2. "Feminism and Economics," *Academe* LXIX (September–October 1983), page 22.
3. Jeanne Dost, "Women [sic] Studies Thrives at Oregon State University," *Northwest Women's Report* II (January–February 1983), page 1.
4. Marcia Westkott, "Women's Studies as a Strategy for Change," *Theories of Women's Studies,* page 213.
5. Adrienne Germain, *Poor Rural Women: A Policy Perspective,* Ford Foundation reprint from *Journal of International Affairs* 30, 2 (Fall–Winter, 1976–77), pages 13–14.
6. Estelle Freedman, "Separatism as Strategy: Female Institution Building and American Feminism, 1870-1930," in *Feminist Studies* V (Fall 1979), pages 512–529. See, too, Martha Vicinus, *Independent Women,* Chicago: University of Chicago Press, 1985.
7. Alice Kessler-Harris, *Out to Work,* New York: Oxford University Press, 1982; Cynthia Fuchs Epstein, *Women in Law,* New York: Basic Books, 1981; Judith H. Stiehm, *Bring Me Men and Women: Mandated Change at the U.S. Air Force Academy,* Berkeley: University of California Press, 1981; Elaine Showalter, *A Literature of Their Own,* Princeton: Princeton University Press, 1977; Jeane J. Kirkpatrick, *Political Women,* New York: Basic Books, 1974. This list is representative, not inclusive.
8. Nancy Chodorow, *The Reproduction of Mothering: Psychoanalysis and the Sociology of Gender,* Berkeley: University of California Press, 1978.
9. "The Economics of Divorce: Social and Economic Consequences of Property, Alimony and Child Support Awards," *UCLA Law Review* XXVIII (August 1981), page 1266.
10. Cynthia Fuchs Epstein, "Ideal Images and Real Roles: The Perpetuation of Gender Inequality," *Dissent* 31 (Fall 1984), page 441.
11. Rossi, "A Biosocial Perspective on Parenting," *Daedalus* (Spring 1977), pages 1–33. For comment, see *Signs* IV, 4 (Summer 1979), pages 695–717.
12. Mary Hartman, "Capitalism and the Sexes" (rev. of Julie A. Matthaei, *An Economic History of Women*), *Raritan Review* 4, 1 (Summer 1984), page 133.
13. Bonnie Thornton Dill, director, Memphis State University Center for Research on Women, personal interview, San Francisco, September 7, 1982, notes how greatly the study of the interaction of race, class, and gender alters the study of gender.
14. Adrienne Rich, "Compulsory Heterosexuality and Lesbian Existences," *Signs* V, 4 (Summer 1980), pages 631–660.
15. Achola O. Pala, "Definitions of Women and Development: An African Perspective," *The Black Woman Cross-Culturally,* ed. Filomina Chioma Steady, Cambridge: Schenkman Publishing, 1981, page 209.

Study/Disussion Questions

1. What are the goals of women's studies, according to Stimpson?
2. How did the content of women's studies courses evolve in the 1970s and 1980s?
3. What is the "minimalist" position on sexual difference?
4. What is the "maximalist" position on sexual difference?

Flash Exercise

"If Men Could Menstruate . . ."

Imagine a man in your life: brother, father, boyfriend, friend, mentor. (Men in the class, imagine a woman you know.) Imagine that, starting today, he has become female. Nothing else has changed, just his sex.

- *What will be different in his everyday life? What will stay the same?*
- *How do you imagine his life will be different twenty years from now than if he had stayed male?*
- *What are the advantages and the disadvantages of this switch for him?*

Fear of Feminism:
Why Young Women Get the Willies

Lisa Marie Hogeland

To many young women today, feminism is something of an "F-word." They often fear what they see as negative connotations of the label: male bashing, "special interest" politics, and lesbianism. Women's Studies professor Lisa Marie Hogeland understands why young women today might feel this way, as she digs beneath the surface of the fear to find the real roots of students' disquietude. In the process, she makes a crucial clarification for all of us engaged in Women's Studies: the distinction between "gender consciousness" and "feminist consciousness." Only the latter, Hogeland says, necessarily engages women in the politics of change. Of course young women fear the potential consequences and the political reprisals that result from challenges to the status quo. That fear is reasonable, but it should not deter us from the personal, political, and societal goals of feminism.

I began thinking about young women's fear of feminism, as I always do in the fall, while I prepared to begin another year of teaching courses in English and women's studies. I was further prodded when former students of mine, now graduate students elsewhere and teaching for the first time, phoned in to complain about their young women students' resistance to feminism. It occurred to me that my response—"Of course young women are afraid of feminism"—was not especially helpful. This essay is an attempt to trace out what that "of course" really means; much of it is based on my experience with college students, but many of the observations apply to other young women as well.

Some people may argue that young women have far less to lose by becoming feminists than do older women: they have a smaller stake in the system and fewer ties to it. At the same time, though, young women today have been profoundly affected by the demonization of feminism during the 12 years of Reagan and Bush—the time when they formed their understanding of political possibility and public life. Older women may see the backlash as temporary and changeable; younger women may see it as how things are. The economic situation for college students worsened over those 12 years as well, with less student aid available, so that young women may experience their situation as extremely precarious—too precarious to risk feminism.

My young women students often interpret critiques of marriage—a staple of feminist analysis for centuries—as evidence of their authors' dysfunctional families. This demonstrates another reality they have grown up with: the increased tendency to pathologize any kind of oppositional politics. Twelve years of the rhetoric of "special interests versus family values" have created a climate in which passionate political commitments seem crazy. In this climate, the logical reasons why all women fear feminism take on particular meaning and importance for young women.

To understand what women fear when they fear feminism—and what they don't—it is helpful to draw a distinction between gender consciousness and feminist consciousness. One measure of feminism's success over the past three decades is that women's gender consciousness—our self-awareness as women—is extremely high. Gender consciousness takes two forms: awareness of women's vulnerability and celebration of women's difference. Fear of crime is at an all-time high in the United States; one of the driving forces behind this fear may well be women's sense of special vulnerability to the epidemic of men's violence. Feminists have fostered this awareness of violence against women, and it is to our credit that we have made our analysis so powerful; at the same time, however, we must attend to ways this awareness can be deployed for nonfeminist and even antifeminist purposes, and most especially to ways it can be used to serve a racist agenda. Feminists have also fostered an awareness of women's difference from men and made it possible for women (including nonfeminists) to have an appreciation of things pertaining to women—perhaps most visibly the kinds of "women's culture" commodified in the mass media (soap operas and romance, self-help

books, talk shows, and the like). Our public culture in the U.S. presents myriad opportunities for women to take pleasure in being women—most often, however, that pleasure is used as an advertising or marketing strategy.

Gender consciousness is a necessary precondition for feminist consciousness, but they are not the same. The difference lies in the link between gender and politics. Feminism politicizes gender consciousness, inserts it into a systematic analysis of histories and structures of domination and privilege. Feminism asks questions—difficult and complicated questions, often with contradictory and confusing answers—about how gender consciousness can be used both for and against women, how vulnerability and difference help and hinder women's self-determination and freedom. Fear of feminism, then, is not a fear of gender, but rather a fear of politics. Fear of politics can be understood as a fear of living in consequences, a fear of reprisals.

The fear of political reprisals is very realistic. There are powerful interests opposed to feminism—let's be clear about that. It is not in the interests of white supremacy that white women insist on abortion rights, that women of color insist on an end to involuntary sterilization, that all women insist on reproductive self-determination. It is not in the interests of capitalism that women demand economic rights or comparable worth. It is not in the interests of many individual men or many institutions that women demand a nonexploitative sexual autonomy—the right to say and mean both no and yes on our own terms. What would our mass culture look like if it didn't sell women's bodies—even aside from pornography? It is not in the interests of heterosexist patriarchy that women challenge our understandings of events headlined MAN KILLED FAMILY BECAUSE HE LOVED THEM, that women challenge the notion of men's violence against women and children as deriving from "love" rather than power. It is not in the interests of any of the systems of domination in which we are enmeshed that we see how these systems work—that we understand men's violence, male domination, race and class supremacy, as systems of permission for both individual and institutional exercises of power, rather than merely as individual pathologies. It is not in the interests of white supremacist capitalist patriarchy that women ally across differences.

Allying across differences is difficult work, and is often thwarted by homophobia—by fears both of lesbians and of being named a lesbian by association. Feminism requires that we confront that homophobia constantly. I want to suggest another and perhaps more subtle and insidious way that fear of feminism is shaped by the institution of heterosexuality. Think about the lives of young women—think about your own. What are the arenas for selfhood for young women in this culture? How do they discover and construct their identities? What teaches them who they are, who they want to be, who they might be? Our culture allows women so little scope for development, for exploration, for testing the boundaries of what they can do and who they can be, that romantic and sexual relationships become the primary, too often the only, arena for selfhood.

Young women who have not yet begun careers or community involvements too often have no public life, and the smallness of private life, of romance as an arena for selfhood, is particularly acute for them. Intimate relationships become the testing ground for identity, a reality that has enormously damaging consequences for teenage girls in particular (the pressures both toward and on sex and romance, together with the culturally induced destruction of girls' self-esteem at puberty, have everything to do with teenage pregnancy). The feminist insistence that the personal is political may seem to threaten rather than empower a girl's fragile, emergent self as she develops into a sexual and relational being.

Young women may believe that a feminist identity puts them out of the pool for many men, limits the options of who they might become with a partner, how they might decide to live. They may not be wrong either: How many young men feminists or feminist sympathizers do you know? A politics that may require making demands on a partner, or that may motivate particular choices in partners, can appear to foreclose rather than to open up options for identity, especially for women who haven't yet discovered that all relationships require negotiation and struggle. When you live on Noah's ark, anything that might make it more difficult to find a partner can seem to threaten your very survival. To make our case, feminists have to combat not just homophobia, but also the rule of the couple, the politics of Noah's ark in the age of "family values." This does not mean that heterosexual feminist women must give up their intimate relationships, but it does mean that feminists must continually analyze those pressures, be clear about how they operate in our lives, and try to find ways around and through them for ourselves, each other, and other women.

For women who are survivors of men's violence—perhaps most notably for incest and rape survivors—the shift feminism enables, from individual pathology to systematic analysis, is empowering rather than threatening. For women who have not experienced men's violence in these ways, the shift to a systematic analysis requires them to ally themselves with survivors—itself a recognition that *it could happen to me.* Young women who have not been victims of men's violence hate being asked to identify with it; they see the threat to their emergent sense of autonomy and freedom not in the fact of men's violence, but in feminist analyses that make them identify with it. This can also be true for older women, but it may be lessened by the simple statistics of women's life experience: the longer you live, the more likely you are to have experienced men's violence or to know women who are survivors of it, and thus to have a sense of the range and scope of that violence.

My women students, feminist and non-feminist alike, are perfectly aware of the risks of going unescorted to the library at night. At the same time, they are appalled by my suggesting that such gender-based restrictions on their access to university facilities deny them an equal education. It's not that men's violence isn't real to them—but that they are unwilling to trace out its consequences and to understand its complexities. College women, however precarious their economic situation, and even despite the extent of sexual harassment and date rape on campuses all over the country, still insist on believing that women's equality has been achieved. And, in fact, to the extent that colleges and universities are doing their jobs—giving women students something like an equal education—young women may experience relatively little overt or firsthand discrimination. Sexism may come to seem more the exception than the rule in some academic settings—and thus more attributable to individual sickness than to systems of domination.

Women of all ages fear the existential situation of feminism, what we learned from Simone de Beauvoir, what we learned from radical feminists in the 1970s, what we learned from feminist women of color in the 1980s: feminism has consequences. Once you have your "click!" moment, the world shifts, and it shifts in some terrifying ways. Not just heterosexism drives this fear of political commitment—it's not just fear of limiting one's partnerpool. It's also about limiting oneself—about the fear of commitment to something larger than the self that asks us to examine the consequences of our actions. Women fear anger, and change, and challenge—who doesn't? Women fear taking a public stand, entering public discourse, demanding—and perhaps getting—attention. And for what? To be called a "feminazi"? To be denounced as traitors to women's "essential nature"?

The challenge to the public-private division that feminism represents is profoundly threatening to young women who just want to be left alone, to all women who believe they can hide from feminist issues by not being feminists. The central feminist tenet that the personal is political is profoundly threatening to young women who don't want to be called to account. It is far easier to rest in silence, as if silence were neutrality, and as if neutrality were safety. Neither wholly cynical nor wholly apathetic, women who fear feminism fear living in consequences. Think harder, act more carefully; feminism requires that you enter a world supersaturated with meaning, with implications. And for privileged women in particular, the notion that one's own privilege comes at someone else's expense—that my privilege is your oppression—is profoundly threatening.

Fear of feminism is also fear of complexity, fear of thinking, fear of ideas—we live, after all, in a profoundly anti-intellectual culture. Feminism is one of the few movements in the U.S. that produce nonacademic intellectuals—readers, writers, thinkers, and theorists outside the academy, who combine and refine their knowledge with their practice. What other movement is housed so substantially in bookstores? All radical movements for change struggle against the anti-intellectualism of U.S. culture, the same anti-intellectualism, fatalism, and disengagement that make even voting too much work for most U.S citizens. Feminism is work—intellectual work as surely as it is activist work—and it can be very easy for women who have been feminists for a long time to forget how hard-won their insights are, how much reading and talking and thinking and work produced them. In this political climate, such insights may be even more hard-won.

Feminism requires an expansion of the self—an expansion of empathy, interest, intelligence, and responsibility across differences, histories, cultures, ethnicities, sexual identities, othernesses. The differences between women, as Audre Lorde pointed out over and over again, are our most precious resources in thinking and acting toward change. Fear of difference is itself a fear of consequences: it is less other women's difference that we fear than our own implication in the hierarchy of differences, our own accountability to other women's oppression. It is easier to rest in gender consciousness, in one's own difference, than to undertake the personal and political analysis required to trace out one's own position in multiple and overlapping systems of domination.

Women have real reasons to fear feminism, and we do young women no service if we suggest to them that feminism itself is safe. It is not. To stand opposed to our culture, to be critical of institutions, behaviors, discourses—when it is so clearly *not* in your immediate interest to do so—asks a lot of a young person,

of any person. At its best, the feminist challenging of individualism, of narrow notions of freedom, is transformative, exhilarating, empowering. When we do our best work in selling feminism to the unconverted, we make clear not only its necessity, but also its pleasures: the joys of intellectual and political work, the moral power of living in consequences, the surprises of coalition, the rewards of doing what is difficult. Feminism offers an arena for selfhood beyond personal relationships but not disconnected from them. It offers—and requires—courage, intelligence, boldness, sensitivity, relationality, complexity, a sense of purpose, and, lest we forget, a sense of humor as well. Of course young women are afraid of feminism—shouldn't they be?

Study/Discussion Questions

1. What is gender consciousness, according to the author?
2. How does she define feminist consciousness?
3. In what ways does feminism challenge or threaten to change American society as it is right now?
4. What does the author mean when she says that a fear of feminism is actually a fear of consequences?
5. What do young women have to lose if they call themselves feminists, according to the author?

Flash Exercise

Perceptions of Feminism

1. *When you think of feminism, what are the first images that come into your mind? Write down the first three or four thoughts you have.*
2. *What would be the first response to the word* feminism *from your: father, mother, brother, sister, child, boyfriend, husband, lover, boss? Pick two of these important people in your life and write down what you think their answers would be.*
3. *Try to trace back your own gut reactions to the word* feminism. *Do you remember hearing about it in the media, or from family or friends when you were younger? If so, what did you hear?*

Bibliography/Filmography for Introduction

WHY WOMEN'S STUDIES?

BOOKS

Beauvoir, Simone de. *The Second Sex.* Trans. and ed. by H. M. Parshley. New York, Knopf, 1953.

Bordo, Susan. *Unbearable Weight: Feminism, Western Culture, and the Body.* Berkeley: University of California Press, 1993.

Butler, Judith. *Gender Trouble: Feminism and the Subversion of Identity.* New York: Routledge, 1990.

Clark, Veve A., Shirley Nelson Garner, Margaret Higonnet, and Ketu Katrak, eds. *Antifeminism in the Academy.* New York: Routledge, 1996.

Conway, Jill K., Susan C. Bourque, and Joan W. Scott, eds. *Learning About Women: Gender, Politics, and Power.* Ann Arbor: University of Michigan Press, 1989.

Cott, Nancy F. *The Grounding of Modern Feminism.* New Haven: Yale University Press, 1987.

Faludi, Susan. *Backlash: The Undeclared War Against American Women.* New York: Doubleday Press, 1991.

Fausto-Sterling, Anne. *Myths of Gender : Biological Theories About Women and Men.* New York: Basic Books, 1992.

Frug, Mari Joe. *Postmodern Legal Feminism.* New York: Routledge, 1992.

Held, Virginia, and Catharine R. Stimpson. *Feminist Morality : Transforming Culture, Society, and Politics.* Chicago: University of Chicago Press, 1993.

Hull, Gloria, Barbara Smith, and Patricia Bell Scott, eds. *But Some of Us Are Brave: Black Women's Studies.* New York: Feminist Press, 1981.

Lakoff, Robin. *Language and Woman's Place.* New York: Harper Colophon, 1975.

Lorber, Judith. *Paradoxes of Gender.* New Haven: Yale University Press, 1994.

Morgan, Robin, ed. *Sisterhood Is Powerful: An Anthology of Writings from the Women's Liberation Movement.* New York: Random House, 1970.

Ortner, Sherry B. *Making Gender: The Politics and Erotics of Culture.* Boston: Beacon Press, 1986.

Richardson, Diane, and Victoria Robinson, eds. *Thinking Feminist: Key Concepts in Women's Studies.* New York: Guilford Press, 1993.

Rosaldo, Michelle Zimbalist, and Louise Lamphere, eds. *Women, Culture and Society.* Stanford, Calif.: Stanford University Press, 1974.

Smith, Joan. *Misogynies: Reflections on Myths and Malice.* New York: Random House, 1989.

Tong, Rosemarie. *Feminist Thought. A Comprehensive Introduction,* 2nd ed. Boulder, CO: Westview Press, 1998.

FILMS

Aliens (U.S., 1986). James Cameron.

Grand Isle (U.S., 1991). Mary Lambert.

Johnny Guitar (U.S., 1954). Nicholas Ray.

Remember My Name (U.S., 1978). Alan Rudolph.

Thelma and Louise (U.S., 1991). Ridley Scott.

THE LIFE CYCLE

PART I

MAKING GIRLS, MAKING WOMEN

Your Life as a Girl

Curtis Sittenfeld

Curtis Sittenfeld, who won Seventeen *magazine's 1992 national fiction award, wrote this essay the next year, just before her eighteenth birthday. Here she describes the startling descent from the freedom of girlhood into the restrictive realities of young womanhood. Exuberant and athletic in elementary school, a girl soon learns to contain her passions in every conceivable way. Written in a second-person voice that invites identification, Sittenfeld's coming-of-age tale depicts a viciousness of the banal that many of us, sadly, recognize well. Her story lends credence to many researchers' observation that early adolescence often traumatizes girls, leading to a sharp decline in self-esteem and school performance.*

In fifth grade, you can run faster than any other girl in your class. One day in the spring, the gym teacher has all of you do a timed mile, and by the third lap, half the girls are walking. You come in seventh, and the boys who are already finished stick up their hands, and you high-five them. When you play kickball you're the first girl to be picked, and when you play capture the flag you're the one who races across the other team's side to free the prisoners. At recess, you're the foursquare queen. You slam the red rubber ball onto your three opponents' patches of pavement, and you gloat when they get disqualified. Sometimes your teacher supervises, standing in a raincoat by the door to the school building. Once, after she's rung the bell to call you inside, you pass her, your body still tense and excited, your face flushed. She says in a low voice, a voice that sounds more like the one she uses with adults and not with the other children in your class, "Anna, aren't you being just a bit vicious?" The next time you're playing, you fumble and let the ball slide beyond the thin white lines that serve as boundaries.

By sixth grade, your friends no longer like foursquare. Neither, really, do you, though you teach the game to your younger sister and sometimes play it with her in your driveway, in the evenings. At school, you sit with the other girls on top of the jungle gym by the swing set, and you argue about how often you're supposed to shave your legs. Your friend Nell says every two days. You probably talk about other things, but later, you can't remember what they are.

Also in the sixth grade, when Nell is spending a Saturday night at your house, Nell's boyfriend Steve calls seven times. At eleven o'clock, you grab the phone from Nell and say: "Steve, we have to go. My parents will be home soon, and they'll be mad if we're still talking to you." He protests but then relents and asks to say good-bye to Nell. You pass her the phone. After she's hung up, she says that he told her to tell you that you're a bitch.

You can't learn how to play football. Early in the winter of your seventh-grade year, you stand with your junior high gym class on the field behind the cafeteria. The gym teacher, whose name is Ted and who has a mustache, goes over various kinds of passes. They all seem alike to you, though, and mid-game, when someone tosses you the ball, you just stand there with no idea of what to do. "Throw it," bellow the boys on your team, so you do, but you don't want to watch where it lands or who catches it. After that, for the remaining weeks of football and even on into basketball and volleyball season, you're careful to station yourself in the back, or at the edges, wherever you're least likely to be accountable.

In the spring, you get moved from the higher to the lower math class, because you have a C-plus average. At first, you don't mind because in lower math you have the best grade in your class. Your teacher, Mr. Willet, asks for the answers to problems he's working out on the chalkboard, and he's pleased when you respond. But sometimes he doesn't call on you, even when you're the only one raising your hand, and he says in a humorless voice: "Well, we all know Anna has the answer. Let's see if anyone else does." On the comments sent home to your parents, Mr. Willet writes that though he appreciates your hard work, he wishes you'd give other students a chance to speak. He says that you're intimidating them.

At the Halloween dance in eighth grade, when you and Nell are standing by the buffet table, Jimmy Wrightson appears from nowhere and says, "Hey, Anna, can I suck your tits?" At first you don't understand what he's said, but

he's coming closer, and Nell is giggling, and then Jimmy is pawing you. You press your fists into his stomach, pushing him away. He smirks at you before he saunters back to where his friends are waiting. You still don't know what he's said, and you have to ask Nell.

You don't tell any teachers, of course. You're not a snitch, and besides, you can take care of yourself. In social studies class the following Monday, you're sitting next to Nate, one of Jimmy's friends. You ask why Jimmy tried to feel you up, and Nate shrugs and says, "Probably someone dared him to." You say, "Yeah, well it was kind of obnoxious." Nate gives you a scornful expression. "It was a joke," he says. "Take it easy."

You hear that Jimmy got ten dollars.

In the summers, you swim for the team at the country club near your house. Before your races, you wander around in a huge T-shirt, and you never eat. You and your friends go on a thousand diets, and you don't say anything else as often as you say that you're fat. In June, your father keeps the air-conditioning blasting through your house. You always wear sweatpants, even though it's 90 degrees outside. You spend the mornings making elaborate desserts: lemon tarts, puddings, pies. You allow yourself to eat the batter but not the finished product. You jog in place, or you do jumping jacks, leaping around your kitchen like a crazy lady. Two or three years later, you find photographs of yourself from that summer when you were 14. The girl you see is grim-looking, pale, and so thin her collarbone sticks out like a rod.

In ninth grade, you go away to boarding school, where you begin to practice making ashamed facial expressions in the mirror. You embarrass yourself on a daily basis, so you want to make sure you're acting appropriately. Everything about you is horrifying: your voice, body, hair, inability to be witty, and panicky desires for approval and companionship. In classes you speak as infrequently as possible, and walk around with your head lowered. You play on the soccer team, but if boys ever watch, you make only halfhearted attempts to kick the ball.

To your mother's dismay, you begin reading romance novels. The covers show chesty, lusty heroines in torn clothing, and men with long hair and fierce stares. The premises of the stories are identical, though the specifics change: the man and woman are attracted to each other, they quarrel, they end up alone together, they have wild sex. The women always say they don't want it, but they really do. The characters live in eighteenth-century France, or on the Scottish moors, or in Hawaii. You start to think that you were born at the wrong time. You would have done better a hundred years ago, when a girl knew that she'd be protected, that she wouldn't have to find a man because one would come to claim her.

When you're in tenth grade the students who write for your high school's yearbook compile a list of people's nicknames and what they're known for. You hear that for your roommate, they're going to write "doesn't like cherries." This is supposed to be a subtly amusing reference to the fact that at a party in the fall, she had sex with a guy she barely knew. You go to the yearbook editor and say, looking at the floor, that you think your roommate would be very upset if that particular line was printed. Afterward you blush, which is something you've just begun to do. You're glad that you got the hang of it because there certainly is a lot for you to be ashamed of. When you walk away from the editor, you hear him murmur, "What a weirdo."

On your grandmother's bed, she has a small pillow that says in needlepoint, "Women are such expensive things." When you and your sister go to your grandmother's house for brunch, your grandmother gives the two of you advice about men. First off, she says, learn to dance. And be a good conversationalist. Read book reviews, and even read the newspaper

from time to time, in case he's an intellectual. Never turn down a date, because he might have a handsome brother. Once when your mother cannot open a jam jar, she passes it to your father, and your grandmother says chirpily, "The women admit their natural inferiority."

"I think I'm going to throw up," says your sister. You laugh as if you agree, but for a minute you're not even sure what she's referring to.

Every day during the summer after your junior year in high school, you run two miles to the country club, then you climb 250 flights on the Stairmaster. You wear spandex shorts that make you feel like your legs are pieces of sausage, and you pant the whole time. Men stick their heads out the windows of their cars and hoot at you as you run past. At first you take their yells as compliments, but you realize how hideous you look, and then you realize that they aren't seeing you, not as a person. They are seeing you as long hair and bare legs, and you are frightened. Recently, you have found yourself wishing that you'd get raped now, and then it would be done with. It will happen sooner or later, you've read the news reports, and you'd rather just get it out of the way.

Senior year, you develop a schedule: Sunday mornings you burn your skin. Not in glory, though, not you: what you do is rub hot wax onto your calves, and then for half a day, your legs are as smooth as pebbles. Or you use rotating silver coils that rip out hair from the root, or you use bleaching cream. You stand in front of the mirror, bleeding and stinging and knowing full well that the boys in your class will never think you're beautiful anyway.

Sometimes the boys are just so rich and handsome and indifferent, drunk on Saturday nights, saying after they've seen a movie with an attractive woman in it, "Hell yeah, I'd do her." It is hard to explain how your insides collapse when they say those words, how far apart from them you start to feel. Maybe they don't know that you want terribly to like them, or maybe they know that you'll like them anyway, however they act. When you protest, even mildly, the boys have words for you: cunt, ho, bitch. They say feminist like it's a nasty insult.

You've changed a little. You've read magazine articles that discuss other teenage girls who get eating disorders and flunk math, and now you know that you're a statistic, not a freak. Somewhere inside, you start to feel a little pissed off. You think of the fairy tales your mother read to you when you were small: Cinderella and Snow White and Rapunzel and the rest of their dippy, flaxen-haired sisters. You think of the songs you chanted with the neighborhood kids, tapping each other to see who had to be "it" when you were playing tag or hide-and-seek: "Inka-binka-bottle-of-ink/The cork falls off and you stink/Not because you're dirty/Not because you're clean/Just because you kissed the boy behind the magazine." Or, "My mother and your mother were hanging up clothes/My mother punched your mother in the nose/What color blood came out?" The world has given you two options: you can be a slut or a matron.

Late at night a kind of sadness descends and grips the girls in your dorm. You watch television shows about men and women who go to work in the morning, who encounter amusing mishaps like getting stuck in elevators with their bosses or having their mother's parakeet die, and then they go on, to sleep or home or to more places where equally witty encounters are had by the handful. The characters' lives unfold in front of you, brisk and brightly colored, and you are sitting on the common room floor or on lumpy, worn couches, you're eating pork-flavored noodles and raw cookie dough, and you have four papers to write before Tuesday. You're waiting for your lives to start.

And maybe the boys can save you. Maybe if you do sit-ups before you go to bed at night your stomach will be flat, and they'll love you

well. Not that you actually believe that, not that you haven't been told a million times about just waiting until college where dozens of guys will treat you nicely. But you want love now, you want to have a boy standing there after you've failed a French test or fought with your roommate. The boy can hold you up with his strong arms and his common sense. You'll start to cry, and he'll get embarrassed and shuffle around and say, "Come on, Anna, don't worry like this." You'll worship his incoherence. You'll wish that you could stay up all night like he does. At two in the morning, guys watch the Home Shopping Network with the younger kids in the dorm, or they set up hockey games with bottles of ketchup, or they play complex tricks involving vacuum cleaners on each other, and the next morning they snore through math class.

Friday night the boy next to you is feeling playful. No one has more than three classes the following morning, so you stay at dinner an hour and a half. The boy keeps saying he's in love with you, he rubs your shoulders and says, "Your hair is magnificently soft," and everyone at the table cracks up. You say, "I forgot to wish you Happy Birthday yesterday," so he says, "Do it now," and he sticks out his cheek for you to kiss. You say, "No way!" You're grinning ferociously, you're practically hyper from the attention, and you think that if he offers you the option of kissing him, you couldn't be that gross after all. And then on Saturday morning, when you pass in the hall, he looks at you exhaustedly and says not a word.

Girls like you are well fed and well clothed and are loved by parents who send checks and say that you don't call home enough. Alumni return to tell you that when God was creating the world, He smiled just a little longer on your campus. On sunny days you believe this. But in the middle of the term, when the sky is gray and your notebooks are shabby and your skin is dry, it gets harder. The weather grows so cold it reminds you of cruelty.

You and your friends get sick with fevers, and you are hungry for something immense. You say, "Let's buy hamburgers, let's order pizza," and you walk to town blowing your noses on your parkas, fantasizing about mittens. At the grocery store you are so overwhelmed by the variety of food that you don't buy anything but Pepsi.

In the morning, after the heater has roared all night, your skin is so dehydrated you tell your roommate you're starting the Roasted Nostrils Club, only boarding school students need apply. You find yourself deliciously witty over toothpaste and Ivory soap, and then at breakfast you start slipping. It's the boys' tiredness. They kill you with their tiredness. You just wish they were more interested, you wish you knew the thing to say to make them stop shoveling oatmeal in their mouths. You want to shout, "Look at me! Dammit!" But you murmur, "I'm worried about the physics quiz/ I heard it's supposed to rain tomorrow."

Once when it snows, you and your friends go to the lower fields and make angels. Other 18-year-olds are enlisting in the army or getting married, but at boarding school, you still open Advent calendars. When a group of boys in your class comes over the hill and down toward where you are standing, you pack the snow into balls and throw them. The boys fly forward, retaliating, smothering you. The air is filled with powdery flakes and everyone is yelling and laughing. One of the boys grabs you around the waist and knocks you down, and he's on top of you, stuffing snow in your mouth. At first you are giggling, and then you are choking and spitting, and you say, "Stop, come on." Your hat has fallen off, and the boy is pressing his arm on your hair so that your head is pulled backward. "Please," you gasp. "Come on." For an instant, your eyes meet his. Your faces are only about three inches apart, and his stare is like a robot's. You think he is breaking your neck, you're going to die or be paralyzed. But then the other boys are want-

ing to leave, and the other girls are already covered with snow, they're still squealing, and the boy pulls away and towers over you.

"What the hell is wrong with you?" you ask. You're still lying on the ground shaking, but you're furious, which is something you haven't been for a long time. Your fury gives you power. "Why did you just do that?"

The boy grins sickeningly and says, "Suck it up, Anna." Then he turns and walks away.

You never tell your friends because you yourself can hardly believe it happened. Later, it seems like a nightmare—rapid, violent, vague. When you were a first-year student, there was a beautiful senior girl in your dorm, and her boyfriend was president of the student council. You heard that they'd go for walks off campus, get in fights, he'd beat her and leave her there, and later, bearing roses or pieces of jewelry, he'd apologize tearfully. It sounded glamorous to you, at the time.

When the sun is out, the boys tease you again. From across the quadrangle, they shout your name in an enthusiastic voice, then they walk over, thrilled to see you, and the golden sky shines down, lighting their hair from behind, and they are wonderfully good-looking and clever, and you think how absolutely happy they sometimes make you.

After class, you are feeling so good that you boldly announce they'd better do their parts of the lab that's due on Monday, and they give you a phony smile and turn away. They are walking with a boy you know less well than the other boys, and they gesture toward you and mutter something to him. You cannot hear everything they say, but you make out your name and the word "nagging." You have overstepped your boundaries, and they have put you in your place.

You've had trouble sleeping lately. You can fall asleep easily enough, but you awaken during the night as many as nine times. Often, your heart is pounding, and you have the sensation that you've narrowly missed something disastrous, but you never can identify what it was. The dark hours pass slowly, and when it's finally light outside, you start to relax. Your bones loosen, your head feels large and soft. You fall asleep again around dawn, and dreams from a long time ago come to you: across all the distance of your life so far, you go back to elementary school, to the afternoon when you ran a timed mile. The air was warm and green, your lungs were burning, and clear, pure lines of sweat fell down the sides of your face. You crossed the finish line, and your eyes met the eyes of the six boys who were already cooling down. For a minute, in the sunlight, they smiled at you, and you smiled back as if you all had something in common.

Study/Discussion Questions

1. What kinds of behavior do adults discourage in the girl in this piece?
2. How do boys influence girls' behavior (and feelings about themselves) in middle school and high school?
3. What messages about themselves do girls internalize as a result of these middle school and high school experiences?
4. Think about your own experiences in middle school, as well as those of your friends, sisters, and brothers. Do your own experiences, memories, and/or observations echo the observations in this essay? If they do, why do you think that is? If they don't, why do you think that is?

Flash Exercise

Children's Books

Take a look at some children's picture books aimed at preschoolers. What images of girls and women do you find in them? Are as many characters female as male (including animal characters)? In what roles do you find characters of each gender? Do you detect gender stereotypes in any of the stories? What would you change to make the books more gender-fair?

The Curse

Karen Houppert

Journalist Karen Houppert's book The Curse *looks at the way American women are taught to view menstruation with shame. In this segment, she talks to a group of preteens about their knowledge of this taboo topic and finds, amidst general ignorance, a sense that menstruation involves something both mysterious and "bad." No wonder girls feel this way, Houppert finds; teen magazines pump out volumes of advertisements and advice that reinforce the view that periods are dirty and embarrassing. Quickly, girls learn that their bodies will "betray" them but that a vast array of products designed just for them can conceal nature's "curse."*

On a warm Saturday in July, I sit beneath a shady tree talking with five giggling nine- and ten-year-olds. I'm spending the weekend at a girls' summer camp in the Catskills, where I'm interviewing campers, aged nine to fifteen, about menstruation. These girls, the youngest of the bunch, have not gotten their periods yet; all are curious about it. The girls trade information and misinformation and worry that their periods will arrive before they've got the facts down. Their knowledge of the facts is indeed sketchy, but their grasp of the message—Shhhh!—is profound.

"Let's talk about menstruation," I begin.

"Which means 'period,'" a ten-year-old translates for her chums. She knows because she just learned the word over lunch yesterday, when the camp director announced that a woman who was writing a book about menstruation would be visiting and did anyone want to sign up to talk to her? Rebecca Rose, who will be entering fifth grade in the fall and who, like all the girls I interviewed, chose her own pseudonym, is delighted to have been granted permission to bandy the term about. "Period! Period!" she says, in a singsong chant. There's something naughty, she's sure, about saying the word aloud.

Her best friend, ten-year-old Rosie Marie (there was a bit of an argument over who owned the coveted name Rose), says that she knows what menstruation is: "It's a thing your mom gets and gets really cranky and says, 'Back off.'"

"It's bad," Rebecca Rose says, then drops her voice to whisper, "Bloody."

"Oh, gross! You said that word!" Rosie Marie shouts.

"Blood," Rebecca repeats timidly. She brushes her cropped blond bangs off her forehead and looks straight at Rosie. She gets defiant. "Blood," she repeats.

Rebecca turns back to me. "My mom said it's bloody. My mom got a book out of the library once and showed me."

"I got a book, *What's Happening to Me?*" interjects a ten-year-old. A plump child with dark, curly hair and olive skin, this fifth-grader would like to be called Anonymous. We settle on Missy for short. Missy is clearly the most well-read of the group. She is a serious and curious child who has already discovered she'll find more complete answers to her questions about menstruation (and sex) in books than from grown-ups. "I found the book at my grandparents' on the bookshelf," she tells me. Clearly, Missy lapped it up, committing whole sections to memory. She sits up straight and recites for me the section on menstruation: "It said, 'It's more of a chore than a pleasure.'"

I'm intrigued. "What is menstruation, exactly?" I ask the girls.

"Blood!" Rosie shouts. Then she smiles guiltily at me, waiting for a reprimand. When none comes, she nudges Rebecca. "Blood," she says again.

But Rebecca doesn't answer. She's conflicted. This topic is steep competition for her attention. She's got lots of questions. Maybe some of them will get answered. "What is periods?" she repeats. She turns away from Rosie, trying to concentrate. "Periods come from . . ." She pauses. She's not sure where they come from or why.

"It's so you can have kids," Rosie says.

"If you don't use one of your eggs, it just comes out in your period," Missy explains.

The other two girls in the group have been silent until this point. When I look at nine-year-old Sandra, a beautiful, self-possessed Hispanic child, to see if she has anything to say, she tells me that her mom talked to her about periods. "She told me that it comes from . . ." Points to crotch. "There." Sandra shrugs. "That's all she told me."

"No one told me," Rosie interjects. She pushes strands of stringy hair off her sweaty face. "No one."

"I told you," Rebecca corrects. "I told the whole cabin last night! You bleed."

"At school they don't talk about it until the fifth grade," Missy laments.

"They don't tell us anything at my school. Nothing," Rebecca says. "Well, nothing gross like that."

"In *Are You There God? It's Me, Margaret* there's a woman who came to their school and showed them a video about it, and she called it *menoooostration*," Missy says, quoting, quite accurately, from the book she later admits she's read five times.

Finally Laura waves her hand to be called on. A heavyset ten-year-old wearing an oversized T-shirt and stretch pants, Laura has held back, not sure what she can contribute to the conversation. But suddenly she's got a story to tell. Her *secret caché*? She's seen "The Movie." All eyes are on her. "We saw the films at school. We were watching them, and . . . well, the boys didn't see our movie because . . ."

"Wait till we get to the fifth grade, Rosie!" Rebecca says. "I wouldn't mind if we talked about it in front of boys as long as I know more what it is."

Laura ignores her. "It was a title like *A Lady to a Girl*. Or something like that."

"How do you know when you're going to get it?" Rebecca interrupts.

"*Girl to a Woman*. It's called *Girl to a Woman*, not *Lady to a Girl*," Missy corrects. "I saw it in *Harriet the Spy*."

"How do you know," Rebecca says again, "when you're going to get it?"

"In the movie, it showed the changes you go through," Laura continues. "And it was about a girl who did have it." Laura lowers her voice and goes into a long story about a girl who went to the store to buy pads but her brother saw her dad giving her money and wanted to know why *she* got money and he didn't, and then when they were in the store her brother snatched the pads out of her hands and they fell on the floor and everybody was looking at them. "It was terrible. It was so embarrassing."

"What? What was terrible? To buy them?" Rebecca wants to know.

No one answers her.

"I have a question," Rebecca says again. "When do you get your period?"

"It just happens one day," Rosie says, impatiently. "It mostly happens at night."

"In *Are You There God?* Margaret's aunt didn't get it until she was sixteen," Missy says.

"Is there a certain age you get it, though?" Rebecca says again.

Missy finally answers her. "Around eleven or twelve."

Ten-year-old Rebecca sighs with relief. "So I have time."

The messages girls internalize about periods start early. Whatever and however girls learn about periods today, by the time they have them as adolescents, they're embarrassed. Nowhere is this clearer than in the teen magazines they devour like junk food.

In 1994, *Seventeen* magazine debuted a new column. Editors called it "Trauma-rama," asking teens to write in about "their most embarrassing moments." "Share your shame," the magazine urged its readers, setting seasonally appropriate themes: a back-to-school "Halls of Shame" warned girls that "crowded classrooms, halls and even bathrooms give you a large, gossipy audience for all your goofiest mistakes"; a Christmas "Shop of Horrors" cautioned teens that "when you shop till you drop, you can fall into some serious embarrassments"; and a less time-specific "Boy Trouble" column warned that "it's extremely embarrassing when girl-meets-boy meets disaster." According to *Seventeen* Senior Features Editor Robert Rorke, "Trauma-rama," which runs on the first content page of every issue, is extremely popular

among its 2.5 million readers. "It's our most read column," he says. Like *Teen* magazine, which runs a similarly hot column called "Why Me? Your Horror Stories and Ultimate Embarrassments" on its last content page, and *YM*'s comparable "Say Anything: Your Most Humiliating Experiences," menstrual mortification is a constant theme.

"*Most* of what I get in the mail is about menstruation," says "Trauma-rama" editor Melanie Mannarino. "Practically every other letter has to do with getting your period. I could sign on to my e-mail tomorrow and I'm sure I'll have a bunch of letters about menstruation and some embarrassing moment." For the most part, Mannarino tosses the letters because her personal policy is to limit "period" stories to one a month. She's sure she'll get more the next day. "And believe it or not, all these letters we run are real," she says.

The stories are revealing. One, titled "Maxi Mortification," in *Seventeen*'s November 1996 issue, reads this way:

> I was getting ready for a date when my period arrived unexpectedly. In a rush, I yelled downstairs to my mother, "I need some pads, I'm leaking everywhere—it's so disgusting!" Little did I know, my date was waiting at the end of the stairs. He hardly touched me all night.

The *YM, Teen,* and *Seventeen* letters are full of such stories, tales in which girls are unwittingly outed, their periods made public, a fact they lament with an I-bleed-therefore-I'm-yucky tagline. In a single, expanded "Why Me?" section in the November 1994 *Teen,* seven out of thirty letters were about periods. These "grossest, most horrifying, mortifying moments" have to do with (1) bleeding through a white dress while meeting your boyfriend's parents for the first time; (2) falling asleep at a slumber party and having your friends stick tampons up your nose, then answering the door with strings hanging out of your nose the next morning . . . and it's your boyfriend!; (3) falling down while roller-skating in a short skirt and being sure your "pad was showing and everything"; (4) being at the drugstore and striking up a conversation with "a really hot guy," then having your little sister convey a message from Mom, a few aisles over, about whether to buy deodorant or nondeodorant tampons; (5) accidentally running into the boys' bathroom at school and shouting out for a *boy* to get you a tampon from the dispenser; (6) sitting on a guy's lap and having your period go through your shorts and onto his shorts; (7) being at cheerleading tryouts, having your pad fall out, and having your chums tease you forever after for being "a bloody Barbie Doll."

Many of the "Trauma-rama" and "Why Me?" letters are leakage stories, which makes sense. Of course it's a drag when you ruin a pair of shorts, bleed onto the living-room couch, stain a pair of panties. What is curious, though, is the number of "I nearly died" stories that have to do with simply acknowledging that you menstruate. Or that you *may* menstruate. Or that you *may have* menstruated in the past. Tampons that fall out of book bags, boys who see you purchasing pads, o.b.s that slip out of pockets—all the accoutrements that make your private shame public are cause for alarm.

Not surprisingly, those studying this phenomenon find it pervasive. Lenore Williams, a nurse-educator who conducted a study of nine-to-twelve-year-old girls in 1983, discovered that 30 percent thought menstruation was embarrassing, 27 percent thought it was disgusting, and 23 percent worried about the fact that it was "uncontrollable." Eighty-five percent thought that girls should not talk to boys about their periods. Though the study is more than a decade old, it's obvious, from the letters in these teen magazines, that the attitude persists.[1]

In one fairly typical letter from the March 1995 *Teen* "Why Me?" column, a girl writes,

> I was at school, when I noticed that I had started my period early. Since I didn't have a pad, my teacher gave me an office pass to get one. When I got to the office, I saw two of the finest guys in school sitting against the wall. I didn't want them to know why I was there, so I whispered my problem in the secretary's ear. To my horror, she turned around and said in a loud voice, "Hey Nancy, could you get this girl a pad please!" She then handed the pad to me right in front of the two guys, and they started to laugh. I could have died!

This letter writer worries that if boys know she bleeds, they won't like her. It's not about the inconveniences of menstruation, it's about the stigma.

With this anecdote, like all of them, I found I had to read it twice. The first time, I read it and thought, "Yeah, that would be embarrassing." The second time, I read it and thought, "Why would this be embarrassing?" Is it because blood is dirty? Is it because it comes from "down there" and "down there" is where sex happens? Is it because your period reminds boys that you touch yourself "down there". . . even if it is only to press a pad into place or push a tampon in?

Maybe. But this seepage also signals a loss of control over the body. It's embarrassing for this girl because her body has betrayed her. Nice girls don't bleed. (Well, of course they do!) Okay then, nice girls don't let on that they bleed. Nice girls control their bodies.

After all, these menstrual moments are nestled among dozens of other "leaky body" stories. Teenage girls, whose bodies have begun to betray them, write about "goo" spilling out of all their orifices. From sweat patches on a prom dress, to vomiting in public, to laughing so hard that soda, snot, or nachos squirt out of their noses. One girl sneezes and farts at the same time . . . in church. Another climbs on a guy's shoulders to hang Christmas ornaments, then laughs so hard she farts. A third slow-dances with the boy of her dreams, giggles when her best friend makes faces from the sidelines, then laughs so hard she farts. (To which her date responds, "Wow! I felt the vibes from that one!")[2] My favorite fart yarn ran in the December 1994 *Teen*. A girl's mother blindfolds her to present her birthday surprise. The girl writes:

> [Mom] brought me to the dining room table and sat me down. The phone rang and she told me not to peek while she answered it. She left the room. Since I had beans at my friend's house earlier, I farted really really loud. I made sure my mom was still on the phone, then I farted again! This time it smelled like rotten eggs! I did this for about five minutes. My mom finally came back and she uncovered my blindfold, and I saw my surprise! Twelve of my best friends and my boyfriend sitting around our table as a birthday surprise! I was mortified! . . .

Farts, of course, always elicit laughs. But somewhere along the way, prepubescent hysteria and girlish giggles turn into "mortification." Your body and its effluents, once the subject of hilarity, become the stuff of nightmares.

This thing, which was once just simply you, has now taken on a life of its own. Your breasts and hips are growing. You leak: your vagina drips, you sweat, you bleed. And everything you read and see on TV tells you to hide these facts. Even the accoutrements you need to attend to these changes are cause for embarrassment. They blow your cover. In the October 1995 *Teen*, "L.G." from Indiana writes:

> I was at softball practice. I had changed right before and stuffed all my clothes, including my bra, in my backpack. My friend and a couple of guys we like were hanging

out, watching me practice. My friend asked to borrow my brush and I told her it was in my backpack. When she went to get it, she pulled everything out, including my bra! . . .

And it's not just undergarments that are embarrassing. One girl, who "wore a strapless black dress to [the] Christmas dance" wrote to *Teen*, "I wanted to die when I got to the dance and my best friend told me that you could see deodorant under my arms!" Another girl was horrified when her dog trotted into the room with a tampon applicator in its mouth. "It wouldn't have been so bad if my boyfriend hadn't been joining us for dinner!" she laments.[3]

Tampon and pad ads—which in *Teen* magazine are often conveniently slotted to appear on the page opposite "Why Me?"—reinforce this. "No one ever has to know: 1. You still use a night-light. 2. You sing show tunes in the shower. 3. Your parents were hippies," Stayfree promises *Teen* readers in ads that run month after month. "And no one ever has to know you have your period." (Advertisers drop the point size down several notches on the word *period*, for emphasis: Shhhhh.)[4] A 1994 Kotex ad in the magazine runs this copy next to a drawing labeled "Your Boyfriend's Sweater": "Hey, when your clothes move around, it's comfortable. When your maxi does, it's gross." (Here, the point-size swells, while the font puffs up and bloats on the last word.) A series of 1994 Tampax ads that run in *Teen* and *Seventeen* borrows a format from the popular advice columns that proliferate in these magazines by having hypothetical teens write in to two "experts" for tampon tips. The "experts" are "Marcia, R.N." (who lends legitimacy with her medical credentials) and "Anne, 19 yrs" (who lends legitimacy with her near-peer colloquialisms). When "Charlene, age 13" writes in, complaining that girls at her school have to carry plastic applicators out of their stalls to the bathroom's sole trash basket, "Anne" commiserates with her. "Taking a pad or plastic applicator to the trash is like wearing a sign that says 'I have my period!'" she laments, reminding Charlene that Tampax Flushable Applicator Tampons are "neater, easier and *much less embarrassing.*"[5]

In some ways, this ad is pushing the concealment element even further than most women go in their everyday lives. After all, while women tend to hide menstruation from men, letting on to other women that you're bleeding is usually fine. In fact, asking to borrow a tampon or some ibuprofen can almost be an overture of friendship, entrusting a colleague or acquaintance with your secrets.

Indeed, author Emily Martin speculates in *The Woman in the Body* that shared confidences in the bathroom occasionally have a subversive effect, this being one of the areas in which women have traditionally gathered to commune with one another and kvetch—though now that more bosses are women, a quick peep beneath the stall doors has been added to the routine. Describing the bathroom as a "complex backstage area in contrast to the school, factory, or firm's public front stage area," Martin notes that documents dating back to the turn of the century contain references to girls in the washroom "fussing over the universe," sobbing over "stolen wages," and "reading union leaflets posted in the washroom during a difficult struggle to organize a clothing factory."[6] "The double-edged nature of the shame of women's bodily functions here works in their favor: if private places must be provided to take care of what is shameful and disgusting, then those private places can be used in subversive ways," Martin says. For young girls today, that tradition is alive and well. They smoke in the girls' room, they hide out there when skipping class, they copy homework there. It's also a haven they use to define themselves by putting on makeup and talking about boys, sex, and teachers they hate. It's one of the few places where girls and women can relax their artifices

for a while. But the Tampax ad pushes the parameters of taboo, suggesting that girls need to hide their menstrual paraphernalia, even in this time-honored "free space."

Part of what makes these fear-of-exposure ads effective is that they play to the subconscious belief on the part of many girls—and women—that they actually look different when they're menstruating. (Remember that the 1981 Tampax report found that 27 percent of Americans believed that women looked different when they were menstruating—and an amazing 49 percent believed they smelled different.)

The sanitary protection industry, of course, capitalizes on these beliefs. Though the 1981 Tampax report is the only one the company ever allowed the public—mostly academics— to get their hands on, we can assume that contemporary marketing surveys are telling them this fear is alive and well. Why else run ads like the one in the September 1997 issue of *Seventeen*? "You know the feeling. It's when you're absolutely positive that everybody in the universe knows you're having your period. You feel different, you feel like you look different . . . and those pads aren't exactly what you'd call discreet. Ugh."

And articles in the magazines also do their part to promote that view. For example, a 1995 *Mademoiselle* article titled "Beauty and the Beast: How Your Period Affects Your Looks" reminds its teenage and twenty-something readers that "you can't look good when you feel like pond scum." Describing "erupting skin" and "raccoon eyes" as a "monthly beauty slump," the magazine concedes that there's "absolutely nothing a woman can't do when she has her period, but, *entre nous,* there are a few things you might want to keep in mind for the sake of your looks . . ." The difference between "looking good and looking like you're on the rag" is nutrition, exercise, stress reduction, and, of course, a few brand-name creams and cleansers like "Aroma Vera Feminine Energy," "Bare

Escentuals," and, for "the offshore rig on your face," "Cetaphil Gentle Cleaning Bar" or "Exact Vanishing Cream." And it's not just your looks; your judgment suffers. Don't make any major decisions, like getting your hair cut because "it may sound brilliant now, but you could regret it later." Follow these steps, though, and "your looks don't have to run amok along with your hormones." And remember, tackling those "dark circles, broken capillaries, puffy eyes" shows character and fortitude. After all, "these are the days that separate the women from the girls."[7]

The "girls," for their part, pick up on the cues. Like Margaret in Judy Blume's *Are You There God?*, they may be excited about getting their period before it happens, but when the reality sets in, with the one-two punch of genuine inconvenience and manufactured embarrassment, they view things differently. A 1988 study by Wellesley College Center for Research on Women discovered a pronounced difference between girls anticipating their periods and those having recently gotten them. The former were excited, the latter were "grossed out."

A group of thirteen-, fourteen-, and fifteen-year-olds whom I interviewed at the camp in the Catskills certainly described their periods in negative terms. They believed they were different when they were menstruating. "You're butt-ugly," fourteen-year-old Tanya explained. But worse than that—or perhaps as a result of that belief—her confidence suffers. "When people say stuff to me, when people are complimenting you, you don't believe them. You doubt everybody then," she said. Her thirteen-year-old friend, Mary, put it more succinctly: "You feel more self-conscious." Tanya agreed. And worried. "Some guys say they can tell [you're having your period]," she said. "But I hope not."

Every bodily function has the potential to betray girls. In the November 1995 "Why Me?" column, "P.C." from Hawaii writes:

One day I went to the movies with my dad and I really had to use the bathroom. While we were walking out of the movie theater, I told my dad I needed to stop at the rest room. I noticed a couple of guys from school waiting near the rest rooms, so I decided not to go in. My dad stopped and said, "I thought you had to use the bathroom!" Even after I told him I didn't, he said, really loud, "But you told me you had to go!" When the guys heard us, they started laughing.

The sheer fact that she has to acknowledge bodily needs, that these boys now realize she pees, devastates her. Puberty—this extended process in which girls' bodies change in ways they cannot control—can cause absolute panic. It's a phenomenon Simone de Beauvoir remarked on nearly fifty years ago in *The Second Sex:*

> The young girl feels that her body is getting away from her, it is no longer the straightforward expression of her individuality; it becomes foreign to her; and at the same time she becomes for others a thing: on the street men follow her with their eyes and comment on her anatomy. She would like to be invisible; it frightens her to become flesh and to show her flesh.

De Beauvoir points to menarche as the moment when bodily realities intrude on any Peter Pan perpetual-child fantasies a girl might have. This hygienic crisis appears like a slap in the face (perhaps explaining the origins of a still-common Jewish ritual: slapping a girl when she gets her first period), an irrefutable sign that girls must move from the relative freedom of childhood into the more restrictive gender roles of womanhood. "Previously the little girl, with a bit of self-deception, could consider herself as still a sexless being," de Beauvoir writes. "Or she could think of herself not at all; she might even dream of awakening changed into a man; but now, mothers and aunties whisper flatteringly: 'She's a big girl now' and the matrons' group has won: she belongs to it." Puberty and menarche are embarrassing for girls, de Beauvoir speculates, because their bodies, unpredictable and out of control, are taking them some place they're loath to go: womanhood. "She is neither gold nor diamond," de Beauvoir writes, "but a strange form of matter, ever-changing, indefinite, deep within which unclean alchemies are in the course of elaboration."[8]

Fueling this anxiety is a culture that feels free to comment on and pick apart a girl's body. Suddenly, people are looking at her body and talking about her body. "She scents danger in her alienated flesh," de Beauvoir writes.

Flash-forward four decades and Paula Vogel is writing about this same phenomenon in her semi-autobiographical 1997 play *How I Learned to Drive*. In a scene that takes place around the supper table, a teenager's breasts become fair game for commentary. The girl, Li'l Bit, is scrutinized and talked about as if she isn't even present. "Look, Grandma. Li'l Bit's getting to be as big in the bust as you are," the mother says. Soon the grandfather chimes in. "Yup," he says. "If Li'l Bit gets any bigger, we're gonna haveta buy her a wheelbarrow to carry in front of her." Later, he suggests, "We could write to Kate Smith. Ask her for somma her used brassieres she don't want anymore—she could maybe give to Li'l Bit here . . ." Li'l Bit, understandably, complains about the direction the conversation's taken. "I tell you, Grandma, Li'l Bit's at that age," says the mother. "She's so sensitive, you can't say boo." Her grandfather goes on: "Well, she'd better stop being so sensitive. 'Cause five minutes before Li'l Bit turns the corner, her tits turn first . . ."[9]

This is a fictional account of growing up in an admittedly bizarre family, but it serves as an overt example of this phenomenon. As girls enter puberty, folks begin to comment on their bodies. They are supposed to both ignore and elicit this reaction. This is not news. Feminists have been putting forward this complaint for several decades: girls (and women) are encouraged to look sexy, but not to act on it; to be the object but not the subject of desire. In an effort to perpetuate this belief, the teen magazines push girls to view themselves as two separate entities, body and self—a contemporary variation of the oppositional patterns of Western thinking, which has traditionally pitted body against soul. The magazines remind girls that there is their baser body—including its fat, pimples, sexual desire, and menstrual effluent—which they must control, and then there is their true self. The teen magazines—and the women's magazines these readers will graduate to—are full of advice on how to "dress up your looks," "brush up on your best beauty bets," and "get a thinner, foxier, cuter body this summer," while simultaneously counseling girls who write to the advice columns to date boys who like them for who they are, not for what they look like.

NOTES

1. Lenore Williams, "Beliefs and Attitudes of Young Girls Regarding Menstruation," in *Menarche: The Transition from Girl to Woman*, ed. Sharon Golub (Lexington, Mass.: Lexington Books, 1983), pp. 139–148.

2. "Why Me?" *Teen* magazine, December 1994, December 1995, and November 1994.

3. "Why Me?" *Teen* magazine, December 1995 and February 1994.

4. *Teen* magazine, October 1994.

5. *Teen* magazine, September 1994.

6. Emily Martin, *The Woman in the Body* (Boston: Beacon Press, 1987), p. 97.

7. "Beauty and the Beast: How Your Period Affects Your Looks." *Mademoiselle*, June 1995, pp. 158–161.

8. Simone de Beauvoir, *The Second Sex,* tr. H. M. Parshley (New York: Random House, Vintage Books, 1974), pp. 345–350.

9 . Paula Vogel, *How I Learned to Drive,* in Paula Vogel, *The Mammary Plays* (New York: Theatre Communications Group, 1998), pp. 14–18.

Study/Discussion Questions

1. How does girls' view of themselves change once they get their first period?
2. How do women feel about their bodies when they are menstruating?
3. In what ways do magazine articles and advertisements play on these feelings?
4. How do boys play on girls' feelings of embarrassment about their bodies, and why do you think they do so?

Flash Exercise

Period Questions

1. *When did you first hear about menstruation? What did you hear? From whom?*
2. *List all the names you've heard for menstruation. Are any of them positive?*
3. *(for women) How did you feel about your period when you first got it?*
4. *Does talking about menstruation embarrass you? In what situations?*

Bearing Witness to Teen Motherhood
The Politics of Violations of Girlhood

Robin A. Robinson

For some teenage girls, passage to womanhood comes with a jolt: They become mothers, sometimes intentionally and sometimes not. Robin A. Robinson's refutation of the stereotypes about teen mothers shows how classist, racist, and sexist stereotypes get parlayed into public policy that punishes teenage mothers and their children with poverty and social ostracism. Instead, Robinson maintains, teenage mothers need to be given the same levels of "social protection" accorded—in theory at least—to all children in our society.

It's like my mother told me, "Don't get pregnant while you're young cause people talk about you. People point their fingers. They say you're no good. They call you all this stuff. And I had that in my head. So I was so embarrassed to go to the doctor . . . I refused to go to the doctor . . . I think I was eight months when I first went to the doctor . . . I was eight months, I think, when I first went to get it checked out . . . I used to think . . . to this day, two people will be sitting, talking, and I'd be paranoid they're gonna talk about me. What is wrong? Is my hair messed up? Cause my mother said I have to be perfect, I have to be what I'm not.
> —*"Tania," 17-year-old mother who abandoned her 2-year-old son*

My mother is mad at me because my daughter doesn't even know her, because I don't live with her and she doesn't want me to tell my daughter, well, you didn't help me much . . . My daughter doesn't really like the juice but I try to give it to her cause her iron level's really low.
> —*"Ashley," 15-year-old mother, who lives in a foster home*

Did I ever have sex with anyone but my boyfriend [age 28]? You mean willingly? Besides that stuff with my father? No, just (my boyfriend). When (my boyfriend) and I would fight, social services would get on his case about statutory rape, and he would say "how do you know I was the only one?" And he always made me look bad. But he was the only guy I was with.
> —*Melina, 15-year-old sent to foster care at age 12 for one year when charges of sexual abuse by her father were substantiated*

From Diane Dujon and Ann Withorn, eds., *For Crying Out Loud: Women's Poverty in the United States,* Boston: South End Press, 1996, pp. 107–119. This article was written by Robin A. Robinson in her private capacity. No official support or endorsement by the Department of Health and Human Services is intended or should be inferred.

In this essay, I bear witness to teen mother-hood. I tell you, from personal and profes-sional perspectives both, how some teen mothers perceive the social world in which they live, and how the social world perceives them. I offer an introductory sociopolitical analysis of responses to teen mothers, of the helping professionals who advocate services and assis-tance, and the welfare reform crusaders who insist upon measures of deterrence and boot-strapping. I conclude with a vision of preven-tion and care, a proposal for assessment of needs of adolescent girls, and an example of what can be achieved in the larger political context. To begin, I offer you a true story of a personal en-counter with an architect of current social policy regarding teen mothers in the United States.

A STORY

A well-regarded economist in the area of wel-fare reform was on the faculty of the graduate school where I did my doctoral work in social welfare policy during the Reagan administra-tion (he has since left). He had received a pres-tigious national award for a set of principles he had formulated, based on the wealth of ag-gregate studies he and others had conducted, on the subject of teenage mothers using wel-fare as an income support. His platform was to substitute his principles of Workfare, child support enforcement, and minimum wage sub-sidies for AFDC income supports; these prin-ciples have since become legion. But here's the story. After receiving the award, he gave a col-loquium at the school on the subject of his work: teenage mothers using welfare as income support. Now this was a subject with which I was quite familiar—I had been a teen mother using welfare and ancillary services as my in-come support. After the economist's talk, he asked me what I had thought of the principles he put forth (I had challenged him in the ques-tion-and-answer period following his talk, ask-ing him where the teen mothers were supposed

to leave their children when they went off to work, childcare being a radical notion at the time in this context.) I told him that in the context of my life experience, his proposed remedies were problematic at best and irrel-evant at worst, and they troubled me, where-upon he told me that I (that is, my experi-ence) didn't count. I asked him to explain.

"Well," he said, "first of all, you are white." I replied that statistics showed that the major-ity of teen mothers in the United States are white. "Well," he said, "you are intelligent." "Did he have evidence to suggest that most teen mothers are stupid?" I queried. "Well," he said, "you got married." I pointed out that a major recent study (at that time) had sug-gested that teen mothers who marry achieve less in terms of educational achievement and income than their unmarried counterparts who remain at home. "Well," he said, "you're at-tractive." "Let me see if I have this straight," I said. "Your profile of teen mothers, upon which you base your considerable influence on policy at the national level, rests on assumptions that we teen mothers are poor, black, dumb, and ugly?" He argued that to address the social problems of teen motherhood, we had to use those assumptions. So I didn't count.

An absurd story, clearly. I do count—my story counts—along with all the other stories of all the different types of women who have been teen mothers. Twenty-five years of direct service experience, formal research, and other scholarly enterprise with and about girls in the social margins tell me that every teen mother's story counts, and that the principal impedi-ments to translation of these stories into con-structive social policy are a rash of racist, classist, and sexist stereotypes that pervade popular and political culture.

AN ANALYSIS

I had been an honor student all my young life, active in school and community services, a volunteer counselor at a camp for developmentally disabled children, a Girl Scout, a volunteer to collect food for poor people. The eldest child and grandchild of a working-class family, I had been the one designated to change the family's status, to go to college, to achieve in my early life the family's transition from working class to professional identity. Upon the discovery of my pregnancy at age 16, the dream was dashed. My family and community of friends, teachers, and other respected adults decided that now I would be nothing, achieve nothing, do nothing. The message from my immediate world and the larger social sphere was clear: Stigma and adversity would prevail over talent, determination, and ambition.

The quotes that introduce this essay, from qualitative research I have done about such girls, are testament to the struggles they face in the personal and social realms. Each quote represents several aspects of teen pregnancy and motherhood that policymakers, authorities, and providers must understand in the formulation of responsible and constructive social policy and services for this population.

Stigmatization and Betrayal

The mantle of stigmatization on girls in this culture and polity is a heavy one; girls are tempted and instructed by the popular culture—television, films, music—to place their sexuality at the forefront of the identity they are developing as they approach adulthood. The concurrent message—in school curricula, religious institutions, messages from political and social leaders, and also the media, through public service announcements and special programming—is that teenage sexuality is dangerous, wrong-headed, morally and socially unacceptable. Add to this confusing formulation the statistics of child sexual abuse and sexual assault: studies, through many methodologies, reveal (1) that one-third to one-half of all females in this country suffer some form of sexual molestation before the age of 18; (2) that one-half to three-quarters of teen mothers endure some form of child sexual maltreatment; (3) that three-quarters or more of delinquent girls were sexually abused as children; and (4) that two-thirds or more female prostitutes were sexually abused as children and prior to prostitution. The model that this compendium of sexual teaching begins to suggest is that sexual attractiveness is desirable, sexual intercourse is wrong, sexual involvement is likely to be involuntary, hurtful, shameful.

Let us focus on teen mothers. Tania's quote of her mother's admonition not to get pregnant while she was young tells a story of the stigma of teen pregnancy. Tania is African American, a good student from a modest home in her early life, sexually abused by a family member and raped as a preadolescent by several acquaintances. Whatever internal messages she had absorbed about avoiding teenage sex and pregnancy had been thwarted by external events; her remark about not being perfect speaks to the self-perception that resulted from her experiences, because perfect girls do not have sex. The stigmatization process had begun, from her own definitions and those of the outside world. She became pregnant at 14, ran away from home, gave birth to a son at 15, abandoned the child—left him at the home of the child's father and his mother, and never told her own mother that she had had a child—and then attempted suicide several times, the last time nearly succeeding. After committing several petty larcenies—according to her a cry for help—she was committed to juvenile corrections. She had experienced betrayal—a traumatic dynamic of child sexual abuse—by those who purportedly loved her, and by the state, whose response to her anguish was to treat her as a criminal. My last knowledge of her was that she was living on the streets, committing petty larceny when she was desperate for a rest from her street life, and trying to convince the youth authorities to let her live as a foster child with her aunt. Tania had fulfilled the social prophecy for African-American girls.

Tania's story raises another effect of stigmatization regarding the plight of teen mothers: her fear of seeking health care during her pregnancy. Her self-described embarrassment, her refusal to see a doctor, boded ill for her own health and that of her child. Studies of adolescent mothers and their children show several conditions of high-risk pregnancies, low birth weights for their babies, prenatal distress, and higher infant mortality. Avoidable prenatal and perinatal problems can lead to later health issues for mothers and children, as well as learning disabilities among the children. But young mothers in crisis either do not know or do not (or cannot) respond to warnings about such matters. These conditions pose challenges of considerable social, moral, and fiscal expense to the larger social realm.

Melina's story tells another story of teenage sexuality and pregnancy. Melina, a bright Caucasian girl from a working-class family—an honor student "when I go to school"—endured six years of forced sexual intercourse by her father, followed by her removal from her family home by social services when she was 12. Thus, her initial sexual identity was created by the experience of an older man forcing himself on her, and her sense of powerlessness to prevent either the violence or the sex. During her one-year stay in a foster home, she continued the only sexual behavior she had known—sex with an older man who controlled the relationship—with a boyfriend twelve years older than she, who used violence to control her. When she became pregnant at 13, her boyfriend pushed her down a flight of stairs in anger. She miscarried. She stayed with the same boyfriend, in fear and in love, for the next two years—turbulent years—during which social services occasionally threatened the boyfriend with statutory rape charges for having sex with a designated Child in Need of Services, the label Melina had gained from her sexual his-

tory. When I last spoke with her, she was still grieving the child that would have been 2 years old, and had been left in her father's care while her mother was ill in the hospital, although her father was under court order not to come within a mile of his daughter.

Melina's formation of sexual identity was that of a precocious awareness of sexuality as the result of early sexual trauma resulting in a confused understanding of what it means to be sexual, or loved; the act of sex alone is confused for love and caring, and elements of betrayal and powerlessness are strong concurrent effects. Melina's story, like Tania's, is illustrative of the betrayal by social protections that label and punish the unwanted sex the girls experience, as well as their powerlessness to cope with their abusers, their personal crises, and the state's mechanisms to attempt to control their sexual activity.

Another important point to be underscored by Melina's story is the finding of several studies that show that the fathers of the children of teenage girls are mostly older men, the majority over the age of 20. Disturbingly, the younger the teen mother, the more consistent this finding is in terms of years difference between the mother's and father's ages. Thus, the suggestion of trauma and powerlessness holds, and education and publicity campaigns to get adolescent boys and girls to just say "no" are undermined.

Responsibility and Determination

One of the principal complaints characteristic of welfare reform rhetoric is the lack of responsibility that teen mothers demonstrate for themselves and their children: financial, emotional, practical. Over years of interviews with girls and women at the social margins, most of whom have had teen pregnancies and/or become teen mothers, a question I have explored with them is, "What makes you feel grownup, or, another way, when does a girl become a woman?" The answers are consistent: "Not sex." "Responsibility" is the most common answer, by far, and responsibility is defined foremost by a devotion to the needs of the child. Teen mothers mourn their lost girlhood and teen social life and fight depression as they speak freely and energetically about their need to continue their education, find a decent place to live, find and keep jobs, find birth control that works. The message of the popular culture that they receive is that they are *de facto* irresponsible because they became pregnant; they struggle to challenge that assumption in what is often the chaos and neediness of their daily lives.

I quoted from Ashley's story at the beginning of this chapter. Ashley, a 15-year-old mother who lived with her 10-month-old daughter in a foster home when I interviewed her, was a shy, soft-spoken girl from a large Italian middle-class family. The woman who fostered Ashley and her baby in her home was an administrator at a local community college, and Ashley was taking classes there toward an Associate's degree, rather than pursue what she considered an inferior course for a General Equivalency Diploma. Ashley had been sexually abused by her grandfather for several years in early childhood, as had her mother, aunt, and sister by the same man. She ran away from home when her father and mother divorced, and her mother and sisters went to live with the sexually abusive grandfather. Ashley eventually picked up charges that led to her commitment to juvenile corrections, and spent time in a residential treatment facility for girls. During that time, she did well in her studies wherever she was, when she could go to school. She ran away again after discharge from the treatment facility to avoid going back to her grandfather's house. When she became pregnant, she went to the foster home.

Determinedly, Ashley avoided bringing her child into the house of the grandfather who had abused her and her female relatives. She told of her responsibility to protect her daugh-

ter from harm, even at the expense of alienating her mother and other family throughout her pregnancy. Her isolation during pregnancy is more common than not in the stories of teen mothers, as babies' fathers abandon their pregnant girlfriends, other friends continue with their own adolescent joys and concerns, and parents—sometimes well-meaning and sometimes not—throw up their hands in symbolic despair at how to cope with their wayward daughters. Many teen mothers are the daughters of teen mothers, and the recapitulation of the burden to mother and daughter is daunting, often, to both. The isolation of pregnant teens and teen mothers is the product of such tension and shame.

Still, most of the teen mothers with whom I have spoken have or find the moral strength and determination to care for their babies as best they can. For better or worse, they do what they can to navigate the social welfare system for food, housing, transportation, childcare, medical care and medicine, and other services. Ashley's comment about the need to feed nutrient-rich juice to her anemic daughter, even though her daughter pushes it away, reveals her understanding of the medical necessity of the nutrients as well as her commitment to care for and guide the development of her daughter. Perhaps this is the salient metaphor to carry into a vision of what the social and political structure can and should do for teen mothers and their babies.

A VISION

In a recent group interview with teen mothers in a prenatal/postpartum clinic, in response to their question to me of what I could do to help them, I asked the girls if they were registered to vote. Only four of many who were 18 or older were registered. The rest looked at me with bewilderment. They did not understand the relationship between the power of their vote—and the power of their need—and the process of policy and law. They did not understand the origins in government, by elected officials, of Medicaid and food stamps and Aid to Families with Dependent Children (AFDC) and Women, Infants, and Children (WIC) nutrition programs and Section Eight housing. They had some vague notion of proposed cutbacks, and a clear understanding of what executed cutbacks had done to their ability to survive. But they did not perceive themselves as citizens with rights and obligations. Often, teen mothers' inexperience with any kind of contact with government or agencies leaves them wanting for basic human needs. Often, young mothers are at odds with a sometimes menacing infrastructure of welfare programs and staff who punish the girls' behaviors by controlling benefits.

Why can't or won't girls just obey the public admonition to abstain from sexual intercourse? Instruction in acceptable social values regarding adolescent sexuality is often a corollary to punishment by scant or withheld benefits, but alien to girls whose life experiences belie the concept of choice, and want for a cohesive, healthy public model of sexuality. The absence of such a model may explain the overall failure of campaigns to promote sexual abstinence among adolescents. I have found that most teen mothers are trying to be responsible about birth control. They are often confused by their experiences with sexuality, with public and private messages. Many babies of teen mothers I have interviewed were the result of birth control failures, or sheer ignorance of family planning methods. Much has been made in the media, in politics, and in social research of a "subculture" of teen mothers who "have babies to get on welfare." My research and that of many others does not support this contention. More likely, it is the case that for many girls, social and political realities fail to provide the protection, nurture, and care they need to pass through adolescence without fear

or experience of sexual assault, economic deprivation, educational and vocational unmet needs, and pregnancy.

The Needs of Teen Mothers

In any case, most adolescent girls who become mothers, whether the pregnancy was intentional or unintentional, quickly develop a mother's sense of the primary need to protect and to provide for their infants. The messages they receive from the larger world are not without impact, however. Such messages of fear, of contempt, of imposed shame, of futility, are not lost on adolescents who are still forming their adult identities. Young mothers still need basic human needs of housing, food, clothing, education, social support, medical care, and legal protection. They need love and kindness. They need respect as human beings and as citizens of the social world in which they live.

Principal areas of welfare reform include the elimination of AFDC, the decrease or elimination of Medicaid, and the decrease or elimination of other supports such as food stamps, WIC, housing, daycare, and education subsidies. The elimination of each of these supports brings young mothers closer to thresholds of desperation. Generous support in the polity for provision of these needs, as teen mothers move toward adulthood and full assumption of adult obligations, will contribute to the general health and productivity of young mothers and their children.

Ironically, the more headway women have made into the labor force, the more stigmatizing AFDC has become. Apparently the social value of women at home rearing their children has all but vanished. But has it? The same political factions that decry the waste and immorality of AFDC tout family values as their prescription for a greater society. Many young mothers with whom I've spoken want to spend some part of their babies' early childhood at home with them, and then resume their education and/or vocational training to become economically self-sufficient. Most have absorbed that notion of family values. Somewhere in this maelstrom of irony are issues of race and class, of privilege and punishment. I submit that the stereotype of poor, minority, dumb, and ugly teen mothers drives the debate in this area of policy more than does clear analysis of the realities.

Most teen mothers with whom I've spoken have an understanding of the responsibility they have for their children's well-being, and hold their education and the attainment of fulfilling work at a living wage as high priorities. With this value, they recognize childcare as an integral part of any plan for them to work or attend school. Even the concept of workfare by conservative proponents of welfare reform has rightly led to the understanding in many segments of the political world that in order to work, mothers need childcare. Whether working for welfare benefits or working for wages, safe, reliable, and available childcare is a necessity. Since so many teen mothers have experienced some form of childhood maltreatment, they fear for the safety of their children, and are reluctant to leave them in the care of others. Policymakers who wish to support teen mothers' move to social and economic self-sufficiency must recognize the need for and provide safe care for the children of teen mothers.

Teen mothers face basic life needs as developing adolescents and as mothers providing for their children. Political rhetoric often focuses only on the needs of teen mothers in terms of services that cost taxpayers money; such rhetoric suggests that there is little but money to address the problems of teen mothers. A larger vision of supporting the needs of teen mothers toward healthy, productive adulthood includes an examination of what a healthy, productive society provides for its citizens.

The Need for Social Protection

"Social protection" is a term often used in the social sciences for the formal systems that constitute economic well-being for citizens of a polity. I will use the term here as a more general concept of the social obligation of the polity to provide all manner of protection for its citizens, including children. First among the principles of social protection is equality, in its most general and accessible sense. Is it not the equal right of every child born among us to claim the provisions of our social contract regarding basic human needs? Is it not further the equal right of every child born among us to claim equal opportunity regarding human worth, work, and achievement, another tenet of our social contract? Agreement on these two basic principles of social protection suggests the following greater vision for teen mothers and their children.

First, we must provide social protection as a context in which children can grow safely. This means that children, including teen mothers, must be equally protected by laws that forbid the abuse or neglect of children under the age of 18, whether that abuse or neglect is perpetrated by a family member, a community, or the policymakers who craft and control services for children and families. To neglect the basic human needs of teen mothers, whatever the social definitions of their sexual deviance or immorality, is still to neglect the basic human needs of children. Further, children must be equally protected by laws that forbid sexual assault and abuse. Child sexual abuse and molestation laws are on the books, but they are prosecuted capriciously, and statistics on this form of violence suggest that enforcement of laws forbidding it is wanting. Since the prevalence of sexual violation in the lives of teen mothers is so great, as mentioned earlier, this concept creates a necessary transition from teen motherhood as a child problem to teen motherhood as an adult problem.

Children, including teen mothers, must be full beneficiaries of a social contract of equal opportunity, so that they may achieve equally in accordance with the effort they are willing to put forth in any life enterprise, while protected in their status as children as described above. A model of education, job training, safe and affordable housing, adequate food, health care, and protection provides opportunity for economic and social self-sufficiency in exchange for children's, including teen mothers', acceptance as they reach adulthood of the responsibilities of the adult society that has nurtured them. These principles are so very basic, but they are missing in current social practice and proposed remedies to the scourge of teen motherhood.

Why does the political agenda identify teen mothers as a threat to the health of society? What is it about teen mothers that people fear? Research has dispelled myths about teen motherhood as principal causes of poverty, delinquency, welfare use, out-of-wedlock births, and other socially unacceptable behaviors. The majority of teen mothers come from the dominant racial group in this country. We must ask ourselves what misinformation or deeply held prejudices are driving social policy to the detriment of children. Moreover, we must ask ourselves what we are doing to teen mothers and their children while the misconceptions and fears persist.

THE NEEDS OF TEEN MOTHERS: A METHOD OF INQUIRY

As I write this, during the Clinton administration, I am heartened by an opportunity to create a clearer understanding of the needs of teen mothers in the context of the federal government. Since 1982, the federal government has funded care and prevention programs in the area of adolescent pregnancy and parenting through its Adolescent Family Life (AFL) Program, located within the Public Health Service of the Department of Health and Human Services. Perceived by some in the field of adolescent pregnancy as conservative in its ap-

proaches, the Office of Adolescent Pregnancy Programs has funded, since its inception, demonstration programs throughout the country that provide health care and ancillary services to pregnant and parenting teens, and that teach pregnancy prevention through abstinence-based curricula that are medically accurate, free of religious content, and neutral on the subject of abortion, in accordance with a related Supreme Court settlement. Within this governmental context, I am directing an evaluation of AFL programs from the perspective of the clients, that is, the adolescents who participated in teen pregnancy care and prevention demonstration programs. This national evaluation is founded methodologically in the traditions of ethnography and phenomenology; by direct observation, by face-to-face intensive interviewing, by seeking the self-perceived meanings of adolescents' life events and program experiences, their stories can emerge in their own voices. Using such stories, we can report to policymakers, in the broadest sense, the needs of adolescent mothers and their children. Using such stories, policymakers can respond with programs that are more closely tailored to those needs, in the name of efficiency and humanity.

So many children lead such hard lives. I have told of some of the hardships they face. In an interview with "Cynthia," a teen mother, I came upon a startling reality. I interviewed Cynthia in her comfortable townhouse in a modest suburb of a major city. She lives there with her husband and her baby daughter. She grew up in a loving family in a comfortable home and reported no abuse or neglect of any kind. She and her husband both finished high school and have full-time jobs at salaries that place them in the lower part of middle-income America. They have had the love and support of their families in building this life. As I asked Cynthia if she had any lost dreams, she began to cry. Of all the teen mothers I have interviewed, she is the only one to cry so uncontrollably. I asked about her tears. "I have no choices now," she sobbed. I later realized that she is the only teen mother I have interviewed who had real dreams and choices.

Perhaps this social world, the United States in the 1990s, blames teen mothers and holds them in contempt because we are afraid that we created these desperate children, and we don't know what to do about them now. Per-haps we are afraid our children will become them. Perhaps we are afraid because we do not know, as adults, how to make it all better, and that is difficult to admit. We cling to myths rather than seek new truths. Perhaps in listening to the stories of teen mothers in their own voices, we can hear their needs and dreams, and answer them with care and choices.

Study/Discussion Questions

1. What stereotypes of teen mothers prevail in the U.S. today?
2. How do these stereotypes influence public policy?
3. What picture does the author present of teen mothers? How does this picture differ from the stereotype?
4. What changes in social policy does the author believe are necessary? How would these changes alter the lives of teen mothers?

Becoming *La Mujer*

Marisa Navarro

Becoming a woman in this society means, among other things, enduring the social purgatory of high school, where girls learn that they must tread a narrow line between sexiness and "slutiness" to gain the acceptance of their peers. Marisa Navarro describes the nuances of that line for a Mexican American girl growing up in East L.A. Surviving the confusing rules imposed by her father and the assaults of male acquaintances and strangers, Navarro emerges into womanhood as la mujer, *a woman comfortable in her own body.*

I used to dream that Superwoman would fly into my life, her legs unshaven and her hair cropped short. She would swoop me up and take me somewhere that made me feel safe and beautiful—a place far from the hell I knew as public high school. In this distant place, I would feel sensual for the first time ever, without feeling dirty. No one would assume I was destined to be a teenage mom, or that my brown skin marked me as a criminal. I wouldn't be "too dark" or "too fat," and my intelligence would never be compromised.

Those were ambitious goals for a Mexican American girl growing up near East Los Angeles. Every year, the drill team girl had a kid, then the prom queen. Pregnancy was so common it was almost a game to guess who the next teenage mother would be. Still, East L.A. is the only place I've lived where the scent of Aqua Net and overprocessed hair mingles with the sounds of English, Spanish, Chinese, Ko-

rean, and Armenian. There was comfort in being surrounded by hundreds of other brown people. I missed that when I went away to college and found my skin color and dark hair made me stand out in class.

I was one of the fortunate at my high school, shielded from some of Los Angeles's harshness by college prep classes. My parents stressed education all my life, so I focused on earning good grades, hoping they would be my ticket to a better life. But there was a price to pay. Since many of my female classmates wouldn't make it to graduation (pregnancy or lack of interest leading them to drop out), girls' actions became dichotomized into right and wrong. There were "good girls" (those who went to college) and "bad girls" (teenage mothers on welfare).

Early on, my parents reinforced that message, and there could be no margin of error. "It's out of love we tell you this, *mijita,*" they'd say. "Be quiet. Study hard. Don't have sex. Go to college, and then get married. A good daughter doesn't dress like a slut. A good daughter doesn't pierce or tattoo herself. A good daughter doesn't rock the boat." If I messed up, my whole future would be over. I must be a good *hijita*.

My parents also grew up in East L.A. I never told them what I faced at school, but I'm sure they knew. That made the parental leash even tighter. As an immigrant (my dad) and a first-generation American (my mom), they stressed hard work and success at any cost. It's a drive I don't think any person who is fourth-generation American or beyond can fully understand. Perhaps it's the stigma of the accent fresh in the memory, the blunter racism and the hard labor not even a distant memory. Either way, it fuels parents' determination that their children will not be like them.

In my family, being a good *hijita* meant more than simply being an obedient daughter. It also meant being desexualized. Being of mind but not of body. Wrapped in that word were my parents' hopes for me—and for themselves. I was to transcend the racism they'd experienced and to surpass society's low expectations.

My father was the success story in the family, and he was proud of it. He came from a small town in Mexico, graduated from college in the United States, and made lots of money. Somehow, my sister and I had to do even better than he had. On top of being supernaturally smart, we had to fulfill his macho idea of sensuality, a classic Madonna/whore tightrope that demanded we be attractive yet pure. We were expected to be skinny, have long hair, and wear clothes that showed our womanliness. Yet, we had to carry this off in a way that let men know we were unavailable for sex.

Sex was the biggest threat to my parents' carefully laid plans. Having sex meant I'd impede my chances to succeed, to achieve an American dream greater than the one offered to my parents. It meant I'd inevitably get pregnant and become a statistic, trapped in a community that was slowly falling apart. My body (and what I did with it) could make or break our family's future. The concept of the body as a battleground had much more meaning than even the most radical feminist could conceive. I needed only to keep my legs tightly locked, and everything would be all right.

Eventually, the word *hijita* left a sour taste in my mouth. It meant I was my parents' daughter. I didn't belong to me.

When I hit puberty, my father took on a form of desexualization with me and my sister. Boys were not humans, but the makers of sperm, waiting to plant their seed in us. For some reason my father saw me as extra fertile ground that he was determined be kept fallow. The only way to accomplish this was to forbid boys into the house and into my social life. If a boy called, I was questioned about his intentions. My father would bend down, squint and stare into my eyes to make sure I wasn't lying.

To further the desexualization process, he inspected me before I went out. If I wore lipstick or a tight shirt that showed my breasts, I was criticized and called a slut. I tried being the dutiful, plain daughter, but still I lost. When I cut off my hair and started wearing baggy pants to avoid his scrutiny, my father called me a boy. Where was this invisible line that would win his acceptance? What did it take to be a good *hijita*?

Since I couldn't figure that out, I looked to my older sister. My father always had a special fondness for her. I think it was because she was just so smart—smarter than all the white kids. In high school, she defied him by experimenting with sexuality, sensuality, and love. She proved she could be smart and sensual and have neither quality compromised. As an intelligent woman, she was unhappy learning about science and literature while knowing nothing about her body. She innocently assumed our father would be okay with this, since it didn't affect her grades.

Instead, he became enraged. Didn't she know that sex led to pregnancy and pregnancy led to welfare, which led to family dishonor? Although my sister didn't agree with his linear thinking, she was powerless to convince him otherwise. He would not have it. My sister became a bad *hijita* and was kicked out of the house. This terrified me; maybe *la familia* wasn't really about unconditional love after all. And if my sister and my father shared a special relationship that I would never have, what would happen to me if I did the same thing? I was too scared to find out.

I played out my teenage years like a script. More than anything, I felt I dressed in drag throughout high school, wearing clothes that would get boys to look at me, but only with vague interest. Avoiding male attention consumed my thoughts so much that men were all I thought about.

In the end, they won. I was constantly concerned that my outfits were too sensual. I had a hard time looking at my face in the mirror much less the rest of my body. Everything was wrong with me. Caught in a paradox, I was always dissatisfied. I hated that men were attracted to me, but I also hated that I didn't have big breasts or a thinner waistline. No guy wanted a fat, small-chested girl.

I lost all sense of ownership and control over my physical self. My memories of that script are vivid, too easy to relive:

Act I: First Year—(Sur)Real World 101

My math teacher walks around the room and then stops and leans his back against mine so that my head and breasts are flattened against the desk. Two boys sitting next to me laugh. I put my head down and silently swear that I'll stick quadratic equations up his ass. Eventually, I stop paying attention in class and drop from an A to barely a B. I chalk it up to the fact that I always hated math.

Act II: Sophomore Year—Boys Will Be Boys

A boy likes me and decides to show it by grabbing me every day. He does it when my back is facing him and I'm trying to be taken seriously. In the beginning, I yell that he's a *fuckin' dick/asshole/no good motherfucker*. He smiles and grabs me again. Eventually, I stop reacting, hoping he'll go away if I don't pay attention to his games. He assumes that means I like it and grabs me even more. Sometimes I think I should fuck him to get it over with, because that's all he really wants. Maybe afterward he'll leave me alone. But I don't. Not because I love myself enough not to fuck an asshole, but because the thought of someone seeing me naked is terrifying.

Act III: Junior Year—Honk If You're Horny

Trying to walk down the street with my head up has become the most political act of my teenage life. I dread major roads and busy intersections because men yell at me or stick out their tongues like deranged lizards. I hate how all they see is long hair and breasts, and how with each honk they take a piece of my self-esteem with them. These are the kind of men that stick silhouettes of women with big tits and tiny waists on their cars. These are the kind of men who smell estrogen and think *fuck*. I start to hate everything that makes me look like a woman—the breasts, the hips, the long hair—because I'm getting lots of attention, but no self-esteem.

Act IV: Senior Year—Stand by Your Man

By now I hate myself for turning men on, for being a "slut." All I want is for someone to love me for my mind. I'm tired of having my body picked apart by my father, being a virgin but made to feel like a whore. I figure since I'm already dirty, having sex won't make it any worse.

In bed, the boy I'm dating pulls my hair and pretends to slap me to make his dick harder. He calls me a slut and a ho'. I lie flat as a board, confused, scared, and sexually unfulfilled. I let him fuck me without a condom, without birth control pills, nothing. My body is too dirty to be worth protecting against AIDS or pregnancy. Everything the men on the street and my father told me seems true.

One day the boy laughs and says that the first time he saw me, he thought I looked ugly because my skin was dark. He doesn't want to take me to the beach or lie down in the park because I could get tan again. Another time, he tells me to shut up because I sound "too Mexican." What race does he think I am? I ask. He smiles, caresses my face, and tells me he doesn't like to think of me as Mexican. He means it as a compliment. At eighteen, I think if this is love, then maybe I was meant to be alone in the world after all.

Act V: Pomp and Circumstance
The most beautiful song I've ever heard. I collect my diploma like a trophy of war and run far away.

I left Los Angeles for Smith College in Northampton, Massachusetts, knowing the distance of a thousand miles had to release the parental leash. I wanted the power to create my identity, a power that I didn't have before. I purposely chose a women's college because I knew I needed time away from men.

School saved my mind and body. In college, I wasn't anyone's *hijita,* and I wouldn't be anyone's slut. I was able to come out of the closet, first to myself and a year later to everyone else. Women told me I was smart and beautiful; neither quality was ever questioned. When I took up smoking and drinking, I wasn't a bad *hijita.* Good and bad vanished, and I was *la mujer.* That phrase sounded beautiful and empowering to me.

At school I met many different types of women who were smart and proud of their bodies. I had a friend who fought boys. One

time she was flyering a concert about a group's homophobic lyrics, and a man shouted "dyke" at her. She grabbed a pool stick, chased him down, and threatened to show him "what a real dyke can do." The guy was so dumbfounded that a woman wasn't going to put her head down and take his shit that he hid underneath a pool table and waited for others to calm her down. I met many women who felt comfortable wearing dresses and grabbing their crotches in public. Others recited Marx to their lovers as they prepared to make passionate love.

I thought racing to be a part of the queer community would save me. I enlisted in the dyke world complete with uniform—short hair, overalls, cap on backwards, and body piercings. As an extra buffer, I gained twenty-five pounds to make sure men wouldn't be interested in me, and to make sure I didn't have the body of a "slut." I walked down the street with pride, knowing that men no longer honked at me. I was undesirable. There was power in that for me. I thought I was screwing the patriarchy, subverting the status quo of femininity.

I didn't realize, however, that I was still blaming myself. At twenty, I had only run away from my problems and never dealt with them. I still felt as if my body was dirty and shameful. I still believed that the unwanted sexual attention I got in high school had been my fault—as though I'd "asked for it" by trying to fit a narrow prescription of femininity.

Soon, I found myself trying to follow the status quo of a different community, complete with confining norms and stereotypes. Now, instead of wanting to be a good *hijita,* I found myself trying to be a good queer girl and a good feminist. The role was just as confining. The feminist and gay communities still had a white/classist/racist framework—one which did nothing to address the multiple-identity dilemmas that came along with being a queer Latina feminist.

When I looked in the mirror, I felt just as much in drag as I had in high school. Finally, after twenty-one years of confusion, I realized I could be happy only when I defined my own idea of beauty and sensuality. My identity had too many layers for me to wrap it into a convenient package. The most political statement I could make was to look the way I wanted and not be ashamed of it. Today, my closet reflects my philosophy with a feather boa, tuxedo shirt, overalls, and platforms all peacefully cohabiting. Such nonsensical words as *butch, femme,* and *drag* have disappeared from my vocabulary and my fashion style.

And naked, I'm just as sensual. I can look at myself and not feel ashamed anymore. Sure, I have stretch marks all over my ass, scars all over my body, and my breasts are lopsided. But that's what being a real *mujer* is all about. Real *mujeres* live life intensely—and their bodies show it. They feast on food, drink with revelry, and play hard. I look forward to watching my body develop more, to becoming more curvaceous. I'm ready for anything that happens, whether it's cellulite or muscle definition.

Now that I wear whatever I like, I feel sensual. I can go to a club and let the beat lead my hips. That's what I like best about dancing. My mind doesn't think. The rhythms dictate how my hips will sway, how my whole body moves. I don't care if men or women are looking. My sensuality is for me.

I need to discover how my body can move. I need to know me before anyone else can. I thought if I reached this epiphany and expressed my sexuality with freedom, that men would see me as a target. I was wrong. It wasn't my body that made men yell and grab me. It was them.

And, in some ways, I have little power to change that. I can't single-handedly overturn messages telling men that women are sex objects. I can't uproot myths casting women of color as wild and sexually available. I also understand my parents' mistakes. Instead of shielding me from boys and sex, they should have prepared me for what I would come to expect. Instead of "protecting" me by teaching me body hatred, they should have taught me to cherish myself. Had I been proud of my body, I may not have let street harassers bring me down so low. I wouldn't have risked my life sleeping with assholes. I would have known how to defend myself.

I accept this now and fight to unlearn twenty-one years of conditioning. So far, I'm doing pretty well. Without realizing it, I've developed a new body language. When I walked with my head down, men picked up on my powerlessness. I believe that my confident new stride actually scares some of those assholes away. Once in a while, I get catcalls, but now those men are sure to get flipped off, barked at, or blown a kiss. I realize why my friend is willing to fight boys, and ultimately, I would fight a man. I spent so many years feeling ashamed of my body that rolling in the dirt might make me feel cleaner.

In the end, no Superfeminist ever flew in from the sky to save me. It took me years to realize that nobody else could rescue me. I didn't have to be a superhero. I just had to allow myself to become *la mujer.*

Study/Discussion Questions

1. What were the advantages of being a "good girl" in the author's community?
2. What were the disadvantages of being a "good girl"?
3. What lessons did Marisa Navarro learn about sexuality and being a girl from her family? What lessons did she learn in high school?
4. What does it mean to Navarro to become *la mujer?*

Dreading It
. . . or how I learned to stop fighting my hair and love my nappy roots

Veronica Chambers

In this essay, first published in Vogue *magazine, Veronica Chambers talks about her hair. As a young African American woman, she knows the cultural significance of hair to black women in particular. Taking place in home kitchens and in beauty parlors, hair care has been central to black women's culture over many generations. Hair is much more than mere adornment, Chambers explains. Its treatment and styling reflect the gender and racial norms of the day. Choosing in the late 1990s to wear natural dreadlocks rather than chemically straighten her hair, Chambers makes a statement of body acceptance that ripples throughout her interactions with family, friends, dates, and strangers.*

There are two relationships I have with the outside world—one is with my hair, and the other is with the rest of me. Sure, I have concerns and points of pride with my body. I like the curve of my butt but dislike my powerhouse thighs. My nose suited me fine for the past 28 years. Then last week, for some strange reason, my nose seemed too big and I started to wonder about a nose job. My breasts, once considered too small, have been proclaimed perfect so often that not only am I starting to believe the hype but I'm booking my next vacation to a topless resort in Greece. But my hair. Oh, my hair.

I have reddish-brown dreadlocks that fall just below shoulder length. I like my hair—a lot. But over the past eight years that I have worn dreadlocks, my hair has conferred upon me the following roles: rebel child, Rasta mama, Nubian princess, drug dealer, unemployed artist, rock star, world-famous comedienne, and nature chick. None of which is really true. It has occurred to me on more than one occasion that my hair is a whole lot more interesting than I am.

Because I am a black woman, I have always had a complicated relationship with my hair. For those who don't know the history, here's a quick primer on the politics of hair and beauty aesthetics in the black community, vis-à-vis race and class in the late twentieth century. "Good" hair is straight and, preferably, long. Think

Excerpted from *Body,* an anthology edited by Steve and Sharon Fiffer (Avon, 1999). Used by permission of the author.

Naomi Campbell. Think Whitney Houston. For that matter, think RuPaul. "Bad" hair is thick and coarse, a.k.a. "nappy," and often short. Think Buckwheat of the Little Rascals. Not the more recent, politically correct version, but the old one, in which Buckwheat looked like Don King's grandson.

Understand that these are stereotypes: broad and imprecise. Some will say that "good" hair versus "bad" hair is outdated. And it's true, it's much less prevalent than it was in the seventies, when I was growing up. Sometimes I see little girls, with their hair in braids and Senegalese twists, sporting cute little T-shirts that read HAPPY TO BE NAPPY and I get teary-eyed. I was born in the sandwich generation between the Black Power Afros of the sixties and the blue contact lenses and weaves of the eighties. In my childhood, no one seemed very happy to be nappy at all.

I knew from the age of four that I had "bad" hair because my relatives and family friends discussed my hair with all the gravity that one might use to discuss a rare blood disease. "Something must be done," they would cluck sadly. "I think I know someone," an aunt would murmur. Some of my earliest memories are of Brooklyn apartments where women did hair for extra money. These makeshift beauty parlors were lively and loud, the air thick with the smell of lye from harsh relaxer, the smell of hair burning as the hot straightening comb did its job. To this day, the sound of a hot comb crackling as it makes its way through a thick head of hair makes me feel at home; the smell of hair burning is the smell of black beauty emerging like a phoenix from metaphorical ashes: transformation.

My hair was so thick that the perms never lasted through the end of the month. Hairdressers despaired like cowardly lion tamers at the thought of training my kinky hair. "This is some hard hair," they would say. As a child, I knew that I was not beautiful and I blamed it on my hair.

The night I began to twist my hair into dreads, I was nineteen years old and a junior in college. It was New Year's Eve, and the boy that I longed for had not called. "We'll all meet at a club," he had said. "I'll call and tell you where." But the phone never rang. A few months before, Alice Walker had appeared on the cover of *Essence,* her locks flowing with all the majesty of a Southern American Cleopatra. I was inspired. It was my family's superstition that the hours between New Year's Eve and New Year's Day were the time to cast spells. "However New Year's catches you is how you'll spend the year," my mother reminded me my whole life long. We spent the days before New Year's cleaning our room, watching as our mother put clean sheets on the bed and stocked the house with groceries. On New Year's Eve, my mother tucked dollar bills into my training bra and into my brother's pants pocket so that the New Year would find us flush. The important thing on New Year's Eve was to set the stage, to make sure you kept close everything you needed and wanted.

Jilted on New Year's Eve, I decided to use the hours that remained to transform myself into the vision that I'd seen on the cover of *Essence.* Unsure of how to begin, I washed my hair, carefully and lovingly. I dried it with a towel, then opened a jar of hair grease. Using a comb to part the sections, I began to twist each section into baby dreads. My hair, at the time, couldn't have been longer than an inch. I twisted for two hours, and in the end was far from smitten with what I saw—my full cheeks dominated my face, now that my hair lay in flat twists around my head. I did not look like the African goddess that I had imagined, but it was a start. I emerged from the bathroom and ran into my aunt Diana, whose headful of luxuriously long, straight black hair always reminded me of Diahann Carroll on *Dynasty*. "Vickie," she said, shaking her head. "Well, well." I knew that night my life would begin to change. I started my dreadlocks and I began the process of seeing beauty where no one had ever seen beauty before. Like Rapunzel, I grew my hair and it freed me, not only from perms that could never quite tame my kinky hair down but from a past in which my crowning glory was anything but.

There are, of course, those who see my hair and still consider it "bad." I have been asked by more than one potential suitor if I had any pictures of myself before "you did that to your hair." One friend was so insistent that I must have been prettier without dreadlocks that I wore a wig to meet him one day. Not only did he not like me in the straight black bob that I wore, he didn't recognize me. "I get it," he said. "Those dreads are really you." I have occasionally thought that I carry all of my personality around on my head. A failure at small talk and countless other social graces, I sometimes walk into a cocktail party and let my hair do the talking for me. I stroll through the room, silently, and watch my hair tell white lies. In literary circles, my hair brands me as "interesting, adventurous." In black middle-class circles, my hair brands me as "rebellious" or "Afrocentric." In predominantly white circles, my hair doubles my level of exotica. My hair says, "Unlike the black woman who reads you the evening news, I'm not even trying to blend in."

That said, it is important to remember that at the end of the day my hair is just hair. "Do you think this could work out?" a man said to me recently. Mind you, it was only our second date and I was pretty convinced that I didn't want there to be a third. "What do you mean?" I asked him, sweetly, even dumbly. "I'm very traditional and you're so wild," he said, reaching out for my hair. "I'm not wild. You only think I'm wild," I wanted to scream. For those who are ignorant enough to think that they can read hair follicles like tea leaves, my hair says a lot of things that it doesn't mean. Taken to the extreme, my hair says that I am a pot-smoking, Rastafarian wannabe who in her off-hours strolls through her house in an African dashiki, lighting incense and listening to Bob Marley. I have been asked to score or smoke pot so often that it doesn't even faze me anymore. Once after a dinner party in Beverly Hills, a white colleague of mine lit up a joint. Everyone at the table passed and when I passed, too, the man proceeded to cajole me relentlessly. "Come on," he kept saying. "Of all people, I thought you'd indulge." I shrugged and said nothing. As we left the party that night, he kissed me good-bye. "Boy, were you a disappointment," he said as if I had been a bad lay. But I guess I had denied him a certain sort of pleasure. It must have been his dream to smoke a big, fat spliff with a real, live Rastafarian.

Similarly, it's such hair judgments that make me a magnet for airport security. I loathe connecting international flights in Miami and London, for I am sure to be stopped and stopped again. On a recent trip from Panama, I was stopped by five officers in one hour; each one took his time poking through my suitcases. Finally, imprudently, I let the last officer have it. "I know what this is," I told him. "This is harassment. And it's because of my hair." He didn't even blink an eye. "We stopped them, too," he said, pointing to a group of white missionaries. "Nothing wrong with their hair." In the Bahamas, a friend and I weren't allowed into a local nightclub because, as the bouncer pointed out, the sign said No Jeans. No Sneakers. No Dreadlocks. I would have laughed if I didn't want to cry. You can change what you're wearing. How do you change the hair on your head? And why should you have to?

I have thought, intermittently, of changing my hairstyle. My hair is too big for me to wear hats, and I sometimes envy women with close-cropped cuts and stylish headgear. The other night, I watched one of my favorite movies, *La Femme Nikita,* and I admired Nikita's no-nonsense bob. "I couldn't be a female assassin with hair like this!" I said, jumping up out of my chair. Even pulled back, my hair is too voluminous to be stark. Then I remembered how

in the movie *Foxy Brown,* Pam Grier pulls a gun out of her Afro, and I was comforted that should I choose the career path of professional ass-kicker, my hair would not be an obstacle. Once, after the end of a great love affair, I watched a man cut all of his dreadlocks off and then burn them in the backyard. This is perhaps the only reason I would ever cut my hair. After all, a broken heart is what started this journey of twisting hair. A broken heart may find me at a new hair road. Because I do not cut my hair, I carry nine years of history on my head. One day, I may tire of this history and start anew. But one thing is for sure, whatever style I wear my hair in, I will live happily—and nappily—ever after.

Study/Discussion Questions

1. What are the messages sent by Chambers' hair to her family when she wears dreads?
2. What messages do men hear? What messages does society (and, in particular, white people) hear?
3. What changed in Chambers' attitude about herself after she started wearing dreads? Did she become a different person when she changed her hairstyle?
4. Why is hair a particularly salient issue for African American women?
5. In what ways do white women have similar hair problems? Are white women in some way exempt from the tensions described by the author?

Flash Exercise

Body Image

1. Name five things you love about your body.
2. Name five things you would like to change about your body.
3. Which of the two lists above was easier for you to complete?

"GIRL FRIENDS": FRIENDS AND SISTERS

The Female World of Love and Ritual
Relations Between Women in Nineteenth-Century America

Carroll Smith-Rosenberg

First published in 1975, this now-classic essay by historian Carroll Smith-Rosenberg both spurred and reflected a new direction in the field of women's history. Much scholarly attention had been paid since the mid-1960s to prescribed roles for women in American culture. Smith-Rosenberg turns to nineteenth-century women's diaries and letters to examine how women felt about themselves and each other. She discovers an emotional world quite apart from the stifling Victorian code of morals and manners prescribed by the advice books and sermons of the day.

The female friendship of the nineteenth century, the long-lived, intimate, loving friendship between two women, is an excellent example of the type of historical phenomena which most historians know something about, which few have thought much about, and which virtually no one has written about.[1] It is one aspect of the female experience which consciously or unconsciously we have chosen to ignore. Yet an abundance of manuscript evidence suggests that eighteenth- and nineteenth-century women routinely formed emotional ties with other women. Such deeply felt, same-sex friendships were casually accepted in American society. Indeed, from at least the late-eighteenth through the mid-nineteenth century, a female world of varied and yet highly structured relationships appears to have been an essential aspect of American society. These relationships ranged from the supportive love of sisters, through the enthusiasms of adolescent girls, to sensual avowals of love by mature women. It was a world in which men made but a shadowy appearance.[2]

Defining and analyzing same-sex relationships involves the historian in deeply problematical questions of method and interpretation. This is especially true since historians, influenced by Freud's libidinal theory, have discussed these relationships almost exclusively

From *Signs: Journal of Women in Culture and Society*, 1, no. 1 (1975), pp. 1–29. Copyright © 1975 University of Chicago Press. Research for this paper was supported in part by a grant from the Grant Foundation, New York, and by National Institutes of Health grant 5 FO3 HD48800-03. I would like to thank several scholars for their assistance and criticism in preparing this paper: Erving Goffman, Roy Schafer, Charles E. Rosenberg, Cynthia Secor, and Anthony Wallace. Judy Breault, who has just completed a biography of an important and introspective nineteenth-century feminist, Emily Howland, served as a research assistant for this paper, and her knowledge of nineteenth-century family structure and religious history proved invaluable.

within the context of individual psychosexual developments or, to be more explicit, psycho-pathology.[3] Seeing same-sex relationships in terms of a dichotomy between normal and abnormal, they have sought the origins of such apparent deviance in childhood or adolescent trauma and detected the symptoms of "latent" homosexuality in the lives of both those who later became "overtly" homosexual and those who did not. Yet theories concerning the nature and origins of same-sex relationships are frequently contradictory or based on question-able or arbitrary data. In recent years such hypotheses have been subjected to criticism both from within and without the psychological professions. Historians who seek to work within a psychological framework, therefore, are faced with two hard questions: Do sound psychodynamic theories concerning the nature and origins of same-sex relationships exist? If so, does the historical datum exist which would permit the use of such dynamic models?

I would like to suggest an alternative approach to female friendships—one which would view them within a cultural and social setting rather than from an exclusively indi-vidual psychosexual perspective. Only by thus altering our approach will we be in the posi-tion to evaluate the appropriateness of particu-lar dynamic interpretations. Intimate friend-ships between men and men and women and women existed in a larger world of social rela-tions and social values. To interpret such friend-ships more fully they must be related to the structure of the American family and to the nature of sex-role divisions and of male-female relations both within the family and in society generally. The female friendship must not be seen in isolation; it must be analyzed as one aspect of women's overall relations with one another. The ties between mothers and daugh-ters, sisters, female cousins, and friends, at all stages of the female life cycle constitute the most suggestive framework for the historian to begin an analysis of intimacy and affection between women. Such an analysis would not only emphasize general cultural patterns rather than the internal dynamics of a particular fam-ily or childhood; it would shift the focus of the study from a concern with deviance to that of defining configurations of legitimate behav-ioral norms and options.[4]

This analysis will be based upon the corre-spondence and diaries of women and men in thirty-five families between the 1760s and the 1880s. These families, though limited in num-ber, represented a broad range of the Ameri-can middle class, from hard-pressed pioneer families and orphaned girls to daughters of the intellectual and social elite. It includes fami-lies from most geographic regions, rural and urban, and a spectrum of Protestant denomi-nations ranging from Mormon to orthodox Quaker. Although scarcely a comprehensive sample of America's increasingly heterogeneous population, it does, I believe, reflect accurately the literate middle class to which the historian working with letters and diaries is necessarily bound. It has involved an analysis of many thousands of letters written to women friends, kin, husbands, brothers, and children at every period of life from adolescence to old age. Some collections encompass virtually entire life spans; one contains over 100,000 letters as well as diaries and account books. It is my contention that an analysis of women's private letters and diaries which were never intended to be pub-lished permits the historian to explore a very private world of emotional realities central both to women's lives and to the middle-class fam-ily in nineteenth-century America.[5]

The question of female friendships is pecu-liarly elusive; we know so little or perhaps have forgotten so much. An intriguing and almost alien form of human relationship, they flour-ished in a different social structure and amidst different sexual norms. Before attempting to reconstruct their social setting, therefore, it might be best first to describe two not atypical friendships. These two friendships, intense, loving, and openly avowed, began during the women's adolescence and, despite subsequent marriages and geographic separation, continued throughout their lives. For nearly half a century these women played a central emotional role in each other's lives, writing time and again of their love and of the pain of separation. Paradoxically to twentieth-century minds, their love appears to have been both sensual and platonic.

Sarah Butler Wister first met Jeannie Field Musgrove while vacationing with her family at Stockbridge, Massachusetts, in the summer of 1849.[6] Jeannie was then sixteen, Sarah fourteen. During two subsequent years spent together in boarding school, they formed a deep and intimate friendship. Sarah began to keep a bouquet of flowers before Jeannie's portrait and wrote complaining of the intensity and anguish of her affection.[7] Both young women assumed nom de plumes, Jeannie a female name, Sarah a male one; they would use these secret names into old age.[8] They frequently commented on the nature of their affection: "If the day should come," Sarah wrote Jeannie in the spring of 1861, "when you failed me either through your fault or my own, I would forswear all human friendship, thenceforth." A few months later Jeannie commented: "Gratitude is a word I should never use toward you. It is perhaps a misfortune of such intimacy and love that it makes one regard all kindness as a matter of course, as one has always found it, as natural as the embrace in meeting."[9]

Sarah's marriage altered neither the frequency of their correspondence nor their desire to be together. In 1864, when twenty-nine, married, and a mother, Sarah wrote to Jeannie: "I shall be entirely alone [this coming week]. I can give you no idea how desperately I shall want you. . . ." After one such visit Jeannie, then a spinster in New York, echoed Sarah's longing: "Dear darling Sarah! How I love you & how happy I have been! You are the joy of my life. . . . I cannot tell you how much hap-

piness you gave me, nor how constantly it is all in my thoughts. . . . My darling how I long for the time when I shall see you. . . ." After another visit Jeannie wrote: "I want you to tell me in your next letter, to assure me, that I am your dearest. . . . I do not doubt you, & I am not jealous but I long to hear you say it once more & it seems already a long time since your voice fell on my ear. So just fill a quarter page with caresses & expressions of endearment. Your silly Angelina." Jeannie ended one letter: "Goodbye my dearest, dearest lover—ever your own Angelina." And another, "I will go to bed . . . [though] I could write all night—A thousand kisses—I love you with my whole soul—your Angelina."

When Jeannie finally married in 1870 at the age of thirty-seven, Sarah underwent a period of extreme anxiety. Two days before Jeannie's marriage, Sarah, then in London, wrote desperately: "Dearest darling—How incessantly have I thought of you these eight days—all today—the entire uncertainty, the distance, the long silence—are all new features in my separation from you, grevious to be borne. . . . Oh Jeannie. I have thought & thought & yearned over you these two days. Are you married I wonder? My dearest love to you wherever and *who*ever you are."[10] Like many other women in this collection of thirty-five families, marriage brought Sarah and Jeannie physical separation; it did not cause emotional distance. Although at first they may have wondered how marriage would affect their relationship, their affection remained unabated throughout their lives, underscored by their loneliness and their desire to be together.[11]

During the same years that Jeannie and Sarah wrote of their love and need for each other, two slightly younger women began a similar odyssey of love, dependence, and—ultimately—physical, though not emotional, separation. Molly and Helena met in 1868 while both attended the Cooper Institute School of Design for Women in New York City. For several years these young women studied and explored the city together, visited each other's families, and formed part of a social network of other artistic young women. Gradually, over the years, their initial friendship deepened into a close intimate bond which continued throughout their lives. The tone in the letters which Molly wrote to Helena changed over these years from "My dear Helena," and signed "your attached friend," to "My dearest Helena," "My Dearest," "My Beloved," and signed "Thine always" or "thine Molly."[12]

The letters they wrote to each other during these first five years permit us to reconstruct something of their relationship together. As Molly wrote in one early letter:

> I have not said to you in so many or so few words that I was happy with you during those few so incredibly short weeks but surely you do not need words to tell you what you must know. Those two or three days so dark without, so bright with firelight and contentment within I shall always remember as proof that, for a time, at least—I fancy for quite a long time—we might he sufficient for each other. We know that we can amuse each other for many idle hours together and now we know that we can also work together. And that means much, don't you think so?

She ended: "I shall return in a few days. Imagine yourself kissed many times by one who loved you so dearly."

The intensity and even physical nature of Molly's love was echoed in many of the letters she wrote during the next few years, as, for instance in this short thank-you note for a small present: "Imagine yourself kissed a dozen times my darling. Perhaps it is well for you that we are far apart. You might find my thanks so expressed rather overpowering. I have that delightful feeling that it doesn't matter much what I say or how I say it, since we shall meet so soon and forget in that moment that we were

ever separated. . . . I shall see you soon and be content."[13]

At the end of the fifth year, however, several crises occurred. The relationship, at least in its intense form, ended, though Molly and Helena continued an intimate and complex relationship for the next half-century. The exact nature of these crises is not completely clear, but it seems to have involved Molly's decision not to live with Helena, as they had originally planned, but to remain at home because of parental insistence. Molly was now in her late twenties. Helena responded with anger, and Molly became frantic at the thought that Helena would break off their relationship. Though she wrote distraught letters and made despairing attempts to see Helena, the relationship never regained its former ardor—possibly because Molly had a male suitor.[14] Within six months Helena had decided to marry a man who was, coincidentally, Molly's friend and publisher. Two years later Molly herself finally married. The letters toward the end of this period discuss the transition both women made to having male lovers—Molly spending much time reassuring Helena, who seemed depressed about the end of their relationship and with her forthcoming marriage.[15]

It is clearly difficult from a distance of 100 years and from a post-Freudian cultural perspective to decipher the complexities of Molly and Helena's relationship. Certainly Molly and Helena were lovers—emotionally if not physically. The emotional intensity and pathos of their love becomes apparent in several letters Molly wrote Helena during their crisis: "I wanted so to put my arms round my girl of all the girls in the world and tell her . . . I love her as wives do love their husbands, as *friends* who have taken each other for life—and believe in her as I believe in my God. . . . If I didn't love you do you suppose I'd care about anything or have ridiculous notions and panics and behave like an old fool who ought to know better. I'm going to hang on to your skirts. . . . You can't get away from [my] love." Or as she wrote after Helena's decision to marry: "You know dear Helena, I really was in love with you. It was a passion such as I had never known until I saw you. I don't think it was the noblest way to love you." The theme of intense female love was one Molly again expressed in a letter she wrote to the man Helena was to marry: "Do you know sir, that until you came along I believe that she loved me almost as girls love their lovers. *I know I loved her so.* Don't you wonder that I can stand the sight of you." This was in a letter congratulating them on their forthcoming marriage.[16]

The essential question is not whether these women had genital contact and can therefore be defined as heterosexual or homosexual. The twentieth-century tendency to view human love and sexuality within a dichotomized universe of deviance and normality, genitality and platonic love, is alien to the emotions and attitudes of the nineteenth century and fundamentally distorts the nature of these women's emotional interaction. These letters are significant because they force us to place such female love in a particular historical context. There is every indication that these four women, their husbands and families—all eminently respectable and socially conservative—considered such love both socially acceptable and fully compatible with heterosexual marriage. Emotionally and cognitively, their heterosocial and their homosocial worlds were complementary.

One could argue, on the other hand, that these letters were but an example of the romantic rhetoric with which the nineteenth century surrounded the concept of friendship. Yet they possess an emotional intensity and a sensual and physical explicitness that is difficult to dismiss. Jeannie longed to hold Sarah in her arms; Molly mourned her physical isolation from Helena. Molly's love and devotion to Helena, the emotions that bound Jeannie and Sarah together, while perhaps a phenomenon

of nineteenth-century society, were not the less real for their Victorian origins. A survey of the correspondence and diaries of eighteenth- and nineteenth-century women indicates that Molly, Jeannie, and Sarah represented one very real behavioral and emotional option socially available to nineteenth-century women.

This is not to argue that individual needs, personalities, and family dynamics did not have a significant role in determining the nature of particular relationships. But the scholar must ask if it is historically possible and, if possible, important, to study the intensely individual aspects of psychosexual dynamics. Is it not the historian's first task to explore the social structure and the world view which made intense and sometimes sensual female love both a possible and an acceptable emotional option? From such a social perspective a new and quite different series of questions suggests itself. What emotional function did such female love serve? What was its place within the hetero- and homosocial worlds which women jointly inhabited? Did a spectrum of love-object choices exist in the nineteenth century across which some individuals, at least, were capable of moving? Without attempting to answer these questions it will be difficult to understand either nineteenth-century sexuality or the nineteenth-century family.

Several factors in American society between the mid-eighteenth and the mid-nineteenth centuries may well have permitted women to form a variety of close emotional relationships with other women. American society was characterized in large part by rigid gender-role differentiation within the family and within society as a whole, leading to the emotional segregation of women and men. The roles of daughter and mother shaded imperceptibly and ineluctably into each other, while the biological realities of frequent pregnancies, childbirth, nursing, and menopause bound women together in physical and emotional intimacy. It was within just such a social framework, I would argue, that a specifically female world did indeed develop, a world built around a generic and unself-conscious pattern of single-sex or homosocial networks. These supportive networks were institutionalized in social conventions or rituals which accompanied virtually every important event in a woman's life, from birth to death. Such female relationships were frequently supported and paralleled by severe social restrictions on intimacy between young men and women. Within such a world of emotional richness and complexity, devotion to and love of other women became a plausible and socially accepted form of human interaction.

An abundance of printed and manuscript sources exists to support such a hypothesis. Etiquette books, advice books on child rearing, religious sermons, guides to young men and young women, medical texts, and school curricula all suggest that late eighteenth- and most nineteenth-century Americans assumed the existence of a world composed of distinctly male and female spheres, spheres determined by the immutable laws of God and nature.[17] The unpublished letters and diaries of Americans during this same period concur, detailing the existence of sexually segregated worlds inhabited by human beings with different values, expectations, and personalities. Contacts between men and women frequently partook of a formality and stiffness quite alien to twentieth-century America and which today we tend to define as "Victorian." Women, however, did not form an isolated and oppressed subcategory in male society. Their letters and diaries indicate that women's sphere had an essential integrity and dignity that grew out of women's shared experiences and mutual affection and that, despite the profound changes which affected American social structure and institutions between the 1760s and the 1870s, retained a constancy and predictability. The ways in which women thought of and interacted with each other remained unchanged.

Continuity, not discontinuity, characterized this female world. Molly Hallock's and Jeannie Fields's words, emotions, and experiences have direct parallels in the 1760s and the 1790s.[18] There are inclinations in contemporary sociological and psychological literature that female closeness and support networks have continued into the twentieth century—not only among ethnic and working-class groups but even among the middle class.[19]

Most eighteenth- and nineteenth-century women lived within a world bounded by home, church, and the institution of visiting—that endless trooping of women to each others' homes for social purposes. It was a world inhabited by children and by other women.[20] Women helped each other with domestic chores and in times of sickness, sorrow, or trouble. Entire days, even weeks, might be spent almost exclusively with other women.[21] Urban and town women could devote virtually every day to visits, teas, or shopping trips with other women. Rural women developed a pattern of more extended visits that lasted weeks and sometimes months, at times even dislodging husbands from their beds and bedrooms so that dear friends might spend every hour of every day together.[22] When husbands traveled, wives routinely moved in with other women, invited women friends to teas and suppers, sat together sharing and comparing the letters they had received from other close women friends. Secrets were exchanged and cherished, and the husband's return at times viewed with some ambivalence.[23]

Summer vacations were frequently organized to permit old friends to meet at water spas or share a country home. In 1848, for example, a young matron wrote cheerfully to her husband about the delightful time she was having with five close women friends whom she had invited to spend the summer with her; he remained at home alone to face the heat of Philadelphia and a cholera epidemic.[24] Some ninety years earlier, two young Quaker girls commented upon the vacation their aunt had taken alone with another woman; their remarks were openly envious and tell us something of the emotional quality of these friendships: "I hear Aunt is gone with the Friend and won't be back for two weeks, fine times indeed I think the old friends had, taking their pleasure about the country . . . and have the advantage of that fine woman's conversation and instruction, while we poor young girls must spend all spring at home. . . . What a disappointment that we are not together."[25]

Friends did not form isolated dyads but were normally part of highly integrated networks. Knowing each other, perhaps related to each other, they played a central role in holding communities and kin systems together. Especially when families became geographically mobile women's long visits to each other and their frequent letters filled with discussions of marriages and births, illness and deaths, descriptions of growing children, and reminiscences of times and people past provided an important sense of continuity in a rapidly changing society.[26] Central to this female world was an inner core of kin. The ties between sisters, first cousins, aunts, and nieces provided the underlying structure upon which groups of friends and their network of female relatives clustered. Although most of the women within this sample would appear to be living within isolated nuclear families, the emotional ties between nonresidenial kin were deep and binding and provided one of the fundamental existential realities of women's lives.[27] Twenty years after Parke Lewis Butler moved with her husband to Louisiana, she sent her two daughters back to Virginia to attend school, live with their grandmother and aunt, and be integrated back into Virginia society.[28] The constant letters between Maria Inskeep and Fanny Hampton, sisters separated in their early twenties when Maria moved with her husband from New Jersey to Louisiana, held their families together, making it possible for their daughters to feel a part of their cousins' network of friends and interests.[29] The Ripley daughters, growing up in western Massachusetts in the early 1800s, spent months each year with their mother's sister and her family in distant Boston; these female cousins and their network of friends exchanged gossip-filled letters and gradually formed deeply loving and dependent ties.[30]

Women frequently spent their days within the social confines of such extended families. Sisters-in-law visited each other and, in some families, seemed to spend more time with each other than with their husbands. First cousins cared for each other's babies—for weeks or even months in times of sickness or childbirth. Sisters helped each other with housework, shopped and sewed for each other. Geographic separation was borne with difficulty. A sister's absence for even a week or two could cause loneliness and depression and would be bridged by frequent letters. Sibling rivalry was hardly unknown, but with separation or illness the theme of deep affection and dependency reemerged.[31]

Sisterly bonds continued across a lifetime. In her old age a rural Quaker matron, Martha Jefferis, wrote to her daughter Anne concerning her own half-sister, Phoebe: "In sister Phoebe I have a real friend—she studies my comfort and waits on me like a child. . . . She is exceedingly kind and this to all other homes (set aside yours) I would prefer—it is next to being with a daughter." Phoebe's own letters confirmed Martha's evaluation of her feelings. "Thou knowest my dear sister," Phoebe wrote, "there is no one . . . that exactly feels [for] thee as I do, for I think without boasting I can truly say that my desire is for thee."[32]

Such women, whether friends or relatives, assumed an emotional centrality in each others' lives. In their diaries and letters they wrote of the joy and contentment they felt in each others' company, their sense of isolation and despair when apart. The regularity of their correspondence underlines the sincerity of their words. Women named their daughters after one another and sought to integrate dear friends into their lives after marriage.[33] As one young bride wrote to an old friend shortly after her marriage: "I want to see you and talk with you and feel that we are united by the same bonds of sympathy and congeniality as ever."[34] After years of friendship one aging woman wrote of another: "Time cannot destroy the fascination of her manner . . . her voice is music to the ear."[35] Women made elaborate presents for each other, ranging from the Quakers' frugal pies and breads to painted velvet bags and phantom bouquets.[36] When a friend died, their grief was deeply felt. Martha Jefferis was unable to write to her daughter for three weeks because of the sorrow she felt at the death of a dear friend. Such distress was not unusual. A generation earlier a young Massachusetts farm woman filled pages of her diary with her grief at the death of her "dearest friend" and transcribed the letters of condolence other women sent her. She marked the anniversary of Rachel's death each year in her diary, contrasting her faithfulness with that of Rachel's husband who had soon remarried.[37]

These female friendships served a number of emotional functions. Within this secure and empathetic world women could share sorrows, anxieties, and joys, confident that other women had experienced similar emotions. One mid-nineteenth-century rural matron in a letter to her daughter discussed this particular aspect of women's friendships: "To have such a friend as thyself to look to and sympathize with her— and enter into all her little needs and in whose bosom she could with freedom pour forth her joys and sorrows—such a friend would very much relieve the tedium of many a wearisome hour." A generation later Molly more informally underscored the importance of this same function in a letter to Helena: "Suppose I come down . . . [and] spend Sunday with you quietly," she wrote Helena ". . . that means talking all the time until you are relieved of all

your latest troubles, and I of mine."[38] These were frequently troubles that apparently no man could understand. When Anne Jefferis Sheppard was first married, she and her older sister Edith (who then lived with Anne) wrote in detail to their mother of the severe depression and anxiety which they experienced. Moses Sheppard, Anne's husband, added cheerful postscripts to the sisters' letters—which he had clearly not read—remarking on Anne's and Edith's contentment. Theirs was an emotional world to which he had little access.[39]

This was, as well, a female world in which hostility and criticism of other women were discouraged, and thus a milieu in which women could develop a sense of inner security and self-esteem. As one young woman wrote to her mother's longtime friend: "I cannot sufficiently thank you for the kind unvaried affection & indulgence you have ever shown and expressed both by words and actions for me. . . . Happy would it be did all the world view me as you do, through the medium of kindness and forbearance."[40] They valued each other. Women, who had little status or power in the larger world of male concerns, possessed status and power in the lives and worlds of other women.[41]

An intimate mother-daughter relationship lay at the heart of this female world. The diaries and letters of both mothers and daughters attest to their closeness and mutual emotional dependency. Daughters routinely discussed their mother's health and activities with their own friends, expressed anxiety in cases of their mother's ill health and concern for her cares.[42] Expressions of hostility which we would today consider routine on the part of both mothers and daughters seem to have been uncommon indeed. On the contrary, this sample of families indicates that the normal relationship between mother and daughter was one of sympathy and understanding.[43] Only sickness or great geographic distance was allowed to cause extended separation. When marriage did result in such separation, both viewed the distance between them with distress.[44] Something of this sympathy and love between mothers and daughters is evident in a letter Sarah Alden Ripley, at age sixty-nine, wrote her youngest and recently married daughter: "You do not know how much I miss you, not only when I struggle in and out of my mortal envelop and pump my nightly potation and no longer pour into your sympathizing ear my senile gossip, but all the day I muse away, since the sound of your voice no longer rouses me to sympathy with your joys or sorrows. . . . You cannot know how much I miss your affectionate demonstrations."[45] A dozen aging mothers in this sample of over thirty families echoed her sentiments.

Central to these mother-daughter relations is what might be described as an apprenticeship system. In those families where the daughter followed the mother into a life of traditional domesticity, mothers and other older women carefully trained daughters in the arts of housewifery and motherhood. Such training undoubtedly occurred throughout a girl's childhood but became more systematized, almost ritualistic, in the years following the end of her formal education and before her marriage. At this time a girl either returned home from boarding school or no longer divided her time between home and school. Rather, she devoted her energies on two tasks: mastering new domestic skills and participating in the visiting and social activities necessary to finding a husband. Under the careful supervision of their mothers and of older female relatives, such late-adolescent girls temporarily took over the household management from their mothers, tended their young nieces and nephews, and helped in childbirth, nursing, and weaning. Such experiences tied the generations together in shared skills and emotional interaction.[46]

Daughters were born into a female world. Their mother's life expectations and sympathetic network of friends and relations were among the first realities in the life of the developing child. As long as the mother's domestic role remained relatively stable and few viable alternatives competed with it, daughters tended to accept their mother's world and to turn automatically to other women for support and intimacy. It was within this closed and intimate female world that the young girl grew toward womanhood.

One could speculate at length concerning the absence of that mother-daughter hostility today considered almost inevitable to an adolescent's struggle for autonomy and self-identity. It is possible that taboos against female aggression and hostility were sufficiently strong to repress even that between mothers and their adolescent daughters. Yet these letters seem so alive and the interest of daughters in their mothers' affairs so vital and genuine that it is difficult to interpret their closeness exclusively in terms of repression and denial. The functional bonds that held mothers and daughters together in a world that permitted few alternatives to domesticity might well have created a source of mutuality and trust absent in societies where greater options were available for daughters than for mothers. Furthermore, the extended female network—a daughter's close ties with her own older sisters, cousins, and aunts—may well have permitted a diffusion and a relaxation of mother-daughter identification and so have aided a daughter in her struggle for identity and autonomy. None of these explanations are mutually exclusive; all may well have interacted to produce the degree of empathy evident in those letters and diaries.

At some point in adolescence, the young girl began to move outside the matrix of her mother's support group to develop a network of her own. Among the middle class, at least, this transition toward what was at the same time both a limited autonomy and a repetition of her mother's life seemed to have most frequently coincided with a girl's going to school. Indeed education appears to have played a crucial role in the lives of most of the families in this study. Attending school for a few months, for a year or longer, was common even among daughters of relatively poor families, while middle-class girls routinely spent at least a year in boarding school.[47] These school years ordinarily marked a girl's first separation from home. They served to wean the daughter from her home, to train her in the essential social graces, and, ultimately, to help introduce her into the marriage market. It was not infrequently a trying emotional experience for both mother and daughter.[48]

In this process of leaving one home and adjusting to another, the mother's friends and relatives played a key transitional role. Such older women routinely accepted the role of foster mother; they supervised the young girl's deportment, monitored her health and introduced her to their own network of female friends and kin.[49] Not infrequently women, friends from their own school years, arranged to send their daughters to the same school so that the girls might form bonds paralleling those their mothers had made. For years Molly and Helena wrote of their daughters' meeting and worried over each others' children. When Molly finally brought her daughter east to school, their first act on reaching New York was to meet Helena and her daughters. Elizabeth Bordley Gibson virtually adopted the daughters of her school chum, Eleanor Custis Lewis. The Lewis daughters soon began to write Elizabeth Gibson letters with the salutation "Dearest Mama." Eleuthera DuPont, attending boarding school in Philadelphia at roughly the same time as the Lewis girls, developed a parallel relationship with her mother's friend, Elizabeth McKie Smith. Eleuthera went to the same school and became a close friend of the Smith girls and eventually married their first cousin. During this period she routinely called Mrs. Smith "Mother." In-

deed Eleuthera so internalized the sense of having two mothers that she casually wrote her sisters of her "Mamma's" visits at her "mother's" house—that is, at Mrs. Smith's.[50]

Even more important to this process of maturation than their mother's friends were the female friends young women made at school. Young girls helped each other overcome homesickness and endure the crises of adolescence. They gossiped about beaux, incorporated each other into their own kinship systems, and attended and gave teas and balls together. Older girls in boarding school "adopted" younger ones, who called them "Mother."[51] Dear friends might indeed continue this pattern of adoption and mothering throughout their lives; one woman might routinely assume the nurturing role of pseudomother, the other the dependency role of daughter. The pseudomother performed for the other woman all the services which we normally associate with mothers; she went to absurd lengths to purchase items her "daughter" could have obtained from other sources, gave advice and functioned as an idealized figure in her "daughter's" imagination. Helena played such a role for Molly, as did Sarah for Jeannie. Elizabeth Bordley Gibson bought almost all Eleanor Parke Custis Lewis's necessities—from shoes and corset covers to bedding and harp strings—and sent them from Philadelphia to Virginia, a procedure that sometimes took months. Eleanor frequently asked Elizabeth to take back her purchases, have them redone, and argue with shopkeepers about prices. These were favors automatically asked and complied with. Anne Jefferis Sheppard made the analogy very explicitly in a letter to her own mother written shortly after Anne's marriage, when she was feeling depressed about their separation: "Mary Paulen is truly kind, almost acts the part of a mother and trys to aid and *comfort me,* and also to *lighten my new cares.*"[52]

A comparison of the references to men and women in these young women's letters is striking. Boys were obviously indispensable to the elaborate courtship ritual girls engaged in. In these teenage letters and diaries, however, boys appear distant and warded off—an effect produced both by the girls' sense of bonding and by a highly developed and deprecatory whimsy. Girls joked among themselves about the conceit, poor looks, or affectations of suitors. Rarely, especially in the eighteenth and early nineteenth centuries, were favorable remarks exchanged. Indeed, while hostility and criticism of other women were so rare as to seem almost tabooed, young women permitted themselves to express a great deal of hostility toward peer-group men.[53] When unacceptable suitors appeared, girls might even band together to harass them. When one such unfortunate came to court Sophie DuPont she hid in her room, first sending her sister Eleuthera to entertain him and then dispatching a number of urgent notes to her neighboring sister-in-law, cousins, and a visiting friend who all came to Sophie's support. A wild female romp ensued, ending only when Sophie banged into a door, lacerated her nose, and retired, with her female cohorts, to bed. Her brother and the presumably disconcerted suitor were left alone. These were not the antics of teenagers but of women in their early and mid-twenties.[54]

Even if young men were acceptable suitors, girls referred to them formally and obliquely: "The last week I received the unexpected intelligence of the arrival of a friend in Boston," Sarah Ripley wrote in her diary of the young man to whom she had been engaged for years and whom she would shortly marry. Harriet Manigault assiduously kept a lively and gossipy diary during the three years preceding her marriage, yet did not once comment upon her own engagement nor indeed make any personal references to her fiance—who was never identified as such but always referred to as Mr. Wilcox.[55] The point is not that these young women were hostile to young men. Far from it; they sought marriage and domesticity. Yet in

these letters and diaries men appear as an other or out group, segregated into different schools, supported by their own male network of friends and kin, socialized to different behavior, and coached to a proper formality in courtship behavior. As a consequence, relations between young women and men frequently lacked the spontaneity and emotional intimacy that characterized the young girls' ties to each other.

Indeed, in sharp contrast to their distant relations with boys, young women's relations with each other were close, often frolicsome, and surprisingly long lasting and devoted. They wrote secret missives to each other, spent long solitary days with each other, curled up together in bed at night to whisper fantasies and secrets.[56] In 1862 one young woman in her early twenties described one such scene to an absent friend: "I have sat up to midnight listening to the confidences of Constance Kinney whose heart was opened by that most charming of all situations, a seat on a bedside late at night, when all the household are asleep & only oneself & one's confidante survive in wakefulness. So she has told me all her loves and tried to get some confidences in return but being five or six years older than she, I know better. . . ."[57] Elizabeth Bordley and Nelly Parke Custis, teenagers in Philadelphia in the 1790s, routinely secreted themselves until late each night in Nelly's attic, where they each wrote a novel about the other.[58] Quite a few young women kept diaries, and it was a sign of special friendship to show their diaries to each other. The emotional quality of such exchanges emerges from the comments of one young girl who grew up along the Ohio frontier:

> Sisters CW and RT keep diaries & allow me the inestimable pleasure of reading them and in turn they see mine—but O shame covers my face when I think of it; theirs is so much better than mine, that every time. Then I think well now I will burn mine but upon second thought it would deprive me the

pleasure of reading theirs, for I esteem it a very great privilege indeed, as well as very improving, as we lay our hearts open to each other, it heightens our love & helps to cherish & keep alive that sweet soothing friendship and endears us to each other by that soft attraction.[59]

Girls routinely slept together, kissed and hugged each other. Indeed, while waltzing with young men scandalized the otherwise flighty and highly fashionable Harriet Manigault, she considered waltzing with other young women not only acceptable but pleasant.[60]

Marriage followed adolescence. With increasing frequency in the nineteenth century, marriage involved a girl's traumatic removal from her mother and her mother's network. It involved, as well, adjustment to a husband, who, because he was male came to marriage with both a different world view and vastly different experiences. Not surprisingly, marriage was an event surrounded with supportive, almost ritualistic, practices. (Weddings are one of the last female rituals remaining in twentieth-century America.) Young women routinely spent the months preceding their marriage almost exclusively with other women—at neighborhood sewing bees and quilting parties or in a round of visits to geographically distant friends and relatives. Ostensibly they went to receive assistance in the practical preparations for their new home—sewing and quilting a trousseau and linen—but of equal importance, they appear to have gained emotional support and reassurance. Sarah Ripley spent over a month with friends and relatives in Boston and Hingham before her wedding; Parke Custis Lewis exchanged visits with her aunts and first cousins throughout Virginia.[61] Anne Jefferis, who married with some hesitation, spent virtually half a year in endless visiting with cousins, aunts, and friends. Despite their reassurance and support, however, she would not

marry Moses Sheppard until her sister Edith and her cousin Rebecca moved into the groom's home, met his friends, and explored his personality.[62] The wedding did not take place until Edith wrote to Anne: "I can say in truth I am entirely willing thou shouldst follow him even away in the Jersey sands believing if thou are not happy in thy future home it will not be any fault on his part. . . ."[63]

Sisters, cousins, and friends frequently accompanied newlyweds on their wedding night and wedding trip, which often involved additional family visiting. Such extensive visits presumably served to wean the daughter from her family of origin. As such they often contained a note of ambivalence. Nelly Custis, for example, reported homesickness and loneliness on her wedding trip. "I left my Beloved and revered Grandmamma with sincere regret," she wrote Elizabeth Bordley. "It was sometime before I could feel reconciled to traveling without her." Perhaps they also functioned to reassure the young woman herself, and her friends and kin, that though marriage might alter it would not destroy old bonds of intimacy and familiarity.[64]

Married life, too, was structured about a host of female rituals. Childbirth, especially the birth of the first child, became virtually a rite of passage, with a lengthy seclusion of the woman before and after delivery, severe restrictions on her activities, and finally a dramatic reemergence.[65] This seclusion was supervised by mothers, sisters, and loving friends. Nursing and weaning involved the advice and assistance of female friends and relatives. So did miscarriage.[66] Death, like birth, was structured around elaborate unisexed rituals. When Nelly Parke Custis Lewis rushed to nurse her daughter who was critically ill while away at school, Nelly received support, not from her husband, who remained on their plantation, but from her old school friend, Elizabeth Bordley. Elizabeth aided Nelly in caring for her dying daughter, cared for Nelly's other children, played a major role in the elaborate funeral arrangements (which the father did not attend), and frequently visited the girl's grave at the mother's request. For years Elizabeth continued to be the confidante of Nelly's anguished recollections of her lost daughter.

These memories, Nelly's letters make clear, were for Elizabeth alone. "Mr. L. knows nothing of this," was a frequent comment.[67] Virtually every collection of letters and diaries in my sample contained evidence of women turning to each other for comfort when facing the frequent and unavoidable deaths of the eighteenth and nineteenth centuries.[68] While mourning her father's death, Sophie DuPont received elaborate letters and visits of condolence—all from women. No man wrote or visited Sophie to offer sympathy at her father's death.[69] Among rural Pennsylvania Quakers, death and mourning rituals assumed an even more extreme same-sex form, with men or women largely barred from the deathbeds of the other sex. Women relatives and friends slept with the dying woman, nursed her, and prepared her body for burial.[70]

Eighteenth- and nineteenth-century women thus lived in emotional proximity to each other. Friendships and intimacies followed the biological ebb and flow of women's lives. Marriage and pregnancy, childbirth and weaning, sickness and death involved physical and psychic trauma which comfort and sympathy made easier to bear. Intense bonds of love and intimacy bound together those women who, offering each other aid and sympathy, shared such stressful moments.

These bonds were often physical as well as emotional. An undeniably romantic and even sensual note frequently marked female relationships. This theme, significant throughout the stages of a woman's life, surfaced first during adolescence. As one teenager from a struggling pioneer family in the Ohio Valley wrote in her diary in 1808: "I laid with my dear R[ebecca]

and a glorious good talk we had until about 4[A.M.]—O how hard I do *love* her . . . "[71] Only a few years later Bostonian Eunice Callender carved her initials and Sarah Ripley's into a favorite tree, along with a pledge of eternal love, and then waited breathlessly for Sarah to discover and respond to her declaration of affection. The response appears to have been affirmative.[72] A half-century later urbane and sophisticated Katherine Wharton commented upon meeting an old school chum: "She was a great pet of mine at school & I thought as I watched her light figure how often I had held her in my arms—how dear she had once been to me." Katie maintained a long intimate friendship with another girl. When a young man began to court this friend seriously, Katie commented in her diary that she had never realized "how deeply I loved Eng and how fully." She wrote over and over again in that entry: "Indeed I love her!" and only with great reluctance left the city that summer since it meant also leaving Eng with Eng's new suitor.[73]

Peggy Emlen, a Quaker adolescent in Philadelphia in the 1760s, expressed similar feelings about her first cousin, Sally Logan. The girls sent love poems to each other (not unlike the ones Elizabeth Bordley wrote to Nellie Custis a generation later), took long solitary walks together, and even haunted the empty house of the other when one was out of town. Indeed Sally's absences from Philadelphia caused Peggy acute unhappiness. So strong were Peggy's feelings that her brothers began to tease her about her affection for Sally and threatened to steal Sally's letters, much to both girls' alarm. In one letter that Peggy wrote the absent Sally she elaborately described the depth and nature of her feelings: "I have not words to express my impatience to see My Dear Cousin, what would I not give just now for an hours sweet conversation with her, it seems as if I had a thousand things to say to thee, yet when I see thee, everything will be forgot thro' joy. . . . I have a very great friendship for several Girls yet it dont give me so much uneasiness at being absent from them as from thee. . . . [Let us] go and spend a day down at our place together and there unmolested enjoy each others company."[74]

Sarah Alden Ripley, a young, highly educated women, formed a similar intense relationship, in this instance with a woman somewhat older than herself. The immediate bond of friendship rested on their atypically intense scholarly interests, but it soon involved strong emotions, at least on Sarah's part. "Friendship," she wrote Mary Emerson, "is fast twining about her willing captive the silken hands of dependence, a dependence so sweet who would renounce it for the apathy of self-sufficiency?" Subsequent letters became far more emotional, and most conspiratorial. Mary visited Sarah secretly in her room, or the two women crept away from family and friends to meet in a nearby woods. Sarah became jealous of Mary's other young woman friends. Mary's trips away from Boston also thrust Sarah into periods of anguished depression. Interestingly, the letters detailing their love were not destroyed but were preserved and even reprinted in a eulogistic biography of Sarah Alden Ripley.[75]

Tender letters between adolescent women, confessions of loneliness and emotional dependency, were not peculiar to Sarah Alden, Peggy Emlen, or Katie Wharton. They are found throughout the letters of the thirty-five families studied. They have, of course, their parallel today in the musings of many female adolescents. Yet these eighteenth- and nineteenth-century friendships lasted with undiminished, indeed often increased, intensity throughout the women's lives. Sarah Alden Ripley's first child was named after Mary Emerson. Nelly Custis Lewis's love for and dependence on Elizabeth Bordley Gibson only increased after her marriage. Eunice Callender remained enamored of her cousin Sarah Ripley for years and rejected as impossible the suggestion by another woman that their love might some day fade away.[76] Sophie DuPont and her childhood friend, Clementina Smith, exchanged letters filled with love and dependency for forty years while another dear friend, Mary Black Couper, wrote of dreaming that she, Sophie, and her husband were all united in one marriage. Mary's letters to Sophie are filled with avowals of love and indications of ambivalence toward her own husband. Eliza Schlatter, another of Sophie's intimate friends, wrote to her at a time of crisis: "I wish I could be with you present in the body as well as the mind & heartμ—I would turn *your good husband out of bed*—and snuggle into you and we would have a long talk like old times in Pine St.—I want to tell you so many things that are not *writable* . . ."[77]

Such mutual dependency and deep affection is a central existential reality coloring the world of supportive networks and rituals. In the case of Katie, Sophie, or Eunice—as with Molly, Jeannie, and Sarah—their need for closeness and support merged with more intense demands for a love which was at the same time both emotional and sensual. Perhaps the most explicit statement concerning women's lifelong friendships appeared in the letter abolitionist and reformer Mary Grew wrote about the same time, referring to her own love for her dear friend and lifelong companion, Margaret Burleigh. Grew wrote, in response to a letter of condolence from another women on Burleigh's death: "Your words respecting my beloved friend touch me deeply. Evidently . . . you comprehend and appreciate, as few persons do . . . the nature of the relation which existed, which exists, between her and myself. Her only surviving niece . . . also does. To me it seems to have been a closer union than that of most marriages. We know there have been other such between two men and also between two women. And why should there not be. Love is spiritual, only passion is sexual."[78]

How then can we ultimately interpret these long-lived intimate female relationships and integrate them into our understanding of Victorian sexuality? Their ambivalent and romantic rhetoric presents us with an ultimate puzzle: the relationship along the spectrum of human emotions between love, sensuality, and sexuality.

One is tempted, as I have remarked, to compare Molly, Peggy, or Sophie's relationships with the friendships adolescent girls in the twentieth century routinely form—close friendships of great emotional intensity. Helena Deutsch and Clara Thompson have both described these friendships as emotionally necessary to a girl's psychosexual development. But, they warn, such friendships might shade into adolescent and postadolescent homosexuality.[79]

It is possible to speculate that in the twentieth century a number of cultural taboos evolved to cut short the homosocial ties of girlhood and to impel the emerging women of thirteen or fourteen toward heterosexual relationships. In contrast, nineteenth-century American society did not taboo close female relationships but rather recognized them as a socially viable form of human contact—and, as such, acceptable throughout a woman's life. Indeed it was not these homosocial ties that were inhibited but rather heterosexual leanings. While closeness, freedom of emotional expression, and uninhibited physical contact characterized women's relationships with each other, the opposite was frequently true of male-female relationships. One could thus argue that within such a world of female support, intimacy, and ritual it was only to be expected that adult women would turn trustingly and lovingly to each other. It was a behavior they had observed and learned since childhood. A different type of emotional landscape existed in the nineteenth century, one in which Molly and Helena's love became a natural development.

Of perhaps equal significance are the implications we can garner from this framework for the understanding of heterosexual marriages in the nineteenth century. If men and women grew up as they did in relatively homogeneous and segregated sexual groups, then marriage represented a major problem in adjustment. From this perspective we could interpret much of the emotional stiffness and distance that we associate with Victorian marriage as a structural consequence of contemporary sex-role differentiation and gender-role socialization. With marriage both women and men had to adjust to life with a person who was, in essence, a member of an alien group.

I have thus far substituted a cultural or psychosocial for a psychosexual interpretation of women's emotional bonding. But there are psychosexual implications in this model which I think it only fair to make more explicit. Despite Sigmund Freud's insistence on the bisexuality of us all or the recent American Psychiatric Association decision on homosexuality, many psychiatrists today tend explicitly or implicitly to view homosexuality as a totally alien or pathological behavior—as totally unlike heterosexuality. I suspect that in essence they may have adopted an explanatory model similar to the one used in discussing schizophrenia. As a psychiatrist can speak of schizophrenia and of a borderline schizophrenic personality as both ultimately and fundamentally different from a normal or neurotic personality, so they also think of both homosexuality and latent homosexuality as states totally different from heterosexuality. With this rapidly dichotomous model of assumption, "latent homosexuality" becomes the indication of a disease in progress—seeds of a pathology which belie the reality of an individual's heterosexuality.

Yet at the same time we are well aware that cultural values can affect choices in the gender of a person's sexual partner. We, for instance, do not necessarily consider homosexual-object choice among men in prison, on shipboard, or in boarding schools a necessary indication of pathology. I would urge that we expand this relativistic model and hypothesize that a number of cultures might well tolerate or even encourage diversity in sexual and nonsexual relations. Based on my research into this nineteenth-century world of female intimacy, I would further suggest that rather than seeing a gulf between the normal and the abnormal we view sexual and emotional impulses as part of a continuum or spectrum. I would like to suggest that the nineteenth century was such a cultural environment. That is, the supposedly repressive and destructive Victorian sexual ethos may have been more flexible and responsive to the needs of particular individuals than those of mid-twentieth century.

NOTES

1. The most notable exception to this rule is now eleven years old: William R. Taylor and Christopher Lasch, "Two 'Kindred Spirits': Sorority and Family in New England, 1839–1846," *New England Quarterly* 36 (1963): 241. Taylor has made a valuable contribution to the history of women and the history of the family with his concept of "sororial" relations. I do not, however, accept the Taylor-Lasch thesis that female friendships developed in the mid-nineteenth century because of geographic mobility and the breakup of the colonial family. I have found these friendships as frequently in the eighteenth century as in the nineteenth and would hypothesize that the geographic mobility of the mid-nineteenth century eroded them as it did so many other traditional social institutions. Helen Vendler (Review of *Notable American Women, 1607–1950,* ed. Edward James and Janet James, *New York Times* [November 5, 1972]: sec. 7) points out the significance of these friendships.

2. I do not wish to deny the importance of women's relations with particular men. Obviously, women were close to brothers, husbands, fathers, and sons. However, there is evidence that despite such closeness, relationships between men and women differed in both emotional texture and frequency from those between women. Women's relations with each other, although they played a central role in the American family and American society, have been so seldom examined either by general social historians or by historians of the family that I wish in this article simply to examine their nature and analyze their implications for our understanding of social relations and social structure. I have discussed some aspects of male-female relationships in two articles: "Puberty to Menopause: The Cycle of Femininity in Nineteenth-Century America," *Feminist Studies* 1 (1973): 572, and, with Charles Rosenberg, "The Female Animal: Medical and Biological Views of Women in 19th Century America," *Journal of American History* 59 (1973): 331–356.

3. See Freud's classic paper on homosexuality, "Three Essays on the Theory of Sexuality," in *The Standard Edition of the Complete Psychological Works of Sigmund Freud,* trans. James Strachey (London: Hogarth Press, 1953), 7:135–172. The essays originally appeared in 1905. Prof. Roy Shafer, Department of Psychiatry, Yale University, has pointed out that Freud's view of sexual behavior was strongly influenced by nineteenth-century evolutionary thought. Within Freud's schema, genital heterosexuality marked the height of human development (Schafer, "Problems in Freud's Psychology of Women," *Journal of the American Psychoanalytic Association* 22 [1974]: 459–485).

4. For a novel and most important exposition of one theory of behavioral norms and options and its application to the study of human sexuality, see Charles Rosenberg, "Sexuality, Class and Role," *American Quarterly* 25 (1973): 131–153.

5. See, e.g., the letters of Peggy Emlen to Sally Logan, 1768–72, Wells Morris Collection, Box I, Historical Society of Pennsylvania; and the Eleanor Parke Custis Lewis Letters Historical Society of Pennsylvania, Philadelphia.

6. Sarah Butler Wister was the daughter of Fanny Kemble and Pierce Butler. In 1859 she married

a Philadelphia physician, Owen Wister. The novelist Owen Wister is her son. Jeannie Field Musgrove was the half-orphaned daughter of constitutional lawyer and New York Republican politician David Dudley Field. Their correspondence (1855–1898) is in the Sarah Butler Wister Papers, Wister Family Papers, Historical Society of Pennsylvania.

7. Sarah Butler, Butler Place, S.C., to Jeannie Field, New York, September 14, 1855.

8. See, e.g., Sarah Butler Wister, Germantown, Pa., to Jeannie Field, New York, September 25, 1862, October 21, 1863; or Jeannie Field, New York, to Sarah Butler Wister, Germantown, July 3, 1861, January 23 and July 12, 1863.

9. Sarah Butler Wister, Germantown, to Jeannie Field, New York, June 5, 1861, February 29, 1864; Jeannie Field to Sarah Butler Wister November 22, 1861, January 4 and June 14, 1863.

10. Sarah Butler Wister, London, to Jeannie Field Musgrove, New York, June 18 and August 3, 1870.

11. See, e.g., two of Sarah's letters to Jeannie: December 21, 1873, July 16, 1878.

12. This is the 1868–1920 correspondence between Mary Hallock Foote and Helena, a New York friend (the Mary Hallock Foote Papers are in the Manuscript Division, Stanford University). Wallace E. Stegner has written a fictionalized biography of Mary Hallock Foote (*Angle of Repose* [Garden City, N.Y.: Doubleday & Co., 1971]). See, as well, her autobiography: Mary Hallock Foote, *A Victorian Gentlewoman in the Far West: The Reminiscences of Mary Hallock Foote,* ed. Rodman W. Paul (San Marino, Calif.: Huntington Library, 1972). In many ways these letters are typical of those women wrote to other women. Women frequently began letters to each other with salutations such as "Dearest," "My Most Beloved," "You Darling Girl," and signed them "tenderly" or "to my dear dear sweet friend, good-bye." Without the least self-consciousness, one woman in her frequent letters to a female friend referred to her

husband as "my other love." She was by no means unique. See, e.g., Annie to Charlene Van Vleck Anderson, Appleton, Wis., June 10, 1871, Anderson Family Papers, Manuscript Division, Stanford University; Maggie to Emily Howland, Philadelphia, July 12, 1851, Howland Family Papers, Phoebe King Collection, Friends Historical Library, Swarthmore College; Mary Jane Burleigh to Emily Howland, Sherwood, N.Y., March 27, 1872, Howland Family Papers, Sophia Smith Collection, Smith College; Mary Black Couper to Sophia Madeleine DuPont, Wilmington, Del.: n.d. [1834] (two letters), Samuel Francis DuPont Papers, Eleutherian Mills Foundation, Wilmington, Del.; Phoebe Middleton, Concordiville, Pa., to Martha Jefferis, Chester County, Pa., February 22, 1848; and see in general the correspondence (1838–1849) between Rebecca Biddle of Philadelphia and Martha Jefferis, Chester County, Pa., Jefferis Family Correspondence, Chester County Historical Society, West Chester Pennsylvania; Phoebe Bradford Diary, June 7 and July 13, 1832, Historical Society of Pennsylvania; Sarah Alden Ripley, to Abba Allyn, Boston, n.d. [1818–1820], and Sarah Alden Ripley, to Sophia Bradford, November 30, 1854, in the Sarah Alden Ripley Correspondence, Schlesinger Library, Radcliffe College; Fanny Canby Ferris to Anne Biddle, Philadelphia, October 11 and November 19, 1811, December 26, 1813, Fanny Canby to Mary Canby, May 27, 1801, Mary R. Garrigues to Mary Canby, five letters n.d., [1802–1808], Anne Biddle to Mary Canby, two letters n.d., May 16, July 13, and November 24, 1806, June 14, 1807, June 5, 1808, Anne Sterling Biddle Family Papers, Friends Historical Society, Swarthmore College; Harriet Manigault Wilcox Diary, August 7, 1814, Historical Society of Pennsylvania. See as well the correspondence between Harriet Manigault Wilcox's mother, Mrs. Gabriel Manigault, Philadelphia, and Mrs. Henry Middleton, Charleston, S.C., between 1810 and 1830, Cadwalader Collection, J. Francis Fisher Section, Historical Society of Pennsylvania. The basis and nature of such friendships can be seen in the comments of Sarah Alden Ripley to her sister-in-law and long-time friend, Sophia Bradford: "Hearing that you are not well reminds me of what it would be to lose your loving society. We have kept step together through a long piece of road in the weary journey of life. We have loved the same beings and wept together over their graves" (Mrs. O. J. Wister and Miss Agnes Irwin, eds., *Worthy Women of Our First Century* [Philadelphia: J. B. Lippincott & Co., 1877], p. 195).

13. Mary Hallock [Foote] to Helena, n.d. [1869–1870], n.d. [1871–1872], Folder 1, Mary Hallock Foote Letters, Manuscript Division, Stanford University.

14. Mary Hallock [Foote] to Helena, September 15 and 23, 1873, n.d. [October 1873], October 12, 1873.

15. Mary Hallock [Foote] to Helena, n.d. [January 1874], n.d. [Spring 1874].

16. Mary Hallock [Foote] to Helena, September 23, 1873; Mary Hallock [Foote] to Richard, December 13, 1873. Molly's and Helena's relationship continued for the rest of their lives. Molly's letters are filled with tender and intimate references, as when she wrote, twenty years later and from 2,000 miles away: "It isn't because you are good that I love you—but for the essence of you which is like perfume" (n.d. [1890s?]).

17. I am in the midst of a larger study of adult gender-roles and gender-role socialization in America, 1785–1895. For a discussion of social attitudes toward appropriate male and female roles, see Barbara Welter, "The Cult of True Womanhood: 1820–1860," *American Quarterly* 18 (Summer 1966): 151–174; Ann Firor Scott, *The Southern Lady: From Pedestal to Politics,* 1830–1930 (Chicago: University of Chicago Press, 1970), chaps. 1–2; Smith-Rosenberg and Rosenberg.

18. See, e.g., the letters of Peggy Emlen to Sally Logan, 1768–1772, Wells Morris Collection, Box 1, Historical Society of Pennsylvania; and the Eleanor Parke Custis Lewis letters, Historical Society of Pennsylvania.

19. See esp. Elizabeth Botts, *Family and Social Network* (London: Tavistock Publications, 1957); Michael Young and Peter Willmott, *Family Kinship in East London*, rev. ed. (Baltimore: Penguin Books, 1964).

20. This pattern seemed to cross class barriers. A letter that an Irish domestic wrote in the 1830s contains seventeen separate references to women but only seven to men, most of whom were relatives and two of whom were infant brothers living with her mother and mentioned in relation to her mother (Ann McGrann, Philadelphia, to Sophie M. DuPont, Philadelphia, July 3, 1834, Sophie Madeleine DuPont Letters, Eleutherian Mills Foundation).

21. Harriett Manigault Diary, June 28, 1814, and passim; Jeannie Field, New York, to Sarah Butler Wister, Germantown, April 19, 1863; Phoebe Bradford Diary, January 30, February 19, March 4, August 11, and October 14, 1832, Historical Society of Pennsylvania; Sophie M. DuPont, Brandywine, to Henry DuPont, Germantown, July 9, 1827, Eleutherian Mills Foundation.

22. Martha Jefferis to Anne Jefferis Sheppard, July 9, 1843; Anne Jefferis Sheppard to Martha Jefferis, June 28, 1846; Anne Sterling Biddle Papers, passim, Biddle Family Papers, Friends Historical Society, Swarthmore College; Eleanor Parke Custis Lewis, Virginia, to Elizabeth Bordley Gibson, Philadelphia, November 24 and December 4, 1820, November 6, 1821.

23. Phoebe Bradford Diary, January 13, November 16–19, 1832, April 26 and May 7, 1833; Abigail Brackett Lyman to Mrs. Catling, Litchfield, Conn., May 3, 1801, collection in private hands; Martha Jefferis to Anne Jefferis Sheppard, August 28, 1845.

24. Lisa Mitchell Diary, 1860s, passim, Manuscript Division, Tulane University; Eleanor Parke

Custis Lewis to Elizabeth Bordley [Gibson] February 5, 1822; Jeannie McCall, Cedar Park, to Peter McCall, Philadelphia, June 30, 1849, McCall Section, Cadwalader Collection, Historical Society of Pennsylvania.

25. Peggy Emlen to Sally Logan, May 3, 1769.

26. For a prime example of this type of letter, see Eleanor Parke Custis Lewis to Elizabeth Bordley Gibson, passim, or Fanny Canby to Mary Canby, Philadelphia, May 27, 1801; or Sophie M. DuPont, Brandywine, to Henry DuPont, Germantown, February 4, 1832.

27. Place of residence is not the only variable significant in characterizing family structure. Strong emotional ties and frequent visiting and correspondence can unite families that do not live under one roof. Demographic studies based on household structure alone fail to reflect such emotional and even economic ties between families.

28. Eleanor Parke Custis Lewis to Elizabeth Bordley Gibson, April 20 and September 25, 1848.

29. Maria Inskeep to Fanny Hampton Correspondence, 1823–1860, Inskeep Collection, Tulane University Library.

30. Eunice Callender, Boston, to Sarah Ripley [Stearnsl, September 24 and October 29, 1803, February 16, 1805, April 29 and October 9, 1806, May 26, 1810.

31. Sophie DuPont filled her letters to her younger brother Henry (with whom she had been assigned to correspond while he was at boarding school) with accounts of family visiting (see, e.g., December 13, 1827, January 10 and March 9, 1828, February 4 and March 10, 1832; also Sophie M. DuPont to Victorine DuPont Bauday, September 26 and December 4, 1827, February 22, 1828; Sophie M. DuPont, Brandywine, to Clementina B. Smith, Philadelphia, January 15, 1830; Eleuthera DuPont, Brandywine, to Victorine DuPont Bauday, Philadelphia, April 17, 1821, October 20,1826; Evelina DuPont [Biderman] to Victorine DuPont Bauday, October 18, 1816).

Other examples, from the Historical Society of Pennsylvania, are Harriet Manigault [Wilcox] Diary, August 17, September 8, October 19 and 22, December 22, 1814; Jane Zook, Westtown School, Chester County, Pa., to Mary Zook, November 13, December 7 and 11, 1870, February 26, 1871; Eleanor Parke Custis [Lewis] to Elizabeth Bordley [Gibson], March 30, 1796, February 7 and March 20, 1798; Jeannie McCall to Peter McCall, Philadelphia, November 12, 1847; Mary B. Ashew Diary, July 11 and 13, August 17, Summer and October 1858, and, from a private collection, Edith Jefferis to Anne Jefferis Sheppard, November 1841, April 5, 1842; Abigail Brackett Lyman, Northampton, Mass., to Mrs. Catling, Litchfield, Conn., May 13, 1801; Abigail Brackett Lyman, Northampton, to Mary Lord, August 11, 1800. Mary Hallock Foote vacationed with her sister, her sister's children, her aunt, and a female cousin in the summer of 1874; cousins frequently visited the Hallock farm in Milton, N.Y. In later years Molly and her sister Bessie set up a joint household in Boise, Idaho (Mary Hallock Foote to Helena, July [1874?] and passim). Jeannie Field, after initially disliking her sister-in-law, Laura, became very close to her, calling her "my little sister" and at times spending virtually every day with her (Jeannie Field [Musgrove] New York, to Sarah Butler Wister, Germantown, March 1, 8, and 15, and May 9, 1863).

32. Martha Jefferis to Anne Jefferis Sheppard, January 12, 1845; Phoebe Middleton to Martha Jefferis, February 22, 1848. A number of other women remained close to sisters and sisters-in-law across a long lifetime (Phoebe Bradford Diary, June 7, 1832, and Sarah Alden Ripley to Sophia Bradford, cited in Wister and Irwin, p. 195).

33. Rebecca Biddle to Martha Jefferis, 1838–1849, passim; Martha Jefferis to Anne Jefferis Sheppard, July 6, 1846; Anne Jefferis Sheppard to Rachael Jefferis, January 16, 1865; Sarah

Foulke Farquhar [Emlen] Diary, September 22, 1813, Friends Historical Library, Swarthmore College; Mary Garrigues to Mary Canby [Biddle], 1802–1808, passim; Anne Biddle to Mary Canby [Biddle], May 16, July 13, and November 24, 1806, June 14, 1807, June 5, 1808.

34. Sarah Alden Ripley to Abba Allyn, n.d., Schlesinger Library.

35. Phoebe Bradford Diary, July 13, 1832.

36. Mary Hallock [Foote] to Helena, December 23 [1868 or 1867]; Phoebe Bradford Diary, December 8, 1832; Martha Jefferis and Anne Jefferis Sheppard letters, passim.

37. Martha Jefferis to Anne Jefferis Sheppard, August 3, 1849; Sarah Ripley [Stearns] Diary, November 12, 1808, January 8, 1811. An interesting note of hostility or rivalry is present in Sarah Ripley's diary entry. Sarah evidently deeply resented the husband's rapid remarriage.

38. Martha Jefferis to Edith Jefferis, March 15, 1841; Mary Hallock Foote to Helena, n.d. [1874–75?]; see also Jeannie Field, New York, to Sarah Butler Wister, Germantown, May 5, 1863, Emily Howland Diary, December 1879, Howland Family Papers.

39. Anne Jefferis Sheppard to Martha Jefferis, September 29, 1841.

40. Frances Parke Lewis to Elizabeth Bordley Gibson, April 29, 1821.

41. Mary Jane Burleigh, Mount Pleasant, S.C., to Emily Howland, Sherwood N.Y., March 27, 1872, Howland Family Papers; Emily Howland Diary, September 16, 1879, January 21 and 23, 1880; Mary Black Couper, New Castle, Del., to Sophie M. DuPont, Brandywine, April 7, 1834.

42. Harriet Manigault Diary, August 15, 21, and 23, 1814, Historical Society of Pennsylvania; Polly [Simmons] to Sophie Madeleine DuPont, February 1822; Sophie Madeleine DuPont to Victorine Bauday, December 4, 1827; Sophie Madeleine DuPont to Clementina Beach Smith, July 24, 1828, August 19, 1829; Clementina Beach Smith to Sophie Madeleine DuPont, April 29, 1831; Mary Black Couper to

Sophie Madeleine DuPont, December 24, 1828, July 21, 1834. This pattern appears to have crossed class lines. When a former Sunday school student of Sophie DuPont's (and the daughter of a worker in her father's factory) wrote to Sophie, she discussed her mother's health and activities quite naturally (Ann McGrann to Sophie Madeleine DuPont, August 25, 1832; see also Elizabeth Bordley to Martha, n.d. [1797], Eleanor Parke Custis [Lewis] to Elizabeth Bordley [Gibson], May 13, 1796, July 1, 1798; Peggy Emlen to Sally Logan, January 8, 1786. All but the Emlen/ Logan letters are in the Eleanor Parke Custis Lewis Correspondence, Historical Society of Pennsylvania).

43. Mrs. S. S. Dalton, "Autobiography" (Circle Valley, Utah, 1876), pp. 21–22, Bancroft Library, University of California, Berkeley; Sarah Foulke Emlen Diary, April 1809; Louisa C. Van Vleck, Appleton, Wis., to Charlena Van Vleck Anderson, Cottingen, n.d. 1875; Harriet Manigault Diary, August 16, 1814, July 14, 1815; Sarah Alden Ripley to Sophy Fisher [early 1860s], quoted in Wister and Irwin (n. 12 above), p. 212. The Jefferis family papers are filled with empathetic letters between Martha and her daughters, Anne and Edith. See, e.g., Martha Jefferis to Edith Jefferis, December 26, 1836, March 11, 1837, March 15, 1841; Anne Jefferis Sheppard to Martha Jefferis, March 17, 1841, January 17, 1847; Martha Jefferis to Anne Jefferis Sheppard, April 17, 1848, April 30, 1849. A representative letter is this of March 9, 1837 from Edith to Martha: "My heart can fully respond to the language of my own precious Mother, that absence has not diminished our affection for each other, but has, if possible, strengthened the bonds that have united us together & I have had to remark how we had been permitted to mingle in sweet fellowship and have been strengthened to bear one another's burdens. . . ."

44. Abigail Brackett Lyman, Boston, to Mrs. Abigail Brackett (daughter to mother), n.d.

[1797], June 3, 1800; Sarah Alden Ripley wrote weekly to her daughter, Sophy Ripley Fisher, after the latter's marriage (Sarah Alden Ripley Correspondence, passim); Phoebe Bradford Diary, February 25, 1833, passim, 1832–33; Louisa C. Van Vleck to Charlena Van Vleck Anderson, December 15, 1873, July 4, August 15 and 29, September 19, and November 9, 1875. Eleanor Parke Custis Lewis's long correspondence with Elizabeth Bordley Gibson contains evidence of her anxiety at leaving her foster mother's home at various times during her adolescence and at her marriage, and her own longing for her daughters, both of whom had married and moved to Louisiana (Eleanor Parke Custis [Lewis] to Elizabeth Bordley [Gibson], October 13, 1795, November 4, 1799, passim, 1820s and 1830s). Anne Jefferis Sheppard experienced a great deal of anxiety on moving two days' journey from her mother at the time of her marriage. This loneliness and sense of isolation persisted through her marriage until, finally a widow, she returned to live with her mother (Anne Jefferis Sheppard to Martha Jefferis, April 1841, October 16, 1842, April 2, May 22, and October 12, 1844, September 3, 1845, January 17, 1847, May 16, June 3, and October 31, 1849; Anne Jefferis Sheppard to Susanna Lightfoot, March 23, 1845, and to Joshua Jefferis, May 14, 1854). Daughters evidently frequently slept with their mothers—into adulthood (Harriet Manigault [Wilcoxl Diary, February 19, 1815; Eleanor Parke Custis Lewis to Elizabeth Bordley Gibson, October 10, 1832). Daughters also frequently asked mothers to live with them and professed delight when they did so. See, e.g., Sarah Alden Ripley's comments to George Simmons, October 6, 1844, in Wister and Irwin, p. 185: "It is no longer 'Mother and Charles came out one day and returned the next,' for mother is one of us: she has entered the penetratice, been initiated into the mystery of the household gods, . . . Her divertissement is to mend the stockings . . . whiten sheets and napkins, . . . and take a stroll at evening with me to talk of our children, to compare our experiences, what we have learned and what we have suffered, and, last of all, to complete with pears and melons the cheerful circle about the solar lamp. . . ." We did find a few exceptions to this mother-daughter felicity (M. B. Ashew Diary, November 19, 1857, April 10 and May 17, 1858). Sarah Foulke Emlen was at first very hostile to her stepmother (Sarah Foulke Emlen Diary, August 9, 1807), but they later developed a warm supportive relationship.

45. Sarah Alden Ripley to Sophy Thayer, n.d. [1861].

46. Mary Hallock Foote to Helena [winter 1873] (no. 52); Jossie, Stevens Point, Wis., to Charlena Van Vleck [Anderson], Appleton, Wis., October 24, 1870; Pollie Chandler, Green Bay, Wis., to Charlena Van Vleck [Anderson], Appleton, n.d. [1870]; Eleuthera DuPont to Sophie DuPont, September 5, 1829; Sophie DuPont to Eleuthera DuPont, December 1827; Sophie DuPont to Victorine Bauday, December 4, 1827; Mary Gilpin to Sophie DuPont, September 26, 1827; Sarah Ripley Stearns Diary, April 2, 1809; Jeannie McCall to Peter McCall, October 27 [late 1840s]. Eleanor Parke Custis Lewis's correspondence with Elizabeth Bordley Gibson describes such an apprenticeship system over two generations— that of her childhood and that of her daughters. Indeed Eleanor Lewis's own apprenticeship was quite formal. She was deliberately separated from her foster mother in order to spend a winter of domesticity with her married sisters and her remarried mother. It was clearly felt that her foster mother's (Martha Washington) home at the nation's capital was not an appropriate place to develop domestic talents (October 13, 1795, March 30, May 13, and [summer] 1796, March 18 and April 27, 1797, October 1827).

47. Education was not limited to the daughters of the well-to-do. Sarah Foulke Emlen, the daughter of an Ohio Valley frontier farmer, for

instance, attended day school for several years during the early 1800s. Sarah Ripley Stearns, the daughter of a shopkeeper in Greenfield, Mass., attended a boarding school for but three months, yet the experience seemed very important to her. Mrs. S. S. Dalton, a Mormon woman from Utah, attended a series of poor country schools and greatly valued her opportunity, though she also expressed a great deal of guilt for the sacrifices her mother made to make her education possible (Sarah Foulke Emlen Journal, Sarah Ripley Stearns Diary, Mrs. S. S. Dalton, "Autobiography").

48. Maria Revere to her mother [Mrs. Paul Revere], June 13, 1801, Paul Revere Papers, Massachusetts Historical Society. In a letter to Elizabeth Bordley Gibson, March 28, 1847, Eleanor Parke Custis Lewis from Virginia discussed the anxiety her daughter felt when her granddaughters left home to go to boarding school. Eleuthera DuPont was very homesick when away at school in Philadelphia in the early 1820s (Eleuthera DuPont, Philadelphia, to Victorine Bauday, Wilmington, Del., April 7, 1821; Eleuthera DuPont to Sophie Madeleine DuPont, Wilmington Del., February and April 3, 1821).

49. Elizabeth Bordley Gibson, a Philadelphia matron, played such a role for the daughters and nieces of her lifelong friend, Eleanor Parke Custis Lewis, a Virginia planter's wife (Eleanor Parke Custis Lewis to Elizabeth Bordley Gibson, January 29, 1833, March 19, 1826, and passim through the collection). The wife of Thomas Gurney Smith played a similar role for Sophie and Eleuthera DuPont (see, e.g., Eleuthera DuPont to Sophie Madeleine DuPont, May 22, 1825; Rest Cope to Philema P. Swayne [niece], West Town School, Chester County, Pa., April 8, 1829, Friends Historical Library, Swarthmore College). For a view of such a social pattern over three generations, see the letters and diaries of three generations of Manigault women in Philadelphia: Mrs. Gabrielle Manigault, her daughter, Harriet Manigault Wilcox, and granddaughter, Charlotte Wilcox McCall.

Unfortunately the papers of the three women are not in one family collection (Mrs. Henry Middleton, Charleston, S.C., to Mrs. Gabrielle Manigault, n.d. [mid 1800s]; Harriet Manigault Diary, vol. I; December 1, 1813, June 28, 1814; Charlotte Wilcox McCall Diary, vol. 1, 1842, passim. All in Historical Society of Philadelphia).

50. Frances Parke Lewis, Woodlawn, Va., to Elizabeth Bordley Gibson, Philadelphia, April 11, 1821, Lewis Correspondence; Eleuthera DuPont, Philadelphia, to Victorine DuPont Bauday, Brandywine, December 8, 1821, January 31, 1822; Eleuthera DuPont, Brandywine, to Margaretta Lammont [DuPont], Philadelphia, May 1823.

51. Sarah Ripley Stearns Diary, March 9 and 25, 1810; Peggy Emlen to Sally Logan, March and July 4, 1769; Harriet Manigault [Wilcox] Diary, vol. I, December 1, 1813, June 28 and September 18, 1814, August 10, 1815; Charlotte Wilcox McCall Diary, 1842, passim; Fanny Canby to Mary Canby, May 27, 1801, March 17, 1804; Deborah Cope, West Town School, to Rest Cope, Philadelphia, July 9, 1828, Chester County Historical Society, West Chester, Pa.; Anne Zook, West Town School, to Mary Zook, Philadelphia, January 30, 1866, Chester County Historical Society, West Chester, Pa.; Mary Gilpin to Sophie Madeleine DuPont, February 25, 1829; Eleanor Parke Custis [Lewis] to Elizabeth Bordley [Gibson], April 27, July 2, and September 8, 1797, June 30, 1799, December 29, 1820; Frances Parke Lewis to Elizabeth Bordley Gibson, December 20, 1820.

52. Anne Jefferis Sheppard to Martha Jefferis, March 17, 1841.

53. Peggy Emlen to Sally Logan, March 1769, Mount Vernon, Va.; Eleanor Parke Custis [Lewis] to Elizabeth Bordley [Gibson], Philadelphia, April 27, 1797, June 30, 1799; Jeannie Field, New York, to Sarah Butler Wister, Germantown, July 3, 1861, January 16, 1863, Harriet Manigault Diary, August 3 and

11–13, 1814; Eunice Callender, Boston, to Sarah Ripley [Stearns], Greenfield, May 4, 1809. I found one exception to this inhibition of female hostility. This was the diary of Charlotte Wilcox McCall, Philadelphia (see, e.g., her March 23, 1842 entry).

54. Sophie M. DuPont and Eleuthera DuPont, Brandywine, to Victorine DuPont Bauday, Philadelphia, January 25, 1832.

55. Sarah Ripley [Stearns] Diary and Harriet Manigault Diary, passim.

56. Sophie Madeleine DuPont to Eleuthera DuPont, December 1827; Clementina Beach Smith to Sophie Madeleine DuPont, December 26, 1828; Sarah Faulke Emlen Diary, July 21, 1808, March 30, 1809; Annie Hethroe, Ellington, Wis., to Charlena Van Vleck [Anderson], Appleton, Wis., April 23, 1865; Frances Parke Lewis, Woodlawn, Va., to Elizabeth Bordley [Gibson], Philadelphia, December 20, 1820; Fanny Ferris to Debby Ferris, West Town School, Chester County, Pa., May 29, 1826. An excellent example of the warmth of women's comments about each other and the reserved nature of their references to men are seen in two entries in Sarah Ripley Stearn's diary. On January 8, 1811 she commented about a young woman friend: "The amiable Mrs. White of Princeton . . . one of the loveliest most interesting creatures I ever knew, young fair and blooming . . . beloved by everyone . . . formed to please & to charm." She referred to the man she ultimately married always as "my friend" or "a friend" (February 2 or April 23, 1810).

57. Jeannie Field, New York, to Sarah Butler Wister, Germantown, April 6, 1862.

58. Elizabeth Bordley Gibson, introductory statement to the Eleanor Parke Custis Lewis Letters [1850s], Historical Society of Pennsylvania.

59. Sarah Foulke [Emlen] Diary, March 30, 1809.

60. Harriet Manigault Diary, May 26, 1815.

61. Sarah Ripley [Stearns] Diary, May 17 and October 2, 1812; Eleanor Parke Custis Lewis to Elizabeth Bordley Gibson, April 23, 1826; Rebecca Ralston, Philadelphia, to Victorine DuPont [Bauday], Brandywine, September 27, 1813.

62. Anne Jefferis to Martha Jefferis, November 22 and 27, 1840, January 13 and March 17, 1841; Edith Jefferis, Greenwich, N.J., to Anne Jefferis, Philadelphia, January 31, February 6 and February 1841.

63. Edith Jefferis to Anne Jefferis, January 31, 1841.

64. Eleanor Parke Custis Lewis to Elizabeth Bordley, November 4, 1799. Eleanor and her daughter Parke experienced similar sorrow and anxiety when Parke married and moved to Cincinnati (Eleanor Parke Custis Lewis to Elizabeth Bordley Gibson, April 23, 1826). Helena DeKay visited Mary Hallock the month before her marriage; Mary Hallock was an attendant at the wedding; Helena again visited Molly about three weeks after her marriage; and then Molly went with Helena and spent a week with Helena and Richard in heir new apartment (Mary Hallock [Foote] to Helena DeKay Gilder [Spring 1874 (no. 61), May 10, 1874 [May 1874], June 14, 1874 [Summer 1874]. See also Anne Biddle, Philadelphia, to Clement Biddle (brother), Wilmington, March 12 and May 27, 1827, Eunice Callender, Boson, to Sarah Ripley [Stearns], Creenfield, Mass., August 3, 1807, January 26, 1808; Victorine DuPont Bauday, Philadelphia, to Evelina DuPont [Biderman], Brandywine, November 25 and 26, December 1, 1813; Peggy Emlen to Sally Logan, n.d. [1769–70?];Jeannie Field, New York, to Sarah Butler Wister, Germantown, July 3, 1861).

65. Mary Hallock to Helena DeKay Gilder [1876] (no. 81); n.d. (no. 83), March 3, 1884; Mary Ashew Diary, vol. 2, September–January, 1860; Louisa Van Vleck to Charlena Van Vleck Anderson, n.d. [1875]; Sophie DuPont to Henry DuPont, July 24, 1827; Benjamin Ferris to William Canby, February 13,1805; Benjamin Ferris to Mary Canby Biddle

December 20, 1825; Anne Jefferis Sheppard to Martha Jefferis, September 15, 1884, Martha Jefferis to Anne Jefferis Sheppard, July 4, 1843, May 5, 1844, May 3, 1847, July 17, 1849; Jeannie McCall to Peter McCall, November 26, 1847, n.d. [late 1840s]. A graphic description of the ritual surrounding a first birth is found in Abigail Lyman's letter to her husband, Erastus Lyman, October 18, 1810.

66. Fanny Ferris to Anne Biddle, November 19, 1811; Eleanor Parke Custis Lewis to Elizabeth Bordley Gibson, November 4, 1799, April 27, 1827; Martha Jefferis to Anne Jefferis Sheppard, January 31, 1843, April 4, 1844; Martha Jefferis to Phoebe Sharpless Middleton, June 4, 1846: Anne Jefferis Sheppard to Martha Jefferis, August 20, 1843, February 12, 1844; Maria Inskeep, New Orleans, to Mrs. Fanny C. Hampton, Bridgeton, N.J., September 22, 1848; Benjamin Ferris to Mary Canby, February 14, 1805; Fanny Ferris to Mary Canhy [Biddle], December 2, 1816.

67. Eleanor Parke Custis Lewis to Elizabeth Bordley Gibson, October-November 1820, passim.

68. Emily Howland to Hannah, September 30,1866; Emily Howland Diary, February 8, 14, and 27, 1880; Phoebe Brandford Diary, April 12 and 13, and August 4, 1833; Eunice Callender, Boston, to Sarah Ripley [Stearns], Greenwich, Mass., September 11, 1802, August 26, 1810; Mrs. H. Middleton, Charleston, to Mrs. Gabrielle Manigault, Philadelphia, n.d. [mid 1800s]; Mrs. H. C. Paul to Mrs. Jeannie McCall, Philadelphia, n.d. [1840s]; Sarah Butler Wister, Germantown, to Jeannie Field [Musgrove], New York, April 22, 1864, Jeannie Field [Musgrove] to Sarah Butler Wister, August 25, 1861, July 6, 1862; S. B. Raudolph to Elizabeth Bordley [Gibson], n.d. [1790s]. For an example of similar letters between men, see Henry Wright to Peter McCall, December 10, 1852; Charles McCall to Peter McCall, January 4, 1860, March 22, 1864; R. Mercer to Peter McCall, November 29, 1872.

69. Mary Black [Couper] to Sophie Madeleine DuPont, February 1827, [November 1, 1834], November 12, 1834, two letters [late November 1834]; Eliza Schlatter to Sophie Madeleine DuPont, November 2, 1834.

70. For a few of the references to death rituals in the Jefferis papers see: Martha Jefferis to Anne Jefferis Sheppard, September 28, 1843, August 21 and September 25, 1844, January 11, 1846, summer 1848, passim; Anne Jefferis Sheppard to Martha Jefferis, August 20, 1843; Anne Jefferis Sheppard to Rachel Jefferis, March 17, 1863, February 9, 1868. For other Quaker families, see Rachel Biddle to Anne Biddle, July 23, 1854; Sarah Foulke Farquhar [Emlen] Diary, April 30, 1811, February 14, 1812; Fanny Ferris to Mary Canhy August 31, 1810. This is not to argue that men and women did not mourn together. Yet in many families women aided and comforted women and men, men. The same-sex death ritual was one emotional option available to nineteenth-century Americans.

71. Sarah Foulke [Emlen] Diary, December 29, 1808.

72. Eunice Callender, Boston, to Sarah Ripley [Stearns] Greenfield, Mass., May 24, 1803.

73. Katherine Johnstone Brinley [Wharton] Journal, April 26, May 30, and May 29, 1856, Historical Society of Pennsylvania.

74. A series of roughly fourteen letters written by Peggy Emlen to Sally Logan (1768–1771) has been preserved in the Wells Morris Collection, Box 1, Historical Society of Pennsylvania (see esp. May 3 and July 4, 1769, January 8, 1768).

75. The Sarah Alden Ripley Collection, the Arthur M. Schlesinger, Sr., Library, Radcliffe College, contains a number of Sarah Alden Ripley's letters to Mary Emerson. Most of these are undated, but they extend over a number of years and contain letters written both before and after Sarah's marriage. The eulogistic biographical sketch appeared in Wister and Irwin (n. 12 above). It should be noted that Sarah Butler Wister was one of the editors who sensitively selected Sarah's letters.

76. See Sarah Alden Ripley to Mary Emerson, November 19, 1823. Sarah Alden Ripley routinely, and one must assume ritualistically, read Mary Emerson's letters to her infant daughter, Mary. Eleanor Parke Custis Lewis reported doing the same with Elizabeth Bordley Gibson's letters, passim. Eunice Callender, Boston, to Sarah Ripley, [Stearnsl, October 19, 1808.

77. Mary Black Couper to Sophie M. DuPont, March 5, 1832. The Clementina Smith—Sophie DuPont correspondence of 1,678 letters is in the Sophie DuPont Correspondence. The quotation is from Eliza Schlatter, Mount Holly, N.J., to Sophie DuPont, Brandywine, August 24, 1834. I am indebted to Anthony Wallace for informing me about this collection.

78. Mary Grew, Providence, R.I., to Isabel Howland, Sherwood, N.Y., April 27, 1892, Howland Correspondence, Sophia Smith Collection, Smith College.

79. Helena Deutsch, *Psychology of Women* (New York: Grune & Stratton, 1944), vol. I, chaps. 1–3; Clara Thompson, *On Women,* ed. Maurice Green (New York: New American Library, 1971).

Study/Discussion Questions

1. How was the structure of the American family different in the nineteenth century? Why were women closer to each other in this society?
2. How were relations between mothers and daughters different?
3. How has friendship between women changed since the nineteenth century?
4. Which aspects of friendship between women no longer exist for heterosexual women?
5. Which aspects have been taken on by other people in women's lives (other than their women friends), and who are these people?

Betrayal

Martha Manning

*Martha Manning writes from within the Catholic tradition of her
girlhood, but her portrayal of young adolescent friendship crosses religious
and cultural boundaries. Pursuing the ever-alluring goal of popularity,
Manning found herself face-to-face with the realities of guilt, sin, and
betrayal as a fifth-grader at Our Lady Queen of Angels. Her dilemma, and
its immediate resolution, remind us with a slap of the interpersonal
agonies that often enter into girls' friendships.*

I was ten when I first experienced real guilt. Until then, the judgment of my behavior existed outside of me: in a parent, a teacher, a neighbor. Even though I knew that certain behaviors like lying and stealing were wrong, I never felt very bad about them, unless I got caught. Then the bad feeling was one of shame and fear, not guilt.

The purpose of guilt in our lives is to make us feel so bad, wrong, anxious, unworthy, shitty, unlovable, and the absolute scum of the earth that we will never, ever want to feel that way again. So a healthy dose of guilt can strengthen our resolve to never sin. Not ever. Well, at least not until the next time the temptation arises, and we forget the pain of it all, just like childbirth, and jump right back into the action.

I learned this lesson in the winter of fifth grade. Right before the Christmas break, Richard Flynn intentionally broke the thermometer on what was optimistically called the "science table" (a Bunsen burner, a beaker, and a compass), the pride and joy of Sister Fatima. That offense, combined with the fact that this was his third year in fifth grade, got him promptly expelled. This finally allowed me to leave public school and take my place among the chosen at Our Lady Queen of Angels.

By the end of the first day, I didn't know the name of the principal, but I could name the three most popular girls in my grade. They clustered together in the schoolyard, linking pinkies as they skipped along the pavement at recess. They passed notes, and clearly had the attention of all the cute boys. Even though we all wore the exact same pleated green-plaid uniforms, with green kneesocks and brown oxfords, they looked almost stylish in theirs. I felt like a freak in mine, and in my vigilant, self-conscious, preadolescent mind, I was sure that everyone could automatically tell that it was a hand-me-down from my next-door neighbor.

Pages 44–52 from *Chasing Grace* by Martha Manning. Copyright © 1996 by Martha Manning. Reprinted by permission of HarperCollins Publishers, Inc.

That night, lying across my bed with a notebook in my hand, I looked like I was doing my homework. And in a way I was. I was exploring the age-old sociological questions of how people enter into groups and, once in, how they develop and maintain their status. This was the beginning of a ten-year period in which the only legitimate purpose of school to me was as a backdrop for playing out my social life.

My targets were Ann Marie, Caroline, and Judy. After several weeks of watching them, I felt I knew them well. But they were so wrapped up in their little group that they wouldn't have recognized me if they had tripped over me in the girls' bathroom. I gave out every signal I knew that I was interested in being their friend. But there was an invisible wall around them that I could not penetrate.

Other girls invited me over after school and I refused, wanting to leave open the possibility that one of the cool girls would call. My mother was puzzled by my reticence at accepting invitations. She had the misinformed notion that as long as a person was "nice," she was "cool." I gave her the same look that my daughter gives me now when a new boy leaves our house and I say, "He seems like a nice boy." My daughter sneers at me with one of those what-rock-did-you-climb-out-from-under looks and I know I will not be laying eyes on that boy again.

There was a girl named Maureen Russell who had been nice to me from my first day of school. She let me look on with her in the books I hadn't gotten yet. She pointed out the relevant information about school that grown-ups never bother to tell you. Maureen had beautiful hair and a body that had clearly gotten a jump on the rest of us. But she still had a round baby face and had not yet adopted any affectations of being "cool." She invited me to her house after school. Unlike everyone I knew—all "walkers"—Maureen lived "on the other side of town," a concept I never really

understood but vaguely felt wasn't good.

But her house looked great to me. It had thick lime-green shag carpeting and modern furniture. She had a white canopy bed with a pink bedspread, something I had longed for my entire life.

Maureen's mother won the award for the person who looked least like a mother of a ten-year-old. She looked more like a Barbie doll, with her hair all teased up and long fingernails with screaming red polish. In the middle of the day, she wore short shorts with backless gold spiked heels. I don't remember her ever without a cigarette dangling from her lips. She smoked in this really elegant way, as if she were emphasizing a point with each exhalation. She held the record for the person who could go the longest without flicking her cigarette ashes. Sometimes I'd get so entranced by her cigarette tip that I'd forget what she was saying. There was always Coke in the refrigerator and potato chips in the cupboard. In a showdown between Maureen and her mother, I would have chosen her mother, but I was growing to like Maureen too.

Over time, we became real friends. We listened to music and argued daily about who was better, Dr. Kildare (me) or Ben Casey (Maureen). We linked pinkies on the playground. I never forgot about the cool girls, and they never strayed from my peripheral vision. But I wasn't alone anymore and that was what mattered.

Maureen encouraged me to join the choir, to which almost every girl belonged. Choir was fun. Sister Margaret Joseph was one of the best nuns, let alone women, that I had ever known. Because I was a second soprano, I was placed next to two of the cool girls, Ann Marie and Caroline. Maureen, being an alto, was a few rows back. As was my tendency in situations I enjoyed, I began to make smart-ass remarks that were, to my great pleasure, thoroughly enjoyed by Ann Marie and Caroline. After a week of acknowledging my existence, Ann

Marie approached me at recess and asked if I wanted to go to the public library with them after school. Going to the Easton Public Library after a long day of school was not a thing that I thought cool people did, but I readily agreed. As an afterthought, I asked if Maureen could come too. Ann Marie wrinkled up her nose and sneered, "No!" as though she couldn't believe my effrontery.

Late in the school day, Maureen passed me a note, confirming the fact that I was still coming over to her house as we had arranged. I wrote back to her saying that I had remembered a dentist appointment and couldn't come. It was a lie. And unlike the lies I told to grown-ups or my brothers and sisters, which didn't count, I could feel this one register somewhere in the pit of my stomach and it didn't feel good. I tried to concentrate on the prized invitation, rather than the fabrication. Maureen wished me good luck at the dentist, and my eyes felt so heavy that it was difficult to meet hers. I waited until she drove off with her mother and then ran to join the girls.

The true reason for the trip to the library was scholastic only in the broadest sense. Judy's older sister, Teresa, had told her about an unbelievable book about "doing it" called *The Group* by Mary McCarthy. Her sister said that all the "good stuff" was in chapter 2. Caroline, who was by far the boldest of us all, went to the geography section and pulled down the biggest atlas she could find. Then she walked right over to the fiction section, scanned the M's, and plucked the book off the shelf, tucking it inside the atlas.

We gathered around her at the table farthest away from the librarian's desk.

And we started to read. Chapter 2 is a graphic, almost clinical, recounting of a woman's first time, and it was like dynamite in the hands of girls who had been given only the most cursory information about menstruation, which was presented to us as all we ever needed to know about sex. We were beside ourselves.

Someone was constantly blushing, giggling, or exclaiming "Oh my God!" as we pored over the pages. I was thrilled to be gaining all this valuable information, but I was even happier that I was sharing this rite of passage with these girls. Jumping from total sexual ignorance to at least partial knowledge through our own guts and wits had a unifying we-all-have-a-secret feeling to it.

As we walked home, the girls began making plans for the next day. Someone had heard that *Peyton Place* was a pretty racy book, and God knows, we figured we needed to get as much knowledge as we could. I couldn't tell whether they were asking me to join them, so I kept my mouth shut. When Caroline asked if I could come, I almost sang out my assent. And then I remembered Maureen. I told them I had made plans to do something with her.

"Why do you hang around with her?" Judy demanded.

Watchful of my every word, I answered, "'Cause she's pretty nice."

"Well, she's a slut," pronounced Ann Marie in that age-old way that girls malign each other.

I was fairly sure that Maureen was equally as inexperienced and probably less knowledgeable than we were.

"How do you know she's a slut?" I ventured.

"Because my brother in the eighth grade said that she let Frankie McManus get to second base with her."

"I don't think she even knows Frankie McManus," I answered.

But then I had all three of them to contend with, "Well, you know about her mother, don't you?"

"What about her?" I asked.

"She *works*," sneered Judy.

"In a *diner*," added Caroline.

And Ann Marie, confident that she held the trump card, concluded, "And . . . she's *divorced!*"

I knew none of those things about Mrs. Russell. All three of them were definite variants in a homogeneous parish in which no one's mother worked, especially in a diner. And no one, no one was divorced.

I wanted to tell them how really cool Mrs. Russell was. But I knew that anything I said to make the Russells look better would make me look worse. I swallowed my words. I swallowed them so hard that they burned in my chest as I experienced, for the second time in two days, the sense that I was involved in something terribly wrong.

Over time, I spent more time with the cool girls and less time with Maureen. There was a silent agreement between Maureen and me that we did not talk about the other girls, as if she knew that if she asked, she would not like the answers.

Though I spent less time with Maureen, my new group was still not content. They set up blatant challenges to my loyalty in all those tiny cruelties that preadolescent girls become expert at inflicting upon one another. If I was talking with Maureen on the playground, one of them would run up to me laughing, tug at my sleeve, yell, "Come here. We've got to tell you something!" and drag me away. I would give Maureen an apologetic look that said "This is all out of my control" and would utter empty words like "I'll be right back." But I never was "right back." That was the point of the whole exercise.

As if to test my loyalty to them, they continually upped the ante, so that I constantly had to choose between Maureen and them. I always chose them, while trying to give Maureen just enough to deceive myself into thinking I was still being a good friend.

One Sunday when we were sitting in the choir loft, an all-out assault was launched. Judy, an alto like Maureen, whispered, "What's that smell?" She began sniffing around Maureen. Between hymns, when Sister Margaret Joseph wasn't looking, Caroline and Ann Marie turned around and said, "I don't know, but I think it's coming from there" and pointed to Maureen.

Caroline poked me to join in. I was silent and kept my head down, pretending to read the text of "Kyrie Eleison," which was our next piece. In a stage whisper, Ann Marie leaned over her pew and hissed, "Martha, you better tell your friend that no amount of perfume is going to cover up the way she smells." Everyone around us was laughing. I kept my head down, still pretending to be engrossed in the hymnal. "Martha! . . . Martha! . . ." Judy demanded. Caroline and Ann Marie were nudging me on both sides—I had to turn around. When I did, I faced not only Judy, but Maureen, who was sitting right next to her. Maureen's face was white, and her eyes were liquid with tears and pain. "Tell her, Martha . . ." chanted the girls in unison. "Tell them, Martha . . ." pleaded Maureen in silence. I looked at Judy and I looked at Maureen. And then I turned around. I looked back down and hid within my hymnal. Mercifully, the acolyte rang the bells on the altar and we all sang in perfect synchrony after the priest:

Kyrie eleison (Lord have mercy)
Christe eleison (Christ have mercy)
Kyrie eleison (Lord have mercy)

I kept my face bent low in the book through the entire mass. I mouthed the words, afraid of any sound that might come from my mouth.

I tried to reassure myself with the technically correct but flimsy excuse that I had been silent because one was not supposed to talk in church. But I knew that by doing nothing, I had done something very wrong. It didn't fit into the catalog of sins I had memorized so well, and certainly didn't feel like anything that a priest could wipe away with a few Hail Marys. I remembered the story of Peter, who denied even knowing his best friend Jesus. Not just once, but three times. At the time when Jesus needed him most, Peter took a hike. For years I had pictured Peter as such a wimp, to deny his connection to Jesus. But now, in my identification with Peter, I reasoned that he probably had a good reason for denying that he knew Christ. He could have gotten himself killed, and how would that have changed anything for Jesus anyway?

It would have been nice if that rationalization had helped me, but it didn't. I knew that even though I sat reverent and straightbacked in that church pew, all the while I was really dancing with the devil. I was saying, "Give me these girls as friends. I won't be cruel. But neither will I be kind. Is that really so bad?"

The joy of belonging was tempered by the guilt of rejecting. It was the first time in my life that I had ever felt truly responsible for my behavior. I was appalled at myself for letting my friend be crucified in that church. No, I never actually used the hammer, but I stood by and held the nails. And that was just as bad. It was then I knew that often the greatest of sins are not the things we do but the things we fail to do. This revelation confused the hell out of me then and continues to plague me now.

Lost in the dark forest without a moral compass, I longed for the times when someone else would judge my behavior, forgive me for it, and provide me with a clear formula for suddenly and magically making everything all better.

Study/Discussion Questions

1. Is this a typical elementary school story? Why or why not?
2. Who were the popular girls in your elementary school? How were they different from the other girls?
3. What do you remember about being friends when you were the age of the girls in the story?

Sisters

Mona Simpson

In Mona Simpson's telling, sisters tend to fall into patterns of relating that persist through a lifetime. The fighters fight; the caregivers care. Simpson herself has no sisters, although she used to have a fantasy of one—an older sister, "knowledgeable, flippant with her dark secrets." But as her observations of sisters' relationships in her lifetime circle of acquaintance suggest, the reality of sisterhood is often more complicated and intimate, if less idyllic, than the fantasy.

My great aunts were six sisters, each with the name of a jewel or semi-precious stone. But they didn't call each other those, they had nicknames. Goody, Heady, Girly, Slavey, Tom Tom, and Baby. Girly was fat. She gave me water once in her square kitchen, a maroon tall metal cup sharp on my lip. They said she went in for antiques. Baby was the wild one. She still wore frills at eighty. Goody could bake, Tom Tom kept a neat house. Slavey lost her hair at the end and had the handsome no-good husband, whom Tom Tom nursed for ten years. They visited each other's houses every day. They had no other friends. They are strangers on their tombstones: Opal, Pearl, Ruby, Sapphire, Coral, Amber.

We knew a family with five sisters, steps besides. A widower married a widow. Two were tall, two less, two blond, two dark, one a redhead look-alike for Hedy Lamarr. If you met them in their sixties you would still know which was the beautiful baby. She'd tell you. They all would. She was still beautiful then too, but not more so. Perhaps in a more regular way. At her wedding, two of the sisters fought. They pulled hair, a lamp was thrown at a head. They bit, scratched, kissed laughing the next day. The steps were mad because the bride wore one of their mother's old dresses she'd found in the basement for her going-away outfit. It was their mother's, not hers. Even though they'd never fit in it. The steps were big girls, all. And the bride did. Fit. She still did the year before she died. She wore it for the costume ball at the home.

When one's husband bought a gift, three or more of the sisters went along.

They eat with each other several times a week, at each other's homes, although there, too, fights erupted over something like a nickname or a shoe or an implication that someone got more fifteen years ago from one parent.

One drove all night from Chicago to reclaim the silver from her mother's attic another had taken home and polished.

You weren't using it.

But it is mine. Still.

The mother, who happened to be kind and fair, one of the beloved women in the world, promised each of the girls silver then, but in time. She needed to buy it on time. She herself worked, baking wedding cakes and taking the festal photographs.

They competed, those girls, all their lives, they envied each other's wardrobes and husbands and houses, but most of all they fought over her.

She had little time with each alone.

They each wanted her only.

Some distant relatives on the Arab side, were four sisters. They were aristocrats. I never knew them well. But I studied the way they were with men.

The oldest was the hook, a dangerous beauty when she was young, one side of the mouth curled down in an almost-sneer. Her lips were big, full, oversized, as if they'd smeared over the border. She lured the men for them all. Men fell for her, mooned over her in a drift and the sisters worked together, laughing at him, at all men. The youngers bided their time.

Three men in turn came to appreciate slower, consoling virtues. The eldest saw her three young sisters married and finally had a baby out of wedlock with an elderly, famous Italian.

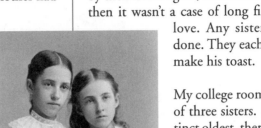

Two sisters, Bertha and Feroline Fox, in their childhood and middle age. (courtesy Schlesinger Library)

The youngest sister died first. The eldest, by then home again, married the husband. By then it wasn't a case of long finally requited love. Any sister would have done. They each knew how to make his toast.

My college roommate was one of three sisters. She was a distinct oldest, there was a middle and a baby. The oldest was Dad, a brilliant but daffy ornithologist, the youngest Mom, a stylishly reckless younger wife who knew one thing and that was how to have fun in life, and the middle was neither, which has given her a life of trouble.

We all know two sisters who are opposites and live miles or a continent or oceans apart. Our town had many of these. The one who stayed and the one who left. My mother and my godmother were each one of these. The one who stayed tended to end up taking care of the aged mother; fathers tending to die first. The one who left did something else and had a life. The one who stayed tended to offer services: the groceries picked up, the odd errand, maybe scrubbing the kitchen floor, picking up a cake on Sundays. Just company. Daily, every day, weather; the other, being. Children. Grandchildren. Arriving in a boisterous mess for a rare holiday when the house was taken apart. Generally, they were represented evenly in the will.

I never had a sister and only sometimes wanted one. Not a younger.

If I had a sister, I would want her to be older and knowledgeable, flippant with her dark secrets. I imagined a room full of underwear and sophisticated underground music, bras on the shower rod.

My old college roommate on the phone to her family, now at thirty-three: a classical lament, everything wrong. How they're wearing pants this year and hers all too wide, sigh, problems of health, her grandfather fell again, oh no, could she do something? Of course he could stay, the couch pulls out. Prices of things.

I listen to her portrait of yoked overworked people and recognize nothing. We've just come in from running. Even her daughter is overburdened in this account, under a melancholy umbrella. "But we're fine," she says at the end. They all did that to each other, each of the daughters, and the mother too. They competed not over joys or accomplishments or even purchases, but over pain. Slights and wrongs of twenty years earlier easily slid into the conversation. What each one got from the father, they came to always at the end of fights, each telling her, the oldest, she got more. She couldn't bear to be alone, but she did love him. "He didn't ask me one question either!" she screamed. Then, later, a hard staccato, "But I call. I call him and I tell him straight, Dad, you didn't hear me."

I whisper to calm down. She holds the phone out for me to hear: "You can ask, that's because you know that he loves you, you were given that sense of entitlement!" Her sister, the always-aggrieved middle.

It was never ending their fight about who got least and they will wage it, I understand, for the rest of their lives.

She is quite snide about her in-laws and their politer conversations.

"Bragging," she calls it. "They brag. That's what they do." Her mother-in-law chronicles the honors and accomplishments her children brought her, starting when the participants were two or three. "Did you hear what Matthew said . . . Three years old," the story always finished.

I envy her family, their bickering and plaintive weeping. My own family assumes a fair evenness in life. Parents set out their children as to sea, at a certain age, with prescribed provisions and from there they expect little. It was assumed your fortune or misfortune, with the exception of dire illness, was your own business.

The sisters compete to suffer because if anyone prospered she would be generally held to owe tithe, they were understood to be on a communal journey, not of their own choosing.

Study/Discussion Questions

1. What do these stories tell us about being sisters?
2. What makes sisters close? What drives them apart?
3. Think about sisters you know yourself. Are they alike or different? Is there a "sisterly" pact to concentrate on the positive or negative?
4. Do they see themselves as being on a communal journey?

The Elder Sister

Sharon Olds

When I look at my elder sister now
I think how she had to go first, down through the
birth canal, to force her way
head-first through the tiny channel,
the pressure of Mother's muscles on her brain,
the tight walls scraping her skin.
Her face is still narrow from it, the long
hollow cheeks of a Crusader on a tomb,
and her inky eyes have the look of someone who has
been in prison a long time and
knows they can send her back. I look at her
body and think how her breasts were the first to
rise, slowly, like swans on a pond.
By the time mine came along, they were just
two more birds in the flock, and when the hair
rose on the white mound of her flesh, like
threads of water out of the ground, it was the
first time, but when mine came
they knew about it. I used to think
only in terms of her harshness, sitting and
pissing on me in bed, but now I
see I had her before me always
like a shield. I look at her wrinkles, her clenched
jaws, her frown-lines—I see they are
the dents on my shield, the blows that did not reach me.
She protected me, not as a mother
protects a child, with love, but as a
hostage protects the one who makes her
escape as I made my escape, with my sister's
body held in front of me.

How It Is

Maxine Kumin

Shall I say how it is in your clothes?
A month after your death I wear your blue jacket.
The dog at the center of my life recognizes
you've come to visit, he's ecstatic.
In the left pocket, a hole.
In the right, a parking ticket
delivered up last August on Bay State Road.
In my heart, a scatter like milkweed,
a flinging from the pods of the soul.
My skin presses your old outline.
It is hot and dry inside.

I think of the last day of your life,
old friend, how I would unwind it, paste
it together in a different collage,
back from the death car idling in the garage,
back up the stairs, your praying hands unlaced,
reassembling the bites of bread and tuna fish
into a ceremony of sandwich,
running the home movie backward to a space
we could be easy in, a kitchen place
with vodka and ice, our words like living meat.

Dear friend, you have excited crowds
with your example. They swell
like wine bags, straining at your seams.
I will be years gathering up our words,
fishing out letters, snapshots, stains,
leaning my ribs against this durable cloth
to put on the dumb blue blazer of your death.

MOTHERS AND DAUGHTERS

Family Structure and
Feminine Personality

Nancy Chodorow

*Why, generation after generation, do girls grow up with "feminine"
personalities and boys with "masculine" ones? How, exactly, do girls learn
to be mothers? These questions lead sociologist and psychoanalyst Nancy
Chodorow to examine the structure of the family and the way people relate
within it. She discovers patterns deeper and less conscious than deliberate
gender socialization. The fact that women care for children in their early
years has an indelible effect on girls' personality development, Chodorow
finds in this classic essay, and that effect has something to do with the
inequality between the sexes that gets perpetuated across generations.*

I propose here a model to account for the reproduction within each generation of certain general and nearly universal differences that characterize masculine and feminine personality and roles.[1] My perspective is largely psychoanalytic. Cross-cultural and social-psychological evidence suggests that an argument drawn solely from the universality of biological sex differences is unconvincing.[2] At the same time, explanations based on patterns of deliberate socialization (the most prevalent kind of anthropological, sociological, and social-psychological explanation) are in themselves insufficient to account for the extent to which psychological and value commitments to sex differences are so emotionally laden and tenaciously maintained, for the way gender identity and expectations about sex roles and gender consistency are so deeply central to a person's consistent sense of self.

This paper suggests that a crucial differentiating experience in male and female development arises out of the fact that women, universally, are largely responsible for early child care and for (at least) later female socialization. This points to the central importance of the mother-daughter relationship for women, and to a focus on the conscious and unconscious effects of early involvement with a female for children of both sexes. The fact that males and females experience this social environment differently as they grow up accounts for the development of basic sex differences in personality. In particular, certain features of the mother-daughter relationship are internalized universally as basic elements of feminine ego

Reprinted from *Women, Culture, and Society,* edited by Michelle Zimbalist Rosaldo and Louise Lamphere, pp. 43–66, with the permission of the publishers, Stanford University Press. © 1974 by the Board of Trustees of the Leland Stanford Junior University.

structure (although not necessarily what we normally mean by "femininity").

Specifically, I shall propose that, in any given society, feminine personality comes to define itself in relation and connection to other people more than masculine personality does. (In psychoanalytic terms, women are less individuated than men; they have more flexible ego boundaries.[3]) Moreover, issues of dependency are handled and experienced differently by men and women. For boys and men, both individuation and dependency issues become tied up with the sense of masculinity, or masculine identity. For girls and women, by contrast, issues of femininity, or feminine identity, are not problematic in the same way. The structural situation of child rearing, reinforced by female and male role training, produces these differences, which are replicated and reproduced in the sexual sociology of adult life.

The paper is also a beginning attempt to rectify certain gaps in the social-scientific literature, and a contribution to the reformulation of psychological anthropology. Most traditional accounts of family and socialization tend to emphasize only role training, and not unconscious features of personality. Those few that rely on Freudian theory have abstracted a behaviorist methodology from this theory, concentrating on isolated "significant" behaviors like weaning and toilet training. The paper advocates instead a focus on the ongoing interpersonal relationships in which these various behaviors are given meaning.[4]

More empirically, most social-scientific accounts of socialization, child development, and the mother-child relationship refer implicitly or explicitly only to the development and socialization of boys, and to the mother-son relationship. There is a striking lack of systematic description about the mother-daughter relationship, and a basic theoretical discontinuity between, on the one hand, theories about female development, which tend to stress the

development of "feminine" qualities in relation to and comparison with men, and on the other hand, theories about women's ultimate mothering role. This final lack is particularly crucial, because women's motherhood and mothering role seem to be the most important features in accounting for the universal secondary status of women (Chodorow, 1971; Ortner, Rosaldo, 1974). The present paper describes the development of psychological qualities in women that are central to the perpetuation of this role.

In a formulation of this preliminary nature, there is not a great body of consistent evidence to draw upon. Available evidence is presented that illuminates aspects of the theory—for the most part psychoanalytic and social-psychological accounts based almost entirely on highly industrialized Western society. Because aspects of family structure are discussed that are universal, however, I think it is worth considering the theory as a general model. In any case, this is in some sense a programmatic appeal to people doing research. It points to certain issues that might be especially important in investigations of child development and family relationships, and suggests that researchers look explicitly at female vs. male development, and that they consider seriously mother-daughter relationships even if these are not of obvious "structural importance" in a traditional anthropological view of that society.

THE DEVELOPMENT OF GENDER PERSONALITY

According to psychoanalytic theory,[5] personality is a result of a boy's or girl's social-relational experiences from earliest infancy. Personality development is not the result of conscious parental intention. The nature and quality of the social relationships that the child experiences are appropriated, internalized, and organized by her/him and come to constitute her/his personality. What is internalized from an on-going relationship continues independent of that original relationship and is generalized and set up as a permanent feature of the personality. The conscious self is usually not aware of many of the features of personality, or of its total structural organization. At the same time, these are important determinants of any person's behavior, both that which is culturally expected and that which is idiosyncratic or unique to the individual. The conscious aspects of personality, like a person's general self-concept and, importantly, her/his gender identity, require and depend upon the consistency and stability of its unconscious organization. In what follows I shall describe how contrasting male and female experiences lead to differences in the way that the developing masculine or feminine psyche resolves certain relational issues.

Separation and individuation (preoedipal development). All children begin life in a state of "infantile dependence" (Fairbairn, 1952) upon an adult or adults, in most cases their mother. This state consists first in the persistence of primary identification with the mother: the child does not differentiate herself/himself from her/his mother but experiences a sense of oneness with her. (It is important to distinguish this from later forms of identification, from "secondary identification," which presuppose at least some degree of experienced separateness by the person who identifies.) Second, it includes an oral-incorporative mode of relationship to the world, leading, because of the infant's total helplessness, to a strong attachment to and dependence upon whoever nurses and carries her/him.

Both aspects of this state are continuous with the child's prenatal experience of being emotionally and physically part of the mother's body and of the exchange of body material through the placenta. That this relationship continues with the natural mother in most societies stems from the fact that women lactate. For convenience, and not because of biological necessity, this has usually meant that mothers, and females in general, tend to take all care of babies. It is probable that the mother's continuing to have major responsibility for the feeding and care of the child (so that the child interacts almost entirely with her) extends and intensifies her/his period of primary identification with her more than if, for instance, someone else were to take major or total care of the child. A child's earliest experience, then, is usually of identity with and attachment to a single mother, and always with women.

For both boys and girls, the first few years are preoccupied with issues of separation and individuation. This includes breaking or attenuating the primary identification with the mother and beginning to develop an individuated sense of self, and mitigating the totally dependent oral attitude and attachment to the mother. I would suggest that, contrary to the traditional psychoanalytic model, the preoedipal experience is likely to differ for boys and girls. Specifically, the experience of mothering for a woman involves a double identification (Klein and Riviére, 1937). A woman identifies with her own mother and, through identification with her child, she (re)experiences herself as a cared-for child. The particular nature of this double identification for the individual mother is closely bound up with her relationship to her own mother. As Deutsch expresses it, "In relation to her own child, woman repeats her own mother-child history" (1944: 205). Given that she was a female child, and that identification with her mother and mothering are so bound up with her being a woman, we might expect that a woman's identification with a girl child might be stronger; that a mother, who is, after all, a person who is a woman and not simply the performer of a formally defined role, would tend to treat infants of different sexes in different ways.

There is some suggestive sociological evidence that this is the case. Mothers in a women's group in Cambridge, Massachusetts (see note 1) say that they identified more with their girl children than with boy children. The perception and treatment of girl vs. boy children in high-caste, extremely patriarchal, patrilocal communities in India are in the same vein. Families express preference for boy children and celebrate when sons are born. At the same time, Rajput mothers in North India are "as likely as not" (Minturn and Hitchcock, 1963) to like girl babies better than boy babies once they are born, and they and Havik Brahmins in South India (Harper, 1969) treat their daughters with greater affection and leniency than their sons. People in both groups say that this is out of sympathy for the future plight of their daughters, who will have to leave their natal family for a strange and usually oppressive postmarital household. From the time of their daughters' birth, then, mothers in these communities identify anticipatorily, by re-experiencing their own past, with the experiences of separation that their daughters will go through. They develop a particular attachment to their daughters because of this and by imposing their own reaction to the issue of separation on this new external situation.

It seems, then, that a mother is more likely to identify with a daughter than with a son, to experience her daughter (or parts of her daughter's life) as herself. Fliess's description (1961) of his neurotic patients who were the children of ambulatory psychotic mothers presents the problem in its psychopathological extreme. The example is interesting, because, although Fliess claims to be writing about people defined only by the fact that their problems were tied to a particular kind of relationship to their mothers, an overwhelmingly large proportion of the cases he presents are women. It seems, then, that this sort of disturbed mother inflicts her pathology predominantly on daughters. The mothers Fliess describes did not allow their daughters to perceive themselves as separate people, but simply acted as if their

daughters were narcissistic extensions or doubles of themselves, extensions to whom were attributed the mothers' bodily feelings and who became physical vehicles for their mothers' achievement of autoerotic gratification. The daughters were bound into a mutually dependent "hypersymbiotic" relationship. These mothers, then, perpetuate a mutual relationship with their daughters of both primary identification and infantile dependence.

A son's case is different. Cultural evidence suggests that insofar as a mother treats her son differently, it is usually by emphasizing his masculinity in opposition to herself and by pushing him to assume, or acquiescing in his assumption of, a sexually toned male-role relation to her. Whiting (1959) and Whiting et al. (1958) suggest that mothers in societies with mother-child sleeping arrangements and post-partum sex taboos may be seductive toward infant sons. Slater (1968) describes the socialization of precarious masculinity in Greek males of the classical period through their mothers' alternation of sexual praise and seductive behavior with hostile deflation and ridicule. This kind of behavior contributes to the son's differentiation from his mother and to the formation of ego boundaries (I will later discuss certain problems that result from this).

Neither form of attitude or treatment is what we would call "good mothering." However, evidence of differentiation of a pathological nature in the mother's behavior toward girls and boys does highlight tendencies in "normal" behavior. It seems likely that from their children's earliest childhood, mothers and women tend to identify more with daughters and to help them to differentiate less, and that processes of separation and individuation are made more difficult for girls. On the other hand, a mother tends to identify less with her son, and to push him toward differentiation and the taking on of a male role unsuitable to his age, and undesirable at any age in his relationship to her.

For boys and girls, the quality of the preoedipal relationship to the mother differs. This, as well as differences in development during the oedipal period, accounts for the persisting importance of preoedipal issues in female development and personality that many psychoanalytic writers describe.[6] Even before the establishment of gender identity, gender personality differentiation begins.

Gender identity (oedipal crisis and resolution). There is only a slight suggestion in the psychological and sociological literature that preoedipal development differs for boys and girls. The pattern becomes explicit at the next developmental level. All theoretical and empirical accounts agree that after about age three (the beginning of the "oedipal" period, which focuses on the attainment of a stable gender identity) male and female development becomes radically different. It is at this stage that the father, and men in general, begins to become important in the child's primary object world. It is, of course, particularly difficult to generalize about the attainment of gender identity and sex-role assumption, since there is such wide variety in the sexual sociology of different societies. However, to the extent that in all societies women's life tends to be more private and domestic, and men's more public and social (Rosaldo, 1974), we can make general statements about this kind of development.

In what follows, I shall be talking about the development of gender personality and gender identity in the tradition of psychoanalytic theory. Cognitive psychologists have established that by the age of three, boys and girls have an irreversible conception of what their gender is (cf. Kohlberg, 1966). I do not dispute these findings. It remains true that children (and adults) may know definitely that they are boys (men) or girls (women), and at the same time experience conflicts or uncertainty about "masculinity" or "femininity," about

what these identities require in behavioral or emotional terms, etc. I am discussing the development of "gender identity" in this latter sense.

A boy's masculine gender identification must come to replace his early primary identification with his mother. This masculine identification is usually based on identification with a boy's father or other salient adult males. However, a boy's father is relatively more remote than his mother. He rarely plays a major caretaking role even at this period in his son's life. In most societies, his work and social life take place farther from the home than do those of his wife. He is, then, often relatively inaccessible to his son, and performs his male role activities away from where the son spends most of his life. As a result, a boy's male gender identification often becomes a "positional" identification, with aspects of his father's clearly or not-so-clearly defined male role, rather than a more generalized "personal" identification—a diffuse identification with his father's personality, values, and behavioral traits—that could grow out of a real relationship to his father.[7]

Mitscherlich (1963), in his discussion of Western advanced capitalist society, provides a useful insight into the problem of male development. The father, because his work takes him outside of the home most of the time, and because his active presence in the family has progressively decreased, has become an "invisible father." For the boy, the tie between affective relations and masculine gender identification and role learning (between libidinal and ego development) is relatively attenuated, He identifies with a fantasied masculine role, because the reality constraint that contact with his father would provide is missing. In all societies characterized by some sex segregation (even those in which a son will eventually lead the same sort of life as his father), much of a boy's masculine identification must be of this sort, that is, with aspects of his father's role, or what he fantasies to be a male role, rather than with his father as a person involved in a relationship to him.

There is another important aspect to this situation, which explains the psychological dynamics of the universal social and cultural devaluation and subordination of women. A boy, in his attempt to gain an elusive masculine identification, often comes to define this masculinity largely in negative terms, as that which is not feminine or involved with women.[8] There is an internal and external aspect to this. Internally, the boy tries to reject his mother and deny his attachment to her and the strong dependence upon her that he still feels. He also tries to deny the deep personal identification with her that has developed during his early years. He does this by repressing whatever he takes to be feminine inside himself, and, importantly, by denigrating and devaluing whatever he considers to be feminine in the outside world. As a societal member, he also appropriates to himself and defines as superior particular social activities and cultural (moral, religious, and creative) spheres—possibly, in fact, "society" (Rosaldo, 1974) and "culture" (Ortner, 1974) themselves.[9]

Freud's description of the boy's oedipal crisis speaks to the issues of rejection of the feminine and identification with the father. As his early attachment to his mother takes on phallic-sexual overtones, and his father enters the picture as an obvious rival (who, in the son's fantasy, has apparent power to kill or castrate his son), the boy must radically deny and repress his attachment to his mother and replace it with an identification with his loved and admired, but also potentially punitive, therefore feared, father. He internalizes a superego.[10]

To summarize, four components of the attainment of masculine gender identity are important. First, masculinity becomes and remains a problematic issue for a boy. Second, it involves denial of attachment or relationship, particularly of what the boy takes to be dependence or need for another, and differentiation of himself from another. Third, it involves the repression and devaluation of femininity on both psychological and cultural levels. Finally, identification with his father does not usually develop in the context of a satisfactory affective relationship, but consists in the attempt to internalize and learn components of a not immediately apprehensible role.

The development of a girl's gender identity contrasts with that of a boy. Most important, femininity and female role activities are immediately apprehensible in the world of her daily life. Her final role identification is with her mother and women, that is, with the person or people with whom she also has her earliest relationship of infantile dependence. The development of her gender identity does not involve a rejection of this early identification, however. Rather, her later identification with her mother is embedded in and influenced by their ongoing relationship of both primary identification and preoedipal attachment. Because her mother is around, and she has had a genuine relationship to her as a person, a girl's gender and gender role identification are mediated by and depend upon real affective relations. Identification with her mother is not positional—the narrow learning of particular role behaviors—but rather a personal identification with her mother's general traits of character and values. Feminine identification is based not on fantasied or externally defined characteristics and negative identification, but on the gradual learning of a way of being familiar in everyday life, and exemplified by the person (or kind of people—women) with whom she has been most involved. It is continuous with her early childhood identifications and attachments.

The major discontinuity in the development of a girl's sense of gender identity, and one that has led Freud and other early psychoanalysts to see female development as exceedingly difficult and tortuous, is that at some point she must transfer her primary sexual object choice from her mother and females to her father and males, if she is to attain her expected heterosexual adulthood. Briefly, Freud considers that all children feel that mothers give some cause for complaint and unhappiness: they give too little milk; they have a second child; they arouse and then forbid their child's sexual gratification in the process of caring for her/him. A girl receives a final blow, however: her discovery that she lacks a penis. She blames this lack on her mother, rejects her mother, and turns to her father in reaction.

Problems in this account have been discussed extensively in the general literature that has grown out of the women's movement, and within the psychoanalytic tradition itself. These concern Freud's misogyny and his obvious assumption that males possess physiological superiority, and that a woman's personality is inevitably determined by her lack of a penis.[11] The psychoanalytic account is not completely unsatisfactory, however. A more detailed consideration of several theorists[12] reveals important features of female development, especially about the mother-daughter relationship, and at the same time contradicts or mitigates the absoluteness of the more general Freudian outline.

These psychoanalysts emphasize how, in contrast to males, the female oedipal crisis is not resolved in the same absolute way. A girl cannot and does not completely reject her mother in favor of men, but continues her relationship of dependence upon and attachment to her. In addition, the strength and quality of her relationship to her father is completely dependent upon the strength and quality of her relationship to her mother. Deutsch suggests that a girl wavers in a "bisexual triangle" throughout her childhood and into puberty, normally making a very tentative resolution in favor of her father, but in such a way that issues of separation from and attachment to her mother remain important throughout a woman's life (1944: 205):

It is erroneous to say that the little girl gives up her first mother relation in favor of the father. She only gradually draws him into the alliance, develops from the mother-child exclusiveness toward the triangular parent-child relationship and continues the latter, just as she does the former, although in a weaker and less elemental form, all her life. Only the principal part changes: now the mother, now the father plays it. The ineradicability of affective constellations manifests itself in later repetitions.

We might suggest from this that a girl's internalized and external object relations become and remain more complex, and at the same time more defining of her, than those of a boy. Psychoanalytic preoccupation with constitutionally based libidinal development, and with a normative male model of development, has obscured this fact. Most women are genitally heterosexual. At the same time, their lives always involve other sorts of equally deep and primary relationships, especially with their children, and, importantly, with other women. In these spheres also, even more than in the area of heterosexual relations, a girl imposes the sort of object-relations she has internalized in her preoedipal and her relationship to her mother.

Men are also for the most part genitally heterosexual. This grows directly out of their early primary attachment to their mother. We know, however, that in many societies their heterosexual relationships are not embedded in close personal relationship but simply in relations of dominance and power. Furthermore, they do not have the extended personal social relations women have. They are not so connected to children, and their relationships with other men tend to be based not on particulristic connection or affective ties, but rather on abstract, universalistic role expectations.

Building on the psychoanalytic assumption that unique individual experiences contribute to the formation of individual personality, culture and personality theory has held that early experiences common to members of a particular society contribute to the formation of "typical" personalities organized around and preoccupied with certain issues: "Prevailing patterns of child-rearing must result in similar internalized situations in the unconscious of the majority of individuals in a culture, and these will be externalized back into the culture again to perpetuate it from generation to generation" (Guntrip, 1961: 378). In a similar vein, I have tried to show that to the extent males and females, respectively, experience similar interpersonal environments as they grow up, masculine and feminine personality will develop directly.

I have relied on a theory which suggests that features of adult personality and behavior are determined, but which is not biologically determinist. Culturally expected personality and behavior are not simply "taught," however. Rather, certain features of social structure, supported by cultural beliefs, values, and perceptions, are internalized through the family and the child's early social object-relationships. This largely unconscious organization is the context in which role training and purposive socialization take place.

SEX-ROLE LEARNING AND ITS SOCIAL CONTEXT

Sex-role training and social interaction in childhood build upon and reinforce the largely unconscious development I have described. In most societies (ours is a complicated exception) a girl is usually with her mother and other female relatives in an interpersonal situation that facilitates continuous and early role learning and emphasizes the mother-daughter identification and particularistic, diffuse, affective relationships between women. A boy, to a greater or lesser extent, is also with women for a large part of his childhood, which prevents continu-

ous or easy masculine role identification. His development is characterized by discontinuity.

Ariès (1962: 61), in his discussion of the changing concept of childhood in modern capitalist society, makes a distinction that seems to have more general applicability. Boys, he suggests, became "children" while girls remained "little women." "The idea of childhood profited the boys first of all, while the girls persisted much longer in the traditional way of life which confused them with the adults: we shall have cause to notice more than once this delay on the part of the women in adopting the visible forms of the essentially masculine civilization of modern times." This took place first in the middle classes, as a situation developed in which boys needed special schooling in order to prepare for their future work and could not begin to do this kind of work in childhood. Girls (and working-class boys) could still learn work more directly from their parents, and could begin to participate in the adult economy at an earlier age. Rapid economic change and development have exacerbated the lack of male generational role continuity. Few fathers now have either the opportunity or the ability to pass on a profession or skill to their sons.

Sex-role development of girls in modern society is more complex. On the one hand, they go to school to prepare for life in technologically and socially complex society. On the other, there is a sense in which this schooling is a pseudo-training. It is not meant to interfere with the much more important training to be "feminine" and a wife and mother, which is embedded in the girl's unconscious development and which her mother teaches her in a family context where she is clearly the salient parent.

This dichotomy is not unique to modern industrial society. Even if special, segregated schooling is not necessary for adult male work (and many male initiation rites remain a form of segregated role training), boys still participate in more activities that characterize them as a category apart from adult life. Their activities grow out of the boy's need to fill time until he can begin to take on an adult male role. Boys may withdraw into isolation and self-involved play or join together in a group that remains more or less unconnected with either the adult world of work and activity or the familial world.

Jay (1969) describes this sort of situation in rural Modjokuto, Java. Girls, after the age of five or so, begin gradually to help their mothers in their work and spend time with their mothers. Boys at this early age begin to form bands of age mates who roam and play about the city, relating neither to adult men nor to their mothers and sisters. Boys, then, enter a temporary group based on universalistic membership criteria, while girls continue to participate in particularistic role relations in a group characterized by continuity and relative permanence.

The content of boys' and girls' role training tends in the same direction as the context of this training and its results. Barry, Bacon, and Child, in their well-known study (1957), demonstrate that the socialization of boys tends to be oriented toward achievement and self-reliance and that of girls toward nurturance and responsibility. Girls are thus pressured to be involved with and connected to others, boys to deny this involvement and connection.

ADULT GENDER PERSONALITY AND SEX ROLE

A variety of conceptualizations of female and male personality all focus on distinctions around the same issue, and provide alternative confirmation of the developmental model I have proposed. Bakan (1966: 15) claims that male personality is preoccupied with the "agentic," and female personality with the "communal." His expanded definition of the two concepts is illuminating:

I have adopted the terms "agency" and "communion" to characterize two fundamental modalities in the existence of living forms, agency for the existence of an organism as an individual and communion for the participation of the individual in some larger organism of which the individual is a part. Agency manifests itself in self-protection, self-assertion, and self-expansion; communion manifests itself in the sense of being at one with other organisms. Agency manifests itself in the formation of separations; communion in the lack of separations. Agency manifests itself in isolation, alienation, and aloneness; communion in contact, openness, and union. Agency manifests itself in the urge to master; communion in noncontractual cooperation. Agency manifests itself in the repression of thought, feeling, and impulse; communion in the lack and removal of repression.

Gutmann (1965) contrasts the socialization of male personalities in "allocentric" milieux (milieux in which the individual is part of a larger social organization and system of social bonds) with that of female personalities in "autocentric" milieux (in which the individual herself/himself is a focus of events and ties).[13] Gutmann suggests that this leads to a number of systematic differences in ego functioning. Female ego qualities, growing out of participation in autocentric milieux, include more flexible ego boundaries (i.e., less insistent self-other distinctions), present orientation rather than future orientation, and relatively greater subjectivity and less detached objectivity.[14]

Carlson (1971) confirms both characterizations. Her tests of Gutmann's claims lead her to conclude that "males represent experiences of self, others, space, and time in individualistic, objective, and distant ways, while females represent experiences in relatively interpersonal, subjective, immediate ways" (p. 270). With reference to Bakan, she claims that men's descriptions of affective experience tend to be in agentic terms and women's in terms of communion, and that an examination of abstracts of a large number of social-psychological articles on sex differences yields an overwhelming confirmation of the agency/communion hypothesis.

Cohen (1969) contrasts the development of "analytic" and "relational" cognitive style, the former characterized by a stimulus-centered, parts-specific orientation to reality, the latter centered on the self and responding to the global characteristics of a stimulus in reference to its total context. Although focusing primarily on class differences in cognitive style, she also points out that girls are more likely to mix the two types of functioning (and also to exhibit internal conflict about this). Especially, they are likely to exhibit at the same time both high field dependence and highly developed analytic skills in other areas. She suggests that boys and girls participate in different sorts of interactional subgroups in their families: boys experience their family more as a formally organized primary group; girls experience theirs as a group characterized by shared and less clearly delineated functions. She concludes (p. 836): "Since embedded responses covered the gamut from abstract categories, through language behaviors, to expressions of embeddedness in their social environments, it is possible that embeddedness may be a distinctive characteristic of female sex-role learning in this society regardless of social class, native ability, ethnic differences, and the cognitive impact of the school."

Preliminary consideration suggests a correspondence between the production of feminine personalities organized around "communal" and "autocentric" issues and characterized by flexible ego boundaries, less detached objectivity, and relational cognitive style, on the one hand, and important aspects of feminine as opposed to masculine social roles, on the other.

Most generally, I would suggest that a quality of embeddedness in social interaction and personal relationships characterizes women's life relative to men's. From childhood, daughters are likely to participate in an intergenerational world with their mother, and often with their aunts and grandmother, whereas boys are on their own or participate in a single-generation world of age mates. In adult life, women's interaction with other women in most societies is kin-based and cuts across generational lines. Their roles tend to be particularistic, and to involve diffuse relationships and responsibilities rather than specific ones. Women in most societies are defined relationally (as someone's wife; mother, daughter, daughter-in-law; even a nun becomes the Bride of Christ). Men's association (although it too may be kin-based and intergenerational) is much more likely than women's to cut across kinship units, to be restricted to a single generation, and to be recruited according to universalistic criteria and involve relationships and responsibilities defined by their specificity.

EGO BOUNDARIES AND THE MOTHER-DAUGHTER RELATIONSHIP

The care and socialization of girls by women ensures the production of feminine personalities founded on relation and connection, with flexible rather than rigid ego boundaries, and with a comparatively secure sense of gender identity. This is one explanation for how women's relative embeddedness is reproduced from generation to generation, and why it exists within almost every society. More specific investigation of different social contexts suggests, however, that there are variations in the kind of relationship that can exist between women's role performance and feminine personality.

Various kinds of evidence suggest that separation from the mother, the breaking of dependence, and the establishment and maintenance of a consistently individuated sense of self remain difficult psychological issues for Western middle-class women (i.e., the women who become subjects of psychoanalytic and clinical reports and social-psychological studies). Deutsch (1944, 1945) in particular provides extensive clinical documentation of these difficulties and of the way they affect women's relationships to men and children and, because of their nature, are reproduced in the next generation of women. Mothers and daughters in the women's group mentioned [in note 1] describe their experience of boundary confusion or equation of self and other, for example, guilt and self-blame for the other's unhappiness; shame and embarrassment at the other's actions; daughters' "discovery" that they are "really" living out their mothers' lives in their choice of career; mothers' not completely conscious reactions to their daughters' bodies as their own (overidentification and therefore often unnecessary concern with supposed weight or skin problems, which the mother is really worried about in herself); etc.

A kind of guilt that Western women express seems to grow out of and to reflect lack of adequate self/other distinctions and a sense of inescapable embeddedness in relationships to others. Tax describes this well (1970: 2; italics mine):

> Since our awareness of others is considered our duty, the price we pay when things go wrong is guilt and self-hatred. And things always go wrong. We respond with apologies; we continue to apologize long after the event is forgotten—*and even if it had no causal relation to anything we did to begin with.* If the rain spoils someone's picnic, we apologize. We apologize for taking up space in a room, for living.

As if the woman does not differentiate herself clearly from the rest of the world, she feels a sense of guilt and responsibility for situations that did not come about through her actions and without relation to her actual ability to determine the course of events. This happens, in the most familiar instance, in a sense of diffuse responsibility for everything connected to the welfare of her family and the happiness and success of her children. This loss of self in overwhelming responsibility for and connection to others is described particularly acutely by women writers (in the work, for instance, of Simone de Beauvoir, Kate Chopin, Doris Lessing, Tillie Olsen, Christina Stead, Virginia Woolf).

Slater (1961) points to several studies supporting the contention that Western daughters have particular problems about differentiation from their mother. These studies show that though most forms of personal parental identification correlate with psychological adjustment (i.e., freedom from neurosis or psychosis, not social acceptability), personal identification of a daughter with her mother does not. The reason is that the mother-daughter relation is the one form of personal identification that, because it results so easily from the normal situation of child development, is liable to be excessive in the direction of allowing no room for separation or difference between mother and daughter.

The situation reinforces itself in circular fashion. A mother, on the one hand, grows up without establishing adequate ego boundaries or a firm sense of self. She tends to experience boundary confusion with her daughter, and does not provide experiences of differentiating ego development for her daughter or encourage the breaking of her daughter's dependence. The daughter, for her part, makes a rather unsatisfactory and artificial attempt to establish boundaries: she projects what she defines as bad within her onto her mother and tries to take what is good into herself. (This, I think, is the best way to understand the girl's oedipal "rejection" of her mother.) Such an arbitrary mechanism cannot break the under-

At the end of the twentieth century, women continue to stay at home with their young children, creating an intense bond between mothers and their children of both sexes.

lying psychological unity, however. Projection is never more than a temporary solution to ambivalence or boundary confusion.

The implication is that, contrary to Gutmann's suggestion (see note 3), "so-called ego pathology" may not be "adaptive" for women. Women's biosexual experiences (menstruation, coitus, pregnancy, childbirth, lactation) all involve some challenge to the boundaries of her body ego ("me"/"not-me" in relation to her blood or milk, to a man who penetrates her, to a child once part of her body). These are important and fundamental human experiences that are probably intrinsically meaningful and at the same time complicated for women everywhere. However, a Western woman's tenuous sense of individuation and of the firmness of her ego boundaries increases the likelihood that experiences challenging these boundaries will be difficult for her and conflictive.

Nor is it clear that this personality structure is "functional" for society as a whole. The evidence presented in this paper suggests that satisfactory mothering, which does not reproduce particular psychological problems in boys and girls, comes from a person with a firm sense

of self and of her own value, whose care is a freely chosen activity rather than a reflection of a conscious and unconscious sense of inescapable connection to and responsibility for her children.

SOCIAL STRUCTURE AND THE MOTHER-DAUGHTER RELATIONSHIP

Clinical and self-analytic descriptions of women and of the psychological component of mother-daughter relationships are not available from societies and subcultures outside of the Western middle class. However, accounts that are primarily sociological about women in other societies enable us to infer certain aspects of their psychological situation. In what follows, I am not claiming to make any kind of general statement about what constitutes a "healthy society," but only to examine and isolate specific features of social life that seem to contribute to the psychological strength of some members of a society. Consideration of three groups with matrifocal tendencies in their family structure (see Tanner, 1974) highlights several dimensions of importance in the developmental situation of the girl.

Young and Willmott (1957) describe the daily visiting and mutual aid of working-class mothers and daughters in East London. In a situation where household structure is usually nuclear, like the Western middle class, grown daughters look to their mothers for advice, for aid in childbirth and child care, for friendship and companionship, and for financial help. Their mother's house is the ultimate center of the family world. Husbands are in many ways peripheral to family relationships, possibly because of their failure to provide sufficiently for their families as men are expected to do. This becomes apparent if they demand their wife's disloyalty toward or separation from her mother: "The great triangle of childhood is mother-father-child; in Bethnal Green the great triangle of adult life is Mum-wife-husband" (p. 64).

Geertz (1961)[15] and Jay (1969) describe Javanese nuclear families in which women are often the more powerful spouse and have primary influence upon how kin relations are expressed and to whom (although these families are formally centered upon a highly valued conjugal relationship based on equality of spouses). Financial and decision-making control in the family often rests largely in the hands of its women. Women are potentially independent of men in a way that men are not independent of women. Geertz points to a woman's ability to participate in most occupations, and to own farmland and supervise its cultivation, which contrasts with a man's inability, even if he is financially independent, to do his own household work and cooking.

Women's kin role in Java is important. Their parental role and rights are greater than those of men; children always belong to the woman in case of divorce. When extra members join a nuclear family to constitute an extended family household, they are much more likely to be the wife's relatives than those of the husband. Formal and distant relations between men in a family, and between a man and his children (especially his son), contrast with the informal and close relations between women, and between a woman and her children. Jay and Geertz both emphasize the continuing closeness of the mother-daughter relationship as a daughter is growing up and throughout her married life. Jay suggests that there is a certain amount of ambivalence in the mother-daughter relationship, particularly as a girl grows toward adulthood and before she is married, but points out that at the same time the mother remains a girl's "primary figure of confidence and support" (1969: 103).

Siegel (1969)[16] describes Atjehnese families in Indonesia in which women stay on the homestead of their parents after marriage and are in total control of the household. Women tolerate men in the household only as long as they provide money, and even then treat them as someone between a child and a guest. Women's stated preference would be to eliminate even this necessary dependence on men: "Women, for instance, envision paradise as the place where they are reunited with their children and their mothers; husbands and fathers are absent, and yet there is an abundance all the same. Quarrels over money reflect the women's idea that men are basically adjuncts who exist only to give their families whatever they can earn" (p. 177). A woman in this society does not get into conflicts in which she has to choose between her mother and her husband, as happens in the Western working class (see above; also Komarovsky, 1962), where the reigning ideology supports the nuclear family.

In these three settings, the mother-daughter tie and other female kin relations remain important from a woman's childhood through her old age. Daughters stay closer to home in both childhood and adulthood, and remain involved in particularistic role relations. Sons and men are more likely to feel uncomfortable at home, and to spend work and play time away from the house. Male activities and spheres emphasize universalistic, distancing qualities: men in Java are the bearers and transmitters of high culture and formal relationships; men in East London spend much of their time in alienated work settings; Atjehnese boys spend their time in school, and their fathers trade in distant places.

Mother-daughter ties in these three societies, described as extremely close, seem to be composed of companionship and mutual cooperation, and to be positively valued by both mother and daughter. The ethnographies do not imply that women are weighed down by the burden of their relationships or by overwhelming guilt and responsibility. On the contrary, they seem to have developed a strong sense of self and self-worth, which continues to grow as they get older and take on their maternal role. The implication is that "ego strength" is not completely dependent on the firmness of the ego's boundaries.

Guntrip's distinction between "immature" and "mature" dependency clarifies the difference between mother-daughter relationships and women's psyche in the Western middle class and in the matrifocal societies described. Women in the Western middle class are caught up to some extent in issues of infantile dependence, while the women in matrifocal societies remain in definite connection with others, but in relationship characterized by mature dependence. As Guntrip describes it (1961: 291): "*Mature dependence* is characterized by full differentiation of ego and object (emergence from primary identification) and therewith a capacity for valuing the object for its own sake and for giving as well as receiving; a condition which should be described not as independence but as mature dependence." This kind of mature dependence is also to be distinguished from the kind of forced independence and denial of need or relationship that I have suggested characterizes masculine personality and

that reflects continuing conflict about infantile dependence (Guntrip, 1961: 293; my italics): "Maturity is not equated with independence though it includes a certain capacity for independence. . . . the independence of the mature person is simply that he does not collapse when he has to stand alone. It is not an independence of needs for other persons with whom to have relationship: *that would not be desired by the mature.*"

Depending on its social setting, women's sense of relation and connection and their embeddedness in social life provide them with a kind of security that men lack. The quality of a mother's relationship to her children and maternal self-esteem, on the one hand, and the nature of a daughter's developing identification with her mother, on the other, make crucial differences in female development.

Women's kin role, and in particular the mother role, is central and positively valued in Atjeh, Java, and East London. Women gain status and prestige as they get older; their major role is not fulfilled in early motherhood. At the same time, women may be important contributors to the family's economic support, as in Java and East London, and in all three societies they have control over real economic resources. All these factors give women a sense of self-esteem independent of their relationship to their children. Finally, strong relationships exist between women in these societies, expressed in mutual cooperation and frequent contact. A mother, then, when her children are young, is likely to spend much of her time in the company of other women, not simply isolated with her children.

These social facts have important positive effects on female psychological development. (It must be emphasized that all the ethnographies indicate that these same social facts make male development difficult and contribute to psychological insecurity and lack of ease in interpersonal relationships in men.) A mother is not invested in keeping her daughter from individuating and becoming less dependent. She has other ongoing contacts and relationships that help fulfill her psychological and social needs. In addition, the people surrounding a mother while a child is growing up become mediators between mother and daughter, by providing a daughter with alternative models for personal identification and objects of attachment, which contribute to her differentiation from her mother. Finally, a daughter's identification with her mother in this kind of setting is with a strong woman with clear control over important spheres of life, whose sense of self-esteem can reflect this. Acceptance of her gender identity involves positive valuation of herself, and not an admission of inferiority. In psychoanalytic terms, we might say it involves identification with a preoedipal, active, caring mother. Bibring points to clinical findings supporting this interpretation: "We find in the analysis of the women who grew up in this 'matriarchal' setting the rejection of the feminine role less frequently than among female patients coming from the patriarchal family culture" (1953: 281).

There is another important aspect of the situation in these societies. The continuing structural and practical importance of the mother-daughter tie not only ensures that a daughter develops a positive personal and role identification with her mother, but also requires that the close psychological tie between mother and daughter become firmly grounded in real role expectations. These provide a certain constraint and limitation upon the relationship, as well as an avenue for its expression through common spheres of interest based in the external social world.

All these societal features contrast with the situation of the Western middle-class woman. Kinship relations in the middle class are less important. Kin are not likely to live near each other, and, insofar as husbands are able to provide adequate financial support for their families, there is no need for a network of mutual aid among related wives. As the middle-class woman gets older and becomes a grandmother, she cannot look forward to increased status and prestige in her new role.

The Western middle-class housewife does not have an important economic role in her family. The work she does and the responsibilities that go with it (household management, cooking, entertaining, etc.) do not seem to be really necessary to the economic support of her family (they are crucial contributions to the maintenance and reproduction of her family's class position, but this is not generally recognized as important either by the woman herself or by the society's ideology). If she works outside the home, neither she nor the rest of society is apt to consider this work to be important to her self-definition in the way that her housewife role is.

Child care, on the other hand, is considered to be her crucially important responsibility. Our post-Freudian society in fact assigns to parents (and especially to the mother[17]) nearly total responsibility for how children turn out. A middle-class mother's daily life is not centrally involved in relations with other women. She is isolated with her children for most of her workday. It is not surprising, then, that she is likely to invest a lot of anxious energy and guilt in her concern for her children and to look to them for her own self-affirmation, or that her self-esteem, dependent on the lives of others than herself, is shaky. Her life situation leads her to an overinvolvement in her children's lives.

A mother in this situation keeps her daughter from differentiation and from lessening her infantile dependence. (She also perpetuates her son's dependence, but in this case society and his father are more likely to interfere in order to assure that, behaviorally, at least, he doesn't act dependent.) And there are not other people around to mediate in the mother-daughter relationship. Insofar as the father is actively involved in a relationship with his daughter and his daughter develops some identification with him, this helps her individuation, but the formation of ego autonomy through identification with and idealization of her father may be at the expense of her positive sense of feminine self. Unlike the situation in matrifocal families, the continuing closeness of the mother-daughter relationship is expressed only on a psychological, interpersonal level. External role expectations do not ground or limit it.

It is difficult, then, for daughters in a Western middle-class family to develop self-esteem. Most psychoanalytic and social theorists[18] claim that the mother inevitably represents to her daughter (and son) regression, passivity, dependence, and lack of orientation to reality, whereas the father represents progression, activity, independence, and reality orientation.[19] Given the value implications of this dichotomy, there are advantages for the son in giving up his mother and identifying with his father. For the daughter, feminine gender identification means identification with a devalued, passive mother, and personal maternal identification is with a mother whose own self-esteem is low. Conscious rejection of her oedipal maternal identification, however, remains an unconscious rejection and devaluation of herself, because of her continuing preoedipal identification and boundary confusion with her mother.

Cultural devaluation is not the central issue, however. Even in patrilineal, patrilocal societies in which women's status is very low, women do not necessarily translate this cultural devaluation into low self-esteem, nor do girls have to develop difficult boundary problems with their mother. In the Moslem Moroccan family, for example,[20] a large amount of sex segregation and sex antagonism gives women a separate (domestic) sphere in which they have a real productive role and control, and also a life situation in which any young mother is in the company of other women. Women do not need to invest all their psychic energy in their children, and their self-esteem is not dependent on their relationship to their children. In this and other patrilineal, patrilocal societies, what resentment women do have at their oppressive situation is more often expressed toward their sons, whereas daughters are seen as allies against oppression. Conversely, a daughter develops relationships of attachment to and identification with other adult women. Loosening her tie to her mother therefore does not entail the rejection of all women. The close tie that remains between mother and daughter is based not simply on mutual overinvolvement but often on mutual understanding of their oppression.

CONCLUSION

Women's universal mothering role has effects both on the development of masculine and feminine personality and on the relative state of the sexes. This paper has described the development of relational personality in women and of personalities preoccupied with the denial of relation in men. In its comparison of different societies, it has suggested that men, while guaranteeing to themselves sociocultural superiority over women, always remain psychologically defensive and insecure. Women, by contrast, although always of secondary social and cultural status, may in favorable circumstances gain psychological security and a firm sense of worth and importance in spite of this.

Social and psychological oppression, then, is perpetuated in the structure of personality. The paper enables us to suggest what social arrangements contribute (and could contribute) to social equality between men and women and their relative freedom from certain sorts of psychological conflict. Daughters and sons must be able to develop a personal identification with more than one adult, and preferably one embedded in a role relationship that gives it a social context of expression and provides some limitation upon it. Most important, boys need to grow up around men who take a major role in child care, and girls around women who, in addition to their child-care responsibilities, have a valued role and recognized spheres of legitimate control. These arrangements could help to ensure that children of both sexes develop a sufficiently individuated and strong sense of self, as well as a positively valued and secure gender identity, that does not bog down either in ego boundary confusion, low self-esteem, and overwhelming relatedness to others, or in compulsive denial of any connection to others or dependence upon them.

REFERENCES

Ariès, Philippe. 1962. *Centuries of Childhood: A Social History of Family Life.* New York.

Bakan, David. 1966. *The Duality of Human Existence: Isolation and Communion in Western Man.* Boston.

———. 1968. *Disease, Pain, and Sacrifice: Toward a Psychology of Suffering.* Boston.

Balint, Alice. 1954. *The Early Years of Life: A Psychoanalytic Study.* New York.

Barry, Herbert, M. K. Bacon, and I. L. Child. 1957. "A Cross-Cultural Survey of Some Sex Differences in Socialization," *Journal of Abnormal and Social Psychology,* 55: 327–332.

Bettelheim, Bruno. 1954. *Symbolic Wounds: Puberty Rites and the Envious Male.* New York.

Bibring, Grete. 1953. "On the 'Passing of the Oedipus Complex' in a Matriarchal Family Setting," in Rudolph M. Lowenstein, ed., *Drives, Affects and Behavior: Essays in Honor of Marie Bonaparte.* New York, pp. 278–284.

Brunswick, Ruth Mack. 1940. "The Preoedipal Phase of the Libido Development," in Robert Fliess, ed., pp. 231–253.

Burton, Roger V., and John W. M. Whiting. 1961. "The Absent Father and Cross-Sex Identity," *Merrill-Palmer Quarterly of Behavior and Development,* 7, no. 2: 85–95.

Carlson, Rae. 1971. "Sex Differences in Ego Functioning: Exploratory Studies of Agency and Communion," *Journal of Consulting and Clinical Psychology,* 57: 267–277.

Chodorow, Nancy. 1971. "Being and Doing. A Cross-Cultural Examination of the Socialization of Males and Females," in Vivian Gornick and B. K. Moran, eds., *Woman in Sexist Society: Studies in Power and Powerlessness.* New York.

Cohen, Rosalie A. 1969. "Conceptual Styles, Culture Conflict, and Nonverbal Tests of Intelligence," *American Anthropologist,* 71: 828–856.

Deutsch, Helene. 1925. "The Psychology of Woman in Relation to the Functions of Reproduction," in Robert Fliess, ed., pp. 165–179.

———. 1930. "The Significance of Masochism in the Mental Life of Women," in Robert Fliess, ed., pp. 195–207.

———. 1932. "On Female Homosexuality," in Robert Fliess, ed., pp. 208–230.

———. 1944, 1945. *Psychology of Women,* Vols. I, II. New York.

Durkheim, Emile. 1897. *Suicide.* New York, 1968.

Erikson, Erik H. 1964. *Insight and Responsibility.* New York.

———. 1965. "Womanhood and the Inner Space," in Robert Jay Lifton, ed., *The Woman in America.* Cambridge, Mass.

Fairbairn, W. Ronald D. 1952. *An Object-Relations Theory of the Personality.* New York.

Fliess, Robert. 1948. "Female and Preoedipal Sexuality: A Historical Survey," in Robert Fliess, ed., pp 159–164.

———. 1961. *Ego and Body Ego: Contributions to Their Psychoanalytic Psychology.* New York, 1970.

Fliess, Robert, ed. 1969. *The Psychoanalytic Reader: An Anthology of Essential Papers with Critical Introductions.* New York. Originally published in 1948.

Freedman, David. 1961, "On Women Who Hate Their Husbands," in Hendrik M. Ruitenbeek, ed., pp. 221–237.

Freud, Sigmund. 1925. "Some Psychological Consequences of the Anatomical Distinction Between the Sexes," in James Strachey, ed., *The Standard Edition of the Complete Psychological Works of Sigmund Freud,* Vol. XIX. London, pp. 248–258.

———. 1931. "Female Sexuality," in Ruitenbeek, ed., pp. 88–105.

———. 1933. "Femininity," in *New Introductory Lectures in Psychoanalysis*. New York, 1961, pp. 112–135.

Geertz, Hildred. 1961. *The Javanese Family: A Study of Kinship and Socialization*. New York.

Guntrip, Harry. 1961. *Personality Structure and Human Interaction: The Developing Synthesis of Psycho-Dynamic Theory*. New York.

Gutmann, David. 1965. "Women and the Conception of Ego Strength," *Merrill-Palmer Quarterly of Behavior and Development*, 2: 229–240.

Harper, Edward B. 1969. "Fear and the Status of Women," *Southwestern Journal of Anthropology*, 25: 81–95.

Jay, Robert R. 1969. *Javanese Villagers: Social Relations in Rural Moddjokuto*. Cambridge, Mass.

Jones, Ernest. 1927. "The Early Development of Female Sexuality," in Ruitenbeek, ed., pp. 21–35.

Klein, Melanie, and Joan Rivière. 1937. *Love, Hate and Reparation*. New York, 1964.

Kohlberg, Lawrence. 1966. "A Cognitive-Developmental Analysis of Children's Sex-Role Concepts and Attitudes," in Eleanor E. Maccoby, ed., *The Development of Sex Differences*. Stanford, Calif., pp. 82–173.

Komarovsky, Mirra. 1962. *Blue-Collar Marriage*. New York, 1967.

Lamp-de Groot, J. 1927. "The Evolution of the Oedipus Complex in Women," in Robert Fliess, ed., pp. 180–194.

LeVine, Robert A. 1971a. "The Psychoanalytic Study of Lives in Natural Social Settings," *Human Development*, 14: 100–109.

———. 1971b. "Rethinking Psychoanalytic Anthropology." Paper presented at the Institute on Psychoanalytic Anthropology, 70th Annual Meeting of the American Anthropological Association, New York.

Mead, Margaret. 1935. *Sex and Temperament in Three Primitive Societies*. New York, 1963.

———. 1949. *Male and Female: A Study of Sexes in a Changing World*. New York, 1968.

Milman, Marcia. 1972. "Tragedy and Exchange: Metaphoric Understandings of Interpersonal Relationships." Ph.D. dissertation, Department of Sociology, Brandeis University.

Minturn, Leigh, and John T. Hitchcock. 1969. "The Rajputs of Khalapur, India," in Beatrice B. Whiting, ed., *Six Cultures: Studies in Child Rearing*. New York.

Mitscherlich, Alexander. 1963. *Society Without the Father*. New York, 1970.

Parsons, Talcott. 1961. *Social Structure and Personality*. New York.

Parsons, Talcott, and Robert F. Bales. 1955. *Family, Socialization and Interaction Process*. New York.

Ruitenbeek, Hendrik M., ed. 1966. *Psychoanalysis and Female Sexuality*. New Haven.

Siegel, James T. 1969. *The Rope of God*. Berkeley, Calif.

Slater, Philip E. 1961. "Toward a Dualistic Theory of Identification," *Merrill Palmer Quarterly of Behavior and Development*, 7: 118–126.

———. 1968. *The Glory of Hera: Greek Mythology and the Greek Family*. Boston.

———. 1970. *The Pursuit of Loneliness: American Culture at the Breaking Point*. Boston.

Tanner, Nancy. 1971. "Matrifocality in Indonesia and Among Black Americans." Paper presented at the 70th Annual Meeting of the American Anthropological Association, New York.

Tax, Meredith. 1970. *Woman and Her Mind: The Story of Daily Life*. Boston.

Thompson, Clara. 1943. "'Penis Envy' in Women," in Ruitenbeek, ed., pp. 215–251.

Whiting, John W. M. 1959. "Sorcery, Sin, and the Superego: A Cross-Cultural Study of Some Mechanisms of Social Control," in Clellan S. Ford, ed., *Cross-Cultural Approaches: Readings in Comparative Research*. New Haven, 1967, pp. 47–68.

Whiting, John W. M., Richard Kluckhohn, and Albert Anthony. 1958 "The Function of Male Initiation Rites at Puberty," in Eleanor E. Maccoby, T. M. Newcomb, and E. L. Hartley, eds., *Readings in Social Psychology*. New York, pp. 359–370.

Winch, Robert F. 1969. *Identification and Its Familial Determinants.* New York.

Young, Michael, and Peter Willmott. 1957. *Family and Kinship in East London.* London, 1966.

NOTES

1. My understanding of mother-daughter relationships and their effect on feminine psychology grows out of my participation beginning in 1971 in a women's group that discusses mother-daughter relationships in particular and family relationships in general. All the women in this group have contributed to this understanding. An excellent dissertation by Marcia Millman (1972) first suggested to me the importance of boundary issues for women and became a major organizational focus for my subsequent work. Discussions with Nancy Jay, Michelle Rosaldo, Philip Slater, Barrie Thorne, Susan Weisskopf, and Beatrice Whiting have been central to the development of the ideas presented here. I am grateful to George Goethals, Edward Payne, and Mal Slavin for their comments and suggestion about earlier versions of this paper.

2. Margaret Mead provided the most widely read and earliest argument for this viewpoint (cf., e.g., 1935 and 1949); see also Chodorow (1971) for another discussion of the same issue.

3. Unfortunately, the language that describes personality structure is itself embedded with value judgment. The implication in most studies is that it is always better to have firmer ego boundaries, that "ego strength" depends on the degree of individuation. Gutmann, who recognizes the linguistic problem, even suggests that "so-called ego pathology may have adaptive implications for women" (1965:231). The argument can be made that extremes in either direction are harmful. Complete lack of ego boundaries is clearly pathological, but so also, as critics of contemporary Western men point out (cf., e.g., Bakan, 1966, and Slater, 1970), is

individuation gone wild, what Bakan calls "agency unmitigated by communion," which he takes to characterize, among other things, both capitalism based on the Protestant ethic and aggressive masculinity. With some explicit exceptions that I will specify in context, I am using the concepts solely in the descriptive sense.

4. Slater (1968) provides one example of such an investigation. LeVine's recent work on psychoanalytic anthropology (1971a,b) proposes a methodology that will enable social scientists to study personality development in this way.

5. Particularly as interpreted by object-relations theorists (e.g., Fairbairn, 1952 and Guntrup, 1961) and, with some similarity, by Parsons (1964) and Parsons and Bales (1955).

6. Cf., e.g., Brunswick, 1940; Deutsch, 1932, 1944; Fliess, 1948; Freud, 1931; Jones, 1927; and Lampl-de Groot, 1928.

7. The important distinction between "positional" and "personal" identification comes from Slater, 1961, and Winch, 1962.

8. For more extensive argument concerning this, cf., e.g., Burton and Whiting (1961), Chodorow (1971), and Slater (1968).

9. The processes by which individual personal experiences and psychological factors contribute to or are translated into social and cultural facts, and, more generally, the circularity of explanations in terms of socialization, are clearly very complicated. A discussion of these issues, however, is not within the scope of his paper.

10. The question of the universality of the oedipus complex as Freud described it is beyond the scope of this paper. Bakan (1966, 1968) points out that in the original Oedipus myth, it was the father who first tried to kill his son, and that the theme of parental infanticide is central to the entire Old Testament. He suggests that for a variety of reasons, fathers probably have hostile and aggressive fantasies and feelings about their children (sons). This more general

account, along with a variety of psychological and anthropological data, convinces me that we must take seriously the notion that members of both generations may have conflicts over the inevitable replacement of the elder generation by the younger, and that children probably feel guilt and (rightly) some helplessness in this situation.

11. These views are most extreme and explicit in two papers (Freud, 1925, 1933) and warrant the criticism that has been directed at them. Although the issue of penis envy in women is not central to this paper, it is central to Freud's theory of female development. Therefore I think it worthwhile to mention three accounts that avoid Freud's ideological mistakes while allowing that his clinical observations of penis envy might be correct.

    Thompson (1943) suggests that penis envy is a symbolic expression of women's culturally devalued and underprivileged position in our patriarchal society; that possession of a penis symbolizes the possession of power and privilege. Bettelheim (1954) suggests that members of either sex envy the sexual functions of the other and that women are more likely to express this envy overtly, because, since men are culturally superior, such envy is considered "natural." Balint (1954) does not rely on the fact of men's cultural superiority, but suggests that a little girl develops penis envy when she realizes that her mother loves people with penises, i.e., her father, and thinks the possession of a penis will help her in her rivalry for her mother's attention.

12. See, e.g., Brunswick, 1940; Deutsch, 1925, 1930, 1932, 1944; Freedman, 1961; Freud, 1931; Jones, 1927.

13. Following Cohen (1969), I would suggest that the external structural features of these settings (in the family or in school, for instance) are often similar or the same for boys and girls. The different kind and amount of adult male and female participation in these settings accounts for their being experienced by children of different sexes as different sorts of milieux.

14. Gutmann points out that all these qualities are supposed to indicate lack of adequate ego strength, and suggests that we ought to evaluate ego strength in terms of the specific demands of different people's (e.g., women's as opposed to men's) dally lives. Bakan goes even further and suggests that modern male ego qualities are a pathological extreme. Neither account is completely adequate. Gutmann does not consider the possibility (for which we have good evidence) that the everyday demands of an autocentric milieu are unreasonable: although women's ego qualities may be "functional" for their participation in these milieux, they do not necessarily contribute to the psychological strength of the women themselves. Bakan, in his (legitimate) preoccupation with the lack of connection and compulsive independence that characterizes Western masculine success, fails to recognize the equally clear danger (which, I will suggest, is more likely to affect women) of communion unmitigated by agency—of personality and behavior with no sense of autonomous control or independence at all.

    I think this is part of a more general social-scientific mistake, growing out of the tendency to equate social structure and society with male social organization and activities within a society. This is exemplified, for instance, in Erikson's idealistic conception of maternal qualities in women (1965) and, less obviously, in the contrast between Durkheim's extensive treatment of "anomic" suicide (1897) and his relegation of "fatalistic" suicide to a single footnote (p. 276).

15. This ethnography, and a reading of it that focuses on strong female kin relations, was brought to my attention by Tanner (1971).

16. See note 15.

17. See Slater (1970) for an extended discussion of the implications of this.

18. See, e.g., Deutsch, 1944, passim; Erikson, 1964: 62; Klein and Rivière, 1937; Parsons, 1970, passim; Parsons and Bales, 1955, passim.

19. Their argument derives from the universal fact that a child must outgrow her/his primary identification with and total dependence upon the mother. The present paper argues that the value implications of this dichotomy grow out of the particular circumstances of our society and its devaluation of relational qualities. Allied to this is the suggestion that it does not need to be, and often is not, relationship to the father that breaks the early maternal relationship.

20. Personal communication from Fatima Mernissi, based on her experience growing up in Morocco and her recent sociological fieldwork there.

Study/Discussion Questions

1. How does Chodorow explain the differences in male and female personalities?
2. What is it about our early experiences with our mothers that pushes boys in one set of directions and girls in another?
3. According to Chodorow, how are men and women different by the time they reach adulthood?
4. If Chodorow is right, what changes in rearing children might make girls and boys less different psychologically? Can you think of ways in which this would be a positive thing for girls?

Who's Irish?

Gish Jen

In China, people say mixed children are supposed to be smart, and definitely my granddaughter Sophie is smart. But Sophie is wild, Sophie is not like my daughter Natalie, or like me. I am work hard my whole life, and fierce besides. My husband always used to say he is afraid of me, and in our restaurant, busboys and cooks all afraid of me too. Even the gang members come for protection money, they try to talk to my husband. When I am there, they stay away. If they come by mistake, they pretend they are come to eat. They hide behind the menu, they order a lot of food. They talk about their mothers. Oh, my mother have some arthritis, need to take herbal medicine, they say. Oh, my mother getting old, her hair all white now.

I say, Your mother's hair used to be white, but since she dye it, it become black again. Why don't you go home once in a while and take a look? I tell them, Confucius say a filial son knows what color his mother's hair is.

My daughter is fierce too, she is vice president in the bank now. Her new house is big enough for everybody to have their own room, including me. But Sophie take after Natalie's husband's family, their name is Shea. Irish. I always thought Irish people are like Chinese people, work so hard on the railroad, but now I know why the Chinese beat the Irish. Of course, not all Irish are like the Shea family, of course not. My daughter tell me I should not say Irish this, Irish that.

How do you like it when people say the Chinese this, the Chinese that, she say.

You know, the British call the Irish heathen, just like they call the Chinese, she say.

You think the Opium War was bad, how would you like to live right next door to the British, she say.

And that is that. My daughter have a funny habit when she win an argument, she take a sip of something and look away, so the other person is not embarrassed. So I am not embarrassed. I do not call anybody anything either. I just happen to mention about the Shea family, an interesting fact: four brothers in the family, and not one of them work. The mother, Bess, have a job before she got sick, she was executive secretary in a big company. She is handle everything for a big shot, you would be surprised how complicated her job is, not just type this, type that. Now she is a nice woman with a clean house. But her boys, every one of them is on welfare, or so-called severance pay, or so-called disability pay. Something. They say they cannot find work, this is not the economy of the fifties, but I say, Even the black people doing better these days, some of them live so fancy, you'd be surprised. Why the Shea family have so much trouble? They are white people, they speak English. When I come to this country, I have no money and do not speak English. But my husband and I own our restaurant before he die. Free and clear, no mortgage. Of course, I understand I am just lucky, come from a country where the food is popular all over the world. I understand it is not the Shea family's fault they come from a country where everything is boiled. Still, I say.

She's right, we should broaden our horizons, say one brother, Jim, at Thanksgiving. Forget about the car business. Think about egg rolls.

Pad thai, say another brother, Mike. I'm going to make my fortune in pad thai. It's going to be the new pizza.

I say, You people too picky about what you sell. Selling egg rolls not good enough for you, but at least my husband and I can say, We made it. What can you say? Tell me. What can you say?

Everybody chew their tough turkey.

I especially cannot understand my daughter's husband John, who has no job but cannot take care of Sophie either. Because he is a man, he say, and that's the end of the sentence.

Plain boiled food, plain boiled thinking. Even his name is plain boiled: John. Maybe because I grew up with black bean sauce and hoisin sauce and garlic sauce, I always feel something is missing when my son-in-law talk.

But, okay: so my son-in-law can be man, I am baby-sitter. Six hours a day, same as the old sitter, crazy Amy, who quit. This is not so easy, now that I am sixty-eight, Chinese age almost seventy. Still, I try. In China, daughter take care of mother. Here it is the other way around. Mother help daughter, mother ask, Anything else I can do? Otherwise daughter complain mother is not supportive. I tell daughter, We do not have this word in Chinese, supportive. But my daughter too busy to listen, she has to go to meeting, she has to write memo while her husband go to the gym to be a man. My daughter say otherwise he will be

depressed. Seems like all his life he has this trouble, depression.

No one wants to hire someone who is depressed, she say. It is important for him to keep his spirits up.

Beautiful wife, beautiful daughter, beautiful house, oven can clean itself automatically. No money left over, because only one income, but lucky enough, got the baby-sitter for free. If John lived in China, he would be very happy. But he is not happy. Even at the gym things go wrong. One day, he pull a muscle. Another day, weight room too crowded. Always something.

Until finally, hooray, he has a job. Then he feel pressure.

I need to concentrate, he say. I need to focus.

He is going to work for insurance company. Salesman job. A paycheck, he say, and at least he will wear clothes instead of gym shorts. My daughter buy him some special candy bars from the health-food store. They say THINK! on them, and are supposed to help John think.

John is a good-looking boy, you have to say that, especially now that he shave so you can see his face.

I am an old man in a young man's game, say John.

I will need a new suit, say John.

This time I am not going to shoot myself in the foot, say John.

Good, I say.

She means to be supportive, my daughter say. Don't start the send her back to China thing, because we can't.

Sophie is three years old American age, but already I see her nice Chinese side swallowed up by her wild Shea side. She looks like mostly Chinese. Beautiful black hair, beautiful black eyes. Nose perfect size, not so flat looks like something fell down, not so large looks like some big deal got stuck in wrong face. Everything just right, only her skin is a brown surprise to John's family. So brown, they say. Even

John say it. She never goes in the sun, still she is that color, he say. Brown. They say, Nothing the matter with brown. They are just surprised. So brown. Nattie is not that brown, they say. They say, It seems like Sophie should be a color in between Nattie and John. Seems funny, a girl named Sophie Shea be brown. But she is brown, maybe her name should be Sophie Brown. She never go in the sun, still she is that color, they say. Nothing the matter with brown. They are just surprised.

The Shea family talk is like this sometimes, going around and around like a Christmas-tree train.

Maybe John is not her father, I say one day, to stop the train.

And sure enough, train wreck. None of the brothers ever say the word brown to me again.

Instead, John's mother, Bess, say, I hope you are not offended.

She say, I did my best on those boys. But raising four boys with no father is no picnic.

You have a beautiful family, I say.

I'm getting old, she say.

You deserve a rest, I say. Too many boys make you old.

I never had a daughter, she say. You have a daughter.

I have a daughter, I say. Chinese people don't think a daughter is so great, but you're right. I have a daughter.

I was never against the marriage, you know, she say. I never thought John was marrying down. I always thought Nattie was just as good as white.

I was never against the marriage either, I say. I just wonder if they look at the whole problem.

Of course you pointed out the problem, you are a mother, she say. And now we both have a granddaughter. A little brown granddaughter, she is so precious to me.

I laugh. A little brown granddaughter, I say. To tell you the truth, I don't know how she came out so brown.

We laugh some more. These days Bess need a walker to walk. She take so many pills, she need two glasses of water to get them all down. Her favorite TV show is about bloopers, and she love her bird feeder. All day long, she can watch that bird feeder, like a cat.

I can't wait for her to grow up, Bess say. I could use some female company.

Too many boys, I say.

Boys are fine, she say. But they do surround you after a while.

You should take a break, come live with us, I say. Lots of girls at our house.

Be careful what you offer, say Bess with a wink. Where I come from, people mean for you to move in when they say a thing like that.

Nothing the matter with Sophie's outside, that's the truth. It is inside that she is like not any Chinese girl I ever see. We go to the park, and this is what she does. She stand up in the stroller. She take off all her clothes and throw them in the fountain.

Sophie! I say. Stop!

But she just laugh like a crazy person. Before I take over as baby-sitter, Sophie has that crazy-person sitter, Amy the guitar player. My daughter thought this Amy very creative—another word we do not talk about in China. In China, we talk about whether we have difficulty or no difficulty. We talk about whether life is bitter or not bitter. In America, all day long, people talk about creative. Never mind that I cannot even look at this Amy, with her shirt so short that her belly button showing. This Amy think Sophie should love her body. So when Sophie take off her diaper, Amy laugh. When Sophie run around naked, Amy say she wouldn't want to wear a diaper either. When Sophie go shu-shu in her lap, Amy laugh and say there are no germs in pee. When Sophie take off her shoes, Amy say bare feet is best, even the pediatrician say so. That is why Sophie now walk around with no shoes like a beggar child. Also why Sophie love to take off her clothes.

Turn around! say the boys in the park. Let's see that ass!

Of course, Sophie does not understand. Sophie clap her hands, I am the only one to say, No! This is not a game.

It has nothing to do with John's family, my daughter say. Amy was too permissive, that's all.

But I think if Sophie was not wild inside, she would not take off her shoes and clothes to begin with.

You never take off your clothes when you were little, I say. All my Chinese friends had babies, I never saw one of them act wild like that.

Look, my daughter say. I have a big presentation tomorrow.

John and my daughter agree Sophie is a problem, but they don't know what to do.

You spank her, she'll stop, I say another day.

But they say, Oh no.

In America, parents not supposed to spank the child.

It gives them low self-esteem, my daughter say. And that leads to problems later, as I happen to know.

My daughter never have big presentation the next day when the subject of spanking come up.

I don't want you to touch Sophie, she say. No spanking, period.

Don't tell me what to do, I say.

I'm not telling you what to do, say my daughter. I'm telling you how I feel.

I am not your servant, I say. Don't you dare talk to me like that.

My daughter have another funny habit when she lose an argument. She spread out all her fingers and look at them, as if she like to make sure they are still there.

My daughter is fierce like me, but she and John think it is better to explain to Sophie that clothes are a good idea. This is not so hard in the cold weather. In the warm weather, it is very hard.

Use your words, my daughter say. That's what we tell Sophie. How about if you set a good example.

As if good example mean anything to Sophie. I am so fierce, the gang members who used to come to the restaurant all afraid of me, but Sophie is not afraid.

I say, Sophie, if you take off your clothes, no snack.

I say, Sophie, if you take off your clothes, no lunch.

I say, Sophie, if you take off your clothes, no park.

Pretty soon we are stay home all day, and by the end of six hours she still did not have one thing to eat. You never saw a child stubborn like that.

I'm hungry! she cry when my daughter come home.

What's the matter, doesn't your grandmother feed you? My daughter laugh.

No! Sophie say. She doesn't feed me anything!

My daughter laugh again. Here you go, she say.

She say to John, Sophie must be growing.

Growing like a weed, I say.

Still Sophie take off her clothes, until one day I spank her. Not too hard, but she cry and cry, and when I tell her if she doesn't put her clothes back on I'll spank her again, she put her clothes back on. Then I tell her she is good girl, and give her some food to eat. The next day we go to the park and, like a nice Chinese girl, she does not take off her clothes.

She stop taking off her clothes, I report. Finally!

How did you do it? my daughter ask.

After twenty-eight years experience with you, I guess I learn something, I say.

It must have been a phase, John say, and his voice is suddenly like an expert.

His voice is like an expert about everything these days, now that he carry a leather briefcase, and wear shiny shoes, and can go shopping for a new car. On the company, he say. The company will pay for it, but he will be able to drive it whenever he want.

A free car, he say. How do you like that.

It's good to see you in the saddle again, my daughter say. Some of your family patterns are scary.

At least I don't drink, he say. He say, And I'm not the only one with scary family patterns.

That's for sure, say my daughter.

Everyone is happy. Even I am happy, because there is more trouble with Sophie, but now I think I can help her Chinese side fight against her wild side. I teach her to eat food with fork or spoon or chopsticks, she cannot just grab into the middle of a bowl of noodles. I teach her not to play with garbage cans. Sometimes I spank her, but not too often, and not too hard.

Still, there are problems. Sophie like to climb everything. If there is a railing, she is never next to it. Always she is on top of it. Also, Sophie like to hit the mommies of her friends. She learn this from her playground best friend, Sinbad, who is four. Sinbad wear army clothes every day and like to ambush his mommy. He is the one who dug a big hole under the play structure, a foxhole he call it, all by himself. Very hardworking. Now he wait in the foxhole with a shovel full of wet sand. When his mommy come, he throw it right at her.

Oh, it's all right, his mommy say. You can't get rid of war games, it's part of their imaginative play. All the boys go through it.

Also, he like to kick his mommy, and one day he tell Sophie to kick his mommy too.

I wish this story is not true.

Kick her, kick her! Sinbad say.

Sophie kick her. A little kick, as if she just so happened was swinging her little leg and didn't realize that big mommy leg was in the way. Still I spank Sophie and make Sophie say sorry, and what does the mommy say?

Really, it's all right, she say. It didn't hurt.

After that, Sophie learn she can attack mommies in the playground, and some will say, Stop, but others will say, Oh, she didn't mean it, especially if they realize Sophie will be punished.

This is how, one day, bigger trouble come. The bigger trouble start when Sophie hide in the foxhole with that shovel full of sand. She wait, and when I come look for her, she throw it at me. All over my nice clean clothes.

Did you ever see a Chinese girl act this way?

Sophie! I say. Come out of there, say you're sorry.

But she does not come out. Instead, she laugh. Naaah, naahna, naaa-naaa, she say.

I am not exaggerate: millions of children in China, not one act like this.

Sophie! I say. Now! Come out now!

But she know she is in big trouble. She know if she come out, what will happen next. So she does not come out. I am sixty-eight, Chinese age almost seventy, how can I crawl under there to catch her? Impossible. So I yell, yell, yell, and what happen? Nothing. A Chinese mother would help, but American mothers, they look at you, they shake their head, they go home. And, of course, a Chinese child would give up, but not Sophie.

I hate you! she yell. I hate you, Meanie!

Meanie is my new name these days.

Long time this goes on, long long time. The foxhole is deep, you cannot see too much, you don't know where is the bottom. You cannot hear too much either. If she does not yell, you cannot even know she is still there or not. After a while, getting cold out, getting dark out. No one left in the playground, only us.

Sophie, I say. How did you become stubborn like this? I am go home without you now.

I try to use a stick, chase her out of there, and once or twice I hit her, but still she does not come out. So finally I leave. I go outside the gate.

Bye-bye! I say. I'm go home now.

But still she does not come out and does not come out. Now it is dinnertime, the sky is black. I think I should maybe go get help, but how can I leave a little girl by herself in the playground? A bad man could come. A rat could come. I go back in to see what is happen to Sophie. What if she have a shovel and is making a tunnel to escape?

Sophie! I say.

No answer.

Sophie!

I don't know if she is alive. I don't know if she is fall asleep down there. If she is crying, I cannot hear her.

So I take the stick and poke.

Sophie! I say. I promise I no hit you. If you come out, I give you a lollipop.

No answer. By now I worried. What to do, what to do, what to do? I poke some more, even harder, so that I am poking and poking when my daughter and John suddenly appear.

What are you doing? What is going on? say my daughter.

Put down that stick! say my daughter.

You are crazy! say my daughter.

John wiggle under the structure, into the foxhole, to rescue Sophie.

She fell asleep, say John the expert. She's okay. That is one big hole.

Now Sophie is crying and crying.

Sophia, my daughter say, hugging her. Are you okay, peanut? Are you okay?

She's just scared, say John.

Are you okay? I say too. I don't know what happen, I say.

She's okay, say John. He is not like my daughter, full of questions. He is full of answers until we get home and can see by the lamplight.

Will you look at her? he yell then. What the hell happened?

Bruises all over her brown skin, and a swollen-up eye.

You are crazy! say my daughter. Look at what you did! You are crazy!

How could you use a stick? I told you to use your words!

She is hard to handle, I say.

She's three years old! You cannot use a stick! say my daughter.

She is not like any Chinese girl I ever saw, I say.

I brush some sand off my clothes. Sophie's clothes are dirty too, but at least she has her clothes on.

Has she done this before? ask my daughter. Has she hit you before?

She hits me all the time, Sophie say, eating ice cream.

Your family, say John.

Believe me, say my daughter.

A daughter I have, a beautiful daughter. I took care of her when she could not hold her head up. I took care of her before she could argue with me, when she was a little girl with two pigtails, one of them always crooked. I took care of her when we have to escape from China, I took care of her when suddenly we live in a country with cars everywhere, if you are not careful your little girl get run over. When my husband die, I promise him I will keep the family together, even though it was just two of us, hardly a family at all.

But now my daughter take me around to look at apartments. After all, I can cook, I can clean, there's no reason I cannot live by myself, all I need is a telephone. Of course, she is sorry. Sometimes she cry, I am the one to say everything will be okay. She say she have no choice, she doesn't want to end up divorced. I say divorce is terrible, I don't know who invented this terrible idea. Instead of live with a telephone, though, surprise, I come to live with Bess.

Imagine that. Bess make an offer and, sure enough, where she come from, people mean for you to move in when they say things like that. A crazy idea, go to live with someone else's family, but she like to have some female company, not like my daughter, who does not believe in company. These days when my daughter visit, she does not bring Sophie. Bess say we should give Nattie time, we will see Sophie again soon. But seems like my daughter have more presentation than ever before, every time she come she have to leave.

I have a family to support, she say, and her voice is heavy, as if soaking wet. I have a young daughter and a depressed husband and no one to turn to.

When she say no one to turn to, she mean me.

These days my beautiful daughter is so tired she can just sit there in a chair and fall asleep. John lost his job again, already, but still they rather hire a baby-sitter than ask me to help, even they can't afford it. Of course, the new baby-sitter is much younger, can run around. I don't know if Sophie these days is wild or not wild. She call me Meanie, but she like to kiss me too, sometimes. I remember that every time I see a child on TV. Sophie like to grab my hair, a fistful in each hand, and then kiss me smack on the nose. I never see any other child kiss that way.

The satellite TV has so many channels, more channels than I can count, including a Chinese channel from the Mainland and a Chinese channel from Taiwan, but most of the time I watch bloopers with Bess. Also, I watch the bird feeder—so many, many kinds of birds come. The Shea sons hang around all the time, asking when will I go home, but Bess tell them, Get lost.

She's a permanent resident, say Bess. She isn't going anywhere.

Then she wink at me, and switch the channel with the remote control.

Of course, I shouldn't say Irish this, Irish that, especially now I am become honorary Irish myself, according to Bess. Me! Who's Irish? I say, and she laugh. All the same, if I could mention one thing about some of the Irish, not all of them of course, I like to mention this: Their talk just stick. I don't know how Bess Shea learn to use her words, but sometimes I hear what she say a long time later. Permanent resident. Not going anywhere. Over and over I hear it, the voice of Bess.

Study/Discussion Questions

1. Who is the narrator? What do mothers owe their daughters, in her view? What do daughters owe their mothers, in her view?
2. How are the narrator's views different from those of her daughter, Natalie?
3. What does Natalie expect from her mother? What does she expect of her daughter, Sophie?

Mothers

Anna Quindlen

Anna Quindlen was nineteen when her mother died. Now an adult, and a Pulitzer Prize–winning journalist, Quindlen observes other grown-up daughters out in New York City with their mothers, and she feels a certain longing. Even while constructing a perfect mother-daughter relationship in her fantasies, Quindlen acknowledges that real life probably would not have delivered anything quite so flawless. Still, the questions she did not know to ask her mother yet, at nineteen, sometimes flood her heart and mind.

The two women are sitting at a corner table in the restaurant, their shopping bags wedged between their chairs and the wall: Lord & Taylor, Bloomingdale's, something from Ann Taylor for the younger one. She is wearing a bright silk shirt, some good gold jewelry; her hair is on the long side, her makeup faint. The older woman is wearing a suit, a string of pearls, a diamond solitaire, and a narrow band. They lean across the table. I imagine the conversation: Will the new blazer go with the old skirt? Is the dress really right for an afternoon wedding? How is Daddy? How is his ulcer? Won't he slow down just a little bit?

It seems that I see mothers and daughters everywhere, gliding through what I think of as the adult rituals of parent and child. My mother died when I was nineteen. For a long time, it was all you needed to know about me, a kind of vest pocket description of my emo-tional complexion: "Meet you in the lobby in ten minutes—I have long brown hair, am on the short side, have on a red coat, and my mother died when I was nineteen."

That's not true anymore. When I see a mother and a daughter having lunch in a res-taurant, shopping at Saks, talking together on the crosstown bus, I no longer want to murder them. I just stare a little more than is polite, hoping that I can combine my observations with a half-remembered conversation, some anecdotes, a few old dresses, a photograph or two, and re-create, like an archaeologist of the soul, a relationship that will never exist. Of course, the question is whether it would have ever existed at all. One day at lunch I told two of my closest friends that what I minded most about not having a mother was the absence of that grown-up woman-to-woman relationship that was impossible as a child or adolescent, and that my friends were having with their mothers now. They both looked at me as though my teeth had turned purple. I didn't need to ask why; I've heard so many times about the futility of such relationships, about women with business suits and briefcases reduced to whining children by their mothers' offhand comment about a man, or a dress, or a homemade dinner.

I accept the fact that mothers and daughters probably always see each other across a chasm of rivalries. But I forget all those things when one of my friends is down with the flu and her mother arrives with an overnight bag to manage her household and feed her soup.

So now, at the center of my heart there is a fantasy, and a mystery. The fantasy is small, and silly: a shopping trip, perhaps a pair of shoes, a walk, a talk, lunch in a good restaurant, which my mother assumes is the kind of place I eat at all the time. I pick up the check. We take a cab to the train. She reminds me of somebody's birthday. I invite her and my father to dinner. The mystery is whether the fantasy has within it a nugget of fact. Would I really have wanted her to take care of the wedding arrangements, or come and stay for a week after the children were born? Would we have talked on the telephone about this and that? Would she have saved my clippings in a scrapbook? Or would she have meddled in my affairs, volunteering opinions I didn't want to hear about things that were none of her business, criticizing my clothes and my children?

Worse still, would we have been strangers with nothing to say to each other? Is all the good I remember about us simply wishful thinking? Is all the bad self-protection?

Perhaps it is at best difficult, at worst impossible for children and parents to be adults together. But I would love to be able to know that.

Sometimes I feel like one of those people searching, searching for the mother who gave them up for adoption. I have some small questions for her and I want the answers: How did she get her children to sleep through the night? What was her first labor like? Was there olive oil in her tomato sauce? Was she happy? If she had it to do over again, would she? When we pulled her wedding dress out of the box the other day to see if my sister might wear it, we were shocked to find how tiny it was. "My God," I said, "did you starve yourself to get into this thing?" But there was no one there. And if she had been there, perhaps I would not have asked in the first place. I suspect that we would have been friends, but I don't really know. I was simply a little too young at nineteen to understand the woman inside the mother.

I occasionally pass by one of those restaurant tables and I hear the bickering about nothing: You did so, I did not, don't tell me what you did or didn't do, oh, leave me alone. And I think that my fantasies are better than any reality could be. Then again, maybe not.

Study/Discussion Questions

1. What kind of relationship does Quindlen imagine she would have with her mother, if her mother were still alive?
2. Why do her friends think she is unrealistic in her expectations?
3. Do you think that she is unrealistic in her expectations?
4. If you are in your late teens or early twenties, how do you hope that your relationship with your mother will change as you get older?
5. If you are older, how has your relationship with your mother changed over the years?

"Bad" Mothers

Molly Ladd-Taylor and Lauri Umansky

Historians Molly Ladd-Taylor and Lauri Umansky trace the tangled roots, and explore the contemporary range, of mother-blaming in American society. They find the phenomenon to be neither recent nor benign. The particular forms mother-bashing has taken in various eras relate directly to the position of women in the family, the state, the economy, and the culture. Recognizing that individual mothers might abuse their children, these authors call for amelioration of the deep social problems masked by the general scapegoating of mothers for society's ills.

It was every parent's nightmare. Five-year old Corinne Erstad disappeared. A massive search found only her blood and a few strands of hair in the home of a family friend, Robert Guevara. DNA evidence linked the girl's blood to Guevara's sweatpants. His fingerprints were found on a plastic bag containing her sundress, her barrette, and a blood-soaked pair of her underpants. The prosecution thought the physical evidence against Guevara was overwhelming. But defense attorneys cast him as a pawn in a scam perpetrated by his lover, Corinne's mother. She was "a scheming welfare mother" who sold her child because she was tired of being poor. The jury found Guevara not guilty.[1]

Sarah and James were engaged in a bitter fight for custody of their six-year-old daughter. Although the two had never married, James believed that he was a more fit parent because of Sarah's hippie lifestyle. Conse-

quently, when the trial court ruled in Sarah's favor, he took his case all the way to the state Supreme Court. As evidence of Sarah's insensitivity to her daughter's needs, James listed her midwife-assisted home birth, advocacy of natural food, preference for home schooling, and opposition to immunization. James also worried about Sarah's unconventional relationships—with a couple who had an "open marriage" and with members of a Native American community. While the court acknowledged that Laural had thrived under her mother's care, it found James a more effective parent, because he was stable, mature—and had a conventional lifestyle. It awarded physical care to the father.[2]

Some mothers are not good mothers. No one can deny that. There are women who neglect their children, abuse them, or fail to provide them with proper psycho-

"Introduction," from Molly Ladd Taylor and Lauri Umansky, editors, *"Bad" Mothers: The Politics of Blame in Twentieth Century America*, New York: NYU Press, 1998, pp. 1–17, 21–28.

logical nurturance. But throughout the twentieth century, the label of "bad" mother has been applied to far more women than those whose actions would warrant the name. By virtue of race, class, age, marital status, sexual orientation, and numerous other factors, millions of American mothers have been deemed substandard.

In the past few decades, "bad" mothers have moved noticeably toward center stage in American culture. The stereotypes are familiar: the welfare mother, the teen mother, the career woman who has no time for her kids, the drug addict who poisons her fetus, the pushy stage mother, the overprotective Jewish mother, and so on. But mother-blaming goes far beyond these stereotypes. It can be found in custody disputes, political speeches, and parent-teacher conferences. It can be found in the glares of disapproval mothers get when their children act out in public. It can be found as well in the guilt feelings of working women who have internalized the "bad" mother label.

The long list of stereotypes and dizzying array of mother-blaming accusations tempt one to conclude that mothers get blamed for everything, pure and simple. Why? Is it just that mothers are there at the center of the nuclear family? Is it that no one can live up to the sentimentalized good-mother ideal? Or is mother-blaming merely a symptom of our society's misogyny?

WHAT MAKES A "BAD" MOTHER?

To most Americans, "bad" mothering is like obscenity: you know it when you see it.[3] Everyone agrees that mothers who beat or kill their children are bad. But beyond that? Americans are divided on whether mothers should stay home with their children, and on whether a "good" parent would spank a child. We even disagree about what age a "good" mother

should be. Most of us agree it's bad to become a mother too young, but at what age does a new mother become too old?[4] Does allowing your baby to sleep in your bed build a more secure child or an overly dependent one? Is it bad to breastfeed a toddler—or to give a newborn a bottle? The proliferation of consumer goods compounds the problem: advertisers make mothers feel bad if they don't buy the right baby products, while advice givers say a sure sign of a "bad" mother is a woman who buys her child too much.[5]

The fact is that all mothers are "bad" sometimes. Who has never spoken too sharply to her child or been too quick to discipline (or not quick enough)? Yet because most mothering takes place at home, away from public scrutiny, truly harmful mothering is not always easy to identify. Countless numbers of abused children fall through the cracks in the child welfare system because no one recognized the danger signs. At the same time, some women get classed as bad mothers, lose custody of their children, and even face criminal charges on astonishingly flimsy evidence.

We do not mean to downplay real violations of parental duty. However, the "bad" mother label does not necessarily denote practices that actually harm children. In fact, it serves to shift our attention away from a specific act to a whole person—and even to entire categories of people. Thus doctors are far more likely to diagnose fetal alcohol syndrome in the child of a Native American than in the child of a WASP, police and social workers are conditioned to look for juvenile delinquency among the sons of welfare mothers, and the media seem stunned when a likable white woman like Susan Smith kills her sons, something we think a drug addict more likely to do.

Over the past century, women classed as "bad" mothers have fallen into three general groups: those who did not live in a "traditional" nuclear family; those who would not or could not protect their children from harm; and those whose children went wrong. The first is the most remarked upon, and the most clearly unjust. Women who did not fit the middle-class family ideal of breadwinning father and stay-at-home mother have born the brunt of mother-blaming throughout most of American history. Wage-earning mothers, single mothers, slave mothers—in short, everyone except middle-class whites—fall outside the narrow good-mother ideal.

Yet the "traditional" two-parent, one-income family so celebrated by conservatives today is the historical exception, not the norm. Prior to the Second World War, few working-class men made enough money to support their families. Working-class mothers took in boarders or washing, did industrial homework such as making cigars or paper flowers—or sent their children off to jobs.[6] Only in the 1950s did a significant number of working-class men earn wages high enough to support their families. Nevertheless, the proportion of married women in the work force continued to grow. By 1960, 30 percent of married women were in the labor force, twice the proportion just twenty years earlier but still far less than the 68 percent of mothers with children at home who are labor force participants today.[7]

Class runs through a second piece of "evidence" of failed motherhood: the refusal (or inability) to protect one's child from danger, or even from disease. Mother-blaming abounds when children suffer untimely deaths. The readiness of the jury to believe that Corinne Erstad's mother had a hand in her death is just one example. The media's callous criticism of Jessica Dubroff's mother after the seven-year-old girl died trying to become the youngest person to copilot a plane across North America is another.[8] Mothers are also faulted when babies die of natural causes, especially when child care practices are identified as risk factors. For example, well-intentioned health reformers of the 1910s and 1920s considered the garlic and spicy food immigrant women fed their babies

to be a significant factor in infant mortality.[9] Similarly, some researchers in the 1990s claim that putting babies to sleep on their stomachs in a crib (instead of letting them sleep with their mothers in the family bed) increases the risk of Sudden Infant Death Syndrome—despite the fact that the majority of SIDS deaths are not associated with any known risk factors.[10]

A host of diseases thought to have psychological origins also get blamed on mothers. Not so long ago the psychiatric establishment considered autism, a neurological condition, to be caused by "refrigerator" mothers who rejected their children. Psychological experts also blamed schizophrenia on maternal rejection; many still associate anorexia with a troubled mother-daughter relationship, describing mothers of anorectics as controlling, perfectionist, frustrated, and nonconfrontational.[11]

Mothers often face blame when their children fall victim to incest or sexual abuse. In some cases, doctors and social workers suspect maternal abuse when a child suffers from a chronic disease. For example, failure to thrive often arouses suspicion of maternal neglect, although it can be caused by a defect in the esophagus. But beware of mothers who seem overly protective of ill children. Medical literature now warns doctors to suspect the mother of a frequently sick child, particularly if she seems "too" versed in medical parlance, of Munchausen's Syndrome by Proxy, a rare psychiatric disorder in which a mother induces illness in her child in order to surround herself with medical personnel and procedures.[12]

Finally, a child "gone wrong" is considered sure-fire evidence of faulty mothering. From the 1890s to the 1950s, independent-minded or overprotective women were thought to have "caused" their sons' homosexuality. Working mothers have long been blamed for juvenile delinquency; black mothers for welfare dependency; and mothers of serial killers for the crimes of their sons.[13] Yet women can be at fault even when sons commit no crimes. Conservatives blamed permissive mothers following the advice of Dr. Spock for an entire generation of flower children![14] Fathers, schools, television—and the environment outside the home—get little if any attention in this frenzy of attribution.

Childrearing advice, which gained unprecedented influence in the twentieth century, further narrows the range of good mothering. Moreover, the advice has changed dramatically over the years. In the 1920s, a "bad" mother raced to pick up her baby when he cried. Babies were to be left alone in their cribs for several hours a day, not overstimulated by too much cuddling, bouncing, or noise. Since doctors emphasized the importance of breaking "bad habits" early, thumbsucking and infant masturbation became signs that the mother had failed.[15] By the 1980s, bestselling author Penelope Leach assured mothers that they could not spoil a baby. She encouraged them to breastfeed on demand, pick up crying children, and even get babies to suck their thumbs. Now only "bad" mothers meted out solace by the clock.[16]

To add to the confusion, the experts in a given era don't agree on the measures of "good" parenting. Most now recommend breastfeeding, but they differ over how long. And there is no agreement about whether parents should sleep with the baby, when they should offer solid food, or when a child should be encouraged to read.[17] No matter. No one could possibly follow all the expert advice, because it often conflicts with real women's lives. For example, although advice givers now encourage women to breastfeed their babies, and for a longer period of time, those who do so in public risk public opprobrium and even arrest.[18] Despite the fact that most mothers of infants work outside the home, the childrearing advice continues to assume that they are home—and to insist that this is best for the children.[19] Indeed, with a minority of American families living the two-parents, one-wage-earner

lifestyle, we all face a discomfiting question: Do most mothers now qualify as "bad" mothers in one way or another?

"BAD" MOTHERS FOR EVERY ERA

Virtually every culture on historical record has had its wicked women, and in many cases their wickedness revolved around the reproductive function. Euripides' Medea, though fictional, epitomizes the evil mother: she slaughtered her own children out of rage over her husband's philandering. Some psychologists surmise that the mysterious power of the womb to bring forth life frightened men, who then projected their fear and aggression onto women in the form of monstrous mythical mothers who abandoned, maimed, slaughtered, or devoured their children (usually sons).[20] Other scholars emphasize the ways "bad" mothers of old threatened the economic status quo. Evil stepmothers, who jeopardized children's inheritance upon the father's death, have populated fairy tales and folklore for centuries.[21] A glance at the "bad" mothers of any age reveals the fate of women who violated the gender norms of their time, whether by choice, by fiat, or by the force of circumstance.

Ultimately, the definition of a "bad" mother intertwines with that of a "good" mother, itself a relatively recent invention. The concept of an instinctive mother love did not exist in the Western world prior to the eighteenth century. Maternal behaviors we take for granted today—such as grieving when your child dies, loving all your kids equally, and physically caring for your own children—were rare, at least among European mothers of the upper classes.[22]

The "bad" mother we recognize today has historical roots in the late eighteenth and early nineteenth century. Her appearance connects to the new ideas about motherhood and childhood innocence that accompanied industrialization, the American Revolution, and Protestant evangelicalism. These historical sea changes continue to inform mothering today: in the beliefs that children are innocent, that good mothering and good government are intertwined, and that nurturing represents woman's essential nature. Vestiges of the Victorian ideal of motherhood persist: the "good" mother remains self-abnegating, domestic, preternaturally attuned to her children's needs; the "bad" mother has failed on one or more of these scores.

Changes in the organization of work provided the basis of the new maternal ideal. As industrialization took hold in North America, "work" was redefined as entrepreneurship and wage earning, and tied to the cash economy. Men went outside the home to "work," while women remained at home, in "woman's sphere," to rear children. The physical differences between men and women supposedly mandated this arrangement.[23]

Political and religious developments, in the form of the American Revolution and Great Awakenings, reinforced the new ideas about women's and children's place. The ideology historians have dubbed Republican Motherhood defined women's place in the new nation and tied "good" mothering to nation building. Women were formally excluded from most rights of citizens (such as voting), but they were assigned informal responsibility for the moral education of their citizen-sons. This education was considered essential to a democracy; citizens' self-control could make or break the American political experiment.[24] In the same years, Calvinism and the belief in original sin gave way to a faith in childhood innocence and malleability. Where children's deaths had once been understood as God's will and their moral failings as the inevitable outcome of innate sinfulness, now the mother could be blamed. She had it in her power to make or break the child.[25]

In many ways, the ideology of woman's sphere signaled an advance for the white middle-class women who most embraced it.

Where previously womanhood was associated with sexuality, cunning, and immorality, the Victorian cult of "true womanhood" defined women as pure, pious, domestic, and submissive. Their supposedly superior moral sensibility gave "true" women dignity, increased their authority at home, justified their education, and defined their role in public life.[26]

Yet the sentimentalized Victorian mother perched on a shaky pedestal. The mother who lifted her voice too loudly or attended too diligently to her own needs felt the sting of familial, clerical, and community disapproval. "The care of children requires a great many sacrifices, and a great deal of self-denial," wrote the author and reformer Lydia Maria Child, "but the woman who is not willing to sacrifice a good deal in such a cause, does not deserve to be a mother."[27]

The ambiguous impact of such beliefs can be seen in the enormous changes to custody law over the nineteenth century. Mothers gained new powers as courts came to accept the view that they should have custody of young children. English common law, which dominated the American legal system until the mid-nineteenth century, gave fathers almost unlimited rights to the custody of their minor legitimate children. By mid-century, however, new ideas about childhood innocence and mother love led courts to emphasize the welfare of the child in custody determinations. By the 1860s, a number of states had adopted the doctrine of tender years, under which mothers, unless they were determined "unfit," automatically received custody of young children. At the same time, however, judicial authority gained force. Ideas about parental fitness, combined with ideas about true womanhood, placed all parents, but especially mothers, at the mercy of judicial assessments of their capacity as childrearers.[28]

The idea of woman's sphere—and the equating of maternal presence with "good" mothering—was not only new to the nineteenth century; it was also specific to middle-class culture. In most societies childrearing responsibilities were shared. Even within the United States, Native Americans, African Americans, and many immigrant groups had more communal childrearing practices that automatically defined the mothers in these groups as "bad" by middle-class Anglo-Saxon standards.[29]

Slave mothers, for example, could not possibly exhibit the hallmarks of "good" Victorian mothering. Slaveowners forced pregnant and nursing women to work long hours in fields, unable to protect their children, who were, after all, the property of the slaveowner. Frequently, slave children were sold away from their mothers, and in general they also suffered high rates of disease and death, as a result of poor nutrition, inadequate housing, and lack of health care. Recent research suggests that many infant deaths, previously explained as infanticide by both contemporaries and historians, may have been due to Sudden Infant Death Syndrome. Thus the high mortality rate among slave infants may well have signified, not slave women's inept mothering or refusal of slave status for their children, but the tragedy that can result from poor nutrition, low birth weight, and inadequate health care.[30]

In spite of these conditions, slave mothers did protect and nurture their children in manifold ways. Yet where the maternal ideal for white women dictated that they nurture their own children exclusively and in private, enslaved mothers developed networks to protect and care for children communally. If force or fatality separated a child from his or her parents, other adults stepped in to see that child through to adulthood. Thus, although slaveowners expropriated women's domestic and maternal labor for the use of their own families, slave children could count on the entire black community for everyday care.

Ironically, the image of the mammy romanticized the "mothering" skills of some black women—as long as these skills were directed to white children. Although proslavery ideologues declared black women to be lacking in maternal feelings for their own children, they sentimentalized the mammy, always there to protect and care for her young white charges. In so doing, they reinforced both the slave system and the gender hierarchy of their own households. The mammy, who was a slave and hence subordinate, epitomized for slaveowners the selfless mother figure; in that way, her image bolstered the notion that good mothering of white children involved submissiveness and domesticity. Since caring for slave children required challenging slaveowners, at least to some extent, the black mother of black children became a "bad" mother in comparison to the mammy.[31]

By the end of the nineteenth century, new scientific thinking had changed how people thought about mothering, and just about everything else. While earlier generations viewed mothering principally through a religious lens, middle-class families increasingly saw child nature as a matter to be investigated, quantified, and studied by psychologists, doctors, and others. Every aspect of children's care and development came under scrutiny.

The late-nineteenth century term "scientific motherhood" captured the new mood. "Good" mothers still had to love their children and be there for them, but now they also had to keep abreast of the latest expert advice. Scientific knowledge (usually provided by men) combined with women's mother love to form the ingredients necessary for successful childrearing in the modern age. A "good" mother joined a child study club. She kept a childrearing manual by her bedside, charted her child's physical and cognitive development, and monitored her own behavior.[32]

Evolutionary theory undergirded notions of good and bad mothering in this period, for it established a hierarchy of races in which only women of Anglo-Saxon or northern European origin could be truly "good" mothers. Women of "superior" heredity could ensure not only the well-being of their families but also the future of the nation (since they raised the next generation of citizens) and the progress of their race! Darwinian ideas thus enhanced the authority and prestige of Anglo-Saxon mothers, even as they turned up the pressure on them.

Women at the top of the evolutionary ladder were at least granted the possibility of being good mothers. Mothers of the so-called lesser races inevitably produced inferior offspring, no matter what they did. Maternal presence, which was considered crucial to the upbringing of middle-class white children, was thought unnecessary for blacks, Native Americans, and most immigrant groups. Darwin's followers thus provided a scientific justification for a two-track social policy, whereby women of so-called inferior races were compelled to leave their children for outside work, while elite mothers were required to remain at home.[33] Conservatives blamed the New Woman—the middle-class woman who sought education, work outside the home, and perhaps even the right to vote—for a host of social ills. Noting the exceedingly low birth rate among college-educated women, they accused graduates (and women's higher education itself) of contributing to the decline of the race. According to one doctor, writing in the *New York Medical Journal* in 1900, the rare "New Woman" who married was a "menace to civilization" and her child. "The weak, plastic, developing cells of the brain are twisted, distorted, and a perverted psychic growth promoted by the false examples and teachings of a discontented mother."[34]

"BAD" MOTHERS IN THE EARLY TWENTIETH CENTURY

As millions of immigrants from southern and eastern Europe poured into the United States in the first two decades of the twentieth cen-

tury, jittery nativists noted the relative diminution of the white Protestant, native-born population and charged elite women who did not produce large crops of children with "race suicide." A good mother was "sacred," proclaimed Theodore Roosevelt, but the woman who "shirks her duty, as wife and mother, earns the right to our contempt."[35]

Three aspects of modern American life exacerbated mother-blaming in the twentieth century: the dominance of childrearing experts, the growth of state power, and the flux in gender roles, manifested in the growing number of women in the work force and in feminist movements. As infant mortality dropped and families gained new hope for the survival of their children, parents began to attribute the deaths or illnesses of their children not to God but to the environment. Infant death was preventable—if the mother kept her home clean and sanitary and followed the experts' advice. With the improvements in infant health and the rise of such professions as psychology and medical pediatrics, the experts' attention moved from physical health to mental development. This shift had dire consequences for the mother.[36]

Prior to the 1920s, childrearing experts told women to combine mother love with scientific advice. By the 1920s, however, they described mother love as a "dangerous instrument" and a "stumbling block" to children's psychological development. Behaviorist psychologist John Watson, who dedicated his influential *Psychological Care of Infants and Children* to the "first mother who brings up a happy child," even wryly suggested that children would be better off never knowing their mothers! [37] According to the experts, industrialization—and the resulting removal of production from the home—led to bored mothers who dominated their children. Moreover, mothers who had little experience beyond the home were limited in their ability to teach children the habits necessary to succeed in business.

How could stay-at-home mothers who followed no strict schedule rear children to live by the clock?[38]

These experts might have had little clout if their rise had not been broadly interwoven with the growth of state power and the "helping professions" in the first third of the century. Public health programs, compulsory schooling, and the growing influence of the social work profession both provided much needed assistance to families and narrowed the range of acceptable behavior. In attempting to "save" children—and make them "American"—social workers frequently engaged in disputes over childrearing with immigrant and working-class mothers. A good American mother, they insisted, did not swaddle her infant or give her a pacifier. She did not feed her baby garlic or sausage or tortillas (or anything other than milk for the first nine months). When her children were sick, she turned to a doctor. A good mother would not place a talisman around her child's neck to ward off the evil eye.[39]

Feminists both challenged and reinforced the good mother/bad mother divide. In the 1910s and 1920s, middle-class women joined together in millions in the social reform movement historians now call maternalism. They attempted to increase women's status and carve out a space in public life by using the rhetoric of good motherhood. Maternalists such as Jane Addams claimed that motherhood (or potential motherhood) united all women, regardless of class, race, or nationality, and that women were uniquely suited to nurturance and care. Maternalists established parent-teacher associations and mothers' clubs and lobbied for numerous "pro-child" policies, such as publicly funded health education for new mothers, the abolition of child labor, and mothers' pensions (which evolved into Aid to Families with Dependent Children).[40]

In invoking the rhetoric of the "good" mother to build welfare services, maternalists unwittingly fostered a more intense criticism of mothers deemed to be bad. Mothers' pensions, for example, were available only for "good" mothers, mostly widows, who were identified as deserving by social workers who came into their homes. The 1935 Social Security Act, which made mothers' pensions (then called Aid to Dependent Children) into a national program, permitted states to deny welfare payments to mothers who did not provide a "suitable home." Many maternalists, like other American reformers, touted education in hygiene or "mothering skills" as solutions to child poverty. Thus, the nation's first welfare measure, the Sheppard-Towner Maternity and Infancy Act of 1921, provided education in nutrition and hygiene, but no medical care, to pregnant women and new mothers and explicitly prohibited monetary aid.[41]

The most egregious antimother laws of the early twentieth century were those permitting the compulsory sterilization of "feebleminded" and insane people considered unfit to bear children. The Supreme Court upheld the principle of compulsory eugenic sterilization in *Buck v. Bell* (1927), a case replete with tragic irony. Scholars now know that Carrie Buck, the allegedly feebleminded white woman whose sterilization the Court endorsed, was not retarded but merely an impoverished single mother who became pregnant as the result of a rape, and was institutionalized. By 1939, more than thirty-three thousand people—mostly women—had been legally sterilized. Yet the definition of "feeblemindedness" was vague. For women, it was tied up with other conditions that made one a "bad" mother, such as having a child out of wedlock, being on welfare, living in poverty.[42]

"BAD" MOTHERS IN THE POSTWAR YEARS

Mother-blaming of the 1920s and 1930s, however fierce, paled in comparison to that of World

War II and the postwar years. Philip Wylie, who coined the term "momism" in 1942, set the mother-bashing tone. To Wylie, "megaloid momworship" was responsible for most problems of modern American society. He and other critics linked the upheaval in gender roles during the war, and American men's responses first to fascism and then to communism, to an apparent crisis of motherhood.[43]

In part this backlash responded to very real concerns that emerged during the war. In the 1940s, war effort propaganda encouraged women to enter the labor force. Real difficulties of combining wage work and family life in the absence of adequate child care or housing combined with hysteria to create media horror stories of juvenile delinquents out of control, children abandoned and uncared for while their mothers worked. Newspapers reported women giving up their children because they could not (or would not?) support them. The Boston liquor licensing board even asked saloon owners to cease serving liquor to women with babies and to discourage the practice of parking baby carriages outside saloons.[44]

Mother-bashers saw the problem as working women's selfishness, not the lack of services. This is partly because of the influence of neo-Freudian thought, which reached its zenith in the 1940s and 1950s, and provided "scientific" justification for mother-blaming. Psychologists believed that in the course of normal development, children had to settle a predictable set of crises as their unbounded inner drives confronted the limitations of real life. To understand the individual, one had to analyze the family of origin. In a therapeutic context, this meant looking for the source of psychic distress in the family configuration. In the renewed craze for domesticity of the postwar economy, the search invariably led to the mother, bound anew to home and children in ideology if not in actuality. And so the question became: What kind of mother led to this person's problems? The answers stretched as far

as the variations on the bad-mother theme could go.

The 1947 publication of Dr. Marynia Farnham and Ferdinand Lundberg's *Modern Woman: The Lost Sex* encapsulated the anti-mother rhetoric of the period. Farnham and Lundberg mentioned the decline of the home, under industrialization, as a contributor to modern problems. But the real culprit was feminism. The proper "feminine mother . . . accepts herself fully as a woman"; that is, she accepted her dependence on a man and sought no fulfillment outside the home. The "good" mother did not need to read books on child care; she knew what to do for her children by keeping attuned to their needs. Yet this "fully maternal" mother was in the minority. A variety of bad mothers—the rejecting mother, the oversolicitous or overprotective mother, the dominating mother, and the overaffectionate mother—produced half the nation's children, and all its delinquents, criminals, and alcoholics.[45]

The bad mother gained a new edge of insidiousness: one could not always tell the difference between the good and the bad at first glance. The overprotective mother might be the model mother of the community whom everyone admired.[46] On closer inspection, one would see that her hovering and intruding ways stunted her children's development. She needed to be pried loose, emotionally. Psychotherapy, and perhaps drug therapy, offered the best solution.

Mother-blaming found its way to Hollywood, as well. Films such as *Mildred Pierce* dramatized the danger and tragedy of the working mother. *Psycho* showed just how crazy a mother could make her son. Women who did not fit the cultural stereotype of passive dependence provided boundless material for comics and caricaturists. The Jewish mother, as the object of derision and ridicule, began to emerge in the general culture as the *ne plus ultra* of hysterical mothering during this period.[47]

British psychiatrist John Bowlby seemed to provide further "scientific" evidence that a good mother did not venture far from the home. Drawing from studies of war orphans and institutionalized children, Bowlby theorized that maternal absence devastated a child's emotional development. Mary Ainsworth took Bowlby's ideas further, assessing the quality of children's attachment to their mothers by a laboratory test. In this test, conducted on twenty-three mother/child pairs, a year-old child first plays with his mother, then with the mother and a stranger, and then is left for a few moments with the stranger. The child's emotional security is measured by the response when the mother first leaves and then reenters the room: if the child protests his mother's departure, the attachment is secure. The studies of Bowlby, Ainsworth, and others fueled the claim that children's mental health depended on mother love—and that mother-love meant being at home with your child. Numerous investigations "proved" that day care damaged children. A good mother stayed out of the work force. She didn't even hire a babysitter too often.[48]

For black women in particular, mother-blaming manifested itself not just in criticism but in public policy. Daniel Patrick Moynihan's report *The Negro Family: The Case for National Action* saw maternal dominance in the black family as the basis of African Americans' societal problems. Noting that one-quarter of all black births were illegitimate, and that welfare rates had increased sharply, Moynihan decried the "tangle of pathology" tied to the black matriarchal family. The solution, Moynihan argued, was to strengthen men's role in the family: by making Aid to Families with Dependent Children available to male-headed families and redesigning the employment structure so that black women gave up their jobs to black men.[49]

Counterculturalists in the 1960s and 1970s both romanticized motherhood for its earthy physicality and rejected the traditional nuclear family arrangement for childrearing. Second Wave feminists, similarly, defined 1950s-style mothering as stultifying to women and to children, yet simultaneously proclaimed the healing power of liberated motherhood; as maternalists had done fifty years before, many feminists harnessed themselves to a notion that women were united by actual or potential motherhood. But the idea that women are naturally nurturing brings its own downside, its own notion of the good mother. For example, feminist health activists who promoted home birth and breastfeeding sometimes defined these as markers of good mothering, with the implication that hospital birth and bottle-feeding were the choices of not-so-good mothers.[50]

Still, any feminist contribution to the "bad" mother rhetoric of today cannot compare to that of the New Right. The Right consistently takes a narrow view of woman's place. Sociologist Kristin Luker, in a study of abortion politics in California in the 1970s, concluded that the debate over abortion was really a "referendum on the place and meaning of motherhood." Where "pro-choice" activists saw motherhood as one of several roles for women, "pro-life" activists seem wedded to the notion that woman's duty and destiny bind her to home and children.[51]

The battles over good motherhood rage particularly forcefully in the area of new reproductive technologies. The famous case of "Baby M," although not really about the use of new technology, first called attention to the issue. Mary Beth Whitehead signed a surrogacy contract, agreeing to be artificially inseminated by William Stern in return for ten thousand dollars if she gave birth to a healthy baby. When the girl was born, however, Whitehead decided she wanted to keep her. The trial judge terminated Whitehead's rights to the child, but the New Jersey Supreme Court reversed his decision.

Since custody decisions are supposed to be based on the best interests of the child, the

Baby M case hinged on whether Mary Beth Whitehead was a "good" or a "bad" mother. Many saw her as good, because she was the "natural" mother and had carried Baby M within her womb. Others saw her as bad, because she had agreed to give away (sell?) her child. Class issues complicated the case. The Sterns had wealth and advanced degrees; the Whiteheads did not. Mother-blaming permeated the trial and Judge Harvey Sorkow's decision: Whitehead was depicted as emotionally unbalanced and "overenmeshed" with her kids.[52] Whatever one's views on surrogacy, it is clear that it taps our culture's deepest notions about motherhood. As legal scholar Carol Sanger puts it, "Surrogacy converts maternal selflessness into profit and transforms maternal devotion into a time-dated offer." In so doing, she says, it undermines the view that motherhood is "natural, sacred, and necessarily long-term."[53]

In the 1980s and 1990s, the battle over mothers' place has been expressed most clearly in debates over "fetal rights." As with mother-blaming in general, science and politics intersect here to provide "scientific" evidence about what is good for children (or fetuses) and the place of a good mother. Accepting the view that the "good" mother is self-sacrificing, proponents of fetal rights want to get the "bad" mother—especially, but not only, the drug addict—to put the interests of the unborn child above her own. As fetal rights critic Cynthia Daniels points out, the pregnant addict is a metaphor for women's alienation from instinctual motherhood—a powerful metaphor strengthened by the popular assumption that motherhood itself is in crisis. Not surprisingly, poor, unmarried mothers of color—the archetypal "bad" mothers in our society—are the predominant victims of the new vigilance over the purity of pregnancy. According to Daniels, fully 76 percent of 167 documented cases of criminal prosecution of women who used illicit drugs or alcohol during pregnancy involved women of color (mostly African American).[54]

In this age of "family values," however, you don't have to be a drug addict to be a "bad" mother. Despite—or perhaps because of—the fact that more than half of all mothers return to work before their children are out of diapers, working mothers too are blamed for our current social ills. Prior to the Civil Rights Act of 1964, which forbade employment discrimination on the basis of sex, women—and especially mothers—were often openly barred from employment. Beginning in 1908 with the landmark case *Muller v. Oregon,* the Supreme Court regulated the hours and wages of women workers, but not of men, on the grounds that healthy motherhood was an object of public interest "to preserve the strength and vigor of the race." School boards routinely fired women teachers when they married or became visibly pregnant. These practices could not continue unchallenged after 1964, but their cultural legacy still affects the lives of working mothers.[55]

Although most mothers now spend significant amounts of time outside the home, in employment or in higher education, popular acceptance of that trend lags, especially if the children are young and in day care. The much publicized custody dispute of Jennifer Ireland is a case in point. Ireland placed her three-year-old daughter in day care so she could attend classes at the University of Michigan, but a judge awarded custody to the father, a student at another university. The judge not only felt that a single parent attending classes at a school as demanding as the University of Michigan could not be a good parent but also preferred the father's plan to keep the child in the care of her grandmother to the mother's out-of-home day care arrangement. Ireland, like Zoe Baird, the ill-fated attorney general nominee, was a "bad" mother in part because she was smart and successful, and did not stay home to rear her child.[56]

As political mother-blaming intensified in the 1990s, single mothers and welfare mothers took center stage. Just as Mom was blamed for American weakness during the Cold War, conservatives now blame single mothers for crime and the growing divisions in American society. Speaker of the House Newt Gingrich saw Susan Smith's desperate drowning of her sons as evidence of "how sick society is getting" and suggested the solution: vote Republican. In a similar leap of logic, Vice President Dan Quayle attributed the 1992 Los Angeles riots to the breakdown of the family, as exemplified in the decision of television character Murphy Brown to bear a child out of wedlock. Conservative author Charles Murray added statistical "proof" to the charge that single motherhood correlates with child poverty, crime, and a host of other ills. In *The Bell Curve,* he and co-author Richard Herrnstein identified "low-intelligence" mothers as the propagators of illegitimacy and urged that welfare benefits be taken away as a disincentive to further childbearing. The 1996 Personal Responsibility Act, which abolished Aid to Families with Dependent Children and established work requirements for single mothers, wrote many of Murray's recommendations into law. While more affluent women are "bad" mothers if they do not stay at home, poor women are "bad" mothers if they do.[57] Mother-blaming unfortunately shows no sign of abating.[58]

GOOD RIDDANCE TO A BAD LABEL

Many mothers do act in ways that are not good for their children. Through those acts, in those moments, they function as bad mothers. That we must acknowledge. But we must also learn to recognize unjust extrapolations from the specific acts of individual mothers.

In many ways, "bad" mothers are not so very different from "good" ones. We all struggle under mountains of conflicting advice that cannot possibly be followed in real life. We all

must find our way in a society that devalues mothering, sees childrearing as a private family responsibility, and pays little heed to what actually happens to kids. Our point, however, is not that the pervasiveness of current mother-blaming creates a rough equality of suffering. One woman's psychic distress over society's harsh judgments cannot be equated with another's loss of legal custody of her children.

Fundamentally, the "bad" mother serves as a scapegoat, a repository for social or physical ills that resist easy explanation or solution. Scapegoating, as a process, does not engage principles of equity or evenhandedness; it seeks pockets of vulnerability. Unfortunately, some of the most vulnerable sometimes use the "bad" mother label themselves. It's a kind of preemptive strike: I'm not the "bad" one, she is!

But the uses of the "bad" mother label go beyond personal confidence boosting. They also have a political purpose. Today that purpose is bound up with government "downsizing." Thus we profess outrage at the death of six-year-old Elisa Izquierdo, allegedly killed by her crack-addicted mother, who got custody when Elisa's father died despite strong evidence that she was abusing the girl. At first glance, Elisa's tragic and well-publicized death highlights the failure of the child welfare system's emphasis on family reunification. Yet it serves another purpose. In deflecting our attention to Elisa's monster mother, it gives us someone to blame for her death, someone not ourselves. Blaming Elisa's death on her mother, and on the welfare agencies that reunited them, allows us to tolerate child poverty and further cuts to the child welfare system. It diverts our attention from the lack of resources for children to a bad mother, an immigrant drug addict.[59]

Blaming Elisa's mother—or at least blaming her exclusively—will not prevent more children's deaths, just as blaming the television show *Murphy Brown* will not prevent more riots in Los Angeles. It is dangerous fantasy to believe that if "they" can be identified and labeled, and then treated or punished, the nation will be somehow purified, made safer for the rest of us. This scapegoating does enormous harm to the women accused of "bad" mothering and serves to intensify already existing social antagonisms, including those of race and class. It also fails as a method of social purification and redounds to the detriment of all women. In other words, the labeling of the "bad" mother narrows for all of us the definition of "good" mothering, while luring us to participate in the limiting of our own options.

We cannot afford to let the cipher of the bad mother stand in for real confrontations with the serious problems of our society. When in fact we need to examine poverty, racism, the paucity of meaningful work at a living wage, the lack of access to day care, antifeminism, and a host of other problems, let us not be diverted by "bad" mothers.

NOTES

1. The trial received wide coverage in the Minnesota press. See, for example, the front-page story, "Guevara Trial Opens with Stunning Assertions," *Star Tribune*, February 3, 1993.
2. *James A. Lambert v. Sarah Everist*, No. 86-1854, Supreme Court of Iowa, January 20, 1988, 418 NW 2d, 40–44. The Supreme Court maintained the lower court's ruling of joint legal custody.
3. Justice Potter Stewart made this point about pornography in *Jacobellis v. Ohio*, 378 U.S. 184, 197 (1964).
4. Margaret Carlson, "Old Enough to Be Your Mother: Technology-Assisted Fertility in Post-Menopausal Women," *Time* 143 (January 10,1994): 41.
5. See Penelope Leach, *Children First: What Society Must Do—and Is Not Doing—for Children Today* (New York: Vintage, 1995).

6. For a general overview of U.S. family history, see Stephanie Coontz, *The Way We Never Were: American Families and the Nostalgia Trap* (New York: Basic Books, 1992). See also Mary Frances Berry, *The Politics of Parenthood: Child Care, Women's Rights, and the Myth of the Good Mother* (New York: Viking, 1993). Books that shed light on the lives of working-class mothers include Eileen Boris, *Home to Work: Motherhood and the Politics of Industrial Homework in the United States* (New York: Cambridge University Press, 1994); Elizabeth Ewen, *Immigrant Women in the Land of Dollars: Life and Culture on the Lower East Side, 1890–1925* (New York: Monthly Review Press, 1985); Linda Gordon, *Heroes of Their Own Lives: The Politics and History of Family Violence* (New York: Viking, 1988). Ellen Ross, *Love and Toil: Motherhood in Outcast London, 1870–1918* (New York: Oxford University Press, 1993) is a brilliant study of the experiences of English working-class mothers.
7. William H. Chafe, *The Paradox of Change: American Women in the Twentieth Century* (New York: Oxford University Press, 1991), 88; Shannon Dortch, "Moms on the Line: The Share of Mothers in the Labor Force Continues to Grow," *American Demographics* 18 (July 1996): 25. According to Dortch, mothers have a higher labor force participation rate than women as a whole.
8. Mary Kay Blakely, "Jessica's Mom," *Ms.* (July–August 1996): 96.
9. See Molly Ladd-Taylor, *Mother-Work: Women, Child Welfare and the State, 1890–1930* (Urbana: University of Illinois Press, 1994), 88.
10. James J. McKenna, "Sudden Infant Death Syndrome: Making Sense of Current Research," *Mothering*, No. 81 (Winter 1996): 74–80. The author notes that the majority of infants who die from SIDS worldwide have no known risk factors.
11. Theodore Lidz, Stephen Fleck, and Alice R. Cornelison, *Schizophrenia and the Family* (New

York: International Universities Press, 1965); Joan Jacobs Brumberg, *Fasting Girls: The Emergence of Anorexia Nervosa as a Modern Disease* (Cambridge: Harvard University Press, 1988), 29–30.

12. On this syndrome, see Herbert A. Schrier and Judith A. Libow, "Munchausen by Proxy—the Deadly Game," *Saturday Evening Post* 268 (July–August 1996): 40; Nancy Wartik, "Fatal Attention," *Redbook* 187 (February 1994): 67; and Skip Hollandsworth, "Hush, Little Baby, Don't You Cry," *Texas Monthly* 23 (August 1995): 70. For medical parent-blaming in Canada, see "The Crime of Being the Parent of a Sick Child," *Globe and Mail,* November 30, 1996.

13 On juvenile delinquency during World War II, see Karen Anderson, *Wartime Women: Sex Roles, Family Relations, and the Status of Women During World War II* (Westport, Conn.: Greenwood, 1970), 95–102. On welfare dependency, see Daniel Patrick Moynihan, *The Negro Family: The Case for National Action* (Washington, D.C.: Government Printing Office, 1965).

14. See Spiro Agnew's famous April 1970 comment on permissive parents, cited in Todd Gitlin, *The Sixties: Years of Hope, Days of Rage* (New York: Bantam, 87), 42.

15. U.S. Children's Bureau, *Infant Care,* 2d ed. (Washington, D.C.: Government Printing Office, 1921); John B. Watson, *Psychological Care of Infant and Child* (New York: W. W. Norton, 1928); "Child Disobedience Blamed on Mothers," *New York Times,* May 4,1937, 28: 2.

16. Penelope Leach, *Your Baby and Child, from Birth to Age Five* (New York: Knopf, 1987).

17. Compare the following childrearing books, written at different times but still widely read: Leach, *Your Baby and Child;* William Sears, *The Baby Book: Everything You Need to Know About Your Baby* (Boston: Little, Brown, 1993); Frank Caplan, *The First Twelve Months of Life: Your Baby's Growth Month by Month* (New York: Bantam 1973); T. Berry Brazleton, *Infants and Mothers: Differences in Development,* rev. ed. (New York: Delta/Seymour Lawrence, 1983); Benjamin Spock and Michael Rothenberg, *Dr. Spock's Baby and Child Care* (New York: Simon & Schuster, 1985). See also David Elkind, *The Hurried Child: Growing Up Too Fast Too Soon* (Reading, Mass.: Addison-Wesley, 1981), 32–34.

18. See Perri Klass, "Decent Exposure: It's Simply Breastfeeding, and as Natural as a Walk on the Beach," *Parenting* 8 (May 1994): 98; and Pete Kotz, "Not for Public Consumption: When Are Breasts Obscene?" *Utne Reader,* No. 76 (July–August 1996): 68.

19. Diane Eyer, *Motherguilt: How Our Culture Blames Mothers for What's Wrong with Society* (New York: Times Books, 1996), 3–7. For a critique of "child-centered moms," see John Rosemond, "Hey, Mom! Get a Life!" *Better Homes and Gardens* 74 (May 1996): 106.

20. Shari Thurer, *The Myths of Motherhood: How Culture Reinvents the Good Mother* (Boston: Houghton Mifflin, 1994); Paula J. Caplan, *Don't Blame Mother: Mending the Mother-Daughter Relationship* (New York: Harper & Row, 1989), 62.

21. Thurer, *The Myths of Motherhood,* 151–152; Louise Bernikow, *Among Women* (New York: Harmony Books, 1980), 26–28. For a fascinating discussion of a particular evil-stepmother myth, see Peter Gossage, "La Maratre: Marie-Anne Houde and the Myth of the Wicked Stepmother in Quebec," *Canadian Historical Review* 76 (December 1995): 563–598.

22. Elizabeth Badinter, *Mother Love, Myth and Reality: Motherhood in Modern History* (New York: Macmillan, 1980).

23. Sara Evans, *Born for Liberty: A History of Women in America* (New York: Free Press, 1989); Nancy F. Cott, *Bonds of Womanhood* (New Haven: Yale University Press, 1977).

24. On Republican Motherhood, see Linda Kerber, *Women of the Republic: Intellect and Ideology in Revolutionary America* (Chapel Hill: University of North Carolina Press, 1980).

25. Mary P. Ryan, *The Empire of the Mother: American Writing about Domesticity, 1830–1860* (New York: Haworth, 1982); Bernard Wishy, *The Child and the Republic: The Dawn of Modern American Child Nurture* (Philadelphia: University of Pennsylvania Press, 1968).

z6. Carroll Smith-Rosenberg, *Disorderly Conduct: Visions of Gender in Victorian America* (New York: Oxford University Press); Cott, *Bonds of Womanhood;* Mary P. Ryan, *The Cradle of the Middle Class: Family and Community in Oneida County, New York, 1780–1865* (New York: Cambridge University Press, 1981).

27. Quoted in Cott, *Bonds of Womanhood,* 91.

28. Michael Grossberg, "Who Gets the Child? Custody, Guardianship, and the Rise of a Judicial Patriarchy in Nineteenth-Century America," *Feminist Studies* 9 (Summer 1983): 235–260. See also Michael Grossberg, *Governing the Hearth: Law and Family in Nineteenth-Century America* (Chapel Hill: University of North Carolina Press, 1985).

29. See Carol Sanger, "Separating from Children," *Columbia Law Review* 96 (March 1996): 375–517.

30. Stephanie J. Shaw, "Mothering Under Slavery in the Antebellum South," in *Mothering: Ideology, Experience, and Agency,* ed. Evelyn Nakano Glenn, Grace Chang, and Linda Rennie Forcey (New York: Routledge, 1994), 237–258. See also Deborah Gray White, *Arn't I a Woman? Female Slaves in the Plantation South* (New York: W. W. Norton, 1985).

31. White, *Arn't I a Woman?* 46–61.

32. On scientific motherhood, see Rima Apple, *Mothers and Medicine: A Social History of Infant Feeding 1890–1950* (Madison: University of Wisconsin Press, 1987); Ladd-Taylor, *Mother-Work,* chap. 2.

33. Sanger, "Separating from Children," 404–405.

34. William Lee Howard. M.D., "Effeminate Men and Masculine Women," *New York Medical Journal* 71 (May 5, 1900); reprinted in *Root of Bitterness: Documents of the Social History of American Women,* 2d ed., ed. Nancy F. Cott et al. (Boston: Northeastern University Press, 1996), 338–340.

35. Theodore Roosevelt, "Address to the Congress on the Welfare of Children," *National Congress of Mothers Magazine* 2 (April 1908): 174.

36. Susan Strasser, *Never Done: A History of American Housework* (New York: Pantheon, 1982); Deirdre English and Barbara Ehrenreich, *For Her Own Good: 150 Years of Advice to Women* (Garden City, N.Y.: Anchor Books, 1978).

37. Watson, *Psychological Care of Infant and Child,* dedication, 5–6; U.S. Children's Bureau, *Child Management* (Washington, D.C.: Government Printing Office, 1925), 3–4.

38. Ernest Groves and Gladys Hoagland Groves, *Parents and Children* (Philadelphia: J. B. Lippincott, 1924), 118. See English and Ehrenreich, *For Her Own Good,* 205.

39. Ewen, *Immigrant Women in the Land of Dollars;* Ladd-Taylor, *MotherWork.*

40. Sonya Michel and Seth Koven, eds., *Mothers of a New World: Maternalist Politics and the Origins of Welfare States* (New York: Routledge, 1993); Ladd-Taylor, *Mother-Work;* Linda Gordon, *Pitied But Not Entitled: Single Mothers and the History of Welfare* (New York: Free Press, 1994); Theda Skocpol, *Protecting Soldiers and Mothers: The Political Origins of Social Policy in the United States* (Cambridge: Harvard University Press, 1992).

41. Ladd-Taylor, *Mother-Work,* 175.

42. Philip R. Reilly, *The Surgical Solution: A History of Involuntary Sterilization in the United States* (Baltimore: Johns Hopkins University Press, 1991); Stephen Jay Gould, "Carrie Buck's Daughter," *Natural History* 93 (1984); Molly Ladd-Taylor, "Saving Babies and Sterilizing Mothers: Eugenics and Welfare

Politics in the Interwar United Sates," *Social Politics* (1997).

43. Philip Wylie, *Generation of Vipers* (New York: Rinehart, 1942), 185. See also Chafe, *The Paradox of Change,* 175–193.

44. See, for example, Eleanor Lake, "Trouble on the Street Corner," *Common Sense* 12 (May 1943): 148; "Mother Left Three Children Thirteen Hours to Gamble Her Husband's Earnings," *New York Times,* January 26, 1944, 21; "Soldier's Wife Who Deserted Baby Says Allotment Was Too Small," *New York Times,* February 16, 1944, 34; "Would Bar Liquor to Mothers," *New York Times,* March 30, 1944, 24.

45. Ferdinand Lundberg and Marynia F. Farnham, *Modern Woman: The Lost Sex* (New York: Grosset & Dunlap, 1947), 298–321.

46. Ibid., 308.

47. E. Ann Kaplan, *Motherhood and Representation: The Mother in Popular Culture and Melodrama* (New York: Routledge, 1992); Thurer, *The Myths of Motherhood,* 257, 270. See also Suzanna Danuta Walters, *Lives Together, Worlds Apart: Mothers and Daughters in Popular Culture* (Berkeley: University of California Press, 1992), 49, 86; and David Everitt, "Mom's the Word," *Entertainment Weekly,* 274 (May 12, 1995): 70.

48. John Bowlby, *Maternal Care and Mental Health,* 2d ed., World Health Organization, Monograph Series no. 2 (Geneva: WHO, 1951); Mary Ainsworth, M. Blehar, E. Waters, and S. Wall, *Patterns of Attachment: A Psychological Study of the Strange Situation* (Hillsdale, N.J.: Lawrence Erlbaum, 1978). Ideas about attachment filtered into popular childrearing manuals; one recent example is Sears, *The Baby Book.* For critiques, see Diane Eyer, *Mother-Infant Bonding: A Scientific Fiction* (New Haven: Yale University Press, 1992); English and Ehrenreich, *For Her Own Good,* 229–230; and Eyer, *Motherguilt,* 77–80.

49. Moynihan, *The Negro Family.*

50. Lauri Umansky, *Reconceiving Motherhood: Feminism and the Legacies of the 1960s* (New York: New York University Press, 1996). One example of a women's health publication that equates breastfeeding with good mothering is the cover graphic with the words "Stamp Out Bottlefeeding" of the Canadian journal *The Compleat Mother,* No. 43 (Fall 1996).

51. Kristin Luker, *Abortion and the Politics of Motherhood* (Berkeley: University of California Press, 1984), 193.

52. Sorkow's decision is reprinted in the appendix of Phyllis Chesler, *The Sacred Bond: The Legacy of Baby M* (New York: Times, 1988). See Katha Pollitt, "Contracts and Apple Pie: The Strange Case of Baby M," *The Nation* 244 (May 23, 1987): 667.

53. Sanger, "Separating from Children," 453, 464.

54. Cynthia R. Daniels, *At Women's Expense: State Power and the Politics of Fetal Rights* (Cambridge: Harvard University Press, 1993), especially chap. 4.

55. Quoted in Lynn Y. Weiner, *From Working Girl to Working Mother: The Female Labor Force in the United States, 1820–1980* (Chapel Hill: University of North Carolina Press, 1985), 45. See also Alice Kessler-Harris, *Out to Work: A History of Wage-Earning Women in the United States* (New York: Oxford University Press, 1982).

56. Susan Jane Gilman, "A Michigan Judge's Ruling Punishes Single Mothers," *Ms.* 5 (November–December 1994): 92–93.

57. Alison Mitchell, "Gingrich's Views on Slayings Draw Fire," *New York Times,* November 3, 1995, B18; "Dan Quayle vs. Murphy Brown: The Vice-President Attacks the Values of a Television Show," *Time* 139 (June 1, 1992): 20; Charles Murray and Richard Herrnstein, *The Bell Curve: Intelligence and Class Structure in American Life* (New York: Free Press, 1994).

58. Anne Roiphe notes the mother-blaming in four Hollywood films released in 1996: "A Quartet of Monstrous Mothers," *Globe and Mail,* January 4, 1997, C4.

59. Katha Pollitt, "The Violence of Ordinary Life," *The Nation,* January 1, 1996, 9.

Study/Discussion Questions

1. What makes a woman a "bad" mother in our society?
2. What constitutes "taking good care" of children in our society? Make two lists: one of things a mother must do in order to be a good mother, and one of things a mother must never do in order to qualify as a good mother.
3. Make the same two lists for fathers. What would make a man a "good" or "bad" father?
4. How are these lists different for mothers and fathers? How are our expectations of mothers and fathers different?

Bad/Good, Good/Bad:
Birth Mothers and Adoptive Mothers

Betty Jean Lifton

Betty Jean Lifton's many writings on adoption have been ground-breaking and moving. Writing as an adoptee, Lifton explains here how she related to the prevailing myths about good and bad mothers as she tried to sort out her feelings about her two mothers—the woman who gave birth to her and the woman who reared her. Neither woman fit the dichotomized role; each played out parts of both scripts. Lifton urges adoptees to write a new script altogether.

Everyone has two mothers, according to Freud: the good mother and the bad mother. The psychological task is to bring them together as two parts of the same woman.

I never knew quite what to do with this Freudian insight, for, as an adoptee, I literally had two mothers: my birth mother[1] and my adoptive mother. Both of them were good, and both of them were bad. Which meant I had four mothers.

But—and this is important—they were each good and bad in their own way.

My adoptive mother existed for me in the real here and now. She was always there for me. In that, she was a good mother. My birth mother existed in the shadowy there and then. She disappeared on me. In that, she was a bad mother.

My birth mother gave me life. Good mother. My adoptive mother couldn't give me life. Bad mother.

Good mother/bad mother. Which is which? What is good? What is bad? It is all in the eyes of the perceiver.

In the eyes of society, the married adoptive mother is good and the unmarried birth mother is bad. The adoptive mother is the virtuous woman who rescues an abandoned child and saves her from the orphanage, or the gutter, by making the child her own. She may tell her daughter (or son) the stock story that Mother loved you so much that she gave you up, but children are not fools. The adopted child senses that she was bad, or that maybe her mother was bad: perhaps a prostitute or a drug addict. Why else has she not been invited to birthday parties or to Thanksgiving dinner?

Even today, when society has relaxed its sexual mores, the birth mother remains cast in the role of the bad mother. She is a loose woman, who not only had a baby out of wed-

From Molly Ladd Taylor and Lauri Umansky, editors, *"Bad" Mothers: The Politics of Blame in Twentieth Century America*, New York: NYU Press, 1998, pp. 191–197. Copyright © B. J. Lifton.

lock but gave that baby away. Yet, here is the devil's bargain: in return for her baby, the "bad" birth mother is allowed to go back into society and pass as a "good" woman. No scarlet letter for her, at least not where it shows. She can pass. Should you meet her in church, in the office, or at the club, you wouldn't be able to tell what she's been through. Unless you happen to catch the sadness that crosses her face in an unguarded moment.

THE PSYCHOLOGY OF THE BAD/ GOOD BIRTH MOTHER

I've known many birth mothers over the years. Some of my best friends are birth mothers.

My own mother was a birth mother.

"You will never know my pain," my mother said in our first meeting after I'd found her.

At the time, I was just learning my own pain, which until then I had effectively split off from consciousness. How could I possibly have the emotional strength to know and hold hers, too?

She did not struggle to articulate her pain. She had become the pain. It was as much a part of her as any vital organ.

I was to learn years later, after her death, that she had tried to keep me against her mother's wishes. My twenty-year-old father was out of there when he learned of her pregnancy, and, having just turned seventeen, she couldn't raise me on her own. She went temporarily blind after signing my relinquishment paper. Fell onto the subway tracks one day. Fell or jumped, who is to say? Someone pulled her out in time.

When she could see again, she, like so many birth mothers, split me off in order to survive: shut me out of her conscious mind. Went psychologically blind. Dissociated. Left me to fester in her unconscious. She kept me a secret from both her husbands, and from the one child she had after me—her only child, in society's eyes.

I saw her just twice. I was the one who disappeared this time. I could not handle my guilt toward my adoptive parents. I could not handle the chaos I felt inside. I did not contact her again for many years.

We were never to meet again. Toward the end of her life, we spoke on the telephone, its wires reuniting mother and daughter like an electrified umbilical cord. She was widowed, living with my unmarried half-brother, dependent on him for everything because she had Meniere's disease, which affected her middle ear. It made her dizzy, unable to venture out alone. Mother and son, inseparable. She was determined from the beginning not to lose this one: her second/first child. She wouldn't tell him about me. She wasn't about to say, "Oh, by the way, there's something I forgot to mention. You have a sister out there."

She just couldn't do it. "Your brother wouldn't understand," she told me repeatedly. Who could? Even Oedipus didn't understand the dire consequences of the secrecy in adoption—until it was too late.

Over the years, I learned to know my mother's pain—not through her words, but through the pain inside of me when I thought of her. It was all so long ago. And yet, I, like all adoptees, still carry within me the child's trauma of losing its mother; of learning it is adopted, rather then born to the people it calls Mom and Dad; of living like a genetic stranger in some other clan; of having to repress the grief, pain, and yearning for that missing bad mother.

THE PSYCHOLOGY OF THE BAD/ GOOD ADOPTIVE MOTHER

My adoptive mother was a good mother. Or, like most mothers, she was, to use Donald Winnicott's term, "a good enough mother." She did all the things that mothers do: she got up in the middle of the night, she fed me, clothed me, worried about me, and loved me—or at least (perhaps like most mothers) she loved the daughter she wanted me to be and the one she thought I was.

But it could be said that she, like so many adoptive mothers of her time, was a bad mother. She never questioned the wisdom of the so-called adoption experts who told her to take me home and live as if I were born to her. She was glad to hear that I did not need to know anything about my antecedents. She allowed herself to believe that I would feel a natural part of my new family and never feel sorrow for the biological kin I had lost. In allowing herself to become psychologically blind, she dissociated her shameful infertility, just as my birth mother had dissociated her shameful fertility.

I don't know if the experts advised my adoptive mother to tell me my parents were dead, but she, again like so many adoptive parents, did. First, she married them off, then she finished them off. She mumbled something about my mother dying of a broken heart after my father's death. Being a child, I believed her. I secretly grieved for my lost parents who, like Romeo and Juliet, died so young. I imagined they were watching over me. It never occurred to me that dead people have names, identities, and family members they have left behind. That's because I didn't let it enter my mind. I did what the adopted child does in order to survive, in order not to lose the only parents she has: I, also, dissociated. I shut them out of my conscious mind.

Like mother, like child. All of us swimming in what Lewis Carroll might have called The Sea of Dissociation.

I would learn that my parents were not married and were very much alive at the time of my adoption. "Your mother lied to you," my husband said when we discovered the truth. I didn't want to think that my adoptive mother lied; that would make her a bad mother. I preferred to think she had confabulated, made up her own fable in order to shape the truth closer to her heart's desire.

THE ADOPTEE'S DILEMMA

Adoptees do not think of their birth mother as good or bad, but rather as good and bad. Good, because she did not abort them at conception; bad, because she, in effect, aborted them at birth. The adoptee's inner baby rages, convinced that a good mother does not abandon her child no matter what the circumstances. The adult adoptee tries to understand the circumstances and even forgive the abandoner.

When the adoptee gets in touch with her need for the mother who gave her life—the need that she had to deny for most of her childhood—there is an overwhelming yearning to see her mother's face, touch her hand, be enfolded in her arms. At such moments the adoptee allows herself to believe that her birth mother has never forgotten her. Her birth mother will offer unconditional love when her child finds her. She will have endless patience for endless questions. She will tell her husband and other children about her child. She will tell her child who her father is. She will get on well with her child's adoptive parents.

For the adoptee, the bad birth mother is the one who "rejects" her, doesn't want contact. Who keeps her a secret from her husband and other children. Who refuses to tell her child who her father is. Who does not ask about her life with her adoptive parents.

I believe—and here is one of the many paradoxes in adoption—that when an adoptee finds her birth mother, she also finds her adoptive mother. She is free to attach more fully to her. Until then, the unknown birth mother has stood like a ghost between them, demanding half her loyalty and all of her fantasy life. When that ghostly birth mother emerges from what I call the "Ghost Kingdom"—located in the adoptee's psychic reality—when she materializes and becomes a real person, with all her virtues and faults, the adoptee can appreciate how good the adoptive mother was, and is. There is no longer the barrier of secrecy that separated adoptive mother and child. The adoptee's feeling of being in psychological bondage is replaced by a real bond.

THE POLITICS OF BAD/GOOD

Adoption is no longer just about parents and children. In recent years, it has been usurped by the political right, which uses it for its own "moral" purposes. The bad birth mother can only become good if she remains missing in action. If she accepts the "confidentiality" that organizations like the Christian Coalition and the National Council for Adoption, a conservative lobby group, call for in her name. As I write this they have slapped a lawsuit on the state of Tennessee for voting to open its records to adult adoptees on July 1, 1996.[2] If Tennessee wins the case, it will be the third state, after Kansas and Alaska, to open adoption records—and the first in almost half a century.

The Christian Coalition and the NCFA are against adoption reform. They claim that open records will make pregnant women choose abortion rather than risk being found some day by the child they put up for adoption. (The truth is just the opposite: pregnant women will abort rather than give a baby up to the closed adoption system.)[3] They also claim that open records violate the "confidentiality" of the birth mother—a woman whom they alternately demonize and protect, depending on the circumstances. (Think of the wolf claiming to protect the constitutional rights of Little Red Riding Hood.)

Birth mothers who change their minds about relinquishment within a few weeks and go to court to try to get their babies back before the adoption is finalized are demonized. We've all heard of the bad birth mothers of Baby Jessica and Baby Richard, who stayed the legal course with the birth fathers for years rather than let other people raise their children. Such mothers are not seen as good mothers, but as spoilsports, stalkers—even terrorists.

While the good birth mother—by the Big Bad Wolf's definition—would never want to see her child again, the bad birth mother cannot forget the child she relinquished in her younger, more vulnerable years. This bad birth mother doesn't want her confidentiality protected. In truth, she was never promised confidentiality;[4] she was never promised anything, not even notification if or when her child was placed in an adoptive home. (Some birth mothers have found that their children languished in foster care throughout their childhood, or were placed in foster care after a failed adoption.)

The bad birth mother has no shame, in the eyes of the anti-adoption reform groups. She's out of the closet. She worries that her son may have been killed in Korea, in Vietnam, in the Gulf War, in Bosnia. She writes articles and books describing how she searched for her child and found him. She is reunited with him on TV. At support groups and on the Internet, she helps other birth mothers who are searching for their children. She redefines herself as good.

THE FUTURE OF BAD/GOOD MOTHERS

As long as adoption reformers come up against the same political conservatism that blocks other social reforms in this country, the closed adoption system, with its secrets and lies, will continue to make potential good mothers into potential bad ones. It can prevent an adoptive mother from giving her beloved child one of the crucial nutrients the child needs in order to feel grounded and whole: access to her birthright. It can close off the open and honest communication that would make her and her child close.

So, too, even today, the secrecy in the closed system keeps many birth mothers in the closet. It discourages them from thinking of themselves as good. It reinforces their shame. It makes them unable to communicate candidly with their family, friends, and subsequent children.

Adoptees must balance everything on their own moral scale when they evaluate the "good" and the "bad" in both their mothers. Many come to see their mothers as neither good nor bad, but as innocent victims, just as they were, of a closed system that they are now working to open for future generations.

I dedicated my book *Journey of the Adopted Self: A Quest for Wholeness* to my two mothers:

> who might have known
> and even liked each other
> in another life
> and another adoption system.[5]

NOTES

1. Adoption has become as much a battle of terminology as of ideology. Historically, the woman who gave birth to a child was known as the "natural" mother. Adoptive parents argued that the use of this term implied that they themselves were "unnatural." They favored "biological mother." However, the mothers who relinquished their children felt that this made them sound as if they were mere biological creatures with no maternal feelings. They favored "birth mother," the term I have used in this article.

2. The new Tennessee legislation to open adoption records on July 1, 1996 allows adopted adults to receive copies of their adoption records and their original birth certificate. If the birth parent does not want to be contacted, he or she can file a "contact veto."

   The law was challenged by a class action suit (*Doe v. Sundquist*) filed on June 25, 1996 by the American Center for Law and Justice (founded by Pat Robertson in 1990 "to defend the rights of believers") against the state of Tennessee on behalf of two birth mothers, an adoptive couple, and an adoption agency affiliated with the National Council For Adoption. The plaintiffs are alleging that it is unconstitutional for any state to open adoption records to adoptees. They claim that opening records to adoptees invades the privacy of both birth parents and adoptive parents.

   The trial was to be held in the District Court in Nashville in the spring of 1997. The decision is expected to be appealed by one side or the other all the way to the Supreme Court. This is a landmark case: if the state of Tennessee wins, it will set a legal precedent for other states to open their records.

3. Research material compiled by the American Adoption Congress from England, Kansas, and Alaska, where adoption records are open, shows that there is no correlation between the confidentiality of adoption and the rate of abortion. Reunion statistics gathered by the American Adoption Congress from six states—Arizona, New Jersey, New Mexico, North Carolina, Washington, and Tennessee—show that in 8,698 reunions, 95 percent of the birth mothers welcomed contact by the adoptee.

4. There were no written promises of confidentiality in the official adoption surrender papers that birth mothers throughout the country were given to sign.

5. *Journey of the Adopted Self: A Quest for Wholeness* (Basic Books, 1994).

Study/Discussion Questions

1. How is a birth mother supposed to behave in our society? (What makes her "bad" or "good" in the eyes of society?)
2. What are the benefits of open records to adopted children, in the author's view?
3. What did Lifton want from her birth mother?
4. What did she want from her adoptive mother?

Christmas Eve: My Mother Dressing

Toi Derricotte

My mother was not impressed with her beauty;
once a year she put it on like a costume,
plaited her black hair, slick as cornsilk, down past her hips,
in one rope-thick braid, turned it, carefully, hand over hand,
and fixed it at the nape of her neck, stiff and elegant as a crown,
with tortoise pins, like huge insects,
some belonging to her dead mother,
some to my living grandmother.
Sitting on the stool at the mirror,
she applied a peachy foundation that seemed to hold her down, to trap her,
as if we never would have noticed what flew among us unless it was
      weighted and bound in its mask.
Vaseline shined her eyebrows,
mascara blackened her lashes until they swept down like feathers,
darkening our thoughts of her.
Her eyes deepened until they shone from far away.

Now I remember her hands, her poor hands, which even then were old
      from scrubbing,
whiter on the inside than they should have been,
and hard, the first joints of her fingers, little fattened pads,
the nails filed to sharp points like old-fashioned ink pens, painted a jolly
      color.
Her hands stood next to her face and wanted to be put away,
prayed
for the scrub bucket and brush to make them feel useful.
And, as I write, I forget the years I watched her
pull hairs like a witch from her chin, magnify
every blotch—as if acid were thrown from the inside.

But once a year my mother
rose in her white silk slip,
not the slave of the house, the woman,
took the ironed dress from the hanger—
allowing me to stand on the bed, so that
my face looked directly into her face,
and hold the garment away from her as she pulled it down.

HEART AND HOME: THE PERSONAL IS POLITICAL

The Problem That Has No Name

Betty Friedan

Many commentators point to the publication of Betty Friedan's The
Feminine Mystique *in 1963 as the start of the modern women's movement. Of course, no single book, and no individual, can create a mass
movement. Yet Friedan's book and her role as a founding member in 1966
of the multi-issue political action group NOW (the National Organization
for Women) do belong in the headlines of twentieth-century feminist
history. As this selection suggests, millions of middle-class American women
in the 1950s and 1960s—and perhaps many still today—felt a void in
their lives that domesticity, marriage, and consumerism could not fill.
While critics have since pointed out the privileged class standing of
Friedan's discontented housewives, none denies the revelatory power of
Friedan's unveiling of "the problem that has no name."*

The problem lay buried, unspoken, for many years in the minds of American women. It was a strange stirring, a sense of dissatisfaction, a yearning that women suffered in the middle of the twentieth century in the United States. Each suburban wife struggled with it alone. As she made the beds, shopped for groceries, matched slipcover material, ate peanut butter sandwiches with her children, chauffeured Cub Scouts and Brownies, lay beside her husband at night—she was afraid to ask even of herself the silent question—"Is this all?"

For over fifteen years there was no word of this yearning in the millions of words written about women, for women, in all the columns, books, and articles by experts telling women their role was to seek fulfillment as wives and mothers. Over and over women heard in voices of tradition and of Freudian sophistication that they could desire no greater destiny than to glory in their own femininity. Experts told them how to catch a man and keep him, how to breastfeed children and handle their toilet training, how to cope with sibling rivalry and adolescent rebellion; how to buy a dishwasher, bake bread, cook gourmet snails, and build a swimming pool with their own hands; how to dress, look, and act more feminine and make marriage more exciting; how to keep their husbands from dying young and their sons from growing into delinquents. They were taught to pity the neurotic, unfeminine, unhappy women who wanted to be poets or physicists or presidents. They learned that truly feminine women do not want careers, higher education, political rights—the independence and the opportunities that the old-fashioned feminists fought for. Some women, in their forties and fifties, still remembered painfully giving up those dreams, but most of the younger women no longer even thought about them. A thousand expert voices applauded their femininity, their adjustment, their new maturity. All they had to do was devote their lives from earliest girlhood to finding a husband and bearing children.

By the end of the nineteen-fifties, the average marriage age of women in America dropped to 20, and was still dropping, into the teens. Fourteen million girls were engaged by 17. The proportion of women attending college in comparison with men dropping from 47 percent in 1920 to 35 percent in 1958. A century earlier, women had fought for higher education; now girls went to college to get a husband. By the mid-fifties, 60 percent dropped out of college to marry, or because they were afraid too much education would be a marriage bar. Colleges built dormitories for "married students," but the students were almost always the husbands. A new degree was instituted for the wives—"Ph.T." (Putting Husband Through).

Then American girls began getting married in high school. And the women's magazines, deploring the unhappy statistics about these young marriages, urged that courses on mar-

riage, and marriage counselors, be installed in the high schools. Girls started going steady at twelve and thirteen, in junior high. Manufacturers put out brassieres with false bosoms of foam rubber for little girls of ten. And an advertisement for a child's dress, sizes 3-6x, in the *New York Times* in the fall of 1960, said: "She Too Can Join the Man-Trap Set."

By the end of the fifties, the United States birthrate was overtaking India's. The birth-control movement, renamed Planned Parenthood, was asked to find a method whereby women who had been advised that a third or fourth baby would be born dead or defective might have it anyhow. Statisticians were especially astounded at the fantastic increase in the number of babies among college women. Where once they had two children, now they had four, five, six. Women who had once wanted careers were now making careers out of having babies. So rejoiced *Life* magazine in a 1956 paean to the movement of American women back to the home.

In a New York hospital, a woman had a nervous breakdown when she found she could not breastfeed her baby. In other hospitals, women dying of cancer refused a drug which research had proved might save their lives: its side effects were said to be unfeminine. "If I have only one life, let me live it as a blonde," a larger-than-life-sized picture of a pretty, vacuous woman proclaimed from newspaper, magazine, and drugstore ads. And across America, three out of every ten women dyed their hair blonde. They ate a chalk called Metrecal, instead of food, to shrink to the size of the thin young models. Department-store buyers reported that American women, since 1939, had become three and four sizes smaller. "Women are out to fit the clothes, instead of vice-versa," one buyer said.

Interior decorators were designing kitchens with mosaic murals and original paintings, for kitchens were once again the center of women's lives. Home sewing became a million-dollar industry. Many women no longer left their homes, except to shop, chauffeur their children, or attend a social engagement with their husbands. Girls were growing up in America without ever having jobs outside the home. In the late fifties, a sociological phenomenon was suddenly remarked: a third of American women now worked, but most were no longer young and very few were pursuing careers. They were married women who held part-time jobs, selling or secretarial, to put their husbands through school, their sons through college, or to help pay the mortgage. Or they were widows supporting families. Fewer and fewer women were entering professional work. The shortages in the nursing, social work, and teaching professions caused crises in almost every American city. Concerned over the Soviet Union's lead in the space race, scientists noted that America's greatest source of unused brain-power was women. But girls would not study physics: it was "unfeminine." A girl refused a science fellowship at Johns Hopkins to take a job in a real-estate office. All she wanted, she said, was what every other American girl wanted—to get married, have four children and live in a nice house in a nice suburb.

The suburban housewife—she was the dream image of the young American women and the envy, it was said, of women all over the world. The American housewife—freed by science and labor-saving appliances from the drudgery, the dangers of childbirth, and the illnesses of her grandmother. She was healthy, beautiful, educated, concerned only about her husband, her children, her home. She had found true feminine fulfillment. As a housewife and mother, she was respected as a full and equal partner to man in his world. She was free to choose automobiles, clothes, appliances, supermarkets; she had everything that women ever dreamed of.

In the fifteen years after World War II, this mystique of feminine fulfillment became the cherished and self-perpetuating core of contemporary American culture. Millions of women lived their lives in the image of those pretty pictures of the American suburban housewife, kissing their husbands goodbye in front of the picture window, depositing their stationwagonsful of children at school, and smiling as they ran the new electric waxer over the spotless kitchen floor. They baked their own bread, sewed their own and their children's clothes, kept their new washing machines and dryers running all day. They changed the sheets on the beds twice a week instead of once, took the rug-hooking class in adult education, and pitied their poor frustrated mothers, who had dreamed of having a career. Their only dream was to be perfect wives and mothers; their highest ambition to have five children and a beautiful house, their only fight to get and keep their husbands. They had no thought for the unfeminine problems of the world outside the home; they wanted the men to make the major decisions. They gloried in their role as women, and wrote proudly on the census blank: "Occupation: housewife."

For over fifteen years, the words written for women, and the words women used when they talked to each other, while their husbands sat on the other side of the room and talked shop or politics or septic tanks, were about problems with their children, or how to keep their husbands happy, or improve their children's school, or cook chicken or make slipcovers. Nobody argued whether women were inferior or superior to men; they were simply different. Words like "emancipation" and "career" sounded strange and embarrassing; no one had used them for years. When a Frenchwoman named Simone de Beauvoir wrote a book called *The Second Sex,* an American critic commented that she obviously "didn't know what life was all about," and besides, she was talking about French women. The "woman problem" in America no longer existed.

If a woman had a problem in the 1950s and 1960s, she knew that something must be wrong with her marriage, or with herself. Other women were satisfied with their lives, she thought. What kind of a woman was she if she did not feel this mysterious fulfillment waxing the kitchen floor? She was so ashamed to admit her dissatisfaction that she never knew how many other women shared it. If she tried to tell her husband, he didn't understand what she was talking about. She did not really understand it herself. For over fifteen years women in America found it harder to talk about this problem than about sex. Even the psychoanalysts had no name for it. When a woman went to a psychiatrist for help, as many women did, she would say, "I'm so ashamed," or "I must be hopelessly neurotic." "I don't know what's wrong with women today," a suburban psychiatrist said uneasily. "I only know something is wrong because most of my patients happen to be women. And their problem isn't sexual." Most women with this problem did not go to see a psychoanalyst, however. "There's nothing wrong really," they kept telling themselves. "There isn't any problem."

But on an April morning in 1959, I heard a mother of four having coffee with four other mothers in a suburban development fifteen miles from New York, say in a tone of quiet desperation, "the problem." And the others knew, without words, that she was not talking about a problem with her husband, or her children, or her home. Suddenly they realized they all shared the same problem, the problem that has no name. They began, hesitantly, to talk about it. Later, after they had picked up their children at nursery school and taken them home to nap, two of the women cried, in sheer relief, just to know they were not alone.

Gradually I came to realize that the problem that has no name was shared by countless women in America. As a magazine writer I often interviewed women about problems with their children, or their marriages, or their houses, or their communities. But after a while

I began to recognize the telltale signs of this other problem. I saw the same signs in suburban ranch houses and split-levels on Long Island and in New Jersey and Westchester County; in colonial houses in a small Massachusetts town; on patios in Memphis; in suburban and city apartments; in living rooms in the Midwest. Sometimes I sensed the problem, not as a reporter, but as a suburban housewife, for during this time I was also bringing up my own three children in Rockland County, New York. I heard echoes of the problem in college dormitories and semi-private maternity wards, at PTA meetings and luncheons of the League of Women Voters, at suburban cocktail parties, in station wagons waiting for trains, and in snatches of conversation overheard at Schrafft's. The groping words I heard from other women, on quiet afternoons when children were at school or on quiet evenings when husbands worked late, I think I understood first as a woman long before I understood their larger social and psychological implications.

Just what was this problem that has no name? What were the words women used when they tried to express it? Sometimes a woman would say "I feel empty somehow . . . incomplete." Or she would say, "I feel as if I don't exist." Sometimes she blotted out the feeling with a tranquilizer. Sometimes she thought the problem was with her husband, or her children, or that what she really needed was to redecorate her house, or move to a better neighborhood, or have an affair, or another baby. Sometimes, she went to a doctor with symptoms she could hardly describe: "A tired feeling . . . I get so angry with the children it scares me . . . I feel like crying without any reason." (A Cleveland doctor called it "the housewife's syndrome.") A number of women told me about great bleeding blisters that break out on their hands and arms. "I call it the housewife's blight," said a family doctor in Pennsylvania. "I see it so often lately in these young women with four, five, and six children who bury themselves in their dishpans. But it isn't caused by detergent and it isn't cured by cortisone."

Sometimes a woman would tell me that the feeling gets so strong she runs out of the house and walks through the streets. Or she stays inside her house and cries. Or her children tell her a joke, and she doesn't laugh because she doesn't hear it. I talked to women who had spent years on the analyst's couch, working out their "adjustment to the feminine role," their blocks to "fulfillment as a wife and mother." But the desperate tone in these women's voices, and the look in their eyes, was the same as the tone and the look of other women, who were sure they had no problem, even though they did have a strange feeling of desperation.

A mother of four who left college at nineteen to get married told me:

> I've tried everything women are supposed to do—hobbies, gardening, pickling, canning, being very social with my neighbors, joining committees, running PTA teas. I can do it all, and I like it, but it doesn't leave you anything to think about—any feeling of who you are. I never had any career ambitions. All I wanted was to get married and have four children. I love the kids and Bob and my home. There's no problem you can even put a name to. But I'm desperate. I begin to feel I have no personality. I'm a server of food and putter-on of pants and a bedmaker, somebody who can be called on when you want something. But who am I?

A twenty-three-year-old mother in blue jeans said:

> I ask myself why I'm so dissatisfied. I've got my health, fine children, a lovely new home, enough money. My husband has a real future as an electronics engineer. He doesn't have any of these feelings. He says maybe I need a vacation, let's go to New York for a weekend. But that isn't it. I always had this idea we should do everything together. I can't sit down and read a book alone. If the children are napping and I have one hour to myself I just walk through the house waiting for them to wake up. I don't make a move until I know where the rest of the crowd is going. It's as if ever since you were a little girl, there's always been somebody or something that will take care of your life: your parents, or college, or falling in love, or having a child, or moving to a new house. Then you wake up one morning and there's nothing to look forward to.

A young wife in a Long Island development said:

> I seem to sleep so much. I don't know why I should be so tired. This house isn't nearly so hard to clean as the cold-water flat we had when I was working. The children are at school all day. It's not the work. I just don't feel alive.

In 1960, the problem that has no name burst like a boil through the image of the happy American housewife. In the television commercials the pretty housewives still beamed over their foaming dishpans and *Time*'s cover story on "The Suburban Wife, an American Phenomenon" protested: "Having too good a time . . . to believe that they should be unhappy." But the actual unhappiness of the American housewife was suddenly being reported—from the *New York Times* and *Newsweek* to *Good Housekeeping* and CBS Television ("The Trapped Housewife"), although almost everybody who talked about it found some superficial reason to dismiss it. It was attributed to incompetent appliance repairmen (*New York Times*), or the distances children must be chauffeured in the suburbs (*Time*), or too much PTA (*Redbook*). Some said it was the old problem—education: more and more women had education, which naturally made them unhappy in their role as housewives. "The road from Freud to Frigidaire, from Sophocles to Spock, has turned out to be a bumpy one," reported the *New York Times* (June 28, 1960). "Many young women—certainly not all—whose education plunged them into a world of ideas feel stifled in their homes. They find their routine lives out of joint with their training. Like shut-ins, they feel left out. In the last year, the problem of the educated housewife has provided the meat of dozens of speeches made by troubled presidents of women's colleges who maintain, in the face of complaints, that sixteen years of academic training is realistic preparation for wifehood and motherhood."

There was much sympathy for the educated housewife. ("Like a two-headed schizophrenic . . . once she wrote a paper on the Graveyard poets; now she writes notes to the milkman. Once she determined the boiling point of sulphuric acid; now she determines her boiling point with the overdue repairman. . . . The housewife often is reduced to screams and tears. . . . No one, it seems, is appreciative, least of all herself, of the kind of person she becomes in the process of turning from poetess into shrew.")

Home economists suggested more realistic preparation for housewives, such as high-school workshops in home appliances. College educators suggested more discussion groups on home management and the family, to prepare women for the adjustment to domestic life. A spate of articles appeared in the mass magazines offering "Fifty-eight Ways to Make Your Marriage More Exciting." No month went by without a new book by a psychiatrist or sexologist offering technical advice on finding greater fulfillment through sex.

A male humorist joked in *Harper's Bazaar* (July 1960) that the problem could be solved by taking away woman's right to vote. ("In the pre-19th Amendment era, the American woman was placid, sheltered and sure of her role in American society. She left all the political decisions to her husband and he, in turn, left all the family decisions to her. Today a

woman has to make both the family and the political decisions, and it's too much for her.")

A number of educators suggested seriously that women no longer be admitted to the four-year colleges and universities: in the growing college crisis, the education which girls could not use as housewives was more urgently needed than ever by boys to do the work of the atomic age.

The problem was also dismissed with drastic solutions no one could take seriously. (A woman writer proposed in *Harper's* that women be drafted for compulsory service as nurses' aides and baby-sitters.) And it was smoothed over with the age-old panaceas: "love is their answer," "the only answer is inner help," "the secret of completeness—children," "a private means of intellectual fulfillment," "to cure this toothache of the spirit—the simple formula of handing one's self and one's will over to God.'"[1]

The problem was dismissed by telling the housewife she doesn't realize how lucky she is—her own boss, no time clock, no junior executive gunning for her job. What if she isn't happy—does she think men are happy in this world? Does she really, secretly, still want to be a man? Doesn't she know yet how lucky she is to be a woman?

The problem was also, and finally, dismissed by shrugging that there are no solutions: this is what being a woman means, and what is wrong with American women that they can't accept their role gracefully? As *Newsweek* put it (March 7, 1960):

> She is dissatisfied with a lot that women of other lands can only dream of. Her discontent is deep, pervasive, and impervious to the superficial remedies which are offered at every hand. . . . An army of professional explorers have already charted the major sources of trouble. . . . From the beginning of time, the female cycle has defined and confined woman's role. As Freud was credited with saying: "Anatomy is destiny." Though no

group of women has ever pushed these natural restrictions as far as the American wife, it seems that she still cannot accept them with good grace. . . . A young mother with a beautiful family, charm, talent and brains is apt to dismiss her role apologetically. "What do I do?" you hear her say. "Why nothing. I'm just a housewife." A good education, it seems, has given this paragon among women an understanding of the value of everything except her own worth . . .

And so she must accept the fact that "American women's unhappiness is merely the most recently won of women's rights," and adjust and say with the happy housewife found by *Newsweek:* "We ought to salute the wonderful freedom we all have and be proud of our lives today. I have had college and I've worked, but being a housewife is the most rewarding and satisfying role. . . . My mother was never included in my father's business affairs . . . she couldn't get out of the house and away from us children. But I am an equal to my husband; I can go along with him on business trips and to social business affairs."

The alternative offered was a choice that few women would contemplate. In the sympathetic words of the *New York Times:* "All admit to being deeply frustrated at times by the lack of privacy, the physical burden, the routine of family life, the confinement of it. However, none would give up her home and family if she had the choice to make again." *Redbook* commented: "Few women would want to thumb their noses at husbands, children and community and go off on their own. Those who do may be talented individuals, but they rarely are successful women."

The year American women's discontent boiled over, it was also reported (*Look*) that the more than 21,000,000 American women who are single, widowed, or divorced do not cease even after fifty their frenzied, desperate search for a man. And the search begins early—

for seventy percent of all American women now marry before they are twenty-four. A pretty twenty-five-year-old secretary took thirty-five different jobs in six months in the futile hope of finding a husband. Women were moving from one political club to another, taking evening courses in accounting or sailing, learning to play golf or ski, joining a number of churches in succession, going to bars alone, in their ceaseless search for a man.

Of the growing thousands of women currently getting private psychiatric help in the United States, the married ones were reported dissatisfied with their marriages, the unmarried ones suffering from anxiety and, finally, depression. Strangely, a number of psychiatrists stated that, in their experience, unmarried women patients were happier than married ones. So the door of all those pretty suburban houses opened a crack to permit a glimpse of uncounted thousands of American housewives who suffered alone from a problem that suddenly everyone was talking about, and beginning to take for granted, as one of those unreal problems in American life that can never be solved—like the hydrogen bomb. By 1962 the plight of the trapped American housewife had become a national parlor game. Whole issues of magazines, newspaper columns, books learned and frivolous, educational conferences and television panels were devoted to the problem.

Even so, most men, and some women, still did not know that this problem was real. But those who had faced it honestly knew that all the superficial remedies, the sympathetic advice, the scolding words and the cheering words were somehow drowning the problem in unreality. A bitter laugh was beginning to be heard from American women. They were admired, envied, pitied, theorized over until they were sick of it, offered drastic solutions or silly choices that no one could take seriously. They got all kinds of advice from the growing armies of marriage and child-guidance counselors, psychotherapists, and armchair psychologists, on how to adjust to their role as housewives. No other road to fulfillment was offered to American women in the middle of the twentieth century. Most adjusted to their role and suffered or ignored the problem that has no name. It can be less painful for a woman, not to hear the strange, dissatisfied voice stirring within her.

It is no longer possible to ignore that voice, to dismiss the desperation of so many American women. This is not what being a woman means, no matter what the experts say. For human suffering there is a reason; perhaps the reason has not been found because the right questions have not been asked, or pressed far enough. I do not accept the answer that there is no problem because American women have luxuries that women in other times and lands never dreamed of; part of the strange newness of the problem is that it cannot be understood in terms of the age-old material problems of man: poverty, sickness, hunger, cold. The women who suffer this problem have a hunger that food cannot fill. It persists in women whose husbands are struggling interns and law clerks, or prosperous doctors and lawyers; in wives of workers and executives who make $5,000 a year or $50,000. It is not caused by lack of material advantages; it may not even be felt by women preoccupied with desperate problems of hunger, poverty or illness. And women who think it will be solved by more money, a bigger house, a second car, moving to a better suburb, often discover it gets worse.

It is no longer possible today to blame the problem on loss of femininity: to say that education and independence and equality with men have made American women unfeminine. I have heard so many women try to deny this dissatisfied voice within themselves because it does not fit the pretty picture of femininity the experts have given them. I think, in fact, that this is the first clue to the mystery: the problem cannot be understood in the gener-

ally accepted terms by which scientists have studied women, doctors have treated them, counselors have advised them, and writers have written about them. Women who suffer this problem, in whom this voice is stirring, have lived their whole lives in the pursuit of feminine fulfillment. They are not career women (although career women may have other problems); they are women whose greatest ambition has been marriage and children. For the oldest of these women, these daughters of the American middle class, no other dream was possible. The ones in their forties and fifties who once had other dreams gave them up and threw themselves joyously into life as housewives. For the youngest, the new wives and mothers, this was the only dream. They are the ones who quit high school and college to marry, or marked time in some job in which they had no real interest until they married. These women are very "feminine" in the usual sense, and yet they still suffer the problem.

Are the women who finished college, the women who once had dreams beyond housewifery, the ones who suffer the most? According to the experts they are, but listen to these four women:

My days are all busy, and dull, too. All I ever do is mess around. I get up at eight—I make breakfast, so I do the dishes, have lunch, do some more dishes, and some laundry and cleaning in the afternoon. Then it's supper dishes and I get to sit down a few minutes, before the children have to be sent to bed. . . . That's all there is to my day. It's just like any other wife's day. Humdrum. The biggest time, I am chasing kids.

Ye Gods, what do I do with my time? Well, I get up at six. I get my son dressed and then give him breakfast. After that I wash dishes and bathe and feed the baby. Then I get lunch and while the children nap, I sew or mend or iron and do all the other things I can't get done before noon. Then I cook supper for the family and my husband watches TV while I do the dishes. After I get the children to bed, I set my hair and then I go to bed.

The problem is always being the children's mommy, or the minister's wife and never being myself.

A film made of any typical morning in my house would look like an old Marx Brothers' comedy. I wash the dishes, rush the older children off to school, dash out in the yard to cultivate the chrysanthemums, run back in to make a phone call about a committee meeting, help the youngest child build a blockhouse, spend fifteen minutes skimming the newspapers so I can be well-informed, then scamper down to the washing machines where my thrice-weekly laundry includes enough clothes to keep a primitive village going for an entire year. By noon I'm ready for a padded cell. Very little of what I've done has been really necessary or important. Outside pressures lash me through the day. Yet I look upon myself as one of the more relaxed housewives in the neighborhood. Many of my friends are even more frantic. In the past sixty years we have come full circle and the American housewife is once again trapped in a squirrel cage. If the cage is now a modern plate-glass-and-broadloom ranch house or a convenient modern apartment, the situation is no less painful than when her grandmother sat over an embroidery hoop in her gilt-and-plush parlor and muttered angrily about women's rights.

The first two women never went to college. They live in developments in Levittown, New Jersey, and Tacoma, Washington, and were interviewed by a team of sociologists studying workingmen's wives.[2] The third, a minister's wife, wrote on the fifteenth reunion questionnaire of her college that she never had any ca-

reer ambitions, but wishes now she had.[3] The fourth, who has a Ph.D. in anthropology, is today a Nebraska housewife with three children.[4] Their words seem to indicate that housewives of all educational levels suffer the same feeling of desperation.

The fact is that no one today is muttering angrily about "women's rights," even though and more women have gone to college. In a recent study of all the classes that have graduated from Barnard College,[5] a significant minority of earlier graduates blamed their education for making them want "rights," later classes blamed their education for giving them career dreams, but recent graduates blamed the college for making them feel it was not enough simply to be a housewife and mother; they did not want to feel guilty if they did not read books or take part in community activities. But if education is not the cause of the problem, the fact that education somehow festers in these women may be a clue.

If the secret of feminine fulfillment is having children, never have so many women, with the freedom to choose, had so many children, in so few years, so willingly. If the answer is love, never have women searched for love with such determination. And yet there is a growing suspicion that the problem may not be sexual, though it must somehow be related to sex. I have heard from many doctors evidence of new sexual problems between man and wife—sexual hunger in wives so great their husbands cannot satisfy it. "We have made women a sex creature," said a psychiatrist at the Margaret Sanger marriage counseling clinic. "She has no identity except as a wife and mother. She does not know who she is herself. She waits all day for her husband to come home at night to make her feel alive. And now it is the husband who is not interested. It is terrible for the woman, to lie there, night after night, waiting for her husband to make her feel alive." Why is there such a market for books and articles offering sexual advice? The kind of sexual orgasm which Kinsey found in statistical plenitude in the recent generations of American women does not seem to make this problem go away.

On the contrary, new neuroses are being seen among women—and problems as yet unnamed as neuroses—which Freud and his followers did not predict, with physical symptoms, anxieties, and defense mechanisms equal to those caused by sexual repression. And strange new problems are being reported in the growing generations of children whose mothers were always there, driving them around, helping them with their homework—an inability to endure pain or discipline or pursue any self-sustained goal of any sort, a devastating boredom with life. Educators are increasingly uneasy about the dependence, the lack of self-reliance, of the boys and girls who are entering college today. "We fight a continual battle to make our students assume manhood," said a Columbia dean.

A White House conference was held on the physical and muscular deterioration of American children: were they being over-nurtured? Sociologists noted the astounding organization of suburban children's lives: the lessons, parties, entertainments, play and study groups organized for them. A suburban housewife in Portland, Oregon, wondered why the children "need" Brownies and Boy Scouts out here. "This is not the slums. The kids out here have the great outdoors. I think people are so bored, they organize the children, and then try to hook everyone else on it. And the poor kids have no time left just to lie on their beds and daydream."

Can the problem that has no name be somehow related to the domestic routine of the housewife? When a woman tries to put the problem into words, she often merely describes the daily life she leads. What is there in this recital of comfortable domestic detail that could possibly cause such a feeling of desperation? Is she trapped simply by the enormous demands of her role as modern housewife: wife,

mistress, mother, nurse, consumer, cook, chauffeur; expert on interior decoration, child care, appliance repair, furniture refinishing, nutrition, and education? Her day is fragmented as she rushes from dishwasher to washing machine to telephone to dryer to station wagon to supermarket, and delivers Johnny to the Little League field, takes Janey to dancing class, gets the lawnmower fixed and meets the 6:45. She can never spend more than 15 minutes on any one thing; she has no time to read books, only magazines; even if she had time, she has lost the power to concentrate. At the end of the day, she is so terribly tired that sometimes her husband has to take over and put the children to bed.

This terrible tiredness took so many women to doctors in the 1950s that one decided to investigate it. He found, surprisingly, that his patients suffering from "housewife's fatigue" slept more than an adult needed to sleep—as much as ten hours a day—and that the actual energy they expended on housework did not tax their capacity. The real problem must be something else, he decided—perhaps boredom. Some doctors told their women patients they must get out of the house for a day, treat themselves to a movie in town. Others prescribed tranquilizers. Many suburban housewives were taking tranquilizers like cough drops. "You wake up in the morning, and you feel as if there's no point in going on another day like this. So you take a tranquilizer because it makes you not care so much that it's pointless."

It is easy to see the concrete details that trap the suburban housewife, the continual demands on her time. But the chains that bind her in her trap are chains in her own mind and spirit. They are chains made up of mistaken ideas and misinterpreted facts, of incomplete truths and unreal choices. They are not easily seen and not easily shaken off.

How can any woman see the whole truth within the bounds of her own life? How can she believe that voice inside herself, when it denies the conventional, accepted truths by which she has been living? And yet the women I have talked to, who are finally listening to that inner voice, seem in some incredible way to be groping through to a truth that has defied the experts.

I think the experts in a great many fields have been holding pieces of that truth under their microscopes for a long time without realizing it. I found pieces of it in certain new research and theoretical developments in psychological, social, and biological science whose implications for women seem never to have been examined. I found many clues by talking to suburban doctors, gynecologists, obstetricians, child-guidance clinicians, pediatricians, high-school guidance counselors, college professors, marriage counselors, psychiatrists, and ministers—questioning them not on their theories, but on their actual experience in treating American women. I became aware of a growing body of evidence, much of which has not been reported publicly because it does not fit current modes of thought about women—evidence which throws into question the standards of feminine normality, feminine adjustment, feminine fulfillment, and feminine maturity by which most women are still trying to live.

I began to see in a strange new light the American return to early marriage and the large families that are causing the population explosion; the recent movement to natural childbirth and breastfeeding; suburban conformity, and the new neuroses, character pathologies, and sexual problems being reported by the doctors. I began to see new dimensions to old problems that have long been taken for granted among women: menstrual difficulties, sexual frigidity, promiscuity, pregnancy fears, childbirth depression, the high incidence of emotional breakdown and suicide among women in their twenties and thirties, the menopause crises, the so-called passivity and immaturity of American men, the discrepancy between women's tested intellectual abilities in child-

hood and their adult achievement, the changing incidence of adult sexual orgasm in American women, and persistent problems in psychotherapy and in women's education.

If I am right, the problem that has no name stirring in the minds of so many American women today is not a matter of loss of femininity or too much education, or the demands of domesticity. It is far more important than anyone recognizes. It is the key to these other new and old problems which have been torturing women and their husbands and children, and puzzling their doctors and educators for years. It may well be the key to our future as a nation and a culture. We can no longer ignore that voice within women that says: "I want something more than my husband and my children and my home."

NOTES

1. See the Seventy-fifth Anniversary Issue of *Good Housekeeping*, May 1960, "The Gift of Self," symposium by Margaret Mead, Jessamyn West, et al.
2. Lee Rainwater, Richard P. Coleman, and Gerald Handel, *Working Man's Wife*, New York, 1959.
3. Betty Friedan, "If One Generation Can Ever Tell Another," *Smith Alumni Quarterly*, Northampton, Mass., Winter 1961. I first became aware of "the problem that has no name" and its possible relationship to what I finally called "the feminine mystique" in 1957, when I prepared an intensive questionnaire and conducted a survey of my own Smith College classmates fifteen years after graduation. This questionnaire was later used by alumnae classes of Radcliffe and other women's colleges with similar results.
4. Jhan and June Robbins, 'Why Young Mothers Feel Trapped," *Redbook*, September 1960.
5. Marian Freda Poverman, "Alumnae on Parade," *Barnard Alumnae Magazine*, July 1957.

Study/Discussion Questions

1. What is the world that Friedan is protesting against?
2. What can we discover about women's lives in the 1950s from this article?
3. One of the criticisms leveled at Friedan is that she only deals with the problems of middle-class women. In what ways do you think this is true?
4. Do you think that Friedan also has a message for women who are not middle class?

The Politics of Housework

Pat Mainardi

Pat Mainardi, writing in 1970 as a member of the New York–based radical feminist group Redstockings, uses humor to critique the internal power dynamics of most marriages when it comes to doing the housework. In keeping with Redstocking's overall analysis of women's oppression in contemporary society —and contrary to several other radical feminist groups of the late 1960s and early 1970s, who thought marriage needed to be eliminated entirely for women to be liberated—Mainardi seeks to alter rather than discard the institution of marriage to make it work for women.

Though women do not complain of the power of husbands, each complains of her own husband, or of the husbands of her friends. It is the same in all other cases of servitude; at least in the commencement of the emancipatory movement. The serfs did not at first complain of the power of the lords, but only of their tyranny.

—*John Stuart Mill,* On the Subjection of Women

Liberated women—very different from women's liberation! The first signals all kinds of goodies, to warm the hearts (not to mention other parts) of the most radical men. The other signals—*housework.* The first brings sex without marriage, sex before marriage, cozy housekeeping arrangements ("You see, I'm living with this chick") and the self-content of knowing that you're not the kind of man who wants a doormat instead of a woman. That will come later. After all, who wants that old commodity anymore, the Standard American Housewife, all husband, home and kids. The New Commodity, the Liberated Woman, has sex a lot and has a Career, preferably something that can be fitted in with the household chores—like dancing, pottery, or painting.

On the other hand is women's liberation—and housework. What? You say this is all trivial? Wonderful! That's what I thought. It seemed perfectly reasonable. We both had careers, both had to work a couple of days a week to earn enough to live on, so why shouldn't we share the housework? So I suggested it to my mate and he agreed—most men are too hip to turn you down flat. "You're right," he said, "It's only fair."

Then an interesting thing happened. I can only explain it by stating that we women have

From *Sisterhood Is Powerful: An Anthology of Writings from the Women's Liberation Movement,* edited by Robin Morgan. Copyright ©1970 Robin Morgan. By permission of Edite Kroll Literary Agency, Inc.

been brainwashed more than even we can imagine. Probably too many years of seeing television women in ecstasy over the shiny waxed floors or breaking down over their dirty shirt collars. Men have no such conditioning. They recognize the essential fact of housework right from the very beginning. Which is that it stinks. Here's my list of dirty chores: buying groceries, carting them home and putting them away; cooking meals and washing dishes and pots; doing the laundry; digging out the place when things get out of control; washing floors. The list could go on but the sheer necessities are bad enough. All of us have to do these things, or get some one else to do them for us. The longer my husband contemplated these chores, the more repulsed he became, and so proceeded the change from the normally sweet considerate Dr. Jekyll into the crafty Mr. Hyde who would stop at nothing to avoid the horrors of—*housework*. As he felt himself backed into a corner laden with dirty dishes, brooms, mops, and reeking garbage, his front teeth grew longer and pointier, his fingernails haggled and his eyes grew wild. Housework trivial? Not on your life! Just try to share the burden.

So ensued a dialogue that's been going on for several years. Here are some of the high points:

"I don't mind sharing the housework, but I don't do it very well. We should each do the things we're best at."

Meaning: Unfortunately I'm no good at things like washing dishes or cooking. What I do best is a little light carpentry, changing light bulbs, moving furniture (*how often do you move furniture?*).
Also Meaning: Historically the lower classes (black men and us) have had hundreds of years experience doing menial jobs. It would be a waste of manpower to train someone else to do them now.
Also Meaning: I don't like the dull stupid boring jobs, so you should do them.

"I don't mind sharing the work, but you'll have to show me how to do it."

Meaning: I ask a lot of questions and you'll have to show me everything every time I do it because I don't remember so good. Also don't try to sit down and read while I'm doing my jobs because I'm going to annoy hell out of you until it's easier to do them yourself.

"We used to be so happy!" (Said whenever it was his turn to do something.)

Meaning: I used to be so happy.
Meaning: Life without housework is bliss. (No quarrel here. Perfect agreement.)

"We have different standards, and why should I have to work to your standards. That's unfair."

Meaning: If I begin to get bugged by the dirt and crap I will say "This place sure is a sty" or "How can anyone live like this?" and wait for your reaction. I know that all women have a sore called "Guilt over a messy house" or "Household work is ultimately my responsibility." I know that men have caused that sore—if anyone visits and the place *is* a sty, they're not going to leave and say, "He sure is a lousy housekeeper." You'll take the rap in any case. I can outwait you.
Also Meaning: I can provoke innumerable scenes over the housework issue. Eventually doing all the housework yourself will be less painful to you than trying to get me to do half. Or I'll suggest we get a maid. She will do my share of the work. You will do yours. It's women's work.

"I've got nothing against sharing the housework, but you can't make me do it on your schedule."

Meaning: Passive resistance. I'll do it when I damned well please, if at all. If my job is doing dishes, it's easier to do them once a week. If taking out laundry, once a month. If washing the floors, once a year. If you don't like it, do it yourself oftener, and then I won't do it at all.

"I *hate* it more than you. You don't mind it so much."

Meaning: Housework is garbage work. It's the worst crap I've ever done. It's degrading and humiliating for someone of my intelligence to do it. But for someone of your intelligence . . .

"Housework is too trivial to even talk about."

Meaning: It's even more trivial to do. Housework is beneath my status. My purpose in life is to deal with matters of significance. Yours is to deal with matters of insignificance. You should do the housework.

"This problem of housework is not a man-woman problem. In any relationship between two people one is going to have a stronger personality and dominate."

Meaning: That stronger personality had better be me.

"In animal societies, wolves, for example, the top animal is usually a male even where he is not chosen for brute strength but on the basis of cunning and intelligence. Isn't that interesting?"

Meaning: I have historical, psychological, anthropological, and biological justification for keeping you down. How can you ask the top wolf to be equal?

"Women's liberation isn't really a political movement."

Meaning: The Revolution is coming too close to home.

Also Meaning: I am only interested in how *I* am oppressed, not how I oppress others. Therefore the war, the draft, and the university are political. Women's liberation is not.

"Man's accomplishments have always depended on getting help from other people, mostly women. What great man would have accomplished what he did if he had to do his own housework?"

Meaning: Oppression is built into the System and I, the white American male, receive the benefits of this System. I don't want to give them up.

POSTSCRIPT

Participatory democracy begins at home. If you are planning to implement your politics, there are certain things to remember.

1. He is feeling it more than you. He's losing some leisure and you're gaining it. The measure of your oppression is his resistance.
2. A great many American men are not accustomed to doing monotonous repetitive work which never ushers in any lasting let alone important achievement. This is why they would rather repair a cabinet than wash dishes. If human endeavors are like a pyramid with man's highest achievements at the top, then keeping oneself alive is at the bottom. Men have always had servants (us) to take care of this bottom strata of life while they have confined their efforts to the rarefied upper regions. It is thus ironic when they ask of women—where are your great painters, statesmen, etc.? Mme. Matisse ran a millinery shop so he could paint. Mrs. Martin Luther King kept his house and raised his babies.

3. It is a traumatizing experience for someone who always thought of himself as being against any oppression or exploitation of one human being by another to realize that in his daily life he has been accepting and implementing (and benefiting from) this exploitation; that his rationalization is little different from that of the racist who says, "Black people don't feel pain" (women don't mind doing the shitwork); and that the oldest form of oppression in history has been the oppression of 50 percent of the population by the other 50 percent.

4. Arm yourself with some knowledge of the psychology of oppressed peoples every-where, and a few facts about the animal kingdom. I admit playing top wolf or who runs the gorillas is silly but as a last resort men bring it up all the time. Talk about bees. If you feel really hostile, bring up the sex life of spiders. They have sex. She bites off his head.

   The psychology of oppressed people is not silly. Jews, immigrants, black men, and all women have employed the same psychological mechanisms to survive: admiring the oppressor, glorifying the oppressor, wanting to be like the oppressor, wanting the oppressor to like them, mostly because the oppressor held all the power.

5. In a sense, all men everywhere are slightly schizoid—divorced from the reality of maintaining life. This makes it easier for them to play games with it. It is almost a cliché that women feel greater grief at sending a son off to war or losing him to that war because they bore him, suckled him, and raised him. The men who foment those wars did none of those things and have a more superficial estimate of the worth of human life. One hour a day is a low estimate of the amount of time one has to spend "keeping" oneself. By foisting this off on others, man gains seven hours week—one working day more to play with

his mind and not his human needs. Over the course of generations it is easy to see whence evolved the horrifying abstractions of modern life.

6. With the death of each form of oppression, life changes and new forms evolve. English aristocrats at the turn of the century were horrified at the idea of enfranchising working men—were sure that it signaled the death of civilization and a return to barbarism. Some working men were even deceived by this line. Similarly with the minimum wage, abolition of slavery, and female suffrage. Life changes but it goes on. Don't fall for any line about the death of everything if men take a turn at the dishes. They will imply that you are holding back the Revolution (their Revolution). But you are advancing it (your Revolution).

7. Keep checking up. Periodically consider who's actually doing the jobs. These things have a way of backsliding so that a year later once again the woman is doing everything. After a year make a list of jobs the man has rarely if ever done. You will find cleaning pots, toilets, refrigerators and ovens high on the list. Use time sheets if necessary. He will accuse you of being petty. He is above that sort of thing (housework). Bear in mind what the worst jobs are, namely the ones that have to be done every day several times a day. Also the ones that are dirty—it's more pleasant to pick up books, newspapers, etc. than to wash dishes. Alternate the bad jobs. It's the daily grind that gets you down. Also make sure that you don't have the responsibility for the housework with occasional help from him. "I'll cook dinner for you night" implies it's really your job and isn't he a nice guy to do some of it for you.

8. Most men had a rich and rewarding bachelor life during which they did not starve or become encrusted with crud or buried under the litter. There is a taboo

that says that women mustn't strain themselves in the presence of men: we haul around 50 pounds of groceries if we have to but aren't allowed to open a jar if there is someone around to do it for us. The reverse side of the coin is that men aren't supposed to be able to take care of themselves without a woman. Both are excuses for making women do the housework.

9. Beware of the double whammy. He won't do the little things he always did because you're now a "Liberated Woman," right? Of course he won't do anything else either . . .

I was just finishing this when my husband came in and asked what I was doing. Writing a paper on housework. Housework? He said, *Housework?* Oh my god how trivial can you get. A paper on housework.

LITTLE POLITICS OF HOUSEWORK QUIZ

- The lowest job in the army, used as punishment is: (a) working 9-5 (b) kitchen duty (K.P.).
- When a man lives with his family, his: (a) father (b) mother does his housework.
- When he lives with a woman, (a) he (b) she does the housework.
- (a) his son (b) his daughter learns in preschool how much fun it is to iron daddy's handkerchief.

- From the *New York Times,* 9/21/69: "Former Greek Official George Mylonas pays the penalty for differing with the ruling junta in Athens by performing household chores on the island of Amorgos where he lives in forced exile" (with hilarious photo of a miserable Mylonas carrying his own water). What the *Times* means is that he ought to have (a) indoor plumbing (b) a maid.
- Dr. Spock said (*Redbook* 3/69): "Biologically and temperamentally I believe, women were made to be concerned first and foremost with child care, husband care, and home care." Think about: (a) *who* made us (b) why? (c) what is the effect on their lives (d) what is the effect on our lives?
- From *Time* 1/5/70, "Like their American counterparts, many housing project housewives are said to suffer from neurosis. And for the first time in Japanese history, many young husbands today complain of being henpecked. Their wives are beginning to demand detailed explanations when they don't come home straight from work, and some Japanese males nowadays are even compelled to do housework." According to *Time,* women become neurotic: (a) when they are forced to do the maintenance work for the male caste all day every day of their lives or (b) when they no longer want to do the maintenance work for the male caste all day every day of their lives.

Study/Discussion Questions

1. Make two lists of the household chores performed by the male and female members of your family when you were growing up. Or, if your living arrangement today includes both men and women, keep a journal for a week of who does what housework, and of conversations about housework.
2. Do men and women have different attitudes toward doing housework?
3. Do men complain more?

4. Do men assume that women will always do certain chores, or do they specialize in fun or infrequent chores, as Mainardi suggests?
5. Do women feel guilty and/or more responsible when the house is a mess?

A Time of Change

Neil Miller

In the 1980s, Neil Miller traversed the United States to investigate the realities of gay life in every corner of the nation. He found, among other things, a veritable lesbian baby boom in several cities. Whether they adopt children, or conceive them through artificial insemination or other methods, or bring with them the children of previous heterosexual partnerships, thousands of lesbian couples are rearing daughters and sons in America. In this excerpt from In Search of Gay America: Women and Men in a Time of Change, *Miller introduces us to lesbian-headed families in Newton, Massachusetts, and Miami, Florida.*

When I returned home to Boston from my trip through small town America, it was as if I was returning to the modern gay world. The gay and lesbian March on Washington was scheduled for the following week; organizers were hoping for a turnout of as many as half a million people. The memorial AIDS quilt—the size of two football fields—was on its way from San Francisco to be unveiled at the march. The film version of *Maurice,* E. M. Forster's novel about homosexuality in Edwardian England, was playing to packed houses in Harvard Square.

In the copy of the *New York Native* that I found in the stack of mail on my desk, the ever-controversial AIDS activist Larry Kramer was blaming the "white middle-class male majority" for the AIDS epidemic—and preaching the gospel of sexual conservatism. "The heterosexual majority has for centuries denied us every possible right of human dignity that the Constitution was framed to provide to all," he argued at a symposium sponsored by the New York Civil Liberties Union. "The right to marry. The right to own property jointly without fear the law would disinherit the surviving partner. The right to hold jobs as an openly gay person. The right to have children. . . . So rightly or wrongly—wrongly, as it turned out—we decided we would make a virtue of the only thing you didn't have control over: our sexuality. Had we possessed these rights you denied us, had we been allowed to live respectably in a community as equals, there would never have been an AIDS. Had we been allowed to marry, we would not have felt the obligation to be promiscuous."

For its part, *GCN* was proudly publishing photographs of five babies born to Boston-area lesbians earlier in the year.

And Mo was seven and a half months pregnant. Mo and her lover, Ellen, are close friends of my friend Katie. Katie and Ellen grew up in the same Cleveland suburb (they met at Girl Scouts) and went to high school together. I had never met Mo or Ellen but Katie kept me closely apprised of developments in their lives. A couple of years ago, they had moved out of the city to suburban Newton—"For the schools," Katie said. Mo had bought a station wagon. Next, I heard that Mo was attempting to get pregnant through artificial insemination. After twelve months of trying, she was finally going to have a baby.

Katie recounted all these events with a mixture of pride and trepidation. She was excited at the prospect of being an "aunt" but was also concerned that her friends were gradually growing more distant—the move to the suburbs, the station wagon, and finally, of course, the baby. She was worried about being left behind. That was a fear that gay people (and childless heterosexuals) often experienced when married friends started raising children; in the past, you could at least have been sure your gay friends wouldn't abandon you for the suburbs, mothers' support groups, and the PTA. I was aware that the number of gay people—primarily lesbians, but some gay men, too—choosing to become parents had grown dramatically in the past few years, especially in the large urban centers. In Boston, it seemed as if virtually every lesbian in her thirties was either having a baby or thinking about it. Gay men were becoming sperm donors to lesbian friends for at-home insemination (although fear of AIDS was making most lesbian parents-to-be turn to sperm banks and "unknown" donors); some gay men and lesbians were involved in complicated co-parenting arrangements.

A friend told me about spending the weekend at the home of a lesbian couple in Boston. One of the women in the household was trying to become pregnant; a gay man in Los Angeles was providing the sperm and would play a role (albeit a distant one) in raising the child. My friend, who was sleeping on the fold-out couch in the living room, was awakened early Saturday morning by the doorbell. It was Federal Express delivering a package. My friend signed for it, assuming it was a pair of khakis from L. L. Bean or the latest lesbian detective novel. When her hosts came down for breakfast, she learned the package contained a sperm specimen, packed in dry ice for transcontinental shipment.

As much as people joked about "turkey-baster babies" and the "lesbian baby boom," the decision of increasing numbers of gay people to become parents outside of heterosexual norms marked a major change in gay and lesbian life. Coming out no longer meant forgoing the option of having children, as had been assumed in the past. By the late eighties, with the aging of the gay baby-boom generation, parenting had unexpectedly emerged as the cutting edge of gay and lesbian liberation. It was a new stage in the development of self-affirmation and identity. But to reach that point, a specific gay and lesbian community had to achieve a certain degree of cohesion and comfort. As a result, the new parenting was primarily a phenomenon of large cities and the East and West coasts, where gay people had developed the most extensive support systems and felt the most secure. Lesbians and gay men I visited in smaller towns wouldn't consider the possibility of having children (although many had them from previous heterosexual marriages); it would be too exposing, call too much attention to themselves.

Most lesbians I knew who were having babies were open about their sexuality and were politically active. Mo and Ellen were, to some degree, in the closet; their neighbors and their co-workers were unaware of their relationship. According to Katie, they intended to continue to live discreetly after the baby was born. I thought the fact that these suburban, relatively closeted lesbians were having a child might indicate that the lesbian baby boom was extending to more mainstream women.

One Saturday, six weeks before their baby was due, I went to visit Mo and Ellen. They were waiting for a changing table to arrive from Sears and would be home all morning, they told me when I phoned. I headed for the land of Dutch Colonials and station wagons, of well-dressed parents pushing well-scrubbed children through the park in Aprica strollers, of the comfortable, child-centered middle class. Traditionally a Jewish middle-class suburb, Newton was increasingly drawing Boston-area Yuppies like Mo and Ellen.

I always felt a pang of nostalgia and sadness when I drove to Newton. When I was growing up, my aunt and uncle and my closest cousins lived there. Visiting them was a treat, to be savored weeks in advance. By the time I was in college, my aunt and uncle were in the middle of an acrimonious divorce and my cousins were estranged from them. My relatives had long since moved out of Newton but I couldn't help but think about the breakup of their family every time I went there.

Mo and Ellen's house was a two-story brick fifties-style dwelling located on a main thoroughfare. The interior was decorated with wall-to-wall carpeting, comfortable furniture, and living-room curtains featuring a pattern of ducks; the clock on the mantelpiece was flanked by framed photographs of Mo and Ellen's families. It was friendly, tasteful, undistinctive—the kind of house where most American middle-class suburban kids have grown up in the past three decades.

Mo and Ellen had been together for more than ten years. They met as sorority sisters at Ohio State. No one in their sorority knew they were involved; they were just best friends who spent all their time together and did their best to hide the truth of their relationship. Later, they found out that most of the officers of the sorority were lesbians and that Mo's former roommate had been having an affair with the woman across the hall.

To me, they seemed quite evenly matched—opinionated, good-humored, a little on the boisterous side. Both looked like they should play rugby or lacrosse. Mo was a tall, dark-haired woman of thirty-one who grew up in rural Ohio. She was dressed in a light blue pullover top and matching; running pants; her outfit was a cross between sweats and pajamas. "The latest in lesbian maternity apparel," she joked. She worked as a career counselor at a nearby college, but was planning to quit once the baby was born. Ellen, thirty, had long, sandy hair and radiated wholesome good cheer. She was in a management position at a Boston computer company and tended to have a somewhat tough-minded, business-like way of viewing things. Katie told me she thought Ellen had softened and begun to express more of her emotional side since Mo's pregnancy.

Mo had always wanted to have kids but once she came out she assumed it wasn't a possibility. Still, she wouldn't give up on the idea entirely. She asked her gay brother (of five siblings in her family, three were gay) if he might consider offering his sperm so Ellen could get pregnant. He was appalled at the notion, she said; he told Mo, somewhat self-righteously, that she and Ellen should adopt a handicapped child. Mo and Ellen started attending meetings of the Choosing Children Network, a Boston-area group that offered information and support to lesbians considering parenthood. They began to lean towards adopting a child. At about that time, the administration of Governor Michael Dukakis issued the controversial regulations that effectively barred gays and lesbians from becoming licensed as foster parents. This policy was widely interpreted as applying to adoption as well, and adoption agencies were running scared. Mo would call up adoption agencies and ask if they would accept applications from gay couples.

"We'll get back to you," they would tell her, but they rarely did.

With possibilities for adoption apparently closed off, Mo and Ellen decided to try artificial insemination (also called AI or alternative insemination, to make it sound less clinical). They began going to a Boston community-health center that performed the procedure. (Under the clinic's policy the identity of donor and recipient remained unknown to each other, donors waived all rights to any child conceived with their sperm.) Mo and Ellen had to wait three months before beginning insemination; in the meantime, they joined a support group of other lesbians who were trying to get pregnant.

The health center permitted them to choose specific characteristics they wanted in a donor—height, hair and eye color, ethnic background, occupation, and the like. But after months of unsuccessful insemination, Mo found herself caring less and less about whether the donor had blue or brown eyes. "After a while," she said, "I was just concerned with getting pregnant. I really didn't care about anything else." In the end, the father turned out to be a six-foot-three Seventh-Day Adventist of Irish extraction from southern California. The health center gave Mo a letter he wrote telling about himself and why he had become a sperm donor; she and Ellen planned to show the note to the child when it got older.

I asked Mo how her parents felt about her pregnancy. She pointed to two large boxes of baby clothes that her mother had sent a few days before, which were still sitting in the front hall. Her parents had known for many years that Mo was a lesbian; that was nothing new. And Mo's baby would be the first grandchild, a fact which made her parents more accepting than they might have been otherwise.

Still, her parents were uncomfortable. Her mother was especially worried about how to explain the pregnancy to her neighbors in the small town where she lived and where the family was quite prominent. Everyone there knew that Mo was unmarried, and her mother had never acknowledged to a soul—not even to her closest friends—that three of her children were gay. But with the baby on the way, her mother had to say something. She began telling neighbors that her daughter was having a child and bringing it up herself. The father, she said, lived in California and would take no part in raising the baby. That was accurate as far as it went. "The disgrace of illegitimacy is better than the truth in her eyes," noted Mo.

Until the couple decided to have a child, Ellen had never told her parents she was gay. But she was seriously thinking about having a baby herself in a couple of years, "to balance things out," as she put it. When Mo began undergoing insemination, Ellen wrote to her parents and revealed the truth of their relationship. Her parents seemed to have responded well. "They offered us a crib," she said. "My mother is buying Christmas ornaments for my sister's child and our child. My father is wondering what he should call the child and how he should talk about it. They are planning to consider it a grandchild."

Mo's mother was preparing to visit after the birth of the baby, and Ellen's parents would follow a couple of weeks later.

That degree of parental support, however qualified, was not typical of the other lesbians (three couples and a single woman) in their childbirth class, they told me. "The other women in the group have parents who are saying, 'This is not our grandchild. We will have nothing to do with this child,'" Mo noted. "We go to these meetings and feel incredibly lucky."

Interestingly, both Mo's and Ellen's parents had become friends, a bond formed before the parents were aware the two young women were lovers. The parents, who lived a few hours' drive from each other, had much in common. Like their daughters, both sets of parents met when they were students at Ohio State, and were active in their alumni organizations; both were members of the same religious denomination. "If I were a guy or you were a guy, it would be a marriage made in heaven," Mo joked to Ellen. The parents had gone to dinner and the theatre together—without their daughters.

After Mo became pregnant, Ellen's parents invited Mo's mother and father to their home, where they discussed the baby. In fact, Ellen's mother had been helping Mo's mother cope with her worries about the situation. "My mother is less inhibited," Ellen explained. "Mo's parents are very uptight about what people think. Mo has been pregnant all this time but her mother only told her own sister-in-law a couple of weeks ago."

The story Mo's mother was giving out to friends and relatives, that "the baby's father lives in California and won't be involved," was identical to what Mo and Ellen were telling people at their jobs, where both kept their relationship a secret. Mo was convinced that her boss would fire her if he learned she was gay; she was planning to leave anyway once the baby was born. People are "one hundred percent more accepting" of a single, heterosexual woman having a baby than a lesbian mother, she maintained. Ellen said that her co-workers were aware she had a female roommate and that the two owned a house together, but apparently made no assumptions beyond that. She had informed the other employees that Mo was pregnant and that she was going to be the birth coach. "They are telling me, 'You are going to be like a father!'" Ellen said. "I think they understand at some level what is going on, even if it is not a conscious level." Still, Ellen was reluctant to come out at work. Acknowledging her sexuality "wouldn't be good for my career," she insisted.

I asked them how they felt about this misrepresentation of their relationship and of the baby's conception. Mo emphasized that her priority was to protect the child as much as possible. If she had to pretend to be heterosexual for the child to have an easier time, she

would do so—to some extent, anyway. "Not to a total extent though," she said. "But I am willing to make some accommodations." What accommodations, I asked. She thought that if her child brought a friend home to stay overnight, there was no reason to make her sexuality known. What about school? About parents of other kids? She just wasn't sure. Of course, they would tell the child about their homosexuality when it was old enough. "Some lesbian mothers are really out," Mo said. "I admire that. But I don't know yet just how open to be. Our big worry is how society will react and how to make it easier for the child. If that means playing a game with people we don't care about, I'll play a game. We're not the most militant people. I think I'll be more middle-of-the-road than most other lesbian mothers. That is how we've lived so far."

I thought that Mo and Ellen might be fooling themselves. I had talked to a number of gay parents who emphasized that a child's comfort with a parent's homosexuality was directly proportional to how relaxed the parent seemed about it. I questioned whether the way Mo and Ellen were planning to handle the issue indicated the necessary degree of ease. How, for example, would the child react to having two mothers in Boston but one mother (and an absent father somewhere in California) when it went to visit its grandmother in Ohio?

In the middle of our talk, the doorbell rang. It was Sears, delivering the changing table. We moved to the front hall, and I thought the deliverymen might assume that, as the only male present, I was the expectant father. But Mo and Ellen immediately took charge, and the men never even looked in my direction. They carried the table upstairs to the guest room, and Mo and Ellen enthusiastically unpacked it. Then, Ellen and I lugged the two boxes of baby clothes from Mo's mother upstairs.

When we sat down again, the conversation shifted. One aspect of child-rearing Mo and

Ellen were sure about was that the child would be both of theirs; they were determined to minimize the primacy of the biological mother as much as possible. "I don't want this to be my child," Mo said firmly. "It is going to have my last name, and when Ellen has a baby that one will have her last name. But they will be our kids and we are going to try to reinforce that in as many ways as we can." They had graduated from college without any money or possessions and had shared everything since then, they said. This would extend to the child. Their biggest problem was what to have the child call them. Most lesbian couples they knew used Mommy and the first name of the co-parent. They rejected this formulation because they felt it reinforced the role of the biological mother as primary parent. But they were unsure what to do instead.

As part of Mo's insistence on downplaying the biological tie, she was determined to bottle-feed the baby. Bottle-feeding would give Ellen an equal role in feeding and prevent her from feeling excluded. The other women in their childbirth class were strong proponents of breast-feeding, however. Mo differed from the rest of the class in still another respect; she was willing to entertain the idea of anesthesia if labor proved too painful, an idea that was totally unacceptable to the other mothers-to-be. In their childbirth class they were "the most mainstream," Mo said. But, always worried about appearing overly conservative, she added, "We are talking about mainstream liberal. Don't get us wrong."

Mainstream liberal or just mainstream, Mo and Ellen were nonetheless pioneers of a sort and they knew it. They emphasized that what they were doing would have been unthinkable ten years ago. As gay people, "We have stopped fighting and started living, really," said Ellen.

Shortly after the first of the year, Katie called me up excitedly. Mo was in the hospital, about to go into labor. For the next day or so, I re-ceived up-to-the-minute bulletins: contractions had begun; Ellen was there by her side; the doctors thought they might have to induce labor. Finally, Katie telephoned to announce that Mo had had the baby, a girl named Emma Claire.

In February, I went to Florida for a few days to visit my own parents, who now live there most of the year. During my stay, I spent an evening with six gay women in the living room of a ranch-style home in the Miami suburb of Kendall. All the women but one had been married before. As a result of these marriages, they had eleven children among them.

The house belonged to two women in their early forties—Rexine Pippinger, who managed a Radio Shack franchise, and her lover of seven years, Becky Anderson, a pediatric nurse. (The other women had just come by for the evening.) Rexine's two red-headed, freckle-faced teenage sons wandered in and out, bantering affectionately with their mother. The family dog, a little black spaniel, was about to give birth and was pacing nervously. Despite the cozy "Leave It to Beaver" atmosphere, the women had horror stories to tell. They were examples of gay parenting the traditional way—coming to terms with sexuality after marriage and childbearing. And the degree of rage in the suburban living room was sometimes frightening.

Four of the five women who had been married had emerged on the losing end of grueling legal battles with their ex-husbands. Becky, the nurse, had lost her house and custody of her two children (now twenty-one and sixteen) in the late seventies, at the height of Anita Bryant's anti-gay crusade. She wound up taking care of the kids for the next eight years anyway. Her lover, Rexine, initially won custody of her children. Later, her alcoholic ex-husband had sued her for fraud—dragging several of her ex-lovers into court as witnesses. As a result, she lost her children for two years and her house, as well.

Another woman had lost custody and even been denied visitation rights. Her former husband had moved out of state with her two children. Now the ex-husband, his new wife, and the kids had moved back to Miami and she got to see the children. But her oldest daughter was pregnant and unwed; her fourteen-year-old was having sex with her boyfriend. She got the blame for the kids' actions; everything they were doing was to show they were not lesbians, according to their stepmother. "I used to think there was some truth in it until I finally learned to stop laying guilt trips on myself," the woman said.

The one parent who had been spared a custody battle nearly lost her children another way. The previous year, Arlie Brice, a graphic designer in her early thirties, had been living in Jacksonville, Florida, with her lover and her two sons, aged nine and eleven. On the children's school forms, Arlie would scratch out "father" and write "co-parent" instead, putting down her lover's name. Both were members of the PTA and baked brownies for school events. One Saturday when Arlie was at work, she got a call from her lover. An investigator from the State Department of Health and Rehabilitative Services had shown up at their door. Someone had accused them of child abuse. After two weeks of investigation, which proved an "utter terror" for the kids (and their parents), they were cleared of any wrongdoing. Still, once you're reported for child abuse, Arlie noted, "you are on a master computer in Tallahassee, whether the accusation is justified or unjustified. Right now if I wanted to work with kids or be a foster parent, I would be denied."

Their accuser, she found out, was the principal of the public school her children attended. He was a religious fundamentalist. When Arlie confronted him, he admitted he had reported them to state authorities, she said. "I know you love your kids," Arlie quoted the principal as saying. "But you are living a lifestyle that is wrong." Arlie's only recourse would have been

to hire an attorney and, as she put it, "make a lot of noise." But in conservative Jacksonville, bringing a court case on such grounds could be "a very dangerous thing to do," she said. "You could lose your job at the drop of a hat." She took her kids out of school immediately; some months later, the family moved to Miami.

After listening to these stories, I turned to the one woman in the group who hadn't been married, a twenty-six year old Cuban-American named Sonia Fandino. Sonia lived at home with her parents and managed a gas station. I asked her facetiously if she ever planned to get married. "No," she laughed. "But I am planning to have a child soon." How did she plan to become pregnant? I asked. "Artificial insemination," she replied, and everyone in the room broke into laughter.

I thought back to that glimpse of old-style gay parenting when I returned to Newton to visit Mo and Ellen two months after Emma Claire was born. Ellen led me upstairs to the baby's room, where Mo was giving Emma Claire a bath. There, on the changing table that had arrived during my previous visit, was a squalling little baby with big blue eyes. The room was now furnished with two cribs—a large one filled with stuffed animals, and a second, smaller one for Emma Claire. Mo dried the baby, put her in a flannel nightgown, and laid her down in the crib. Ellen and I headed downstairs to the living room, now equipped with a baby's swing chair and decorated with a mobile depicting various animals.

Once Emma Claire had fallen asleep, Mo joined us. The two filled me in on events since I had last seen them. Childbirth was the toughest thing she had ever done in her life, Mo said. In the middle of the contractions Mo shouted to Ellen, who was holding Mo's legs as she worked to push the baby out, "This is really going to be hard for you when it's your turn!"

In general, the hospital staff had been at ease with them, they said. By coincidence, another lesbian who had become pregnant through AI was in the next room. When Mo mentioned to one nurse that they knew the woman next door, the nurse apparently assumed Mo was a lesbian. She began barraging her with questions: How did she get pregnant? What was AI, anyway? Did she know the baby's father?

According to the hospital rules, only husbands could spend all day in the room with the woman during and after labor, but Ellen remained and no one objected. Another regulation said no visitors except husbands could bring a baby from the nursery to the mother's room. Ellen went in and asked to take Emma Claire. The nurse balked. "I'm a partner," she insisted. The nurse relented, eyeing her suspiciously as she walked out the door with the baby.

Mo's mother came up from Ohio for the birth and stayed for two weeks. Mo had lost a lot of blood during childbirth and was too weak and exhausted to be very enthusiastic about holding Emma Claire. Her mother tried to get her to bond with the baby. But she went to such lengths that Ellen felt she was deliberately trying to freeze her out of any role. Mo's mother was constantly sending Ellen out of the house on errands. She would call Mo "Mommy" in the baby's presence, something Mo and Ellen had agreed not to do. At one point, the grandmother grabbed the baby right out of Ellen's arms and gave her to Mo to hold. Ellen became increasingly convinced that the mother's intention was to make it clear that the baby was Mo's, not Mo and Ellen's.

Caught between her mother and her lover, Mo was trying not to take sides. Her mother would come around, she was convinced; she just had to get used to the situation. And she had been helpful during the two weeks after the birth of the baby. The following weekend, Mo and Ellen were planning to bring the baby to visit Mo's parents. But if her mother persisted in trying to demonstrate that Emma Claire was Mo's and Mo's alone, her daughter was ready to insist she "cut the 'Mommy' crap."

Our mutual friend Katie, a social worker by profession, suspected that Mo's relations with her parents were about to undergo a major change. Mo, in her view, had always been the family mediator, listening patiently as her mother complained about the travails of having three gay children. Now, with the birth of Mo's baby, Katie thought that Mo would have to become more outspoken in defending the child and affirming her own relationship.

Meanwhile, Ellen reported that people at work were bringing her gifts for her "roommate's" baby. One co-worker gave her a bib; another bought a suit for Emma Claire. Everyone was asking her how the baby was doing. "I've been getting some weird questions," she said. "One of my co-workers asked me, 'Is your roommate being a surrogate mother?' But generally, people seem to go along with it and understand that I come home after work and help take care of the baby. In fact, a male co-worker had called earlier that week to ask Ellen out on a date. "I'm involved," she told him.

A month after the baby was born, a disquieting incident occurred. Ellen's brother-in-law, who held a highly sensitive post in the navy, had been called into his superior's office. "Do you know your sister-in-law is a lesbian?" he was asked. Of course, he knew, he replied. "Just as long as you are aware of it," his superior told him. Apparently, the navy was afraid of a potential blackmail situation.

Ellen's sister had called her up and told her about what had happened. She and Mo were upset and angry. They were puzzled about how the navy could have known about their relationship. Both their names appeared on the home mortgage, they noted. They were also on the mailing lists of the *Gay Community News* and a gay hiking club. Was the military spying on gay organizations? "It could have ruined our lives if we weren't 'out' to our families," said Ellen. Added Mo, her middle-of-the-road approach veering towards militance, "I'd like to know how national security is compromised by my love life!" Ironically, the same week, a federal court of appeals panel in San Francisco had struck down the army's ban on homosexuals.

At the time the United States Navy was questioning Ellen's brother-in-law, rumors were flying in the small Ohio town where Mo's parents live. Mo received a letter of congratulations from a high-school friend; in the letter, the woman noted that her grandmother had heard about the baby at her bridge club. She added that the grandmother had heard that Mo had gotten pregnant through "artificial whatever," a fact that Mo's mother had never revealed. Mo had no idea how the woman could have known. "I was floored," she said. "Information about our personal lives seemed to be sweeping the land. The government was spying on us, and everyone in Ohio was talking about us!"

Despite these minor but dramatic incidents, the new gay parenting as exemplified by Mo and Ellen was still worlds apart from the horrors related by the lesbian mothers in Miami. In Mo and Ellen's case, there would be no ugly custody battles, no ex-husbands exacting revenge, and (one assumed) in liberal Newton, no overzealous school principals alleging child abuse. But clearly the future would not be easy. The tension between how open or discreet to be about their sexuality and the difficulties of dealing with parents, schools, and society in general were something that Mo and Ellen would have to face squarely.

So far, most of these challenges lay in the future. Parents and baby were doing reasonably well. Ellen's mother and father had been up to visit; some of the neighbors had come by to see Emma Claire. Ellen was still quite determined to have another baby within the next year or two; the sleepless nights since Emma Claire's arrival had not dampened her enthusiasm. On the Friday night after my visit, six lesbian couples, all with babies, were coming by for a potluck.

Still, I couldn't help but speculate on how Emma Claire and all the children of these unusual parenting arrangements would turn out. Would they feel embarrassed about their parents? Protective? Proud? How important would the "absent (and unknown) father" issue be for them as they got older? Would they perceive themselves as different from the other kids? Or would growing up in a community like Newton, where divorced and single-parent families were commonplace, help them feel accepted? Would they be rebellious adolescents trying to prove they weren't gay? No one knew. The only studies of children of gay and lesbian parents had been done about traditional gay parenting (after heterosexual marriage), with its complicating factors of divorce and late coming out. Those studies had all been quite positive, but there was no doubt that psychologists and sociologists would have an interesting future studying the children of the lesbian baby boom.

Study/Discussion Questions

1. What hinders gay people from leading traditional family lives?
2. If you worked with Mo or Ellen, do think you would be more or less comfortable if they were more candid about their relationship?
3. Should women be more or less open about being lesbians when they have children together?
4. What happens to women who come out as lesbians after they have children in relationships with men? What effect does it have on their lives as women and mothers?

The Business of Selling Mail-Order Brides

Venny Villapando

Not all marriages begin with a typical romance, Venny Villapando reminds us. For thousands of Asian women, the "picture bride" system is still in effect. Originally a way for immigrant men to bring a bride of their family's choosing to the United States, the "mail order" bride system now specializes in bringing Asian women from impoverished circumstances to marry wealthier Caucasian males who tend to be "much older than the bride they choose, politically conservative, frustrated by the women's movement, and socially alienated." The new wife finds herself in a vulnerable position in a strange land.

The phenomenon is far from new. Certainly in the Old West and in other frontier situations such as the labor camps at the sugar farms in Hawaii, the colonization of Australia, or even in the early Irish settlements of New York, there were always lonely men who would write to their homeland for a bride. These women would come on the next train or on the next boat to meet their husbands for the very first time.

For Japanese immigrants traditional marriages were arranged in Japan between relatives of the man and the prospective bride. Information was exchanged between the two families about the potential union, and photographs were exchanged between the couple. If both parties agreed, then the marriage was legalized in the home country, and the bride came to America.

While these marriages occurred in less than ideal situations, a number of them were successful. For example the Japanese sugar worker who once waited at the Honolulu pier for the arrival of his picture bride today enjoys the company of a family clan that spans at least two generations. That is indeed an achievement considering the picture bride of yesteryear, just like the contemporary mail-order bride, has always been at a disadvantage. She comes to the marriage from far away, without the nearby support of her family or a familiar culture. The distance that she has traveled is measured not so much in nautical as in emotional miles. She is not quite the happy bride who has been courted and wooed, freely choosing her groom and her destiny.

Today's mail-order brides are products of a very complex set of situations and contradictions. They are confronted by far more complicated conditions than the picture brides of years past. They do not quite fit the simple pattern of a marriage between a lonely man stranded in a foreign land and a woman who accepts him sight unseen.

In the present matches brides-to-be are generally Asian and husbands-to-be are Caucasians, mostly American, Australian, and Canadian. A majority of the women are poor and because of economic desperation become mail-order brides. Racial, as well as economic, factors define the marriage however. The new wife is relegated to a more inferior position than her picture bride counterpart. Plus the inequity of the partnership is further complicated by the mail-order bride's immigrant status. Consequently she is a foreigner not only to the culture, language, and society, but to her husband's race and nationality as well.

WHY MEN CHOOSE MAIL-ORDER BRIDES

"These men want women who will feel totally dependent on them," writes Dr. Gladys L. Symons of the University of Calgary. "They want women who are submissive and less intimidating." Aged between thirty and forty, these men grew up most likely before the rise of the feminist movement, adds Symons. She partially attributes the resurgence of the mail-order bride to a backlash against the 1980s high-pressure style of dating.[1]

Dr. Davor Jedlicka, a sociology professor from the University of Texas, notes in his study of 265 subscribers of mail-order bride catalogues that "very many of them had extremely bitter experiences with divorce or breakups or engagements." His research also shows the

median income of these men to be higher than average—65 percent of them had incomes of over $20,000. According to Jedlicka, the average age was thirty-seven, average height five feet seven inches, and most were college educated. Only five percent never finished high school.[2]

The Japanese American Citizens League, a national civil rights group, confirms this general profile of the typical male client and adds other findings. According to its recent position paper on mail-order brides, the group found that the men tend to be white, much older than the bride they choose, politically conservative, frustrated by the women's movement, and socially alienated. They experience feelings of personal inadequacy and find the traditional Asian value of deference to men reassuring.[3]

In her interview in the Alba Report, Symons points out that the men are also attracted to the idea of buying a wife, since all immigration, transportation, and other costs run to only about two thousand dollars. "We're a consumer society," says Symons. "People become translated into commodities easily."[4] And commodities they are.

GOLD AT THE END OF THE RAINBOW

Contemporary traders in the Asian bride business publish lists sold for twenty dollars for a catalogue order form to twenty thousand dollars for a deluxe videotaped presentation. Perhaps the most successful company is Rainbow Ridge Consultants run by John Broussard and his wife, Kelly Pomeroy. They use a post office box in Honakaa, Hawaii. Explains Broussard:

> Basically, we just sell addresses. . . . We operate as a pen pal club, not a front for the slave trade, although some people get the wrong idea. We're not a Sears catalogue from

which you buy a wife. You have to write and win the heart of the woman you desire.[5]

For providing this service, Broussard and Pomeroy reported a net profit in 1983 of twenty-five thousand dollars, which catapulted to sixty-five thousand in 1984.

Rainbow Ridge Consultants distribute three different publications, of which the top two are *Cherry Blossoms* and *Lotus Blossoms*. These differ from the Sears catalogue only because an issue is only twenty-eight pages long, not several hundred, and photos are black and white, not glossy color. A typical entry reads: "If you like 'em tall, Alice is 5'9", Filipina, social work grad, average looks, wants to hear from men 25-40. $4." For the stated dollar amount, interested men can procure an address and a copy of her biographical data. Broussard and Pomeroy's sister publication *Lotus Blossoms* has twice the number of names, but Broussard admits that *Lotus* is a "second string" brochure, offering pictures of women who do not have the same looks as those in *Cherry Blossoms.*[6]

Six months of subscription to the complete catalogues of Rainbow Ridge will cost the wife-seeker $250. A special service will engage Broussard and Pomeroy in a wife hunt at the rate of $50 per hour and includes handling all details, even writing letters and purchasing gifts when necessary. Should the match succeed, the business pockets another fee of $1,000.

Kurt Kirstein of Blanca, Colorado, runs Philippine-American Life Partners, which offers one thousand pictures of Filipino women looking for American men. Louis Florence of the American Asian Worldwide Service in Orcutt, California, provides men with a similar catalogue for $25; another $630 will permit the bride-seeker to correspond with twenty-four women, of whom any fifteen will be thoroughly investigated by the service. The California business reports an annual gross income of $250,000.

Selling Asian women is a thriving enterprise because the number of American men who seek Asian brides continues to grow. Broussard estimates the total number of daily inquiries is five hundred. In 1984 the Gannett News Service reported that seven thousand Filipino women married Australians, Europeans, and Americans. The *Wall Street Journal* noted that in 1970, only 34 Asians were issued fiancée-petitioned visas; while in 1983, the figure jumped dramatically to 3,428.[7]

Broussard says that he receives one hundred letters a day from Asian and other women. He publishes about seven hundred pictures every other month in his catalogues. Still, Broussard reports that the chances of a man finding a wife through his service is only about one in twenty.

When he receives a letter and the appropriate fees from a prospective groom, Broussard sends off a catalogue. One of his correspondents describes the process: "I selected fourteen ladies to send introductory letters to. To my amazement, I received fourteen replies and am still corresponding with twelve of them."[8] One of the reasons why letters so often succeed is the detailed coaching both parties receive. For instance, Broussard and Pomeroy publish a 130-page pamphlet entitled "How to Write to Oriental Ladies." There is also one for women called "The Way to an American Male's Heart."

The Japanese American Citizens League points out the disadvantage to women in these arrangements because of the inequality of information disseminated. Under the traditional arranged marriage system, family investigation and involvement insured equal access to information and mutual consent. Now only the women must fill out a personality evaluation which asks very intimate details about their life style and history, and is then shared with the men. Prospective grooms do not have to submit similar information about themselves. Some companies, in fact, even discourage their male clients from disclosing certain types of personal facts in their correspondence, including such potentially negative characteristics as being black or having physical disabilities.[9]

THE ECONOMICS OF ROMANCE

Coaching or no coaching, the mail-order brides business succeeds partly because it takes advantage of the economic deprivation faced by women in underdeveloped Asian countries. The Broussard brochure categorically states:

> We hear lots of stories about dishonest, selfish and immature women on both sides of the Pacific. Perhaps women raised in poverty will have lower material expectations and will be grateful to whoever rescues them and offers a better life.

One Caucasian man who met his wife through the mail says: "They don't have a whole lot of things, so what they do have they appreciate very much. They appreciate things more than what the average American woman would." In other words, they are properly grateful for whatever the superior male partner bestows on them.

"Filipinas come because their standard of living is so low," asserts Pomeroy. In 1984 the per capita income in the Philippines was $640. "Most of the women make no secret of why they want to marry an American: money."[10] An Australian reporter who has studied the influx of Filipino mail-order brides to her country agrees: "Most Filipinas are escaping from grinding poverty."[11] Indeed most Asian governments that are saddled with chronic unemployment, spiraling cost of living, malnutrition, and political turmoil are faced with the problem of emigration and a diminishing labor force. In contrast, Japan, the economic and technological leader of Asia, has very few women listed in mail-order catalogues.

The *Chicago Sun-Times* describes Bruce Moore's visit to the family home of his mail-order bride, Rosie, in Cebu, Philippines:

> "All of a sudden, we were driving through the jungle. There was nothing but little huts. I really started worrying about what I got myself into." . . . The house turned out to be an unpainted concrete building with no doors, plumbing or electricity. . . . Rosie had worked in a factory, eight hours a day, making 75 to 80 cents a day.[12]

Because the Filipinas who avail themselves of mail-order bride services may not have much, Broussard's instructional brochures advise men to use caution in describing their financial status. The woman may turn out to be "a con artist after your money or easy entry into the United States."[13] Despite the poverty, though, many of the women are truly sincere in their responses. The Broussard customer who is still writing to twelve of the fourteen women who wrote him notes:

> They all appeared genuine, and not one has asked me for money or anything else. In fact, in two instances, I offered to help with postage, and in both cases, it was declined. One of the ladies said she could not accept postal assistance, as that would lessen the pleasure she felt in the correspondence.[14]

Regardless of the sincerity of the parties involved, one women's rights group in the Philippines has denounced the promotion of relationships through "commerce, industry, negotiation or investment." Their protests, however, do not seem to affect the business.

RACIAL IMAGES AND ROMANCE

Added to economic exploitation, a major cornerstone of the mail-order bride business is the prevalence of racial stereotypes. They have a widespread effect on the treatment of women and influence why so many men are attracted to mail-order romance. "These men believe the stereotypes that describe Oriental women as docile, compliant and submissive," says Jedlicka. His 1983 survey showed that 80 percent of the respondents accept this image as true.

One Canadian male, who asked not to be identified, was quoted as saying: "Asian girls are not as liberated as North American or Canadian girls. They're more family-oriented and less interested in working. They're old-fashioned. I like that."[16]

The California-based American Asian Worldwide Service perpetuates the stereotypes when it says in its brochure: "Asian ladies are faithful and devoted to their husbands. When it comes to sex, they are not demonstrative, however, they are inhibited. They love to do things to make their husbands happy."[17]

This company began after owner Louis Florence began his search for a second wife. He says that friends had touted how their Asian wives "love to make their men happy" and finally convinced him to find a wife from Asia.

Another mail-order pitch describes Asian women as "faithful, devoted, unspoiled and loving."[18] Broussard confirms this popular misconception by saying these women are "raised to be servants for men in many Oriental countries." Referring to the Malaysian and Indonesian women who have recently joined his list of registrants, Broussard insists "Like the Filipinas, they are raised to respect and defer to the male. . . . The young Oriental woman . . . derives her basic satisfaction from serving and pleasing her husband."[19]

Virginity is a highly sought virtue in women. Tom Fletcher, a night worker in Ottawa, Canada, who dislikes North American women because they "want to get out [of the house] and work and that leads to break-ups," is especially appreciative of this sign of purity. "These women's virginity was a gift to their husbands and a sign of faithfulness and trust." One mail-order service unabashedly advertises virginity in a brochure with photos, home addresses, and descriptions of Filipino women, some of whom are as young as seventeen. "Most, if not all are very feminine, loyal, loving . . . and virgins!" its literature reads.[20]

Many of the Asian countries affected by the revived mail-order bride business have a history of U.S. military involvement. Troops have either fought battles or been stationed in Korea, the Philippines, and countries in Southeast Asia. During their stays, the soldiers have often developed strong perceptions of Asian women as prostitutes, bargirls, and geishas. Then they erroneously conclude that Asian American women must fit those images, too. Consequently the stereotype of women servicing and serving men is perpetuated.

The Japanese American Citizens League objects to the mail-order bride trade for that very reason. "The marketing techniques used by the catalogue bride companies reinforce negative sexual and racial stereotypes of Asian women in the U.S. The negative attitude toward Asian women affects all Asians in the country." Further, the treatment of women as "commodities" adds to the "non-human and negative perception of all Asians."[21]

ROMANCE ON THE ROCKS

A marriage made via the mail-order bride system is naturally beset by a whole range of problems. In her testimony before the U.S. Commission on Civil Rights, professor Bok-Lim Kim, then with the University of Illinois, noted that negative reactions and attitudes toward foreign Asian wives "exacerbates marital problems," which result in incidences of spouse abuse, desertion, separation, and divorce.[22] In addition, writes an Australian journalist, most of the men they marry are social misfits. "Many of them drink too much; some beat their wives and treat them little better than slaves."[23]

The Japanese American Citizens League asserts:

> Individually, there may be many cases of couples meeting and marrying through these arrangements with positive results. We believe, however, that for the women, there are many more instances in which the impetus for leaving their home countries and families, and the resulting marriage relationships, have roots and end results which are less than positive.[24]

Many of the Caucasian men who marry what they believe are stereotypical women may be in for some surprises. Psychiatry professor Joe Yamamoto of the University of California at Los Angeles says: "I've found many Asian women acculturate rather quickly. These American men may get a surprise in a few years if their wives pick up liberated ways."[25]

One legally blind and hard-of-hearing American, married to a Korean woman, was eventually bothered by the same problems that plague other couples: in-laws and lack of money. "She gets frustrated because I don't hear her," complains the man about his soft-spoken Asian wife. In response, she says, "The main problem is [his] parents. I can't adapt to American culture. I was going to devote my life for him, but I can't."[26]

Another area which specifically affects foreign-born brides is their immigrant status. According to the Japanese American Citizens League, "these foreign women are at a disadvantage." This civil rights group targets the women's unfamiliarity with the U.S. immigration laws as one of the most disturbing aspects of the business. "As a result [of the ignorance], they may miss an opportunity to become a naturalized citizen, forfeit rights as a legal spouse, or live under an unwarranted fear of deportation which may be fostered by their spouse as a means of control."[27]

CONCLUSION

Despite the constant stream of criticism, the mail-order bride system will prevail as long as there are consumers and profit, and as long as underdeveloped countries continue failing to meet the economic, political, and social needs of their people. Indications show the business is not about to collapse now.

Erroneous ideas continue to thrive. An Asian woman dreams she will meet and marry someone rich and powerful, someone to rescue her and free her from poverty-stricken bondage. She hopes to live the rest of her life in a land of plenty. An American man dreams he will meet and marry someone passive, obedient, nonthreatening, and virginal, someone to devote her entire life to him, serving him and making no demands. Only a strong women's movement, one tied to the exploited underdeveloped country's struggle for liberation and independence, can challenge these ideas and channel the aspirations and ambitions of both men and women in a more positive and realistic direction.

NOTES

1. Interview with Calgary sociologist Gladys L. Symons in "Mail-Order Marriage Boom: Submissive Foreign Women Are Just Dying to Meet Albertans," *Alberta Report,* 18 December 1981.
2. "Mates by Mail: This Couple Catalogs Affairs of the Heart," *Chicago Sun Times,* 12 August 1984. Statistics based on a 1983 survey ("American Men in Search of Oriental Brides") of 265 American men "actively seeking a partner from the 'Orient.'"

3. Japanese American Citizens League (JACL), "Mail-Order Asian Women Catalogues" (Report issued by the Japanese American Citizens League, Spring 1985), 4.

4. *Alberta Report,* 18 December 1981.

5. John Broussard and Kelly Pomeroy, telephone interview with author, 1985.

6. Hugh Paterson, "Brides Jump from Pages of Pamphlet," *The Citizen,* Ottawa, Canada, 3 March 1982.

7. Karen Peterson, "Mail-Order Brides from the Unliberated East," Gannett News Service; Raymond A. Joseph, "American Men Find Asian Brides Fill the Unliberated Bill: Mail-Order Firms Help Them Look for the Ideal Women They Didn't Find at Home," *Wall Street Journal,* 25 January 1984.

8 . Letter to Broussard and Pomeroy from *Cherry Blossoms* customer who asked to remain anonymous, 27 December 1984.

9. See JACL, "Mail-Order" (Questions and Answers section), 1–2.

10. Rita Calvano, "Mail-Order Marriages Blossom: Western Men Turn to Catalog Listing Oriental Women," *The Tribune,* San Diego, 6 September 1984; and Jack Lessenberry, "Brides to Go: Mail-Order Service Aids Hunt for Good Wives," *The Detroit News,* 8 July 1984.

11. Lloyd Shearer, "Mail-Order Brides," *Parade,* 10 October 1982.

12. Pat Tremmel, "Mates by Mail: Love Letters Spell Trouble," *Chicago Sun Times,* 12 August 1984.

13. Calvano, *The Tribune,* 6 September 1984.

14. Letter to Broussard and Pomeroy from *Cherry Blossoms* customer, 27 December 1984.

15. Peterson, Gannett News Service.

16. Paterson, *The Citizen,* 3 March 1982.

17. American Asian Worldwide Service brochure quoted in JACL, "Mail-Order," 2.

18. Peterson, Gannett News Service.

19. Paterson, *The Citizen,* 3 March 1982; and Shearer, *Parade,* 10 October 1982.

20. Paterson, ibid.; and JACL, "Mail-Order," 2. Many women listed in the catalogues include virginity as one of their positive traits, writing, "I am still a virgin." See *Cherry Blossoms,* September/October 1981.

21. JACL, "Mail-Order," (Questions and Answers), 3.

22 . Quoted in JACL, "Mail-Order," 5.

23. Shearer, *Parade,* 10 October 1982.

24. JACL, "Mail-Order," 4.

25. Peterson, Gannett News Service.

26. Calvano, *The Tribune,* 6 September 1984.

27. JACL, "Mail-Order," 3.

Study/Discussion Questions

1. What motivates Asian women to become mail-order brides?
2. What stereotypes of Asian women make mail-order brides appealing to American men?
3. What kind of marriage do these men think they will have if they marry a mail-order bride?
4. How do they think it will be an improvement on marriage to a white American woman, according to Villapando?

Working at Single Bliss

Mary Helen Washington

This essay was published in Ms. Magazine *in 1982, just as the American media had begun to dwell on a purported man shortage that would leave single women alone with their biological clocks ticking loudly. Here Mary Helen Washington writes about the societal pressures on women to get married and have children. Living as a happy, fulfilled adult single woman, Washington defies the negative stereotypes of unmarried women. She surveys those stereotypes here, in all their vacuousness and malintent. The life decisions of women who refuse to be "defined by the presence or absence of a man" need to be honored at the same level as those of women who choose to marry men, Washington contends.*

I

Last year I was asked to be on the "Tom Cottle Show," a syndicated television program that originates here in Boston. The psychiatrist-host wanted to interview six single women about their singleness. I hesitated only a moment before refusing. Six single women discussing the significance of their lives? No, I instinctively knew that the interview would end up being an interrogation of six unmarrieds (a pejorative, like coloreds)—women trying to rationalize lives of loss. Losers at the marriage game. *Les femmes manqués.*

I watched the program they put together without me, and sure enough, Cottle asked a few perfunctory questions about singleness and freedom, and then moved on rapidly to the real killer questions. I found it painful to watch these very fine women trapped in the net he'd laid. "Don't you ever come home from these glamorous lives of freedom [read selfishness] and sit down to dinner alone and just cry?" "What about sex?" "What about children?" The women struggled to answer these insulting questions with dignity and humor, but clearly the game was rigged against them. Imagine the interviewer lining up six couples and asking them the same kinds of questions: "Well, what about your sex lives?" "Why don't you have any children?" (or "Why do you have so many?") "Don't you ever come home at night, sit down to dinner, and wonder why you ever married the person on the other side of the table?" Of course, this interview would never take place—the normal restraint and politeness that are reserved for people whose positions are socially acceptable assure married folks some measure of protection and, at least, common decency.

"You're so lucky, footloose and fancy-free, with no responsibilities," a friend with two children once said to me. Ostensibly that's a compliment, or at least, it's supposed to be. But underneath it is really a critique of single people, implying that their lives do not have the moral stature of a life with "responsibilities." It's a comment that used to leave me feeling a little like a kid, a failed adult; for what's an adult with no responsibilities? A kid. I have had to learn to recognize and reject the veiled contempt in this statement because, of course, single people do have responsibilities.

At age 40, I have been a single adult for 20 years. No, I am neither widowed nor divorced. I am single in the pristine sense of that word—which unleashes that basic fear in all of us, "What will I do if I'm left by myself?" As I have more or less successfully dealt with that fear over the years, I am somewhat indignant at being cast as an irresponsible gadfly, unencumbered by the problems of Big People. I have earned a living and "kept myself," and I have done that without being either male or white in a world dominated by men and corroded by racism. I've sat up nights with students' papers and even later with their problems. Without any of the social props married people have, I have given many memorable parties. Like my aunts before me, I've celebrated the births, birthdays, first communions, graduations, football games, and track meets of my 10 nephews. And not a hair on my mother's head changes color without my noticing it.

As Zora Hurston's Janie says, "Two things everybody's got tuh do fuh theyselves. They got tuh go tuh God, and they got tuh find out about livin' fuh theyselves." If anything, a single person may be more aware of the responsibility to discover and create meaning in her life, to find community, to honor her creativity, to live out her values, than the person whose life

is circumferenced by an immediate and intimate family life.

II

To some extent my adolescent imagination was bewitched by the myth that marriage is the vertical choice in a woman's life—one that raises her status, completes her life, fulfills her dreams, and makes her a valid person in society. In the 1950s, all the movies, all the songs directed us to this one choice: to find our worldly prince and go two by two into the ark. Nothing else was supposed to matter quite as much and it was a surprise to discover that something else matters just as much, sometimes more.

But in spite of the romance-marriage-motherhood bombardment, I grew up in a kind of war-free zone where I heard the bombs and artillery all around me but was spared from a direct attack. I was raised in two very separate but mutually supportive communities—one black, one Catholic, both of which taught me that a woman could be her own person in the world.

In the all-women's Catholic high school and college in Cleveland, Ohio where I put in eight formative years, we were required to think of ourselves as women with destinies, women whose achievements mattered—whether we chose marriage or religious life or, as it was called then, a life of "single blessedness." In fact, marriage and the single life seemed to my convent-honed ninth-grade mind to have a clearly equal status: they were both inferior to the intrinsically superior religious life.

The program of spiritual, intellectual, social, and physical development the nuns demanded of us allowed an involvement with myself I craved even in the ninth grade. Some dating was encouraged at Notre Dame Academy (ninth through twelfth grades)—not as a consuming emotional involvement but as part of a "normal social development." Boys had their place on the periphery of one's life. (A girl who came to school with her boyfriend's taped class ring on her finger was subject to expulsion.) You were expected to be the central, dominant figure in the fabric of your own life.

The nuns themselves were vivid illustrations of that principle. For me they were the most powerful images of women imaginable—not ladies-in-waiting, not submissive homebodies, not domestic drudges, not deviants. They ran these women-dominated universes with aplomb and authority. Even if "Father" appeared on Monday morning for our weekly religious lesson, his appearance was tolerated as a kind of necessary token of the male hierarchy, and, when he left, the waters ran back together, leaving no noticeable trace of his presence.

Nuns were the busiest people I knew then. No matter how graceful and dignified the pace, they always seemed to be hurrying up and down the corridors of Notre Dame planning something important and exciting. Sister Wilbur directed dramatics and went to New York occasionally to see the latest Off-Broadway productions. Sister Kathryn Ann wrote poetry and went to teach in Africa. Another sister coached debate and took our winning teams to state championships in Columbus. Though technically nuns are not single, they do not have that affiliation with a male figure to establish their status. (After Mary Daly it should not be necessary to point out that God is not a man.) They also have to ward off the same stigma of being different from the norm as single people do. So it's only a little ironic that I got some of my sense of how a woman could be complete and autonomous and comfortable in the world—sans marriage—from the Sisters of Notre Dame.

The message I got from the black community about single life was equally forceful. So many black girls heard these words, they might have been programmed tapes: "Girl, get your-self an education, you can't count on a man to take care of you." "An education is something no one can take from you." "Any fool can get married, but not everyone can go to school."

I didn't know it then, but this was my feminist primer. Aim high, they said, because that is the only way a black girl can claim a place in this world. Marriage was a chancy thing, not dependable like diplomas: my mother and aunts and uncles said that even if you married a Somebody—a doctor or a lawyer—there was no assurance that he'd have a good heart or treat you right. They thought that the worst thing a woman could do was to get into financial dependency with a man—and it was not that they hated or distrusted men so much as they distrusted any situation that made an already vulnerable woman more powerless.

There was such reverence in my mother's voice for women of achievement that I never connected their social status with anything as mundane as marriage. The first black woman with a Ph.D., first black woman school principal, the first woman doctor—I knew their names by heart and wanted to be one of them and do important things.

My third-grade teacher, the first black teacher at Parkwood Elementary in Cleveland, Ohio, was a single woman in her thirties. At age nine, I saw her as a tall, majestic creature who wore earrings, drove her own car, and made school pure joy. To my family and the neighborhood, Miss Hilliard was like a totem of our tribe's good fortune: an independent, self-sufficient educated woman bringing her treasures back to their children. She was a part of that tradition of 19th-century black women whose desire for "race uplift" sent them to teach in the South and to schools like Dunbar High in Washington, D.C., and the School for Colored Youth in Philadelphia. Though many of these women were married, the majority of them were widowed for a great many years and those were often the years of achievement for them.

One of these 19th-century stellar examples, Anna Julia Cooper, dismissed the question of marriage as a false issue. The question should not be "How shall I so cramp, stunt, simplify, and nullify myself as to make me eligible for the horror of being swallowed up into some little man," but how shall a generation of women demand of themselves and of men "the noblest, the grandest and the best" in their capacities.

III

I learned early about being single from my five aunts. By the time I was old enough to notice, four were widowed and one divorced, so from my 12-year-old perspective, they were single women for a good part of their lives. They ran their own households, cooked, entertained, searched for spirituality, helped my mother to raise eight children, traveled some, went to work, cared for the sick, planned picnics. In short, they made up their lives by themselves, inventing the forms that satisfied them. And in the course of their "scheming" they passed on to me something about the rituals and liturgy of single life.

The eldest of these aunts, Aunt Bessie, lived as a single woman for 26 years. Her husband of 40 years died when she was 60 and she began to live alone for the first time since she was 18. She bought a huge old house, painted, decorated, and furnished every room with Oriental rugs and secondhand furniture purchased at estate sales. (Black people discovered this bonanza in the 1940s long before it became a middle-class fad.) She put in a new lawn, grew African violets, and started a whole new life for herself on Ashbury Avenue.

Aunt Bessie was secretly proud of how well she was doing on her own, and she used to tell me slyly how many of these changes she could not have made as a married woman: "Uncle wouldn't have bought this house, baby; he wouldn't have wanted this much space. He wouldn't have changed neighborhoods." She was finally doing exactly what pleased her, and the shape of her life as she had designed it in her singularity was much more varied, dynamic, and daring. What I learned from her is symbolized by that multilevel house on Ashbury Avenue. She had three bedrooms—she needed them for guests; on the third floor she made hats, which she sold for a living; the huge old basement was for her tools and lawn work. All this room was essential to the amount of living she planned to do.

Since she willed all of her furniture to me, my own flat resembles that house in many ways, and her spirit came with the furnishings: I have the sense of inhabiting every corner of my life just as she lived in all 10 rooms of her house. Even my overstocked refrigerator is a reflection of something I learned from her about taking care of your life. Another aunt, Hazel, died only a few years after she was widowed, and I remember Aunt Bessie's explanation of her untimely death as a warning about the perils of not taking your life seriously. "Hazel stopped cooking for herself after her husband died, just ate snacks and junk food instead of making a proper dinner for herself. And she got that cancer and died." The message was clear to me—even at age 12—that single life could be difficult at times and that living it well required some effort, but you were not supposed to let it kill you.

IV

Girded up with all of this psychological armament from my past, I still entered adult life without the powerful and sustaining myths and rituals that could provide respect and support for single life. Terms like "old maid" and "spinster," not yet redefined by a feminist consciousness, could still be used to belittle and oppress single women. By the time I was 35, I had participated in scores of marriage ceremonies, and even had begun sending anniversary cards to my married friends. But never once did I think of celebrating the anniversary of a friendship—even one that was by then 25 years old. (Aren't you entitled to gifts of silver at that milestone?)

Once, about 10 years ago, five of us single women from Cleveland took a trip to Mexico together. (Actually only four of the group were single; the fifth, Ernestine, was married and three months pregnant.) I remember that trip as seven days and eight nights of adventure, laughter, discovery, and closeness.

We were such typical tourists—taking snapshots of ancient ruins, posing in front of cathedrals, paying exorbitant sums to see the cliff divers (whose entire act took about 20 seconds), floating down debris-filled waterways to see some totally unnoteworthy sights, learning the hard way that in the hot Acapulco sun even us "killer browns" could get a sunburn. We stayed up at night talking about our lives, our dreams, our careers, our men, and laughing so hard in these late-night sessions that we hardly had the energy for the next morning's tour.

It was the laughter and the good talk (remember Toni Cade Bambara's short story "The Johnson Girls") that made the trip seem so complete. It was so perfect that even in the midst of the experience I knew it was to be a precious memory. Years later I asked my friend, Ponchita, why she thought the five of us never planned another trip like that, why we let such good times drift out of our lives without an attempt to recapture them. "Because," she said, "it wasn't enough. It was fun, stimulating, warm, exciting, but it wasn't 'The Thing That Made Life Complete,' and it wasn't leading us in that direction; I guess it was a little like 'recess.'" We wanted nests, not excitement. We wanted domestic bliss, not lives lived at random, no matter how thrilling, how wonderful. So there was the potential— those "dependable and immediate supports" existed. But

without the dependable myths to accompany them, we couldn't seriously invest ourselves in those experiences.

When my friend Meg suggested we celebrate Mother's Day this year with a brunch for all our single, childless women friends, and bring pictures of the nieces and nephews we dote on, I recognized immediately the psychic value in honoring our own form of caretaking. We were establishing rituals by which we could ceremonially acknowledge our particular social identities.

My oldest friend Ponchita and I did exchange gifts last year on the twenty-fifth anniversary of our friendship, and never again will the form "anniversary" mean only a rite (right) of the married. My journey through the single life was beginning to have its own milestones and to be guided by its own cartography.

v

Our Mexico trip was in 1971. In the next 10 years, I earned a Ph.D., became director of black studies at the University of Detroit, edited two anthologies, threw out my makeshift bricks-and-board furniture, began to think about buying a house and adopting a child, and in the process, decided that my life was no longer "on hold." These deliberate choices made me begin to regard my single status as an honorable estate. But you know, when I look back at that checklist of accomplishments and serious life plans, I feel resentful that I had to work so hard for the honor that naturally accompanies the married state. Overcompensation, however, sometimes has its rewards: I had established a reputation in my profession that brought the prospect of a fellowship year at Radcliffe and a new job in Boston.

When I was leaving Detroit, I was acutely aware of my single status. What kind of life was it, I wondered, if you could start all over again in a new city with nothing to show for your past except your furniture and your diplomas? I didn't even have a cat. Where were the signs and symbols of a coherent, meaningful life that others could recognize? What was I doing living at random like this? I had made this "pure" decision and was honoring my inclination to live in another city, to take a job that offered excitement and challenge. As I packed boxes alone, signed contracts with moving companies, and said good-bye at numerous dinners and going-away parties to all the friends I had made over 10 years, I felt not so very different from a friend who was moving after separating from his wife: "like a rhinoceros being cut loose from the herd."

I think it was the wide-open, netless freedom of it all that scared me, because I was truly not alone. I moved into a tripledecker in Cambridge where I live in a kind of semi-cooperative with two other families. Here, I feel secure, but independent and private. The journalist on the second floor and I read each other's work, and I exchange ideas about teaching methods with the three other professors in the house. We all share meals occasionally; we've met one another's extended families; and we celebrate one another's assorted triumphs. I have put together another network of friends whose lives I feel intimately involved in, and who, like me, are interested in making single life work—not disappear.

But I do not yet have the solid sense of belonging to a community that I had in Cleveland and Detroit, and sometimes I am unsettled by the variousness and unpredictableness of my single life. This simply means that I still have some choices to make—about deepening friendships, about having children (possibly adopting them), about establishing closer ties with the black community in Boston. If and when I do adopt a child, she or he will have a selection of godparents and aunts and uncles as large and varied as I had. That is one of the surest signs of the richness of my single life.

VI

Last year Elizabeth Stone wrote an article in the *Village Voice* called "A Married Woman" in which she discussed how much her life had changed since she married at the age of 33. Somewhat boastfully, she remarked at the end that she had hardly made any reference in the whole article to her husband. But if a single woman describes her life without reference to romance—no matter how rich and satisfying her life may be; no matter what she says about wonderful friends, exciting work, cultural and intellectual accomplishments—in fact, the *more* she says about these things—the more skeptical people's reactions will be. That one fact—her romantic involvement—if it is not acceptable can cancel out all the rest. This is how society keeps the single woman feeling perilous about her sense of personal success.

Still, everybody wants and needs some kind of special alliance(s) in her life. Some people have alliances called marriage. (I like that word *alliance:* it keeps marriage in its proper—horizontal—place.) I'd like an alliance with a man who could be a comrade and kindred spirit, and I've had such alliances in the past. Even with the hassles, they were enriching and enjoyable experiences for me, but I have never wanted to forsake my singularity for this kind of emotional involvement. Whatever psychic forces drive me have always steered me toward autonomy and independence, out toward the ocean's expanse and away from the shore.

I don't want to sound so smooth and glib and clear-eyed about it all, because it has taken me more than a decade to get this sense of balance and control. A lot of rosaries and perpetual candles and expensive long-distance calls have gotten me through the hard times when 1 would have chosen the holy cloister over another day of "single blessedness." The truth is that those hard times were not caused by being single. They were part of every woman's struggle to find commitment and contentment for herself. Singleness does not define me, is not an essential characteristic of me. I simply wish to have it acknowledged as a legitimate way to be in the world. After all, we started using Ms. instead of Mrs. or Miss because *none* of us wanted to be defined by the presence or absence of a man.

VII

Apart from the forest
a single tree will sometimes grow awry
in brave and extraordinary search
for its own shape.
—*Paulette Childress White,* "A Tree
Alone"

When I first started running in 1972, I ran regularly with a man. As long as I had this male companion, the other men passing by either ignored me or gave me slight nods to show their approval of my supervised state. Eventually I got up the nerve to run alone around Detroit's Palmer Park, and then the men came out of the trees to make comments—usually to tell me what I was doing wrong ("Lift your legs higher" or "Stop waving your arms"), or to flirt ("Can I run with you, baby?" was by far the most common remark, though others were nastier).

Once a carload of black teenagers who were parked in the lot at the end of my run started making comments about my physical anatomy, which I started to dismiss as just a dumb teenage ritual. But on this particular day, something made me stop my run, walk over to the car, and say, "You know, when you see a sister out trying to get some exercise, as hard as that is for us, you ought to be trying to support her, because she needs all the help she can get." I didn't know how they would respond, so I was surprise when they apologized, and somewhat shamefaced, one of them said: "Go on, sister; we're with you."

Now, that incident occurred because I was alone, and the image has become part of my self-definition: I am woman in the world—single and powerful and astonished at my ability to create my own security, "in brave and extraordinary search for my own shape."

Study/Discussion Questions

1. How is Washington's life different from that of a married woman in her 30s or 40s?
2. What are the advantages for her of having remained single?
3. What are the disadvantages?
4. Think about how Washington experiences her life and compare her feelings about being single to the media stereotypes of single women. How are they different?

they're always curious

Irena Klepfisz

they're always curious about what you eat as if you were
some strange breed still unclassified by darwin & whether
you cook every night & wouldn't it be easier for you to
buy frozen dinners but i am quick to point out that my intravenous tubing has been taken out and they back up saying i
could never just cook for one person but i tell them it's
the same exactly the same as for two except half

but more they're curious about what you do when the urge
is on & if you use a coke bottle or some psychedelic dildo
or electric vibrator or just the good old finger or whole
hand & do you mannipppppulllaaatttte yourself into a clit
orgasm or just kind of keep digging away at yourself & if
you mind it & when you have affairs doesn't it hurt when it's
over & it certainly must be lonely to go back to the old finger

& they always cluck over the amount of space you require
& certainly the extra bedroom seems unnecessary & i try to
explain that i like to move around & that i get antsy when
i have the urge so that it's nice to have an extra place
to go when you're lonely & after all it seems small compensation for using the good old finger & they're surprised because they never thought of it that way & it does seem reasonable come to think of it

& they kind of probe about your future & if you have a will or
why you bother to accumulate all that stuff or what you plan
to do with your old age & aren't you scared about being put
away somewhere or found on your bathroom floor dead after
your downstairs neighbor has smelled you out but then of course
you don't have the worry of who goes first though of course
you know couples live longer for they have something to live
for & i try to explain i live for myself even when in love but
it's a hard concept to explain when you feel lonely

WOMEN WORKING

Work

Germaine Greer

Thirty years after publishing The Female Eunuch, *a controversial treatise on women's status and feminism, Australian writer Germaine Greer has written a sequel:* The Whole Woman. *In this chapter of the new book, Greer surveys the landscape of women's work. As her discussion makes clear, women perform myriad duties that are not considered work in a conventional sense but that need to be if women are ever to achieve equality with men. From housework to child care to arguments about comparable worth, Greer explores the economic and social significance of women's labors.*

As women do all the work in human reproduction, so they have always done most of the work required for human survival. While the male hunter-gatherer strolled along burdened with no more than his spear and throwing stick, his female mate trudged along after him carrying their infant, their shelter, their food supplies, and her digging stick. She collected firewood and carried water. She prepared their food. The universal "division of labour" between the sexes was in fact the apportioning of daily drudgery to the female, so that the male could indulge his appetite for sport, play, dreaming, ritual, religion, and artistic expression. When beasts were domesticated, men drove them. If the beast died, the woman pulled the plough and the man directed her. Even today, in many agricultural households, the valuable beasts are treated with more consideration than the replaceable women. The heaviness of work has never been a reason for women's not doing it; rather, women were not admitted to jobs that required brain-power or management skills, even when the only thing being managed was a donkey. In some parts of the world you may still see the male peasant riding his donkey as his wife walks alongside. In the rich world the equivalent is the husband who drives a car with a wife who walks or catches the bus. All over the world women do the heavy, mindless, repetitive labour. Women gather scarce firewood over many miles and carry it home on their backs or on their heads. Water is heavy but men will not carry it. As soon as a source of energy is found that makes work lighter, men take it over. When cultivation is done with mattocks and hoes women do it; when a tractor comes along, men drive it. When a U.N. project made bicycles available to women traders in Asia, men took them for their own use and their wives walked to the market as they had always done, carrying their heavy produce on their heads.

Women are the labouring sex. From the time girls are very small they learn that work is what time is for. Comparison of women's work-load with men's is difficult because a good deal of women's effort is not even recognized as work. Time spent with the children is not classified as work, although the mother does not use it to read the paper while the kid crawls between her legs, but to teach her child to speak, to advance its social skills, to answer its questions, to deal with its preoccupations, to prepare it for school activities. A woman who bears a child does so knowing that any leisure time she might have had in the past is effectively cancelled for the next sixteen years; yet, if she is not earning pay of any kind, she will appear in statistics as idle, economically inactive. Conventional economic analyses, being based upon the "gross national product" or "gross domestic product," can take account only of activities that involve cash flow. In 1995 the U.N. Development Program published a Human Development Report which for the first time attempted to provide a picture of women's unpaid contribution, estimating its value

> ALL SCHOLARS AGREE THAT EVEN IN STUDIES SUGGESTING THAT HUSBANDS OF EMPLOYED WIVES DO STATISTICALLY MORE [HOUSE-WORK], THE INCREASE IS SMALL IN ABSOLUTE MAGNITUDE, AND EMPLOYED WIVES CONTINUE TO DO THE BULK OF THE FAMILY WORK.
> *JOSEPH H. PLECK, SOCIOLOGIST*[1]

worldwide as $11 trillion; men's unpaid work was valued at $5 trillion, less than half. Much of women's work remains as invisible to conventional data collection methods as the work of animals; recent attempts to compile comparisons of contrasting kinds of activity in widely varying economic circumstances, in response to feminist pressure to acknowledge women's contribution, have not been entirely successful. In *The World's Women 1995* U.N. analysts attempted to provide a picture of women's time-use rather than labour-force participation, but the raw data emanating from the different countries were difficult to interpret. A French study came to the odd conclusion that employed men do two hours of housework a day throughout the life cycle, while women's unpaid work takes up 3.4 hours a day, rising to 4.5 hours a day at ages fifty-five to sixty-four. Equally baffling were statistics about women's work week, which appears as longer than men's in all developed countries except the U.S. When we read that a Spanish woman's working week is twenty-three hours longer than a man's while a British woman's is only six hours longer, we have to conclude that different notions of "working week" are being applied. Unpaid work the world over is starkly gendered; in the developed world women do three-quarters of all meal preparation and clean-up; in some countries the proportion rises to 90 percent. According to a recent Canadian study, 52 percent of Canadian women working full-time got no help with housework, and 28 percent did most of it; only 10 percent had partners who took equal responsibility, which seems about par.

All studies show that leisure is a masculine privilege. What is more, men are permitted to alienate money coming into the household to spend on their leisure pursuits; when recent floods in Cambridgeshire swept away the angling gear of a father, his friend, and their sons camped on the bank of a river, the replacement cost was estimated at £7,000. All the attempts of record companies to get women to invest in their products fail because women, even if they consider themselves entitled to spend so much money on themselves, do not have the time to listen to CDs. The contrast between male and female patterns of spending is not limited to the developed world. In November 1996 Leena Kirjavainen, director of the women and population division of the FAO, pointed out that "If [aid] money is given to women, it is generally used for better nutrition, better clothing, and for the welfare of the household. If it's given to men, it tends to be spent on electronic goods, a new bicycle maybe, or—if we're to be really frank—on prostitution, alcohol and other forms of consumption that don't help the family."[2]

Men regard weekends as time off, when they play sport in a more or less serious way, or watch it, or not, as they please. Working women use weekends to catch up with the tasks left over from an exhausting week. They are grateful if their partner takes the kids out with him, so they can get on with their work, but if he does it is not for long.

Women have been conditioned to believe that men's work is harder and more stressful than theirs, which is a con. The truth seems to be that men resent having to work and harbour a positive ambition to do nothing, which women do not share. A love of idleness is another characteristic that male *Homo sapiens* has inherited from his anthropoid ancestors; an animal behaviour researcher observed "that she would find it exceedingly difficult to observe a lone male gorilla for 8 hours because he does so little."[3] Females, be they gorillas or worker bees, are naturally busy, which suggests another cause of men's irritability with women who penetrate their territories. They do not want the myth of male energy and purposiveness to be exploded. They might find themselves having to do some serious work, with concomitant loss of status among the other alpha males. In male hierarchies idleness is associated with status. Angling is the most popular sport in Britain because it is an excuse to do absolutely nothing for days on end.

When I was a little girl, little girls were kept in to do the housework while little boys were sent out to play. Half a century later boys aren't sent out to play because the outdoors is thought unsafe for children of either sex. Even so boys are not sharing the work around the house; they are playing in their rooms with their boys' toys (which is why they are so much further into computers than girls are). Conscientious mothers might try to teach their boys not to expect women to do their chores for them, but they are notably unsuccessful. When women were admitted to King's College, Cambridge, a cynical don was heard to remark, "Now the men will get their laundry done free." The men say that they don't mind if their digs are filthy and smell of unwashed clothes; the women who share those digs end up doing the housework out of self-defence. "I'm not bothered about the state of the kitchen. You want the kitchen clean—you clean it," goes the masculine script. Little girls are still expected to be tidy and keep themselves clean and big girls continue the tradition. A good deal of the unpaid work younger women do is maintenance of a hairless, odourless, band-box self. The boys are under no such obligation. In March 1998 little girls' mag *Mizz* ran a story on "Super Slobs." Slob No. 1 boasted, "I never clean up my mess," Slob No. 2, "Some days I don't get up!" Slob

> EXCLUDING STUDENTS, THE NUMBER OF UNEMPLOYED MEN WHO ARE NOT SEEKING WORK ROSE FROM 800,000 IN 1979 TO 2.3 MILLION IN 1997.
>
> *EMPLOYMENT POLICY INSTITUTE*

No. 2's "fave slobby outfit" was "a tracksuit I wear when I go fishing—it's covered in holes and has dried fish slime all over it. I also own a pair of very smelly trainers." Slob No. 3 liked to "hog the couch and lay [sic] there for hours with the remote control, channel surfing."

International surveys tell us the proportion of unpaid work done by men in the developed world is rising but it remains low, even though in these calculations no attempt is made to differentiate between gardening and do-it-yourself, both hobbies, and the unavoidable repetitive daily tasks that fall to women. Recent British surveys that tell us that 26 percent of women *never* wash their own clothes contrasted with 57 percent of men, and 7 percent of women *never* wash dishes as against 21 percent of men, give a very distorted impression of the difference in men's and women's contributions. Women may spend up to sixty-two hours a week on housework, men a third of that time. Though equal pay legislation has been in operation in all the developed countries for thirty years, women continue to earn less than men because the kinds of work that women do are considered to be of less value. Women are not only paid less, they are also disadvantaged in pensions, sickness benefits, conditions, in-service training, and opportunities for promotion. The 1995 New Earning Survey showed that women were 70 percent of the lowest earners and only 10 percent of the highest. The age-old spectacle of women supplying the hard graft and men directing their efforts can be seen as clearly in universities, schools, and hospitals as it can in the case of Um Sara photographed for the *National Geographic* in 1993 as she pulled the heavy oars of her husband's boat, with her baby asleep under the thwart, for eight hours a day, as he did the lighter work of casting his net into the Nile and pulling it up again.

In December 1997 consultants Towers Perrin reported back to the Universities and Colleges Employers Association, a consortium of 110 organizations that feared it might be vulnerable on the grounds of consistently paying women less than men, that, across all types of work in higher education—academic, administrative, manual, and technical—62 percent of the jobs done by women were consistently undervalued as against 37 percent of the jobs done by men. The skills and knowledge deployed by women, whether as nursery coordinators, secretaries, or cleaning supervisors, were worth less than the skills and knowledge of security guards, building managers, and mechanics. Other studies have shown that over a lifetime a woman's earnings will be significantly lower than those of men in the same professions; a female nurse, for example, will earn £50,000 less in her working life than a male nurse. The difference is not only the consequence of different rates of pay, but also of restrictions on access to overtime and promotion. Women have no spare time to devote to the employer. Women don't allow themselves any spare time. Lots of women don't give themselves time for sufficient sleep. Women rushing to catch up with the day's complement of tasks are usually anxious and guilty, afraid that they are spreading themselves too thin, maybe skimping this or fudging that, not giving a child or a husband or a project enough attention.

Women carry their worry about the quality of their contribution into negotiations with the employer, where it places them at a definite disadvantage. Employment analysts say that a job advertised with a salary of £40,000 a year will get no female applicants but women will gladly apply for the same job if it is advertised at £20,000. Successful entrepreneur Jane Wellesley was quoted as saying, "I think women are less concerned with perks and getting up the ladder than with job satisfaction. Men are, by and large, better at promoting themselves." Who would want a mere salary when she could have job satisfaction? Many women behave as if they feel a real sense of gratitude to their employer and act delighted as more and more work is heaped upon them, never pausing to ask if their male colleagues are doing anywhere near as much. If women themselves put a lower value on their own contribution than on that of men, personnel managers will seize the cue to employ them as low in the pay scale as they can.

Job evaluation is a subtle business, because work has no intrinsic value. Work is worth what the worker can force the employer to pay for it, no more and no less. Women's occupations have never developed effective collective strategies to protect pay and conditions, let alone to force up wages, which is why women are more welcome than men in the deconstructed workforce of the nineties. Job evaluation plus legal action might have the effect of equalizing the perceived value of men's and women's jobs; the employer meanwhile uses an array of strategies to keep workers' pay and power at the lowest level possible. The traditional trade unions insisted on recognition for self-defining elites within the workforce and overvalued the work of their male members by contrast with the ancillary female workers in their own administrations. In the 1980s labour was "emasculated"; in the 1990s the sex-change procedure continued as the workforce became more than 50 percent female. The trade unions had only themselves to blame. Their defeat was only possible because they never recognized the necessity of organizing all workers, women included, to fight for decent pay and conditions or of defending the right of all workers to a living wage and fair conditions of employment. Women who downed tools in protest against inhuman treatment picketed for years without any sign of solidarity from the labour hierarchy. In the most recent case fifty-three women cleaners of Hillingdon Hospital who refused to sign new contracts for reduced rates of pay and were sacked were originally supported by their union

"YOUR WORK IS IMPORTANT BUT NOT VALUABLE"

FOR THIS AND OTHER EXAMPLES OF EMPLOYER BLOODINESS SEE HTTP://WWW.DISGRUNTLED.COM/ AND HTTP://WWW.MYBOSS.COM/

which then negotiated a settlement without securing the women's agreement. As the settlement did not include reinstatement, most of the women rejected it. The union withdrew its support; the women lost their case for unfair dismissal as a consequence. At the time of writing their picket outside Hillingdon Hospital was still in place.

In understanding male power it is important to understand that masculine oligarchies exclude not only all women but most men. Male elites are as interested in exercising sway over other males in the same organization as they are in defending the organization as a whole. The labour movement, engrossed in the "dick thing" of jockeying for power within its own organizations and at the same time resisting any erosion of its own elite status, allowed a huge pool of workers to remain unrepresented. Capital had only to hold off the organized onslaughts on its embedded power long enough to undermine old systems of collective bargaining when it would find itself in a position to replace unionized labour with a biddable workforce recruited largely from undemanding female workers. The vast mass of female workers in modern industry, which is mostly service industry, have no job security, few privileges, and little or no insurance. In Britain more than six million women workers, half the female workforce, are paid less than what is defined by the Council of Europe as the "decency threshold." The new Labour government, committed by its election manifesto to bringing in a national minimum wage, has set it at a level well below decency, having accepted the Tory argument that if employers were to be forced to pay a living wage they would sack vast numbers of workers. Thirty years ago a working man could keep his family on what he earned; now it takes two working people to afford a decent standard of living for a household with children. Higher paid workers in Britain might be able to support a household from their own earnings alone, but the penalty is the longest working week in Europe. They might be able to pay the bills, but paying the bills is all they can do. There is no time for anything else.

It is difficult to reconcile the powerlessness of the workforce of the twenty-first century with the triumphalism of "the future is female" lobby.

Women may be doing better in the workplace, but the workplace is not what it was. The fact that more men than women complained to the Equal Opportunities Commission in 1995 has less to do with the actual amount of sex discrimination in the job market than it does with men's readiness to use the existing instruments for redress of grievance, their readiness to fight. Men's lives are still organized in such a way that they have the time and energy to fight; women's lives, by and large, are not. Practically all the half-million British outworkers, nowadays as often called home workers, are female. Outworkers are employed by manufacturers to work in their own homes for piecework rates. The average outworker has children, works over thirty hours a week, and can earn as little as £56 for her week's toil. Now that part-time workers are assured the same entitlements as full-time workers an outworker is quite likely to be forced by her employer to register herself as self-employed, which means that, instead of using factory equipment and being on the factory pay-roll, she must lease-hire her equipment and pay her own expenses before she can earn a penny.

Full acceptance of women in the workplace has been hampered by the rise of male unemployment. Though a 1996 Cambridge University study found that support for the belief that

WOMEN ARE DOING BETTER THAN EVER IN THE WORKPLACE WHERE, FINALLY, SEXIST ATTITUDES APPEAR TO BE ON THE DECLINE—IN 1995 MORE MEN THAN WOMEN COMPLAINED TO THE EQUAL OPPORTUNITIES COMMISSION ABOUT JOB ADVERTISEMENTS.[4]

it was the man's role to earn money fell from 65 percent in 1984 to 43 percent in 1994, men still objected to mothers working outside the home. Both men and women believe that women's family responsibilities, especially if young children are involved, must come first. Relatively few men or women agreed that a woman and her family would all be happier if she went out to work. One wonders how they would answer if they were asked how happy they would be to do without the central heating or the VCR or the computer games or the holiday that the working mother's money helps to pay for. One thing is certain; very little of the money that a working mother earns will be spent on herself, and none of it on any form of recreation. Most of the 45 percent of British mothers who are in paid work do not actually have the choice of staying home; they must earn money to help service the family debt. If their children suffer it is because working mothers do not have access to affordable childcare. Nearly half of them have to rely on unpaid help from friends or family members. Only a quarter of British working mothers pay for childcare, professional or informal. In Britain, with six million children under eight years of age, there are only 700,000 regulated childcare places; the cost of such care is in the region of £3,000 per child per year. Only 2 percent of care for children aged between three and five and 5 percent of care for children between six and eleven is publicly funded. Only 2 percent of employers offer workplace creches; another 2 percent offer childcare vouchers. Four out of five mothers told BSA researchers in 1996 that they would work and a quarter of mothers working part-time said they would work longer hours, if they could get the right childcare arrangements. The Labour government is offering credits to working mothers to pay for childcare but at a level which would pay only a fraction of the cost of professional, properly monitored care, supposing that it were available.

When a woman without other responsibilities is not earning her living she is working on her body, her appearance, her clothes. Staying in to wash her hair means staying in to work on her appearance. If she works out, she is still working. When she has a house to run she will work long hours on that. When she is in a relationship she will work much harder on that than her male partner will; when she has a child the work of raising it will devolve on her. If she has an older dependent relative she will work to care for her or him. Only a tiny fraction of the work that women do produces an income. The rest is done because somebody has to do it, if life is to be livable. Women's industriousness need not be seen as oppression as long as they enjoy what they are doing while they are doing it. Work and play are manifestations of the same basic human urge to activity. Very few women can sit without something in their hands to work on; all men can sit for hours relaxing. Women cannot go out without something to carry; men keep their hands free and move about unburdened as much as possible. Women are busy; men are idle. Men have dispensed with any necessity to work on their appearance, beyond the choice of shaving or not. Their hair is low maintenance; their clothes are durable and suitable for cleaning by others; their domestic arrangements are of the simplest.

Women are worker bees; males are drones. Lionesses do the hunting to feed their cubs and their father; apesses do all the child-rearing. Male animals are conspicuously less busy than females, yet somehow the human male has convinced the human female that he, not she, is the worker. His work is real work; her work is vicarious leisure. Just how much work men actually do when they are "at work" is an interesting and inscrutable question. How much of men's long work-days is spent in the pub, in

the bar on the train, playing squash or golf, lunching? Despite all the media hype about working women, the lunchers in London restaurants who sit over their snifters well into the afternoon are still men. Men have still not realized that letting women do so much of the work for so little reward makes a man in the house an expensive luxury rather than a necessity. Many of the women who will this year shed a husband who thinks that he has behaved as well as could be expected will do so because he is just too much trouble. The cost in human terms of feeding him, grooming him, humouring him, and financing his recreation is way out of proportion to the contribution that he makes in return, even if he is an attentive and sensitive lover. As things stand at the end of the century women are clear that they are doing all the work without having a fair share of the reward. Less work for the same reward must become an irresistible option. If men want the pleasure of living with women and children they are going to have to shape up. All work and no play may have made Jill too dull to understand a football game, but all play and no work will make Jack that most vulnerable of creatures, a redundant male.

NOTES

1. From Helen Z. Lopata and Joseph H. Pleck, *Research into the interweave of jobs and families,* 3 (Greenwich CT, JAI Press, 1983), p. 39.

2. *All work and no play: The sociology of women and leisure* (Milton Keynes, Open University Press, 1986); E. Green, S. Hebron, and D. Woodward, *Women's Leisure, What Leisure?* (London, Macmillan, 1990).

3. Irene Elia, *The Female Animal* (Oxford, Oxford University Press, 1985), p. 210, quoting Kelly Stewart, "The birth of a wild mountain gorilla."

4. Charlotte Raven, "Me, myself, I," *Guardian,* 9 September 1996.

Study/Discussion Questions

1. What evidence does Greer present that women work more than men?
2. Make a list of the kinds of unpaid labor women do, according to Greer.
3. In what ways are women at a disadvantage in negotiations in the workplace?
4. What "fun" activities do men define as part of their work, according to the author?

It's a Family Affair:
Women, Poverty, and Welfare

Randy Albelda and Chris Tilly

"Why are so many single-mother families poor?" ask economic rights activists Randy Albelda and Chris Tilly. In response to that question, they tackle the myths and misunderstandings surrounding women, poverty, and welfare. Punitive and misguided welfare reform, they say, will not create the kind of fundamental institutional change needed to break the connection between gender and poverty. Here the authors suggest seven basic steps toward severing that link.

Hating poor women for being poor is all the rage—literally. Radio talk show hosts, conservative think tanks, and many elected officials bash poor single mothers for being too "lazy," too "dependent," and too fertile. Poor mothers are blamed for almost every imaginable economic and social ill under the sun. Largely based on anecdotal information, mythical characterizations, and a recognition that the welfare system just isn't alleviating poverty, legislatures across the land and the federal government are proposing and passing draconian welfare "reform" measures.

It is true that current welfare policies do not work well—but not for the reasons usually presented. Welfare "reform" refuses to address the real issues facing single-mother families, and is heavily permeated by myths.

Aid to Families with Dependent Children (AFDC), the government income transfer pro-gram for poor non-elder families in the United States, serves only about 5 percent of the population at any given time, with over 90 percent of those receiving AFDC benefits being single mothers and their children. In 1993, 14 million people (two-thirds of them children) in the United States received AFDC. That same year, just under 40 million people were poor. Despite garnering a lion's share of political discussion, AFDC receives a minuscule amount of funding: It accounts for less than 1 percent of the federal budget and less than 3 percent of the state budgets.

Single mothers work. Not only do they do the unpaid work of raising children, they also average the same number of hours in the paid labor force as other mothers do—about 1,000 hours a year (a full-time, year-round job is about 2,000 hours a year).[1] And while close to 80 percent of all AFDC recipients are off in

From Diane Dujon and Ann Withorn, eds., *For Crying Out Loud: Women's Poverty in the United States,* Boston: South End Press, 1996, pp. 79–85.

two years, over half of those return at some later point—usually because their wages in the jobs that got them off welfare just didn't match the cost of health care and childcare needed so they could keep the jobs. In fact, most AFDC recipients "cycle" between relying on families, work, and AFDC benefits to get or keep their families afloat.[2] That means that, for many single mothers, AFDC serves the same function as unemployment insurance does for higher-paid, full-time workers.

And, contrary to a highly volatile stereotype, welfare mothers, on average, have fewer kids than other mothers. And once on AFDC, they are less likely to have another child.

POVERTY AND THE "TRIPLE WHAMMY"

Poverty is a persistent problem in the United States. People without access to income are poor. In the United States, most people get access to income by living in a family with one or more wage-earners (either themselves or others). Income from ownership (rent, dividends, interest, and profits) provides only a few families with a large source of income. Government assistance is limited—with elders getting the bulk of it. So wages account for about 80 percent of all income generated in the United States. Not surprisingly, people whose labor market activity is limited, or who face discrimination, are the people most at risk for poverty. Children, people of color, and single mothers are most likely to be poor.

In 1993, 46 percent of single-mother families in the United States were living in poverty, but only 9 percent of two-adult families with children were poor.[3]

Why are so many single-mother families poor? Are they lazy, do they lack initiative, or are they just unlucky? The answer to all of these is a resounding "No." Single-mother families have a very hard time generating enough in-

come to keep themselves above the poverty line for a remarkably straightforward reason: One female adult supports the family—and one female adult usually does not earn enough to provide both childcare expenses and adequate earnings.

To spell it out, single mothers face a "triple whammy." First, like all women, when they do paid work they often face low wages—far lower than men with comparable education and experience. In 1992, the median income (the midpoint) for all women who worked full-time was $13,677. That means that about 40 percent of all working women (regardless of their marital status) would not have made enough to support a family of three above the poverty line. Even when women work year-round full-time, they make 70 percent of what men do.

Second, like all mothers, single mothers must juggle paid and unpaid work. Taking care of healthy and, sometimes, sick children and knowing where they are when at work requires time and flexibility that few full-time jobs afford. All mothers are more likely to earn less and work less than other women workers because of it.

Finally, unlike married mothers, many single mothers must juggle earning income and taking care of children without the help of another adult. Single-mother families have only one adult to send into the labor market. And that same adult must also make sure children get through their day.

The deck is stacked—but not just for single mothers. All women with children face a job market which has little sympathy for their caregiving responsibilities and at the same time places no economic value on their time spent at home. The economic activity of raising children is one that no society can do without. In our society, we do not recognize it as work worth paying mothers for. For a married mother, this contradiction is the "double day." For a single mother, the contradiction frequently results in poverty for her and her children.

DENYING THE REAL PROBLEMS

The lack of affordable childcare, the large number of jobs that fail to pay living wages, and the lack of job flexibility are the real problems that face all mothers (and increasingly everyone). For single mothers, these problems compound into crisis.

But instead of tackling these problems head on, politicians and pundits attack AFDC. Why? One reason is that non-AFDC families themselves are becoming more desperate and resent the limited assistance that welfare provides to the worst-off. With men's wages falling over the last 30 years, fewer and fewer families can get by with only one wage earner. The government is not providing help for many low-income families who are struggling but are still above the AFDC eligibility threshold. This family "speed-up" has helped contribute to the idea that if both parents in a two-parent household can work (in order to be poor), then all AFDC recipients should have to work too.

Instead of facing the real problems, debates about welfare reform are dominated by three dead ends. First, politicians argue that single mothers must be made to work in the paid labor market. But, most single mothers already work as much as they can. Studies confirm that AFDC recipients already do cycle in and out of the labor force. Further, as surveys indicate, mothers receiving AFDC would like to work. The issue is not whether or not to work, but whether paid work is available, how much it pays, and how to balance work and childcare.

Second, there is a notion of replacing the social responsibilities of government assistance with individual "family" responsibilities: Make men pay child support, demand behavioral changes of AFDC recipients, or even pressure

single women to get married. While child support can help, for most single mothers it offers a poor substitute for reliable government assistance. Penalizing women and their children for ascribed behaviors (such as having more children to collect welfare) that are supported by anecdotes but not facts is at best mean-spirited.

Third, there is an expectation that people only need support for a limited amount of time—many states and some versions of federal welfare reform limit families to 24 months of aid over some period of time (from a lifetime to five years). Yet, limiting the amount of time women receive AFDC will not reduce or limit the need for support. Children do not grow up in 24 months, nor will many women with few skills and little education necessarily become job ready. But more important, many women who do leave AFDC for the workplace will not make enough to pay for childcare or the health insurance they need to go to work.

In short, welfare "reform" that means less spending and no labor market supports will do little beyond making poor women's lives more miserable.

BEYOND WELFARE REFORM

What could be done instead? Welfare reform in a vacuum can solve only a small part of the problem. To deal with poverty among single-mother families, to break the connection between gender and poverty, requires changing the world of work, socializing the costs of raising children, and providing low-wage supports.

If we as a nation are serious about reducing the poverty of women and children, we need to invest in seven kinds of institutional changes:

- *Create an income-maintenance system that recognizes the need for full-time childcare.* Policies that affect families must acknowledge the reality of children's needs. To truly value families means to financially support those (women or men) who must provide full-time childcare at home or to provide dependable, affordable, and caring alternative sources of childcare for those who work outside the home.

- *Provide support for low-wage workers.* If leaving welfare and taking a job means giving up health benefits and childcare subsidies, the loss to poor families can be devastating. Although high-salary workers receive (or can afford) these benefits, low-wage workers often don't. Government should provide these supports; universal health care and higher earned income tax credits (EITC) are a first step in the right direction.
- *Close the gender pay gap!* One way to achieve pay equity is to require employers to re-evaluate the ways that they compensate comparable skills. Poor women need pay equity most, but all women need it. Another way to close the pay gap is to increase the minimum wage. Most minimum-wage workers are women. An increase from the current $4.25 an hour to $5.50 would bring the minimum wage to 50 percent of the average wage.
- *Create jobs.* Create the opportunity to work, for poor women and poor men as well. Full employment is an old idea that still makes sense.
- *Create jobs that don't assume you have a "wife" at home to perform limitless unpaid work.* It's not just the welfare system that has to come to terms with family needs; it's employers as well. With women making up 46 percent of the workforce—and men taking on more childcare responsibilities as well—a change in work styles is overdue.
- *Make education and training affordable and available for all.* In an economy where the premium on skills and education is increasing, education and training are necessities for young people and adults, women and men.
- *Fix the tax structure.* Many of these proposals

require government spending consistent with the ways our industrial counterparts spend money. Taxes must be raised to pay for these programs: the alternative—not funding child allowances, health care, and training—will prove more costly to society in the long run. But it is critically important to make the programs universal and to fund them with a fairer tax system. Federal, state, and local governments have taxed middle- and low-income families for too long without assuring them basic benefits. Taxes paid by the wealthiest families as a percentage of their income have fallen dramatically over the last 15 years, while the burden on the bottom 80 percent has risen; it's time to reverse these trends.

The changes proposed are sweeping, but no less so than those proposed by the Republican Contract with America. With one out of every four children in this nation living in poverty, all our futures are at stake.

NOTES

1. These data, and others throughout the paper, were calculated by the authors using current population survey tapes.
2. Five recent studies have looked at welfare dynamics and all come to these conclusions. LaDonna Pavetti, "The Dynamics of Welfare and Work: Exploring the Process by Which Young Women Work Their Way Off Welfare," paper presented at the APPAM Annual Research Conference, 1992; Kathleen Harris, "Work and Welfare Among Single Mothers in Poverty," *American Journal of Sociology,* vol. 39 (2), September 1993, pp. 317–352; Roberta Spalter-Roth, Beverly Burr, Heidi Hartmann, and Lois Shaw, "Welfare That Works: The Working Lives of AFDC Recipients," Institute for Women's Policy Research, 1995; Rebecca Blank and Patricia Ruggles, "Short-Term

Recidivism Among Public Assistance Recipients," *American Economic Review,* vol. 84 (2), May 1994, pp. 49–53; and Peter David Brandon, "Vulnerability to Future Dependence Among Former AFDC Mothers," Institute for Research on Poverty discussion paper DP1005-95, University of Wisconsin, Madison, Wis., 1995.

3. U.S. Department of Commerce, Census Bureau, "Income, Poverty and Valuation of Noncash Benefits," *Current Populations Reports,* 1995, pp. 60–188. p. D-22.

Study/Discussion Questions

1. What is the "triple whammy" that keeps single mothers poor?
2. What problems are most likely to lead single mothers to need welfare?
3. In what ways are these also the problems of married mothers?
4. Of Albelda and Tilly's list of necessary changes, which seem the most likely to be implemented in the U.S. today? Which would be the easiest to implement?

Comparable Worth: When Do Two Jobs Deserve the Same Pay?

Carolyn J. Aman and Paula England

The wage gap separating men's and women's earnings still has not been closed, write Carolyn J. Aman and Paula England. Women earn only 70 percent of what men earn in the United States. With legislation forbidding overt sex discrimination in hiring and wage determination (equal pay for equal work) already in existence, what can still be done? Comparable worth legislation might provide the remedy needed. Men and women are often not doing the same jobs, and those jobs typically performed by men get higher remuneration, on average. The pay levels of various kinds of work can be rated according to the value of the work performed, the demands of the job, supporters of comparable worth laws reason; that way, the work itself and not the sex of the worker who typically performs the job will determine the pay level.

In an office I used to have before the lab moved to this hospital, we had windows and I would look outside and I would see a fellow out there mowing a lawn, raking leaves, and he was paid $300 to $500 more a month than I was. His job specifications did not require that he could read or write. They only required that he could push a lawn mower and rake leaves.

—*Hospital secretary, quoted in Willborn (1989, p. 1)*

The wage gap between women and men has decreased in the past 10 years, from a female-male earnings ratio of around 60 percent in the early 1980s to nearly 70 percent in 1991. Yet, with women who hold full-time jobs making only 70 percent of what men do, the remaining gap is still large (Institute for Women's Policy Research, 1993). This gap cannot be explained by women having less education than men. The distribution of women and men across all levels of education is similar (with slightly more men than women at both very low and very high educational levels), but men earn far more at each educational level than women. The sex gap in pay stems from many factors, only some of which are under the control of employers. Discrimination of various types by employers is among the factors causing the gap. Our focus here will be on one very subtle type of wage discrimination—that at issue in "comparable worth" (sometimes called "pay equity"). We begin by contrasting this form of discrimination with other better known types.

LEGAL STATUS OF TYPES OF DISCRIMINATION AFFECTING PAY

There are three types of sex discrimination that can affect the sex gap in pay: (a) discrimination in hiring or job placement, affecting which jobs women and men work in; (b) wage discrimination, in which women and men are paid differently even though they work in the same job; and (c) the distinct type of wage discrimination at issue in comparable worth, in which the sex of the typical worker in a job affects the pay employers set for all workers in the job. Federal legislation prohibits the first two types of discrimination. The third, comparable worth discrimination, perhaps because it is so subtle, remains legal in the United States.

The first type of discrimination, discrimination in hiring or job placement, affects the sex gap in pay whenever employers won't hire or promote women into better-paying jobs simply because of their sex. This type of discrimination is prohibited by Title VII of the 1964 Civil Rights Act, which forbids discrimination in hiring, benefits, and other personnel decisions, on the basis of sex, race, color, national origin, or religion, by employers with 15 or more employees (Kay, 1988). Executive Order 11246 (affirmative action), which affects organizations that sell goods or services to the federal government or get federal grants or aid, also has the goal of ensuring women and minorities the right to enter higher-paying positions if they have the qualifications. The executive order requires these employers to take proactive steps to recruit, hire, and pro-

mote qualified women and minorities (Kay, 1988).

The second type of discrimination, wage discrimination within a job, occurs when women and men are in the same job and are doing the same work, but do not receive the same pay. This is what people commonly call "lack of equal pay for equal work." The Equal Pay Act of 1963 made this illegal. It prohibits employers from paying men more than women (or vice versa) when they are doing the same work, unless the pay difference is because of differences between the individual men and women in question in their seniority, merit, quality or quantity of production, or some factor other than sex (Kay, 1988). Title VII of the Civil Rights Act of 1964 also prohibits this (among many other forms of) discrimination.

But this prohibition of wage discrimination within jobs can only have a limited effect on the overall sex gap in pay because women and men are often not in the same jobs. In the United States and most other nations, jobs show a substantial degree of sex segregation. Many occupations are predominantly female—for example, secretaries, child care workers, nurses, elementary school teachers, and dental hygienists. Other occupations are almost entirely male-segregated enclaves—for example, pilots, engineers, fire fighters, and unskilled laborers. Although segregation has decreased somewhat since about 1970 as more women have moved into male-dominated fields such as law, medicine, engineering, and management, it is still quite pervasive. An index of segregation shows that for each occupation to have the same sex composition as the labor force as a whole, over 60 percent of men and/ or women would have to change occupations (Blau, 1988; England, 1992). If very detailed job categories are used, segregation is shown to be even more pervasive. Because of this extensive job segregation by sex, a large sex gap in pay can persist even when women receive equal pay for equal work in the same job, because men and women are rarely in the same jobs and predominantly male jobs generally pay more.

Federal legislation prohibiting lack of equal pay for equal work in the same job does not do anything about the inequity the woman quoted at the beginning of this chapter is complaining about—that as a medical secretary she earns much less than a groundskeeper. Although it would be illegal (under Title VII's prohibition of hiring and placement discrimination) for her employer not to let her compete for the groundskeeper job, once she has taken the job of medical secretary, no equal pay legislation requires the employer to pay her job as much as a predominantly male job—even if her job requires more education and skill. The secretary's complaint of discrimination is based on the idea that she is being paid less than the groundskeeper despite the fact that her work is more demanding in many ways. Her complaint embodies the third type of discrimination, the type at issue in comparable worth. Proponents of comparable worth argue that equal pay should be given to work of equal value (and unequal pay to work of unequal value). Failure to do this permits sex discrimination, because jobs often pay less not because of a difference in skill level or work conditions but simply because the jobs are filled by women.

In a number of court cases, plaintiffs have tried to get federal courts to treat this type of discrimination as a violation of Title VII of the Civil Rights Act since this law contains very general language about prohibiting sex discrimination in any of the terms of employment. To date, however, the federal appellate courts have not accepted this interpretation of the law, arguing that requiring comparable worth was not the intent of Congress. It is only where there is a "smoking gun" that the between-job pay inequity in comparable worth has been interpreted by the courts as a violation of Title VII (England, 1992). An example of a smoking gun would be a memo in which an em-

ployer explicitly stated that one job was being paid less than another because it was filled by women, and not for any other reason. By contrast, statistical proofs with no smoking gun are permitted in hiring-discrimination cases. Because employers are seldom stupid enough to write smoking-gun memos, in effect there is no legal redress for the sort of discrimination at issue in comparable worth.

THE SUBTLETY OF COMPARABLE WORTH COMPARISONS

The idea behind comparable worth is simple. It is that the pay level of a job should not be affected by the sex of those doing the work, but it may be affected by the demands of the job. Despite the simplicity of this principle, comparable worth discrimination is a very subtle form of sex discrimination that is invisible to most people. The subtlety and invisibility may be because people seldom make comparisons between the pay in "female" and "male" jobs.

A proportional definition of justice underlies the principle of comparable worth. According to proportional justice, a situation is just if the ratio of a person's (or group's) rewards to inputs is equal to the ratio for a "comparison other" (Adams, 1965). A *comparison other* refers to any person or group to whom the first person or group is compared. One theory in social psychology states that this conception underlies many judgments about what reward distributions are just (Adams, 1965). For example, many people believe that jobs requiring more education should pay more because, to qualify for these jobs, workers have to expend the effort and cost to obtain the education. The higher pay makes rewards proportional with the inputs of effort and cost that education requires. A similar argument is sometimes made for jobs that require more responsibility or effort or involve more danger.

If most people believe in "proportional justice," then why don't people notice that many predominantly female occupations pay much less than male occupations requiring a similar (or even smaller) amount of input such as education, training, or effort? And why don't they question such injustice? Researchers in social psychology suggest an explanation for this blind spot. A clue comes from their studies of the sorts of individuals, groups, and positions to which people usually compare their own situation. Similarity is the general principle that has been found to affect the selection of comparison others (Major, 1989). We tend to make comparisons between phenomena that are similar. Thus, men and women generally compare themselves with others in the same job, or a job that is very similar—not only in terms of amount of education, effort, skill, or difficulty involved but in terms of the types of tasks done and perhaps the sex of those holding the job. Given extensive sex segregation, this means that women in predominantly female jobs will usually compare their pay to others in the same or a similar job that is also filled by women, and men in male jobs will compare their pay to that of others in the same job they hold or other male jobs. In addition, the similarity principle means that women are likely to compare themselves mostly to other women and men to other men. Again, this makes it less likely that the pay of women in mostly female jobs will ever be compared to that of men in mostly male jobs. In both these ways, the similarity principle mitigates against comparisons between male and female jobs. As a result, many employers, the public, and even workers themselves rarely draw the conclusion that lack of equal pay for jobs of comparable worth is unjust. Until relevant comparisons are made, comparable worth discrimination goes unnoticed. With this type of discrimination seldom noticed and not against the law, its prevalence is not surprising.

PREVALENCE OF VIOLATIONS OF THE PRINCIPLE OF COMPARABLE WORTH

The quote with which we opened, featuring the secretary paid much less than a groundskeeper whose job does not require literacy, is not an isolated example of comparable worth discrimination. When relevant comparisons are made between female and male occupations, female occupations are often shown to be relatively underpaid. Consider some further examples: Women workers for the city of San Jose discovered that secretaries, most of whom had high school degrees and some years of college, were generally earning less than workers in male jobs that required no more than an eighth-grade education, including men who washed cars for the city (Blum, 1991). Nurses (with their science- and math-intensive college degrees) sued the city of Denver because their jobs paid less than male jobs such as tree trimmer and sign painter (Blum, 1991). The California School Employees Association complained that the largely female job category of school librarian (often requiring a master's degree) paid less than custodians and groundskeepers, predominately male jobs requiring no more than a high school degree (Steinberg, 1990). In each of these cases, the workers in the largely female jobs had made the comparisons between male and female jobs and were shocked by the injustice of the pay differences.

But even a long list of examples does not tell us how widespread this type of discrimination really is. Researchers have used two types of studies, those using national data and job evaluation studies for a single employer, to determine the prevalence of comparable worth discrimination.

Studies using national data have shown that the sex composition of a job affects its wages. These analyses include all occupations, using data for a particular nation (most studies have been done for the United States). Of course, such studies must take into account the demands of jobs. If predominantly female jobs pay less than predominantly male jobs because women's jobs do not require as much skill, education, or endurance of difficult working conditions, then the pay difference would not be an instance of comparable worth discrimination. National studies investigate the effect of a job's sex composition on its wages through a statistical technique called multiple regression analysis that determines the extent to which each of many factors affects the pay level of jobs. The factors used to explain jobs' pay include requirements of the jobs for various skills, working conditions, and education. After ascertaining statistically how much the differences between occupations' pay levels are explained by differences on these factors, the analysis determines whether the sex composition of the occupation affects its pay over and above what can be explained by the factors mentioned above. Such studies virtually always find that predominantly female occupations pay less (relative to predominantly male occupations) than would be expected considering the demands of the jobs (England, 1992; Sorensen, 1989; Treiman & Hartmann, 1981).

Job evaluation studies differ from national studies in that they focus on jobs within one organization, such as a business or a government. These studies generally use the "point factor system." Jobs are assigned points based on "compensable factors." Compensable factors are characteristics of jobs that employers think should—and do—affect which jobs pay more than others. Most commonly, they relate to the skill, effort, responsibility, and working conditions of each job. The scores on compensable factors are weighted to reflect which compensable factors will count more in pay. For example, the mental effort required by a job may be rated as twice as important (and weighted twice as much) as the physical effort (Beuhring, 1989). Sometimes the weights are obtained from a statistical analysis of the existing pay system. This is accomplished by working backward from the existing pay and skill demands of jobs to determine the relative importance (weight) of each skill or factor. Other times, employers do not use data, but rather decide a priori which factors they want to weight more heavily. Then each job is given a total point score—the sum of its score on each factor times the weight for that factor. Job evaluation studies commonly find that female jobs pay less than male jobs that were given the same number of points by the job evaluation, indicating a systematic pay bias against female jobs relative to male jobs (England, 1992).

WHAT HAS BEEN DONE AND CAN BE DONE TO PROMOTE COMPARABLE WORTH

A variety of comparable worth bills has been introduced in the U.S. Congress since 1980 (Bureau of National Affairs, 1981; Paul, 1989). They range from comprehensive measures that would prohibit this sort of discrimination by any employers in the nation to more limited bills that would mandate a study of the pay system for federal government workers. None of the bills has survived to become law, however. None has even made it out of committees for a floor vote. Comparable worth discrimination wlll only become illegal for most employers if there is new legislation at the federal or state levels prohibiting it.

The one type of legislative action that has been successful at the state level is passage of bills that mandate comparable worth principles be used to set pay in state government jobs. Somewhat less than half of all states have done job evaluation studies and then implemented comparable worth pay adjustments where female jobs have been found underpaid due to discrimination (National Committee on Pay Equity, 1989; Sorensen, 1994). In vir-

While women have moved into the workforce in increasing numbers and at all levels since the 1970s, they still have not reached the goal of equal pay for equal work.

tually every state where such studies have been done, they have revealed systematic underpayment of female jobs. But because these adjustments only affect those who work for government agencies, they have had a limited effect on the overall sex gap in pay among workers in those states because most people work in the private sector (Blum, 1991; Lowe & Wittig, 1989). Not including Minnesota, which has mandated pay equity adjustments at the local level, over 90 counties, cities, and school districts have either implemented pay equity plans or made comparable worth adjustments (Cook, 1985, 1986; National Committee on Pay Equity, 1989). Many of these localities are in California (e.g., Long Beach, Los Angeles, San Jose, Santa Cruz), but cities as diverse as Colorado Springs, Spokane, Minneapolis, and Chicago have also implemented comparable worth policies (Cook, 1985, 1986; National Committee on Pay Equity, 1989). Again, however, pay adjustments have affected only public sector workers.

In the private sector, any job evaluation studies focusing on comparable worth adjustments are voluntary at this point: No law requires comparable worth in wage setting in the United States. Many workplaces already use job evaluation studies in decisions about pay; between one half to two thirds of U.S. workers are in jobs where wages are affected by job evaluations (Belcher, 1974; Schwab, 1984). Yet the job evaluations are seldom used to ensure equal pay for male and female jobs given the same number of points by a job evaluation. One way employers avoid equal pay is by doing a separate job evaluation study for each job group in the company. One common strategy is to compare clerical jobs only to other clerical jobs, managerial jobs only to other managerial jobs, and blue-collar jobs only with other blue-collar jobs. In this way, there is no comparison between male and female jobs (Treiman & Hartmann, 1981). Comparable worth proponents endorse such evaluations to eradicate gender bias in setting wages.

In contrast to the United States, comparable worth legislation has been enacted in half of the jurisdictions in Canada, a majority of which require that employers in both public and private sectors set the relative job pay levels in accordance with comparable worth standards (Gunderson, 1989). Despite the lack of federal legislation making comparable worth discrimination illegal for all employers in the United States, awareness of the issue sometimes helps employee groups in women's jobs to push for wage increases. Unions representing workers in predominantly female jobs have used evidence of comparable worth discrimination in their negotiations with some employers (Lowe & Wittig, 1989). Knowledge of comparable worth discrimination among the women (and the few men) in predominantly female jobs can be a powerful force for political organizing; such action led to a strike in San Jose and a lawsuit in San Diego (Blum, 1991). Occasionally employers voluntarily undertake job evaluation with the intention of setting pay equal for male- and female-dominated jobs of comparable worth.

THE PROS AND CONS OF COMPARABLE WORTH

The basic argument for laws that would mandate comparable worth in wage setting is that it is simple justice. If the wages in women's jobs are low simply because the jobs are filled by women rather than because of greater demands in male jobs, this is discrimination. Such practices are as unfair as discrimination in hiring or unequal pay for equal work in the same job, both of which Congress decided to make illegal. Another argument in favor of comparable worth is that women are spending more of their lives in paid employment today than in past decades. This discrimination, then, affects more people now than in the past when fewer women were employed. Also an increasing proportion of women are single mothers who provide the major or sole financial support for their children. The pay increases could thus bring many children out of poverty. Finally, if the bargaining power of husbands and wives is affected by their relative earnings, by raising women's pay, comparable worth would make marriages more egalitarian.

The most frequent argument against comparable worth is that wages should be set by the free market rather than by the government (Paul, 1989). Of course, proponents of comparable worth do not propose that the government should stipulate a wage that employers

must pay for each job title. Rather, they argue for laws mandating that employers take steps to ensure that the relative wages they pay in various jobs are not systematically biased against predominantly female jobs. Otherwise, employers should be held legally accountable if plaintiffs can prove that such bias exists. But for some critics, even this is too much governmental regulation.

To put the issue in perspective, many current laws put certain limits on the decisions employers can make. This is true of minimum-wage laws, the Equal Pay Act that prohibits sex discrimination in wages among those doing the same job, and Title VII of the Civil Rights Act (which makes many forms of race and sex discrimination illegal). Thus, unless one opposes all these laws, the issue is not whether government should regulate employment relations but which kinds of regulation are warranted. We think comparable worth legislation is necessary because the pervasiveness of such discrimination has been well documented by research.

A related argument against comparable worth states that employers do not control what wage they pay a particular job. Instead, they have no choice but to pay "market wages"—the going rate in the overall labor market for a given job. Economists sometimes make this argument. According to the most orthodox version of neoclassical economic theory, wages are determined by supply and demand in a competitive labor market. Because employers are in competition with each other, they must pay at least the going rate in a given job or no one will work for them. In this view, employers cannot pay less than the going wage, and they will not pay more because they want to maximize profits.

This view of how labor markets work ignores discrimination, however, by claiming that market forces will eliminate discrimination in the long run. (The theory also does not say how long the long run is, and it may be very long.) But if there is discrimination of various types in the labor market, this discrimination will affect the market wages. The going rate in various jobs will be lower relative to skill levels in female jobs. According to national and job evaluation studies, the effect of occupational sex composition on wages suggests that discrimination is occurring and is affecting market wages. If discrimination has affected the wage many employers are willing to pay in an occupation because the workers are women, then the market wage itself embodies discrimination (England, 1992; Grune, 1984; Treiman & Hartmann, 1981).

Employers' different responses to shortages in male and female occupations provide further evidence that a gender-neutral picture of "supply and demand" is not the whole story. When there is a shortage of employees in a male occupation, the wage is often raised. But when it is a female occupation, often greater effort is expended to find a new source of cheap labor rather than raising pay. For example, U.S. hospitals have complained of a shortage of nurses for over two decades but have often imported foreign nurses instead of raising pay (Grune, 1984). In our view, when market wages embody discrimination, governmental regulation is needed to rid the market of such inequity.

Another argument against comparable worth states that it is the segregation of women in "women's jobs," not the lower payment of such jobs, that is the real problem. Our response to this is that discriminatory barriers that keep women out of "men's jobs" and the discriminatory pay in women's jobs at issue in comparable worth are both real problems and deserve legal remedies. If it is wrong for sex to affect whether one will be hired in a job, then it is also wrong for the sex of job incumbents to affect the pay offered in the job. Both arguments flow from a simple principle of nondiscrimination. One should not have to change jobs (with all the attendant costs of new training and possibly losing a pension or health

benefits) to escape a discriminatory wage.

A final argument against comparable worth policies is that they will be too costly for employers. This is why many employers oppose comparable worth proposals. (Of course, employers and their lobbyists also opposed all existing antidiscrimination legislation, including the Equal Pay Act, but they have learned to live with it.) Opponents argue that the resulting costs will hurt both employers and the economy as a whole. That is, if employers pass on any increased labor costs to consumers by raising the prices of goods, this may cause inflation and make American products more expensive and less competitive in international markets. Opponents of comparable worth also maintain that governmental enforcement mechanisms would be expensive. One response to this complaint is simply to say that if comparable worth is a matter of justice, costs should be irrelevant (Williams & Kessler, 1984). Another response is that the costs are surprisingly low. In states that have implemented comparable worth wage adjustments for government workers, the costs have usually been somewhere in the range of 1 percent to 9 percent of the payroll budget (Sorensen, 1994).

CONCLUSION

There is strong evidence from national data and job evaluation studies that compared to jobs filled largely by men, jobs filled largely by women are systematically underpaid relative to their demands for skill, effort, responsibility, education, and difficult working conditions. This discrimination contributes to the sex gap in pay. It directly affects millions of women (and the fewer number of men in predominantly female jobs). It indirectly affects the spouses and children in the families of those discriminated against.

Yet the United States has no comprehensive legislation prohibiting this form of discrimination. Over 30 years ago, when the Equal Pay Act and the Civil Rights Act were passed, Congress outlawed two types of sex discrimination. Congress decided that sex should not affect pay differences among people doing the same work and that sex should not affect hiring decisions. Instead, qualifications should govern pay and hiring. Comparable worth policies would extend this simple principle of nondiscrimination to decisions employers make about the relative pay of different jobs. Pay differences among jobs could be based on factors measuring the demands of the job, applied conistently across all jobs, but the sex of those holding the job should not be a consideration. Unfortunately, however, this subtle but pervasive type of sex discrimination remains prevalent today.

NOTE

1. Updated information on the status of comparable worth in individual cities can be obtained from the National Committee on Pay Equity, 1201 16th Street, N.W., Suite 411, Washington, DC 20036.

REFERENCES

Adams, J. S. (1965). Inequity in social exchange. In L. Berkowitz (Ed.), *Advances in experimental social psychology: Vol. 2* (pp. 267–299). New York: Academic Press.

Beatty, R. W., & Beatty, J. R. (1984). Some problems with contemporary job evaluation systems. In H. Remick (Ed.), *Comparable worth and wage discrimination* (pp. 59–78). Philadelphia: Temple University Press.

Belcher, C. W. (1974). *Compensation administration.* Englewood Cliffs, NJ: Prentice Hall.

Beuhring, T. (1989). Incorporating employee values in job evaluation. *Journal of Social Issues, 45,* 169–189.

Blau, F. (1988, December). *Occupational segregation by gender: A look at the 1980s.* Paper presented at the annual meetings of the American Economic Association, New York.

Blum, L. (1991). *Between feminism and labor: The significance of the comparable worth movement.* Berkeley: University of California Press.

Bureau of National Affairs. (1981). *The comparable worth issue.* Washington, DC: Author.

Cook, A. H. (1985). *Comparable worth: A case book of experiences in states and localities.* Manoa: University of Hawaii at Manoa, Industrial Relations Center.

Cook, A. H. (1986). *Comparable worth: A case book . . . 1986 supplement.* Manoa: University of Hawaii at Manoa, Industrial Relations Center.

England, P. (1992). *Comparable worth: Theories and evidence.* New York: Aldine de Gruyter.

Grune, J. A. (1984). Pay equity is a necessary remedy for wage discrimination. In U.S. Commission on Civil Rights (Ed.), *Comparable worth: Issue for the 80's: A consultation of the U.S. Commission on Civil Rights* (pp. 165–176). Washington, DC: U.S. Commission on Civil Rights.

Gunderson, M. (1989). Implementation of comparable worth in Canada. *Journal of Social Issues, 45,* 209–222.

Hochschild, A. R. (1983). *The managed heart: Commercialization of human feeling.* Berkeley: University of California Press.

Institute for Women's Policy Research. (1993). *The wage gap: Women's and men's earnings* (Briefing paper). Washington, DC: Author.

Kay, H. H. (1988). *Text, cases, and materials on sex-based discrimination* (3rd ed.). St. Paul, MN: West.

Lowe, R. H., & Wittig, M. A. (1989). Comparable worth: Individual, interpersonal, and structural considerations. *Journal of Social Issues, 45,* 223–246.

Major, B. (1989). Gender differences in comparisons and entitlement: Implications for comparable worth. *Journal of Social Issues, 45,* 99–115.

National Committee on Pay Equity. (1989). *Pay equity activity in the public sector, 1979–1989.* Washington, DC: Author.

Paul, E. F. (1989). *Equity and gender: The comparable worth debate.* New Brunswick, NJ: Transaction Books.

Schwab, D. P. (1984). Using job evaluation to obtain pay equity. In U.S. Commission on Civil Rights (Ed.), *Comparable worth: Issue for the 80's: A consultation of the U.S. Commission on Civil Rights* (pp. 83–92). Washington, DC: U.S. Commission on Civil Rights.

Sorensen, E. (1989). The wage effects of occupational sex composition: A review and new findings. In M. A. Hill & M. R. Killingsworth (Eds.), *Comparable worth: Analyses and evidence* (pp. 57–79). Ithaca, NY: Industrial and Labor Relations Press.

Sorensen, E. (1994). *Comparable worth: Is it a worthy policy?* Princeton, NJ: Princeton University Press.

Steinberg, R. (1990). Social construction of skill: Gender, power, and comparable worth. *Work and Occupations, 17,* 449–482.

Treimnn, D. J., & Hartmann, H. I. (1981). Women, work, and wages: Equal pay for jobs of equal value. Washington, DC: National Academy Press.

U.S. Bureau of the Census. (1993). *Money income of households, families, and persons in the United States: 1992* (Current population reports, Series P-60, No. 184). Washington, DC: Government Printing Office.

U.S. Department of Labor, Women's Bureau. (1994). *1993 handbook on women workers: Trends and issues.* Washington, DC: Government Printing Office.

Willborn, S. L. (1989). *A secretary and a cook: Challenging women's wages in the courts of the United States and Great Britain.* Ithaca, NY: Industrial Labor Relations Press.

Williams, R. E., & Kessler, L. L.(1984). *A closer look at comparable worth: A study of the basic questions to be addressed in approaching pay equity.* Washington, DC: National Foundation for the Study of Equal Employment Policy.

Study/Discussion Questions

1. What is comparable worth discrimination?
2. In what other ways are women discriminated against in the workplace?
3. How has comparable worth been promoted in the United States? How could it be promoted more effectively?
4. What arguments are made against comparable worth?

Flash Exercise

What's a Job Worth?

Estimate the salaries of five typical "men's" jobs and five typical "women's" jobs, keeping the education and/or training level necessary for each set of jobs roughly even. Then imagine switching the salaries. Which gender would benefit most from such a switch?

Women and Men Talking on the Job

Deborah Tannen

Can we talk? Apparently not, according to best-selling author Deborah Tannen. In Talking from 9 to 5, *Tannen, who earlier analyzed the miscommunications between women and men in personal relationships, turns her gaze on the workplace. Women's speaking and negotiating styles, which often differ radically from men's, place women at a disadvantage in a business world structured around male communication patterns, Tannen says. In her controversial view, the wage gap might be better understood as a communication gap.*

Amy was a manager with a problem: She had just read a final report written by Donald, and she felt it was woefully inadequate. She faced the unsavory task of telling him to do it over. When she met with Donald, she made sure to soften the blow by beginning with praise, telling him everything about his report that was good. Then she went on to explain what was lacking and what needed to be done to make it acceptable. She was pleased with the diplomatic way she had managed to deliver the bad news. Thanks to her thoughtfulness in starting with praise, Donald was able to listen to the criticism and seemed to understand what was needed. But when the revised report appeared on her desk, Amy was shocked. Donald had made only minor, superficial changes, and none of the necessary ones. The next meeting with him did not go well. He was incensed that she was now telling him his report was not acceptable and accused her of having misled him. "You told me before it was fine," he protested.

Amy thought she had been diplomatic; Donald thought she had been dishonest. The praise she intended to soften the message "This is unacceptable" sounded to him like the message itself: "This is fine." So what she regarded as the main point—the needed changes—came across to him as optional suggestions, because he had already registered her praise as the main point. She felt he hadn't listened to her. He thought she had changed her mind and was making him pay the price.

Work days are filled with conversations about getting the job done. Most of these conversations succeed, but too many end in impasses like this. It could be that Amy is a capricious boss whose wishes are whims, and it could be that Donald is a temperamental employee who can't hear criticism no matter how it is phrased. But I don't think either was the case

Excerpted from pp. 21–24, 29–32 of *Talking from 9 to 5* by Deborah Tannen. Copyright © 1994 by Deborah Tannen. Reprinted by permission of William Morrow and Company, Inc., and Virago Press, London, UK.

in this instance. I believe this was one of innumerable misunderstandings caused by differences in conversational style. Amy delivered the criticism in a way that seemed to her self-evidently considerate, a way she would have preferred to receive criticism herself: taking into account the other person's feelings, making sure he knew that her ultimate negative assessment of his report didn't mean she had no appreciation of his abilities. She offered the praise as a sweetener to help the nasty-tasting news go down. But Donald didn't expect criticism to be delivered in that way, so he mistook the praise as her overall assessment rather than a preamble to it.

This conversation could have taken place between two women or two men. But I do not think it is a coincidence that it occurred between a man and a woman. Conversational rituals common among men often involve using opposition such as banter, joking, teasing, and playful put-downs, and expending effort to avoid the one-down position in the interaction. Conversational rituals common among women are often ways of maintaining an appearance of equality, taking into account the effect of the exchange on the other person, and expending effort to downplay the speakers' authority so they can get the job done without flexing their muscles in an obvious way.

When everyone present is familiar with these conventions they work well. But when ways of speaking are not recognized as conventions, they are taken literally, with negative results on both sides. Men whose oppositional strategies are interpreted literally may be seen as hostile when they are not, and their efforts to ensure that they avoid appearing one-down may be taken as arrogance. When women use conversational strategies designed to avoid appearing boastful and to take the other person's feelings into account, they may be seen as less confident and competent than they really are. As a result, both women and men often feel they are not getting sufficient credit for what

they have done, are not being listened to, are not getting ahead as fast as they should.

When I talk about women's and men's characteristic ways of speaking, I always emphasize that both styles make sense and are equally valid in themselves, though the difference in styles may cause trouble in interaction. In a sense, when two people form a private relationship of love or friendship, the bubble of their interaction is a world unto itself, even though they both come with the prior experience of their families, their community, and a lifetime of conversations. But someone who takes a job is entering a world that is already functioning, with its own characteristic style already in place. Although there are many influences, such as regional background, the type of industry involved, whether it is a family business or a large corporation, in general, workplaces that have previously had men in positions of power have already established male-style interaction as the norm. In that sense, women, and others whose styles are different, are not starting out equal, but are at a disadvantage. Though talking at work is quite similar to talking in private, it is a very different enterprise in many ways.

NEGOTIATING FROM THE INSIDE OUT

Two co-workers who were on very friendly terms with each other were assigned to do a marketing survey together. When they got the assignment, the man began by saying, "I'll do the airline and automobile industry, and you can do the housewares and direct-mail market." The woman was taken aback. "Hey," she said. "It sounds like you've got it all figured out. As a matter of fact, I'd like to do airlines and autos. I've already got a lot of contacts in those areas." "Oh," he said, a little chagrined and a lot surprised. She continued, "I wish you wouldn't come on so strong." "Well, how would you have started?" he asked. She said, "I wouldn't have just said what I wanted to do. I would have asked, 'What parts do you want to do?'" This made no sense to him. "Then what are you complaining about? If you had asked me what parts I wanted to do, I would have said, 'I'll do the airlines and autos.' We would have ended up in the same place anyway."

The woman saw his point. But if the conversation had gone that way, she still would have been frustrated. To her, the question "What parts of the survey would you like to do?" is not an invitation to grab the parts he wants and run away with them. It's an invitation to talk about the various parts—which ones interest him, which he has experience in, which he would like to learn more about. Then he would ask, "What do you want to do?" and she would say what interests her, where her experience lies, and where she'd like to get more experience. Finally, they would divvy up the parts in a way that gave them both some of what they wanted, while taking advantage of both their expertise.

Making decisions is a crucial part of any workday. Daily, weekly, monthly, decisions must be made with never enough information and never enough time. People have very different ways of reaching decisions, and none is clearly better than others. But when two people with different styles have to make decisions together, both styles may have worse results than either would have if their styles were shared, unless the differences are understood and accommodated.

Beginning by stating what you will do is a style of negotiating that starts inside and works its way out. If others have different ideas, you expect them to say so, and you'll negotiate. Opening with a question like "What would you like to do?" or "What do you think?" is a style that begins by being vague and works its way in. It specifically invites others to express their perspective. Either style can work well.

What makes the machine go TILT! is the difference in styles. Someone who expects negotiation to proceed from the inside and work its way out hears a vague question as an invitation to decide; someone who tends to negotiate from the outside in hears a specific claim as a nonnegotiable demand. In this sense, both styles are indirect—they depend on an unspoken understanding of how the subsequent conversation is expected to go. This is a sense in which conversation is ritualized: It follows a preset sequencing scheme that seems self-evidently appropriate.

WHEN IS THE WAGE GAP A COMMUNICATION GAP?

There are those who claim that what's really important is economic issues like the salary gap—equal pay for equal work. Why do women still make less than men, on the average, and why, if efforts are made to equalize salaries in a given setting, is it only a few years before the women's pay once again falls behind? This too can be a matter of ways of speaking, since anything you get depends on talking.

Marjorie and Lawrence Nadler suspected that getting raises, promotions, and other advantages depends on people's ability to negotiate, and that women might be at a disadvantage in this regard. They tested this by asking 174 students to role-play negotiations for salary, and sure enough, they found that the women in their study ended up with lower raises than men. The researchers turned up a slew of other fascinating results too: On the average, male students role-playing supervisors gave lower raises than females in the same role, even though the males started out by offering more than the females. In other words, the women playing supervisors raised their offers much more as a result of negotiation. Even more interesting, and more worrisome, male students playing supervisors ended up giving higher raises to male student-subordinates, though this may be related to the fact that male student subordinates made higher initial demands than females did. In the end, the lowest raises were negotiated by female students playing subordinates in negotiation with males as bosses.

This does not mean that differences in ways of speaking are the only reason for the salary gap. Nadler and Nadler found not only that men in their role-plays ended up with higher raises than women as the outcome of negotiation, but that men were offered higher raises *to start with, before* negotiation. Most distressing, the lowest initial offers were made by female students playing supervisors negotiating with females as subordinates. It could be that the women started with low offers to women because they knew they would raise the offers as a result of negotiation. In the end, the researchers found that higher final offers were made when the negotiators were of the same sex.[1]

A real-life incident sheds light on another phenomenon that could affect relative wages. Doreen had advanced gradually but inexorably up the ladder in her company, until she held one of the highest positions in the firm. She had advanced at each stage along with Dennis, who had been hired at the same time as she. It seemed that the executives at the top were reluctant to give her a promotion or raise unless they felt that Dennis merited the same recognition, even though their jobs were by now quite different, and hers involved more responsibility as well as a higher operating budget. At one point, when she asked for a raise to bring her salary up to that of the other managers who had jobs comparable to hers, she was told that the firm couldn't manage raises for her and Dennis at that time. Doreen was taken aback by the reference to Dennis; she had simply asked about her own salary. But she was also enlightened; this tipped her off that her bosses regarded the two of them together and did not feel they could let her salary get ahead of his.

It may well be that some people have a gut-level, not-logically-thought-out sense that women should get less, either because they are expected to have lower abilities, or because they do not display their abilities, or because their rank and salaries are being measured against those of other women rather than their male peers. There may also be an unarticulated sense that women need less: Whether or not an individual woman is self-supporting or the main or sole support of her family, the image of a woman does not readily suggest "breadwinner."

All of this is to say that results like the salary gap may result from a range of factors, including ways of speaking as well as preconceptions about women and men.

NOTE

1. Lawrence B. Nadler, Marjorie Keeshan Nadler, & William R. Todd-Mancillas, eds., *Advances in Gender Communication Research* (Lanham, MD: University Press of America, 1987), p. 189.

Study/Discussion Questions

1. What are women's aims in workplace conversation? What rules do they follow?
2. How are men's aims different from women's? What are their goals in workplace conversation?
3. How might the "feminine" style described by Tannen put women at a disadvantage in the workplace?

The Low Road

Fanny Howe

Soon she headed into the wind. Sepulveda Boulevard would lead her to the cornfields and crows of Scripture, a field gullied by rainfall, and parking lots where men sat in cars smoking. Sometimes they got out of their cars and went to the bathroom in a cement barrack. This action scared her back to creation. Rows of electric lights burned white in the daylight under a plastic tent. A model airplane buzzed across the field, but she was forbidden entrance to that nature preserve because she walked with a dog. Encircled by mountains, the valley was a catcher for fog. Early mist dreamed over the dam. Brittle twigs screened her vista. Berries bled blue but were gray with dew too. Two bodies had lain in mud the night before as she bolted across the San Diego Freeway. Yellow canvas covered them and she flinched to avoid a blue raindrop heading for her eye. Police lights were on the way. She had noticed earlier that angels, like mourning doves, coo to a Pyhrric meter. Later she would take the square bread soaked in wine from an Eastern Orthodox priest and pray for those bodies. But that night she continued on past the end of their lives to the recycling center with her daily bag of cans.

ARE THERE NO GREAT WOMEN ARTISTS?

If Shakespeare Had a Sister

Virginia Woolf

In this excerpt from A Room of One's Own, *first published in 1929, Virginia Woolf responds to an age-old question, usually asked in a tone of disparagement: "Why have there been no great women artists?" The reason for women's failure to reach the heights has nothing to do with their intrinsic nature or inherent capabilities, Woolf implies. She makes her point by asking us to imagine what would have happened if Shakespeare had had a sister. Suppose this Judith Shakespeare had been as gifted as her brother William. Would she have been able to write her plays? How would she have been received? Woolf's short response to her own hypothetical question offers a grim lesson in the history of women as artists.*

It would have been impossible, completely and entirely, for any woman to have written the plays of Shakespeare in the age of Shakespeare. Let me imagine, since facts are so hard to come by, what would have happened had Shakespeare had a wonderfully gifted sister, called Judith, let us say. Shakespeare himself went, very probably—his mother was an heiress—to the grammar school, where he may have learnt Latin—Ovid, Virgil and Horace—and the elements of grammar and logic. He was, it is well known, a wild boy who poached rabbits, perhaps shot a deer, and had, rather sooner than he should have done, to marry a woman in the neighbourhood, who bore him a child rather quicker than was right. That escapade sent him to seek his fortune in London. He had, it seemed, a taste for the theatre; he began by holding horses at the stage door.

Very soon he got work in the theatre, became a successful actor, and lived at the hub of the universe, meeting everybody, knowing everybody, practising his art on the boards, exercising his wits in the streets, and even getting access to the palace of the queen.

Meanwhile his extraordinarily gifted sister, let us suppose, remained at home. She was as adventurous, as imaginative, as agog to see the world as he was. But she was not sent to school. She had no chance of learning grammar and logic, let alone of reading Horace and Virgil. She picked up a book now and then, one of her brother's perhaps, and read a few pages. But then her parents came in and told her to mend the stockings or mind the stew and not moon about with books and papers. They would have spoken sharply but kindly, for they were substantial people who knew the conditions of life for a woman and loved their daughter—indeed, more likely than not she was the apple of her father's eye. Perhaps she scribbled some pages up in an apple loft on the sly, but was careful to hide them or set fire to them. Soon, however, before she was out of her teens, she was to be betrothed to the son of a neighbouring wool-stapler. She cried out that marriage was hateful to her, and for that she was severely beaten by her father. Then he ceased to scold her. He begged her instead not to hurt him, not to shame him in this matter of her marriage. He would give her a chain of beads or a fine petticoat, he said; and there were tears in his eyes. How could she disobey him? How could she break his heart?

The force of her own gift alone drove her to it. She made up a small parcel of her belongings, let herself down by a rope one summer's night and took the road to London. She was not seventeen. The birds that sang in the hedge were not more musical than she was. She had the quickest fancy, a gift like her brother's, for the tune of words. Like him, she had a taste for the theatre. She stood at the stage door; she wanted to act, she said. Men laughed in her face. The manager—a fat, loose-lipped man—guffawed. He bellowed something about poodles dancing and women acting—no woman, he said, could possibly be an actress. He hinted—you can imagine what. She could get no training in her craft. Could she even seek her dinner in a tavern or roam the streets at midnight? Yet her genius was for fiction and lusted to feed abundantly upon the lives of men and women and the study of their ways. At last—for she was very young, oddly like Shakespeare the poet in her face, with the same grey eyes and rounded brows—at last Nick Greene the actor-manager took pity on her; she found herself with child by that gentleman and so—who shall measure the heat and violence of the poet's heart when caught and tangled in a woman's body?—killed herself one winter's night and lies buried at some crossroads where the omnibuses now stop outside the Elephant and Castle.

Study/Discussion Questions

1. Virginia Woolf is addressing a question often posed by men: If women and men have equal ability, why are there no great women writers (or composers or philosophers . . .)? How does she answer this question?
2. How is Judith Shakespeare's life different from that of William Shakespeare? How do her parents treat her differently? How is she treated differently when she goes out into the world?
3. What does Woolf say prevented women from doing creative work in the sixteenth century?
4. What makes it difficult for women to pursue creative work today?

In Search of Our Mothers' Gardens

Alice Walker

Alice Walker celebrates the wellspring of creative spirituality that has allowed black women, through years of oppression, to be artists. Their art might not be recognizable to the eye trained toward high culture— meaning elite white male culture—but it has always existed. In quilts made from rags, stories and blues songs wrung from life experience, and gardens raised from rocky soil, black women for generations have passed down to their daughters a need and ability to create art and beauty from the artifacts of daily life. Walker describes her own mother, gardening, as "ordering the universe in the image of her personal conception of Beauty."

I described her own nature and temperament. Told how they needed a larger life for their expression. . . . I pointed out that in lieu of proper channels, her emotions had overflowed into paths that dissipated them. I talked, beautifully I thought, about an art that would be born, an art that would open the way for women the likes of her. I asked her to hope, and build up an inner life against the coming of that day. . . . I sang, with a strange quiver in my voice, a promise song.

—*Jean Toomer, "Avey," Cane*

The poet speaking to a prostitute who falls asleep while he's talking—

When the poet Jean Toomer walked through the South in the early twenties, he discovered a curious thing: black women whose spirituality was so intense, so deep, so unconscious, that they were themselves unaware of the richness they held. They stumbled blindly through their lives: creatures so abused and mutilated in body, so dimmed and confused by pain, that they considered themselves unworthy even of hope. In the selfless abstractions their bodies became to the men who used them, they became more than "sexual objects," more even than mere women: they became "Saints." Instead of being perceived as whole persons, their bodies became shrines: what was thought to be their minds became temples suitable for worship. These crazy Saints stared out at the world, wildly, like lunatics—or quietly, like suicides; and the "God" that was in their gaze was as mute as a great stone.

Who were these Saints? These crazy, loony, pitiful women?

Some of them, without a doubt, were our mothers and grandmothers.

In the still heat of the post-Reconstruction

South, this is how they seemed to Jean Toomer: exquisite butterflies trapped in an evil honey, toiling away their lives in an era, a century, that did not acknowledge them, except as "the mule of the world." They dreamed dreams that no one knew—not even themselves, in any coherent fashion—and saw visions no one could understand. They wandered or sat about the countryside crooning lullabies to ghosts, and drawing the mother of Christ in charcoal on court-house walls.

They forced their minds to desert their bodies and their striving spirits sought to rise, like frail whirlwinds from the hard red clay. And when those frail whirlwinds fell, in scattered particles, upon the ground, no one mourned. Instead, men lit candles to celebrate the emptiness that remained, as people do who enter a beautiful but vacant space to resurrect a God.

Our mothers and grandmothers, some of them: moving to music not yet written. And they waited.

They waited for a day when the unknown thing that was in them would be made known; but guessed, somehow in their darkness, that on the day of their revelation they would be long dead. Therefore to Toomer they walked, and even ran, in slow motion. For they were going nowhere immediate, and the future was not yet within their grasp. And men took our mothers and grandmothers, "but got no pleasure from it." So complex was their passion and their calm.

To Toomer, they lay vacant and fallow as autumn fields, with harvest time never in sight: and he saw them enter loveless marriages, without joy; and become prostitutes, without resistance; and become mothers of children, without fulfillment.

For these grandmothers and mothers of ours were not Saints, but Artists; driven to a numb and bleeding madness by the springs of creativity in them for which there was no release. They were Creators, who lived lives of spiritual waste, because they were so rich in spirituality—which is the basis of Art—that the strain of enduring their unused and unwanted talent drove them insane. Throwing away this spirituality was their pathetic attempt to lighten the soul to a weight their work-worn, sexually abused bodies could bear.

What did it mean for a black woman to be an artist in our grandmothers' time? In our great-grandmothers' day? It is a question with an answer cruel enough to stop the blood.

Did you have a genius of a great-great-grandmother who died under some ignorant and depraved white overseer's lash? Or was she required to bake biscuits for a lazy backwater tramp, when she cried out in her soul to paint watercolors of sunsets, or the rain falling on the green and peaceful pasturelands? Or was her body broken and forced to bear children (who were more often than not sold away from her)—eight, ten, fifteen, twenty children—when her one joy was the thought of modeling heroic figures of rebellion, in stone or clay?

How was the creativity of the black woman kept alive, year after year and century after century, when for most of the years black people have been in America, it was a punishable crime for a black person to read or write? And the freedom to paint, to sculpt, to expand the mind with action did not exist. Consider, if you can bear to imagine it, what might have been the result if singing, too, had been forbidden by law. Listen to the voices of Bessie Smith, Billie

Holiday, Nina Simone, Roberta Flack, and Aretha Franklin, among others, and imagine those voices muzzled for life. Then you may begin to comprehend the lives of our "crazy," "Sainted" mothers and grandmothers. The agony of the lives of women who might have been Poets, Novelists, Essayists, and Short-Story Writers (over a period of centuries), who died with their real gifts stifled within them.

And, if this were the end of the story, we would have cause to cry out in my paraphrase of Okot p'Bitek's great poem:

> *O, my clanswomen*
> *Let us all cry together*
> *Come,*
> *Let us mourn the death of our mother,*
> *The death of a Queen*
> *The ash that was produced*
> *By a great fire!*
> *O, this homestead is utterly dead*
> *Close the gates*
> *With lacari thorns,*
> *For our mother*
> *The creator of the Stool is lost!*
> *And all the young women*
> *Have perished in the wilderness!*

But this is not the end of the story, for all the young women—our mothers and grandmothers, ourselves—have not perished in the wilderness. And if we ask ourselves why, and search for and find the answer, we will know beyond all efforts to erase it from our minds, just exactly who, and of what, we black American women are.

One example, perhaps the most pathetic, most misunderstood one, can provide a backdrop for our mothers' work: Phillis Wheatley, a slave in the 1700s.

Virginia Woolf, in her book *A Room of One's Own,* wrote that in order for a woman to write fiction she must have two things, certainly: a room of her own (with key and lock) and enough money to support herself.

What then are we to make of Phillis Wheatley, a slave, who owned not even herself? This sickly, frail black girl who required a servant of her own at times—her health was so precarious—and who, had she been white, would have been easily considered the intellectual superior of all the women and most of the men in the society of her day.

Virginia Woolf wrote further, speaking of course not of our Phillis, that "any woman born with a great gift in the sixteenth century [insert "eighteenth century," insert "black woman," insert "born or made a slave"] would certainly have gone crazed, shot herself, or ended her days in some lonely cottage outside the village, half witch, half wizard [insert "Saint"], feared and mocked at. For it needs little skill and psychology to be sure that a highly gifted girl who had tried to use her gift for poetry would have been so thwarted and hindered by contrary instincts [add "chains, guns, the lash, the ownership of one's body by someone else, submission to an alien religion"], that she must have lost her health and sanity to a certainty."

The key words, as they relate to Phillis, are "contrary instincts." For when we read the poetry of Phillis Wheatley—as when we read the novels of Nella Larsen or the oddly false-sounding autobiography of that freest of all black women writers, Zora Hurston—evidence of "contrary instincts" is everywhere. Her loyalties were completely divided, as was, without question, her mind.

But how could this be otherwise? Captured at seven, a slave of wealthy, doting whites who instilled in her the "savagery" of the Africa they "rescued" her from . . . one wonders if she was even able to remember her homeland as she had known it, or as it really was.

Yet, because she did try to use her gift for poetry in a world that made her a slave, she was "so thwarted and hindered by . . . contrary instincts, that she . . . lost her health." In the last years of her brief life, burdened not only with the need to express her gift but also with a penniless, friendless "freedom" and several small children for whom she was forced to do strenuous work to feed, she lost her health, certainly. Suffering from malnutrition and neglect and who knows what mental agonies, Phillis Wheatley died.

So torn by "contrary instincts" was black, kidnapped, enslaved Phillis that her description of "the Goddess"—as she poetically called the Liberty she did not have—is ironically, cruelly humorous. And, in fact, has held Phillis up to ridicule for more than a century. It is usually read prior to hanging Phillis's memory as that of a fool. She wrote:

The Goddess comes, she moves divinely fair,
Olive and laurel binds her golden hair.
Wherever shines this native of the skies,
Unnumber'd charms and recent graces rise.
[My emphases]

It is obvious that Phillis, the slave, combed the "Goddess's" hair every morning; prior, perhaps, to bringing in the milk, or fixing her mistress's lunch. She took her imagery from the one thing she saw elevated above all others.

With the benefit of hindsight we ask, "How could she?"

But at last, Phillis, we understand. No more snickering when your stiff, struggling, ambivalent lines are forced on us. We know now that you were not an idiot or a traitor, only a sickly little black girl, snatched from your home and country and made a slave; a woman who still struggled to sing the song that was your gift, although in a land of barbarians who praised you for your bewildered tongue. It is not so much what you sang, as that you kept alive, in so many of our ancestors, *the notion of song.*

Black women are called, in the folklore that so aptly identifies one's status in society, "the mule of the world," because we have been handed the burdens that everyone else—everyone else— refused to carry. We have also been called

"Matriarchs," "Superwomen," and "Mean and Evil Bitches." Not to mention "Castraters" and "Sapphire's Mama." When we have pleaded for understanding, our character has been distorted; when we have asked for simple caring, we have been handed empty inspirational appellations, then stuck in the farthest corner. When we have asked for love, we have been given children. In short, even our plainer gifts, our labors of fidelity and love, have been knocked down our throats. To be an artist and a black woman, even today, lowers our status in many respects, rather than raises it: and yet, artists we will be.

Therefore we must fearlessly pull out of ourselves and look at and identify with our lives the living creativity some of our great-grandmothers were not allowed to know. I stress some of them because it is well known that the majority of our great-grandmothers knew, even without "knowing" it, the reality of their spirituality, even if they didn't recognize it beyond what happened in the singing at church—and they never had any intention of giving it up.

How they did it—those millions of black women who were not Phillis Wheatley, or Lucy Terry or Frances Harper or Zora Hurston or Nella Larsen or Bessie Smith; or Elizabeth Catlett, or Katherine Dunham, either—brings me to the title of this essay, "In Search of Our Mothers' Gardens," which is a personal account that is yet shared, in its theme and its meaning, by all of us. I found, while thinking about the far-reaching world of the creative black woman, that often the truest answer to a question that really matters can be found very close.

In the late 1920s my mother ran away from home to marry my father. Marriage, if not running away, was expected of seventeen-year-old girls. By the time she was twenty, she had two children and was pregnant with a third. Five children later, I was born. And this is how I came to know my mother: she seemed a large, soft, loving-eyed woman who was rarely impatient in our home. Her quick, violent temper was on view only a few times a year, when she battled with the white landlord who had the misfortune to suggest to her that her children did not need to go to school.

She made all the clothes we wore, even my brothers' overalls. She made all the towels and sheets we used. She spent the summers canning vegetables and fruits. She spent the winter evenings making quilts enough to cover all our beds.

During the "working" day, she labored beside—not behind—my father in the fields. Her day began before sunup, and did not end until late at night. There was never a moment for her to sit down, undisturbed, to unravel her own private thoughts; never a time free from interruption—by work or the noisy inquiries of her many children. And yet, it is to my mother—and all our mothers who were not famous—that I went in search of the secret of what has fed that muzzled and often mutilated, but vibrant, creative spirit that the black woman has inherited, and that pops out in wild and unlikely places to this day.

But when, you will ask, did my overworked mother have time to know or care about feeding the creative spirit?

The answer is so simple that many of us have spent years discovering it. We have constantly looked high, when we should have looked high—and low.

For example: in the Smithsonian Institution in Washington, D.C., there hangs a quilt unlike any other in the world. In fanciful, inspired, and yet simple and identifiable figures, it portrays the story of the Crucifixion. It is considered rare, beyond price. Though it follows no known pattern of quilt-making, and though it is made of bits and pieces of worthless rags, it is obviously the work of a person of powerful imagination and deep spiritual feel-

ing. Below this quilt I saw a note that says it was made by "an anonymous Black woman in Alabama, a hundred years ago."

If we could locate this "anonymous" black woman from Alabama, she would turn out to be one of our grandmothers—an artist who left her mark in the only materials she could afford, and in the only medium her position in society allowed her to use.

As Virginia Woolf wrote further, in *A Room of One's Own:*

> Yet genius of a sort must have existed among women as it must have existed among the working class. [Change this to "slaves" and "the wives and daughters of sharecroppers."] Now and again an Emily Bronte or a Robert Burns [change this to "a Zora Hurston or a Richard Wright"] blazes out and proves its presence. But certainly it never got itself on to paper. When, however, one reads of a witch being ducked, of a woman possessed by devils [or "Sainthood"], of a wise woman selling herbs [our root workers], or even a very remarkable man who had a mother, then I think we are on the track of a lost novelist, a suppressed poet, of some mute and inglorious Jane Austen. . . . Indeed, I would venture to guess that Anon, who wrote so many poems without signing them, was often a woman.

And so our mothers and grandmothers have, more often than not anonymously, handed on the creative spark, the seed of the flower they themselves never hoped to see: or like a sealed letter they could not plainly read.

And so it is, certainly, with my own mother. Unlike "Ma" Rainey's songs, which retained their creator's name even while blasting forth from Bessie Smith's mouth, no song or poem will bear my mother's name. Yet so many of the stories that I write, that we all write, are my mother's stories. Only recently did I fully realize this: that through years of listening to my mother's stories of her life, I have absorbed not only the stories themselves, but something of the manner in which she spoke, something of the urgency that involves the knowledge that her stories—like her life—must be recorded. It is probably for this reason that so much of what I have written is about characters whose counterparts in real life are so much older than I am.

But the telling of these stories, which came from my mother's lips as naturally as breathing, was not the only way my mother showed herself as an artist. For stories, too, were subject to being distracted, to dying without conclusion. Dinners must be started, and cotton must be gathered before the big rains. The artist that was and is my mother showed itself to me only after many years. This is what I finally noticed:

Like Mem, a character in *The Third Life of Grange Copeland,* my mother adorned with flowers whatever shabby house we were forced to live in. And not just your typical straggly country stand of zinnias, either. She planted ambitious gardens—and still does—with over fifty different varieties of plants that bloom profusely from early March until late November. Before she left home for the fields, she watered her flowers, chopped up the grass, and laid out new beds. When she returned from the fields she might divide clumps of bulbs, dig a cold pit, uproot and replant roses, or prune branches from her taller bushes or trees—until night came and it was too dark to see.

Whatever she planted grew as if by magic, and her fame as a grower of flowers spread over three counties. Because of her creativity with her flowers, even my memories of poverty are seen through a screen of blooms—sunflowers, petunias, roses, dahlias, forsythia, spirea, delphiniums, verbena . . . and on and on.

And I remember people coming to my mother's yard to be given cuttings from her flowers; I hear again the praise showered on her because whatever rocky soil she landed on, she turned into a garden. A garden so brilliant with colors, so original in its design, so magnificent with life and creativity, that to this day people drive by our house in Georgia—perfect strangers and imperfect strangers—and ask to stand or walk among my mother's art.

I notice that it is only when my mother is working in her flowers that she is radiant, almost to the point of being invisible—except as Creator: hand and eye. She is involved in work her soul must have. Ordering the universe in the image of her personal conception of Beauty.

Her face, as she prepares the Art that is her gift, is a legacy of respect she leaves to me, for all that illuminates and cherishes life. She has handed down respect for the possibilities—and the will to grasp them.

For her, so hindered and intruded upon in so many ways, being an artist has still been a daily part of her life. This ability to hold on, even in very simple ways, is work black women have done for a very long time.

This poem is not enough, but it is something, for the woman who literally covered the holes in our walls with sunflowers:

They were women then
My mama's generation
Husky of voice—
Stout of
Step
With fists as well as
Hands
How they battered down
Doors
And ironed
Starched white
Shirts
How they led
Armies
Headragged Generals
Across mined
Fields
Booby-trapped
Kitchens
To discover books

Desks
A place for us
How they knew what we
Must know
Without knowing a page
Of it
Themselves.

Guided by my heritage of a love of beauty and a respect for strength—in search of my mother's garden, I found my own.

And perhaps in Africa over two hundred years ago, there was just such a mother; per-haps she painted vivid and daring decorations in oranges and yellows and greens on the walls of her hut; perhaps she sang—in a voice like Roberta Flack's—sweetly over the compounds of her village; perhaps she wove the most stunning mats or told the most ingenious stories of all the village storytellers. Perhaps she was herself a poet—though only her daughter's name is signed to the poems that we know.

Perhaps Phillis Wheatley's mother was also an artist.

Perhaps in more than Phillis Wheatley's biological life is her mother's signature made clear.

Study/Discussion Questions

1. What has prevented women, and particularly African American women, from acting on their creative impulses?
2. If women can't always exercise their creativity in the same ways that men do, how does Alice Walker say that women express themselves?
3. Have you seen examples of this in your life, or in the lives of your mothers or grandmothers?
4. What aspects of women's lives today still hinder them from doing creative work?

Flash Exercise

Where's the Art?

Imagine that you are the curator of a museum exhibit of women's "everyday art." What items or artifacts would you place in the exhibit? How would you justify your selections to critics?

"Mary Cassatt" and "The Case of Berthe Morisot"

Mary Gordon

Mary Gordon, best-selling novelist, in these two essays reflects on the lives and works of two women artists, Mary Cassatt and Berthe Morisot. Each woman struggled to be taken seriously as a painter, and each, Gordon says, left a stunning tribute to "the feminine," to women—especially mothers and daughters—as the subjects of art. While Cassatt faced the blatant opposition of a father who declared he'd rather see her die than pursue a career as an artist, Morisot met a more subtle subversion of her artistic agency in her transformation into a subject of art in Manet's Le Repos.

MARY CASSATT

When Mary Cassatt's father was told of her decision to become a painter, he said: "I would rather see you dead." When Edgar Degas saw a show of Cassatt's etchings, his response was: "I am not willing to admit that a woman can draw that well." When she returned to Philadelphia after twenty-eight years abroad, having achieved renown as an Impressionist painter and the esteem of Degas, Huysmans, Pissarro, and Berthe Morisot, the *Philadelphia Ledger* reported: "Mary Cassatt, sister of Mr. Cassatt, president of the Pennsylvania Railroad, returned from Europe yesterday. She has been studying painting in France and owns the smallest Pekingese dog in the world."

Mary Cassatt exemplified the paradoxes of the woman artist. Cut off from the experiences that are considered the entitlement of her male counterpart, she has access to a private world a man can only guess at. She has, therefore, a kind of information he is necessarily deprived of. If she has almost impossible good fortune—means, self-confidence, heroic energy and dedication, the instinct to avoid the seductions of ordinary domestic life, which so easily become a substitute for creative work—she may pull off a miracle: she will combine the skill and surety that she has stolen from the world of men with the vision she brings from the world of women.

Mary Cassatt pulled off such a miracle. But if her story is particularly female, it is also American. She typifies one kind of independent American spinster who keeps reappearing in our history in forms as various as Margaret Fuller and Katharine Hepburn. There is an astringency in such women, a fierce discipline, a fearlessness, a love of work. But they are not inhuman. At home in the world, they embrace it with a kind of aristocratic greed that knows nothing of excess. Balance, proportion, an instinct for the distant and the formal, an exuberance, a vividness, a clarity of line: the genius of Mary Cassatt includes all these elements. The details of the combination are best put down to grace; the outlines may have been her birthright.

She was one of those wealthy Americans whose parents took the children abroad for their education and medical care. The James family comes to mind and, given her father's attitude toward her career, it is remarkable that Cassatt didn't share the fate of Alice James. But she had a remarkable mother, intelligent, encouraging of her children. When her daughter wanted to study in Paris, and her husband disapproved, Mrs. Cassatt arranged to accompany Mary as her chaperone.

From her beginnings as an art student, Cassatt was determined to follow the highest standards of craftsmanship. She went first to Paris, then to Italy, where she studied in Parma with Raimondi and spent many hours climbing up scaffolding (to the surprise of the natives) to study the work of Correggio and Parmigianino. Next, she was curious to visit Spain to look at the Spanish masters and to make use of the picturesque landscape and models. Finally, she returned to Paris, where she was to make her home, and worked with Degas, her sometime friend and difficult mentor. There has always been speculation as to whether or not they were lovers; her burning their correspondence gave the rumor credence. But I believe that they were not; she was, I think, too protective of her talent to make herself so vulnerable to Degas as a lover would have to be. But I suppose I don't believe it because I cherish, instead, the notion that a man and a woman can be colleagues and friends without causing an excuse for raised eyebrows. Most important, I want to believe they were

not lovers because if they were, the trustworthiness of his extreme praise grows dilute.

She lived her life until late middle age among her family. Her beloved sister, Lydia, one of her most cherished models, had always lived as a semi-invalid and died early, in Mary's flat, of Bright's disease. Mary was closely involved with her brothers and their children. Her bond with her mother was profound: when Mrs. Cassatt died, in 1895, Mary's work began to decline. At the severing of her last close familial tie, when her surviving brother died as a result of an illness he contracted when traveling with her to Egypt, she broke down entirely. "How we try for happiness, poor things, and how we don't find it. The best cure is hard work—if only one has the health for it," she said, and lived that way.

Not surprisingly, perhaps, Cassatt's reputation has suffered because of the prejudice against her subject matter. Mothers and children: what could be of lower prestige, more vulnerable to the charge of sentimentality. Yet if one looks at the work of Mary Cassatt, one sees how triumphantly she avoids the pitfalls of sentimentality because of the astringent rigor of her eye and craft. The Cassatt iconography dashes in an instant the notion of the comfortable, easily natural fit of the maternal embrace. Again and again in her work, the child's posture embodies the ambivalence of his or her dependence. In *The Family,* the mother and child exist in positions of unease; the strong diagonals created by their postures of opposition give the pictures their tense strength, a strength that renders sentimental sweetness impossible. In *Ellen Mary Cassatt in a White Coat* and *Girl in the Blue Arm Chair,* the children seem imprisoned and dwarfed by the trappings of respectable life. The lines of Ellen's coat, which create such a powerful framing device, entrap the round and living child. The sulky little girl in the armchair seems about to be swallowed up by the massive cylinders of drawing room furniture and the strong curves of emptiness that are the floor. In *The Bath*, the little girl has all the unformed charming awkwardness of a young child: the straight limbs, the loose stomach. But these are not the stuff of Gerber babies—even of the children of Millais. In this picture, the center of interest is not the relationship between the mother and the child but the strong vertical and diagonal stripes of the mother's dress, whose opposition shape the picture with an insistence that is almost abstract.

Cassatt changed the iconography of the depiction of mothers and children. Hers do not look out into and meet the viewer's eye; neither supplicating nor seductive, they are absorbed in their own inner thoughts. Minds are at work here, a concentration unbroken by an awareness of themselves as objects to be gazed at by the world.

The brilliance of Cassatt's colors, the clarity and solidity of her forms, are the result of her love and knowledge of the masters of European painting. She had a second career as adviser to great collectors: she believed passionately that America must, for the sake of its artists, possess masterpieces, and she paid no attention to the outrage of her European friends, who felt their treasures were being sacked by barbarians. A young man visiting her in her old age noted her closed mind regarding the movement of the moderns. She thought American painters should stay home and not become "cafe loafers in Paris. Why should they come to Europe?" she demanded. "When I was young it was different. . . . Our Museums had not great paintings for the students to study. Now that has been corrected and something must be done to save our young over here."

One can hear the voice of the old, irascible, still splendid aunt in that comment and see the gesture of her stick toward the Left Bank. Cassatt was blinded by cataracts; the last years of her life were spent in a fog. She became ardent on the subjects of suffragism, socialism, and spiritualism; the horror of the First World

War made her passionate in her conviction that mankind itself must change. She died at her country estate near Grasse, honored by the French, recipient of the Legion d'honneur, but unappreciated in America, rescued only recently from misunderstanding, really, by feminist art critics. They allowed us to begin to see her for what she is: a master of line and color whose great achievement was to take the "feminine" themes of mothers, children, women with their thoughts alone, to endow them with grandeur without withholding from them the tenderness that fits so easily alongside the rigor of her art.

THE CASE OF BERTHE MORISOT

Losing My Temper in the National Gallery, and Types of Feminist Shame

It is the first one-woman show of hers in America. The National Gallery, a place where I have been happy. Official nineteenth-century America built these marble halls, these splashing pools so you can hear the sound of water while you're looking at the pictures, the pictures of the great collectors, making their money God knows how. I have never seen many of Morisot's paintings, and the ones I saw I found rather disappointing, a secret I don't tell anyone, but they seem pale to me, with nothing of Cassatt's draftsmanship or bold coloration—although it may be unfair to compare them simply because they were contemporaries and friends. And of course, female. Renoir said female painters were like a five-legged calf, a version of Dr. Johnson's dancing dog (I wonder if he knew it). But Morisot was important because there is no doubt that she is a serious and highly accomplished painter, and unless one is comparing her to the greatest geniuses—Manet and Monet and Degas (I am not easy saying Cassatt, although I mean it)—as good as the best of her age. I'd rather look at most Morisots than at most Renoirs

Le Repos, 1870 (Portrait of Berthe Morisot) by Edouard Manet. (Museum of Art, Rhode Island School of Design; bequest of the Estate of Mrs. Edith Stuyvesant Vanderbilt Gerry)

and Sisleys and Pissarros; the faults I find in her I find in them, and I find her subject matter more interesting.

But before I am allowed to look at the work of Morisot I am forced to look at her image. "Forced" sounds like a highly ungrateful language for the privilege of being allowed to look at a very beautiful painting: Manet's *Le Repos.* The curves of the sofa and the female figure (Morisot), the creaminess of the white dress—it is a beautiful picture of a beautiful woman. But it is a portrait *of* Berthe Morisot, not *by* Berthe Morisot. I feel angry for her, insulted, as if a virtuoso had been invited to her first recital and stole the audience's attention by perfectly playing a solo before she got on stage. I enjoy the Morisots, particularly the pictures of her daughter, and I am compelled by a self-portrait she does in late middle age: the face is serious, heavy, matronly, the eyes are deep-set, the hair is severely pulled back. But I keep thinking about *Le Repos.* Nothing Morisot has painted is as beautiful as this portrait of her. I have to keep thinking about her as a female body, as the object of an erotically charged vision greater than her own. I didn't want to have to think about her that way. Just for one afternoon, I wanted to think of her as a painter, dislodged from her biography, from

her physical beauty—separated from the admiring and powerful male gaze.

I keep thinking of another painter who was a famous object of male artistic vision: Georgia O'Keeffe. I had an odd reaction to seeing Steiglitz's photographs of her, a reaction unshared by anyone I knew. I resented Steiglitz for presenting her to me as so much the object of his desire. I resented her for *posing.* I didn't understand why she did it. It must have taken up a lot of her time. And to *pose,* to make oneself immobile, fixed, seemed to me an act of obedience, a loss of autonomy I couldn't forgive. In those photographs, the immediacy of the camera's eye means that the subject of the photograph, particularly when she is photographed incessantly, has something of the aspect of pornography. I was ashamed of these feelings. But I didn't want O'Keeffe lolling

A Girl Arranging Her Hair, 1885–86 by Berthe Morisot. Oil on canvas. (Sterling and Francine Clark Art Institute, Williamstown, Massachusetts)

around on sheets for Steiglitz, her hair loose, her breasts unflatteringly droopy. I wanted her up, girt, on her feet, her hair pulled back, her eye not resting on the camera's but on something in the world she could make the object of her own vision: the heart of a flower, red stones in the desert, a window frame of a Lake George house. Of course, Steiglitz's photographs of O'Keeffe helped make her famous; they made her 1924 show a cause célèbre: no one could separate the paintings from the body of the painter. Did she use that, consciously? Was it a strategy, an opening up of a private erotic contract to the art-buying world?

I see those photographs and I'm angry. K. suggests that this may be because of a severe puritanism about female exhibitionism; I suspect she's right. She says that in *Chanson de Roland*, which she's now teaching, there's pas-

sage after passage about male military posing. And no one judges that harshly. H. thinks O'Keeffe is a lousy painter: too full of self-love. I find her great. H. likes the photographs better than the paintings. For me, it is no contest, so I can forget about them, dislodge the object of male vision from the painter when I see her work. But I cannot dislodge the memory of her face: so arresting it appeared in *Vogue* as often as a model's. Is it possible to separate the image of the beautiful woman's face and body from her work? The question is more difficult for a visual artist. We know, for example, that Virginia Woolf was a beautiful woman, but because the visual aspects of her art are privately apprehended and symbolically rendered by black signs on a white page, we can forget that a physical woman held a pen in her fleshly hand to make these impressions. The writer is always more ghostly than the painter; there is a possible modesty in the hiddenness, the abstraction, of our re-creation of the world.

I try to think if all this could ever be an issue for a male artist. I cannot think of a male artist whose appearance is so much connected to his work that we would have to look at it differently if he looked different. I try to think of a male artist who existed with equal importance as the object of artistic vision and the creator of art. I cannot think of one possible example, nor can I easily imagine it for the future. The primacy of the female body as the locus of erotic charge seems immutable as long as the male heterosexual's is the dominant vision.

The truth is that for me—and I feel ashamed of it—Berthe Morisot's biography, as well as her physical beauty, is inseparable for me from her art. Perhaps this wouldn't be true if I loved the art more purely, as I do Cassatt's and O'Keeffe's. And the fact is that what is important for me is not Morisot's beauty, or her happy erotic and marital life, but her maternity. Morisot introduces into the artistic language the daughter as object of the mother's adoring gaze. Julie is painted in all her stages of babyhood and young womanhood. Was that sensuous mouth an anxiety to the mother, even as the painter rejoiced in it? Mothers desire their daughters' flesh, we desire it to be near our own with an ardor we are afraid to speak of—largely for the daughters' sakes. We have been told over and over again that mothers are jealous of their daughters' youth, and this is perhaps the truth in many cases. But we also rejoice in our daughters' growing and their beauty, and there is an extraordinary poignance to me in Morisot's depicting herself as a sober matron at the same time that she paints her daughter at the dreamy brink of her sexual ascent. I love the drawing of Julie looking over Morisot's shoulder as she sketches, interested in her mother's work but also luxuriating in

her usually forbidden nearness to the body of the working mother. This combination of art and life makes me much more emotionally engaged with Morisot's paintings than I am with what I know to be a greater work, Manet's *Le Repos.* Trained in the modern tradition, I react by feeling uneasy, immature. I am supposed to know better. But it shakes up, as well, the notion of modernist purity, because like it or not, what I know about Morisot's life has deepened my experience of her work.

A final admission: nothing of her work moves me as deeply as her final letter to her daughter. Morisot died young, at fifty-four. Julie was only seventeen.

> My little Julie, I love you as I die; I shall love you even when I am dead; I beg you not to cry, this parting was inevitable. I hoped to live until you were married. . . . Work and be good, as you have always been; you have not caused me one sorrow in your little life. You have beauty, money; make good use of them. I think it would be best for you to live with your cousins . . . but I do not wish to force you to do anything. . . . Do not cry; I love you more than I can tell you. . . .

So that in the end, both the physical beauty and the depth and tenderness of the connection between mother and daughter were cut down by death. Inevitable, yes, but still unbearable, and worse because we have such palpable evidence of intensely lived physical and affective life.

Study/Discussion Questions

1. What aspects of Mary Cassatt's family life and background helped her to become an artist?
2. What nineteenth-century assumptions about middle-class women hindered her?
3. How does Manet's portrait of Berthe Morisot as a beautiful young woman shape our view of her?
4. Why doesn't that portrait belong in an exhibit of Morisot's paintings, in Gordon's view?
5. What is the connection between how a woman looks and what we think of her creative work?

My Struggle as a Woman Artist

Judy Chicago

The work of artist Judy Chicago gained international fame in the 1970s, with her multimedia exhibition, The Dinner Party. *In this project, as in future work, Chicago sought to elucidate the history and experience of women in Western civilization. With her belief that an artist's gender affects not only choice of subject matter but also artistic point of view, Chicago has been at the forefront of a feminist art movement in the United States and abroad for more than thirty years. In this excerpt from her autobiography, Chicago details the obstacles women faced in establishing themselves as serious artists in the early 1960s. The piece starts in 1962, just after the apparent suicide of Chicago's first husband, Jerry.*

After Jerry's death, I worked in my studio constantly, trying to make images out of my feelings. I did drawings that contained shapes tumbling down the page, like Jerry's body falling through the air and down the cliff. I made images of death and resurrection and frozen contact; shapes trying to touch, forever held in the agony of separation. I wasn't always conscious of the meaning of these images, but in the process of struggling to come to terms with my circumstances, I made myself into the artist I was always determined to be. It was in the year and a half after Jerry's death that I learned what it meant to make art seriously. I also began to understand what difficulties I was going to face as an artist because I was a woman.

When I was an undergraduate, I had noticed that most of the serious students were men, and because I wanted to be taken seriously, I sought the friendship of these men. They often told me that I was "different" from other women. I felt a warm glow of pride in my "specialness" and enjoyed the status that I had as the result of being the only woman they took seriously. I can remember the men at school putting other women down, calling them "chicks" and "cunts." Occasionally, I joined in, feeling a little guilty, but wanting to be "in" with them. I didn't understand at the time why other women weren't interested in the things I was, and I slowly and unknowingly began to absorb the culture's contempt for women, rationalizing my own femaleness, as the men did, by the fact that I was somehow "different."

I had had women teachers before I went to college, but at the university, the respected

Excerpt from *Through the Flower: My Struggle as a Woman Artist,* Garden City, N.Y.: Doubleday, 1975, pp. 27–43. © 1975 by Judy Chicago.

members of the studio faculty were all male. There were two older women teaching in the painting department; however, they were discounted by the male teachers and students. I can remember talking to one of the women and discovering that she was a fascinating person. She had lived a very independent life, had studied with John Dewey and traveled widely. The other female instructor had a collection of women's art that everyone laughed about and that I never made an effort to see. It makes me feel sad to know that I did not pursue relationships with these women because of male peer pressure. But the men didn't respect them, so how could I?

By the time that I entered graduate school, I was becoming more conscious of my situation as a female student. Continuing hostile comments from men and the absence of other serious women combined to make me conclude that some men didn't seem to like women who had aspirations as artists. I remember discussing teaching assistantships with my sculpture teacher, commenting that I was afraid that my sex would disqualify me, having heard that the department didn't give teaching assistantships to women. He assured me that, although there was discrimination in the painting department, he did not practice it, and he was sure that I could get an assistantship in sculpture (an unusual event in 1962). As I remember this period of my life, I realize that there was a knowing and a not-knowing going on within me simultaneously. I was coming to recognize that there was a serious gap between the way I saw myself and the way I was seen by the world. At the same time, I tried to deny the significance of that gap, because I did not want to feel how alienated I really was as a woman who took herself seriously. I was having enough trouble, first coping with the struggle to recover from my father's death, and then, after Jerry died, trying to put my life back together.

Fortunately, I had a tendency to pursue my own objectives regardless of the messages I received. This came partly from my irrepressible confidence that whatever I did was "terrific," partly from my drive and determination, and partly as a result of my life experience with my father. I had learned early that the world's perceptions of a person are not necessarily true, so I tended to discount comments and attitudes that conflicted with my own sense of what was right. My self-confidence, combined with the pressure of my personal problems, tended to make me somewhat oblivious to the social pressures in high school and college that came down on the women of my generation.

Several years after I left college, a school friend told me that she and most of the other young women we knew always felt that the discussions that took place in academic classes were intended to be between male faculty and male students. I had always noticed that most of the other female students were quiet in class, but I had no idea why. I know I felt annoyed that other women didn't take an active role in my classes, but I attributed it to the fact that I was "different" and acted as I wished. As we talked, I remembered that, often, when I raised my hand to speak, I wasn't called on right away, but I just figured that the instructor didn't see my hand. So I kept on waving it around until he called on me. It suddenly dawned upon me, in the context of that conversation, that I had simply refused to "read the signs" that pervaded the college atmosphere, signs that told women to be "good girls" and to accept the inevitable second-class status of our sex. Since I never understood this message, I continued to behave in terms of my own self-expectations and according to the standards of equality I had absorbed from my family.

Nonetheless, I couldn't entirely escape the realization that my ambition, aspiration, and dedication was somewhat unusual in women of my generation. But because I always demanded and got a place for myself in my classes, in my relationships, and in my work, I was able to separate myself from that social conditioning that prompted other women to relinquish their goals. I had what seemed at the time to be good relationships with some of the male students, but even those ultimately forced me into greater consciousness of my situation as a developing woman artist. One day in 1963, I visited my friend Lloyd Hamrol's studio. We had been close since I was a freshwoman and he a junior in college. We were always drawn together by our mutual interest in art and by some sense of identification with each other. I don't think the issue of my sex ever came up while we were in school together. He accepted me and my level of ambition, which was very much like his own. We used to joke about being Braque and Picasso. We had dated occasionally and Lloyd always wanted to have a serious relationship. But I tended to see him as my "soul mate," which, somehow, in my eyes, precluded the possibility of any romance. Lloyd continued to visit me when I was married to Jerry and stood by me throughout the period surrounding Jerry's death. After Jerry and I had married, Lloyd had become involved with another woman, whom he married. But his marriage was short-lived.

Lloyd and I had not seen each other for a while because he was working on his Master's show. When I went to his studio, I was shocked. He had changed his way of working and had built a series of large sculptures with techniques that I didn't even realize he knew. They were made of plywood and were entirely different from anything he had done before. When I looked at his work, I felt as if a large gulf had opened up between me and my "soul mate." All those years at school together—drawing, taking classes, sharing ideas. Now, he had begun to work in a way that I knew nothing about. And what differentiated us was sex-role conditioning. He, a male, had grown up learning to put things together, use tools, processes, and techniques that were completely outside my cultural orientation as a woman. When he showed the work in a gallery, people

continually commented on his good craftsmanship. I didn't even understand why it was the least bit important how one's "craft" was. In fact, someone at school had told Lloyd that he liked the "deliberately uncraftsmanlike approach" in my work, and I had laughed. Later, when Lloyd and I shared a studio, I never could relate to the idea of building something "right," with which he was always concerned. As long as the piece held together, I couldn't see what difference it made if it was "right" or not. The whole idea of artmaking as an involvement with materials, process, forms, or "craft" was entirely foreign to me. When, in sculpture class, the teacher had given lectures on long, elaborate, technical processes, I had barely been able to contain my boredom. My male friends, although as bored as I was, took voluminous notes—preparations, I later discovered, for the time when they would get jobs teaching sculpture and setting up sculpture shops. No one had ever even suggested to me that I would have to "make a living," so I was not involved with "preparing" myself for a job. (I suppose I just assumed that "somehow I would get along.") Besides, there were certainly no women who ran sculpture departments, at least none that I knew of, so it seemed clear that the lectures had no value at all for me.

I was visiting the galleries often by then, and I could see that many people in the art scene were more concerned with how something was made than with what it meant. Lloyd's orientation seemed more consistent with the attitudes of the art scene than mine. It was very confusing to me that something could be considered "good" just because it was well made, independent of its meaning. Yet, in the world of art galleries, museums, and art magazines, there seemed to be a set of standards by which art was measured that was very different from anything I had ever known, standards that had to do not only with craft and process, but with "newness," "issues," and the "formal properties of the work," whatever that meant. Since I wanted to do "important" work, I felt obliged to internalize these new and foreign standards.

I began to realize that in order to be taken seriously as an artist, I would have to develop some knowledge of craft, process, and technique. I felt extremely uncomfortable with the tools and machines of sculpture, my cultural orientation as a woman combining with my upbringing, which stressed the Jewish intellectual's disdain for physical work. But, as I was determined to be taken seriously, I forced myself to learn how to use tools that I had never seen before, much less used. I didn't want to admit that I didn't know the first thing about the mechanical world, because I knew that my "status" in the art department depended upon the fact that I was "different" from other women, who were "weak" or "dumb." I couldn't exhibit either of those traits or I would be just "another cunt." So I pretended to know what I was doing in the shop. Even when I almost lost a breast in the table saw, I wouldn't ask for help. Instead, I just maintained a "brave front" and bumbled my way through the problems.

In my second year in graduate school, I had a confrontation with my male painting instructors. Although I was working in the sculpture department, I was also painting. The work that I did in the summer after Jerry died had led me to a series of paintings on masonite. As I had begun to learn something about tools by then, I built some large panels to paint on. Lloyd's work and success had influenced me and I had copied the symmetrical, frontal format he was using and stuffed all my falling, tumbling shapes into a position of stasis and formal organization. But I was filling the framework with images that came out of my deepest emotions.

The images in the paintings were biomorphic and referred to phalluses, vaginas, testicles, wombs, hearts, ovaries, and other body parts. The first one, "Bigamy," held a double vagina/heart form, with a broken heart below and a frozen phallus above. The subject matter was the double death of my father and husband, and the phallus was stopped in flight and prevented from uniting with the vaginal form by an inert space. Another of the paintings, "Birth," had an abstract body form composed of reproductive parts that hunched over, as in the birth process. The other paintings were similar in imagery, and although abstract, were very graphic in their expression. There was no emphasis on craft in this work, although by that time, my craftsmanship was adequate. Rather, all of the energy was focused on the images, which grew out of direct feeling and were very overt in their femaleness.

When I showed these paintings to the two painting instructors on my thesis committee, they became irate and began to make irrational objections to the work. I didn't understand why they were upset, and obviously neither did they. They threatened to withdraw their support if I continued to make works like these. One sputtered out something about not being able to show the paintings to his family, and they left, leaving me more confused than ever about standards in art. However, I was getting one message loud and clear. I was putting something into my work that wasn't supposed to be there. Thinking about it, I remembered male instructors making comments about some of my earlier works, drawings and sketches that contained references to female anatomy. "Iccch," one man had said, "that looks like a womb." Perhaps, I thought, they didn't like work that looked too womanly.

Looking at the work of graduate candidates that the faculty liked, and whose work bore some relation to mine, I could see that it tended to be more abstract and less graphic in its description of emotional or sexual subject matter, like the work at the better galleries around town, which seemed to be more about painting itself and less about any internal or personal reality. I made some pieces in which the subject matter was less obvious, and my teachers were pleased. I became intimidated and began to hide my subject matter from them, trying to find a way to still be involved with my own content without making it so graphic that the male teachers would respond negatively.

Halfway through my last year in graduate school, I became involved with a gallery run by a man named Rolf Nelson. He used to take me to the artists' bar, Barney's Beanery, where all the artists who were considered "important" hung out. They were all men, and they spent most of their time talking about cars, motorcycles, women, and their "joints." I knew nothing about cars or motorcycles, couldn't really join in on their discussions about women, and obviously didn't have a "joint." They made a lot of cracks about my being a woman and repeatedly stated that women couldn't be artists. I was determined to convince them, as I had convinced the men at school, that I was serious. In an effort to be accepted, I began to wear boots and smoke cigars. I went to the motorcycle races and tried to act "tough" whenever I saw them.

By the time I left school, I had incorporated many of the attitudes that had been brought to bear on me and my work, both in school and in the art scene. I had abandoned the paintings that my graduate advisers disliked so intensely, leaving them in a garage to be destroyed. I had begun to compensate for my situation as a woman by trying to continually prove that I was as tough as a man, and I had begun to change my work so that it would be accepted by men. I used to have dreams about being on a battlefield with bullets zinging across the field in front of me. I felt that I had to get across, but I didn't know how, having never been trained for warfare. I was terrified. Finally, an anonymous hand reached out and helped me across the field safely. The dream symbolized my need to learn how to survive in the rough and-tumble male world in order to become visible as an artist. I didn't want to run away or hide in a closet, pursuing my work in total privacy and isolation.

After I finished college, I decided to go to auto body school to learn to spray paint, something several of the male artists had discussed doing. I was the only woman among 250 men, all of whom lined up to see me do my final project, which was spraying an old Ford truck with metallic chartreuse paint. I learned quite a bit that was actually beneficial to me as an artist, the most important being an understanding of the role of craft. I had never actually seen artmaking in terms of "making an object," and learning this concept improved my work. The problem was that I had gone there partly to prove something to the male artists. Recently, a male artist told me that he had held me up as an example to his female students, saying: "You see, if you want to be taken seriously, you've really got to dig in there, like Judy." It may be true about digging in there, but it is a shame that I was made to feel that "digging in" could be measured only in terms of "tough talk," spray paint, and motorcycles.

What I have described is a voyage that I was forced to make out of the female world and into the male world where, I was told, "real" art was made. I learned that if I wanted my work to be taken seriously, the work should not reveal its having been made by a woman. One of the best compliments a woman artist could receive then was that "her work looked like it was made by a male." A sculpture like "In My Mother's House," done while I was in graduate school, was smilingly referred to as "one of Judy's cunts" by male artists. (The imagery was obviously feminine and vaginal.) In "Car Hood," which I made at auto body school, the vaginal form, penetrated by a phallic arrow, was mounted on the "masculine" hood of a car, a very clear symbol of my state of mind at this time.

The next few years were confusing to me both in terms of my life as an artist and my relationships with men in the art world. On the one hand, there were men who were very supportive, but not without reservations. One man, an art critic, used to bring me paint and canvas, mention my work occasionally in his articles, and take me out to dinner. But then he would say, in the middle of a discussion, "You know, Judy, you have to decide whether you're going to be a woman or an artist." One time, when I was going to New York, he suggested that I visit a critic friend of his and said that he would mention that I was coming for a visit in his next letter. When I reached the city, I called him and mentioned our mutual friend. He responded warmly and invited me over to his loft. As I climbed the stairs to his upstairs loft, I was very excited at the idea of meeting a man who was so well-known. I imagined him writing an article on my work, introducing me to artists in New York, taking me to galleries and museums. When I walked into his place, I saw a large man, who limped toward me on what appeared to be a wooden leg. He shook my hand and invited me to sit down. We began to talk, and I asked him if he'd like to see slides of my work. He nodded, but as I reached into my purse for a box of slides, I saw him look me up and down, and I suddenly felt very anxious. He barely looked at my slides, and ignoring my attempts to discuss my work with him, began to try to caress me and push me down on the couch. I moved away from him and suggested that we go to dinner. He agreed, but I knew that the evening was ruined and that I had been totally deluded into thinking that this man was interested in anything but a sexual encounter. I never knew whether my friend, the critic, had made him think, in the note that he had written, that he was sending me to see him so that he could get laid or so he could see my work.

After I returned from New York, Lloyd and I became increasingly more involved with each other. After Jerry's death, I had several affairs, all of which depressed me enormously and made me think that I would have to spend the rest of my life alone. The men with whom I became involved either used me sexually, expected me to "take care" of them, were threatened by my work, or, if they could relate to my work, were unable to relate to me personally. Lloyd seemed to be the only man I knew who cared about me, who could relate to my work, and who wanted to be involved with me in other ways as well. At the beginning of 1965, we moved into a loft in Pasadena. At that time, we began a slow struggle to build a loving and equalized relationship, in which we could both be ourselves. For the next few years, my energies were divided between my work in the studio and developing a mature relationship with Lloyd.

It was after I left school that my professional life really began. With it came another dose of discrimination, this time worse than before. It seemed that as my work got better, the resistance to acknowledging that a woman could be an artist grew stronger. After we moved to Pasadena, male artists came to visit and made it clear that they were interested in Lloyd, not me. Gallery and museum people refused to see my work, or if they did, ignored it, or at most, gave me an inappropriate or patronizing response. One museum curator dropped by our studio almost every month. One time, Lloyd asked him if he had seen my new work, and when he said "No," suggested that he go into the studio we shared. My piece, which was quite large, was against one wall. As we walked into the room, the curator went over to a sculpture of Lloyd's that he had seen many times and became completely absorbed in looking at it, asking Lloyd if he had changed the color. Embarrassed, Lloyd said "No" and asked him why he wasn't looking at my piece. When the man still refused to turn around, Lloyd covered his sculpture and demanded that the man look at my work. Finally, he looked at it and mumbled something about it being very beautiful. But by this time I was too hurt to respond, and just fled from the studio crying. Later, when the piece was in a show in New York and much acclaimed, this same man went around bragging about how he visited me all the time. Earlier, he had told me that neither he nor his wife wanted much to do with me because I was too "direct."

During the next five years, I was continually made to feel by men in the art world that there was something "wrong" with me. They'd say things like "Gee, Judy, I like your work, but I just can't cut it that you're a woman." Or male artists who lived in the neighborhood would come over and be astonished that I wouldn't cook for them or cater to their needs. I heard stories from people about how someone said that I was a "bitch" or a "castrater," which hurt me deeply. If I showed work and Lloyd didn't, then I was held responsible for his not being shown, and I was accused of having "cut his balls off." The same thing applied if I did a good work and he did a work that wasn't as good as his last piece. It seemed like I couldn't win. But I wouldn't give up. I knew that what I was confronting came out of the fact that I was a woman, but whenever I tried to talk about that openly, I would be put down with statements like, "Come on, Judy, the suffrage movement is over," and treated as if I were a leper.

All through this period, I worked and I showed my work in galleries and museums. The two people who helped me most were my dealer and Lloyd; they supported me and stood up for me. My earlier naiveté about my situation as a woman artist was giving way to a clear understanding that my career was going to be a long, hard struggle. Fortunately, I knew that I was okay—that the problem was in the culture and not in me, but it still hurt. And I still felt that I had to hide my womanliness and be tough in both my personality and my work. My imagery was becoming increasingly more "neutralized." I began to work with formal rather than symbolic issues. But I was

never interested in "formal issues" as such. Rather, they were something that my content had to be hidden behind in order for my work to be taken seriously. Because of this duplicity, there always appeared to be something "not quite right" about my pieces according to the prevailing aesthetic. It was not that my work was false. It was rather that I was caught in a bind. In order to be myself, I had to express those things that were most real to me, and those included the struggles I was having as a woman, both personally and professionally. At the same time, if I wanted to be taken seriously as an artist, I had to suppress anything in my work that would mark it as having been made by a woman. I was trying to find a way to be myself, still function within the framework of the art community, and be recognized as an artist. This required focusing upon issues that were essentially derived from what men had designated as being important, while still trying to make my own way. However, I certainly do not wish to repudiate the work that I made in this period, because much of it was good work within the confines of what was permissible.

By 1966, I had had a one-woman show, had been in several group and museum shows, and had made a lot of work that could be classified as "minimal," although hidden behind that facade were a whole series of concerns that I did not know how to deal with openly without "blowing my cover," as it were, and revealing that I was, in fact, a woman with a different point of view from my male contemporaries. At that time, I firmly believed that if my difference from men were exposed, I would be rejected, just as I had been in school. It was only by being different from women and like men that I seemed to stand a chance of succeeding as an artist. There was beginning to be a lot of rhetoric in the art world then to the effect that sex had little to do with art, and if you were good, you could make it.

Lloyd had moved into another studio on the same street, leaving me with a five thousand-square-foot studio to myself. He and I had been having a lot of trouble working together, and we decided it would be better if we each had our own place. This need was particularly strong in me because I felt that if people came to my loft and I was alone, they would be less apt to see me in relation to Lloyd. I felt convinced that the only way to make any progress in the art world was to stay unmarried, without children, live in a large loft, and present myself in such a way that I would have to be taken seriously.

In 1967, I was working on a piece for a big sculpture show. The piece was called "Ten Part Cylinder" and was made from the forms in which freeway pillars are cast. I needed a large amount of money to finish the piece, and a collector friend of mine introduced me to a man who, he said, was interested in helping me. This man owned a large company that dealt in plastics, and I thought his involvement in plastics was the reason for his interest in my sculpture, which was to be finished with Fiberglas. We went to lunch, and at lunch I discovered the real reason for his offered help. He felt that women "needed help" from men because they were inferior, and he "liked to help women." He went on to say that if a male artist were to ask him for help, it would be very degrading to the artist, and he would refuse, because "men should take care of themselves."

I can remember my throat constricting and my stomach becoming tight. On the one hand, this man was willing to give me all the money I needed to finish my piece, but it meant that I would have to live with the fact that I accepted help from a person who considered me inferior and was only helping me as a way of proving that inferiority since, by accepting the money, I would be reinforcing his belief. I felt a painful and familiar conflict.

Perhaps today I would tell him off and walk out. Then, because I had accepted the

idea that I had to be "tough enough" to do whatever I had to in order to get my work done, I accepted his offer, feeling terrible about it. Was it any wonder that in my work I was trying to move as far away as possible from revealing that I was a woman? Being a woman and being an artist spelled only one thing: pain.

Although I was struggling to deny anything in my work that could mark me as a woman, some aspects of my femaleness were intrinsically involved with both my day-to-day activity as an artist and in my developing aesthetic. In fighting for my rights in the art world I was acting out of a feminist consciousness before I knew what to call my point of view. When I worked in my studio I came into contact with those areas of my personality structure that had been crippled by female role conditioning. This was particularly true in relation to my expectations of the male art authorities, who I tended to see as a child sees a parent. I kept expecting to gain approval from them, particularly since I had grown up expecting to be loved for whatever I did. It was a continual shock to me to discover that instead of love and approval, I encountered hostility and rejection. Now it is clear to me that to expect men to validate one for challenging male dominance (which is what a woman artist implicitly does, simply by being a woman and an artist) is entirely fantastic. But, at the time, I kept going out into the world with my vulnerability and my need for love and acceptance, only to slowly and painfully realize that I had to change my expectations. Instead of looking to the male world to approve of me and my work, I had to learn to approve of myself and to see myself, not as a child to be approved of by someone "out there," but rather as a creator with something to give to the world. In some strange way, the rejection I faced strengthened me, but only because it forced me to learn to live on my own hook, to use my values, instincts, and judgments as my guides.

Study/Discussion Questions

1. What assumptions did Chicago's male teachers make about their female students?
2. How do these assumptions shape women's development as artists?
3. In what ways was Chicago's art considered "unfeminine," and why?
4. In what ways did the men in her life support her art?
5. In what ways did they hinder her from realizing her artistic vision?

Poetry Is Not a Luxury

Audre Lorde

In the daily round of living, women have been taught to squelch their innermost feelings, to block off their deepest stores of creativity, writes Audre Lorde. Lorde, whose poetry and prose have inspired many thousands of feminists in the past thirty years, says that through poetry, women can reclaim their feelings, their spirits, and their lives. Poetry, she says, is a "revelatory distillation of experience," and as such, it is far too meaningful to be considered a "luxury."

The quality of light by which we scrutinize our lives has direct bearing upon the product which we live, and upon the changes which we hope to bring about through those lives. It is within this light that we form those ideas by which we pursue our magic and make it realized. This is poetry as illumination, for it is through poetry that we give name to those ideas which are—until the poem—nameless and formless, about to be birthed, but already felt. That distillation of experience from which true poetry springs births thought as dream births concept, as feeling births idea, as knowledge births (precedes) understanding.

As we learn to bear the intimacy of scrutiny and to flourish within it, as we learn to use the products of that scrutiny for power within our living, those fears which rule our lives and form our silences begin to lose their control over us.

For each of us as women, there is a dark place within, where hidden and growing our true spirit rises, "beautiful/and tough as chestnut/stanchions against (y)our nightmare of weakness/"[1] and of impotence.

These places of possibility within ourselves are dark because they are ancient and hidden; they have survived and grown strong through that darkness. Within these deep places, each one of us holds an incredible reserve of creativity and power, of unexamined and unrecorded emotion and feeling. The woman's place of power within each of us is neither white nor surface; it is dark, it is ancient, and it is deep.

When we view living in the european mode only as a problem to be solved, we rely solely upon our ideas to make us free, for these were what the white fathers told us were precious.

But as we come more into touch with our own ancient, non-european consciousness of living as a situation to be experienced and interacted with, we learn more and more to cherish our feelings, and to respect those hidden sources of our power from where true knowledge and, therefore, lasting action comes.

At this point in time, I believe that women carry within ourselves the possibility for fusion of these two approaches so necessary for survival, and we come closest to this combination in our poetry. I speak here of poetry as a revelatory distillation of experience, not the sterile word play that, too often, the white fathers distorted the word *poetry* to mean—in order to cover a desperate wish for imagination without insight.

For women, then, poetry is not a luxury. It is a vital necessity of our existence. It forms the quality of the light within which we predicate our hopes and dreams toward survival and change, first made into language, then into idea, then into more tangible action. Poetry is the way we help give name to the nameless so it can be thought. The farthest horizons of our hopes and fears are cobbled by our poems, carved from the rock experiences of our daily lives.

As they become known to and accepted by us, our feelings and the honest exploration of them become sanctuaries and spawning grounds for the most radical and daring of ideas. They become a safe-house for that difference so necessary to change and the conceptualization of any meaningful action. Right now, I could name at least ten ideas I would have found intolerable or incomprehensible and frightening, except as they came after dreams and poems. This is not idle fantasy, but a disciplined attention to the true meaning of "it feels right to me." We can train ourselves to respect our feelings and to transpose them into a language so they can be shared. And where that language does not yet exist, it is our poetry which helps to fashion it. Poetry is not only dream and vision; it is the skeleton architecture of our lives. It lays the foundations for a future of change, a bridge across our fears of what has never been before.

Possibility is neither forever nor instant. It is not easy to sustain belief in its efficacy. We can sometimes work long and hard to establish one beachhead of real resistance to the deaths we are expected to live, only to have that beachhead assaulted or threatened by those canards we have been socialized to fear, or by the withdrawal of those approvals that we have been warned to seek for safety. Women see ourselves diminished or softened by the falsely benign accusations of childishness, of nonuniversality, of changeability, of sensuality. And who asks the question: Am I altering your aura, your ideas, your dreams, or am I merely moving you to temporary and reactive action? And even though the latter is no mean task, it is one that must be seen within the context of a need for true alteration of the very foundations of our lives.

The white fathers told us: I think, therefore I am. The Black mother within each of us—the poet—whispers in our dreams: I feel, therefore I can be free. Poetry coins the language to express and charter this revolutionary demand, the implementation of that freedom.

However, experience has taught us that action in the now is also necessary, always. Our children cannot dream unless they live, they cannot live unless they are nourished, and who else will feed them the real food without which their dreams will be no different from ours? "If you want us to change the world someday, we at least have to live long enough to grow up!" shouts the child.

Sometimes we drug ourselves with dreams of new ideas. The head will save us. The brain alone will set us free. But there are no new ideas still waiting in the wings to save us as women, as human. There are only old and forgotten ones, new combinations, extrapolations and recognitions from within ourselves along with the renewed courage to try them out. And we must constantly encourage ourselves and each other to attempt the heretical actions that our dreams imply, and so many of our old ideas disparage. In the forefront of our move toward change, there is only poetry to hint at possibility made real. Our poems formulate the implications of ourselves, what we feel within and dare make real (or bring action into accordance with), our fears, our hopes, our most cherished terrors.

For within living structures defined by profit, by linear power, by institutional dehumanization, our feelings were not meant to survive. Kept around as unavoidable adjuncts or pleasant pastimes, feelings were expected to kneel to thought as women were expected to kneel to men. But women have survived. As poets. And there are no new pains. We have felt them all already. We have hidden that fact in the same place where we have hidden our power. They surface in our dreams, and it is our dreams that point the way to freedom. Those dreams are made realizable through our poems that give us the strength and courage to see, to feel, to speak, and to dare.

If what we need to dream, to move our spirits most deeply and directly toward and through promise, is discounted as a luxury,

then we give up the core—the fountain—of our power, our womanness; we give up the future of our worlds.

For there are no new ideas. There are only new ways of making them felt—of examining what those ideas feel like being lived on Sunday morning at 7 A.M., after brunch, during wild love, making war, giving birth, mourning our dead—while we suffer the old longings, battle the old warnings and fears of being silent and impotent and alone, while we taste new possibilities and strengths.

NOTE

1. From "Black Mother Woman," first published in *From a Land Where Other People Lie* (Broadside Press, Detroit, 1973), and collected in *Chosen Poems: Old and New* (W. W. Norton and Company, New York, 1982) p. 53.

Study/Discussion Questions

1. What does Audre Lorde mean when she says that poetry is not a luxury?
2. What role does she think that poetry can play in women's lives?
3. Have you read poems (in this book or elsewhere) that allow you to face challenging ideas, as Lorde suggests?
4. Pick a poem (in this book or elsewhere) and think about how writing that poem might have empowered the poet.

IN SICKNESS AND IN HEALTH

Women as Healers

Boston Women's Health Book Collective

The modern women's health movement blossomed in the 1970s in the United States. One of its first projects was to unearth the buried history of women as healers. More than two centuries of a male-dominated medical profession covered that history. As the Boston-area activists who wrote Our Bodies, Ourselves *(first published in 1971) note, the recovery of this portion of women's history of self-help and self-empowerment constitutes a political act intended to incite change in the medical care system. Toward that end, the Boston Women's Health Book Collective offers the following montage of writings by and about women healers.*

The history of women as healers is our history. It tells us where we have come from and casts a revealing light on our present condition. It puts us in touch with a power that has rightfully belonged to women throughout the ages and which we now legitimately reclaim. Without a past, our image is incomplete, and part of our deepest selves is lost.

We are just beginning to discover the true history of women and healing, because history as men have written it ignores women. In particular, midwives and "wise women" (healers) have been primarily poor and working class and as such have not been recognized as significant matter for history. Women's research is uncovering the missing pieces of our story, and so we learn about ourselves from the way churchmen and medical men viewed women. Many of us have internalized these views.

What has happened in the evolution and suppression of women as healers is critical to our understanding of the relationship between medicine and women today. It helps us to see the vast difference between healing and medicine.

Below are a few selections from early writings by and about women healers and from recent historical works by women. *This is our history. These are our historians.*

FOREWORD

Medicine, like war, is an extension of politics. The story of the old wife is not the story of an inferior practice losing ground with the advances of medical science and technology; rather, it is a story which concerns the politics of medicine—a story of control and access.

—*Mary Chamberlain, a modern historian*[1]

THE HEALERS

About 3000 B.C., Near East

The practitioners of healing in the preclassical cultures of the Near and Middle East were also the religious guardians.

In nearly all areas of the world, goddesses were extolled as healers, dispensers of curative herbs, roots, plants and other medical aids, casting the priestesses who attended the shrines into the role of physicians of those who worshipped there.

—*Merlin Stone*

In Sumer, Assyria, Egypt and Greece until about the third millennium the practice of healing was almost exclusively in the hands of priestesses.

—*Mary Chamberlain*[2]

About 1550 B.C., Egypt

The Ebers Papyrus, which contains guidance on midwifery, indicates that knowledge of gynaecology and obstetrics was quite advanced, including not only childbirth and abortion but a range of other problems from breast cancer to prolapse of the womb.

—*Mary Chamberlain*[3]

About 129–201 A.D., Rome

The conversion of the Roman empire to Christianity crystallised attitudes towards women and women healers. The Roman gods were replaced by one all-powerful God whose duties included healing, and who delegated the role of healing to His chosen successors. Thus men were confirmed in their role as official healer and Galenic medicine . . . was confirmed as Christian medicine.

—*Mary Chamberlain*[4]

11th–12th Century, Europe

In fact, the wise woman, or witch, as the authorities labeled her, did possess a host of remedies which had been tested in years of use. *Liber Simplicis Medicinae,* the compendium of natural healing methods written by St. Hildegarde of Bingen (A.D. 1098–1178), gives some idea of the scope of women healers' knowledge in the early middle ages. Her book lists the healing properties of 213 varieties of plants and 55 trees, in addition to dozens of minerals and animal derivatives.

—*Barbara Ehrenreich and Deirdre English,
modern historians*[5]

14th–16th Century, Europe

For all but the very rich healing had traditionally been the prerogative of women. The art of healing was linked to the tasks and spirit of motherhood; it combined wisdom and nurturance, tenderness and skill. All but the most privileged women were expected to be at least literate in the language of herbs and healing techniques; the most learned women traveled widely to share their skills. The women who distinguished themselves as healers were not only midwives caring for other women, but "general practitioners," herbalists, and counselors serving men and women alike.

—*Barbara Ehrenreich and Deirdre English*[6]

15th Century, England

And although women have various maladies and more terrible sicknesses than any man knows as I said, they are ashamed for fear of reproof in times to come and of exposure by discourteous men who love women only for physical pleasure and for evil gratification. And if women are sick, such men despise them and fail to realize how much sickness women have before they bring them into this world. And so, to assist women, I intend to write of how to help their secret maladies so that one woman may aid another in her illness and not divulge her secrets to such discourteous men.

> —*Unknown writer 14th–16th century, England*[7]

14th–16th Century, England

They [Old Wives] were the custodians of communal and community medical knowledge. But this knowledge was free and freely given. With little or no money at stake there was no need to preserve a "closed" profession in terms of entry, training and dissemination of knowledge.

> —*Mary Chamberlain*[8]

SUPPRESSION

THE WITCH TRIALS

14th Century, Europe

An acquaintance of herbs soothing to pain, or healing in their qualities, was then looked upon [by the Church] as having been acquired through diabolical agency. In the fourteenth century the Church decreed that any woman who healed others without having studied, was duly a witch and should suffer death.

> —*A 19th-century feminist historian*[9]

14th Century, Europe

The exclusion of women from the universities, and therefore from access to learning, was justified on the grounds that their intellects were deficient, largely because they were governed by the senses rather than by reason.

> —*Mary Chamberlain*[10]

All witchcraft comes from carnal lust which is in women insatiable. . . . Wherefore for the sake of fulfilling their lusts they consort even with devils. . . . It is sufficiently clear that it is no matter for wonder that there are more women than men found infected with the heresy of witchcraft. . . . And blessed be the Highest who has so far preserved the male sex from so great a crime.

> —*Dominican monks Frs. Sprenger and Kramer, authors of the Inquisition's Malleus Maleficarum*[11]

1484–1700s, Europe and England

And if it is asked how it is possible to distinguish whether an illness is caused by witchcraft or by some natural physical defect, we answer that there are various methods. And the first is by means of the judgment of doctors.

> —*Frs. Sprenger and Kramer*[12]

Moreover. . . it was shown . . . that the greatest injuries to the Faith as regards the heresy of witches are done by midwives: and this is made clearer than daylight itself by the confessions of some who were afterwards burned.

> —*Frs. Sprenger and Kramer*[13]

1608, England

For this must always be remembered, as a conclusion, that by Witches we understand not only those which kill and torment, but all diviners, charmers, jugglers, all Wizards, commonly called wise men and wise women . . . and in the same number we reckon all good Witches, which do no hurt but good, which do not spoil and destroy, but save and deliver. . . . It were a thousand times better for the land if Witches, but especially the blessing Witch, might suffer death.

> —*William Perkins, the leading English Witch Hunter*[14]

15th–16th Century, Europe

The extent of the witch craze is startling: in the late fifteenth and early sixteenth centuries there were thousands upon thousands of executions—usually live burnings at the stake—in Germany, Italy, and other countries. In the mid-sixteenth century the terror spread to France, and finally to England. One writer has estimated the number of executions at an average of six hundred a year for certain German cities—one or two a day, leaving out Sundays. In the Bishopric of Trier, in 1585, two villages were left with only one female inhabitant each. Many writers have estimated the total number killed to have been in the millions. Women made up 85 percent of those executed—old women, young women, and children.

The targets of the witch hunts were, almost exclusively, peasant women, and among them female lay healers were singled out for prosecution.

—*Barbara Ehrenreich and Deirdre English*[15]

15th–16th Century, Europe and England

Because the Medieval Church, with the support of kings, princes and secular authorities, controlled medical education and practice, the Inquisition constitutes, among other things, an early instance of the "professional" repudiating the skills and interfering with the rights of the "nonprofessional" to minister to the poor.

—*Thomas Szasz, a modern psychiatrist and historian*[16]

The witch trials established the male physician on a moral and intellectual plane vastly above the female healer. It placed him on the side of God and the Law, a professional on a par with lawyers and theologians, while it placed her on the side of darkness, evil, and magic. The witch hunts prefigured—with dramatic intensity—the clash between male doctors and female healers in nineteenth-century America.

—*Barbara Ehrenreich and Deirdre English*[17]

THE INTELLECTUAL ARGUMENTS

17th Century, Europe and England

Between the twelfth and seventeenth centuries the theological arguments which held that

the spiritual deficiency of women laid them open to temptation by the Devil were translated into lay terms. By the seventeenth century spiritual deficiency had become intellectual deficiency: women were not merely open to the temptations of sensuality but were motivated by illogicality and irrationality. In both arguments, women's bodies were seen to be the cause of their fundamental weakness.

—*Mary Chamberlain*[18]

The Hippocratic (medical) tradition held that women were governed by the womb and were therefore "naturally" incapable of logic and reason. Moreover . . . women took advantage of the sick!

—*Mary Chamberlain*[19]

1612, England

Such persons are the curse of God and the sinne of man [for they that] persuade the sicke that they have no needs of the Physition, call God a lyar, who expressly saith otherwise! And make themselves wiser than their creator, who hath ordained the Physition for the good of man.

—*John Cotta, an early 17th-century physician*[20]

18th Century, England and Europe

The intellectual mood of the eighteenth century meant a move away from the "arts" of the Middle Ages and towards the cognitive sciences and ideas of progress and enlightenment. With this came the desire to protect those areas of knowledge from those unable to comprehend its complexities. Knowledge itself began to be institutionalized, and became expertise. Knowledge without expertise became skilled deceit. "Cunning" changed its meaning from "knowledge" to "craftiness," and the cunning woman, once an expert, was now a charlatan.

—*Mary Chamberlain*[21]

NORTH AMERICA

18th–19th Century, U.S.A.

The North American female healer, unlike the European witch-healer, was not eliminated by violence. No Grand Inquisitors pursued her; flames did not destroy her stock of herbs or the knowledge of them. The female healer in North America was defeated in a struggle which was, at bottom, economic. Medicine in the nineteenth century was being drawn into the marketplace, becoming—as were needles, or ribbons, or salt already—a thing to be bought and sold. Healing was female when it was a neighborly service based in stable communities, where skills could be passed on for generations and where the healer knew her patients and their families. When the attempt to heal is detached from personal relationships to become a commodity and a source of wealth in itself—then does the business of healing become a male enterprise.

—*Barbara Ehrenreich and Deirdre English*[22]

Late 19th Century, U.S.A.

But the American medical profession would settle for nothing less than the final solution to the midwife question: they would have to be eliminated—outlawed. The medical journals urged their constituencies to join the campaign: "Surely we have enough influence and friends to procure the needed legislation. Make yourselves heard in the land; and the ignorant meddlesome midwife will soon be a thing of the past."

—*Barbara Ehrenreich and Deirdre English*[23]

Late 19th–Early 20th Century, U.S.A.

The obstetrician thought of her as ". . . The typical, old, gin-fingering, guzzling midwife with her pockets full of forcing drops, her mouth full of snuff, her fingers full of dirt and her brains full of arrogance and superstition" (Gerwin, 1906); "filthy and ignorant and not far removed from the jungles of Africa" (Underwood, 1926); "a relic of barbarism" (deLee, 1915); "pestiliferous" (Garrigues, 1898); "vicious" (Titus in Huntington, 1913); "often malicious" (Emmons and Huntington 1911), "[with] the overconfidence of half-knowledge . . . unprincipled and callous of the feelings and welfare of her patients and anxious only for her fee" (Emmons and Huntington, 1912); "[earning] $5,888,888 . . . which should be paid to physicians and nurses for doing the work properly" (Ziegler, 1913); and lastly "un-American" (Mabbott, 1907).

—*Neal Devitt, modern physician and historian*[24]

THE CONSEQUENCES

20th Century, U.S.A. and the Western World

With the elimination of midwifery, all women—not just those of the upper class—fell under the biological hegemony of the medical profession. In the same stroke, women lost their last autonomous role as healers. The only roles left for women in the medical system were as employees, customers, or "material.". . . The male takeover of healing had weakened the communal bonds among women—the networks of skill and information sharing—and had created a model for professional authority in all areas of domestic activity.

—*Barbara Ehrenreich and Deirdre English*[25]

It is perhaps inevitable that childbirth and areas related to women's sexuality should have become those areas most susceptible to aggressive medical techniques. For not only are these areas ones in which the old wife remained a challenge but they are also areas in which women, as women, remain a challenge to men.

—*Mary Chamberlain*[26]

The medical system we have inherited today has certain intrinsic features which were accentuated in the struggle for dominance over what came to be termed "illegitimate" practitioners. These practitioners were largely women and the struggle for dominance was, I believe, fundamentally a gender struggle. To that extent, modern medicine is "masculine" medicine and some of its most dominant features are reactions against healers' practice.

—*Mary Chamberlain*[27]

AN ALTERNATIVE

The Year 2000 and Beyond

This is the vision that is implicit in feminism—a society that is organized around human needs: a society in which healing is not a commodity distributed according to the dictates of profit but is integral to the network of community life . . . in which wisdom about daily life is not hoarded by "experts" or doled out as a commodity but is drawn from the experience of all people and freely shared among them.

—*Barbara Ehrenreich and Deirdre English*[28]

NOTES

1. Mary Chamberlain. *Old Wives' Tales: Their History, Remedies, and Spells.* London: Virago Press, Ltd., 1981, p. 139.
2. Mary Chamberlain. *Old Wives' Tales,* p. 11. (Contains a quote from Merlin Stone, *The Paradise Papers,* London: Virago/Quartet, 1976, p. 19.)
3. Mary Chamberlain. *Old Wives' Tales,* p. 13.
4. Mary Chamberlain. *Old Wives' Tales,* p. 29.
5. Barbara Ehrenreich and Deirdre English. *For Her Own Good: 150 Years of the Experts' Advice to Women.* Garden City, NJ: Anchor Books/Doubleday, 1979, p. 36.
6. Barbara Ehrenreich and Deirdre English. *For Her Own Good,* p. 34.
7. Richard Smith. "A Fifteenth Century 'Our Bodies Ourselves,'" *British Medical Journal,* Vol. 283, No. 28 (November 1981), pp. 1452–1453.
8. Mary Chamberlain. *Old Wives' Tales,* p. 3.
9. Matilda Joslyn Gage. *Woman, Church and State: The Original Exposé of Male Collaboration Against the Female Sex.* Watertown, MA: Persephone Press, 1980 (original ed. 1893), p. 104.
10. Mary Chamberlain. *Old Wives' Tales,* p. 44.
11. Jacob Sprenger and Heinrich Kramer. *Malleus Maleficarum (The Hammer of Witches).* Germany, 1484. Translated by Montague Summers. London: John Rodker, Publisher, 1928, p. 47.
12. Jacob Sprenger and Heinrich Kramer. *Malleus Maleficarum,* p. 87.
13. Jacob Sprenger and Heinrich Kramer. *Malleus Maleficarum,* p. 140.
14. William Perkins. *A Discourse of the Damned Art of Witchcraft.* England, 1608. As quoted in Christina Hole, New York: Collier Books, 1966, p. 130.
15. Barbara Ehrenreich and Deirdre English. *For Her Own Good,* p. 35.
16. Thomas Szasz. *The Manufacture of Madness: A Comparative Study of the Inquisition and the Mental Health Movement.* New York: Harper & Row, 1970; Harper Torchbooks, 1984 (paper), p. 91.
17. Barbara Ehrenreich and Deirdre English. *For Her Own Good,* pp. 31–32.
18. Mary Chamberlain. *Old Wives' Tales,* pp. 31–32.
19. Mary Chamberlain. *Old Wives' Tales,* p. 46.
20. John Cotta. *A Short Discoverie of the Unobserved Dangers of Severall Sorts of Ignorant and Unconsiderable Practisers of Physicken in England.* London, 1612, p. 29.
21. Mary Chamberlain. *Old Wives' Tales,* p. 79.
22. Barbara Ehrenreich and Deirdre English. *For Her Own Good,* p. 41.

23. Ann Sablosky. "The Power of the Forceps: A Study of the Development of Midwifery in the United States." Master's thesis, Graduate School of Social Work and Social Research, Bryn Mawr College, May 1975, p. 17. Quoted in Barbara Ehrenreich and Deirdre English, *For Her Own Good*, pp. 96–97.

24. Neal Devitt. "The Transition from Home to Hospital," in *The Elimination of Midwifery*, *1900–1935*, p. 8. Unpublished manuscript, Information Center, Boston Women's Health Book Collective, Somerville, MA.

25. Barbara Ehrenreich and Deirdre English. *For Her Own Good*, pp. 98, 191.

26. Mary Chamberlain. *Old Wives' Tales*, pp. 153–154.

27. Mary Chamberlain. *Old Wives' Tales*, p. 139.

28. Barbara Ehrenreich and Deirdre English. *For Her Own Good*, p. 324.

Study/Discussion Questions

1. How did women become healers in the ancient world?
2. What medical help have women healers provided for other women since the middle ages?
3. What methods have men used to exclude women from the healing professions?
4. What differences have there been between male doctors and females healers in recent centuries?

The Cancer Journals

Audre Lorde

Poet, activist, and essayist Audre Lorde writes here about the breast cancer that eventually took her life. Devastated by the diagnosis, Lorde regathers her strength, and applies all of her self to the task of being fully human while dealing with both serious illness and the medical system that shapes much of the experience of illness in our day. Lorde's difficult but successful struggle to hold on to her love of her body, her sexuality, and all her life-wisdom reflects the profound impact of feminism on our current understandings of "health." Lorde herself played a pivotal role in shaping that feminism.

March 25, 1978

The idea of knowing, rather than believing, trusting, or even understanding, has always been considered heretical. But I would willingly pay whatever price in pain was needed, to savor the weight of completion; to be utterly filled, not with conviction nor with faith, but with experience—knowledge, direct and different from all other certainties.

October 10, 1978

I want to write about the pain. The pain of waking up in the recovery room which is worsened by that immediate sense of loss. Of going in and out of pain and shots. Of the correct position for my arm to drain. The euphoria of the 2nd day, and how it's been downhill from there.

I want to write of the pain I am feeling right now, of the lukewarm tears that will not stop coming into my eyes—for what? For my lost breast? For the lost me? And which me was that again anyway? For the death I don't know how to postpone? Or how to meet elegantly?

I'm so tired of all this. I want to be the person I used to be, the real me. I feel sometimes that it's all a dream and surely I'm about to wake up now.

November 2, 1978

How do you spend your time, she said. Reading, mostly, I said. I couldn't tell her that mostly I sat staring at blank walls, or getting stoned into my heart, and then, one day when I found I could finally masturbate again, making love to myself for hours at a time. The flame was dim and flickering, but it was a welcome relief to the long coldness.

"Breast Cancer: A Black Lesbian Feminist Perspective," from *The Cancer Journals,* San Francisco, Spinster Ink, 1980. Used with permission of the Charlotte Sheedy Agency.

December 29, 1978

What is there possibly left for us to be afraid of, after we have dealt face to face with death and not embraced it? Once I accept the existence of dying, as a life process, who can ever have power over me again?

This is work I must do alone. For months now I have been wanting to write a piece of meaning words on cancer as it affects my life and my consciousness as a woman, a black lesbian feminist mother lover poet all I am. But even more, or the same, I want to illuminate the implications of breast cancer for me, and the threats to self-revelation that are so quickly aligned against any woman who seeks to explore those questions, those answers. Even in the face of our own deaths and dignity, we are not to be allowed to define our needs nor our feelings nor our lives.

I could not even write about the outside threats to my vision and action because the inside pieces were too frightening.

This reluctance is a reluctance to deal with myself, with my own experiences and the feelings buried in them, and the conclusions to be drawn from them. It is also, of course, a reluctance to living or re-living, giving life or new life to that pain. The pain of separation from my breast was at least as sharp as the pain of separating from my mother. But I made it once before, so I know I can make it again.

Trying to even set this all down step by step is a process of focusing in from the periphery towards the center.

A year ago I was told I had an 80% chance of having breast cancer. That time, the biopsy was negative. But in that interim of three weeks between being told that I might have cancer and finding out it was not so, I met for the first time the essential questions of my own mortality. I was going to die, and it might be a lot sooner than I had ever conceived of. That knowledge did not disappear with the diagnosis of a benign tumor. If not now, I told my lover, then someday. None of us have 300 years. The terror that I conquered in those three weeks left me with a determination and freedom to speak as I needed, and to enjoy and live my life as I needed to for my own meaning.

During the next summer, the summer of 1978, I wrote in my journal:

> Whatever the message is, may I survive the delivery of it. Is letting go a process or a price? What am I paying for, not seeing sooner? Learning at the edge? Letting go of something precious but no longer needed?

So this fall I met cancer, as it were, from a considered position, but it still knocked me for a hell of a loop, having to deal with the pain and the fear and the death I thought I had come to terms with once before. I did not recognize then how many faces those terms had, nor how many forces were aligned within our daily structures against them, nor how often I would have to redefine the terms because other experiences kept presenting themselves. The acceptance of death as a fact, rather than the desire to die, can empower my energies with a forcefulness and vigor not always possible when one eye is out unconsciously for eternity.

Last month, three months after surgery, I wrote in my journal:

I seem to move so much more slowly now these days. It is as if I cannot do the simplest thing, as if nothing at all is done without a decision, and every decision is so crucial. Yet I feel strong and able in general, and only sometimes do I touch that battered place where I am totally inadequate to any thing I most wish to accomplish. To put it another way, I feel always tender in the wrong places.

In September 1978, I went into the hospital for a breast biopsy for the second time. It all happened much faster this time than the year before. There was none of the deep dread of the previous biopsy, but at the same time there was none of the excitement of a brand new experience. I said to my surgeon the night before—"I'm a lot more scared this time, but I'm handling it better." On the surface, at least, we all expected it to be a repeat. My earlier response upon feeling this lump had been—"I've been through this once before. What do we do for encore?"

Well, what we did for encore was the real thing.

I woke up in the recovery room after the biopsy colder than I can remember ever having been in my life. I was hurting and horrified. I knew it was malignant. How, I didn't know, but I suspect I had absorbed that fact from the operating room while I still was out. Being "out" really means only that you can't answer back or protect yourself from what you are absorbing through your ears and other senses. But when I raised my hand in the recovery room and touched both bandaged breasts, I knew there was a malignancy in one, and the other had been biopsied also. It was only for affirmation. I would have given anything to have been warmer right then. The gong in my brain of "malignant," "malignant," and the icy sensations of that frigid room, cut through the remnants of anesthesia like a fire hose trained on my brain. All I could focus upon was getting out of that room and getting warm. I yelled and screamed and complained about the cold and begged for extra blankets, but none came. The nurses were very put out by my ruckus and sent me back to the floor early.

My doctor had said he would biopsy both breasts if one was malignant. I couldn't believe this hospital couldn't shut off the air-conditioning or give me more blankets. The Amazon girls were only 15, I thought, how did they handle it?

Frances was there by the door of my room like a great sunflower. I surfaced from anesthesia again as she took my hand in her deliciously warm ones, her dear face bent over mine. "It is malignant, isn't it, Frances, it is malignant," I said. She squeezed my hand and I saw tears in her eyes. "Yes, my love, it is," she said, and the anesthesia washed out of me again before the sharp edge of fact. "Baby, I'm so cold, so cold," I said. The night before I had said to her, crying, before she left, "The real victory will be my waking up out of the anesthetic."

The decisions seemed much easier. The whole rest of that day seemed a trip back and forth through the small pain in both breasts and my acute awareness of the fact of death in the right one. This was mixed with the melting and chewing over of the realities, between Frances and me. Our comforting each other—"We'll make it through this together"—and the cold, the terrible cold of that first hour. And between us both, our joint tears, our rich loving. I swam in and out of sleep, mostly out.

Our friends came and were there, loving and helpful and there, brought coats to pile upon my bed and then a comforter and blankets because the hospital had no spare blankets, they said, and I was so desperately chilled from the cold recovery room.

I remember their faces as we shared the knowledge and the promise of shared strength in the trial days to come. In some way it was as if each of the people I love most dearly came one by one to my bedside where we made a silent pledge of strength and sisterhood no less sacred than if it had been pledged in blood rather than love.

Off and on I kept thinking. I have cancer. I'm a black lesbian feminist poet, how am I going to do this now? Where are the models for what I'm supposed to be in this situation? But there were none. This is it, Audre. You're on your own.

In the next two days, I came to realize as I agonized over my choices and what to do, that I had made my decision to have surgery if it were needed even before the biopsy had been done. Yet I had wanted a two-stage operation anyway, separating the biopsy from the mastectomy. I wanted time to re-examine my decision, to search really for some other alternative that would give me good reasons to change my mind. But there were none to satisfy me.

I wanted to make the decision again, and I did, knowing the other possibilities, and reading avidly and exhaustively through the books I ordered through Frances and Helen and my friends. These books now piled up everywhere in that wretched little room, making it at least a little bit like home.

Even before the biopsy, from the time I was admitted into the hospital Monday afternoon, the network of woman support had been begun by our friends. Blanche and Clare arrived from Southampton just in time before visiting hours were over bearing a gorgeous French rum and mocha cake with a marzipan banner that said "we love you, audre," outrageously rich and sinfully delicious. When the findings were malignant on Tuesday, this network swung into high gear. To this day, I don't know what Frances and I and the children would have done without it.

From the time I woke up to the slow growing warmth of Adrienne's and Bernice's and Deanna's and Michelle's and Frances' coats on the bed, I felt Beth Israel Hospital wrapped in a web of woman love and strong wishes of faith and hope for the whole time I was there, and it made self-healing more possible, knowing I was not alone. Throughout the hospitalization and for some time after, it seemed that no problem was too small or too large to be shared and handled.

My daughter Beth cried in the waiting room after I told her I was going to have a mastectomy. She said she was sentimentally attached to my breasts. Adrienne comforted her, somehow making Beth understand that hard as this was, it was different for me from if I had been her age, and that our experiences were different.

Adrienne offered to rise early to park the car for Frances so she could be with me before the operation. Blanche and Clare took the children shopping for school clothes, and helped give them a chance to cut up and laugh in the midst of all this grimness. My sister Helen made chicken soup with homemade dumplings. Bernice gathered material and names and addresses and testimonials for alternative treatments for breast cancer. And through those three days between the biopsy and the mastectomy, good wishes came pouring in by mail and telephone and the door and the psychic ether.

To this day, sometimes I feel like a corporate effort, the love and care and concern of so many women having been invested in me with such open-heartedness. My fears were the fears of us all.

And always, there was Frances, glowing with a steady warm light close by to the island within which I had to struggle alone.

I considered the alternatives of the straight medical profession, surgery, radiation, and chemotherapy. I considered the holistic health approaches of diet, vitamin therapy, experimental immunotherapeutics, west german pancreatic enzymes, and others. The decision whether or not to have a mastectomy ultimately was going to have to be my own. I had always been firm on that point and had chosen a surgeon with that in mind. With the various kinds of information I had gathered together before I went into the hospital, and the additional information acquired in the hectic three days after biopsy, now more than ever before I had to examine carefully the pros and cons of every possibility, while being constantly and acutely aware that so much was still not known.

And all the time as a background of pain and terror and disbelief, a thin high voice was screaming that none of this was true, it was all a bad dream that would go away if I became totally inert. Another part of me flew like a big bird to the ceiling of whatever place I was in, observing my actions and providing a running commentary, complete with suggestions of factors forgotten, new possibilities of movement, and ribald remarks. I felt as if I was always listening to a concert of voices from inside myself, all with something slightly different to say, all of which were quite insistent and none of which would let me rest.

They very effectively blotted out the other thin high voice that counseled sleep, but I still knew it was there, and sometimes in the middle of the night when I couldn't sleep, I wondered if perhaps it was not the voice of wisdom rather than despair.

I now realize that I was in a merciful state akin to shock in those days. In a sense it was my voices—those myriad pieces of myself and my background and experience and definitions of myself I had fought so long and hard to nourish and maintain—which were guiding me on automatic, so to speak. But it did not feel so at the time. I felt sometimes utterly calm cool and collected, as if this whole affair was an intellectual problem to be considered and solved: should I have a mastectomy or not? What was the wisest approach to take having a diagnosis of breast cancer and a history of cystic mastitis? Other times, I felt almost overwhelmed by pain and fury, and the inadequacies of my tools to make any meaningful decision, and yet I had to.

I was helped by the fact that one strong voice kept insisting that I had in truth made this decision already, all I had to do was remember the pieces and put them together. That used to annoy me sometimes, the feeling that I had less to decide than to remember.

I knew the horror that I had lived with for a year since my last biopsy had now become a reality, and in a sense that reality, however difficult, was easier to deal with than fear. But it was still very hard for me not only to face the idea of my own fragile mortality, but to anticipate more physical pain and the loss of such a cherished part of me as my breast. And all these things were operating at the same time I was having to make a decision as to what I should do. Luckily, I had been in training for a long time.

I listened to my voices, considered the alternatives, chewed over the material that concerned women brought to me. It seems like an eternity went by between my returning from the biopsy and my making a decision, but actually it was only a day and a half.

On Wednesday afternoon I told Frances that I had decided to have surgery, and tears came to her eyes. Later she told me that she had been terrified that I might refuse surgery, opting instead for an alternative treatment, and she felt that she was prepared to go along with whatever I would decide, but she also felt surgery was the wisest choice.

A large factor in this decision was the undeniable fact that any surgical intervention in a cystic area can possibly activate cancer cells that might otherwise remain dormant. I had dealt with that knowledge a year ago when deciding whether or not to have a biopsy, and with the probabilities of a malignancy being as high as they were then, I felt then I had no choice but to decide as I did. Now, I had to consider again whether surgery might start another disease process. I deluged my surgeon with endless questions which he answered in good faith, those that he could. I weighed my options. There were malignant cells in my right breast encased in a fatty cyst, and if I did not do something about that I would die of cancer in fairly short order. Whatever I did might or might not reverse that process, and I would not know with any certainty for a very long time.

When it came right down to deciding, as I told Frances later, I felt inside myself for what I really felt and wanted, and that was to live and to love and to do my work, as hard as I could and for as long as I could. So I simply chose the course that I felt most likely to achieve my desire, knowing that I would have paid more than even my beloved breast out of my body to preserve that self that was not merely physically defined, and count it well spent.

Having made that decision, I felt comfortable with it and able to move on. I could not choose the option of radiation and chemotherapy because I felt strongly that everything I had read about them suggested that they were in and of themselves carcinogenic. The experimental therapies without surgery were interesting possibilities, but still unproven. Surgery, a modified radical mastectomy, while traumatic and painful would arrest any process by removal. It was not in and of itself harmful at this point, since whatever process might have been started by surgery had already been begun by the biopsy. I knew that there might come a time when it was clear that surgery had been unnecessary because of the efficacy of alternate therapies. I might be losing my breast in vain. But nothing else was as sure, and it was a price I was willing to pay for life, and I felt I had chosen the wisest course for me. I think now what was most important was not what I chose to do so much as that I was conscious of being able to choose, and having chosen, was empowered from having made a decision, done a strike for myself, moved.

Throughout the three days between the mastectomy and the biopsy I felt positively possessed by a rage to live that became an absolute determination to do whatever was necessary to accomplish that living, and I remember wondering if I was strong enough to sustain

that determination after I left the hospital. If I left the hospital. For all the deciding and great moral decisions going on, I was shit-scared about another bout with anesthesia. Familiarity with the procedures had not lessened my terror.

I was also afraid that I was not really in control, that it might already be too late to halt the spread of cancer, that there was simply too much to do that I might not get done, that the pain would be just too great. Too great for what, I did not know. I was afraid. That I would not survive another anesthesia, that the payment of my breast would not be enough; for what? Again, I did not know. I think perhaps I was afraid to continue being myself.

The year before, as I waited almost four weeks for my first biopsy, I had grown angry at my right breast because I felt as if it had in some unexpected way betrayed me, as if it had become already separate from me and had turned against me by creating this tumor which might be malignant. My beloved breast had suddenly departed from the rules we had agreed upon to function by all these years.

But on the day before my mastectomy I wrote in my journal:

September 21, 1978
The anger that I felt for my right breast last year has faded, and I'm glad because I have had this extra year. My breasts have always been so very precious to me since I accepted having them it would have been a shame not to have enjoyed the last year of one of them. And I think I am prepared to lose it now in a way I was not quite ready to last November, because now I really see it as a choice between my breast and my life, and in that view there cannot be any question.

Somehow I always knew this would be the final outcome, for it never did seem like a finished business for me. This year between was like a hiatus, an interregnum in a battle within which I could so easily be a casualty, since I certainly was a warrior. And in that brief time the sun shone and the birds sang and I wrote important words and have loved richly and been loved in return. And if a lifetime of furies is the cause of this death in my right breast there is still nothing I've never been able to accept before that I would accept now in order to keep my breast. It was a 12 month reprieve in which I could come to accept the emotional fact/truths I came to see first in those horrendous weeks last year before the biopsy. If I do what I need to do because I want to do it, it will matter less when death comes, because it will have been an ally that spurred me on.

I was relieved when the first tumor was benign, but I said to Frances at the time that the true horror would be if they said it was benign and it wasn't. I think my body knew there was a malignancy there somewhere, and that it would have to be dealt with eventually. Well, I'm dealing with it as best I can. I wish I didn't have to, and I don't even know if I'm doing it right, but I sure am glad that I had this extra year to learn to love me in a different way.

I'm going to have the mastectomy, knowing there are alternatives, some of which sound very possible in the sense of right thinking, but none of which satisfy me enough. . . . Since it is my life that I am gambling with, and my life is worth even more than the sensual delights of my breast, I certainly can't take that chance.

7:30 p.m. And yet if I cried for a hundred years I couldn't possibly express the sorrow I feel right now, the sadness and the loss. How did the Amazons* of Dahomey feel? They were only little girls. But they did this willingly, for something they believed in. I suppose I am too but I can't feel that now.

Eudora Garrett was not the first woman with whom I had shared body warmth and wildness, but she was the first woman who to-tally engaged me in our loving. I remember the hesitation and tenderness I felt as I touched the deeply scarred hollow under her right shoulder and across her chest, the night she finally shared the last pain of her mastectomy with me in the clear heavy heat of our Mexican spring. I was 19 and she was 47. Now I am 44 and she is dead.

Eudora came to me in my sleep that night before surgery in that tiny cold hospital room so different from her bright hot dishevelled bedroom in Cuernavaca, with her lanky snapdragon self and her gap-toothed lopsided smile, and we held hands for a while.

The next morning before Frances came I wrote in my journal:

September 22, 1978
Today is the day in the grim rainy morning and all I can do now is weep. Eudora, what did I give you in those Mexican days so long ago? Did you know how I loved you? You never talked of your dying, only of your work.

Then through the dope of tranquilizers and grass I remember Frances' hand on mine, and the last sight of her dear face like a great sunflower in the sky. There is the horror of those flashing lights passing over my face, and the clanging of disemboweled noises that have no context nor relationship to me except they assault me. There is the dispatch with which I have ceased being a person who is myself and become a thing upon a Guerney cart to be delivered up to Moloch, a dark living sacrifice in the white place.

I remember screaming and cursing with pain in the recovery room, and I remember a disgusted nurse giving me a shot. I remember a voice telling me to be quiet because there were sick people here, and my saying, well, I have a right, because I'm sick too. Until 5:00 A.M. the next morning, waking was brief seas of local-

---

*It is said that the Amazon warriors of Dahomey have their right breasts cut off to make themselves more effective archers.

ized and intense pain between shots and sleep. At 5:00 a nurse rubbed my back again, helped me get up and go to the bathroom because I couldn't use the bedpan, and then helped me into a chair. She made me a cup of tea and some fruit juice because I was parched. The pain had subsided a good deal.

I could not move my right arm nor my shoulder, both of which were numb, and wrapped around my chest was a wide Ace bandage under which on my left side the mound of my left breast arose, and from which on the right side protruded the ends of white surgical bandages. From under the Ace bandage on my right side, two plastic tubes emerged, running down into a small disc-shaped plastic bottle called a hemovac which drained the surgical area. I was alive, and it was a very beautiful morning. I drank my tea slowly, and then went back to bed.

I woke up again at about 7:30 to smell Frances outside my door. I couldn't see her because the sides of my bed were still up, but I sat up as best I could one-armed, and peeped around the corner and there she was, the person I needed and wanted most to see, and our smiles met each other's and bounced around the room and out into the corridor where they warmed up the whole third floor.

The next day the sun shone brilliantly, and for ten days steadily thereafter. The autumn equinox came—the middle—the sun now equidistant, then going away. It was one of those rare and totally gorgeous blue New York City autumns.

That next day after the operation was an incredible high. I now think of it as the euphoria of the second day. The pain was minimal. I was alive. The sun was shining. I remember feeling a little simple but rather relieved it was all over, or so I thought. I stuck a flower in my hair and thought "This is not as bad as I was afraid of."

During the first two days after surgery, I shared thanksgiving with beautiful and beloved women and slept. I remember the children coming to visit me and Beth joking, but how both of their faces were light with relief to see me so well. I felt as if there was grey smoke in my head and something I wasn't dealing with, but I wasn't sure what. Once I put a flower in my hair and walked through the halls looking for Frances who had gone into the waiting room with Michelle and Adrienne to let me rest.

From time to time I would put my hand upon the flattish mound of bandages on the right side of my chest and say to myself my right breast is gone, and I would shed a few tears if I was alone. But I had no real emotional contact yet with the reality of the loss; it was as if I had been emotionally anesthetized also, or as if the only feelings I could reach were physical ones, and the scar was not only hidden under bandages but as yet was feeling little pain. When I looked at myself in the mirror even, the difference was not at all striking, because of the bulkiness of the bandages.

And my friends, who flooded me with love and concern and appreciation and relief gave me so much energy that for those first 48 hours I really felt as if I was done with death and pain, and even loss, and that I had for some unknown reason been very very lucky. I was filled with a surety that everything was going to be all right, in just those indeterminate phrases. But it was downhill from there.

On the morning of the third day, the pain returned home bringing all of its kinfolk. Not that any single one of them was overwhelming, but just that all in concert, or even in small repertory groups, they were excruciating. There were constant ones and intermittent ones. There were short sharp and long dull and various combinations of the same ones. The muscles in my back and right shoulder began to screech as if they'd been pulled apart and now were coming back to life slowly and against their will. My chest wall was beginning to ache and burn and stab by turns. My breast which was no longer there would hurt as if it were being squeezed in a vise. That was perhaps the worst pain of all, because it would come with a full complement of horror that I was to be forever reminded of my loss by suffering in a part of me which was no longer there. I suddenly seemed to get weaker rather than stronger. The euphoria and numbing effects of the anesthesia were beginning to subside.

My brain felt like grey mush—I hadn't had to think much for the past two days. Just about the time that I started to feel the true quality of the uphill climb before me—of adjustment to a new body, a new time span, a possible early death—the pains hit. The pain grew steadily worse and I grew more and more furious because nobody had ever talked about the physical pain. I had thought the emotional and psychological pain would be the worst, but it was the physical pain that seemed to be doing me in, or so I wrote at that time.

Feeling was returning to the traumatized area at the same time as I was gradually coming out of physical and emotional shock. My voices, those assorted pieces of myself that guided me between the operations were settling back into their melded quieter places, and a more and more conscious part of me was struggling for ascendancy, and not at all liking what she was finding/feeling.

In a way, therefore, the physical pain was power, for it kept that conscious part of me away from the full flavour of my fear and loss, consuming me, or rather wearing me down for the next two weeks. That two week period of time seems like an age to me now, because so many different changes passed through me. Actually the course of my psychic and physical convalescence moved quite quickly.

I do not know why. I do know that there was a tremendous amount of love and support flowing into me from the women around me, and it felt like being bathed in a continuous tide of positive energies, even when sometimes I wanted a bit of negative silence to complement the pain inside of me.

But support will always have a special and vividly erotic set of image/meanings for me now, one of which is floating upon a sea within a ring of women like warm bubbles keeping me afloat upon the surface of that sea. I can feel the texture of inviting water just beneath their eyes, and do not fear it. It is the sweet smell of their breath and laughter and voices calling my name that gives me volition, helps me remember I want to turn away from looking down. These images flow quickly, the tangible floods of energy rolling off these women toward me that I converted into power to heal myself.

There is so much false spirituality around us these days, calling itself goddess-worship or "the way." It is false because too cheaply bought and little understood, but most of all because it does not lend, but rather saps, that energy we need to do our work. So when an example of the real power of healing love comes along such as this one, it is difficult to use the same words to talk about it because so many of our best and most erotic words have been so cheapened.

Perhaps I can say this all more simply; I say the love of women healed me.

It was not only women closest to me, although they were the backbone. There was Frances. Then there were those women whom I love passionately, and my other friends, and my acquaintances, and then even women whom I did not know.

In addition to the woman energy outside of me, I know that there must have been an answering energy within myself that allowed me to connect to the power flowing. One never really forgets the primary lessons of survival, if one continues to survive. If it hadn't been for a lot of women in my lifetime I'd have been long dead. And some of them were women I didn't even like! (A nun; the principal of my high school; a boss.)

I had felt so utterly stripped at other times within my life for very different reasons, and survived, so much more alone than I was now. I knew if I lived I could live well. I knew that if the life spark kept burning there would be fuel; if I could want to live I would always find a way, and a way that was best for me. The longer I survive the more examples of that I have, but it is essentially the same truth I knew the summer after my friend Genevieve died. We were sixteen.

To describe the complexities of interaction between the love within and the love without is a lifetime vocation.

Growing up Fat Black Female and almost blind in america requires so much surviving that you have to learn from it or die. Gennie, rest in peace. I carry tattooed upon my heart a list of names of women who did not survive, and there is always a space left for one more, my own. That is to remind me that even survival is only part of the task. The other part is teaching. I had been in training for a long time.

After I came home on the fifth day after surgery, the rest of those two weeks were permeated with physical pain and dreams. I spent the days mostly reading and wandering from room to room, or staring at blank walls, or lying outdoors in the sun staring at the insides of my eyelids. And finally, when at last I could again, masturbating.

Later, as the physical pain receded, it left room for the other. But in my experience, it's not true that first you cry. First you hurt, and then you cry.

For me, there was an important interim period between the actual event and my beginning to come to terms emotionally with what having cancer, and having lost a breast, meant and would mean to my life. The psychic self created a little merciful space for physical cellular healing and the devastating effects of anesthesia on the brain. Throughout that period, I kept feeling that I couldn't think straight, that there was something wrong with my brain I couldn't remember. Part of this was shock, but part of it was anesthesia, as well as conversations I had probably absorbed in the operating room while I was drugged and vulnerable and only able to record, not react. But a friend of mine recently told me that for six months after her mother died, she felt she couldn't think or remember, and I was struck by the similarity of the sensations.

My body and mind had to be allowed to take their own course. In the hospital, I did not need to take the sleeping pills that were always offered. My main worry from day three onward for about ten more was about the developing physical pain. This is a very important fact, because it is within this period of quasi-numbness and almost childlike susceptibility to ideas (I could cry at any time at almost anything outside of myself) that many patterns and networks are started for women after breast surgery that encourage us to deny the realities of our bodies which have just been driven home to us so graphically, and these old and stereotyped patterns of response pressure us to reject the adventure and exploration of our own experiences, difficult and painful as those experiences may be.

On the second day in the hospital I had been crying when the head nurse came around, and she sent in another woman from down the hall who had had a mastectomy a week ago and was about to go home. The woman from down the hall was a smallbodied feisty redhead in a pink robe with a flower in her hair. (I have a permanent and inexplicable weakness for women with flowers in their hair.) She was about my own age, and had grown kids who, she said, wanted her to come home. I knew immediately they must be sons. She patted my hand and gestured at our bandages.

"Don't feel bad," she said, "they weren't that much good anyway." But then she threw open her robe and stuck out her almost bony chest dressed in a gay printed pajama top, saying, "Now which twin has the Toni?" And I had to laugh in spite of myself, because of her energy, and because she had come all the way down the hall just to help make me feel better.

The next day, when I was still not thinking too much, except about why was I hurting more and when could I reasonably expect to go home, a kindly woman from Reach for Recovery came in to see me, with a very upbeat message and a little prepared packet containing a soft sleep-bra and a wad of lambswool pressed into a pale pink breast-shaped pad. She was 56 years old, she told me proudly. She was also a woman of admirable energies who clearly would uphold and defend to the death those structures of a society that had allowed her a little niche to shine in. Her message was, you are just as good as you were before because you can look exactly the same. Lambswool now, then a good prosthesis as soon as possible, and nobody'll ever know the difference. But what she said was, "You'll never know the difference," and she lost me right there, because I knew sure as hell I'd know the difference.

"Look at me," she said, opening her trim powder-blue man-tailored jacket and standing before me in a tight blue sweater, a gold embossed locket of no mean dimension provocatively nestling between her two considerable breasts. "Now can you tell which is which?"

I admitted that I could not. In her tight foundation garment and stiff, up-lifting bra, both breasts looked equally unreal to me. But then I've always been a connoisseur of women's breasts, and never overly fond of stiff uplifts. I looked away, thinking, "I wonder if there are any black lesbian feminists in Reach for Recovery?"

I ached to talk to women about the experience I had just been through, and about what might be to come, and how were they doing it and how had they done it. But I needed to talk with women who shared at least some of my major concerns and beliefs and visions, who shared at least some of my language. And this lady, admirable though she might be, did not.

"And it doesn't really interfere with your love life, either, dear. Are you married?"

"Not anymore," I said. I didn't have the moxie or the desire or the courage maybe to say, "I love women."

"Well, don't you worry. In the 6 years since my operation I married my second husband and buried him, god bless him, and now I have a wonderful friend. There's nothing I did before that I don't still do now. I just make sure I carry an extra form just in case, and I'm just like anybody else. The silicone ones are best, and I can give you the names of the better salons."

I was thinking, "What is it like to be making love to a woman and have only one breast brushing against her?"

I thought, "How will we fit so perfectly together ever again?"

I thought, "I wonder if our love-making had anything to do with it?"

I thought, "What will it be like making love to me? Will she still find my body delicious?"

And for the first time deeply and fleetingly a groundswell of sadness rolled up over me that filled my mouth and eyes almost to drowning. My right breast represented such an area of feeling and pleasure for me, how could I bear never to feel that again?

The lady from Reach for Recovery gave me a book of exercises which were very very helpful to me, and she showed me how to do them. When she held my arm up to assist me, her grip was firm and friendly and her hair smelled a little like sun. I thought what a shame such a gutsy woman wasn't a dyke, but they had gotten to her too early, and her grey hair was dyed blond and heavily teased.

After she left, assuring me that Reach for Recovery was always ready to help, I examined the packet she had left behind.

The bra was the kind I was wearing, a soft front-hooking sleep-bra. By this time, the Ace bandage was off, and I had a simple surgical bandage taped over the incision and the one remaining drain. My left breast was still a little sore from having been biopsied, which is why I was wearing a bra. The lambswool form was the strangest part of the collection. I examined it, in its blush-pink nylon envelope with a slighter, darker apex and shaped like a giant slipper-shell. I shuddered at its grotesque dryness. (What size are you, she'd said. 38D I said. Well I'll leave you a 40C she said.)

I came around my bed and stood in front of the mirror in my room, and stuffed the thing into the wrinkled folds of the right side of my bra where my right breast should have been. It perched on my chest askew, awkwardly inert and lifeless, and having nothing to do with any me I could possibly conceive of. Besides, it was the wrong color, and looked grotesquely pale through the cloth of my bra. Somewhere, up to that moment, I had thought, well perhaps they know something that I don't and maybe they're right, if I put it on maybe I'll feel entirely different. I didn't. I pulled the thing out of my bra, and my thin pajama top settled back against the flattened surface on the right side of the front of me.

I looked at the large gentle curve my left breast made under the pajama top, a curve that seemed even larger now that it stood by itself. I looked strange and uneven and peculiar to myself, but somehow, ever so much more myself, and therefore so much more acceptable, than I looked with that thing stuck inside my clothes. For not even the most skillful prosthesis in the world could undo that reality, or feel the way my breast had felt, and either I would love my body one-breasted now, or remain forever alien to myself.

Then I climbed back into bed and cried myself to sleep, even though it was 2:30 in the afternoon.

On the fourth day, the other drain was removed. I found out that my lymph nodes had shown no sign of the spread of cancer, and my doctor said that I could go home on the following day, since I was healing so rapidly.

I looked down at the surgical area as he changed the dressing, expecting it to look like the ravaged and pitted battlefield of some major catastrophic war. But all I saw was my same soft brown skin, a little tender-looking and puffy from the middle of my chest up into my armpit, where a thin line ran, the edges of which were held closed by black sutures and two metal clamps. The skin looked smooth and tender and untroubled, and there was no feeling on the surface of the area at all. It was otherwise quite unremarkable, except for the absence of that beloved swelling I had come so to love over 44 years, and in its place was the strange flat plain down across which I could now for the first time in my memory view the unaccustomed bulge of my rib-cage, much broader than I had imagined it to be when it had been hidden beneath my large breasts. Looking down now on the right side of me I could see the curve of the side of my stomach across this new and changed landscape.

I thought, "I wonder how long it was before the Dahomean girl Amazons could take their changed landscapes for granted?"

I cried a few times that day, mostly, I thought, about inconsequential things. Once I cried though simply because I hurt deep down inside my chest and couldn't sleep, once because it felt like someone was stepping on my breast that wasn't there with hobnailed boots.

I wanted to write in my journal but couldn't bring myself to. There are so many shades to what passed through me in those days. And I would shrink from committing myself to paper because the light would change before the word was out, the ink was dry.

In playing back the tapes of those last days in the hospital, I found only the voice of a very weakened woman saying with the greatest difficulty and almost unrecognizable:

September 25th, the fourth day. Things come in and out of focus so quickly it's as if a flash goes by; the days are so beautiful now so golden brown and blue; I wanted to be out in it, I wanted to be glad I was alive, I wanted to be glad about all the things I've got to be glad about. But now it hurts. Now it hurts. Things chase themselves around inside my eyes and there are tears I cannot shed and words like cancer, pain, and dying.

Later, I don't want this to be a record of grieving only. I don't want this to be a record only of tears. I want it to be something I can use now or later, something that I can remember, something that I can pass on, something that I can know came out of the kind of strength I have that nothing nothing else can shake for very long or equal.

My work is to inhabit the silences with which I have lived and fill them with myself until they have the sounds of brightest day and the loudest thunder. And then there will be no room left inside of me for what has been except as memory of sweetness enhancing what can and is to be.

I was very anxious to go home. But I found also, and couldn't admit at the time, that the very bland whiteness of the hospital which I railed against and hated so, was also a kind of protection, a welcome insulation within which I could continue to non-feel. It was an erotically blank environment within whose undifferentiated and undemanding and infantalizing walls I could continue to be emotionally vacant—psychic mush—without being required by myself or anyone to be anything else.

Going home to the very people and places that I loved most, at the same time as it was welcome and so desirable, also felt intolerable, like there was an unbearable demand about to be made upon me that I would have to meet. And it was to be made by people whom I loved, and to whom I would have to respond. Now I was going to have to begin feeling, dealing, not only with the results of the amputation, the physical effects of the surgery, but also with examining and making my own, the demands and changes inside of me and my life. They

would alter, if not my timetable of work, at least the relative pieces available within that timetable for whatever I was involved in or wished to accomplish.

For instance, there were different questions about time that I would have to start asking myself. Not, for how long do I stand at the window and watch the dawn coming up over Brooklyn, but rather, how many more new people do I admit so openly into my life? I needed to examine and pursue the implications of that question. It meant plumbing the depths and possibilities of relating with the people already in my life, deepening and exploring them.

The need to look death in the face and not shrink from it, yet not ever to embrace it too easily, was a developmental and healing task for me that was constantly being sidelined by the more practical and immediate demands of hurting too much, and how do I live with myself one-breasted? What posture do I take, literally, with my physical self?

I particularly felt the need—craved the contact, really—of my family, that family which we had made of friends, which for all its problems and permutations was my family, Blanche and Clare and Michelle and Adrienne and Yolanda and Yvonne and Bernice and Deanna and Barbara and Beverly and Millie, and then there were the cousins and surely Demita and Sharon and them, even Linda, and Bonnie and Cessie and Cheryl and Toi with her pretty self and Diane and even my sister Helen. All through that time even the most complicated entanglements between other family members—and there were many not having to do directly with me—all those entanglements and fussings and misunderstandings and stubbornnesses felt like basic life-pursuits, and as such were, no matter how annoying and tiresome, fundamentally supportive of a life force within me. The only answer to death is the heat and confusion of living; the only dependable warmth is the warmth of the blood. I can feel my own beating even now.

In that critical period the family women enhanced that answer. They were macro members in the life dance, seeking an answering rhythm within my sinews, my synapses, my very bones. In the ghost of my right breast, these were the micro members from within. There was an answering rhythm in the ghost of those dreams which would have to go in favor of those which I had some chance of effecting. The others had lain around unused and space-claiming for a long time anyway, and at best needed to be re-aired and re-examined.

For instance, I will never be a doctor. I will never be a deep-sea diver. I may possibly take a doctorate in etymology, but I will never bear any more children. I will never learn ballet, nor become a great actress, although I might learn to ride a bike and travel to the moon. But I will never be a millionaire nor increase my life insurance. I am who the world and I have never seen before.

Castaneda talks of living with death as your guide, that sharp awareness engendered by the full possibility of any given chance and moment. For me, that means being—not ready for death—but able to get ready instantly, and always to balance the "I wants" with the "I haves." I am learning to speak my pieces, to inject into the living world my convictions of what is necessary and what I think is important without concern (of the enervating kind) for whether or not it is understood, tolerated, correct or heard before. Although of course being incorrect is always the hardest, but even that is becoming less important. The world will not stop if I make a mistake.

And for all that, I wish sometimes that I had still the myth of having 100 years in this frame, and this hunger for my sister stilled.

Women who speak with my tongue are lovers; the woman who does not parry yet matches my thrust, who will hear; the woman I hold in my arms, the woman who arms me whole . . .

I have found that people who need but do not want are far more difficult to front than people who want without needing, because the latter will take but sometimes give back, whereas the former simply absorb constantly while always looking away or pushing against and taking at the same time. And that is a wasting of substance through lack of acknowledgement of both our energies, and waste is the worst. I know this because I have done them both.

Coming home from the hospital, it was hard not to feel like a pariah. There were people who avoided me out of their own pain or fear, and others who seemed to expect me to suddenly become someone other than who I have always been, myself, rather than saint or buddha. Pain does not mellow you, nor does it ennoble, in my experience. It was hard not to feel pariah, or sometimes too vulnerable to exist. There were women who were like the aide in the hospital who had flirted so nicely with me until she heard my biopsy was positive. Then it was as if I had gone into purdah; she only came near me under the strictest of regulatory distance.

The status of untouchable is a very unreal and lonely one, although it does keep everyone at arm's length, and protects as it insulates. But you can die of that specialness, of the cold, the isolation. It does not serve living. I began quickly to yearn for the warmth of the fray, to be good as the old even while the slightest touch meanwhile threatened to be unbearable.

The emphasis upon wearing a prosthesis is a way of avoiding having women come to terms with their own pain and loss, and thereby, with their own strength. I was already dressed to go home when the head nurse came into my room to say goodbye. "Why doesn't she have a form on?" she asked Frances, who by this time was acknowledged by all to be my partner.

"She doesn't want to wear it," Frances explained.

"Oh you're just not persistent enough," the head nurse replied, and then turned to me with a let's-have-no-nonsense-now look, and I was simply too tired. It wasn't worth the effort to resist her. I knew I didn't look any better.

At home I wept and wept and wept, finally. And made love to myself, endlessly and repetitively, until it was no longer tentative.

Where were the dykes who had had mastectomies? I wanted to talk to a lesbian, to sit down and start from a common language, no matter how diverse. I wanted to share dyke-insight, so to speak. The call went out. Sonny and Karyn came to the house that evening and the four of us shared our fears and our stories across age and color and place and difference and I will be forever grateful to Sonny and Karyn.

"Take it easy," Sonny said. "Remember you're not really as strong now as you feel." I knew what she meant because I could tell how easily I fell apart whenever I started to believe my own propaganda and overdo anything.

But still she told me about her going to an educational conference three weeks after her surgery, and that she thought now that it probably had been a mistake. But I knew why she had done it and so did she, and we both speechlessly acknowledged that she would probably do it again. It was the urge, the need, to work again, to feel a surge of connection begin with that piece of yourself. To be of use, even symbolically, is a necessity for any new perspective of self, and I thought of that three weeks later, when I knew I needed to go to Houston to give a reading, even though I felt weak and inadequate.

I will also be always grateful to Little Sister. My brother-in-law, Henry, who lives in Seattle and whom I had not seen for seven years, was working in Virginia and had come up to New York to see my mother, passing through Philadelphia where he had grown up to pick up his youngest sister who was called Little Sister, actually Li'l Sister.

Li'l Sister had been quite a hell-raiser in her younger days, but now was an established and matronly black lady of Philadelphia with a college-bound son and rimless glasses. I had never met her before but she knew my mother quite well. When they got to New York my mother told Henry and Li'l Sister that I had had a mastectomy and was home just now from the hospital, so they decided to drop by and see me on their way back to Philadelphia which is only 1 1/2 hours south of Staten Island.

Over the phone my mother said to me, with the slightest air of reproach in her voice, "I didn't know all these years that Li'l Sister had had that same operation!" Li'l Sister had had a mastectomy 10 years ago, and neither her brother nor her in-laws had known any thing about it.

Henry is one of the gentlest men I have ever met, although not the most tactful. "Howya doing, girl?" he said, giving me a kiss and settling down to his beer.

I welcomed Li'l Sister, we shared perfunctory remarks and inquiries about each other's children, and very soon the three of us were seated around the dining room table, Henry with his hat and his beer, Li'l Sister proper, reticent and elegantly erect, and me, rather disheveled in a lounging robe. Li'l Sister and I were deeply and busily engaged in discussing our surgeries, including pre- and post-mastectomy experiences. We compared notes on nurses, exercises, and whether or not cocoa-butter retarded black women's tendencies to keloid, the process by which excess scar tissue is formed to ward off infection.

At one point brother Henry sort of wrinkled up his nose and said plaintively, "Can't y'all talk about somethin' else now? Ya kinda upsetting' my stomach."

Lil Sister and I just looked at him for a moment, and then returned to our conversation. We disagreed about prostheses, but she was very reassuring, and told me what to look out for, like rainy days and colds in the chest. We did every thing but show each other our scars.

At the end of an hour, having refused another cup of tea, Li'l Sister got up, smoothed down her jacket and adjusted her glasses.

"Well, it's been real nice to meet you, Audre," she said, "I've sure enjoyed talking with you. C'mon, Henry, we have to get back to Philly, now."

And they left. Somehow, I had the distinct feeling that she had never talked to anyone about her mastectomy before, for 10 years. I could be wrong.

Even propped up on pillows I found I couldn't sleep more than three or four hours at a time because my back and shoulder were paining me so. There were fixed pains, and moveable pains, deep pains and surface pains, strong pains and weak pains. There were stabs and throbs and burns, gripes and tickles and itches. I would peep under the bandage when I changed it; the scar still looked placid and inoffensive, like the trussed rump of a stuffed goose, and once the stitches were out, even the puffiness passed.

I would sleep for a few hours and then I would get up, go to the john, write down my dreams on little scraps of paper without my glasses, take two aspirin, do my hand exercises, spider-crawling up the wall of the bathroom, and then go back to bed for another few hours and some more dreams.

I pretty much functioned automatically, except to cry. Every once in a while I would think, "what do I eat? how do I act to announce or preserve my new status as temporary upon this earth?" and then I'd remember that we have always been temporary, and that I had just never really underlined it before, or acted out of it so completely before. And then I would feel a little foolish and needlessly melodramatic, but only a little.

On the day after the stitches came out and I got so furious with the nurse who told me I was bad for the morale of the office because I did not wear a prosthesis, I wrote in my journal:

October 5, 1978
I feel like I'm counting my days in milliseconds never mind hours. And it's a good thing, that particular consciousness of the way in which each hour passes, even if it is a boring hour. I want it to become permanent. There is so much I have not said in the past few days, that can only be lived now—the act of writing seems impossible to me sometimes, the space of time for the words to form or be written is long enough for the situation to totally alter, leaving you liar or at search once again for the truth. What seems impossible is made real/ tangible by the physical form of my brown arm moving across the page; not that my arm cannot do it, but that something holds it away.

In some way I must aerate this grief, bring heat and light around the pain to lend it some proportion, and god knows the news is nothing to write home about—the new pope is dead, the yankees won the game . . .

Later

If I said this all didn't matter I would be lying. I see this as a serious break in my work/ living, but also as a serious chance to learn something that I can share for use. And I mourn the women who limit their loss to the physical loss alone, who do not move into the whole terrible meaning of mortality as both weapon and power. After all, what could we possibly be afraid of after having admitted to ourselves that we had dealt face to face with death and not embraced it? For once we accept the actual existence of our dying, who can ever have power over us again?

Now I am anxious for more living—to sample and partake of the sweetness of each moment and each wonder who walks with me through my days. And now I feel again the large sweetness of the women who stayed open to me when I needed that openness like rain, who made themselves available.

I am writing this now in a new year, recalling, trying to piece together that chunk of my recent past, so that I, or anyone else in need or desire, can dip into it at will if necessary to find the ingredients with which to build a wider construct. That is an important function of the telling of experience. I am also writing to sort out for myself who I was and was becoming throughout that time, setting down my artifacts, not only for later scrutiny, but also to be free of them. I do not wish to be free from their effect, which I will carry and use internalized in one way or another, but free from having to carry them around in a reserve part of my brain.

But I am writing across a gap so filled with death—real death, the fact of it—that it is hard to believe that I am still so very much alive and writing this. That fact of all these other deaths heightens and sharpens my living, makes the demand upon it more particular, and each decision even more crucial.

Breast cancer, with its mortal awareness and the amputation which it entails, can still be a gateway, however cruelly won, into the tapping and expansion of my own power and knowing. We must learn to count the living with that same particular attention with which we number the dead.

February 20, 1979
I am often afraid to this day, but even more so angry at having to be afraid, of having to spend so much of my energies, interrupting my work, simply upon fear and worry. Does my incomplete gall bladder series mean I have cancer of the gall bladder? Is my complexion growing yellow again like it did last year, a sure sign, I believe, of the malignant process that had begun within my system? I resent the time and weakening effect of these concerns—they feel as if they are available now for diversion in much the same way the FBI lies are available for diversion, the purpose being to sway us from our appointed and self-chosen paths of action.

I must be responsible for finding a way to handle those concerns so that they don't enervate me completely, or bleed off the strength I need to move and act and feel and write and love and lie out in the sun and listen to the new spring birdsong.

I think I find it in work, being its own answer. Not to run away from the fear, but to use it as fuel to help me along the way I wish to go. If I can remember to make the jump from impotence to action, then working uses the fear as it drains it off, and I find myself furiously empowered.

Isn't there any other way, I said.

In another time, she said.

28 February 1979

Study/Discussion Questions

1. Is facing breast cancer a different experience for women than dealing with other forms of cancer?
2. Why does Lorde decide not to wear a prosthesis after her surgery?
3. How is Lorde's experience of cancer different because she is a feminist?
4. How is Lorde's experience of cancer different because she is a lesbian?

HIV: The National Scandal

Peg Byron

"The concept that women's health counts as much as men's is long over-due," writes journalist Peg Byron. In this article, Byron exposes the disparities in the detection and treatment of HIV infection and AIDS in men and women. Although women make up the fastest-growing segment of the AIDS epidemic in the United States, Byron reports, they have been grossly underrepresented in drug trials and other cutting-edge treatments. This neglect speaks to deep social inequalities.

Harlem Hospital's HIV outpatient clinic was emptying into the gray afternoon and Wilda Correa was waiting to see the doctor. Nervous, but trying to be cooperative, she had already waited three months for the appointment since taking the blood test for HIV, the human immunodeficiency virus responsible for AIDS. Inside the crowded clinic, Correa, a 43-year-old mother of three, knew it would take a lot to keep the once-silent virus from totally destroying her immune system.

In many ways, Correa epitomizes the people who are at a great risk yet most ignored in the U.S. AIDS epidemic: poor women of color and IV drug users, who, because of sex, race, and class, are viewed as the "throwaways" of society. But Harlem is not the only place in the U.S. where women must wait too long to get HIV care. And delays mean deterioration as the infection destroys the immune system and spirals into devastating diseases and, often, death.

AIDS might be described most accurately as a late stage of HIV disease. There are some long-term AIDS survivors, but the outlook for most women is bleak. One small New Jersey survey found that women diagnosed with AIDS live an average of barely four months, while white gay men with AIDS live 1.3 to 1.7 years; studies conducted in New York and San Francisco corroborate the differential. African American women in 1988 died at nine times the rate of European American women. Does this reflect the difference in the quality of health care available to these groups? Is HIV affecting women in different ways? Are different epidemics striking different communities? Experts say they don't know.

They don't know because these questions remain unexplored. But the lack of interest and the high death rate for women are two sides of the same crime: women are being ignored in the AIDS epidemic.

Women continue to get the attention of most AIDS researchers only as possible infectors of children and men. It is as if HIV-infected women are viewed solely as carriers of disease. Seen as pregnancy risks and troublesome with their child care and transportation problems, women also are widely excluded from experimental drug trials—making up only 7 percent of the enrollment in AIDS treatment research. Yet such drug trials are usually the only sources of potentially crucial medicine for this as yet incurable condition.

More often than men, women with HIV/AIDS suffer from lack of money or insurance for basic care. Yet without the data to define how they get sick with HIV differently from men, many women are denied desperately needed disability benefits.

Still, no major research has addressed the question of whether women may experience any symptoms different from men's. Dr. Daniel Hoth, AIDS division director for the National Institute of Allergy and Infectious Diseases (NIAID), a man who controls millions of research dollars, reluctantly concedes he has sponsored no studies about women's health. And the situation is the same at the National Cancer Institute; together, the two institutes get the bulk of U.S. AIDS research dollars, but neither has gotten around to asking what AIDS looks like in women.

According to Dr. Kathryn Anastos, director of HIV primary care services at Bronx-Lebanon Hospital Center in New York, one third to one half of all HIV-infected women have gynecological complications before the appearance of any other symptoms, except possibly fatigue; 32 percent to 86 percent of HIV-infected women have abnormal Pap smears and are at risk for cervical cancer; there is some evidence that pelvic inflammatory disease (PID) is more aggressive and caused by a wider array of organisms; irregular periods and infertility have been reported, suggesting unknown hormonal effects.

For at least three years, reports in medical journals have warned about severe, hard-to-treat gynecological infections linked to HIV (see *Ms.*, July 1988). But not a single female genital complication is included in the federal guidelines set by the Centers for Disease Control (CDC) for AIDS diagnoses or even as signs of HIV infection.

"It's a major problem," said Dr. Mardge Cohen, who is the director of the Women and Children with AIDS Project at Cook County Hospital in Chicago. "It would make more sense to consider gynecological manifestations as representative of the clinical spectrum of AIDS. If it's not AIDS by the official definition, we see women who are desperate for those benefits."

The very definition of AIDS, as set forth by the federal government, excludes women. The CDC has characterized AIDS based on what government scientists knew when clusters of gay men were stricken in the early 1980s. Originally called GRID, for Gay-Related Immune Deficiency, AIDS was gradually defined. If many women or intravenous drug users were dying in similar ways then, they were not noticed and their particular symptoms were not included in the AIDS definition. The human cost of that exclusion continues today each time a woman confronts her HIV problems.

"Look at my hands," Correa says, still waiting for her clinic appointment. They are covered with strange, reddish-brown spots, a few of which faintly scatter her cheek. "It feels like something crawling up my face. They itch." The spots appeared during the summer when Correa first got sick and lost 30 pounds with a severe bout of diarrhea.

She saw a doctor about fatigue and shortness of breath just two years earlier. He did not suggest an HIV test, though intravenous drug use accounts for over 50 percent of all U.S. women who have been diagnosed with AIDS and he knew she had a ten-year-long heroin habit. He diagnosed an enlarged heart and warned her to clean up her lifestyle. Since then, she's been off both heroin and methadone.

Dr. Wafaa El-Sadr calls Correa into one of the clinic's examining rooms and decides to hospitalize her to get her heart and blood pressure under control before starting HIV treatment. Chief of the hospital's infectious disease department, El-Sadr says Correa does not have what is officially AIDS. She will try an antibacterial ointment on Correa's rash, which she says is not Kaposi's sarcoma lesions (common among gay men with AIDS but almost never seen on others diagnosed with AIDS).

Did Correa have any unusual gynecological symptoms? The doctor says she doesn't know. While the city-run clinic supplies at no cost an expensive regimen of drugs, it does not have the equipment to do pelvic exams. The examining tables don't even have stirrups.

The doctor describes the clinic's almost 600 patients as "desperately poor," many of them homeless. Women make up 30 percent of her AIDS caseload—triple the national AIDS rate for women. The Egyptian-born El-Sadr says the high percentage of women she treats are the leading edge of the epidemic. "We're seeing the evolution of the epidemic."

Women throughout the country are the fastest growing part of the AIDS epidemic. Several years ago, they made up 7 percent of all those who were diagnosed. Now, women with AIDS number about 15,000; of these, 72 percent are African American or Latina. "If AIDS has done anything for us, it has magnified the other social and health problems that exist for women of color," said Dazon Dixon, executive director of SISTERLOVE, an affiliate of the National Black Women's Health Project.

By 1993, women will make up 15 percent of the people with AIDS in the U.S., according to the CDC; several AIDS researchers argue that the CDC's figures on women are a least 40 percent too low, in part because of its failure to count many of women's HIV-induced illnesses as AIDS.

Even when examining tables have stirrups, most researchers aren't interested in the woman, but in the fetus she is bearing.

For a new, national AZT study called protocol 076, 700 pregnant women are being sought to determine if the drug reduces the chance of an infected woman transmitting the virus to the baby. The protocol, still under review, as recently as last March included no evaluation of the women's health or the drug's impact on the mothers. A letter from NIAID's Hoth explained that protocol 076 "was not designed to be a study of pregnant women, although this topic is most important. . . ." NAIAD has since revised the study to include a maternal health component, but it is not for purposes of the women's health.

Hoth said in an interview, "As we move on in our thinking, we realize we have two patients to account for in pregnancy studies." This startling revelation is a chilling reminder of the history of interference with women's reproductive choices, from forced sterilizations and denial of abortions to the current concern for fetal rights.

For a woman with HIV, pregnancy poses a dilemma: if she wants to deliver (the odds of having a healthy baby are estimated to be 70 percent), she may be pressured to end the pregnancy. But if she chooses to abort, many clinics refuse to assist anyone who has HIV, and 37 states do not allow Medicaid or other public funds to be used for abortion.

In the limited studies that do involve pelvic exams, abnormal cervical Pap smears have been detected at rates five to eight times greater than in non-HIV women in the same communities. Other studies suggest a dangerous synergy between HIV and a common virus that causes genital warts, called the human papillomavirus, or HPV. Women with both HIV and HPV infections are 29 times more likely than non-HIV women to have cervical cancer, one study found.

"HPV is a ubiquitous virus. It is found in the inner cities, the upper classes. Some studies suggest that it is found in a third of all adolescents in the inner cities and a quarter of all women," said Dr. Sten Vermund, chief of epidemiology for NIAID. He warns that once HIV-infected women start reaching the same life expectancy as HIV-infected men, an epidemic in cervical cancer may emerge due to the HIV-HPV combination.

Doctors who treat many women with HIV infections (in clinics with properly equipped examining tables) say they already see higher rates of abnormal cervical conditions rapidly progressing to invasive cancers.

Advanced HPV with HIV, argues Vermund, should be considered one of the opportunistic infections that define AIDS—making many more women count in both the AIDS toll and benefit programs. "I'm having trouble getting people's attention on this matter. I have had a paper about it in review at the *American Journal of Obstetrics and Gynecology* for a god-awful long time," said Vermund.

Dr. Mathilde Krim of the American Foundation for AIDS Research (AmFAR) says how women are counted "matters a lot when it comes to entitlement to disability payments or Medicare. The rest of the government relies on this definition. And where women are left out of the system, the lack of treatment can shorten their lives."

There are conflicts over the hierarchy of AIDS illnesses, which not only affects who qualifies for limited disability benefits but how the shape and scope of the epidemic is defined. And that affects how both public and private agencies must respond.

The battles pit the sick against the dying in a fight over money. Scientists and doctors, for example, are in a fierce competition for limited research funding: the scientists are focused on long-range goals to stop HIV with the development of antiviral drugs and a vaccine, while doctors are desperate for ways to treat people already infected. But President Bush and the Congress—which will spend a projected $800 billion on the S&L crisis and $2.2 billion a month in the Persian Gulf—have capped NIAID's AIDS research funding at $432.6 million and NCI's at $161 million for fiscal year 1991.

AIDS activist Maxine Wolfe, who demonstrated and sat in at CDC and NIAID offices as part of the Women's Caucus of AIDS Coalition to Unleash Power (ACT UP), says: "The whole size of the epidemic is being squashed. Can you imagine if they added TB with HIV, or vaginal thrush with HIV, or PID or syphilis with HIV? The number of cases out there would be enormous. By not having that number, they [the feds] justify so little government money for research and treatment."

Following pressure from activists as well as the Congressional Caucus for Women's Issues, NIAID sponsored a special conference on women and HIV in December to help prioritize women's needs. At another meeting at NIAID last year, Wolfe, a professor at the City University of New York Graduate Center, and other ACT UP activists confronted NIAID chief Dr. Anthony Fauci, Hoth, and other officials to demand that "women be treated as women and not as fetus-bearers." Even Fauci had to concede that there had been few women included in AIDS drug trials.

Not surprisingly, the blind sexism of the NIH establishment is also reflected in the institute's attitudes toward women researchers. According to Dr. Deborah Cotton, an assistant professor of medicine at Harvard Medical School who chaired the session on women in clinical trials at NIAID's December conference, condescension was the typical response to criticisms from her and other women of the Food and Drug Administration committee reviewing protocol 076.

"As a woman, part of the problem in talking about clinical trials in women is that people don't listen," said Cotton. "They consider it a political statement . . . as if we are overstating what the scientific issues are." Pressure from women's advocates has helped, she said. "I think it did take that kind of advocacy to put women at the top of the agenda."

Legal pressure may also help. A class-action lawsuit has been filed against Health and

Human Services Secretary Louis Sullivan, who oversees the Social Security Administration as well as CDC, NIH, and NCI. The suit seeks to grant disability benefits for a broader range of HIV diseases, including HIV-induced gynecological diseases. Legal services attorney Theresa McGovern filed the case from her cramped New York City office after hearing from dozens of people like S.P., a 23-year-old with two children in foster care.

S.P. said she can't have her name published because she must keep her HIV condition a secret from her father, with whom she shares a tiny, dilapidated apartment. She can't afford her own apartment unless she receives Social Security Disability insurance and Supplemental Security Income benefits. Without adequate housing, she has been unable to convince the family court to return her children.

"I get headaches, throw up a lot. I've got a lot of pain in my side," S.P. said. She has outbreaks of painful pelvic inflammatory disease for which she has been hospitalized. Her immune system is nearly depleted.

The benefits would mean a monthly grant of $472 instead of the $113 she gets from local assistance programs. Despite her own doctor's testimony at a hearing last fall that she is unable to work, an administrative law judge deemed the rail-thin woman's testimony "not credible" and denied her claim. The class-action suit, in U.S. District Court in Manhattan, could affect thousands of women as well as male IV drug users.

"This should have been a national class action but we just didn't have the money to do it," McGovern says. Other nonprofit legal service groups joined in the suit, including the gay-rights oriented Lambda Legal Defense and Education Fund. But McGovern said that support from major AIDS groups has been slower in coming.

McGovern's lawsuit—like the Women's AIDS Network in San Francisco and the handful of other such efforts for women—has been run on a shoestring. These groups get little of the money that flows, for example, to New York's Gay Men's Health Crisis (GMHC), the country's biggest AIDS service group. GMHC, for its part, did not join the lawsuit, though it made a small donation.

Even when better funded AIDS groups sponsor programs needed by women with HIV, they may set entrance criteria women can't meet. Even large groups like GMHC have restricted their client services to serve only those diagnosed with AIDS or AIDS-related conditions, as set by the male-oriented CDC definition; GMHC has long refused services to anyone still using drugs. Given the barriers women face getting diagnosed correctly, plus the high percentage who get AIDS from IV drug use, women are falling through the cracks even in community HIV service groups.

Some doctors are uneasy about women bringing new demands into the fray. They are critical of demands to include women's genital tract infections among AIDS-defining illnesses. "Some of these infections are very common," said Dr. Paula Shuman, infectious disease specialist at Wayne State University School of Medicine in Detroit. "It would terrify a lot of women into thinking it means they have HIV." No one wants to promote unnecessary anxiety, but viewing women as hysterics who would place extra demands on doctors is a common reason given to deny better research and medical care to women.

Women's organizations themselves are also guilty of ignoring the threat of HIV to women. Center for Women Policy Studies Executive Director Leslie Wolfe says her group will be pushing women's organizations to start giving AIDS priority, after years of groups insisting HIV is not a women's issue.

"If women don't fit some stereotype, HIV won't be considered," said Cohen of Chicago's Cook County Hospital. For women of color, the poor, and IV drug users who are the majority of women with AIDS, HIV adds a grim dimension to the neglect they always have experienced; for middle-class European American women, HIV is often missed because AIDS is what happens to other people.

Older women also suffer from doctor biases. According to Dr. Mary A. Young, who sees scores of infected women at her office in the Georgetown University Medical Center in Washington, D.C., one 62-year-old was given cancer tests for a year before anyone thought to take her sexual history and recommend an HIV test. It was positive. "No one had considered this widow might be sexually active," Young said.

But women with HIV have been organizing among themselves to try to answer the questions that the AIDS establishment has ignored. Michelle Wilson, 39, a legal services aide from Washington, D.C., started a newsletter and an organization called "The Positive Woman" for women like herself who live with the virus. Sex is one of the toughest topics.

"Initially, it made me feel unclean," she said about trying to have sex after learning of her infection last year. "I felt like my husband couldn't touch me without infecting himself." For a while, he didn't wear a condom because he thought it would make her feel bad. "It was hard to relax and feel good. I couldn't keep feeling sexually aroused because I knew what that condom meant. But at some point, a coping mechanism kicks in and you feel, 'Now what a guy—our lovemaking remains unchanged because he really loves me.' And that keeps us a loving and sexual couple."

Wilson gets calls from around the country about the newsletter. Many women describe frustrations when they look for support from male-oriented service groups. "You're reluctant if you're in a room filled with men to raise your hand and say, 'I have lesions on my vagina,'" Wilson said.

Lesbians with HIV find their existence even more widely denied. Drug use, alternative methods of fertilization, blood transfusions,

and sex with infected men are known routes of HIV into the lesbian population. As for lesbian sexual HIV transmission, several possible cases have been reported in letters to medical journals, but the risk remains unclear. CDC epidemiologist Susan Chu, the lead author of a recent report that looked for AIDS in lesbians, said she found no cases of female-to-female transmission.

But Chu states flatly her study did not rule out HIV risks in lesbian sex. Notably, the study used the CDC's narrow definition of AIDS, not a cross section of HIV-infected women. And the authors defined "lesbian" more strictly than would many lesbian women: they omitted any women mentioned in CDC AIDS reports through 1989 who had had sex with men since 1977, leaving 79 lesbians, or 0.8 percent of all reported adult women with AIDS in the country. Almost all were intravenous drug users and 5 percent were described as infected through transfusions. This gives no help for lesbians who, for whatever reason, are infected. The CDC has not found the question of lesbian risk significant enough to warrant safer sex guidelines.

As far as menstrual blood is concerned, Chu said she doesn't know if it is as HIV-laden as circulating blood in infected women. She could not say if sex during menses was riskier for one's sex partner, although the menstruating woman might be at more risk of infection herself, because her cervix is more open.

In trying to assess their own risk, women probably should consider the geographic prevalence of the virus where they or their sexual partners have had sex, shared hypodermic needles, had blood transfusions, maybe even had tattoos and electrolysis performed since the late 1970s. Perhaps most tangled is the daisy chain of sex tied to everyone's history that is both invisible and sometimes distorted by guilt.

The answer to uncertain risk—"just wear a condom"—ignores the fact that women don't wear condoms. Men do and most don't like it; some admit it gives them performance anxiety and others say it is "unnatural." For some, says Dooley Worth, Ph.D., an anthropologist and adviser to New York's Health and Hospitals Corporation, condoms are unwelcome symbols of extra-relationship activity. Worth also warns that no relationship is static and commitment to condom use can diminish over time. And condom campaigns ignore the real pressures in women's relationships that sometimes make unsafe sex seem the less risky alternative.

"Women may be getting battered, or fear the possibility of battery or of losing the relationship," said Sally Jue, the mental health program manager for AIDS Project Los Angeles. "For many Asian and Hispanic women, being assertive and getting their men to wear condoms is a ludicrous idea."

In one study of women in prostitution, only 4 percent of nearly 600 women reported they regularly had customers use condoms. In a more encouraging study, the Alan Guttmacher Institute recently reported that levels of condom use among Latino teenagers had tripled during the 1980s.

But if condoms are not known as perfect birth control, why are they so great when it comes to a question of life and death? After all, condom failure in pregnancy prevention ranges between 3 percent for older, white married women and 36 percent for younger, nonmarried women of color. With HIV protection, less is known. One study concluded that condom use reduces HIV infection risk for women by a factor of 10.

There are mixed recommendations about antiviral spermicides, containing nonoxynol 9, sodium oxychlorosene, or benzalkonium chloride. Although these are in the woman's control, they are less effective than condoms. Also, spermicides can irritate mucous membranes lining the vagina and anus, making them more vulnerable to infection.

As a long-term public health strategy, condoms are not the answer for women wanting control over their health. But federal officials were dumbfounded when Representative Constance Morella (R.-Md.) and other congresswomen asked what was being done to give women control of HIV protection. "They have not been doing anything," said Morella, whose district includes the NIH's sprawling research campus.

The concept that women's health counts as much as men's is long overdue. Last summer, the Congressional Caucus for Women's Issues forced the formation of an Office of Research on Women's Health at NIH. The caucus also introduced the Women's Health Equity Act, which includes AIDS initiatives written by the Center for Women Policy Studies in Washington.

"The activists are right," said AmFAR's Krim. "But unless politicians also feel pressure from the mainstream, from groups like NOW and the League of Women Voters, they won't do it for women." Certainly, scientists and doctors, when asked to spend time and money on women's health, must stop reacting like men who have been asked to wear condoms.

Women cannot afford to let the Health Equity Act follow the path of the ERA. Unless true health equity is addressed, thousands and thousands of women, especially in the inner cities and gradually across the country, are sentenced to death as HIV in the U.S. begins to take on the global pattern of AIDS.

VOICES

Carolyn Wilson, Detroit, Michigan
Age 42

I've been off drugs for four years. I have a 24-year-old son, a 23-year-old daughter, and two grandchildren. Never been married. I found out I was HIV-infected in April 1990 when I got sick with pneumonia and was in the hospital for a month. That's when devastation came in. My pastor helped, and I was able to get focused on Carolyn again.

The system is so outrageous—first the nurses and the doctors shook my hand, and then they came in with gloves, masks. I was moved to an isolated room and they talked to me long distance. They wouldn't change my sheets for days—one day I would have toilet paper, one day not. After I told people from an AIDS support group, my treatment got better.

Now I've been doing outreach for a month. We pass out condoms, take surveys, do STD and HIV presentations in schools, correctional centers, churches, drug rehabilitation centers, and girls' homes. I feel great because I can tell people that I'm HIV-positive, and, yes, you can live with this virus. You just pray that somebody will hear that you don't have to die if you don't want to.

But if I depended on this system, I'm sure I would die. You know what a revolving door is like? All my doctor would do is write a prescription and take some blood. No thoroughness in it. I wouldn't go back to him. A woman doctor who then saw me for free said I had thrush in my throat and a yeast infection.

That's what so good about my support group—different individuals have gone through these things. When the women meet separately we talk about having a mate and telling them we're infected, dealing with rejection, that women want women doctors, children telling mothers how much they hate them.

The women I speak to think prostitution and drug use are the only ways for AIDS to be transmitted. When we tell them that all women are at risk, their eyes bug. Women focus on men, and they need to wake up. When a woman says to me, "My first priority is a man," I say, "Uh-uh. Think about yourself. Once you get this virus, it belongs to you—lock, stock, and barrel."

Gloria Boyd, New York, New York
Age 52

I definitely got AIDS through needles. I'm hard core—I never took anything in my life but heroin. In 1985 1 broke out, from head to toe. I went to the hospital, they said it was scabies. But I knew then.

With any catastrophic illness, the hard part is to hear it's incurable. After that, you're fine, you just live your life. People have cancer, they have TB. There are people with no legs. I'm no better or no worse than anyone else. I never went through a period of devastation. I've been through so many situations in my life, this is no worse.

I was brought up Italian Catholic. My mother died when I was eight. When I was 13 they said I was incorrigible and sent me to reform school. When I was 18, 1 went to California—I was shooting dope and I was hustling. I'm not religious, but I'm very spiritual. I believe there's a god—there are no accidents. I'm at the point I'm supposed to be. With all the things I've done in my life—and I'm still alive—something is telling me I have some work to do.

I'm supposed to soak twice a day for my skin condition. I live in a welfare hotel—there's no bathtub. All I want is an apartment with a refrigerator, a stove, a tub. I'd put in a typewriter, a tape deck, a Walkman, and music. That's all I need—to be in a quiet place for my music, my writing, my work.

I never think of dying, never. But I do think about getting sick. I have so many things to do—if I get laid up four or five days I couldn't stand it. I have no fear. I love life. I plan to live to be 99 and a half, to write a book and be successful.

Suzanne Wilson, Dallas, Texas
Age 29

I met Cragg in a restaurant/bar four and a half years ago. It was love at first sight. I walked right up to him and said, "You are the sexiest man I've ever seen in my life." We got married three months later.

Even with my knowledge that Cragg had been an IV drug user, I still did not think it was going to happen to me. He had been clean for almost four years when I met him. You just don't think it's going to touch your life. If I knew then what I know now, I would not be infected. I still would have married Cragg, but I would have used a rubber.

I quit my job at Neiman-Marcus after almost six years to work on renovating this house Cragg and I got three years ago. That's what we were doing when he got sick last January. We're both asymptomatic now. We're both on AZT.

When people ask me what's different between our lifestyle and somebody else's, I tell them our biggest difference is that on our kitchen table, instead of just salt and pepper, we have a bottle of AZT. Ninety percent of the time, Cragg and I lead a very normal life. There's that 10 percent where we sit down and cry.

But I don't look at what's been taken away from me now. I look at things that God gives me every day. That's real hard to do when you've got one set of dreams that have been smashed. You say, O.K., they're smashed, what do we do? Well, you set new ones, except on a day-to-day basis. I don't project two years from now.

My mother calls me an innocent victim. I got this because I fell in love with someone. I can look at it like that, and I can cry about it and feel real sorry for myself, but I can't dwell on it. I think that everybody who contracts AIDS is an innocent victim.

"Alice," San Francisco, California
Age 45

Being a third-generation Japanese American had a lot to do with my accepting that I have this disease and also communicating that to the family, because of the need not to bring shame on your family or yourself. My parents, brother, and sister-in-law know finally. They were tremendously supportive. My anonymity is because my extended family doesn't know and in the community there's still that negative stigma.

About a year ago I went to one of the local street fairs in Japantown, and parked a few feet away from a table for the Asian AIDS Project. I watched people of my own community whiz past the table like they didn't even see it. If this is happening in my community, how can I expect to get any help? But this year there were a lot more Asian faces staffing the table and more active involvement by the people walking by. It made me feel good that there were changes—slow—but little victories count.

My partner was bisexual, I'm heterosexual. I'm not promiscuous, and I thought I was pretty selective.

The idea that women are promiscuous is a biggie with the media. I want to tell women that they shouldn't stop having sex. It's one of the most beautiful things in the world for two people to share. But we need to arm ourselves—with education, and with a sense of our own responsibility and our partners'.

I found out I had HIV in 1987 and worked as an accountant until the winter of 1988. Social Security—I swear to God—almost made me commit suicide. I applied in March and didn't get a determination until June. This involved numerous bus trips downtown, and here I am in pain. I said, "I am a person with AIDS and I was told you could expedite things." And they said, "Well, ma'am, we're sorry, we can't be expediting applications for everybody with AIDS." In my frustration and anger I said, "You're just going to drag your feet and hope we die in the meantime."

I have what is called peripheral neuropathy, which is numbness in my lower extremities. When I have food cravings, I jump on them because I've lost about ten pounds. Every day I want a hamburger, even if it gets monotonous, and a real, homemade-style milk shake. It's just a little game you play with your body. You've got to keep your sense of humor, or you'll go stir-crazy. Friends ask me how I get around, and I say, "Very slowly"—but I get there eventually.

Migdalia Ayala, Miami, Florida
Age 38

I've been on disability for years. I'm a diabetic and a chronic asthmatic and have arthritis, and now I have AIDS. They first told me on May 22. I was in the hospital with pneumonia, which was then diagnosed as PCP [pneumocystis carinii pneumonia]. It was a shock. I started screaming and crying and ran out of the hospital. Now I've had PCP three times already.

I'm real scared of dying. One reason is that I have 12 beautiful grandchildren. I was divorced a long time ago, but I live with one of my grandkids, who has HIV. His mother abandoned him at the hospital when he was two days old, and now he's three. He's so beautiful. My oldest son is going to keep him if I die, but nobody's going to treat him like I do.

At the beginning it was very hard on me. I didn't want to accept my life, accept being a person with AIDS. Now I accept my life. I don't do anything about it. I just stay here and cry and cry and cry, take my pills and go to sleep. But sometimes I have a feeling when I go to sleep that I'm not going to wake up. Now when I get scared like that I play solitaire.

A lot of people are staying away from me now, friends I used to know. My son's godmother saw me in the store and got away from me. When you see things like that, when people treat you unfair, you just try to keep away from people. So I don't associate with too many people anymore.

I don't think I have any more future since I was diagnosed with AIDS, because you live today to die tomorrow. Before, I would say, when I get older, I'll do this or do that. I don't think like that anymore, because I never know if I'm going to live that long.

Bernice Thompson, Boston, Massachusetts
Age 56

My son Charles died in 1984. He started getting sick in 1981–82, when he was 29 or 30. I would take care of him. My husband and I did everything for him, and when my husband died in 1969, there was only Charles. When Charles got sick, I stopped my world. I did nothing else. Everything was Charles.

Charles and I had a good time. We'd play cards. He'd say, "Ma, you always cheat." I bathed him, I took him to the bathroom. I rubbed his legs and turned him over. And then there were the bedsores. They were horrible. He stopped eating. But one day he called me and said he was hungry. I ran out and bought a bunch of grapefruits and ran to the hospital, telling everybody, "My Charles is hungry." I was so happy.

When he died there were a lot of things. Like the health department and the undertakers didn't want the body because they knew he had AIDS. Then the health department wanted to do tests, and they came to the cemetery to make sure that he was buried.

Then there was nothing else. I had nothing to live for. And then I brought him back. In my mind I brought him back. I talked with him, played with him—I got sick. I was in a mental hospital. I didn't know Charles was dead. I lived in a different world. I was in there for so long, without going out.

One day, I was sitting in the lobby, and I heard the word "AIDS," and it stuck in my mind. So I left the hospital and I came to the AIDS Action Committee. I wanted to help . . . I think I wanted to find Charles. They told me I couldn't be a buddy because I couldn't take care of myself, but they found me something easier to do, stuffing envelopes. Then one day they put me on the front desk—I was so afraid,

I was really down. It's sad what society does to you. But the people at AIDS Action took me by the hand.

It's hard to see the people at AIDS Action who are sick. I've been there, and I know what they're going through. That's why I tell them jokes and I want to make them laugh and to know that I love them.

When I was in the hospital, no one talked to me about AIDS. The only reason I came back was I heard that word AIDS. I was determined to find out what killed my son. I want it never to hurt anyone else. Every time I hear about the loneliness from kids whose parents have cast them aside because they have AIDS, it makes me so angry. I just can't stand it.

Study/Discussion Questions

1. How does HIV research neglect women?
2. What AIDS illnesses do women tend to suffer from?
3. How are women's symptoms of HIV and AIDS different from those of men?
4. In what ways do women suffer more from their illnesses because of the focus on men and children with HIV and AIDS?

Ruth's Song
(Because She Could Not Sing It)

Gloria Steinem

Gloria Steinem was founding editor of Ms. *magazine, and for many Americans not directly involved in women's liberation organizations, she represented the very face of feminism in the 1970s and 80s. "Ruth's Song," published for the first time in Steinem's 1983 essay collection,* Outrageous Acts and Everyday Rebellions, *impressed thousands of readers with its frank but tender recounting of Steinem's mother's mental illness. Steinem wrote this piece more than a decade after the publication of Phyllis Chesler's devastating book,* Women and Madness *(1972); during that decade, women's health activists fervently analyzed the social and political, as well as medical, dimensions of women's physical, emotional, and mental health. Nonetheless, when Steinem proffered this intimate portrayal of her mother's struggle to be whole, her words still made a difference.*

Happy or unhappy, families are all mysterious. We have only to imagine how differently we would be described— and will be, after our deaths—by each of the family members who believe they know us. The only question is, Why are some mysteries more important than others?

The fate of my Uncle Ed was a mystery of importance in our family. We lavished years of speculation on his transformation from a brilliant young electrical engineer to the town handyman. What could have changed this elegant, Lincolnesque student voted "Best Dressed" by his classmates to the gaunt, unshaven man I remember? Why did he leave a young son and a first wife of the "proper" class and religion, marry a much less educated woman of the "wrong" religion, and raise a second family in a house near an abandoned airstrip; a house whose walls were patched with metal signs to stop the wind? Why did he never talk about his transformation?

For years, I assumed that some secret and dramatic events of a year he spent in Alaska had made the difference. Then I discovered that the trip had come after his change and probably been made because of it. Strangers he worked for as a much-loved handyman talked about him as one more tragedy of the Depression, and it was true that Uncle Ed's father, my paternal grandfather, had lost his money in the stock-market Crash and died of (depending on who was telling the story) pneumonia or a broken heart. But the Crash of 1929 also had come long after Uncle Ed's transformation. Another theory was that he was afflicted with a mental problem that lasted most of his life, yet he was supremely competent at his work, led an independent life, and asked for help from no one.

Perhaps he had fallen under the spell of a radical professor in the early days of the century, the height of this country's romance with socialism and anarchism. That was the theory of another uncle on my mother's side. I do remember that no matter how much Uncle Ed needed money, he would charge no more for his work than materials plus 10 percent, and I never saw him in anything other than ancient boots and overalls held up with strategic safety pins. Was he really trying to replace socialism-in-one-country with socialism-in-one-man? If so, why did my grandmother, a woman who herself had run for the

school board in coalition with anarchists and socialists, mistrust his judgment so much that she left his share of her estate in trust, even though he was over fifty when she died? And why did Uncle Ed seem uninterested in all other political words and acts? Was it true instead that, as another relative insisted, Uncle Ed had chosen poverty to disprove the myths of Jews and money?

Years after my uncle's death, I asked a son in his second family if he had the key to this family mystery. No, he said. He had never known his father any other way. For that cousin, there had been no question. For the rest of us, there was to be no answer.

For many years I also never imagined my mother any way other than the person she had become before I was born. She was just a fact of life when I was growing up; someone to be worried about and cared for; an invalid who lay in bed with eyes closed and lips moving in occasional response to voices only she could hear; a woman to whom I brought an endless stream of toast and coffee, bologna sandwiches and dime pies, in a child's version of what meals should be. She was a loving, intelligent, terrorized woman who tried hard to clean our littered house whenever she emerged from her private world, but who could rarely be counted on to finish one task. In many ways, our roles were reversed: I was the mother and she was the child. Yet that didn't help her, for she still worried about me with all the intensity of a frightened mother, plus the special fears of her own world full of threats and hostile voices.

Even then I suppose I must have known that, years before she was thirty-five and I was born, she had been a spirited, adventurous young woman who struggled out of a working-class family and into college, who found work she loved and continued to do, even after she was married and my older sister was there to be cared for. Certainly, our immediate family and nearby relatives, of whom I was by far the youngest, must have remembered her life as a whole and functioning person. She was thirty before she gave up her own career to help my father run the Michigan summer resort that was the most practical of his many dreams, and she worked hard there as everything from bookkeeper to bar manager. The family must have watched this energetic, fun-loving, book-loving woman turn into someone who was afraid to be alone, who could not hang on to reality long enough to hold a job, and who could rarely concentrate enough to read a book.

Yet I don't remember any family speculation about the mystery of my mother's transformation. To the kind ones and those who liked her, this new Ruth was simply a sad event, perhaps a mental case, a family problem to be accepted and cared for until some natural process made her better. To the less kind or those who had resented her earlier independence, she was a willful failure, someone who lived in a filthy house, a woman who simply would not pull herself together.

Unlike the case of my Uncle Ed, exterior events were never suggested as reason enough for her problems. Giving up her own career was never cited as her personal parallel of the Depression. (Nor was there discussion of the Depression itself, though my mother, like millions of others, had made potato soup and cut up blankets to make my sister's winter clothes.) Her fears of dependence and poverty were no match for my uncle's possible political beliefs. The real influence of newspaper editors who had praised her reporting was not taken as seriously as the possible influence of one radical professor.

Even the explanation of mental illness seemed to contain more personal fault when applied to my mother. She had suffered her first "nervous breakdown," as she and everyone else called it, before I was born and when my sister was about five. It followed years of trying to take care of a baby, be the wife of a kind but financially irresponsible man with show-business dreams, and still keep her much-loved job as reporter and newspaper editor. After many months in a sanatorium, she was pronounced recovered. That is, she was able to take care of my sister again, to move away from the city and the job she loved, and to work with my father at the isolated rural lake in Michigan he was trying to transform into a resort worthy of the big dance bands of the 1930s.

But she was never again completely without the spells of depression, anxiety, and visions into some other world that eventually were to turn her into the nonperson I remember. And she was never again without a bottle of dark, acrid-smelling liquid she called "Doc Howard's medicine": a solution of chloral hydrate that I later learned was the main ingredient of "Mickey Finns" or "knockout drops," and that probably made my mother and her doctor the pioneers of modern tranquilizers. Though friends and relatives saw this medicine as one more evidence of weakness and indulgence, to me it always seemed an embarrassing but necessary evil. It slurred her speech and slowed her coordination, making our neighbors and my school friends believe she was a drunk. But without it, she would not sleep for days, even a week at a time, and her feverish eyes began to see only that private world in which wars and hostile voices threatened the people she loved.

Because my parents had divorced and my sister was working in a faraway city, my mother and I were alone together then, living off the meager fixed income that my mother got from leasing her share of the remaining land in Michigan. I remember a long Thanksgiving weekend spent hanging on to her with one hand and holding my eighth-grade assignment of *Tale of Two Cities* in the other, because the war outside our house was so real to my mother that she had plunged her hand through a window, badly cutting her arm in an effort to help us escape. Only when she finally agreed to swallow the medicine could she sleep, and only then could I end the terrible calm that comes with crisis and admit to myself how afraid I had been.

No wonder that no relative in my memory challenged the doctor who prescribed this medicine, asked if some of her suffering and hallucinating might be due to overdose or withdrawal, or even consulted another doctor about its use. It was our relief as well as hers.

But why was she never returned even to that first sanatorium? Or to help that might come from other doctors? It's hard to say. Partly, it was her own fear of returning. Partly, it was too little money, and a family's not-unusual assumption that mental illness is an inevitable part of someone's personality. Or perhaps other family members had feared something like my experience when, one hot and desperate summer between the sixth and seventh grade, I finally persuaded her to let me take her to the only doctor from those sanatorium days whom she remembered without fear.

Yes, this brusque old man told me after talking to my abstracted, timid mother for twenty minutes: She definitely belongs in a state hospital. I should put her there right away. But even at that age, *Life* magazine and newspaper exposes had told me what horrors went on inside those hospitals. Assuming there to be no other alternative, I took her home and never tried again.

In retrospect, perhaps the biggest reason my mother was cared for but not helped for twenty years was the simplest: her functioning was not that necessary to the world. Like women alcoholics who drink in their kitchens while costly programs are constructed for executives who drink, or like the homemakers subdued with tranquilizers while male patients get therapy and personal attention instead, my mother was not an important worker. She was not even the caretaker of a very young child, as she had been when she was hospitalized the first time. My father had patiently brought home the groceries and kept our odd household going until I was eight or so and my sister went away to college. Two years later when wartime gas rationing closed his summer resort and he had to travel to buy and sell in summer as well as winter, he said: How can I travel and take care of your mother? How can I make a living? He was right. It was impossible to do both. I did not blame him for leaving once I was old enough to be the bringer of meals and answerer

of my mother's questions. ("Has your sister been killed in a car crash?" "Are there German soldiers outside?") I replaced my father, my mother was left with one more way of maintaining a sad status quo, and the world went on undisturbed.

That's why our lives, my mother's from forty-six to fifty-three, and my own from ten to seventeen, were spent alone together. There was one sane winter in a house we rented to be near my sister's college in Massachusetts, then one bad summer spent house-sitting in suburbia while my mother hallucinated and my sister struggled to hold down a summer job in New York. But the rest of those years were lived in Toledo where both my mother and father had been born, and on whose city newspapers an earlier Ruth had worked.

First we moved into a basement apartment in a good neighborhood. In those rooms behind a furnace, I made one last stab at being a child. By pretending to be much sicker with a cold than I really was, I hoped my mother would suddenly turn into a sane and cheerful woman bringing me chicken soup à la Hollywood. Of course, she could not. It only made her feel worse that she could not. I stopped pretending.

But for most of those years, we lived in the upstairs of the house my mother had grown up in and that her parents left her—a deteriorating farm house engulfed by the city, with poor but newer houses stacked against it and a major highway a few feet from its sagging front porch. For a while, we could rent the two downstairs apartments to a newlywed factory worker and a local butcher's family. Then the health department condemned our ancient furnace for the final time, sealing it so tight that even my resourceful Uncle Ed couldn't produce illegal heat.

In that house, I remember:

. . . lying in the bed my mother and I shared for warmth, listening on the early morning radio to the royal wedding of Princess Elizabeth and Prince Philip being broadcast live, while we tried to ignore and thus protect each other from the unmistakable sounds of the factory worker downstairs beating up and locking out his pregnant wife.

. . . hanging paper drapes I had bought in the dime store; stacking books and papers in the shape of two armchairs and covering them with blankets; evolving my own dishwashing system (I waited until all the dishes were dirty, then put them in the bathtub); and listening to my mother's high praise for these housekeeping efforts to bring order from chaos, though in retrospect I think they probably depressed her further.

. . . coming back from one of the Eagles' Club shows where I and other veterans of a local tap-dancing school made ten dollars a night for two shows, and finding my mother waiting with a flashlight and no coat in the dark cold of the bus stop, worried about my safety walking home.

. . . in a good period, when my mother's native adventurousness came through, answering a classified ad together for an amateur acting troupe that performed Biblical dramas in churches, and doing several very corny performances of Noah's Ark while my proud mother shook metal sheets backstage to make thunder.

. . . on a hot summer night, being bitten by one of the rats that shared our house and its back alley. It was a terrifying night that turned into a touching one when my mother, summoning courage from some unknown reservoir of love, became a calm, comforting parent who took me to a hospital emergency room despite her terror at leaving home.

. . . coming home from a local library with the three books a week into which I regularly escaped, and discovering that for once there was no need to escape. My mother was calmly planting hollyhocks in the vacant lot next door.

But there were also times when she woke in the early winter dark, too frightened and disoriented to remember that I was at my usual afterschool job, and so called the police to find me. Humiliated in front of my friends by sirens and policemen, I would yell at her—and she would bow her head in fear and say "I'm sorry, I'm sorry, I'm sorry," just as she had done so often when my otherwise-kindhearted father had yelled at her in frustration. Perhaps the worst thing about suffering is that it finally hardens the hearts of those around it.

And there were many, many times when I badgered her until her shaking hands had written a small check to cash at the corner grocery and I could leave her alone while I escaped to the comfort of well-heated dime stores that smelled of fresh doughnuts, or to air-conditioned Saturday-afternoon movies that were windows on a very different world.

But my ultimate protection was this: I was just passing through, a guest in the house; perhaps this wasn't my mother at all. Though I knew very well that I was her daughter, I sometimes imagined that I had been adopted and that my real parents would find me, a fantasy I've since discovered is common. (If children wrote more and grownups less, being adopted might be seen not only as a fear but also as a hope.) Certainly, I didn't mourn the wasted life of this woman who was scarcely older than I am now. I worried only about the times when she got worse.

Pity takes distance and a certainty of surviving. It was only after our house was bought for demolition by the church next door, and after my sister had performed the miracle of persuading my father to give me a carefree time before college by taking my mother with him to California for a year, that I could afford to think about the sadness of her life. Suddenly, I was far away in Washington, living with my sister and sharing a house with several of her friends. While I finished high school and discovered to my surprise that my classmates felt sorry for me because my mother wasn't there, I also realized that my sister, at least in her early childhood, had known a very different person who lived inside our mother, an earlier Ruth.

She was a woman I met for the first time in a mental hospital near Baltimore, a humane place with gardens and trees where I visited her each weekend of the summer after my first year away in college. Fortunately, my sister hadn't been able to work and be our mother's caretaker, too. After my father's year was up, my sister had carefully researched hospitals and found the courage to break the family chain.

At first, this Ruth was the same abstracted, frightened woman I had lived with all those years; though now all the sadder for being approached through long hospital corridors and many locked doors. But gradually she began to talk about her past life, memories that doctors there must have been awakening. I began to meet a Ruth I had never known.

. . . A tall, spirited, auburn-haired high-school girl who loved basketball and reading; who tried to drive her uncle's Stanley Steamer when it was the first car in the neighborhood; who had a gift for gardening and who sometimes, in defiance of convention, wore her father's overalls; a girl with the courage to go to dances even though her church told her that music itself was sinful, and whose sense of adventure almost made up for feeling gawky and unpretty next to her daintier, dark-haired sister.

. . . A very little girl, just learning to walk, discovering the body places where touching was pleasurable, and being punished by her mother who slapped her hard across the kitchen floor.

. . . A daughter of a handsome railroad-engineer and a schoolteacher who felt she had married "beneath her"; the mother who took her two daughters on Christmas trips to faraway New York on an engineer's free railroad pass and showed them the restaurants and theaters they should aspire to—even though they could only stand outside them in the snow.

. . . A good student at Oberlin College, whose freethinking traditions she loved, where friends nicknamed her "Billy"; a student with a talent for both mathematics and poetry, who was not above putting an invisible film of Karo syrup on all the john seats in her dormitory the night of a big prom; a daughter who had to return to Toledo, live with her family, and go to a local university when her ambitious mother—who had scrimped and saved, ghost-written a minister's sermons, and made her daughters' clothes in order to get them to college at all—ran out of money. At home, this Ruth became a part-time bookkeeper in a lingerie shop for the very rich, commuting to classes and listening to her mother's harsh lectures on the security of becoming a teacher; but also a young woman who was still rebellious enough to fall in love with my father, the editor of her university newspaper, a funny and charming young man who was a terrible student, had no intention of graduating, put on all the campus dances, and was unacceptably Jewish.

I knew from family lore that my mother had married my father twice: once secretly, after he invited her to become the literary editor of his campus newspaper, and once a year later in a public ceremony, which some members of both families refused to attend as the "mixed marriage" of its day.

And I knew that my mother had gone on to earn a teaching certificate. She had used it to scare away truant officers during the winters when, after my father closed the summer resort for the season, we lived in a house trailer and worked our way to Florida or California and back by buying and selling antiques.

But only during those increasingly adventurous weekend outings from the hospital—going shopping, to lunch, to the movies—did I realize that she had taught college calculus for a year in deference to her mother's insistence that she have teaching "to fall back on." And only then did I realize she had fallen in love with newspapers along with my father. After graduating from the university paper, she wrote a gossip column for a local tabloid, under the name "Duncan MacKenzie," since women weren't supposed to do such things, and soon had earned a job as society reporter on one of Toledo's two big dailies. By the time my sister was four or so, she had worked her way up to the coveted position of Sunday editor.

It was a strange experience to look into those brown eyes I had seen so often and realize suddenly how much they were like my own. For the first time, I realized that she might really be my mother.

I began to think about the many pressures that might have led up to that first nervous breakdown: leaving my sister whom she loved very much with a grandmother whose values my mother didn't share; trying to hold onto a job she loved but was being asked to leave by her husband; wanting very much to go with a woman friend to pursue their own dreams in New York; falling in love with a co-worker at the newspaper who frightened her by being more sexually attractive, more supportive of her work than my father, and perhaps the man she should have married; and finally, nearly bleeding to death with a miscarriage because her own mother had little faith in doctors and refused to get help.

Did those months in the sanatorium brainwash her in some Freudian or very traditional way into making what were, for her, probably the wrong choices? I don't know. It almost doesn't matter. Without extraordinary support to the contrary, she was already convinced that divorce was unthinkable. A husband could not be left for another man, and certainly not for a reason as selfish as a career. A daughter could not be deprived of her father and certainly not be uprooted and taken off to an uncertain future in New York. A bride was supposed to be virginal (not "shopworn," as my euphemistic mother would have said), and if your husband turned out to be kind, but innocent of the possibility of a woman's pleasure, then just be thankful for kindness.

Of course, other women have torn themselves away from work and love and still survived. But a story my mother told me years later has always symbolized for me the formidable forces arrayed against her.

"It was early spring, nothing was open yet. There was nobody for miles around. We had stayed at the lake that winter, so I was alone a lot while your father took the car and traveled around on business. You were a baby. Your sister was in school, and there was no phone. The last straw was that the radio broke. Suddenly it seemed like forever since I'd been able to talk with anyone—or even hear the sound of another voice.

"I bundled you up, took the dog, and walked out to the Brooklyn road. I thought I'd walk the four or five miles to the grocery store, talk to some people, and find somebody to drive me back. I was walking along with Fritzie running up ahead in the empty road—when suddenly a car came out of nowhere and down the hill. It hit Fritzie head on and threw him over to the side of the road. I yelled and screamed at the driver, but he never slowed down. He never looked at us. He never even turned his head.

"Poor Fritzie was all broken and bleeding, but he was still alive. I carried him and sat down in the middle of the road, with his head cradled in my arms. I was going to make the next car stop and help.

"But no car ever came. I sat there for hours, I don't know how long, with you in my lap and holding Fritzie, who was whimpering and looking up at me for help. It was dark by the time he finally died. I pulled him over to the side of the road and walked back home with you and washed the blood out of my clothes.

"I don't know what it was about that one day—it was like a breaking point. When your father came home, I said: 'From now on, I'm going with you. I won't bother you. I'll just sit in the car. But I can't bear to be alone again.'"

I think she told me that story to show she had tried to save herself, or perhaps she wanted to exorcise a painful memory by saying it out loud. But hearing it made me understand what could have turned her into the woman I remember: a solitary figure sitting in the car, perspiring through the summer, bundled up in winter, waiting for my father to come out of this or that antique shop, grateful just not to be alone. I was there, too, because I was too young to be left at home, and I loved helping my father wrap and unwrap the newspaper around the china and small objects he had bought at auctions and was selling to dealers. It made me feel necessary and grown-up. But sometimes it was hours before we came back to the car again and to my mother who was always patiently, silently waiting.

At the hospital and later when Ruth told me stories of her past, I used to say, "But why didn't you leave? Why didn't you take the job? Why didn't you marry the other man?" She would always insist it didn't matter, she was lucky to have my sister and me. If I pressed hard enough, she would add, "If I'd left you never would have been born." I always thought but never had the courage to say: *But you might have been born instead.*

I'd like to tell you that this story has a happy ending. The best I can do is one that is happier than its beginning.

After many months in that Baltimore hospital, my mother lived on her own in a small apartment for two years while I was in college and my sister married and lived nearby. When she felt the old terrors coming back, she returned to the hospital at her own request. She was approaching sixty by the time she emerged from there and from a Quaker farm that served as a halfway house, but she confounded her psychiatrists' predictions that she would be able

to live outside for shorter and shorter periods. In fact, she never returned. She lived more than another twenty years, and for six of them, she was well enough to stay in a rooming house that provided both privacy and company. Even after my sister and her husband moved to a larger house and generously made two rooms into an apartment for her, she continued to have some independent life and many friends. She worked part-time as a "salesgirl" in a china shop; went away with me on yearly vacations and took one trip to Europe with relatives; went to women's club meetings; found a multi-racial church that she loved; took meditation courses; and enjoyed many books. She still could not bear to see a sad movie, to stay alone with any of her six grandchildren while they were babies, to live without many tranquilizers, or to talk about those bad years in Toledo. The old terrors were still in the back of her mind, and each day was a fight to keep them down.

It was the length of her illness that had made doctors pessimistic. In fact, they could not identify any serious mental problem and diagnosed her only as having "an anxiety neurosis": low self-esteem, a fear of being dependent, a terror of being alone, a constant worry about money. She also had spells of what now would be called agoraphobia, a problem almost entirely confined to dependent women: fear of going outside the house, and incapacitating anxiety attacks in unfamiliar or public places.

Would you say, I asked one of her doctors, that her spirit had been broken? "I guess that's as good a diagnosis as any," he said. "And it's hard to mend anything that's been broken for twenty years."

But once out of the hospital for good, she continued to show flashes of the different woman inside; one with a wry kind of humor, a sense of adventure, and a love of learning. Books on math, physics, and mysticism occupied a lot of her time. ("Religion," she used to say firmly, "begins in the laboratory.") When she visited me in New York during her sixties and seventies, she always told taxi drivers that she was eighty years old ("so they will tell me how young I look"), and convinced theater ticket sellers that she was deaf long before she really was ("so they'll give us seats in the front row"). She made friends easily, with the vulnerability and charm of a person who feels entirely dependent on the approval of others. After one of her visits, every shopkeeper within blocks of my apartment would say, "Oh yes, I know your mother!" At home, she complained that people her own age were too old and stodgy for her. Many of her friends were far younger than she. It was as if she were making up for her own lost years.

She was also overly appreciative of any presents given to her—and that made giving them irresistible. I loved to send her clothes, jewelry, exotic soaps, and additions to her collection of tarot cards. She loved receiving them, though we both knew they would end up stored in boxes and drawers. She carried on a correspondence in German with our European relatives, and exchanges with many other friends, all written in her painfully slow, shaky handwriting. She also loved giving gifts. Even as she worried about money and figured out how to save pennies, she would buy or make carefully chosen presents for grandchildren and friends.

Part of the price she paid for this much health was forgetting. A single reminder of those bad years in Toledo was enough to plunge her into days of depression. There were times when this fact created loneliness for me, too. Only two of us had lived most of my childhood. Now, only one of us remembered. But there were also times in later years when, no matter how much I pled with reporters not to interview our friends and neighbors in Toledo, not to say that my mother had been hospitalized, they published things that hurt her very much and sent her into a downhill slide.

On the other hand, she was also her mother's daughter, a person with a certain amount of social pride and pretension, and some of her objections had less to do with depression than false pride. She complained bitterly about one report that we had lived in a house trailer. She finally asked angrily: "Couldn't they at least say 'vacation mobile home'?" Divorce was still a shame to her. She might cheerfully tell friends, "I don't know why Gloria says her father and I were divorced—we never were." I think she justified this to herself with the idea that they had gone through two marriage ceremonies, one in secret and one in public, but been divorced only once. In fact, they were definitely divorced, and my father had briefly married someone else.

She was very proud of my being a published writer, and we generally shared the same values. After her death, I found a mother-daughter morals quiz I once had written for a women's magazine. In her unmistakably shaky writing, she had recorded her own answers, her entirely accurate imagination of what my answers would be, and a score that concluded our differences were less than those "normal for women separated by twenty-odd years." Nonetheless, she was quite capable of putting a made-up name on her name tag when going to a conservative women's club where she feared our shared identity would bring controversy or even just questions. When I finally got up the nerve to tell her I was signing a 1972 petition of women who publicly said we had had abortions and were demanding the repeal of laws that made them illegal and dangerous, her only reply was sharp and aimed to hurt back. "Every starlet says she's had an abortion," she said. "It's just a way of getting publicity." I knew she agreed that abortion should be a legal choice, but I also knew she would never forgive me for embarrassing her in public.

In fact, her anger and a fairly imaginative ability to wound with word increased in her last years when she was most dependent, most focused on herself, and most likely to need the total attention of others. When my sister made a courageous decision to go to law school at the age of fifty, leaving my mother in a house that not only had many loving teenage grandchildren in it but a kindly older woman as a paid companion besides, my mother reduced her to frequent tears by insisting that this was a family with no love in it, no home-cooked food in the refrigerator; not a real family at all. Since arguments about home cooking wouldn't work on me, my punishment was creative and different. She was going to call up *The New York Times,* she said, and tell them that this was what feminism did: it left old sick women all alone.

Some of this bitterness brought on by failing faculties was eventually solved by a nursing home near my sister's house where my mother not only got the twenty-four-hour help her weakening body demanded, but the attention of affectionate nurses besides. She charmed them, they loved her, and she could still get out for an occasional family wedding. If I ever had any doubts about the debt we owe to nurses, those last month laid them to rest.

When my mother died just before her eighty-second birthday in a hospital room where my sister and I were alternating the hours in which her heart wound slowly down to its last sounds, we were alone together for a few hours while my sister slept. My mother seemed bewildered by her surroundings and the tubes that invaded her body, but her consciousness cleared long enough for her to say: "I want to go home. Please take me home." Lying to her one last time, I said I would. "Okay, honey," she said. "I trust you." Those were her last understandable words.

The nurses let my sister and me stay in the room long after there was no more breath. She had asked us to do that. One of her many fears came from a story she had been told as a child about a man whose coma was mistaken for death. She also had made out a living will requesting that no extraordinary measures be used to keep her alive, and that her ashes be sprinkled in the same stream as my father's.

Her memorial service was in the Episcopalian church that she loved because it fed the poor, let the homeless sleep in its pews, had members of almost every race, and had been sued by the Episcopalian hierarchy for having a woman priest. Most of all, she loved the affection with which its members had welcomed her, visited her at home, and driven her to services. I think she would have liked the Quaker-style informality with which people rose to tell their memories of her. I know she would have loved the presence of many friends. It was to this church that she had donated some of her remaining Michigan property in the hope that it could be used as a multiracial camp, thus getting even with those people in the tiny nearby town who had snubbed my father for being Jewish.

I think she also would have been pleased with her obituary. It emphasized her brief career as one of the early women journalists and asked for donations to Oberlin's scholarship fund so others could go to this college she loved so much but had to leave.

I know I will spend the next years figuring out what her life has left in me.

I realize that I've always been more touched by old people than by children. It's the talent and hopes locked up in a failing body that gets to me; a poignant contrast that reminds me of my mother, even when she was strong.

I've always been drawn to any story of a mother and a daughter on their own in the world. I saw *A Taste of Honey* several times as both a play and a film, and never stopped feeling it. Even *Gypsy* I saw over and over again, sneaking in backstage for the musical and going to the movie as well. I told myself that I was learning the tap-dance routines, but actually my eyes were full of tears.

I once fell in love with a man only because we both belonged to that large and secret club of children who had "crazy mothers." We traded stories of the shameful houses to which we could never invite our friends. Before he was born, his mother had gone to jail for her pacifist convictions. Then she married the politically ambitious young lawyer who had defended her, stayed home and raised many sons. I fell out of love when he confessed that he wished I wouldn't smoke or swear, and he hoped I wouldn't go on working. His mother's plight had taught him self-pity—nothing else.

I'm no longer obsessed, as I was for many years, with the fear that I would end up in a house like that one in Toledo. Now, I'm obsessed instead with the things I could have done for my mother while she was alive, or the things I should have said.

I still don't understand why so many, many years passed before I saw my mother as a person and before I understood that many of the forces in her life are patterns women share. Like a lot of daughters, I suppose I couldn't afford to admit that what had happened to my mother was not all personal or accidental, and therefore could happen to me.

One mystery has finally cleared. I could never understand why my mother hadn't been helped by Pauline, her mother-in-law; a woman she seemed to love more than her own mother. This paternal grandmother had died when I was five, before my mother's real problems began but long after that "nervous breakdown," and I knew Pauline was once a suffragist who addressed Congress, marched for the vote, and was the first woman member of a school board in Ohio. She must have been a courageous and independent woman, yet I could find no evidence in my mother's reminiscences that Pauline had encouraged or helped my mother toward a life of her own.

I finally realized that my grandmother never changed the politics of her own life, either. She was a feminist who kept a neat house for a husband and four antifeminist sons, a vegetarian among five male meat eaters, and a woman who felt so strongly about the dangers of alcohol that she used only paste vanilla; yet she served both meat and wine to the men of the house and made sure their lives and comforts were continued undisturbed. After the vote was won, Pauline seems to have stopped feminist activity. My mother greatly admired the fact that her mother-in-law kept a spotless house and prepared a week's meals at a time. Whatever her own internal torments, Pauline was to my mother a woman who seemed able to "do it all." "Whither thou goest, I shall go," my mother used to say to her much-loved mother-in-law, quoting the Ruth of the Bible. In the end, her mother-in-law may have added to my mother's burdens of guilt.

Perhaps like many later suffragists, my grandmother was a public feminist and a private isolationist. That may have been heroic in itself, the most she could be expected to do, but the vote and a legal right to work were not the only kind of help my mother needed.

The world still missed a unique person named Ruth. Though she longed to live in New York and in Europe, she became a woman who was afraid to take a bus across town. Though she drove the first Stanley Steamer, she married a man who never let her drive.

I can only guess what she might have become. The clues are in moments of spirit or humor.

After all the years of fear, she still came to Oberlin with me when I was giving a speech there. She remembered everything about its history as the first college to admit blacks and the first to admit women, and responded to students with the dignity of a professor, the accuracy of a journalist, and a charm that was all her own.

When she could still make trips to Washington's wealth of libraries, she became an expert genealogist, delighting especially in finding the rogues and rebels in our family tree.

Just before I was born, when she had cooked one more enormous meal for all the members of some famous dance band at my father's resort and they failed to clean their plates, she had taken a shotgun down from the kitchen wall and held it over their frightened heads until they had finished the last crumb of strawberry shortcake. Only then did she tell them the gun wasn't loaded. It was a story she told with great satisfaction.

Though sex was a subject she couldn't discuss directly, she had a great appreciation of sensuous men. When a friend I brought home tried to talk to her about cooking, she was furious. ("He came out in the kitchen and talked to me about *stew!*") But she forgave him when we went swimming. She whispered, "He has wonderful legs!"

On her seventy-fifth birthday, she played softball with her grandsons on the beach, and took pride in hitting home runs into the ocean.

Even in the last year of her life, when my sister took her to visit a neighbor's new and luxurious house, she looked at the vertical stripes of a very abstract painting in the hallway and said, tartly, "Is that the price code?"

She worried terribly about being socially accepted herself, but she never withheld her own approval for the wrong reasons. Poverty or style or lack of education couldn't stand between her and a new friend. Though she lived in a mostly white society and worried if I went out with a man of the "wrong" race, just as she had once married a man of the "wrong" religion, she always accepted each person as an individual.

"Is he *very* dark?" she once asked worriedly about a friend. But when she met this very dark person, she only said afterward, "What a kind and nice man!"

My father was the Jewish half of the family, yet it was my mother who taught me to have pride in that tradition. It was she who encouraged me to listen to a radio play about a concentration camp when I was little. "You should know that this can happen," she said. Yet she did it just enough to teach, never enough to frighten.

It was she who introduced me to books and a respect for them, to poetry that she knew by heart, and to the idea that you could never criticize someone unless you "walked miles in their shoes."

It was she who sold that Toledo house, the only home she had, with the determination that the money be used to start me in college. She gave both her daughters the encouragement to leave home for four years of independence that she herself had never had.

After her death, my sister and I found a journal she had kept of her one cherished and belated trip to Europe. It was a trip she had described very little when she came home: she always deplored people who talked boringly about their personal travels and showed slides. Nonetheless, she had written a descriptive essay called "Grandma Goes to Europe." She still must have thought of herself as a writer. Yet she showed this long journal to no one.

I miss her, but perhaps no more in death than I did in life. Dying seems less sad than having lived too little. But at least we're now asking questions about all the Ruths and all our family mysteries.

If her song inspires that, I think she would be the first to say: It was worth the singing.

Study/Discussion Questions

1. What was Ruth like before her mental illness?
2. What does Ruth need from her husband and daughters once she becomes ill?
3. How does this make her daughter a different child? How does it change her as an adult?
4. Would Ruth have been treated differently for her mental illness if she had been a man? If she had had money? What does Gloria Steinem think?

Having It Out with Melancholy

Jane Kenyon

*If many remedies are prescribed for an illness, you may be certain that the
illness has no cure.*
　—A. P. Chekhov, The Cherry Orchard

1　FROM THE NURSERY

*When I was born, you waited
behind a pile of linen in the nursery,
and when we were alone, you lay down
on top of me, pressing the bile of desolation
into every pore.*

*And from that day on
everything under the sun and moon
made me sad—even the yellow
wooden beads that slid and spun
along a spindle on my crib.*

*You taught me to exist without gratitude.
You ruined my manners toward God:
"We're here simply to wait for death;
the pleasures of earth are overrated."*

*I only appeared to belong to my mother,
to live among blocks and cotton undershirts
with snaps; among red tin lunch boxes
and report cards in ugly brown slipcases.
I was already yours—the anti-urge,
the mutilator of souls.*

2 BOTTLES

Elavil, Ludiomil, Doxepin,
Norpramin, Prozac, Lithium, Xanax,
Wellbutrin, Parnate, Nardil, Zoloft.
The coated ones smell sweet or have
no smell; the powdery ones smell
like the chemistry lab at school
that made me hold my breath.

3 SUGGESTION FROM A FRIEND

You wouldn't be so depressed
if you really believed in God.

4 OFTEN

Often I go to bed as soon after dinner
as seems adult
(I mean I try to wait for dark)
in order to push away
from the massive pain in sleep's
frail wicker coracle.

5 ONCE THERE WAS A LIGHT

Once, in my early thirties; I saw
that I was a speck of light in the great
river of light that undulates through time.

I was floating with the whole
human family. We were all colors—those
who are living now, those who have died,
those who are not yet born. For a few

moments I floated, completely calm,
and I no longer hated having to exist.

Like a crow who smells hot blood
you came flying to pull me out
of the glowing stream.
"I'll hold you up. I never let my dear
ones drown!" After that, I wept for days.

6 IN AND OUT

The dog searches until he finds me
upstairs, lies down with a clatter
of elbows, puts his head on my foot.

Sometimes the sound of his breathing
saves my life—in and out, in
and out; a pause, a long sigh . . .

7 PARDON

A piece of burned meat
wears my clothes, speaks
in my voice, dispatches obligations
haltingly, or not at all.
It is tired of trying
to be stouthearted, tired
beyond measure.

We move on to the monoamine
oxidase inhibitors. Day and night
I feel as if I had drunk six cups
of coffee, but the pain stops
abruptly. With the wonder
and bitterness of someone pardoned
for a crime she did not commit
I come back to marriage and friends,
to pink-fringed hollyhocks; come back
to my desk, books, and chair.

8 CREDO

Pharmaceutical wonders are at work
but I believe only in this moment
of well-being. Unholy ghost,
you are certain to come again.

Coarse, mean, you'll put your feet
on the coffee table, lean back,
and turn me into someone who can't
take the trouble to speak; someone
who can't sleep, or who does nothing
but sleep; can't read, or call
for an appointment for help.

There is nothing I can do
against your coming.
When I awake, I am still with thee.

9 WOOD THRUSH

High on Nardil and June light
I wake at four,
waiting greedily for the first
notes of the wood thrush. Easeful air
presses through the screen
with the wild, complex song
of the bird, and I am overcome

by ordinary contentment.
What hurt me so terribly
all my life until this moment?
How I love the small, swiftly
beating heart of the bird
singing in the great maples;
its bright, unequivocal eye.

GETTING OLDER

Blood Ties
Standing at Different Points in the Creative Cycle

Alma Luz Villanueva

Poet and novelist Alma Luz Villanueva views menopause (which she calls "menostop," a more accurate term for the cessation of menses) as part of a cycle connected physically and spiritually with menarche and childbirth. At age eleven, when she first got her period, she felt drained, angry, and powerless. At forty-nine, experiencing her "menostop," Villanueva revels in the sense of power and wholeness gained through her years as a mother, a grandmother, a seeker of truth, and an artist.

FIRST BLOOD

My daughter calls this morning,
* her voice in wonder:*
*   "Ashley has her menstrual."*

My granddaughter: Yesterday
* I bled old blood, between*
*   my cycles, to honor*

your new blood, the Most Sacred.
* The Goddess in your Body.*
*   The Goddess in your Womb.*

Your mother weeps with happiness.
* Your grandmother smiles with*
*   joy and nods to sorrow,*
child and companion.
* To Ashley*

Whenever I think of menostop (no, not pause, but stop) now, I think of my granddaughter, her first menstruation, and what that evoked in me—this poem. She, the child; and companion, her woman's blood. Creativity. Her power to create. I want her (and all young women) to know this early on: they have the power. To create: children, books, paintings, cities, science, music, dance, worlds without end. But who will tell her (and all the young, bleeding women)?

It should be us, the older women, the women in menostop, the women (like myself) approaching menostop, the women who have created children, books, paintings, cities, science, music, dance, worlds without end. There aren't many of us (if all the menostop women be counted), but the numbers are definitely growing.

At 49, at the edge of 50, at the edge of menostop, I pause to look at my beautiful, strong daughter, Antoinette, through her to my beautiful, strong granddaughter, Ashley (who also writes poems), and to myself at 11 when I began to bleed.

It was the year my grandmother, Jesus Villanueva, died that I became a woman. It was Indian summer (close to my twelfth birthday) in San Francisco. It was sunset and I was alone. I decided to climb a building's steel scaffold, though it terrified me to climb alone. Usually I did these daring things with my friend Judy, who was a tomboy like myself. She was blond, blue-eyed, and had a strong, muscular, boyish body; I had thick, dark, unruly hair (that I kept short or it defied me and became a bush of curls), dark-hazel eyes, and a skinny, surprisingly strong body that, in a pinch (as when defending my mother from my abusive stepfather), exploded with what I thought of as "super girl energy."

And so, the sun had set, and the sky rotated above me with bands of pink to red to purple, violet. I knew if I climbed to the top I would

see everything so clearly. Like a picture. There might be seagulls in my picture. Or an airplane making a thin trail of smoke. The clouds might form into a familiar face, or into ones that might want to kill me. How did I know. When you're alone anything could happen. What if one of the workmen returned for a wrench, or just to see if some kid was climbing his steel structure. I knew, at 11, that I was trespassing on masculine territory. Men came here in the daytime, when the sun was out, and created buildings that pierced the sky.

Judy and I climbed the steel structures, never complaining about the coldness that numbed our hands (we climbed at night), or the heights, as we left the ground. It was nonverbal, never said, but we felt this was how we became boys, became like men, and therefore we deserved to be on their territory.

As I stood on the exposed earth, not yet covered with cement, I looked up to the 12 floors of steel. I knew in my body if I climbed by myself, this picture would be mine. No one else's. If I fell, it would be my fault. If a workman returned and caught me, it would be my fault. If the sky was empty, it would be my fault.

I had to do it. The signal for me was fear. And excitement. That small, dark voice—deep, deep inside me—that persistently said, "I want you to," over and over, until it drowned out all the usual, logical reasons why I shouldn't. Dare.

I began to climb, and the steel didn't feel cold like it did later, at night. It still felt warm from the sun. But I had to concentrate: hand to hand, foot to foot, stretching myself higher toward the top, to that faraway sliver of steel that looked unreachable as I stood on the second-story beam, alone, and the soft night (the faint smell of steel, oil, and men) surrounded me.

Suddenly, I felt unfamiliar, secretive, as though I didn't really care if I died. It was that super girl energy, but I had nothing to protect or defend. It was just me.

My grandmother, *mi mamacita,* who had taught me to dream (but never told me, in words, anything about being a woman), had died. My mother was living with her husband, my stepfather, whom I hated (I'd knocked him out cold, nearly killing him, when he tried to strangle her). I was living with a woman I barely knew. I felt utterly alone in the world, and it seemed as though something waited for me at the top of this incomplete 12-story building, its skeleton of steel. So, I kept climbing. The words, "I want you to," the command, had become my breath filling my lungs, the blood that pumped my heart. (Now, writing this, I remember Mamacita's words, *"No te dejes!"* which translates, "Don't take any shit!" Or more politely, "Take care of yourself!" She would tell me this, from time to time, when I came in complaining about some mistreatment, and out I'd go to defend myself.) Air to lungs, blood to heart, girl to woman.

My mind was empty when I reached the top. The sky was nearly dark. Soon it would be completely dark. The only sound I heard was a steady wind, occasionally a car horn far away on Earth, below. This night, alone, without Judy, I saw the first star appear, then the others, separate and alone. In school they said the stars were the Hunter, the Lion, things like that. All I saw was each star, alone, bravely shining in the dark, it seemed for me. They gave me light, each one, separately, and I thought of my grandmother's words, *"El obscuro es la ausencia de la luz"* ("Darkness is the absence of light"). I wasn't afraid anymore.

Then I felt it. An unfamiliar wetness on my leg, trailing down into my rough, dirty jeans. I sat down on the thin, steel beam, clutching the scaffolding with my arms and legs. I didn't even think it, *blood,* but I knew. For a long, long time, I sat there absolutely still. I saw myself in the years to come, not in distinct events, but in a blur of feeling—strong, overpowering feeling—as though I were flying

through my life wide awake, terrified yet undisturbed. I saw that it was going to be hard, for *her.*

I remember that the stars receded, and that the darkness was complete. I remember that my body was utterly unfamiliar. And so, I turned and climbed down as fast as I could, trying to touch the ground. But I had seen the picture. My picture. And I thought I had no one to blame but myself.

I was changed. I was different. I was unfamiliar. Now, I was able. To create. Like a woman. My womb had opened up and swallowed me whole.

This is what happened, but I had no one to translate this experience, this picture (vision) for me. Mamacita, who raised me, was dead, but she, a full-blood Yaqui Indian from Sonora, Mexico, had taught me to *dream,* and to know more than I could say in words. And so, I stumbled on without the sustained guidance of older women (it was just your period, the business, the curse, a mess, a taboo mess that stained your clothes and smelled bad, and, worse, it was now impossible to *be* a boy and trespass on masculine territory, that measure of freedom I'd stolen in my disguise). I stumbled into my teens without a clue to this power. To create. Worlds.

Now, approaching 50, I see I stumbled, fell, and danced, occasionally, onto the hazardous path of my power. To create. A baby at 15, the others at 17, 21, and finally 36. The poems and stories that had come to me mysteriously at 11 and 12 died out at 13, resurfacing with a vengeance at 30. Poetry and stories in my thirties. My first novel at 40. The endless struggle (and endless joy) to raise my first four creations, each one a novel, each one a world. And my daughter, Antoinette, whom I had at 15 (child and companion), was the mirror to my girlchild, my lost dreams of creativity (she who creates worlds without end), until I reclaimed my lost dreams, firmly and fiercely, in my thirties.

My other children are sons; those privileged by birth, biology, and patriarchal culture to have a wider horizon of freedom. They gave me many years to observe an *unspoiled,* a kind of pure, masculinity (which I love and admire and also recognize in myself as necessary, treasured, and hard-won).

Three years ago I was experiencing a rush of menostop symptoms. I was beginning to feel dire warnings from my body. I was losing some vital strength, some vital energy. I vividly felt my body beginning to cave in on itself. This was at the end of writing two novels and a collection of short stories—a lot of sitting. Though I've always hiked, swum, biked, the *balance* just wasn't right. So I started a "body program" that included, first, acupuncture, then a take-it-to-the-limit workout and weight lifting program. Three years later, I've lost 16 pounds, gained muscles where I forgot I had them (coaxing my strength, the energy, back). Now I experience the occasional hot flash, but it feels friendly, welcome, and I just let myself sweat, shift gears, let whatever it is, this new energy, do its job—cleanse me. Change me.

As Vicki Noble says in *Shakti Woman* (warning against hormone replacement therapy to avoid hot flashes and menostop symptoms): "Hot flashes happen for a reason, besides the fact that we're toxic and need the release of heat and sweat to relieve the body. *Menopause is preparing us to be healthy old women!* It gives our body a raised temperature during the transition, which probably heals it of potential ills, such as the pervasive cancers that exist in the present moment." Now, coupled with my occasional hot flashes, I also experience my own self-induced sweating/cleansing rituals of exercise.

I also see that my warrior rose up in me, guiding me to that super girl energy that was beginning to become a memory. Who was I at 11? Where was all that energy coming from, fairly unimpeded? What was all that energy preparing me to do? What if I (and all the other

11-year-old girls) had lived in a woman-loving, Goddess/God-loving culture? What if there had been (and were now widely accepted) rituals for this transition, this huge leap into this crucial phase (girl to woman) of creativity? The challenge of creativity.

These same questions are also for boys (boy to man). Rather than the rituals of drugs, drinking, violence—some media-induced version of patriarchal masculinity—the rituals of creativity and challenge, real challenge, like sports, rock climbing, a musical instrument, poetry, stories, a mountain, a mentor, a vision quest *to keep the unspoiled essence* of their masculinity, which is not encouraged by patriarchal culture. In fact, this essence is under almost constant attack, even as women are under attack (as the girl becoming a woman knows in her bleeding body).

Once, when I was taking a walk with my 13-year-old son, Jules, he asked me, as we paused to gaze at the ocean: "Is the phallic symbol all the bad stuff like missiles and rifles?" We'd been talking about phallic symbols in our patriarchal culture and how the media use them for exploitation. I knew, instantly, how crucial this moment was for him, at 13, as he approached becoming a man. I said, "Absolutely not. The *real* phallic symbol, the penis, is the symbol of potency and *life*. Like creation, you know?" I saw his face expand, then relax with the sensuality of knowledge, and I knew his body, if not his mind, would always remember this moment. This answer.

Now, at 49, with my 13-year-old son and my 12-year-old granddaughter in mind, I pause at the edge of menostop, and I see that the bleeding 11-year-old girl at the top of the steel structure, at sunset, in Indian summer, in San Francisco, was androgynous (in the dictionary: "*andr* man + *gyne* woman—more at QUEEN"). She was a girl and a boy. She was whole, naturally, in a way that I had to learn (step by excruciating step) to become whole again. Always a woman. But androgynous. Whole. Like a girl or boy is whole. This time learned. Earned.

At 35 I moved with my then 14-year-old son, Marc, to the Sierras and lived in an isolated cabin for four years. A failing second marriage, my grown daughter leaving to live on her own, symbols of the circle that had seemed to appear everywhere I looked (seaweed in a circle, a perfectly round stone, a full moon ringed by a circle of light, on and on). Everything had seemed to prod me, go. But where? I had a series of dreams, ending with a clear dream of the cabin, exactly the way it would look.

This dream appeared as a black dot (a dark, tight circle), which I had to pull open, painfully, with both my hands. First, I had to find my hands in the dream and then with a great conscious effort—pain running up and down my arms—I instructed my hands not to let go, not for anything. I pulled open the dark, tight circle as wide as I could, and saw a cabin surrounded by boulders and trees, with a small meadow in front. The light was strange; not sunlight or moonlight, but dream light. It didn't attract me; it compelled me (the words, "I want you to," filled my dreaming body). Fear and excitement, dread and curiosity, terror and wonder—my old, familiar allies—simultaneously commanded and challenged me, dared me to do what I felt was impossible at that time. *Where* was this cabin? (I'd never lived in a remote place on my own—and with the responsibility of a teenage son?) And *why* was I supposed to go there? Because of the circle? Because of the dream?

I found the way, the mountain, and the cabin, and I moved, and also found I was pregnant with my third son, my fourth and final child, Jules. So, I was also going to experience the most primal feminine condition (after deciding, painstakingly, against abortion), in what seemed to be the most primal masculine conditions (hermit on the mountain, snow-buried cabin, town 15 miles away, as well as

rattlers, mountain lions, bears, coyotes—and the local cowboys, but that's another story).

My first journey up to the Sierras, in Plumas (Feathers) County, prompted by a letter from an old friend in Quincy, was true to the black dot, circle dream. My car's engine caught on fire. Two men, passing me in both directions, jumped out of their trucks with fire extinguishers (help from the masculine) and put out the fire so quickly my engine suffered only minor damage. I asked myself, should I continue? After minor repairs, replacing all hoses and burned parts, I continued.

I had come to that place of transition (as I had on the steel structure 24 years before), that leap into the unknown: creativity. That power. And just as I had as a girl, I felt hunted and unsafe as a woman in the crowded cities of the patriarchal culture. I had to do this leap or die. I simply couldn't bear to be a coward. I couldn't bear to give in. To accept my limits. To be a good girl, a "normal" woman (all the time knowing that my family, and most of my friends, thought I'd gone too far this time. "And to top it off, she's pregnant, belongs with her husband, for God's sake." I could hear their thoughts).

I desired, at 35, to be *whole* like a bodily need (thirst, hunger, sex) and I knew if I backed away from this inner demand I would die. Perhaps not physically but, most important, spiritually. In my soul.

I went looking for my wholeness, looking for the Goddess. I couldn't *see* her in the crowded places where patriarchal time reigned. I couldn't see her, bodily. I had to see her or myself. For my self.

So I stayed on my mountain, in my cabin, and learned to walk at night with "night eyes" over rocks, downed branches, following the sound and curve of a creek (the first few months, it was challenge enough to turn off all the lights in the cabin, fall asleep, and dream). Then a year later, I realized walking back to my cabin in the dark by myself: *This darkness, this forest, swallows my cabin, my sons, and me, completely. No wonder I dream these amazing dreams.* I remember smiling, engulfed by the scent of pine and cedar and so many night smells I couldn't identify. Yet they all merged into one scent: freedom.

I didn't wander in naive bliss through the night, through the forest. I strapped on my Buck knife or packed it in a readily available pouch. There were times I would actually forget to take my knife, and a few times my shields were tested in dangerous situations (once by a growling mountain lion, another time by two heavily armed men I met on a lonely trail). Looking back on these incidents, I realize I was meant "to forget" my knife and rely only on my shields (fluidity, intuition, strength, innocence). And the shields held, firmly.

My stance was to gather as much awareness as possible (like a circle of light, a radar) and tune myself to its continuous message of *what was there.* The forest, the mountains, the night, and the day, taught me this. I learned to trust my self (the feminine, the masculine). I learned that though I was the hunted, I was also the hunter; and that beyond survival, I was loved, and I was the lover. I was loved by the Earth herself. And the Sky. As well as the Cosmos. That I *belonged* in the Cosmos, and that weakness and strength, hatred and love, coward and hero, male and female (the whole) were born in me.

Two months after Jules was born, prematurely, a blizzard blew in that I thought was going to take off the cabin's roof and knock down the walls. My teenager, Marc, was staying the night with a teacher in town; this blizzard stopped all travel. The worst in a century, I read later in the paper. Immense pines and cedars bent to the fierce winds like toothpicks, and the sound of a hundred freight trains roared by my small cabin. I fed Jules every 30 minutes (his preemie schedule), facing, simultaneously, the fire I kept going all night and the night outside the windows that merged wind, trees, and snow (Sky and Earth) in a perfect and terrifying balance.

Exhausted, but alive, in the dawn, drinking my first cup of coffee, facing my wide kitchen window, I saw her: the Goddess. The sight was blinding. She was entirely surrounded by cold, cold diamonds: snow. I could see her clearly: high cheekbones, downcast eyes (looking inward), Mayan, utterly serene. Her strength and power flew through my body. I wept with gratitude, relief. Joy. There was no wind at all; it was absolutely still, but it was freezing out there where she was, no more than 15 feet away. All day I fed Jules within the diamond. All day she stayed with me, utterly perfect. The Goddess.

I had the following dream in the Sierras on February 12, New Moon, 1983 (I keep dream journals, which I write in poetry form). I'm shown a basket cradle with chunks of turquoise dangling in a circle, obscuring the contents of the cradle. It's the most beautiful thing I've ever seen, and I'm overjoyed that it's also mine (though I know it ultimately belongs to the Goddess—and the God). The dream poem ends:

> *I have gathered*
> *turquoise for the*
> *cradle of my*
> *power.*
> *It is empty, dark*
> *and full. No human*
> *child sleeps in this,*
> *but the Child of knowledge*
> *and possibility exists*
> *within.*

At the edge of menostop, I look at all my perfect creations: my 34-year-old daughter, Antoinette; my three sons—Ed, 32, Marc, 28, and Jules, 13. I also look at my *im*perfect creations: five books of poetry, three novels, a book of short stories, the next novel, the new poems. Then I shut my eyes and I see the basket cradle. It's so beautiful I want to weep and laugh.

I hear the words, "I want you to," but I don't know the exact nature of this command/challenge. I've begun the dreaming (which always translates into living), so I trust this ongoing path of power, my creativity.

I see my future 59-year-old self (thick gray hair, loose to my shoulders), strengthened by exercise and weight lifting, climbing the steel structure. It's Indian summer, close to my sixtieth birthday. It's sunset, and bands of color—pink, red, purple, violet—wash the sky, changing from moment to moment. I'm terrified, but I'm old enough, and wise enough (at last), to know the twin natures of terror and wonder, how they melt in my mouth, bitter/sweet, and so I simply taste it and sniff the night wind, its many scents, that blur into one scent: freedom.

I see *her* (her short dark hair, cut like a boy's). My 11-year-old self, waiting. There's new, warm blood oozing down her leg, and she's terrified, ashamed, angry. But she's fearless. In her terror, she's absolutely fearless.

She turns to face me. She waits. Child and companion. I feel something on my back, and I know it's the basket cradle. I no longer bleed, so I gather my creations in this mysterious basket, encircled with perfect chunks of turquoise. The turquoise sways in the night wind as I walk toward the bleeding girl. I take her hand (virgin/maiden, virgin/crone) in mine. Her grip is firm. How strong she is. How eager she is to leap. How eager she is for the journey of her life.

Holding hands, we turn and face the western horizon. We leap. And instead of falling, we fly. The basket cradle is magic (of course), and we have grown feathers/*plumas*.

Together (child and companion), we will create worlds without end. And I know that, though I don't want to die, I'm not afraid of dying ("I want you to").

Menostop is my (further) door, my challenge to accept the mystery of creation. *And I do.*

Study/Discussion Questions

1. In what ways does the author see menopause as a good thing?
2. In what ways is the author at 49 like her 11-year-old self?
3. What does she feel that she has gained from her life experience since she was an 11-year-old?

How Was It for You?

Margaret Forster

Prolific author of sixteen novels, and mother of three grown children, British writer Margaret Forster reveals how "the menopause" was for her, when she was forty-six years old. Contrary to the cultural mandate to preserve and celebrate youth at all costs, Forster finds the post-menopausal phase of her life gratifying in many ways. Her thoughts on beauty, sex, work, younger women, grandchildren, and hormone replacement therapy read like a paean to self-acceptance.

My mother never mentioned the word "menopause" to me, but then she did not mention a great many other words: periods, menstruation, puberty, sex, womb . . . There was a whole hidden vocabulary learned later from friends and books. She used to send me, as a young child, to a shop nearby with a note which said: "One packet of Dr White's, please." I'd be given a plain brown paper package which I would trot home with, not having the least idea what was in it. I asked, of course, being an intensely curious child, and was told either "Things" or "You'll know in good time," both of which answers drove me mad.

When I was ten, and my mother was forty-six, the collecting of the mysterious packages stopped. My mother went into hospital for "an operation," and when she came out she never needed me to go again. Naturally, I'd no idea what the operation was for. "Something inside," I was told.

The more I pressed to be told exactly what, the more distressed my mother became. So I stopped asking. I watched her with great anxiety instead. She put on weight rapidly, after always being slim, and her hair seemed to turn white in the space of a few months. She was depressed even melancholic, but then she often had been. Whatever it was that had happened inside was obviously not good news.

Another word was added to those not used: "hysterectomy." I heard a neighbour say, "Well, you were at the change anyway, so what's the odds?" It sounded such an unemotive word that I risked asking, "What's the change?" "Nothing," I was told.

But do not deduce from this that my mother was a silly or ignorant woman. On the contrary, she was highly intelligent, one of that generation of working-class women who were cheated of the higher education they should have had (and which we, their daughters, then received). So the explanation for

From *A Certain Age: Reflecting on Menopause*, edited by Joanna Goldsworthy, New York: Columbia University Press, 1993, pp. 147–158.

why she kept everything to do with menstruation virtually secret had more to do with psychological reasons than anything else. She believed, I think (because it was never discussed), that talking about "intimate problems" was somehow indelicate. It upset her without her being able to say why. There was embarrassment and even misplaced pride mixed up in her furtive attitudes—she wanted this side of her life ignored, to pretend it did not exist.

Now this had a good as well as a bad effect on me. The bad effect is all too obvious and hardly needs to be stated but the good effect was more subtle. Because my mother believed in concealing everything to do with menstruation, including its ending, the menopause, it never loomed large in my thoughts. My mother did not moan and groan every month or fill me full of dire warnings about pains and aches and floodings and all the other things many of my friends' mothers frightened them with. I grew up believing this "something" that happened to women could be risen above and need not feature too much in their lives. I had no fear of the menopause because I did not associate it with my mother after her operation. This operation was one thing; the aftermath, during which she visibly aged, another. I made no connection.

This attitude to the menopause continued after I left home and right up to my own menopause. I never had the slightest fear of it; it didn't loom over me or cause me any apprehension. But I was aware, all the same, that I was ridiculously ill-informed: I really hadn't the faintest idea what happened beyond periods stopping. I'd slide my eyes occasionally over articles in newspapers and magazines to do with the menopause, but never had the interest I had in similar features about, say, pregnancy. As far as I was concerned it was just something that happened naturally and I couldn't see any reason to worry about it until it happened, and preferably not even then.

So I went into my own menopause quite blithely. I first thought it might be starting when, over a year, my periods were not only lighter and shorter but had longer gaps between them. Well, thought I, if this is the jolly old menopause then hurrah. I was forty-six at the time, the same age my mother had her strange operation, and I found myself wondering why she had had what I by then knew was a hysterectomy. (She was dead, so I couldn't ask.)

The next thing that signalled a menopause in progress was faint—very faint—feelings of heat in the face and neck. It took me quite a while to realize these were the famous hot flushes of all the jokes, and once more I was amazed at how harmless they were. And so I found myself wondering, at the age of forty-seven, when menstruation had ceased, in the immortal words of Bob Geldof, "Is that it, then?"

For me it was, but I don't make the mistake of deducing that the menopause is a doddle for everyone. Mine was, yours might be, but certainly others' won't be. Like childbirth, it's all a matter of luck, or a great deal of it. I have had three children and know very well how violently different the experience of giving birth can be, ranging from simple and ecstatic to absolute torture and horrible complications. The menopause, that other great female watershed, is the same: some, like me, sail through it, hardly aware it is happening; others have their lives wrecked. But so vociferous are those who back HRT [hormone replacement therapy] that it is perhaps worth reminding women that they ought at least to wait and see before embarking on it. Nature, sometimes, can manage perfectly well on its own.

Even easier to manage, for me, has been the transition to post-menopausal woman—but then, again, I would say that, wouldn't I? If I had had no children, and had wanted them, then the menopause would have been a time of wistfulness, and perhaps even real despair. Fine for me that my childbearing years are over—I was actually glad to see them go. It struck me as wonderfully neat that just as my children were all more or less off on their own I should suddenly be given all this extra energy to work harder and better than I had ever been able to. During my pre-menopausal years I was so often exhausted, whereas in my post-menopausal ones I am rested and fitter. I'm able to be so good to myself. A little tired? Fine, I put my feet up and read a novel in the middle of the day if I want to. I am another creature, and the physical benefits are enormous.

But of course, so far as looks go—ah, looks! —I am also another creature, and have to face up to it. Face is the word. I've never in my life worn make-up of any sort, so there is nothing to hide behind. The lines and wrinkles are there, and sometimes I do catch sight of myself and get a slight shock. Whether, after I've recovered, I mind or not is difficult to answer truthfully. On balance, I have to admit I do mind, and that I do regret the disappearance of a smooth skin and good complexion, but what I do not mind so much is what it signifies—I don't mind looking like what I am: a middle-aged woman. If, when young, I had been beautiful or glamorous, then I think I would have been depressed by the change in my facial appearance—hard, surely, to have had a lovely, glowing face and then have to adapt to wrinkled skin. Older faces can have a beauty of their own, and glow in a different way, but they are not attractive in the *same* way.

And this, of course, is what is regarded as the crux: attraction. Post-menopausal women are thought of as not sexually attractive, and that is what they are supposed to mind most of all. It is no good wheeling out Joan Collins or Jane Fonda or Cher because the whole point of women like that is that they attempt to defy the menopause and stay young-looking and therefore, allegedly, attractive. But women who do that are exactly those women whose whole life has been built on this physical attraction of theirs. Mine has not been. If I'm attractive

to the one man who loves me, and whom I love, and am attracted by, then the rest of the world doesn't matter.

But there we go again—luck. If there was no one man with whom I was able to be so secure, then my whole perspective might change. I could not be so relaxed about the lines, the general ageing, if I had to go out into the world and hope to attract. And some women do have to, and want to, do that— post-menopausal or not. Sex can't simply be cut out of one's life because one is post-menopausal, even if it is true—which I think it is— that it occupies a different place.

This is certainly the aspect of the menopause talked about least—something not quite nice about thinking about sex and the menopause, it seems. Germaine Greer got it only half-right in *The Change,* and the half she got wrong was dangerous. It is not, as she suggested, that post-menopausal women should rejoice because sex means nothing to them any more, but that they should recognize it doesn't mean the same. Sex doesn't dominate life as it used to, nor is the need for it so intense, but it does not disappear, nor are its pleasures and joys gone forever. I think there *is* some sadness in this, but it's tolerable just so long as paradise can be regained sometimes.

As in so many parts of ageing, nature tries to help by arranging for what would, at one stage of life, be far, far too little to be sufficient. It is not so much the waning of desire as the spacing of it. The bit Germaine Greer got right was how satisfactory it is not to be dictated to by hormones *all the time* so that nothing else mattered, for so many years, but sex.

Other things now matter just as much, and one of them is work. Throughout my adult life I've had to scheme and battle to find time and energy to work. I got married young, at twenty-two, and had children young: my first at twenty-five. My first novel was published weeks before my first child was born. For the next twenty years it was a case of the familiar juggling act: wife, mother and, trailing a poor third, writer. I chose this. I wanted this. I regretted none of it. I wouldn't have had it any other way. But the fact remains that, self-inflicted or not, the load was heavy, and carrying it was a strain.

In my own case I made it heavier than it might have been and the strain greater by doing everything myself without help—no cleaners, no nannies, no au pairs. But equally, the consequence of the load being lifted, because it was so heavy, was dramatic. I am thrilled with my post-menopause status so far as work goes. I find my output has doubled and I love saying "yes" to things when always before I had to say "no" because one more job and I'd have cracked. And because I am suddenly available I am more in demand: certainly I can whip in today and do a review for "Kaleidoscope," a pleasure to take part in a "Bookshelf" discussion; absolutely no problem about appearing in a book program on some TV channel.

Naturally, when I get to these places, all the producers are younger. Much younger. Young enough to be my children exactly. This could make me feel an Old Bat. But it doesn't —or rather, it does, but I like it. These young things have enthusiasm and energy which, you would suppose, would be matched by my—perhaps—experience and gravitas—but not at all. Yes, I do have experience and a certain weight which comes from it, but I've never yet found any of them outstripped me for enthusiasm or intellectual energy.

That, yet again—and I never forget it—is my luck: to have work which takes virtually no regard of age. A literary critic is, if anything, of more value older rather than younger. The younger critic, inevitably, has a mark to make, and wants to make it; the older critic doesn't have to worry, and can enjoy herself more. And I cannot deny that I like being thought of as dependable, as professional, because I've been tried and tested. They know what I can do, and this leads to a lovely welcome.

When I was young and a slashing attacker, at times the tension could be acute on both sides. I'd be worked up because I wanted to blast something, and the producer would be anxious I'd overdo it. All that has gone from this fringe work of mine. It is a pure pleasure, and has become that only with age.

One thing that has not yet come with age—and it is something heavily associated with menopausal women—is the change of status from mother to grandmother. I am not, thank heaven, a grandmother, though most of my contemporaries are. I don't say "thank heaven" because the thought of being a grandmother depresses me—on the contrary, I'm sure I'd love it—but because none of my children seems to me anything like ready to have children.

But I don't find, as people seem to expect me to, that I yearn for grandchildren. I don't think this is an automatic part of being post-menopausal—unable to breed myself, but wanting my children to do it for me. I haven't become in the least haunted by visions of myself holding a beloved grandchild. In a way I feel I want the gap: motherhood is only just over, in the practical if not emotional sense, and I'm in no hurry to start grandmotherhood even if it is—or so I'm told—not so arduous and all-consuming a calling.

It may also be because I relish what I am at the moment, more my own person than I have ever been. "Fifty is the heyday of a woman's life," said Elizabeth Cady Stanton, one of the early-nineteenth-century feminists. It feels my heyday. What surprises me is the increase of my sense of ambition: I thought it would desert me, but it hasn't. I've always been ambitious, but during my childbearing years I could feel this desire to write a great book fading away, becoming unimportant beside the bearing and rearing of children. There was some definite loss of motivation. What was a book, after all, compared to a child? How could I want to be a good writer when it was so much more absorbing and gratifying trying to be a good mother?

But the ambition came back as my youngest child reached around thirteen, and now. it is fierce again. Curiously, it doesn't yet seem to dismay me that I haven't fulfilled this ambition—I simply like having it. I don't, as a writer, have to look at myself only halfway up a ladder, as I would have to if I were in another profession, and see that at my age I'll now never reach the top. That probably would depress me, and I'd see the menopause as an awful tolling of a bell telling me I was doomed never to reach my potential. But no bells toll for writers, not until the final hour of their lives.

Nor does that final hour, or its approach, cause me much concern. When I was young, I thought about death a great deal. Now, when it is bound to be so much nearer, I rarely think of it, and when I do it is without fear. For the post-menopausal woman, with this "dying" of one part of herself, this running down of a system which has operated for some forty years, there should be an inescapable sense of being reminded that death is coming. But I don't feel it. I don't believe I am blocking out or suppressing fears of death so much as appreciating and revelling in all that feels vigorously alive in myself.

The menopause has brought with it a better adjustment to myself, and I'm grateful for it. I haven't found myself an easy person to live with, ever—too irritable, too demanding, too impatient, too critical, too moody; the list is endless. I've spent far too many years wishing I was different, and some few trying to make myself so, all to no avail. Now, I've accepted myself and I get on with myself better. This may very well be due to hormonal changes; if so they happened naturally, and I'm charmed by them. If they do exist, these changes, and had not happened for me, and if as a result I'd been even more irritable, and so on, then maybe I would have tried HRT.

I am not entirely anti-HRT, but I am very wary of how it is used—of the propaganda,

if you like. If a woman has appalling menopausal symptoms, then fine, try it, but what I cannot go along with is its use *before* any symptoms have appeared in order to "stay young." The idea is that "We all want to stay young and sexy if we can," said Teresa Gorman (to me, during a television discussion). But no, I don't think that we all either do or should.

What we do all want to do is not suffer terrible hot flushes, sweats and all the other things I never had, but neither do we (or some of us) want to use drugs, forever, to evade the appearance of growing old. That is to falsify ourselves in the worst possible way, to place an even greater emphasis on looks than there already is. The menopause would then become a time when the great pretence would have to begin and be maintained until death—and death not even HRT could halt.

It would also rob me, at least, of the benefit of looking an older woman. I love the fact that my obvious age makes me reassuring and trusted. I have clearly "seen life," and this draws forth all kinds of confidences and requests for advice. I love it. I've always liked listening to anyone's problems, but never have I had to listen so hard as during the last few years when suddenly I am meant to be wise, as befits my age. I have run the whole female race from start to finish, and this makes me useful to younger women. Howling babies? Troublesome teenagers? My dear, I've seen and dealt with the lot—just try me. On love affairs I am not so hot, only ever having had one, but even then I am a safe person to confide in, and ever ready to listen and come up with what I think is considered judgement.

And I love the young women who sometimes confide in me. I cannot imagine where this legendary competitiveness between younger and older women comes from, this jealousy there is supposed to be. "You look beautiful," I tell them, and, "You're so talented," I remind them, and, "Go for it," I urge.

The young, instead of appalling me, or making me envious, fascinate me.

Sometimes, one of them will groan, "I'll be thirty next year, oh God, thirty!" and I am reminded of the panic of youth. To be thirty and not to have achieved what one wanted—not, perhaps, to have got anywhere near it—is enough to make the blood run cold. At thirty, there is no way of knowing if whatever one wants ever will be gained, especially if it is to do with lovers and children. So I do not fool myself: I am relaxed, as a post-menopausal woman, because I am, on the whole, happy with how my life has turned out.

I remember, with pain, the unhappiness of women who, at the menopause, had to face the fact that life had not given them what they wanted. In those days, a mere forty years ago, there were so many more of them. Life was motherhood, put plainly. When the children left home, and especially if they moved away, all meaning in one's days was virtually over. My mother had no career: we were her career. When we left she felt useless. She joined various church clubs and tried to fulfill herself in other ways, but she did not succeed. The menopause to her meant the end of everything she cared about.

But my generation has been more fortunate. Most of us have careers of one sort or another, most of us have not been complete slaves to our children, most of us have worn better be-cause our lives have been physically easier: we haven't scrubbed stone floors, stood over sinks washing clothes by hand, raked out fires, toiled home with heavy bags of shopping, or any of those other household tasks which aged women so. We have had infinitely better pregnancies and childbirths, and we have approached the menopause physically in far better shape.

All this should be something to rejoice over; it should remove the stigma of the dreaded menopause to know the better condition we are all in. But it has not done so—not yet. It amuses me, when I ask a contemporary, "Are you through the menopause yet?" to be met quite often with the indignant reply, "Certainly not!" as though I'd insulted her. No other inquiry of a middle-aged woman is so resented.

Nor does any, except the rare woman, ever advertise the fact that she is post-menopausal. Women will rush to tell you they are pregnant, or even to discuss miscarriages and abortions, but they seek to hide their menopauses. No one ever says, "Isn't it great—I'm post-menopausal and I feel terrific." If the menopause is talked about at all, it is in whispers, and always to complain.

Only the attitudes of women themselves can change this. The more women make it known that the process itself can be perfectly easy, and the change which takes place hugely beneficial, as well as nothing to fear, the more the menopause will cease to be a thing of dread.

Study/Discussion Questions

1. How has Forster's life changed as she has aged?
2. What are the advantages of middle age for her?
3. How have her feelings about herself and her work changed?
4. Why does the author oppose HRT (hormone replacement therapy)?
5. What is her purpose in telling her story of getting older happily and easily? What, besides good luck, has made it easier for her?

Ageism and the Politics of Beauty

Cynthia Rich

Ageism and sexism combine to make a potent brew of disdain for the bodies of old women. That is why, explains Cynthia Rich, it remains acceptable in our society, even among those who pride themselves on sensitivity to issues of diversity, to speak with disgust about old women's looks. Confronting ageism means grappling with the "politics of beauty" as surely as it means fighting more blatant forms of discrimination, Rich argues.

If you are a younger woman, try to imagine what everything in society tells you not to imagine: that you are a woman in your seventies, eighties, nineties, or older, and yet you are still you. Even your body is yours. It is not, however, in the language of the embalmers, "well-preserved," and though the male world gives you troubles for it, you like it that way. Apart from those troubles, you find sometimes a mysterious integrity, a deep connection to life, that comes to you from having belonged to a body that has been large and small, thin and fat, with breasts and hips of many different sizes and shapes, and skin of different textures.

In your fifties and sixties when your eyebrows and pubic hair and the hair on your head began to thin, it bothered you at first. But then you remembered times when you tweezed your eyebrows, shaved your pubic hair and legs and underarms, or took thinning shears to your head. "Too much" hair, "too little" hair—now you know that both are male messages.

One day you pick up a book that you find rich and nourishing, published by a feminist press. It is a political book and a sensuous book, and you like the way its politics and its sensuality seem merged. One of the authors is a poet in her fifties, with a warmth of connection to other people, especially women. It is when you come to a section about aging that abruptly the connection—with you—is broken. You find the poet writing with dread and loathing at the thought that one day she must live inside the body of a woman who looks like you.

Stop!
I don't want my scalp
shining through a few thin hairs.
Don't want my neck skin to hang—
neglected cobweb the corner of my chin.
Stop![1]

It shouldn't take this guided tour for any of us to recognize that an old woman must find

From *Look Me in the Eye,* by Barbara MacDonald with Cynthia Rich. San Francisco: Spinsters Ink, 1983. Available from Spinsters Ink, 32 East First Street #330, Duluth, MN 55802. Reprinted by permission.

it insulting, painful, personally humiliating, to be told in print that other women in her community find her body disgusting.

What you—the old woman—find especially painful is that the feminist newspaper where this excerpt was first printed, the feminist publisher, the poet herself, would surely protest if Jewish features, Black features, or the features of any other marginalized group were described—whether in the form of the outsider's contempt or the insider's self-hatred—with this kind of revulsion. They would not think of their protest as censorship of literary expression. They would know that such attitudes do deep damage to a work artistically, as well as humanly and politically.

Yet clearly there are not the same standards about speaking with disgust about the bodies of old women. So the message has a double sting. The "ugliness" of your physical being is not a cruel opinion but an accepted fact; you have not even the right to be insulted. How is it that you, the old woman, find yourself in this place?

I believe the revulsion towards old bodies is only in part a fear of death, as the poet suggests—she ends the poem, *"No quiero morir."* (Of course there is no reason why women over 60 should have to hear such insults whether they remind us of death or not.) Or else everybody would find soldiers going to battle repugnant, young women with leukemia disgusting, the tubercular Violetta in *La Traviata* loathsome. This is a death-obsessed and death-fearing society, that's true enough. But the dying young woman has always been a turn-on.

No, there is another more deeply anti-woman source for this disgust. Once again it is men who have defined our consciousness and, as Susan Sontag noted ten years ago, in aging as in so much else a double standard reigns. True, old men who are quite powerless are sometimes viewed by younger men as if they were old women. But old men routinely seek out much younger women for erotic companions and usually find them. In white Western society, the old woman is distasteful to men because she is such a long way from their ideal of flattering virginal inexperience. But also she outlives them, persists in living when she no longer serves them as wife and mother, and if they cannot make her into Grandma, she is—like the lesbian—that monstrous woman who has her own private reasons for living apart from pleasing men. On the one hand she is a throwaway, on the other a threat.

White men have provided the world with little literature, sculpture, or painting in which the old woman's body is seen through the eyes of desire, admiration, love, wonder, playfulness, tenderness. Instead they have filled our minds with an extensive literature and imagery of disgust, which includes a kind of voyeuristic fascination with what they see as the obscenity of female aging. Men's disgust for old women's bodies, with its language of contempt (shriveled, sagging, drooping, wizened, ravaged, liver spots, crow's feet, old bag, etc.) is so familiar to us that it feels like home.

Still, if this were all, how is it that twenty years of ground-breaking feminism have not led us to rise up to challenge such a transparent, gross form of woman-hating? An honest answer to that question is painful but essential, and Barbara Macdonald has named the key to our resistance. Younger women can no longer afford to ignore the fact that we learned early on to pride ourselves on our distance from, and our superiority to, old women.

While I was thinking about this article, the picture of an old woman caught my eye from the comic pages. The three frames of "The Wizard of Id" show an old woman with thin hair pulled to a tiny topknot on her head, her breasts and hips a single balloon. The Wizard, her jaunty old husband, hand debonairly on hip, legs crossed with a flair, has bragged: "The king and I are judging a beauty contest tonight." She wags her finger. "That's degrading!" she exclaims through her down-turned, toothless mouth. "My lady friends and I will picket!" The Wizard gets in the last word, which of course leaves her speechless: "That'll make a nice contrast."

This slice of mainstream media is jammed with political messages. Old women are ugly. Their view of things can be dismissed as just a way of venting their envy of young women. The old men, who have status and power, and therefore are the judges who matter, prize the young women's beauty and judge old women's bodies to be contemptible. The old woman has no defense since she, too, knows old women are ugly. And: the young woman's body in fact gains in value when set beside that of an old woman.

Images like this accustom younger women to unthinkingly adopting an ageist stance and woman-hating language from men. But also the old woman's low currency temporarily drives up our own. Just as the "plain" white woman is at least not Black, the "plainest" younger woman is at least not old. The system gives us a vested interest in maintaining the politics of beauty and in joining in the oppression of old women.

The principal source of the distaste for old women's bodies should be perfectly familiar. It is very similar to the distaste anti-Semites feel toward Jews, homophobes feel toward lesbians and gays, racists toward Blacks—the drawing back of the oppressor from the physical being of the oppressed. This physical revulsion travels deep; it is like fear. It feels entirely "natural" to the oppressor; he/she believes that everybody who claims to feel differently is simply hiding it out of politeness or cowardice.

When I was twelve, I had an argument with my grandmother. (Because of ageism, I feel a need to point out that she was no more racist than most white Baltimoreans of all ages in the 1940s.) It was probably my first political argument, and I felt both shaky and strong. Buttressed by a book on what in the '40s was called "tolerance," I didn't see why little Black girls couldn't go to my school. I can still remember her voice as she bypassed the intelli-

gence argument. "But just think—would you want one to come to your house and spend the night?" Yes, but would you want to marry one? Physical revulsion is an ideal tool for maintaining oppressive systems, an instant check whenever reason or simple fairness starts to lead us onto more liberal paths.

To treat old women's minds as inconsequential or unstable is in one sense more serious, more dangerous, than disgust for their bodies. But most women find that the more our bodies are perceived as old, the more our minds are dismissed as irrelevant. And if we are more than our bodies (whatever that means), we also are our bodies. If you find my body disgusting, no promises that you admire or love my mind can assure me that I can trust you.

No, the issue of "beauty" and "ugliness" is not frivolous. I think of two white women who are in their sixties. One, a lesbian psychologist from a working-class, radical home, has written about the compelling urge she felt to have a facelift—until she became aware that what she was dealing with was not her own ugliness but the ugly projections of others, and became instead an activist against ageism. The other, a former airplane pilot and now a powerful photographer, has made a series of self-portraits that document, mercilessly, the bruises and scars of her own facelift. These are not conforming Nancy Reagans. These are creative, independent, gutsy women, and they heard the message of society quite accurately: the pain of an operation for passing is less than the pain of enduring other people's withdrawal.

One example of how the danger increases when an old woman's body is seen as less valuable than a younger woman's is that the old woman is unlikely to receive equal treatment from medical practitioners, male or female. Old women attest to this fact. Recent research agrees: a UCLA study confirms that old women with breast cancer are treated less thoroughly than younger women, so that their lives are "needlessly shortened."

In her pamphlet, *Ageism in the Lesbian Community* (Crossing Press), Baba Copper points to the daily erosions of "ugly." She observes that the withdrawal of eroticism between women "which takes place after middle age (or at the point when a woman no longer passes for young) *includes withdrawal of the emotional work which women do to keep the flow of social interactions going:* teasing, touching, remembering details, checking back, supporting" (emphasis mine).

I hear a voice: "All of this may be true. But aren't you trying to place the heavy boot of political correctness on the mysteries of attraction?" No. But obviously the fewer women we can be drawn to because they are "too" Jewish or fat or Asian or old, the more impoverished our lives. And also: if we can never feel that mysterious attraction bubbling up towards an old woman, a disabled woman, an Hispanic woman, we can pretty well suspect that we are oppressive to such women in other ways.

Sometimes I sense a presumption that the fact that each of us is growing older gives us all license to speak of old women's bodies in insulting and degrading ways—or even makes this particular form of woman-hating somehow admirable and honest. Yet the fact that one of us may well in the next twenty years become disabled or fat doesn't make feminist editors eager to hear the details of any "honest" loathing we may feel for the bodies of disabled or fat women.

It does not surprise me that ageism is still with us, since eradicating oppressive attitudes is hard, ongoing, embarrassing, painful, gut work. But as a movement we have developed many sensitivities that are at least well beyond those of the mainstream. And we are quite familiar by now with the basic dynamics that almost all oppressions have in common (most of which we learned from the insights of the civil rights movement and applied to feminism and other liberation movements). Erasure. Stereotyping. Internalized self-hatred, including passing when possible. The attempt to prove the oppression is "natural." Impugning of the mental and emotional capacities. Blame-the-victim. Patronizing. Tokenizing. Segregation. Contempt mingled with fear. And physical revulsion. So it seems almost incredible that we have not learned to identify these most flagrant signals of ageism.

How can we begin to change? We—especially those of us in our forties and fifties—can stop the trend of examining in public how disgusted we are at the thought of the bodily changes of growing old. Such examinations do not display our moral courage. They reveal our insensitivity to old women who have to hear once more that we think their bodies are the pits. We can recognize that ideas of beauty are socialized into us and that yes, Virginia, we can begin to move in the direction of resocializing ourselves. We can work, for ourselves and for any revolution we might imagine, to develop a deeper and more resonant—dare I say more *mature*—concept of beauty.

I am looking at two photographs. One is of Septima Clark, on the back of the book she wrote in her late eighties about her early and ongoing work in the civil rights movement. The other is a postcard of Georgia O'Keeffe from a photo taken twenty years before her death. The hairs on their scalps are no longer a mass, but stand out singly. O'Keeffe's nose is "too" strong, Clark's is "too" broad. O'Keeffe's skin is "wizened," Clark's is "too" dark. Our task is to learn: not to look insultingly beyond these features to souls we can celebrate, but instead to take in these bodies as part of these souls—exciting, individual, beautiful.

NOTE

1. The poem excerpted here is "Old," by Rosario Morales, from *Getting Home Alive* by Aurora Levins Morales and Rosario Morales (Firebrand Books, 141 The Commons, Ithaca, NY 14850, 1986), p.188.

Study/Discussion Questions

1. In what ways are older women discriminated against in our society?
2. What role does looks play in this discrimination?
3. Do women suffer more than men from prejudice against the old?
4. In what ways are women more vulnerable than men?
5. Rich suggests that younger women and men are afraid of and revolted by older women. Do you think that this is true, and, if so, why do you think that is?

Flash Exercise

Brainstorm!

Make two lists: one for everything that comes to mind when you hear the phrase "old man" and one for everything that comes to mind when you hear the phrase "old woman." How much overlap do you have in your lists? Is one more positive than the other? How do you account for the differences in the lists?

A Poem on Getting Up Early in the Morning (or Even Late in the Morning), When One Is Old

Kay Boyle

Wake, yes, wake (the Irish have a grimmer meaning
For the word and—so like the Irish—magic the verb
Into a noun.) Yes, wake and cross the Bridge of Sighs
Into the menage of the day. The buckling knees
Betray the thighs and hammer toes reduce their size,
Outraged that they are called upon to stride. "Fall, fall,"
The ankles urge, eager to sprain or to be sprained while,
Whether it rains now or has just rained, Tom's voice
Across the wire decrees that one must walk at least
Two miles a day; also that this pill or another be ingested
(Furosemide, or Lasix) on "arising," seemingly unaware that
Rising in the morning is the final chapter of despair.

As the curtain of fog descends (instead of "rising"), bull-frogs
Take on the operatic roles of tenor and baritone, their voices
Hoarse and the libretto lost in the morass. Useless to care
Whether or not the willows cease their weeping
As they braid and unbraid their long green tangled hair.

Gift for My Mother's 90th Birthday

Maude Meehan

BURCHAM HOSPITAL

We watched the rain sluice down
against the window of your sterile room
and listened as you told of childhood's
summer showers at the farm; how you ran out
a colt unpenned, into their sudden soaking bliss.

Now you, aged changeling mother,
emptied and clean as a cracked china cup
on the wrong shelf, whisper, "What I would give
to feel that rain pelt hard against my face."

But you had nothing left, so we
conspirators of love, locked the white door
and your granddaughter wheeled you to the bath
where we unclothed your little sack of bones
and lifted you beneath the shower.

She held you up, your legs pale stalks a-dangle
and clasped your wasted body, bracing her taut
young flesh to your slack folds.
And you clung laughing, joyous as a child
to feel the clear fresh rivulets
course down your upturned face.

From *Washing the Stones: Selected Poems 1975–1995*, Watsonville, Calif.: Papier-Mache Press. © 1999 Maude Meehan.

Bibliography/Filmography for Part I

MAKING GIRLS, MAKING WOMEN

BOOKS

American Association of University Women. *Gender Gaps: Where Schools Still Fail Our Children.* New York: Marlowe and Company, 1999.

Angelou, Maya. *I Know Why the Caged Bird Sings.* New York: Random House, 1969.

Barbieri, Maureen. *Sounds from the Heart: Learning to Listen to Girls.* Portsmouth, NY: Heinemann, 1995.

Blais, Madeleine. *In These Girls, Hope Is a Muscle.* New York: The Atlantic Monthly Press, 1995.

Brady, Jeanne. *Schooling Young Children: A Feminist Pedagogy for Liberatory Learning.* Albany: State University of New York Press, 1995.

Brumberg, Joan Jacobs. *Fasting Girls: The Emergence of Anorexia Nervosa as a Modern Disease.* Cambridge: Harvard University Press, 1988.

Chernin, Kim. *The Obsession: Reflections on the Tyranny of Slenderness.* New York: Harper & Row, 1981.

Delaney, Janice, Mary Jane Lupton, and Emily Toth, eds. *The Curse: A Cultural History of Menstruation.* Urbana: University of Illinois, 1988.

Douglas, Susan. *Where the Girls Are: Growing Up Female with the Mass Media.* New York: Random House, 1994.

Gilligan, Carol. *In a Different Voice: Psychological Theory and Women's Development.* Cambridge: Harvard University Press, 1982.

Hesse-Biber, Sharlene. *Am I Thin Enough Yet? The Cult of Thinness and the Commercialization of Identity.* New York: Oxford University Press, 1996.

Hall, Brian. *The Saskiad.* Boston: Houghton Mifflin, 1997.

Kincaid, Jamaica. *Annie John.* New York: Farrar, Straus, Giroux, 1985.

Lee, Andrea. *Sarah Phillips.* New York: Random House, 1984.

Luker, Kristen. *Dubious Conceptions: The Politics of Teenage Pregnancy.* Cambridge: Harvard University Press, 1996.

Mann, Judy. *The Difference: Discovering the Hidden Ways We Silence Girls—Finding Alternatives That Can Give Them a Voice.* New York: Warner Books, 1994.

Morrison, Toni. *The Bluest Eye.* New York: Plume Books, 1994.

Orenstein, Peggy. *Schoolgirls: Young Women, Self-Esteem, and the Confidence Gap.* New York: Doubleday, 1994.

Porter, Connie. *Imani All Mine.* Boston: Houghton Mifflin, 1999.

Rooks, Noliwe M. *Hair Raising: Beauty, Culture, and African American Women.* New Brunswick, NJ: Rutgers University Press, 1996.

Sadker, Myra and David Sadker. *Failing at Fairness: How Our Schools Cheat Girls.* New York: Scribner's, 1994.

Smith, Betty. *A Tree Grows in Brooklyn* (1943). New York: Perennial Classics, 1998.

Thorne, Barrie. *Gender Play: Girls and Boys in School.* New Brunswick, N.J.: Rutgers University Press, 1993.

Walkerine, Valerie. *Daddy's Girl: Young Girls and Popular Culture.* Cambridge: Harvard University Press, 1997.

Wolf, Naomi. *The Beauty Myth: How Images of Beauty Are Used Against Women.* New York: Morrow, 1991.

FILMS

Anne Frank Remembered (Great Britain, 1995). Jon Blair.

Eating (U.S., 1990). Henry Jaglom.

Fly Away Home (U.S., 1996). Carroll Ballard.
Hair Piece: A Film For Nappy-Headed People (U.S., 1985). Ayoka Chenzira.
The Incredibly True Adventures of Two Girls in Love (U.S., 1995). Maria Maggenti.
The Last Days of Disco (U.S., 1998). Whit Stilman.
The Littlest Rebel (U.S., 1935). David Butler.
Metropolitan (U.S., 1990). Whit Stilman.
My Brilliant Career (Australia, 1979). Gillian Armstrong.
Peppermint Soda (France, 1977). Diane Kurys.
Rambling Rose (U.S., 1991). Martha Coolidge.
The Secret Garden (U.S., 1993). Agnieszka Holland.
The Secret of Roan Inish (U.S., 1994). John Sayles.
The Snapper (Great Britain, 1993). Stephen Frears.

"GIRLFRIENDS": FRIENDS AND SISTERS

BOOKS

Apter, Terri, Ruthellen Josselson, and Jaimie Baron. *Best Friends: The Pleasures and Perils of Girls' and Women's Friendships.* New York: Crown Publishers, 1998.
Bechdel, Alison. *Dykes to Look Out For: The Sequel.* Ithaca, NY: Firebrand Books, 1992.
Berry, Carmen Renee and Tamara Traeder. *Girlfriends: Invisible Bonds, Enduring Ties.* Berkeley, CA: Wildcat Canyon Press, 1995.
Boyd, Julia. *Embracing the Fire: Sisters Talk About Sex and Relationships.* New York: Dutton, 1997.
Cott, Nancy F. *The Bonds of Womanhood: 'Woman's Sphere' in New England, 1780–1835.* New Haven: Yale University Press, 1978.
Fishel, Elizabeth. *Sisters: Shared Histories, Lifelong Ties.* New York: Morrow, 1979.
Lindsey, Karen. *Friends as Family.* Boston: Beacon Press, 1981.
McCullough, Mary W. *Black and White Women as Friends: Building Cross-Race Friendships.* Cresskill, NJ: Hampton Press, 1999.
Peterson, Brenda. *Sister Stories: Taking the Journey Together.* New York: Viking Press, 1996.
Raymond, Janice. *A Passion for Friends: Toward a Philosophy of Female Affection.* Boston: Beacon Press, 1986.

FILMS

All About Eve (U.S., 1950). Joseph L. Mankiewicz.
Antonia and Jane (Great Britain, 1991). Beeban Kidron.
Black Widow (U.S., 1987). Bob Rafelson.
Desperately Seeking Susan (U.S., 1985). Susan Seidelman.
Girlfriends (U.S., 1978). Claudia Weill.
Go Fish (U.S., 1994). Rose Troche.
High Art (U.S., 1998). Lisa Cholodenko.
Entre Nous (France, 1983). Diane Kurys.
Little Women (U.S., 1994). Gillian Armstrong.
Maedchen in Uniform (Germany, 1931). Leontine Sagan.
Marianne and Juliane (Germany, 1981). Margarethe von Trotta.
The Prime of Miss Jean Brodie (U.S., 1969). Ronald Neame.

MOTHERS AND DAUGHTERS

BOOKS

Bell-Scott, Patricia, Beverly Guy-Sheftall, Jacqueline Jones Royster, Janet Sims-Wood, Miriam DeCosta-Willis, and Lucie Fultz, eds. *Double Stitch: Black Women Write About Mothers and Daughters*. New York: HarperCollins, 1991.

Blakely, Mary Kay. *American Mom: Motherhood, Politics, and Humble Pie*. Chapel Hill, N.C.: Algonquin Books, 1994.

Chodorow, Nancy. *The Reproduction of Mothering: Psychoanalytic Feminism and the Sociology of Gender*. Berkeley: University of California Press, 1978.

Eyer, Diane. *Motherguilt: How Our Culture Blames Mothers for What's Wrong with Society*. New York: Random House, 1996.

Kincaid, Jamaica. *The Autobiography of My Mother*. New York: Farrar, Straus, Giroux, 1996.

Ladd-Taylor, Molly and Lauri Umansky, eds. *"Bad" Mothers: The Politics of Blame in Twentieth-Century America*. New York: New York University Press, 1998.

Lessing, Doris. *The Fifth Child*. London: Cape, 1988.

Lewin, Ellen. *Lesbian Mothers: Accounts of Gender in American Culture*. Ithaca, NY: Cornell University Press, 1993.

Moskowitz, Faye, ed. *Her Face in the Mirror: Jewish Women on Mothers and Daughters*. Boston: Beacon Press, 1994.

Olsen, Tillie. *Tell Me a Riddle*. New York: Dell Publishing, 1994.

Rich, Adrienne. *Of Woman Born: Motherhood as Experience and Institution*. New York: Norton, 1976.

Rosenzweig, Linda W. *The Anchor of My Life: Middle-Class American Mothers and Daughters, 1880–1920*. New York: New York University Press, 1993.

Ruddick, Sara. *Maternal Thinking: Towards a Politics of Peace*. Boston: Beacon Press, 1989.

Slovo, Shawn. *A World Apart*. London: Faber & Faber, 1988.

FILMS

A Cry in the Dark (U.S.-Australia, 1988). Fred Schepisi.

Dim Sum (U.S., 1985). Wayne Wang.

Germany Pale Mother (Germany, 1980). Helma Sanders-Brahms.

The Good Mother (U.S., 1988). Leonard Nimoy.

Kramer vs. Kramer (U.S., 1979). Robert Benton.

The Hand That Rocks the Cradle (U.S., 1992). Curtis Hanson.

Imitation of Life (U.S., 1934). John M. Stahl.

Imitation of Life (U.S., 1959). Douglas Sirk.

Little Voice (Great Britain and U.S., 1998). Mark Herman.

Mildred Pierce (U.S., 1945). Michael Curtiz.

The Official Story (Argentina, 1985). Luis Puenzo.

Secrets and Lies (Great Britain, 1996). Mike Leigh.

A World Apart (U.S., 1988). Chris Menges.

HEART AND HOME: THE PERSONAL IS POLITICAL

BOOKS

Anshaw, Carol. *Aquamarine*. Boston: Houghton Mifflin, 1992.

Anshaw, Carol. *Seven Moves*. Boston: Houghton Mifflin, 1996.

Bartholet, Elizabeth. *Family Bonds: Adoption and the Politics of Parenting*. Boston: Houghton Mifflin, 1993.

Bechdel, Alison. *Split-level Dykes to Watch Out For.* Ithaca, NY: Firebrand Books, 1998.

Chopin, Kate. *The Awakening* (1899). New York: Modern Library, 1996.

Faderman, Lillian. *Odd Girls and Twilight Lovers: A History of Lesbian Life in Twentieth-Century America.* New York: Penguin, 1991.

Faderman, Lillian. *Surpassing the Love of Men: Romatic Friendship and Love Between Women from the Renaissance to the Present.* New York: Morrow, 1981.

Franzen, Trisha. *Spinsters and Lesbians: Independent Womanhood in the United States.* New York: New York University Press, 1996.

Minow, Martha, ed. *Family Matters: Readings on Family Lives and the Law.* New York: New Press, 1993.

Omolade, Barbara. *It's a Family Affair: The Real Lives of Black Single Mothers.* New York: Kitchen Table-Women of Color Press, 1986.

Pollack, Sandra and Jeanne Vaughn, eds. *Politics of the Heart: A Lesbian Parenting Anthology.* Ithaca, NY: Firebrand Press, 1987.

Reilly, Lee. *Women Living Single: Thirty Women Share Their Stories of Navigating Through a Married World.* Boston: Faber & Faber, 1996.

Stacey, Judith. *Brave New Families: Stories of Domestic Upheaval in Late Twentieth Century America.* New York: Basic Books, 1990.

Stephens, Brooke, ed. *Men We Cherish: African American Women Praise the Men in Their Lives.* New York: Anchor, 1997.

Texier, Catherine. *Breakup: The End of a Love Story.* New York: Doubleday, 1998.

Thorne, Barrie, ed. *Rethinking the Family: Some Feminist Questions,* rev. ed. Boston: Northeastern University Press, 1992.

Weitzman, Lenore. *The Divorce Revolution: The Unexpected Social and Economic Consequences for Women and Children in America.* New York: Free Press, 1987.

FILMS

Alice Doesn't Live Here Anymore (U.S., 1974). Martin Scorsese.

Another Woman (U.S., 1988). Woody Allen.

The Best Years of Our Lives (U.S., 1946). William Tyler.

Desert Hearts (U.S., 1985). Donna Dietch.

Fatal Attraction (U.S., 1987). Adrian Lyne.

Fire (India, 1996). Deepa Mehta.

Lianna (U.S., 1983). John Sayles.

Making Mr. Right (U.S., 1987). Susan Seidelman.

Scenes from a Marriage (Sweden, 1973). Ingmar Bergman.

An Unmarried Woman (U.S., 1978). Paul Mazursky.

WOMEN WORKING

BOOKS

Abramovitz, Mimi. *Under Attack, Fighting Back: Women and Welfare in the United States.* New York: Monthly Review Press, 1996.

Amott, Teresa and Julie Matthaei. *Race, Gender, and Work: A Multicultural Economic History of Women in the United States,* rev. ed. Boston: South End Press, 1996.

Berry, Mary Frances. *The Politics of Parenthood: Child Care, Women's Rights, and the Myth of the Good Mother.* New York: Viking, 1993.

Blum, Linda. *Between Feminism and Labor: The Significance of the Comparable Worth Movement.* Berkeley: University of California Press, 1991.

Cobble, Dorothy Sue, ed. *Women and Unions: Forging a Partnership.* Ithaca, NY: ILR Press, 1993.

Eisenberg, Susan. *We'll Call If We Need You: Experiences of Women Working Construction.* Ithaca, NY: ILR, 1998.

Friedman, Sara Ann. *Work Matters: Women Talk About Their Jobs and Their Lives.* New York: Viking Press, 1996.

Hochschild, Arlie. *The Second Shift.* New York: Avon Books, 1990.

Howe, Louise Kapp. *Pink-Collar Workers: Inside the World of Women's Work.* New York: Putnam, 1977.

Kessler-Harris, Alice. *Out to Work: A History of Wage-Earning Women in the United States.* New York: Oxford University Press, 1982.

Parker, Gwendolyn M. *Trespassing: My Sojourn in the Halls of Privilege.* Boston: Houghton Mifflin, 1997.

Romero, Mary. *Maid in the USA.* New York: Routledge, 1992.

Samuels, Suzanne Uttaro. *Fetal Rights, Women's Rights: Gender Equality in the Workplace.* Madison: University of Wisconsin Press, 1995.

Scott, Hilda. *Working Your Way to the Bottom: The Feminization of Poverty.* Boston: Pandora Press, 1985.

Sidel, Ruth. *Keeping Women and Children Last: America's War on the Poor.* New York: Penguin Books, 1996.

FILMS

Adam's Rib (U.S., 1949). George Cukor.

His Girl Friday (U.S., 1940) Howard Hawks.

The Life and Times of Rosie the Riveter (U.S., 1980). Connie Field.

Norma Rae (U.S., 1979). Martin Ritt.

Union Maids (U.S., 1976). Julia Reichert and Miles Mogulescu.

With Babies and Banners (U.S., 1978). Lyn Goldfarb and Lorraine Gray.

ARE THERE NO GREAT WOMEN ARTISTS?

BOOKS

Berger, John. *Ways of Seeing.* New York: Penguin, 1977.

Carson, Diane, Linda Dittmar, and Janice R. Welsch, eds. *Multiple Voices in Film Criticism.* Minneapolis and London: University of Minnesota Press, 1994.

Erens, Patricia, ed. *Issues in Feminist Film Criticism.* Bloomington and Indianapolis: Indiana University Press, 1990.

Greer, Germaine. *The Obstacle Race: The Fortunes of Women Painters and Their Work.* New York: Farrar, Straus, Giroux, 1979.

Haskell, Molly. *From Reverence to Rape: The Treatment of Women in the Movies,* 2nd ed. Chicago: University of Chicago Press, 1987.

Haskell, Molly. *Holding My Own in No Man's Land: Women and Men and Film and Feminists.* New York: Oxford University Press, 1997.

Heilbrun, Carolyn G. *Hamlet's Mother and Other Women.* New York: Columbia University Press, 1990.

Heilbrun, Carolyn G. *Writing a Woman's Life.* New York: Random House, 1989.

Higonnet, Anne. *Berthe Morisot.* New York: Harper & Row, 1990.

Hooks, Bell. *Outlaw Culture: Resisting Representations.* New York: Routledge,1994.

Hooks, Bell. *Reel to Real: Race, Sex and Class at the Movies.* New York: Routledge, 1996.

Kay, Karyn and Gerald Peary, eds. *Women and the Cinema: A Critical Anthology.* New York: Dutton, 1977.

Lesser, Wendy. *His Other Half: Men Looking at Women Through Art.* Cambridge: Harvard University Press, 1991.

Nochlin, Linda. *Women, Art, and Power: And Other Essays.* New York: Harper & Row, 1988.

Olsen, Tillie. *Silences.* New York: Dell, 1979.

Raphael, Amy. *Grrrls: Viva Rock Divas.* New York: St. Martin's Press, 1996.

Russo, Vito. *The Celluloid Closet: Homosexuality in the Movies,* rev. ed. New York: Harper & Row, 1987.

Sheriff, Mary D. *The Exceptional Woman: Elisabeth Vigée-Lebrun and the Cultural Politics of Art.* Chicago: University of Chicago Press, 1996.

Woolf, Virginia. *Orlando: A Biography* (1928). New York: Harcourt Brace, 1993.

FILMS

Artemisia (France-Italy-Germany, 1997). Agnés Merlet.

Daughters of the Dust (U.S., 1991). Julie Dash.

Meshes in the Afternoon (U.S., 1943). Maya Derens.

Orlando (Great Britain, 1993). Sally Potter.

The Piano (New Zealand-France, 1993). Jane Campion.

The Story of Adèle H. (France, 1975). Francois Truffaut.

Sweetie (Australia, 1989). Jane Campion.

IN SICKNESS AND IN HEALTH

BOOKS

Bair, Barbara and Susan Cayleff, eds. *Wings of Gauze: Women of Color and the Experience of Health and Illness.* Detroit: Wayne State University Press, 1993.

Boston Women's Health Book Collective. *Our Bodies, Ourselves for the New Century.* New York: Simon and Schuster, 1998.

Candib, Lucy M. *Medicine and the Family: A Feminist Perspective.* New York: Basic Books, 1995.

Chavkin, Wendy, ed. *Double Exposure: Women's Health Hazards on the Job and at Home.* New York: Monthly Review Press, 1984.

Chesler, Phyllis. *Women and Madness.* New York: Avon, 1972.

Corea, Gina. *The Invisible Epidemic: The Story of Women and AIDS.* New York: HarperCollins, 1992.

Doyal, Lesley. *What Makes Women Sick: Gender and the Political Economy of Health.* New Brunswick, NJ: Rutgers University Press, 1995.

Ehrenreich, Barbara and Deirdre English. *Witches, Midwives, and Nurses: A History of Women Healers.* Old Westbury, NY: Feminist Press, 1973.

Gilman, Charlotte Perkins. *The Yellow Wallpaper* (1892). Old Westbury, NY: Feminist Press, 1973.

Hepburn, Cuca. *Alive and Well: A Lesbian Health Guide.* Freedom, CA: Crossing Press, 1988.

Lee, Scout Cloud. *The Circle Is Sacred: A Medicine Book for Women.* Tulsa, Okla.: Council Oak Books, 1995.

Showalter, Elaine. *The Female Malady: Women, Madness, and English Culture, 1830–1980.* New York: Pantheon Books, 1985.

Taylor, Verta A. *Rock-a-By Baby: Feminism, Self-Help and Postpartum Depression.* New York: Routledge, 1996.

Todd, Alexandra Dundas. *Intimate Adversaries: Cultural Conflicts Between Doctors and Women Patients.* Philadelphia: University of Pennsylvania Press, 1989.

White, Evelyn C., ed. *The Black Women's Health Book: Speaking for Ourselves.* Seattle: Seal Press, 1990.

GETTING OLDER

BOOKS

Banner, Lois W. *In Full Flower: Aging Women, Power, and Sexuality.* New York: Random House, 1993.

Bird, Caroline. *Lives of Our Own: Secrets of Salty Old Women.* Boston: Houghton Mifflin, 1995.

Boston Women's Health Book Collective. *The New Ourselves Growing Older.* New York: Simon and Schuster, 1994.

Davis, Nancy, Ellen Cole, and Esther Rothblum, eds. *Faces of Women and Aging.* New York: Haworth Press, 1993.

Dowling, Colette. *Red Hot Mamas: Coming into Our Own at Fifty.* New York: Bantam Books, 1996.

Friedan, Betty. *The Fountain of Age.* New York: Simon and Schuster, 1993.

Greer, Germaine. *Women, Changing, and the Menopause.* New York: Knopf, 1992.

The Hen Coop. *Growing Old Disgracefully: New Ideas for Getting the Most Out of Life.* Freedom, CA: Crossing Press, 1993.

Meyerhoff, Barbara. *Remembered Lives: The Work of Ritual, Storytelling, and Growing Older.* Ann Arbor: University of Michigan Press, 1992.

Pogrebin, Letty Cottin. *Getting Over Getting Older: An Intimate Journey.* New York: Berkley Books, 1996.

Sarton, May. *At Eighty-Two: A Journal.* New York: Norton, 1995.

FLASHPOINTS

PART II

REPRODUCTIVE RIGHTS

Pregnancy and Power Before
Roe v. Wade, 1950–1970

Rickie Solinger

Historian Rickie Solinger has written widely on single pregnant girls and women in the decades before the historic Roe v. Wade *decision legalizing abortion in the United States. In this article, she discusses the complex reproductive politics of the post–World War II era. Today's conflicts over reproductive rights trace meaningfully to that period, Solinger shows; only by understanding the politics and policies of the recent past can we comprehend the ferocity of the current struggle over "who will control women's bodies and their fertility."*

In the late 1980s, when the legal right to abortion seemed desperately threatened, I decided to find out as much as I could about the experiences of single mothers and unwillingly pregnant girls and women in the decades immediately preceding *Roe v. Wade.* I imagined that in uncovering these experiences, I would find patterns reflecting literally millions of instances of danger, coercion, humiliation, and basic degradation of females in the United States. And indeed I did. I believed then that writing about these patterns—laying out the proof of degradation—would help dissipate legislative and judicial efforts to reenslave girls and women to their fertility.

Today, with the threat to reproductive freedom still a virulent strain in our political culture, I am painfully aware of the romanticism of my original intention, based as it was on the simple conviction that history is transformative. Having had such high hopes for the evidence I found in archives and trial transcripts, I neglected to consider how difficult it is to communicate history, perhaps especially this recent, decidedly unglamorous history of the politics of female fertility.

But even now that my perspective on the power of history is more clear-sighted, in the sense that I know more about how hard it is to bring history into the political and policy arenas, I remain just as certain that knowledge of the history of reproductive politics in the United States is crucial, for a number of reasons. One of the most important reasons is that history does teach that most transformative lesson: progressive social change is possible and occurs most surely and swiftly in eras of progressive activism. And, when we know the his-

From *Abortion Wars: A Half Century of Struggle, 1950–2000,* Berkeley: University of California Press, 1998, pp. xi–xvi, 15–32. Reprinted by permission of the Regents of the University of California.

tory of reproductive politics, we can better understand the roots of current conflicts in this arena. Then we who believe in women's reproductive rights can use this understanding to define our goals and shape our strategies.

In this essay I consider how reproductive politics in the immediate pre-*Roe v. Wade* decades illuminates the roots—and helps explain the persistence of—some of the more hideous impulses that bedevil reproductive politics today. Specifically, I look at why abortion practitioners were targeted and demonized in the postwar decades, an era when, of course, most of them operated outside of the law. Then I consider one of the many ways that women were coerced in the 1950s and 1960s to cede control over their bodies to "experts," in this case to doctors sitting on hospital abortion boards. And finally, I review how reproductive politics after World War II divided women against each other by race.

In addition to exposing the roots of contemporary conflicts, these historical aspects of the politics of female fertility, taken together, reveal the variety and complexity of the forces arrayed against women—including municipal, medical, and federal politics and policies. The material also points to the depth and force of women's determination to control their own fertility, even in the face of so many obstacles. It is important to note that this history most

decidedly does not validate the central claim of Randall Terry and other leaders of the opposition to reproductive rights: that, before legalization, women did not seek and did not obtain abortions. The truth is that even when blocked by laws, institutions, and authorities, up to one million women a year sought and obtained abortions in the illegal era—though not without a struggle.

Women and the state have been engaged in a series of overlapping and ongoing struggles to determine who will control women's bodies and their fertility. In this regard three great struggles waged individually and collectively by women in the twentieth century have been for legalization of contraception, for legalization of abortion, and—most intractably—for nonracist and non-class-based policies supporting access to reproductive self-determination.[1] The history of these struggles reveals that women's bodies and their fertility have repeatedly provided rich opportunities for U.S. politicians and policy makers determined to preserve both male and white supremacy.

The contemporary history of reproductive politics in the United States begins immediately after World War II, after a period when women had joined the paid workforce in unprecedented numbers, and at a point when the issue of race was emerging as a central concern of the polity and its citizens. In the late 1940s

---

Chronology of Abortion Politics

Late 1940s–early 1950s
Experts estimate 200,000 to 1.3 million illegal abortions in United States annually.
Rise of hospital abortion boards, formed to adjudicate women's appeals for permission to obtain legal "therapeutic abortions."

1953
Alfred Kinsey's *Sexual Behavior in the Human Female* reports that 9 out of 10 premarital pregnancies end in abortion and 22 percent of married women have had an abortion while married.

and into the 1950s, cultural arbiters and authorities—psychiatrists, lawyers and judges, educators and employers, journalists and politicians, advertisers, the clergy, fashion designers, social service providers, and others—used the media as never before to address what had become a set of burning questions: Who is the American woman? What is a woman? Who is a mother?[2] Most prominently published responses to these questions claimed not just that motherhood was a defining attribute of womanhood, but that for motherhood to be an authentic expression of femininity (a postwar synonym for womanhood), it must occur within marriage. A woman, they claimed, must passively receive and submit to the "gifts" of marriage, especially pregnancy. Sensationalized public censure of females who got pregnant without being married or were otherwise unwillingly pregnant, combined with greatly increased prosecutions of illegal abortion practitioners, gave bite to prevailing definitions of womanhood and warned all women about the wages of transgression.[3] It was in this context that various power centers mobilized to clamp down on women seeking to control their fertility and on those willing to help them do so.

Today, abortion practitioners in the United States are targeted and reviled by the radical right and isolated by their communities. Many wear bulletproof vests in public, and almost all have unlisted home telephone numbers. The need for such precautions is relatively recent. During the illegal era (from the mid-nineteenth century until 1973), abortion practitioners operated with varying degrees of secrecy, but they did not fear for their lives. In fact, a number of abortionists in the illegal era provided their services for years—twenty, thirty, forty years, and more—completely unimpeded by the law. In many communities, the local abortion practitioner's name and address were well known, not only to women who might require the service but also to police and politicians, who generally regarded the presence of a good abortionist as a public health asset. For decades after the American Medical Association worked with state legislatures in the nineteenth century to outlaw abortion, abortion prosecutions were rare relative to the number of abortions performed. In most communities an unwritten agreement prevailed between law enforcement and practitioners: no death, no prosecution.[4]

But after World War II the old agreement was rather suddenly canceled, and practitioners—chiefly the female ones (presumed by law enforcement to be unskilled, untrained, and unprotected in comparison to their male counterparts, and therefore more likely to be convicted)—were arrested, convicted, and sent to

---

1955

Mary S. Calderone, medical director of Planned Parenthood, organizes high-profile conference, "Abortion in America"; conference volume published in 1958.

1960

American Medical Association observes that laws against abortion are unenforceable.
American Law Institute (ALI) endorses liberalization of abortion laws.

1962

In highly publicized incident, Sherri Finkbine, denied an abortion in Phoenix, goes to Stockholm to abort a fetus damaged by thalidomide; according to Gallup Poll, 52 percent of Americans approve.
In California, Pat Maginnis founds women's-rights-based Citizens for Humane Abortion Laws.

jail in unprecedented numbers, even when there was no evidence of a botched abortion. Many of these practitioners were highly skilled and experienced, having performed twenty some abortions a day, year after year.

If we look at when and how these arrests were carried out and at how abortion trials were conducted, we can get a sense of what was at issue and begin to understand the agendas of the district attorneys, judges, and politicians who managed the postwar crackdowns. In many cities what stands out is that everything about these prosecutions—the sensationalized media coverage of police raids, arrests, and trials—transformed abortion from an everyday, if semi-secret, occurrence into a crime. Often scandal-tainted mayors and police forces were looking for opportunities to demonstrate that municipal governance and law enforcement were not ineffectual or corrupt, as charged. Many police chiefs, in concert with a district attorney's office, an eager crime-busting reporter, or a clutch of city fathers concerned with civil probity, scouted for fodder for municipal exposés. Theirs was a peculiarly postwar–cold war project: to root out the "hidden" enemy within and "cleanse" the city in the process. In Los Angeles, San Francisco, Cincinnati, St. Louis, Trenton, Portland, Oregon, and other cities, even though there was no expressed anti-abortion agenda (nobody raised the spec-

ter or even the subject of unborn babies), women abortionists and their clients became attractive targets. These women represented a political opportunity because they were vulnerable, with almost no recourse to credible defense. Moreover, given the associations of sex and secrecy, the arrests were exciting; the lurid headlines sold newspapers and made law enforcement appear well deployed.[5]

What one finds in the abortion courtroom is that in the postwar decades such trials became first-rate occasions for men—doctors, lawyers, judges, police, jury members—to gather in a public place and affirm their right to govern women's bodies, to define women's rights, and to enforce women's vulnerability. In addition, these trials were titillating dramas that pitted one woman against another—the alleged abortionist (cast most often as a perverse and mercenary harridan) against her putative client (the slut). The whole event was drenched in sex. Wherever it occurred, the trial emerged day by day as a species of pornography, a cryptoporn show in which, in the name of the law and public morality, men invoked women's naked bodies, their sexuality, and their vulnerability in a style that was both contemptuous and erotic.[6]

In the largest sense, the abortion trials became arenas to address the culturally crucial question: Who is not a "real" woman? By de-

---

1965

New York Times endorses abortion law reform, February 13.

Rubella epidemic leads to abortions performed on grounds of "mental health crisis."

In *Griswold v. Connecticut* Supreme Court rules, 7-2 that Connecticut law banning contraception infringes on married couples' right to privacy.

Mid-1960s

Abortion law repeal (vs. reform) efforts gain momentum.

1966

National Organization for Women (NOW) formed.

Association to Repeal Abortion Laws in California started.

fining female abortionists and their clients as perverse and unwomanly, the qualities of real womanhood were reaffirmed. The lawyers, doctors, and judges in command of these trials met no resistance as they defined the female transgressors before them. The political context made it easy to interpret an act of "exposing deviance" as an act of concern for the safety of the community. The social context sanctioned efforts to reinforce rigid gender roles in the aftermath of the war. To promote their defensive ends, the men who ran the show almost always adopted an offensive mode: cryptoporn, titillating the crowd while at the same time provoking shame and repugnance.

The men in charge at the courthouse shared a dreadful sense that the gender roles and relations they had depended on were threatening to give way. That they conducted the proceedings so brutally indicates how strongly they felt this. Women were on trial; the script called for them to be degraded, humiliated, divided against each other, and exposed. The most private facts of their lives were publicly revealed and reviled: their bodies (even their wombs), their sexuality, the intimate sources of their personal dignity. At the same time, the script allowed for men—doctors, lawyers, judges, journalists, and myriad expert witnesses—to stand up, one by one, and reaffirm their prerogatives over women's bodies and lives.[7]

These scenarios were enacted against a backdrop of demands for the domestication of women after the Depression and war years, during which women had shouldered economic and social responsibilities outside their homes. Cultural arbiters of every sort ordered women to go back home, to be proper wives and mothers, to be content.[8] The incidence of abortion after the war provided distressing evidence that many women were resisting some parts—or all—of this prescription. The trials provided the opportunity to humiliate resisters, to reiterate the injunction, and to underscore an important source of cultural as well as legal authority.[9]

The politicians and the law enforcement officers who canceled the old arrangement that had tolerated abortion as long as nobody got hurt, together with the courthouse men in charge of naming women's guilt and setting their punishment, were fighting the prospect of a community in which women could decide when and whether to associate sex and marriage, sex and maternity, marriage and maternity. In the 1950s these men had the institutional power to mount their opposition by targeting individual women. And their leverage extended even farther: the newspaper headlines and the courtroom dramas carried powerful cultural messages to the general citizenry.

1967

Journal of the American Medical Association prints pro-reform editorial.

Abortion reform bills considered by at least 25 state legislatures.

Colorado enacts ALI-style abortion reform law, followed by North Carolina and California.

Twenty-one New York clergymen establish Clergy Consultation Service on Abortion, an abortion referral network.

Federal government spends over $70 million a year on contraceptive programs in United States.

Modern Medicine magazine reports 87 percent of American physicians favor liberalization of country's anti-abortion policies.

These spectacles announced the danger and the just desserts for any woman associated with abortion. They also announced that the law was predicated on a willingness to place women in danger and on a contempt for women's self-determination. Anyone could see that enforcing anti-abortion laws involved the degradation of women. Every woman, whether she ever had or ever would climb up on the abortionist's table, was endangered by the statutes that criminalized abortion.

The prosecutions (and our memories of them) also carried the message that abortion practitioners were vulnerable vermin—an attitude that lives on in the anti-abortionists' hit list, as well as in the pro-choice claim that the chief function of *Roe v. Wade* has been to protect women from the back-alley butchers of the past, despite the historical reality that most illegal abortions were performed by highly skilled and experienced practitioners, who compiled an astonishing record of successful procedures under extremely difficult conditions. In actuality, the power of *Roe v. Wade* has been, since 1973, to diminish the danger and the degradation of women mandated by the anti-abortion statutes of the criminal era.

At the same time that police and politicians were busy burnishing their reputations by cracking down on illegal abortionists, medical doctors were experimenting with opportunistic and oppressive supervisory structures of their own. In the late 1940s doctors designed these structures—hospital abortion boards—to govern the meaning and the course of the pregnancies of millions of women. The boards ensured that experts, not women themselves, had final control over the abortion decision.[10]

In the postwar era, after several generations of performing abortions themselves, looking the other way, or facilitating, through referrals, illegal abortions, a great many doctors adopted an aggressive position against abortion.[11] Before the war many women had found cooperative doctors, as evidenced by the vast number of approved medical indications for "therapeutic abortion" (a list that kept expanding through the 1930s).[12] Even a woman who did not have a medical problem had little trouble finding one of the hundreds of illegal practitioners who practiced undisturbed, in the shadows of cities and towns across the country. One way or another, thousands and thousands of women each year who wanted to end their pregnancies found a way.[13] But after the war things changed. Many doctors said abortion was no longer necessary.

For one thing, the list of illnesses that doctors had defined as incompatible with pregnancy began to shrink year by year with the advent of new therapies and technologies. By

1969

Jane, an underground abortion services network, formed in Chicago.

First National Conference on Abortion Laws held; National Association for Repeal of Abortion Laws (NARAL) founded there.

Radical feminist group Redstockings holds first speak-out on abortion.

1970

New York state legislature legalizes abortion; Hawaii and Washington follow.

the early 1950s, influential physicians were standing up to make the claim that almost no medical contraindications to pregnancy remained.[14] Even a woman with breast cancer or cardiovascular disease, who could have gotten a routine hospital abortion in the 1930s, was now told not to worry about having a baby.

The doctors' turnabout, however, did not stop the many women who had grown accustomed to a certain degree of abortion availability from coming to their offices, begging for abortions or referrals to abortionists. It was an awkward situation all around. Most doctors were simply not willing to break the law, no matter what their private thoughts might be about abortion. But they still had to find a way to deal with the women in their offices seeking help.

Doctors dealt with these women by explaining to them and to each other that pregnancy no longer represented an added burden or an increased strain on a woman, even on a woman with a preexisting illness. In many cases, of course, this rationale had the effect of diminishing the relevance of a pregnant woman's condition and her own assessment of it. Doctors implied now that pregnancy was an event that transcended a woman's body and had, in an odd way, ceased to be a medical issue.

In these postwar years, pregnancy became fundamentally a moral issue. As new imaging technology allowed doctors to construct the fetus as a "little person," they tended to describe pregnancy first as a process of fulfillment and realization for the fetus, and to refer to the pregnant woman's body in terms that suggested a safe reproductive container. Now the pregnant woman, along with her physician, had the moral duty to keep the container fit. As one obstetrician put it: "Woman is a uterus surrounded by a supporting mechanism and a directing personality." Completely effaced, the woman-as-uterus simply housed the child.[15]

As doctors adopted and promoted these ideas, the number and the rate of therapeutic abortions performed in U.S. hospitals plummeted.[16] But women did not necessarily accede to the new medical definition of pregnancy. They did not stop seeking abortions. Underground abortionists knew that. And so did hospital-affiliated obstetricians and gynecologists, whose dilemma was graver than ever.[17] In some ways the situation was paradoxical. On the one hand, many people believed that doctors were scientific and humanitarian heroes for subduing the dangers of pregnancy and for developing methods to conquer diseases that threatened pregnancy and the pregnant female. On the other hand, state laws still required that a pregnant woman's life had to be endangered for her to get an abortion. Medical advances had seemingly wiped

---

1971

National poll shows that over half of Americans favor legalizing abortion.

American Bar Association officially supports a woman's right to choose abortion up to 20th week of pregnancy.

Supreme Court hears first round of oral arguments in *Roe v. Wade*.

Abele v. Markle filed in Connecticut; 858 plaintiffs.

Dr. Jane Hodgson convicted for performing in-hospital abortion; only U.S. physician ever convicted for this reason.

Feminist Women's Health Center set up in Los Angeles; teaches women how to perform "menstrual extractions."

out any legal grounds for demanding abortion—but they had not changed women's determination to get abortions, the law and their doctors' proscriptions notwithstanding.

There is no question that doctors were feeling the squeeze from all sides and from within their own ranks as well. Any two doctors might disagree about which woman should be given permission for an abortion, under which conditions.[18] Nevertheless, doctors still had a legal responsibility to make the decision. And they were still interested in holding on to their medical authority to do so. The result was that many physicians struggled to find new grounds for making medical decisions about abortions. To a significant extent, psychiatrists helped out in the crisis, providing myriad esoteric ways of selecting who should and who should not be permitted an abortion. It must be added that most of these ways were based on providing a clinical answer to the question, "was this woman psychologically fit to be a mother?" Answers in the negative—those that gave women permission to abort—defined the petitioner as unfit, unwomanly, to some degree depraved. The means and the ends here were both degrading to women seeking to control their fertility.[19]

Beyond this help from psychiatrists, though, physicians felt a need to create institutional structures to strengthen their position as abor-

tion decision makers. In the late 1940s and early 1950s, they began to assemble hospital-based abortion committees.[20] From these official groups, professional, expert diagnoses and decisions regarding individual women could be issued in one voice. The abortion committees gave doctors legal protection and ensured that the "right" ratio of births to abortions was maintained in the hospital. The ratio varied from hospital to hospital, but doctors everywhere believed that a high ratio of births to abortions would protect the reputation of their hospital.[21]

By associating abortion decisions with the scientific objectivity of the group of doctors, and with the probity of the profession, all committee members could disassociate themselves personally from widespread concerns that an unreasonable number of abortions—legal and illegal—were being performed. Through the committee, doctors could diminish their individual vulnerability and perhaps their crises of conscience. And they could promote the aura of medical solidarity and legal compliance. For all these reasons, many doctors were satisfied that hospital abortion committees were a good solution.

As might be expected, women seeking abortions were not so thrilled with them. Imagine the physically exhausted pregnant woman, already the mother of three little ones and de-

---

1972

Connecticut's abortion law declared unconstitutional; Meskill bill reinstates law; Women versus Connecticut files new suit with 2,000 plaintiffs.

1973

Supreme Court's *Roe v. Wade* decision legalizes abortion, as does its ruling in companion case, *Doe v. Bolton*. NARAL becomes National Abortion Rights Action League in response to anti-*Roe* backlash.
First edition of National Right to Life Committee's newsletter editorializes, "We must work for the passage of a constitutional Human Life Amendment."
Religious Coalition for Abortion Rights founded.

termined to have no more children, being told by her doctor that abortion was unnecessary and immoral. Imagine that the woman was determined enough to persist and to make an application to the abortion committee (a humiliating and coercive innovation, from her point of view, which no one had even heard of the previous year). What if she were turned down?

Today we can look back at how the committees functioned and understand the pain and humiliation with which women remember these ordeals. At the time Dr. Alan Guttmacher, a great champion of these committees, described how his committee worked at Mt. Sinai Hospital in New York:

> The director of the obstetrical and gynecological service is chairman of the permanent abortion committee. The other members are the chief, or a senior attending, from the departments of medicine, surgery, neuropsychiatry, and pediatrics. The board has a scheduled weekly meeting-hour, and convenes routinely whenever a case is pending. No case is considered unless the staff ob-gyn desiring to carry out the procedure presents affirmative letters from two consultants in the medical field involved. Five copies of each letter must be filed at least forty-eight hours in advance of the meeting. The ob-gyn

whose case it is, and one of the two consultants who made the recommendation must make themselves available at the meeting for further information when desired. In addition, if the chairman feels that an expert from some other department would be helpful in arriving at a proper decision, this specialist is requested to attend as a non-voting member. The case is then carefully discussed and if any member of the five on the committee opposes therapeutic interruption, the procedure is disallowed.[22]

The fact is, many women whose unwanted pregnancies were vetted by abortion boards in the 1950s and 1960s say that these experiences were among the most awful of their lives. Many could not bring themselves to submit to such a process and went off on their own, in search of an abortionist. Other women did apply to the board, were denied an abortion, but emerged with their determination undiminished. These women, too, often went into the so-called back alley.

It is a shocking fact that many women who were "successful" with the committee found out, to their horror, that they could have the abortion only if they agreed to be sterilized at the same time. One doctor explained, "A serious effort is made to control the need for dealing with the same problem in the same patient

1975
National Women's Health Network founded.

1976
Hyde Amendment enacted, prohibiting Medicaid-funded abortions except "where the life of the mother would be endangered."

twice." A doctor who objected to this practice chose a pointed analogy to explain why: "For some while now, I have called attention to this irrational policy of insisting that a patient be sterilized at the time of the therapeutic abortion as a guarantee that the patient will not return again pregnant seeking another therapeutic abortion. Such an argument possesses hardly less logic to recommend it than one which advocates amputation of the penis along with routine leutic therapy because, unless this is done, the patient may return with another chancre sore." Another doctor, equally angry at his colleagues for their hostility to women seeking abortions, declared, "The fairly common practice of insisting on sterilization if an abortion is permitted may have arisen from dealing with epileptics or feebleminded women. It carries on as a punishment or a threat—as if the physician is saying: 'All right, if you do not want this baby, you are not capable of having any.'"[24]

Studies conducted in the early 1950s showed that, indeed, sterilization had become a fairly common practice. Over 53 percent of teaching hospitals made simultaneous sterilization a condition of approval for abortion, and in all U.S. hospitals, the rate was 40 percent.[24] One doctor, unhappy that unwillingly pregnant women were being forced to accept sterilization, observed that the practice was driving women to illegal abortionists because dealing with law-abiding physicians was likely to entail the permanent loss of their fertility. He added, "I would like to point out because the package [therapeutic abortion/sterilization] is so frequent, I therefore consider them fortunate to have been illegally rather than therapeutically aborted and thus spared sterilization."[25]

This doctor had a good point, although it was a point rarely made at the time. Many of his colleagues knew it was true but proceeded, week after week, to gather in their abortion tribunals and warn each other that, as one put it, "The physician must have a high index of suspicion for the patient who tries to pull a fast one." Another doctor spoke for many committee members when he raised the specter of the "clever, scheming women, simply trying to hoodwink the psychiatrist and obstetrician" when they appealed for permission to abort.[26]

Despite what they could plainly see in their own offices and at the weekly committee meetings about the determination of ordinary women to make their own decisions, doctors bolstered their personal righteousness about intervention by referring to the hefty and growing body of literature affirming that women's role on earth was to have children and that a woman's healthy sex life was predicated on her desire to have children. Leading postwar experts in the psychology of women argued that

---

1980

Republican Party platform calls for appointment of anti-abortion-rights judges at every level of the federal judiciary.

In *Harris v. McRae* Supreme Court rules that although the government "may not place obstacles in the path of a woman's exercise of her freedom of choice, it need not remove those not of its own creation. Indigence falls within the latter category."

1983

National Black Women's Health Project founded.

1985

Women of Color Partnership Program created by Religious Coalition for Abortion Rights.

women who insisted on separating sex and procreation, for example, by deciding to abort, were consigned to the hell of "sexual limbo." A Portland, Oregon, doctor expressed his pleasure when an illegal abortionist in town was arrested by explaining that he believed in stamping out abortion because the operation caused guilt complexes, frigidity, and divorce. Stamp out abortion, he said, and these neurotic symptoms would disappear naturally.[27] Many doctors told each other about women like "Laura," whose case exemplified the problem. After her abortion, Laura "lost her sexual desire and moved to a separate bedroom. So seriously was her marriage affected that Laura was sent to a psychiatrist for treatment. She was on the brink of divorce. And all this was caused by interrupting the most vital biologically sacred function of womanhood—conception."[28] In line with this 1950s orthodoxy, the committee doctors forced a woman who did not want to carry any given pregnancy to term to declare herself insane. That was what the structure demanded.

Doctors also justified their committee work by referring to the force of women's will to have children. They basically accepted the adage that nobody gets pregnant who doesn't want to be. In this way, any and every pregnancy became a choice. It may well have been an unconscious choice (a favorite Freudian explanation in the 1950s), but it was a choice nonetheless, despite what the woman herself might think she wanted. (A doctor said at the time, "If we have learned anything in psychiatry, we have learned to respect the unconscious far more than the conscious and we have learned not to take abortion requests at face value.")[29] In a cruel twist on the meaning of choice today, a woman who said she wanted an abortion could be understood to be proposing to violate her own choice to be pregnant.

As they made their way through this nightmarish maze of new psychological and cultural ideas about pregnancy and abortion, many pregnant women declined the opportunity to become supplicants before the abortion panels.[30] They did not accept the new definition of pregnancy that granted primacy to the fetus, nor did they give up the idea that a particular pregnancy could be dangerous to them, or damaging. So while abortion boards were sitting in hospitals around the country, hundreds of thousands of pregnant women each year did the only thing they could. They sought out abortionists elsewhere.

The physicians who developed hospital abortion committees were not, it should be noted, primarily concerned with the issue of when life begins. They were, however, very concerned with what they took to be their cultural mandate in postwar America to protect

---

1987
Reproductive Health Technologies Project founded.
Randall Terry leads first "rescue."

1988
Operation Rescue formally established.
In *Bowen v. Kendrick* Supreme Court upholds Adolescent Family Life Act's denial of funding to programs that "advocate, promote, or encourage abortion."

and preserve the links between sexuality, femininity, marriage, and maternity. They were also deeply concerned about their professional dignity and about devising strategies to protect and preserve the power, the prerogatives, and the legal standing of the medical profession.

An important strategy of many doctors in this era was to draw on the vulnerability of pregnant women to construct a definition of pregnancy that effaced the personhood of the individual pregnant woman. This definition created a safe place for the fetus and also for the doctor forced by law to adjudicate the extremely personal decisions of women, many of whom were resisting effacement. The subordination of the pregnant woman to the fetus revitalized medical participation in the abortion decision because the doctor was now required to make sure that the woman stayed moral, that is, served her fetus correctly. These postwar ideas are powerful demonstrations of the prevailing relationship then between scientific advances and ideological positions on women, pregnancy, and fetuses.[31]

While mayors and police chiefs and obstetricians and psychiatrists were using the abortion issue to resolve issues of municipal and medical politics in cities and towns across the country, the role of reproductive politics on the national political scene in the postwar years is in many ways even more terrifying. What we can learn from examining the point at which female fertility emerged as a national political preoccupation is that, from the start, reproductive politics provided legislators and the judiciary with rich opportunities to support agendas hostile to female autonomy and racial equality.

The postwar experiences of white and black females who were unmarried and pregnant make it clear, first of all, that when lawmakers take the right to regulate and control female fertility—to answer the question "Who is a mother?"—all women are degraded. And beyond that, when lawmakers take this right, they simultaneously and quite "naturally" take the additional right to treat different groups of women differently, in this case depending on the race of the woman and her "illegitimate" child.

I have written extensively in *Wake Up Little Susie: Single Pregnancy and Race Before Roe v. Wade* about the different treatments and experiences of white and black unwed mothers in this country at midcentury. Briefly, after World War II tens of thousands of white girls and women who became pregnant outside of marriage each year were unable to determine either the course of their pregnancies or the conditions of their maternity. They were, in astonishing numbers, deeply shamed by their families, removed from school, diagnosed as

---

1989

In *Webster v. Reproductive Health Services* Supreme Court upholds Missouri law stating "human life begins at conception" and placing restrictions on access to abortion; Court comes within one vote of overturning *Roe v. Wade.*

Teenager Becky Bell, afraid to obey parental-notification statute, dies after septic illegal abortion.

1989–1992

Over 700 anti-abortion-rights bills introduced in state legislatures across the country.

Late 1980s–early 1990

Anti-abortion violence aimed at abortion clinics escalates.

psychologically disturbed, and defined as not-mothers without husbands.[32] They were pressed, even coerced, into giving up their "valuable" white babies for adoption to infertile, white, married couples prescreened and judged by social workers to be eager and proper parents.[33]

In contrast, black girls and women who were unmarried and pregnant kept their "illegitimate" children, often with the help of their families and community-based institutions.[34] But politicians in every region of the country began to blame unwed black mothers for producing "excessive" numbers of "unwanted" black babies. Politicians and journalists said these babies created burdens for white taxpayers. Worse, many politicians, policy makers, and ordinary citizens began claiming at midcentury that the wombs of poor black women, excessively and wantonly fertile, were the source of all problems in the black community (including poverty, juvenile delinquency, and urban disorders) and, by extension, in America as a whole.[35]

Consequently, beginning in the late 1940s and continuing with increasing determination throughout the postwar decades, politicians threatened unwed mothers of color with incarceration, sterilization, and removal from welfare rolls. Social scientists and social commentators of diverse political persuasions be-

gan—at a time when the whole country was a battleground in the war of integrationists versus segregationists—to use the out-of-wedlock pregnancies of some women of color to bolster policies of white supremacy. Many used these "illegitimate" pregnancies to justify stands against school integration and for restrictive public housing policies. Numerous politicians associated welfare with oversexed black women who had too many children, thus giving focus to white opposition to government aid to poor mothers and their children, especially African Americans.[36]

This review of some of the ways that players on the terrains of municipal, medical, and national politics opportunistically targeted, constrained, and degraded millions of American women on the basis of their gender and reproductive capacity in our recent past illuminates how deeply vulnerable fertile women may be in an era lacking a collective, vibrant, feminist political culture. To the degree that such a political culture is weakened or unrealized in the contemporary United States, many politicians and others are seizing the same opportunities today as they did in the 1950s.

We can find additional roots (and lessons) in this history. To begin with, it seems to me that the poisonous attacks and deathly threats against abortion providers today depend

---

1990

In *Hodgson v. Minnesota* Supreme Court upholds state law that no abortion should be performed on a minor woman for 48 hours after both parents are notified; statute also provides for "judicial bypass."

1991

RU 486 approved for use in Britain.

Operation Rescue stages massive blockades throughout summer in Wichita, Kansas.

In *Rust v. Sullivan* Supreme Court rules 5-4 that since the government had not discriminated on the basis of viewpoint, but had "merely chosen to fund one activity [childbirth] to the exclusion of another [abortion], the 'gag rule' prohibiting physicians and other employees of abortion-providing facilities from counseling pregnant women about abortion or engaging in activities that encourage, promote, or advocate abortion as a method of family planning" did not violate the free-speech rights of doctors, their staffs, or their patients.

heavily on a continuing cultural hostility to women who take the right to separate sex and maternity. The attacks also depend, just as heavily, on a misreading of the past, a misreading that says that cravenly greedy back-alley butchers were the chief source of danger to helpless women in the criminal era. Given the salacious and sensational prosecutions of illegal abortionists in the postwar decades, it is easy to understand why so many people on all sides of the abortion issue find it reasonable to marginalize or target practitioners. They forget that it was the law, not illegal abortionists, that created, even mandated, danger for all women before *Roe v. Wade*.

When we also consider the history and the projects of hospital abortion boards in the 1950s we can clearly recognize the dangers fertile women faced when male authorities (who often ignored these women's perspective) had the right to control pregnancy-related decisions. The history of hospital abortion boards strikes a particularly chilling note at the end of the twentieth century when, for the first time since legalization, congressional Republicans, free from substantial opposition by the medical establishment, are determined to legislate medical matters and to start outlawing abortions by type, thus once again forcing women (any woman, all women) into roles of supplication and obedience.

Perhaps most resonant today is the history of the ways that politicians have used race-based reproductive politics to shore up and advance a politics of male supremacy and white supremacy. It is sad, frustrating, and frightening that these politics are still dividing women against each other.

The lessons of midcentury reproductive politics are not, however, all cautionary and grim. For example, it is instructive to know that in the late 1950s, among broadly middle-class white girls and women who got pregnant while unmarried, over 95 percent gave their babies up for adoption. Today the rate for all such girls and women is 3 percent. This is a startling change and suggests that with *Roe v. Wade,* women won more than the right to decide whether to stay pregnant. They also won the overlapping but distinct right to decide whether to become a mother. With the dramatic decline of coerced adoptions and the advent of legal abortion, many women in the United States have rights and choices that were virtually unimaginable in the recent past and certainly unobtainable. Social change is possible and, in the case of reproductive politics, was realized largely during the resurgence of the feminist movement from 1965 to 1980.

At the end of the twentieth century, racism, misogyny, and prejudice against poor people are factors that deeply stain our national cul-

---

1992

President Clinton lifts "gag rule."

National Network of Abortion Funds established.

Eighty-four percent of counties in United States have no physician willing to perform abortions.

In *Planned Parenthood v. Casey* Supreme Court rules, 5-4, to "retain and reaffirm" women's right to abortion but also upholds Pennsylvania restrictions.

In wake of *Casey* decision, Mississippi becomes first state to introduce a mandatory delay and biased-information requirement.

ture and consequently stain the politics of female fertility. Against this culture, women have been and are determined, whenever and however they can, to control their own bodies and their lives, and to answer for themselves the questions: What is a woman? And who is a mother? In the future American women will continue to exercise the same determination. The task before us is to revitalize a vast feminist movement so that women's determination can be exercised in a climate that honors the relationship between reproductive autonomy and citizenship rights for each and every female.

NOTES

1. Some relatively recent—and excellent— treatments of these twentieth-century struggles include Carole Joffe, *Doctors of Conscience: The Struggle to Provide Abortion Before and After* Roe v. Wade (Boston: Beacon Press, 1995); Leslie Reagan, *When Abortion Was a Crime: Women, Medicine, and Law in the United States, 1867–1973* (Berkeley: University of California Press, 1997); Laura Kaplan, *The Story of Jane: The Legendary Underground Feminist Abortion Service* (New York: Pantheon, 1995); Carole R. McCann, *Birth Control Politics in the United States, 1916–1945* (Ithaca, N.Y.: Cornell University Press, 1994); Ellen Chesler, *Woman of Valor: Margaret Sanger and the Birth Control Movement in America* (New York: Simon and Schuster, 1992); David J. Garrow, *Liberty and Sexuality: The Right to Privacy and the Making of* Roe v. Wade (New York: Macmillan, 1994); *From Abortion to Reproductive Freedom: Transforming a Movement,* ed. Marlene Gerber Fried (Boston: South End Press, 1990); *The Politics of Pregnancy: Adolescent Pregnancy and Public Policy,* ed. Annette Lawson and Deborah Rhode (New Haven: Yale University Press, 1993); *Conceiving the New World Order,* ed. Faye Ginsburg and Rayna Rapp (Berkeley: University of California Press, 1995). Also see Rickie Solinger, *Wake Up Little Susie: Single Pregnancy and Race Before* Roe v. Wade (New York: Routledge, 1992); and *The Abortionist: A Woman Against the Law* (New York: Free Press, 1994).

2. See Rickie Solinger, "The Smutty Side of LIFE: Picturing 'Babes' as Icons of Gender Difference in the 1950s," in *Looking at LIFE: Rethinking America's Favorite Picture Magazine,* ed. Erika Doss (Washington, D.C.: Smithsonian Press).

3. See Solinger, *Wake Up Little Susie* and *ZAbortionist.*

4. Solinger, *Abortionist,* 16.

5. Ibid., ch. 6 and 7.

6. Ibid., ch. 8.

7. See, for example, *State of California v. Geraldine Rhoades* (1948), Superior Court, Sacramento

---

1993
NARAL changes name to National Abortion and Reproductive Rights Action League.
National Black Women's Health Project takes lead in fight against Hyde Amendment.
Dr. David Gunn, an abortion practitioner, murdered in Florida.
Congress expands Hyde Amendment to provide federal funding for abortions in cases of rape and incest.

County, transcript in California State Archives, Sacramento, and *State of Oregon v. Ruth Barnett* (1966), no. 15959, transcript in Oregon State Archives, Salem.

8. See, for example, Robert Coughlan, "Changing Roles of Modern Marriage," *Life,* December 4, 1956, 109–118; and, of course, Ferdinand Lundberg and Marynia Farnham, *Modern Woman: The Lost Sex* (New York: Harper and Brothers, 1947).

9. This tendency can be found in almost all the abortion trials of the postwar era, including *State of North Carolina v. Geneva Phifer Hoover and Florence Stallworth* (1960), Superior Court, Mecklenburg County, transcript in North Carolina State Supreme Court Law Library, Raleigh.

10. Rickie Solinger, "A Complete Disaster: Abortion and the Politics of Hospital Abortion Committees, 1950–1970," *Feminist Studies* 19 (Summer 1993): 241–268.

11. See Dr. X as told to Lucy Freeman, *The Abortionist* (Garden City, N.Y.: Doubleday, 1962), and Joffe, *Doctors of Conscience.*

12. Quinten Scherman, "Therapeutic Abortion," *Obstetrics and Gynecology* 11 (March 1958): 333–335.

13. To get a sense of the flavor and frequency of abortion in the illegal era, see Rickie Solinger, "Extreme Danger: Women Abortionists and Their Clients Before *Roe v. Wade*," in *Not June*

Cleaver: Women and Gender in Postwar America, 1945–1960, ed. Joanne Meyerowitz (Philadelphia: Temple University Press, 1994), 335–357.

14. Mary Calderone, ed., *Abortion in the United States* (New York: Harper and Brothers, 1958), 84.

15. Ibid., 118. Also see the images in "The Drama of Life before Birth," *Life,* April 30, 1965, 54 ff. For discussion of these images, see Solinger, "A Complete Disaster," 55–56.

16. Lawrence Lader, *Abortion* (Indianapolis: Bobbs-Merrill, 1966), 26–27.

17. Herbert L. Packer and Ralph J. Campbell, "Therapeutic Abortion: A Problem in Law and Medicine," *Stanford Law Review* 11 (May 1959): 417–455.

18. Keith P. Russell, "Changing Indications for Therapeutic Abortion: Twenty Years' Experience at Los Angeles Community Hospital," *Journal of the American Medical Association* 151 (January 10, 1953): 108; Myrna Loth and H. Close Hesseltine, "Therapeutic Abortion at the Chicago Lying-ln Hospital," *American Journal of Obstetrics and Gynecology* 7 (August 1956): 304–311; Harry A. Pearse and Harold A. Ott, "Hospital Control of Sterilization and Therapeutic Abortion," *American Journal of Obstetrics and Gynecology* 60 (August 1950): 85.

19. Harold Rosen, "The Psychiatric Implications of Abortion: A Case Study in Hypocrisy," in

---

1994

Supreme Court rules RICO may be used to prosecute perpetrators of abortion clinic violence.

FACE Act passed, restricting protest activity near clinic entrances.

After circulating his "justifiable homicide" petition, Paul Hill murders abortion provider Dr. John Britton and his volunteer escort, James Barrett, in Florida; Dr. Gary Romalis shot at his home in British Columbia.

Republicans attain majority in Congress; move quickly to bar health insurance coverage of abortion for federal employees, outlaw use of U.S. military hospitals for abortions, ban federal funding of abortions for federal prisoners, and abolish federal subsidies for international family-planning agencies that provide abortions or abortion-related information.

Attorney General Janet Reno convenes grand jury to investigate clinic violence.

Medical Students for Choice founded.

Abortion and the Law, ed. David T. Smith (Cleveland: Press of Case Western Reserve University, 1967), 105.

20. Lewis E. Savel, "Adjudication of Therapeutic Abortion and Sterilization," in *Therapeutic Abortion and Sterilization,* ed. Edmund W. Overstreet (New York: Harper and Row, 1964); *Journal of the Indiana Medical Association* 40 (1947): 16; Pearse and Ott, "Hospital Control."

21. See, for example, John Johnson, Termination of Pregnancy on Psychiatric Grounds," *Medical Gynecology and Sociology* 2 (1966): 2.

22. Dr. Alan Guttmacher described the Mt. Sinai committee in several places, including Calderone, *Abortion in the United States,* 9, 139; and Alan F. Guttmacher, "Therapeutic Abortion: The Doctor's Dilemma," *Journal of Mt. Sinai Hospital* 21 (1954): 111.

23. Johan W. Eliot, Robert E. Hall, J. Robert Willson, and Carolyn Hauser, "The Obstetrician's View," in *Abortion in a Changing World,* vol. I, ed. Robert E. Hall (New York: Columbia University Press, 1970), 93; Kenneth R. Niswander, "Medical Abortion Practices in the United States," in *Abortion and the Law,* ed. Smith, 57. A Chicago study of 209 aborted patients showed that doctors at the Lying-In Hospital in that city determined, "In the majority of cases when therapeutic abortion is indicated, the patient's medical condition warrants the prevention of future gestations";

69.4 percent of these women were sterilized. Loth and Hesseltine, "Therapeutic Abortion," 306; see also Pearse and Ott, "Hospital Control."

24. Eliot et al., "The Obstetrician's View," and Niswander, "Medical Abortion Practice."

25. Calderone, *Abortion in the United States,* 131.

26. Nicholson J. Eastman, "Obstetric Foreword," in *Therapeutic Abortion,* ed. Harold Rosen (New York: Julian Press, 1954), xx.

27. *Oregon Journal,* July 11 1951.

28. Hans Lehfeldt, "Willful Exposure to Unwanted Pregnancy," *American Journal of Obstetrics and Gynecology* 78 (1959): 665; also see the statement of Dr. Iago Goldston defining the desire for abortion in a "so-called adult woman" as an indication of "a sick person and a sick situation . . . which could be relieved, or ameliorated [by the abortion] like cutting off a gangrenous foot" (Calderone, *Abortion in the United States,* 118–119).

29. Sidney Bolter, "The Psychiatrist's Role in Therapeutic Abortion: The Unwitting Accomplice," *American Journal of Psychiatry* 119 (September 1962): 315.

30. For estimates regarding the decline in the abortion rate after the institution of hospital abortion boards, see, for example, Niswander, "Medical Abortion Practices in the United States." Niswander lists a number of studies that also found a substantial decline.

1995

Two clinic employees, Shannon Lowney and Leanne Nichols, murdered in Brookline, Massachusetts. Ohio bans abortions carried out by dilation and extraction method ("partial birth abortions").

1996

Both houses of Congress take the unprecedented step of passing a bill that criminalizes the performance of abortion by a specific method, so-called partial birth abortions. Legislation is vetoed by President Clinton and efforts to override veto fail; however, Congress and state legislatures continue attempts to ban this infrequently used method, properly called intact dilation and extraction.

FDA issues letter finding RU486 "approvable," but subsequent business and legal complications render U.S. distribution plans unclear.

31. See Edwin M. Gold et al., "Therapeutic Abortions in New York City: A Twenty Year Review," *American Journal of Public Health* 55 (July 1965): 969; J. A. Harrington, "Psychiatric Indications for the Termination of Pregnancy," *Practitioner* 185 (November 1960): 654–658; J. G. Moore and J. H. Randall, "Trends in Therapeutic Abortion: A Review of 137 Cases," *American Journal of Obstetrics and Gynecology* 63 (January 1952):

18–40; Roy J. Heffernan and William Lynch, "What Is the Status of Therapeutic Abortion in Modern Obstetrics?" *American Journal of Obstetrics and Gynecology* 66 (August 1953): 335.

32. See Solinger, *Wake Up Little Susie,* ch. 3.
33. Ibid., ch. 5.
34. Ibid., ch. 2.
35. Ibid., ch. 6.
36. Ibid., see ch. 2, 6, 7.

Study/Discussion Questions

1. According to Solinger, what attitude did women take toward abortion in the 1930s?
2. How did abortion become a moral issue after World War II? What changed? How did this view of abortion change ideas about pregnant women?
3. How did the response to abortion of the police, politicians, and doctors change after World War II?
4. How were black and white women treated differently when they did have "illegitimate" children?
5. In reading Solinger's "Chronology of Abortion Politics," pick out two items that you find surprising or particularly interesting and write about why.

To Bear or Not to Bear

Childbearing Rights Information Project

With the passage of the Supreme Court's Roe v. Wade *decision in 1973, the struggle for reproductive rights in the United States did not end. The courts, the legislatures, and a growing militant antiabortion movement throughout the nation chipped away at these rights. Moreover, many supporters of women's "right to choose" began to incorporate into their understanding of reproductive rights the message that African American and Latino activists had stressed for many years: Reproductive freedom means the freedom to have children, as well as the freedom not to. Here the Childbearing Rights Information Project explains the race and class dimensions of the closely linked battles for abortion rights and against sterilization abuse.*

The right to decide when and if to bear children is central to the wide range of childbearing rights that women and their families need. This right is being attacked viciously today from many sides. But the most significant attacks are on the one hand, on the right to abortion, to terminate an unwanted pregnancy, and on the other hand, on the right to bear children, attacked through forced sterilization. These two attacks go hand-in-hand. Aimed first at minority and poor women, they affect all women by slowly eroding the rights of all women to choose.

And there is every indication that the loss of abortion rights will increase the incidence of sterilization abuse. For if a woman cannot terminate an unwanted pregnancy, and cannot afford more children, how will her welfare worker or doctor sound when they "suggest" sterilization? How will they view "one more welfare child" when she comes in to give birth?

For these reasons, the abortion rights struggle is the critical battle in the overall fight for childbearing rights at this time. It has been made so by government attacks, the rightwing anti-abortion movement, and the worsening living conditions that force many women and working-class families to "choose" to terminate an unwanted pregnancy simply because they cannot afford another child.

Yet another factor makes the defense of abortion rights critical. This right was won through hard struggle in the late sixties and the early seventies by the reemerging movement for women's rights. The women's movement understood that women had to be free

From *For Ourselves, Our Families and Our Future: The Struggle for Childbearing Rights,* copyright 1981 by the Childbearing Rights Information Project.

from compulsory pregnancy and compulsory motherhood if women were to fight for all the other rights they need. Because as long as a woman is able to conceive, her life can be seriously disrupted and permanently changed by an unwanted pregnancy. Winning the right to abortion has meant that women's options regarding their standard of living, their ability to work and become self-supporting, and their ability to fight for other rights and for their community's needs, have increased .

Abortion rights crucially affect the position of women. This is why there is such a furor and public debate surrounding abortion, not because of its "moral" nature, or because of the emotional questions it raises, although these factors are involved and do cloud the issue. It is because the winning and defending of abortion rights signals women's fierce determination to have control over their lives and to have an effect on the world around them. Those who would have women back in the kitchen, or off the streets, are those who would condemn women to endless and unwanted childbearing.

Then there are those, the population controllers, who would simply have some people disappear from the face of the earth, or limit their numbers to what they can easily exploit. The genocidal nature of sterilization abuse becomes clear in the case of a country like Puerto Rico, where one-third of all women of childbearing age have been sterilized. This threat hangs over all women in the United States. Women and poor people can become a force for social change, placing demands on the system and educating their children to do the same. Those who would thwart that change benefit from limiting the very numbers of the poor. . . .

Sterilization is an operation which permanently ends a person's reproductive life, eliminating all possibility that they will ever bear children. Female sterilization is done by cutting or "tying" the women's fallopian tubes (tubal ligation), by removing the uterus, the ovaries, or both.

The widespread nature of sterilization abuse has become evident in the last few years, and awareness of the problem is increasing. In the winter of 1978, public outrage at sterilization abuse was expressed over and over at regional HEW hearings on proposed sterilization guidelines. These hearings were themselves the result of the efforts of anti-abuse activists since the early 1970s.

Just what is sterilization abuse, and how does it happen?

Tens of thousands of women are sterilized each year with the use of government funds. The targets of sterilization have been poor, Black, Native American, and Latin women. Abuse occurs when women are pressured into sterilization by doctors or welfare agencies who threaten to withdraw services and benefits unless the woman agrees to be sterilized.

Sterilization abuse occurs when the woman is not informed of the permanence of the procedure, or is told that her tubes can be "untied" at some point in the future. Sterilization abuse occurs when the woman is not spoken to in her primary language and when forms for consent are also in a language she does not read—as has been the case for many Puerto Rican and Chicana women. Abuse occurs when informed consent is not obtained prior to surgery, and when women are coerced into signing forms without discussions, explanations, or counseling, as often happens when women go to a hospital for the purpose of giving birth. Some women have left hospitals without even knowing they have been sterilized, because they were too groggy from anesthesia to realize what they were signing or what was happening to them. Other women have been told upon awakening from surgery or childbirth that they have been sterilized—as was a Native American woman in Massachusetts whose doctor informed her that he had sterilized her in the course of performing an appendectomy "because you are Native American." Abuse occurs when doctors unnecessarily remove women's reproductive organs (uterus, ovaries and fallopian tubes) for "contraceptive" purposes—when in fact, this is often for the training and experimentation purposes of the doctors involved.

But sterilization abuse is most on the rise in the case of women who "choose" sterilization because they are victims of unemployment, discrimination, poverty, cutbacks in welfare and child care, inadequate housing, and poor health care. It is increasing for women who must "choose" sterilization because the Hyde Amendment denies poor women abortion. Forced to "choose" between the risk of unwanted children, the dangers of self-induced or otherwise unsafe abortions, or sterilization, more and more women are encouraged by a racist and sexist health care and welfare system to "choose" sterilization as a means of controlling fertility.

The genocidal nature of sterilization abuse was revealed in a 1970 National Fertility Study which reported that 20% of all Black married women have been sterilized. Latin women have been sterilized at a rate six times that of white women. At least 19% of all Native American women in the U.S. have been sterilized. In the U.S. colony of Puerto Rico, 35.3% of all women of childbearing age have been sterilized. This staggering statistic is related, first and foremost, to Puerto Rico's colonial status. It is also related to the lack of health care, abortion and birth control services for Puerto Rican women, as well as to the massive funding for "family planning" supplied by the U.S. government.

A 1973 HEW study showed the connection between sterilization abuse and poverty when it revealed that the rate of sterilization for low-income women is twice that for higher-income women. The government pays for sterilizations done on welfare recipients in the U.S., and pays in full. It will not, on the other hand,

pay for a poor women's abortion. The message is that poor women are either supposed to endure punitive and compulsory pregnancy, or just not reproduce at all. Between 1969 and 1974, at the height of the welfare rights and civil rights movements, HEW's "family planning" budget increased from $51 million to $250 million. The Boston Committee to End Sterilization Abuse reports that sterilization of women increased three-fold between 1970 and 1975.

Many cases of abuse have been taken to court, packing the dockets in state after state as in the cases of ten Chicanas in California, of Native American Norma Jean Serena, and of Norma James who had to become sterilized in order to keep her job in a battery factory. These women have all made public their terrible loss and have helped to make people aware that sterilization abuse is a serious national problem. . . .

Whenever we deal with an issue so basic as a people's ability to reproduce, we must address the whole gamut of social and political problems a society faces. The only real long-term solution to the problem of sterilization abuse is elimination of the conditions of poverty and racial and sexual discrimination in which sterilization abuse thrives. In the meantime, work to gain legislative tools to deal with abuse, community education and organizing, and vigilant pressure on the government regarding its sterilization practices, can all help to build the kind of movement which will be able to wage the long-term struggle for childbearing rights.

"I just want them to put me back like they found me," says Valerie Cliett, who was sterilized against her will and without her knowledge while she was on welfare. Valerie Cliett will never be back like they found her. But the work of the anti-abuse movement can insure that one day there will be no more bitter statements from women like her, and sterilization abuse will be a thing of the past.

Study/Discussion Questions

1. Who is most likely to be sterilized in our society, and why?
2. What examples of sterilization abuse do the authors cite?
3. Why is the right to choose an abortion critical to women's fight for other rights, in the authors' view?
4. What connections do the authors see between abortion rights and forced sterilization?

Choosing Disability

Laura Hershey

Laura Hershey has been an activist for both disability rights and reproductive rights. Yet these two sets of basic human rights, and the movements surrounding them, are often seen as antithetical to each other. Hershey argues against this hostile pairing, while also urging that reproductive rights activists confront the deep-seated prejudices against people with disabilities that pervade feminist thinking no less than that of the society at large.

In 1983, when I was in college, local anti-abortion protesters commemorated the tenth anniversary of *Roe v. Wade* with a rally. Our student feminist organization held a small counterdemonstration. Frantic in their zeal, anti-choice protesters assailed us with epithets like "slut" and "bitch." But the most hostile remark was directed at me. I was confronted by an angry nun whose "Abortion Is Murder" sign hung tiredly at her side. She stopped in front of me and aimed a pugnacious finger. "You see." she announced. "God even let you be born!"

I'm not sure the sister realized that I had been part of the pro-choice demonstration. All she saw in me was a poster child for her holy crusade. I must have seemed to her an obvious mistake of nature: a severely disabled person, who, through a combination of divine intervention and legal restrictions, had been born anyway.

That was my first inkling of how attitudes about disability function in the volatile debate over reproductive rights. I understood that the nun and her co-crusaders were no friends of mine. To her, I was a former fetus who had escaped the abortionists. No room in that view for my identity as an adult woman; no room for the choices I might make. Now, more than a decade later, antiabortion groups are courting the disability community. The approach has become less clumsy, emphasizing respect for the lives of people with disabilities, and some activists have accepted the anti-choice message because they find it consistent with the goals of the disability rights movement. As a feminist, however, I recoil at the "pro-life" movement's disregard for the lives and freedom of women.

But I cannot overlook the fact that when a prenatal test reveals the possibility of a "major defect," as the medical profession puts it, the pregnancy almost always ends in "therapeutic abortion." The prospect of bearing a child with disabilities causes such anxiety that abortion has become the accepted outcome—even

Disabled rights activists participating in a pro-choice rally in Boston, 1989.

among people who oppose abortion rights in general.

Indeed, fear of disability played a key role in the legalization of abortion in the United States in the 1960s. When thousands of pregnant women who had taken thalidomide (a drug used in tranquilizers) or had contracted rubella (German measles) gave birth to children with "defects," doctors called for easing abortion laws.

Today, despite three decades of activism by the disability community, and substantial disability rights legislation, avoiding disability is an important factor in the use and regulation of abortion. In a 1992 Time/CNN survey, for example, 70 percent of respondents favored abortion if a fetus was likely to be born deformed.

This is the quandary we face: the choices we all seek to defend—choices individual women make about childbirth—can conflict with efforts to promote acceptance, equality, and respect for people with disabilities. I am inseparably committed to the empowerment of both people with disabilities and women. Therefore, my pro-choice stance must lie somewhere in the common ground between feminism and disability rights. I want to analyze

social and scientific trends, and to vocalize my troubled feelings about where all of this may lead. I want to defy patriarchy's attempts to control women, and also to challenge an age-old bias against people with disabilities. I want to discuss the ethics of choice—without advocating restrictions on choice. To draw a parallel, feminists have no problem attacking sex-selective abortion used to guarantee giving birth to a child of the "right" sex (most often male), but we try to educate against the practice, rather than seek legislation.

In an effort to clarify my own thinking about these complex, interlocking issues, I have been reading and listening to the words of other disabled women. Diane Coleman, a Nashville-based disability rights organizer, is deeply concerned about the number of abortions based on fetal disability. Coleman sees this as "a way that society expresses its complete rejection of people with disabilities, and the conviction that it would be better if we were dead." I find myself sharing her indignation.

Julie Reiskin, a social worker in Denver who is active in both disability rights and abortion rights, tells me, "I live with a disability, and I have a hard time saying, 'This is great.' I think that the goal should be to eliminate disabilities." It jars me to hear this, but Reiskin makes a further point that I find helpful. "Most abortions are not because there's something wrong with the fetus," she says. "Most abortions are because we don't have decent birth control." In other words, we should never have to use fetal disability as a reason to keep abortion legal: "It should be because women have the right to do what we want with our bodies, period," says Reiskin.

We are a diverse community, and it's no surprise to find divergent opinions on as difficult an issue as abortion. Our personal histories and hopes, viewed through the lens of current circumstances, shape our values and politics. Like all the women I interviewed, I must be guided by my own experiences of living with disability. At two years old, I still could not walk. Once I was diagnosed—I have a rare neuromuscular condition—doctors told my parents that I would live only another year or two. Don't bother about school, they advised; just buy her a few toys and make her comfortable until the end.

My parents ignored the doctors' advice. Instead of giving up on me, they taught me to read. They made sure I had a child-size wheelchair and a tricycle. My father built a sled for me, and when the neighborhood kids went to the park to fly downhill in fresh snow, he pulled me along. My mother performed much of my physical care, but was determined not to do all of it; college students helped out in exchange for housing. She knew that her own wholeness and my future depended on being able to utilize resources outside our home.

Now my life is my own. I have a house, a career, a partner, and a community of friends with and without disabilities. I rely on a motorized wheelchair for mobility, a voice-activated computer for my writing, and the assistance of Medicaid-funded attendants for daily needs—dressing, bathing, eating, going to the bathroom. I manage it all according to my own goals and needs.

My life contradicts society's stereotypes about how people with disabilities live. Across the country, thousands of other severely disabled people are surviving, working, loving, and agitating for change. I don't mean to paint a simplistic picture. Most of us work very hard to attain independence, against real physical and/or financial obstacles. Too many people are denied the kind of daily inhome assistance that makes my life possible. Guaranteeing such services has become a top priority for the disability rights movement.

Changes like these, amounting to a small revolution, are slow to reach the public consciousness. Science, on the other hand, puts progress into practice relatively quickly. Prenatal screening seems to give pregnant women more power—but is it actually asking women to ratify social prejudices through their reproductive "choices"? I cannot help thinking that in most cases, when a woman terminates a previously wanted pregnancy expressly to avoid giving birth to a disabled child, she is buying into obsolete assumptions about that child's future. And she is making a statement about the desirability or the relative worth of such a child. Abortion based on disability results from, and in turn strengthens, certain beliefs: children with disabilities (and by implication adults with disabilities) are a burden to family and society; life with a disability is scarcely worth living; preventing the birth is an act of kindness; women who bear disabled children have failed.

Language reinforces the negativity. Terms like "fetal deformity" and "defective fetus" are deeply stigmatizing, carrying connotations of inadequacy and shame. Many of us have been called "abnormal" by medical personnel, who view us primarily as "patients," subject to the definitions and control of the medical profession. "Medical professionals often have countless incorrect assumptions about our lives," says Diane Coleman. "Maybe they see us as failures on their part." As a result, doctors who diagnose fetuses with disabilities often recommend either abortion or institutionalization. "I really haven't heard very many say, 'It's O.K. to have a disability, your family's going to be fine,'" Coleman says.

The independent living movement, which is the disability community's civil rights movement, challenges this medical model. Instead of locating our difficulties within ourselves, we identify our oppression within a society that refuses to accommodate our disabilities. The real solution is to change society—to ensure full accessibility, equal opportunity, and a range of community support services—not to attempt to eliminate disabilities.

The idea that disability might someday be permanently eradicated—whether through prenatal screening and abortion or through medical research leading to "cures"—has strong appeal for a society wary of spending resources on human needs. Maybe there lurks, in the back of society's mind, the belief—the hope?—that one day there will be no people with disabilities. That attitude works against the goals of civil rights and independent living. We struggle for integration, access, and support services, yet our existence remains an unresolved question. Under the circumstances, we cannot expect society to guarantee and fund our full citizenship.

My life of disability has not been easy or carefree. But in measuring the quality of my life, other factors—education, friends, and meaningful work, for example—have been decisive. If I were asked for an opinion on whether to bring a child into the world, knowing she would have the same limitations and opportunities I have had, I would not hesitate to say, "Yes."

I know that many women do not have the resources my parents had. Many lack education, are poor, or are without the support of friends and family. The problems created by these circumstances are intensified with a child who is disabled. No woman should have a child she can't handle or doesn't want. Having said that, I must also say that all kinds of women raise healthy, self-respecting children with disabilities, without unduly compromising their own lives. Raising a child with disabilities is difficult, but raising any child is difficult; just as you expect any other child to enrich your life, you can expect the same from a child with disabilities. But the media often portray raising a child with disabilities as a personal martyrdom. Disabled children, disabled people, are viewed as misfortunes.

I believe the choice to abort a disabled fetus represents a rejection of children who have disabilities. Human beings have a deep-seated fear of confronting the physical vulnerability that is part of being human. This terror has been dubbed "disabiliphobia" by some activists. I confront disabiliphobia every day: the usher who gripes that I take up too much room in a theater lobby; the store owner who insists that a ramp is expensive and unnecessary because people in wheelchairs never come in; the talk-show host who resents the money spent to educate students with disabilities. These are the voices of an age-old belief that disability compromises our humanity and requires us to be kept apart and ignored.

Disabiliphobia affects health care reform too. In the proposed Clinton health plan only people disabled through injury or illness—not those of us with congenital disabilities—will be covered. Is this exclusion premised on the assumption that those of us born with disabilities have lesser value and that our needs are too costly?

People with severe disabilities do sometimes require additional resources for medical and support services. But disabiliphobia runs deeper than a cost-benefit analysis. Witness the ordeal of Bree Walker, a Los Angeles newscaster with a mild physical disability affecting her hands and feet. In 1990, when Walker became pregnant with her second child, she knew the fetus might inherit her condition, as had the first. She chose to continue the pregnancy, which led talk-show hosts and listeners to feel they had the right to spend hours debating whether Walker should have the child (most said no). Walker received numerous hostile letters. The callers and letter writers seemed to be questioning her right to exist, as well as her child's.

Walker's experience also pointed out how easily disabiliphobia slips from decisions about fetuses with disabilities to decisions about people with disabilities. That's why abortion is an area where we fear that the devaluation of our lives could become enshrined in public policy. Pro-choice groups must work to ensure that they do not support legislation that sets different standards based on disability.

A case in point is Utah's restrictive 1991 antiabortion law (which has since been declared unconstitutional). The law allowed abortions only in cases of rape, incest, endangerment of the woman's life, a profound health risk to the woman—or "fetal defect." According to Susanne Millsaps, director of Utah's NARAL affiliate, some disability rights activists wanted NARAL and other pro-choice groups to join in opposing the "fetal defect" exemption. The groups did not specifically take a stand on the exemption; instead they opposed the entire law. I would agree that the whole statute had to be opposed on constitutional and feminist grounds. But I would also agree that there should have been a stronger response to the fetal disability exemption.

To group "fetal defect" together with rape, incest, and life-endangering complications is to reveal deep fears about disability. As Barbara Faye Waxman, an expert on the reproductive rights of women with disabilities, says: "In this culture, disability, in and of itself, is perceived as a threat to the welfare of the mother. I find that to be troublesome and offensive."

There is more at stake here than my feelings, or anyone else's, about a woman's decision. Rapidly changing reproductive technologies, combined with socially constructed prejudices, weigh heavily on any decision affecting a fetus with possible disabilities. While some women lack basic prenatal and infant care, huge amounts of money are poured into prenatal screening and genetic research. Approximately 450 disorders can now be predicted before birth. In most cases the tests reveal only the propensity for a condition, not the condition itself. The Human Genome Project aims to complete the DNA map, and to locate hundreds more physical and developmental attributes. There is little public debate about the worth or ultimate uses of this federally funded multibillion-dollar program. But there are issues with regard to abortion that we can no longer afford to ignore:

- Does prenatal screening provide more data for women's informed choices, or does it promote the idea that no woman should risk having a disabled child?
- Who decides whether a woman should undergo prenatal screening, and what she should do with the results?
- Are expensive, government-funded genetic research projects initiated primarily for the benefit of a society unwilling to support disability-related needs?
- Is society attempting to eradicate certain disabilities? Should this ever be a goal? If so, should all women be expected to cooperate in it?

The January/February 1994 issue of *Disability Rag & Resource,* a publication of the disability rights movement, devoted several articles to genetic screening. In one, feminist lawyer Lisa Blumberg argues that women are being coerced into accepting prenatal tests, and then pressured to terminate their pregnancies when disabling conditions appear likely. "Prenatal testing has largely become the decision of the doctor," Blumberg writes, and "the social purpose of these tests is to reduce the incidence of live births of people with disabilities."

A woman faced with this choice usually feels pressure from many directions. Family, friends, doctors, and the media predict all kinds of negative results should her child be disabled. At the same time, she is unlikely to be given information about community resources; nor is she encouraged to meet individuals who have the condition her child might be born with. This lack of exposure to real-life, nonmedical facts about living with a disability should make us wonder whether women are really making "informed" choices about bearing children with disabilities.

Few outside the disability community have dealt with these issues in any depth. "We are all aware of the potential for abuses in reproductive technology and in genetic testing," says Marcy Wilder, legal director for NARAL's national office in Washington, D.C. "I don't see that there have been widespread abuses—but we're certainly concerned." That concern has not led to any coalition-building with disability rights groups, however.

Many feminist disability rights activists report chilly responses when they attempt to network with pro-choice groups. Too often, when we object to positions that implicitly doubt the humanity of children born disabled, we are accused of being anti-choice. One activist I know recently told me about her experience speaking at a meeting of a National Organization for Women chapter. She mentioned feeling discomfort about the widespread abortion of disabled fetuses—and was startled by the members' reactions. "They said, 'How could you claim to be a feminist and pro-choice and even begin to think that there should be any limitations?' I tried to tell them I don't think there should be limitations, but that our issues need to be included."

On both sides, the fears are genuine, rational, and terrifying—if not always articulated. For the pro-choice movement, the fear is that questioning the motives and assumptions behind any reproductive decision could give ammunition to antiabortionists. Defenders of disability rights fear that the widespread use of prenatal testing and abortion for the purpose of eliminating disability could inaugurate a new eugenics movement. If we cannot unite and find ways to address issues of reproductive screening and manipulation, we all face the prospect that what is supposed to be a private decision—the termination of a pregnancy—might become the first step in a campaign to eliminate people with disabilities.

I am accusing the pro-choice movement not of spurring these trends, but of failing to address them. Most pro-choice organizations do not favor the use of abortion to eliminate disabilities, but their silence leaves a vacuum in which fear of disability flourishes.

Disabiliphobia and the "genetics enterprise," as activist Adrienne Asch calls it, have also had legal implications for the reproductive rights of all women. The tendency to blame social problems such as poverty and discrimination on individuals with disabilities and their mothers has made women vulnerable to the charge that they are undermining progress toward human "perfectibility"—because they insist on a genuine choice. Some legal and medical experts have developed a concept called "fetal rights," in which mothers can be held responsible for the condition of their unborn or newborn children. According to Lisa Blumberg, "fetal rights" could more accurately be called "fetal quality control." For women with hereditary disabilities who decide to have children this concept is nothing new. Society and medical professionals have often tried to prevent us from bearing and raising children. Disabled women know, as well as anyone, what it means to be deprived of reproductive choice. More broadly, decisions involving our health care, sexuality, and parenting have been made by others based on assumptions about our inabilities and/or our asexuality.

The right to control one's body begins with good gynecological care. Low income, and dependence on disability "systems," restrict access to that care. Like many women of disability, my health care choices are limited by the accessibility of medical facilities, and by providers' attitudes toward disability and their willingness to accept the low reimbursement of Medicaid. And Medicaid will not cover most abortions, a policy that discriminates against poor women and many women with disabilities.

Paradoxically, policy is often undermined by practice. Although public funding rarely pays for abortions, many women with disabilities are encouraged to have them—even when they would prefer to have a child. Doctors try to convince us an abortion would be best for "health reasons"—in which case, Medicaid will pay for it after all. "Abortions are easier for disabled women to get," says Nancy Moulton, a health care advocate in Atlanta, "because the medical establishment sees us as not being fit parents." Most women grow up amid strong if subtle pressures to become mothers. For those of us with disabilities, there is an equal or greater pressure to forgo motherhood. This pressure has taken the form of forced sterilization, lost custody battles, and forced abortion.

Consequently, for women with disabilities, reproductive freedom means more than being able to get an abortion. It is hard for many of us to relate to those in the reproductive rights movement whose primary concern is keeping abortions legal and available. But I believe our different perspectives on reproductive freedom are fundamentally compatible, like variations on a single theme.

Whatever the reason, feminist organizations seem inclined to overlook disability concerns. Feminist speakers might add "ableism" to their standard list of offensive "isms," but they do little to challenge it. Now more than ever, women with disabilities need the feminist movement's vigorous support. We need you to defend our rights as if they were your own—which they are. Here are a few suggestions:

- Recognize women with disabilities' equal stake in the pro-choice movement's goals. That means accepting us as women, not dismissing us as "other," or infirm, or genderless. Recognize us as a community of diverse individuals whose health needs, lifestyles, and choices vary.
- Defend all our reproductive rights: the right to appropriate education about sexuality and reproduction; to gynecological care, family planning services, and birth control; the right to be sexually active; to have children and to keep and raise those children, with assistance if necessary; and the right to abortion in accessible facilities, with practitioners who are sensitive to our needs.
- Remove the barriers that restrict the access of women with disabilities to services. Help to improve physical accessibility, arrange disability awareness training for staff and volunteers, and conduct outreach activities to reach women with disabilities.
- Continue struggling to build coalitions around reproductive rights and disability issues. There is plenty of common ground, although we may have to tiptoe through dangerous, mine-filled territory to get to it.
- Question the assumptions that seem to make bearing children with disabilities unacceptable.

Despite our rhetoric, abortion is not strictly a private decision. Individual choices are made in a context of social values; I want us to unearth, sort out, and appraise those values. I wouldn't deny any woman the right to choose abortion. But I would issue a challenge to all women making a decision whether to give birth to a child who may have disabilities.

The challenge is this: consider all relevant information, not just the medical facts. More important than a particular diagnosis are the conditions awaiting a child—community acceptance, access to buildings and transportation, civil rights protection, and opportunities for education and employment. Where these things are lacking or inadequate, consider joining the movement to change them. In many communities, adults with disabilities and parents of disabled children have developed powerful advocacy coalitions. I recognize that, having weighed all the factors, some women will decide they cannot give birth to a child with disabilities. It pains me, but I acknowledge their right and their choice.

Meanwhile, there is much work still to be done.

Study/Discussion Questions

1. Why does the author think that abortion should be legal?
2. Why does she think that women should not choose abortion to avoid giving birth to a child with a disability?
3. What problems does Hershey see in prenatal testing for disabilities? How is it biased, in her view?
4. What reproductive rights do women with disabilities deserve, according to Hershey, and how are their reproductive rights limited in our society?
5. Think about whether you fear having a child with a disability. If so, have you questioned any of your assumptions about what that would be like since reading this article?

Nonmothers as Bad Mothers
Infertility and the "Maternal Instinct"

Elaine Tyler May

In "Nonmothers as Bad Mothers," an excerpt from her book Barren In the Promised Land, *historian Elaine Tyler May looks at two particular waves of pronatalism in the recent American past. In the height of the post–World War II baby boom, women faced intense pressure to become mothers. Those who were infertile often received psychological diagnoses and treatments designed to reduce their putative masculine, aggressive tendencies. During the 1980s backlash against feminism, societal pressure to bear children built up again.*

For conception to take place a woman must be a woman. Not only must she have the physical structure and hormones of a woman but she must feel she is a woman and accept it. A girl child becomes and feels herself a developing woman if she has made a proper identification with her own mother and has also learned to accept her femininity and also masculinity as represented by her father and later, by her husband. Being a woman means acceptance of her primary role, that of conceiving and bearing a child. Every woman has a basic urge and need to produce a child. Being a woman means a complete readiness to look forward to the delivery of that child when it is sufficiently nourished by her to take its place as an infant in the outside world. Being a woman means her feeling of her own readiness and capability to rear that child and aid in its physical, emotional and mental development.[1]

> —*Abraham Stone, medical director of the Margaret Sanger Research Foundation, 1950*

In the years following World War II, as the baby boom exploded and a powerful ideology of domesticity gripped the nation, the definition of womanhood articulated by Dr. Abraham Stone gained widespread acceptance. Some medical experts, particularly specialists in the growing field of infertility, frequently based their diagnoses and treatments on the theory that women often caused their own infertility by a subconscious rejection of their maternal instinct. Unless they could be restored to psychological health—which meant a full and eager acceptance of motherhood—such

From Molly Ladd Taylor and Lauri Umansky, editors, *"Bad" Mothers: The Politics of Blame in Twentieth Century America*, New York: NYU Press, 1998, pp. 198–229. This essay originally appeared in *Barren in the Promised Land: Childless Americans and the Pursuit of Happiness* (New York: Basic Books, 1995), chapters 5 and 7.

women were not considered to be good candidates for infertility treatment. According to these neo-Freudian theorists, if such women were helped to conceive, they would become bad mothers. The first step in treating them was to help them become psychologically ready for motherhood.

Margaret Valen encountered this theory when she consulted a physician in 1945 to discover why she was not getting pregnant. She was twenty-five and her husband was twenty-seven, and they had been married only a year, but since they married "late" by 1945 standards, most of her friends no doubt had children already. Medical experts encouraged childless couples to seek help early, warning that "the longer sterility has existed, the harder it is to correct. Only a qualified physician can answer for each man and wife the question of when they should undergo examination." Margaret went through the usual infertility workup and tried "everything kookie," but nothing worked. The physicians could find no physiological cause for the Valens' childlessness.

The Valens were among the 50 percent of infertile couples at the time who could not be diagnosed.[2] But that did not prevent her physician from suggesting treatment. When no physiological cause could be found, some physicians looked for psychological explanations. As a working woman in the postwar era, Margaret was not behaving in an appropriately feminine way. Perhaps, the theory went, she was inhibiting her own fertility because she held a job—an unwomanly thing to do and evidence that maybe she did not really want a child. Particular warnings were directed toward employed women, who allegedly put their fertility at risk: "The pressures of modern living and the strains of occupations in which women have been engaging are . . . significant causes" of infertility, cautioned a leading expert. "The same can be said of men, but to a lesser extent."[3] In keeping with such theories, Margaret's physician told her she

should quit her job, so she did. Like most infertile women who sought medical advice, she did whatever her physician told her to do, even if she thought it was "kookie." But Margaret never got pregnant. Quitting her job did not do the trick.

Advising a woman to quit her job was not a standard treatment for infertility, but it was one approach to a problem that was still difficult to diagnose and treat. Researchers had found that stress could be a factor in infertility, by causing fallopian tubes to contract or by affecting the motility of sperm. If employment was a cause of stress, it was not entirely "kookie" for physicians to suggest quitting a job to relieve stress. The problem, however, is that there was no way to be certain that job-related stress caused a woman's tubes to contract. It was just as likely that stress at work affected a man's fertility. But it was unthinkable to suggest that a male breadwinner should quit his job. The woman's job during these years appeared to be expendable. Moreover, in most cases it was the woman, not the man, who sought treatment. . . .

Most infertility practitioners were specialists in female reproductive medicine. The vast majority of the members of the American Society for the Study of Sterility, for example, were in the field of obstetrics and gynecology, followed by urology, with a few in related fields, such as internal medicine, endocrinology, general practice, and pathology.[4] At its annual meeting in 1963, Herbert H. Thomas, the president of the society, justified the continued focus on the female patient: "This does not indicate that we are unaware of the responsibility of the male in the problem of infertility, but the incidence of primary male infertility is variable but relatively low and, in our culture, it is usually the women who initiate the request for assistance." Surely, the president of the society knew the widely published statistics by its own members indicating that approximately half the infertility cases involved a problem with the man. Yet he remained focused on the woman as the patient:

> In seeking counsel with us, she . . . admits to frustration and failure . . . as we endeavor to probe and explore the innermost secrets of her life in order to alleviate her barrenness. As she bares her personal life before us and submits to many indignities and both painful and somewhat hazardous diagnostic procedures . . . we must not betray this trust. . . . The responsibility to our frustrated patient and her husband is a great one.[5]

The definition of the patient as female extended into medical language itself, which cast the female body as inherently flawed. Medical texts, as well as physicians and their patients, routinely described infertility in terms of "failure," "blame," and "fault." One woman, for example, who wrote to a noted specialist about her repeated miscarriages, wondered whether he agreed with her local physician that surgery might correct her "defective cervix." The specialist agreed that surgery might solve the difficulty, but referred to the condition not as a "defective cervix," as the woman's letter had, but as an "incompetent cervix."[6] Medical terminology was filled with metaphors of the "incompetent" female body, while presenting the male reproductive system as robust. This cultural casting of biological phenomena not only described women's physiology as weak and flawed, it also disadvantaged men, whose reproductive systems might need attention and repair.

The anthropologist Emily Martin analyzed the language of reproduction in standard twentieth-century medical textbooks that have been used routinely in medical schools. She found such statements as these: Ovaries "shed" eggs but testicles "produce" sperm, unfertilized eggs "degenerate" and are "wasted," and "menstruation is the uterus crying for lack of a baby." In contrast, although millions of sperm that do not fertilize eggs die within a few hours, the textbooks never called them "wasted," "failed," or "degenerating"; rather, they described the male reproductive physiology as a "remarkable cellular transformation . . . amazing characteristic of spermatogenesis is its sheer magnitude." Descriptions of fertilization in these textbooks reflect cultural ideas about male aggressiveness and female passivity. Although research documented the active role of the egg in traveling through the tube and showed that the process of fertilization involves mechanisms in both the sperm and the egg that make them "mutually active partners," the loaded language persisted. As if cast as a villain in a film noir, the advancing egg "captures and tethers" the sperm and "clasps" the sperm to its nucleus. The egg has become the femme fatale or the overbearing Mom, devouring its male victim.[7]

PSYCHOLOGICAL DIAGNOSES

Infertility treatment was frequently unsuccessful, because half the cases eluded diagnosis. Clinical research continued to focus on the development of more precise diagnostic methods and more effective treatments. Practitioners did not all agree about the basic underlying causes of infertility. Some staunchly believed that if a physiological cause could not be identified, it simply had not been discovered yet. Most, however, agreed that emotional factors could be involved. Researchers had already established that stress could affect hormonal secretions, tubal contractions, and even sperm motility. But the causes of the emotional stresses that led to these physiological outcomes, as well as the prescriptions for reducing these stresses, were a subject of considerable debate. Some leading physicians downplayed the psychological factor. "It is easy to overestimate its importance," said the medical director of the Planned Parenthood Center of Los Angeles. "Admittedly, emotional disturbances can play a part in infertility, but physical conditions are a more frequent cause.[8] Others, however, emphasized psychological causes.

At the extreme end of this debate in the 1940s and 1950s were the psychoanalytically oriented practitioners. If they could find no physiological cause for a couple's childlessness, they often looked for evidence of their patients' unconscious desires to avoid parenthood. This psychological scrutiny was generally directed toward women. Although men were more likely than women to resist treatment, physicians rarely considered the possibility that reluctant men had a psychological difficulty that contributed to their impaired fertility or that they "subconsciously" did not really want children. Stress caused by pressure at work was the only psychological factor mentioned in the medical literature on the evaluation of male patients. Experts in the field never suggested that men thwarted their own potential for parenthood by "unconscious wishes" or "a rejection of their masculinity." On the contrary, specialists frequently reassured men that infertility did not mean they were lacking in masculinity. Clearly, most physicians believed that masculinity was not something that men were likely to avoid. But psychoanalytically oriented physicians claimed that some women contributed to their own infertility by their reluctance, consciously or unconsciously, to "accept their femininity." According to these practitioners, even the most eager and cooperative female patient might "subconsciously" wish to avoid motherhood.

As infertility continued to gain attention from the popular media, as well as the scientific community, these psychoanalytic perspectives began to infuse the discussion of childlessness. The postwar years witnessed a romance with all forms of psychology, especially Freudian and neo-Freudian theories. Psychoanalytic jargon appeared everywhere, from scientific journals to popular articles, and even in casual conversations. Some neo-Freudian theorists breathed new life into prescriptions that were first voiced by their Victorian forebears about the importance of women attending to their proper role. Old notions that education and careers hindered women's reproductive potential resurfaced, as did exhortations about women's sexual behavior. Although many infertility experts were skeptical of psychoanalytic explanations, neo-Freudian practitioners received a remarkable amount of attention in both the medical and popular literature.[9]

One example of this approach was a 1951 article by a sociologist, a psychologist, and a gynecologist that was published in the *Journal of the American Medical Association*. The authors began with the premise that normal, healthy adults naturally desire children. "Most people who do not truly want them probably have personality defects—for example, infantilism. . . . . Women totally lacking the desire for children are so rare that they may be considered as deviants from the normal." Infertile women, they reasoned, might subconsciously thwart their own fertility by rejecting their femininity. They described three "types" of such women:

> The masculine-aggressive woman insists on having a child of her own body, cost what it may. She is a ready, though rarely ideal, candidate for donor insemination, sometimes obtaining her husband's reluctant consent by a species of emotional blackmail. Second, there is the wife who accepts childlessness and lives on good terms with her sterile husband but demands from him constant proofs of his masculinity in the way of achievement and material success. And, third, the truly motherly woman compensates for her lack of children by directing her motherliness toward other persons or objects, real or symbolic.

The three male authors asserted that whatever intrusive procedures were required to enable a woman to get pregnant, including artificial insemination with the sperm of an anonymous donor, the women did not mind. In fact, they argued, the women may even enjoy it.

> The patients are seldom troubled by any notion of violation of their bodies; indeed, some of them derive a peculiar satisfaction from the coldly scientific nature of the operation. Successful results create a feeling of superiority and triumph over the male, as well as a sense of fulfillment.[10]

Some specialists who agreed with these psychological theories warned other practitioners not to treat "neurotic" women for infertility. One advised: "The wise physician will be able to ascertain the psychic health of his patients. He will then be in an enviable position to determine whether or not attempts should be made to relieve sterility." It was important to do so, he argued, for "allowing an emotional [sic] immature woman to become fertile may open up the proverbial hornet's nest. The repercussions may result in neurotic children, broken homes, and divorce."[11] Some gynecologists, as well as psychologists and psychiatrists, pointed to "personality" factors in infertility. "The emotional maturity of the patient, that is, her ability adequately to meet the demands of pregnancy as well as motherhood, should always be considered in the treatment of sterility," argued W. S. Kroger, director of Psychosomatic Gynecology at Mount Sinai Hospital in Chicago and one of the leading voices in the application of psychoanalytic theories to infertility treatment. Kroger urged his fellow practitioners to take note of "those unhealthy attitudes and personality factors likely to complicate or contraindicate pregnancy." To determine if a woman should be treated for infertility, the physician should "seek answers to the following questions":

1. Is the patient a cold, selfish, demanding person, or is she a warm, giving woman?

2. What is her motivation for becoming pregnant?
3. Could the absence of so-called "motherliness" be due to environmental factors, permanent or temporary, and does this account for her sterility?
4. How much does her emotional past . . . influence her attitudes toward motherhood?
5. What are the deeper meanings underlying her surface attitudes toward pregnancy, motherhood, and sterility?

Those who should be rejected for treatment included "the aggressive and masculine women who are competitive, strong, ambitious, and dominating. They 'wear the pants in the family' and are usually successful career women, possessing considerable executive ability." The greatest exemplar of the maladjusted female was the career woman. "We have all seen a long-desired pregnancy follow the renunciation of a career. This may be the result of the development of 'motherliness' and the consequent hormonal changes." Kroger concluded that "it should not be necessary for every physician to have training in psychoanalysis" to understand these basic principles. In other words, physicians who were not trained in psychology should make a psychological diagnosis that would determine whether the personality of the patient disqualified her for motherhood, in which case the physician should refuse treatment.[12] Kroger ended with a word of caution to the physician who might unwittingly treat a woman who was emotionally unqualified to become a mother: "If such a woman finally does conceive, the same psychological difficulties which once prevented conception, may adversely affect the child's psychic development, and . . . another individual is added to an endless procession of neurotics."[13] . . .

Psychoanalytic ideas moved easily from the medical journals to the popular press. An article in *Coronet* magazine in 1953, entitled

"Sterility Can Be a State of Mind," asserted that emotional states—hatred, fear, anxiety, poor adjustment to marriage—could inhibit fertility in from one-fourth to one-third of all cases of involuntary childlessness. According to the author, infertility often resulted from "high-strung women"; "strong parental prohibitions against sex"; and other psychological inhibitions, such as unresolved Oedipal conflicts. "Some specialists point out that to many persons, the doctor has become the highest authority in the conduct of their personal lives. . . . [He] has taken the place of the father of their childhood." Sometimes a visit to such a physician "may be reassuring to the wife and lead to a relaxation of her Fallopian tubes." The author also argued for the importance of sexual adjustment. "The 'act of love' must, in truth, be an act of love, rather than just an act of sex, if fruitful union is to ensue." Repeating a common refrain, the article concluded, "If the wife is working, perhaps she can take a leave of absence for a while, or quit her job and stay at home. Rest and relax, and just forget all about doctors for a while. And see what happens."[14]

Some experts claimed that mere association with children would bring out a woman's "maternal instinct," which could stimulate fertility. *American Magazine* suggested a "plan that sometimes does wonders for childless couples. This is to go out babysitting. . . . [A] woman's maternal instincts are tremendously stimulated when there are children around." This was also the argument frequently given for the alleged "cure" of infertility by adoption. "Sometimes the adoption of a child is the secret," wrote an observer. "In the sunlight of a new happiness, the adoptive mother bears a child of her own." In one case, a psychoanalyst argued that the reason pregnancy followed adoption was because the wife quit her job after adopting a baby.

Her conflict . . . resolved [sic] around the fact that if she became pregnant, she would

have to stop working outside the home and abandon the masculine role. The decision to adopt a baby solved this unconscious conflict by making it absolutely necessary for her to give up her job. This, in some strange way, added to her femininity, and allowed her to conceive. Cases in which pregnancy follows the adoption of a baby are by no means rare. Everyone knows of similar instances.[15]

Some physicians were skeptical of these explanations. One cautioned those who believed that adoption often leads to biological parenting. "This popular belief has no justification. Some couples adopt a child, then subsequently have children of their own, and when this occurs, there's a lot of comment. But we don't hear about the many more couples who do not have children subsequent to adoption." This physician was also cautious about placing too much emphasis on emotional factors in infertility. He noted that emotional tension was as likely to be a result of infertility as a cause, since trying to conceive a child and seeking medical help in the effort were stressful activities in themselves: "Many childless couples are emotionally upset because of their failure to have children, but often the tensions have been built up as a result of years of frustration and hence may be an effect rather than a cause of the problem."[16]

This physician had a point. Infertile couples in the postwar years faced tremendous stresses. First, there was the stigma of childlessness at a time when having many children, at a young age, was the norm. Next was the suggestion, reinforced by psychoanalytic theories and echoed in the popular press, that infertile women were to blame for their own condition. Women were labeled abnormal if they were ambivalent about having children, they were suspected of not really wanting children even if they truly believed that they did, they were accused of unconscious wishes to remain childless, they were chastised for holding jobs or aspiring to careers, and they were admonished if they were not adequately passive and submissive. They were made to feel guilty if they had an abortion, held a job or pursued a career, or found sexual satisfaction in any way other than through a vaginal orgasm resulting from male penetration.

Since researchers had determined that stress might affect fertility, some of these pressures may have had the ironic effect of contributing to infertility. Women who were accused of being "abnormal," "selfish," "neurotic," or "immature" as a result of normal and healthy ambivalence toward or resistance to the accepted female role of full-time wife and mother may indeed have suffered enough stress to cause their fallopian tubes to contract. Meanwhile, in spite of the efforts of many specialists to improve the treatment of male infertility and the recognition that most infertility cases involved some problem with the male partner, infertility remained defined as a female complaint.

THE NEW PRONATALISM

According to feminist author Susan Faludi, the renewed push toward parenthood in the 1980s took the form of a media blitz aimed at educated career women, warning them that if they delayed childbearing, they were likely to find themselves infertile. Few of the alarmists who pointed to a new "infertility epidemic" took note of studies showing a troubling trend in male fertility: the decline in the average sperm count by more than half in the past thirty years. Nor did they mention the fact that less-educated poor women were more likely than professional women to be infertile, as a result of pelvic inflammatory disease, caused frequently by sexually transmitted diseases. Rather, many articles claimed that the alleged increase in infertility resulted from women postponing motherhood until they were in their thirties, when it might be too late to conceive.[17]

In 1987, NBC correspondent Maria Shriver called childlessness "the curse of the career woman." In the same year, *Life* published a special report entitled "Baby Craving." Headlines warned against "Having It All: Postponing Parenthood Exacts a Price" and bemoaned "The Quiet Pain of Infertility: For the Success-Oriented, It's a Bitter Pill." A columnist for the *New York Times* described the infertile woman as "a walking cliché" of the feminist generation, "a woman on the cusp of forty who put work ahead of motherhood." *Newsweek* noted the "trend of childlessness," and *Mademoiselle* warned, "Caution: You Are Now Entering the Age of Infertility."[18] . . .

Many observers assume that infertility is on the rise. But there is no evidence that the proportion of infertile Americans has increased. There is evidence, however, that the number of people who are seeking treatment has risen dramatically. The number of visits to physicians for infertility treatment rose from 600,000 in 1968 to 1.6 million in 1984. The increase has been due, in part, to the huge baby-boom generation; the infertile among them are a large and visible group. But there are other reasons as well. Even if the chances for successful treatment are not much better than they were a half-century ago, dramatic new technological interventions are now available. High-tech approaches, such as in-vitro fertilization (IVF, fertilization of the egg in a laboratory petri dish and then its insertion directly into the uterus), first successfully used in the birth of Louise Brown in England in 1978, appear to offer "miracle babies" to the childless. Treatments using assisted reproduction techniques jumped 30 percent from 1990 to 1991, even though the chance of ending up with a "take-home baby" from these procedures was only about 15 percent.[19]

The promise of a technological fix, combined with a faith in medical progress, led many Americans to believe that they could triumph over most physical limitations. Physicians have responded to the demand. Studies have shown that American physicians are more likely than British practitioners to resort to heroic measures for treating infertility, probably because their patients request such intervention.[20] But reproductive medicine, despite its many advances over the past century, remains an imperfect art, available only to those who can afford it. Nor does it guarantee success. Infertility treatment is a high-stakes gamble: It is possible to lose all the money, time, and effort invested and gain nothing in return. If all the efforts of modern science, human struggle, and economic sacrifice do not result in the desired child, the rage, desperation, and anguish can be overwhelming.

Because birth control and reproductive choice are widely taken for granted, the infertile experience extreme frustration. Reproductive choice is much easier to achieve if the goal is to avoid pregnancy. Contraceptive technologies offer a success rate of nearly 100 percent, and legal abortion provides a backup when birth control methods fail. But infertile couples who seek treatment have only a 50 percent chance for success in the 1990s, odds that have not dramatically improved since the 1950s.[21] The inability to "control" one's reproductive fate is among the most exasperating experiences of infertility, especially for those who have put so much effort into the struggle. As the reporter Susan Sward wrote of her struggle with infertility, "As an organized, energetic person, I was used to getting what I wanted in life most of the time. To a major extent, I was also used to feeling in control of my life and knowing what I did would produce results if I tried hard enough. When it came to making babies, I found I had a lot to learn."[22]

Those who become pregnant while using birth control tend to blame the technology. But infertility patients who do not conceive often blame themselves. They feel unable to control their bodies or their destinies, even with medical intervention. For Roberta O'Leary, "It gets more and more difficult to pick up the pieces after each failure. I also don't like the feeling of having no control over what happens." Amanda Talley "felt like a freak of nature . . . embarrassed and shameful. . . . I felt as though my body betrayed me." Dierdre Kearney explained, "My feelings of helplessness have been hard to handle. We humans like to have control over our own lives and the one thing we think we can control is our body." She has done everything to have a baby and

> still my body betrays me and deprives me of one of the things I want most in life. I cannot make my body do what I want. . . . I've heard some women say that being infertile makes them feel less like a woman. I've never really felt this. I guess, this has made me feel all too much like a woman because it's what makes me a woman that has caused my problem— PERIODS and HORMONES! I just feel helpless in determining my own future. Sometimes I feel like a ship at sea and just when I am close to land, a huge wave washes me out to sea again.[23]

The inability to control one's reproductive functions often leads to feelings of shame and worthlessness, especially for women. Maureen Wendell explained, "I began to feel defective, ashamed. I can't do a 'normal' biological function that most anyone else could do. I had to reevaluate my life, my hopes, my dreams and my identity as a woman. I am blessed to have a very supportive husband but even with that I felt inadequate as a wife." Feelings of inadequacy were magnified by the association of fertility with sexuality. In a taped message, Patricia Painter used the language of sexual potency when describing her husband's healthy sperm. "My husband has this, you know, magnificent, I guess he's extremely virile. He has like super sperm. . . . Everybody from the lab technicians to the receptionist at the doctor's office was always so amazed at the amount and the virility of this sperm. It's like super-human sperm." When they accidentally spilled some of the semen sample, a physician replied,

> "It doesn't matter. He could impregnate the whole block with what's left in here. It's amazing." Which made me feel absolutely horrible because he couldn't impregnate me. Well, it was real obvious who had the problem in this relationship, as far as who was the one responsible for us not getting pregnant, and that was me. So I felt extremely terrible about that. This resulted in my being very embarrassed around people. I felt very defective. . . . It was just really such a blow . . . I would get physically ill . . . 'cause I felt so defective and so embarrassed.

Laura Lerner also felt "abnormal," even though she was not infertile. But she was single, and her singleness deprived her of the opportunity to become a mother. "I am a woman. I am supposed to have children, right? What am I if I don't produce children?" She considered adopting as a single parent or trying donor insemination. But she could not bring herself to do it: "Withdrawing some sperm from the sperm bank sounds so cold and mechanical." Without children, she felt "unnatural. . . . I have had these damn menstrual cycles since age 11 and I have nothing to show for it. . . . I get so I hate the cycle when it comes. . . . I have the most trouble trying to determine why I am here. I feel very incomplete, and very abnormal."

Before she discovered she was infertile, Leila Ember felt that "Life was good! Most importantly I was in control of it!" When she did not get pregnant, however, she began treatment, even though she recoiled at the invasive procedures: "For a person who had never had so much as a band-aid applied to any part of their body I found it quite difficult to endure the poking and prodding and exploratory procedures which were both financially and emo-

tionally expensive." But her body remained uncooperative. Infertility destroyed her peace of mind and self-confidence: "I remember sitting on the floor of my bathroom for what seemed like hours and sobbing. I'd look at my husband and begin to scream how sorry I was that I 'messed up again!'" Blaming herself, she wrote, "My biological clock isn't ticking; it isn't working at all!"

Many childless women who wanted children questioned their own womanhood. Suzanna Drew felt "less of a woman—somehow not complete." Kate Foley felt "barren." Paula Kranz described feelings of "failure . . . it's like an empty space within yourself that you cannot fill." Marie Gutierrez blamed herself when her husband's semen analysis

> came back ok, then O Boy! All fingers pointed to me, wow was I ever so unhappy, people don't know what it is like to try and try and never succeed. . . . I told no one . . . we were both embarrassed, marked, hurt. My husband is a very supportive husband, a good man and tells me that he accepts whatever happens, but . . . I can't accept the fact that I feel like some sort of alien, all women who are "normal" have children.

Along with at least four other women and men who wrote me, Marie offered to release her spouse from the marriage so that he could find a fertile partner and have children. . . .

One reason why infertility is so wrenching is that treatment holds out the possibility of a "miracle cure," making it difficult to give up, grieve, and find acceptance. To pursue medical intervention means to hold out hope and experience disappointment month after month, while the possibility of pregnancy still exists.[24] Many infertility patients described the experience as an "emotional roller coaster." Marie Gutierrez explained, "After each surgery and taking the fertility drug Clomid still trying and holding onto every good word from the Doctor that it could possibly happen this time, what a real drop in my Soul and a real letdown for my husband's ego, every test, every pill still no hope."

Amelia Monterey described the cycles of hope and disappointment. A thirty-three-year-old medical secretary married fifteen years to a construction worker, she lives in a trailer house in rural Minnesota. Like many others, she and her husband planned, dreamed, worked hard, saved, and assumed that they would achieve their goals. "We're poor," she wrote, but they pursued every possible treatment available before they finally gave up, heartbroken. Amelia wrote: "I've always been a caretaker. . . .I had no plans for college or even a career. . . . My whole childhood was built on the dream of becoming a wife and more—a Mother. I had no other life goals." When she did not become pregnant,

> I tried EVERYTHING! I took Clomid, got [hormone] shots, took my [temperature] every morning for years and even put an experimental drug up my nose. . . . I even had major surgery. They removed part of my ovaries. . . . What I want to get across is the feelings and the heartbreak of all these years of poking and probing that I went through. Looking at that thermometer every morning and not seeing it rise. . . . I went through that hurt, ache and devastation EVERY month. . . . [It] was like killing a small part of my womanhood.

In a similar cycle of hope and devastation, Susan Delmont had eight miscarriages and one failed adoption attempt. "I feel like a failure," she wrote. The experience destroyed her self-confidence; she quit her job, because she did not have "time enough to cry." She doubts her ability to raise a child. "I can't seem to apply for adoption. I don't know if I'm fit to be a mother or not, and I can't just say that I am. If God or whoever won't let me have my babies, why should an adoption agency?" Still, de-

pressed as she was, she knew when she was getting the wrong advice from experts. One psychiatrist told her "just having 8 miscarriages couldn't make me as sad as I was. He was sure that my father sexually abused me as a child, and that my subconscious covered it up. Needless to say, I dumped him." But she was still left with her anguish. "I don't feel like I've had miscarriages, I feel like I've lost children. . . . I have 'phantom' children—you know, like an amputee has a phantom limb."

RAGE

Along with pain and frustration, many infertile respondents expressed almost bottomless rage—at themselves, their bodies, and the fertile world. Carey Van Camp described feeling "almost hateful" and feeling "a burning rage inside me," especially toward pregnant women or infants. Lydia Sommer said infertility

> came as a shock to us—like being punched in the stomach and not being able to catch your breath. . . . The world turns and we stand still. . . . I detest all pregnant women—whether they are my friends or not. They carry their pregnancy like a badge of honor, when they did nothing special to achieve it. Honestly, they make me sick. Sounds pretty bad, doesn't it? I'm becoming more cynical about it as I get older and my clock ticks away.

For many, the sight of their desired goal did not bring out warm feelings toward children. Rather, they felt hateful—even murderous. As Patricia Painter explained,

> It was so painful to see anybody that was pregnant or had a baby. . . . I was the proverbial woman that was leaving the fertility doctor's office and saw the pregnant lady with two kids, a baby and a, you know, a toddler, in the crosswalks, and wanted to run over

them all. God I felt so guilty for feeling that way until I got involved with Resolve. I really thought I was a horrible person. I thought God was punishing me or something. . . . I really wanted to run them over very badly with my car. . . . And I knew that every pregnant woman, every woman that had a new baby . . . got pregnant just to hurt my feelings. And God knows they did!

Patricia realized that her initial motivation for pursuing infertility treatment, her "love for children," virtually vanished. "I had a point where I could not see children at all. It was so painful." One friend, to protect her feelings when her toddler ran to the door, "looked around in her house, grabbed a newspaper, and put it in front of his face. Wasn't that nice? So I didn't have to see the kid. I thought that was nice. I'm sure my friends thought I was nuts." She even began to question her own sanity. "My values got real distorted and screwed up. . . . It felt very weird. . . . I had the ability to stand back and say, 'You're getting real strange, Patricia.' . . . And yet I couldn't seem to stop it. Kind of like trying to stop an avalanche, I think. The flood of emotion was so difficult."

Many of the desperately infertile expressed their most intense rage and disdain toward those who they believed neither wanted nor deserved their children, especially the young and the poor. Sonia Everly wrote, "It just doesn't seem fair . . . that young girls are getting pregnant when they have no desire to be parents." Daisy Posner's hatred went in all directions. As a nurse, she worked in labor and delivery. "I hated all the patients, even more so the ones with 3-4 kids who were on cocaine. I was sick with envy and hated God for being so unfair to me." In 1990, after infertility treatment, Daisy had a healthy daughter. But

having one child isn't enough. . . . I still feel like a failure for all the miscarriages. I hate my

body—it has felt empty and useless ever since my daughter was born. I hate reading about all the pregnant teenagers in the paper . . . All my friends here are pregnant with their second child. It is all I can do to stay friendly with them—I hate them so much. . . . I pray all the time for another baby but God must hate me. He gives lots of babies to poor drug addicts and only one to me. . . . And I still hated my labor and delivery patients for having more kids. Needless to say I work elsewhere now . . . but I am still stuck in anger and despair.

Some infertile women expressed anger at women who had abortions. Paula Kranz felt "anger, bitterness and jealousy. . . . And then there are women out there being blessed with babies, and they are killing them with abortions." Dierdre Kearney wrote, "Each time I read of a child abuse case or of a woman having a third abortion, I cannot help but question, 'Why?'" But many infertile women saw abortion as a choice, much like infertility treatment. Karen Pasmore found it ironic that "so many women become pregnant without even thinking about it, many when they'd rather not," but she was nevertheless "strongly pro-choice. Many of my friends don't understand my position but if another woman becomes pregnant against her wishes, my infertility is not affected. I guess the grass is always greener."

Infertile women who had abortions themselves often felt guilty for years. Sue Kott got pregnant when she was twenty-five. Although she wanted to have the baby, her boyfriend wanted her to have an abortion. Two years later they married, and she has not been able to conceive again. She never forgave herself for the abortion. After years of infertility treatment, she is still childless, and her husband "refuses to adopt." Sonia Everly, on the other hand, has forgiven herself. Between her two marriages, she became pregnant while in graduate school and had an abortion.

The abortion was traumatic, as it always is; never an easy decision, but the right one for me, and my partner, at the time. I obviously did not know that would be my only pregnancy. Would my choice have been different had I known? I think so, but I made my decision based on what I knew at that time. I still assumed I could become pregnant when I wanted to, when I was ready.

If abortion was difficult for some infertile women to accept, others found the fecundity of the poor unbearable. Some who believed that they had earned their right to reproductive self-determination were quick to deny the same right to others. Several shared the sentiments of Lisa Brown, who wrote, "I don't appreciate females having more kids than they can provide for and go on welfare. . . . I think there should be a law of 2 kids on welfare only. I think there should be sterilization inforced after the 2nd child."

Lisa's fury was directed toward the wrong target. Poor women on welfare were not responsible for her infertility, but she blamed them, rather than the real villains. In her case, as in many others, there were real villains. She was one of several respondents whose infertility resulted from severe damage to their bodies caused by sexual abuse when they were children. These respondents well understood the source of their problem, but did not express anger directly toward the men who raped them. None, in fact, mentioned whether their molesters had been apprehended. Thirty-one respondents, including two men, specifically mentioned abuse as a direct cause of their childlessness, ranging from emotional abuse to physical and sexual abuse.[25] The most horrifying were the stories of women like Lisa whose reproductive organs were damaged because they were raped when they were young children.

Lisa did not mention the rapes until the end of her letter. She began without a standard salutation, asking "if your some weirdo, getting off on others pain." She described years of infertility treatment, including several reconstructive surgeries, tubal pregnancies, and miscarriages. She and her husband tried to adopt, but they learned that it would take approximately ten years, because they wanted a child under age two. At age forty-three, Lisa had lost her struggle to have a child and lost her marriage as well. She explained,

When your husband goes out and gets a bar whore pregnate after 12 years of marriage and 4 miscarriages and tubal pregnancies and the loss of 7 children, your mom says, "what do you expect? He wants kids, you can't give him any." So the marriage is gone and death looks good! What good am I to anyone? . . . Bitter? VERY! Being a female has not been fun for me. . . . Why did God see fit to take my kids but lets whores, child beaters and molesters have kids? And hurt or kill them?

Lisa was on the list for IVF when her husband "got a bar whore pregnant" and the marriage ended. "That was the hardest phone call I had to make in my life—calling and cancelling my only sure promise of a child." Although it was certainly far from a "sure promise," she was prepared to pay the $4,500 to try it. It was not until a brief postscript added after she signed her letter that she revealed the source of her difficulty: She was repeatedly raped by her step-grandfather and half-uncle from ages four through seven. "And by the way the rapes were performed (on the top of the bathroom toilet tank lid with my legs drawn up like I was squatting). It tilted my uterus so severely it caused all my future female problems."

Trudy Mayer, a white married factory worker, was also a victim of incest as a child and cannot carry a baby. She wrote three letters explaining her experience and her anguish, expressing anger not toward her molester but toward herself.

When I first found out that I may never have a child I tryed to kill myself because I was raised to believe that women are to reproduce so that made me feel like if I can't do what God intend women to do then I didn't belong. After that I felt very angry I was angry at me, at God at my Mother for having Me I was looking for some one to hate or blame I still have these feelings.

But the true villain remained unnamed.

Doctors and friends and family say oh just keep trying it will happen even my husband says we will just keep trying. Me I'm tired of it I want a baby but I don't want to keep going throw the hurt I have been pregnant seven times and each one I have lost and everyone says oh I understand but there is no way that they can understand what I go throu. I read the paper and see where some parents kill there kids or leave them in a trash can or something and stop and say to myself why would someone do such a thing to their own child but how can I understand I have never been in there shoes the same as you, you could never understand no matter how much you would like to.

She has seen specialists and had many surgeries, "so many that my stomach looks like a war zone." It was not until the end of her letter that she gave the reason for her misery: "I was molested very young . . . but it did not stop there it continued until I was 10 years old because I did not know that this was wrong."

Trudy did not name her abuser until her second letter: "I was molested when I was five years old by my father and it went on for years and I thought of suicide many of times through the years." She lived with her husband seven years before she finally married him

because if he can handle all these things we have been throu then I would be dum not to

marrie him. . . . he has been at every doctors appointment been write there with every miscarriage he has cryed throu them with me he has been my clown but even with all this he new that he could leave and be with some one who can have children but he wanted to be with me even thou being with me hurts him a little of him dies every day because of are childless problem we have a specialist we go to and even with insurance it hurts the pocket book and we have looked in to adoption but they want you to be millionaire just to adopt a child this is what kills us every day a little to a time but what can you do.

In cases of sexual violence, the cause of infertility was grimly evident. But brutality surfaced in the letters of only a minority of respondents. In other cases, the very technologies that were developed to improve individual control over reproduction led to infertility. Ironically, many infertile individuals turned to medical experts to cure a problem that medical technology had created. Vivian Johnson discovered that her tubes were scarred from her previous use of an intrauterine device (IUD), and surgery did not correct the problem. Ultimately, high-tech reproductive medicine overcame the problem created by high-tech contraception. She had twins from her first IVF attempt. Karen Pasmore had a problem shared by tens of thousands of her peers: she was infertile because her mother was treated with diethylstilbestrol, or DES, during pregnancy. The drug was used widely in the 1940s and 1950s to prevent miscarriages.[26] In college, "DES became the specter in my life that it remains today." She turned to invasive high-tech infertility treatment, with no luck. Lorraine Pascasio was luckier. She, too, was a DES daughter. Initially she felt, "I'm defective . . . Damaged goods." But she finally had a "miracle baby" and wrote her story for the *Ladies Home Journal*.[27]

It is now nearly fifty years since Dr. Abraham Stone offered his definition of a woman as one who accepts "her primary role, that of conceiving and bearing a child." Today most physicians, as well as most women, I know that infertility can result from a wide range of factors, affecting both male and female. But the power of that psychological and behavioral definition of womanhood has persisted long after its scientific validity has been questioned. Articles in the popular press still blame career women for an "infertility epidemic," even though infertility continues to affect poor people to a much greater extent than the affluent. This fact should be obvious, since infertility, like other health problems, is more likely to plague those with fewer resources and less access to good medical care.

Nevertheless, in spite of all evidence to the contrary, infertility still carries a stigma suggesting that women are to blame for their own inability to conceive.

NOTES

1. "Psychological Aspects of Fertility," manuscript draft, dated November 8, 1950, *New York Times,* Stone File, Countway Library of Medicine, Rare Books and Manuscripts, Harvard University, Boston (hereafter Stone File, Countway Library).

2. By 1990, only 20 percent of infertility remained unexplained, yet only half of all infertile couples undergoing medical treatment would achieve pregnancies. See Margarete J. Sandelowski, "Failures of Volition: Female Agency and Infertility in Historical Perspective," *Signs: Journal of Women in Culture and Society* 15 (1990): 475–499.

3. I. C. Rubin, M.D., as told to Margaret Albrecht, "Childlessness and What Can Be Done About It," *Parents,* March 1957, 46ff.

4. Herbert H. Thomas, M.D., "Thirty-Two Years of Fertility Progress," Presidential Address, *Fertility and Sterility* 27 (October 1976): 1125–1131.

5. Edward T. Tyler, M.D., as told to Roland H. Berg, "Childless Couples Can Have Babies," *Look,* September 17, 1957, 41–50; and Willis E. Brown, M.D., "Privilege and Responsibility: Presidential Address," *Fertility and Sterility* 14 (1963): 475–481.

6. Mrs. Gary B., Hurst, Texas, January 14, 1964, to Dr. Rock; reply from Robert E. Wheatley, M.D., March 23,1964, Rock Papers, Countway Library.

7. Emily Martin, "The Egg and the Sperm: How Science Has Constructed a Romance Based on Stereotypical Male-Female Roles," *Signs: Journal of Women in Culture and Society* 16 (1991): 485–501; see also Emily Martin, *The Woman in the Body: A Cultural Analysis of Reproduction* (Boston: Beacon Press, 1987), 45–48.

8. Tyler, "Childless Couples Can Have Babies."

9. For an excellent study of the transformation of psychiatry during the early twentieth century and its cultural significance, see Elizabeth Lunbeck, *The Psychiatric Persuasion: Knowledge, Gender, and Power in Modern America* (Princeton: Princeton University Press, 1994).

10. Herbert D. Lamson, Willem J. Pinard, and Samuel R. Meaker, "Sociologic and Psychological Aspects of Artificial Insemination with Donor Semen," *Journal of the American Medical Association* 145 (April 7, 1951): 1062–1063.

11. "Program: American Society for the Study of Sterility, Eighth Annual Conference," June 7 and 8, 1952, Chicago, 10 and 11; and descriptions of papers by Therese Benedek, M.D., "Infertility as a Psychosomatic Defense," and W. S. Kroger, M.D., "The Evaluation of Personality Factors in the Treatment of Infertility," in Tyler Clinic Archives, Los Angeles.

12. Sandelowski, "Failures of Volition," 475–499.

13. W. S. Kroger, M.D., "Evaluation of Personality Factors in the Treatment of Infertility," *Fertility and Sterility* 3 (November–December 1952): 542–551.

14. Vera G. Kinsler, "Sterility Can Be a State of Mind," *Coronet,* April 1953, 109–112.

15. "Family Problems," *American Magazine,* August 1951, 108; William Engle, "Maybe You Can Have a Baby," *American Weekly,* November 8, 1953, 8; J. D. Ratcliff, "Clinics for the Childless," *Hygeia* 19 (October 1941): 854; Joseph D. Wassersug, "More Help for Childless Couples," *Hygeia* 25 (November 1947): 384–385.

16. Tyler, "Childless Couples Can Have Babies."

17. Susan Faludi, *Backlash: The Undeclared War Against American Women* (New York: Crown, 1991), 24–27. On the declining sperm count, see Amy Linn, "Male Infertility: From Taboo to Treatment," *Philadelphia Inquirer,* May 31, 1987, A1, cited in Faludi, *Backlash,* 31–32. On the new pronatalism, see also Margarete J. Sandelowski, *With Child in Mind: Studies of the Personal Encounter with Infertility* (Philadelphia: University of Pennsylvania Press, 1993), 9.

18. Articles cited in Faludi, *Backlash,* 104–110.

19. On the proportion of the infertile, see Arthur L. Greil, *Not Yet Pregnant: Infertile Couples in Contemporary America* (New Brunswick, N.J.: Rutgers University Press, 1991), 27–28; data on physicians visits from Office of Technology Assessment, in Philip Elmer-Dewitt, "Making Babies," *Time,* September 30, 1991, 56–63; see also David Perlman, "The Art and Science of Conception: Brave New Babies," *San Francisco Chronicle,* March 3, 1990, B3; on the success of IVF, see Nancy Wartik, "Making Babies," *Los Angeles Times Magazine,* March 6,1994, 18ff.

20. Study cited in Greil, *Not Yet Pregnant,* 11.

21. Most estimates gave infertile couples a 50 percent chance, as they did in the 1950s and 1960s, although some physicians were more conservative. One physician in 1962, for example, gave infertile couples a 40 percent chance of a cure, saying that "more could be helped if husbands would cooperate completely with medical examination and treatment." See Grace Naismith, "Good News for Childless Couples," *Today's Health* 40 (January 1962):

24ff. For 1990 data, see Greil, *Not Yet Pregnant,* 11.

22. Susan Sward, "I Thought Having a Baby Would Be Easy," *San Francisco Chronicle,* March 5, 1990, B4. See also Miriam D. Mazor, "Barren Couples," *Psychology Today,* May 1979,101–112.

23. The quotations from infertile women, unless otherwise indicated, were gathered using an author's query sent to newspapers and journals across the country. The query letter, addressed to the editors, asked individuals who had experienced childlessness at some point in their lives to write to me about their experiences and feelings. We had no way of knowing which journals published the query, but more than five hundred people wrote back from all over the country. None of the respondents is identified by his or her real name. For a more detailed discussion of the sample, see "Appendix: A Note on the Sample of Letters," in May, *Barren in the Promised Land,* 261–265.

24. See Greil, *Not Yet Pregnant,* esp. chap. 4.

25. The abuse mentioned included psychological or physical abuse that the respondents did not wish to perpetuate or made them feel they would be bad parents. Some said that they had only recently "discovered" their childhood sexual abuse in therapy, by retrieving repressed memories. Although these approaches are highly controversial in the professional therapeutic community, it is noteworthy that several childless people mentioned these "repressed memories" in relation to their childlessness. Other cases, however, like those quoted in this chapter, were not repressed memories. They were well-remembered rapes that continued for years.

26. See Philip Elmer Dewitt, "Making Babies," *Time,* September 30, 1991, 56–62. DES Action and other groups have been formed by and on behalf of women who have been harmed by DES, the Dalkon Shield, and other medical products. See Karen M. Hicks, *Surviving the Dalkon Shield IUD: Women v. The Pharmaceuti-*

cal Industry (New York: Teachers College Press, 1994).

27. Lorraine Pascasio, "A Christmas Baby," *Ladies Home Journal,* December 1991, 14–17.

Study/Discussion Questions

1. In what ways were women seen as responsible for their own infertility in the post–World War II era?
2. What personality traits were thought to make a woman emotionally unfit for motherhood in the 1940s and 1950s?
3. How do women feel today when they are infertile?
4. How do media reports magnify these feelings?

Checkbook Maternity
When Is a Mother Not a Mother?

Katha Pollitt

The word "mother" cannot be understood by its mere dictionary definition, Katha Pollitt, acclaimed poet and associate editor of The Nation, *writes in this article that appeared in the wake of several controversial court decisions about high-tech pregnancy, surrogacy, and adoption. Who gets to be a mother in our society today has as much to do with "underlying ideas about class, race, children, and, above all, women that the new maternities rely on." Reproductive technologies do not reside in some realm of scientific purity, but rather get mediated through familiar channels of privilege and prejudice. The alarming result, Pollitt finds, is that courts tend to choose parents with the money and social status to "buy" the right to rear children over the poor women whose bodies "incubate" those children for nine months.*

To the small and curious class of English words that have double and contradictory meanings—"moot," for example, and "cleave"—the word "mother" can now be added. Within the space of a single dazzling week this fall, this hoary old noun was redefined so thoroughly, in such mutually exclusive ways, that what it means now depends on which edition of the newspaper you read.

On October 23, in Orange County, California, Superior Court Judge Richard Parslow decided that the rightful mother of Baby Boy Johnson was not Anna Johnson, the black "gestational surrogate" who, for $10,000, carried him and birthed him, but Crispina Calvert, the wombless Asian-born woman who provided the egg from which, after in vitro fertilization with her (white) husband's sperm and implantation in Ms. Johnson, the baby grew. Declining, he said, to play Solomon and put the baby in the "crazy-making" position of having "two mothers"—or to follow California law, which defines the mother as the woman who gives birth to the child—Judge Parslow ruled that genes make the mom, as they do the dad. Anna Johnson was merely a kind of foster mother, a "home," an "environment."

One wonders what Judge Parslow would make of a headline two days later. "Menopause Is Found No Bar to Pregnancy" announced *The*

New York Times, reporting that doctors had succeeded in making six prematurely menopausal women pregnant by implanting each with donated eggs fertilized in vitro with her husband's sperm. By Judge Parslow's reasoning, of course, those women are merely foster mothers, homes and environments, but so far no one has suggested this, much less called for a reevaluation of Johnson's claim in the light of new information about the value women place on pregnancy and childbirth and the persistent (if apparently erroneous) belief that the resultant babies belong to them.

To their credit, commentators have not regarded these developments with unalloyed rapture. Perhaps they learned something from the Baby M fracas. In that dispute, you will remember, many intelligent people persuaded themselves that the baby's rightful mother was a woman who had no biological connection to it, and that its real mother, Mary Beth Whitehead, was a grasping madwoman because she did not think she was, as child psychologist Lee Salk put it, a "surrogate uterus." The New Jersey Supreme Court disagreed, restored Whitehead's parental rights, which the lower court had abrogated, and, lo and behold, none of the confidently predicted dire consequences ensued. Women are not regarded as too emotional to make binding contracts, as some feminists feared, nor has motherhood been more deeply consigned to the realm of instinct and mystification. The child, now a toddler, has not been destroyed or corrupted by contact with her mother: Mary Beth Whitehead, the supposed Medea of the Meadowlands, turns out to be such a good mom, in fact, that *New York Times* columnist Anna Quindlen, who observed one of the child's visits, felt moved to renounce her earlier anti-Whitehead position. Indeed, the only consequences have been positive: The child knows both her parents; paid Baby M-style arrangements have been outlawed in two states, the contracts declared unenforceable in three; Noel Keane, the infamous baby broker who boasted that he had made $300,000 in fees the year of the Baby M contract, has found another métier.

As our Eastern European friends are now reminding us, however, markets must be served. The New Jersey Supreme Court put a damper on Baby M-style contract motherhood—now known as "traditional surrogacy," as if it had come over with the Pilgrims—but it seems to have spurred science and commerce on to more ingenious devices. And so we have Baby Boy Johnson. Thanks to Baby M, we are a little sheepish, a little wiser. Ellen Goodman has called for the banning of gestational surrogacy for pay; like millions of other middle-aging moms, she wonders if being able to bear a child in one's fifties is really an unmitigated blessing. But we have not yet, as a society, begun to face the underlying ideas about class, race, children and, above all, women that the new maternities rely on.

Take class. By upholding the Johnson-Calvert contract, Judge Parslow opens the door to the sale of poor women's bodies to well-off couples. It is disingenuous to claim, as does Polly Craig of the Los Angeles Center for Surrogate Parenting, that $10,000 is not enough money to motivate a woman to sell her womb, and that gestational surrogates simply enjoy being pregnant, want to help others, or wish to atone for a past abortion. Why offer payment at all, if it serves no function? And why, if gestational surrogacy is such an occasion for pleasure, altruism and moral purification, don't prosperous women line up for it? The Calverts—she a nurse, he an insurance broker—presumably possess a wide female acquaintanceship in their own income bracket, none of whom felt friendship required of them that they turn over their bodies to the Calvertian zygote. Instead the couple approached Johnson, a sometime welfare recipient, single mother and low-paid worker at Crispina Calvert's hospital.

No, money is the motivator here. Ten thousand dollars may not seem like a lot to Craig and her clients, but it's a poor person's idea of major cash—as much as 25 percent of American women earn in a whole year of full-time employment. It's quite enough to becloud good judgment. "You wave $10,000 in front of someone's face," said Anna Johnson, "and they are going to jump for it." By "someone," Johnson meant women like herself, shuttling between welfare and dead-end jobs, single, already supporting a child, with a drawerful of bills and not much hope for the future.

In a particularly nasty wrinkle, gestational surrogacy invites the singling out of black women for exploitation. It's not just that blacks are disproportionately poor and desperate, more likely to be single mothers and more likely to lack the resources to sue. It's that their visible lack of genetic connection with the baby will argue powerfully against them in court. (Indeed, about the Baby Boy Johnson case hovers the suggestion that the Calverts chose Johnson for precisely this reason.) Judge Parslow's comparison of Johnson to a foster mother is interesting in view of the fact that foster mothers who grow attached to their charges and try to keep them are regarded with much popular sympathy and sometimes even succeed. But it is safe to say that few American judges are going to take seriously the claims of a black woman to a nonblack child. Black women have, after all, always raised white children without acquiring any rights to them. Now they can breed them, too.

There are those who worry about the social implications of gestational surrogacy but who still think Judge Parslow made the right choice of homes for Baby Boy Johnson. Be that as it may, Anna Johnson wasn't suing for custody but for visitation. She wanted to be a small part of the child's life, for him to know her and for her to know him. Why would that be so terrible? As Dr. Michelle Harrison, who testified for Johnson, wrote in *The Wall Street Journal,* Judge Parslow wasn't being asked to divide the child between three parents; the

Calverts had in fact so divided him when they chose to produce a baby with Johnson's help. Recent court decisions (not to mention social customs like open adoption, blended families, and gay and lesbian co-parenting) have tended to respect a widening circle of adult relationships with children. Every state, for instance, gives grandparents access to grandchildren in the case of a divorce, regardless of the wishes of the custodial parent. Stepparents and lesbian co-parents are demanding their day in court. In 1986, California state courts upheld the right of a sperm donor to sue for parental rights when the artificial insemination did not involve a doctor (the old turkeybaster method). Why isn't that prospect too "crazy-making" for California? Or, for that matter, mandatory joint custody, an innovation that California pioneered? Given the increasing number of children living outside the classic nuclear-family arrangement, and the equanimity with which the courts divide them up among competing adults, it seems rather late in the day to get all stuffy about Anna Johnson.

The most important and distressing aspect of Judge Parslow's decision, however, is that it defines, or redefines, maternity in a way that is thoroughly degrading to women. By equating motherhood with fatherhood—that is, defining it solely as the contribution of genetic material—he has downgraded the mother's other contributions (carrying the fetus to term and giving birth) to services rather than integral components of biological parenthood. Under this legal definition, a normally pregnant woman is now baby-sitting for a fetus that happens to be her own. "In a debate over nature vs. nurture, the winner is nature" read the *New York Times* pullquote. But why define "nature" as DNA rather than as the physiological events of pregnancy and birth? There's nothing "natural" about egg donation, which involves the hormonal priming of an infertile woman, the extraction of an egg by delicate technology, fertilization in a dish with masturbated sperm, and implantation of the zygote in another. And to call pregnancy and childbirth "nurture" seems a feeble way to describe the sharing of the body and the risking of health, well-being and even life itself that is required to bring another life into existence. Like "parenting," another fashionable buzzword, "nurture" is a bland social-sciency word that belittles a profound relationship and masks the role of women in gender-neutral language.

The picture of pregnancy as biological baby-sitting has many sources. It's as old as Aeschylus, who had Athena acquit Orestes of matricide in the *Eumenides* on the ground that mothers are merely "nurses" of men's seed, and as new as those ubiquitous photos of fetuses seeming to float in empty space. But its major proponents today are the antiabortionists. In order to maximize the claims of the fetus to personhood, they must obscure the unique status of the pregnant woman: She is not making a person, because the fertilized egg already is a person; she's only caring for it, or housing it, or even (as one imaginative federal judge recently wrote) holding it captive. Ironically, the movement that claims to celebrate motherhood is led by its own logic to devalue the physical, emotional and social experience of pregnancy. If unwanted pregnancy is just an "inconvenience," how serious an occasion can a wanted pregnancy be? If mass adoption is the answer to 1.6 million annual abortions, how strong can the ties be between mother and newborn? When ethicists fret that professional women may resort to gestational surrogacy to avoid "putting their careers on hold," they betray more than antiquated views about the capacities of pregnant women to get out of bed in the morning. They reveal their own assumption that pregnancy is a trivial, empty experience with nothing positive about it except the end product, the genetically connected baby. They then compound the insult by attributing this view to a demonized fantasy of working women—cold, materialistic, selfish, corrupted by "male values"—

that is, those held by the ethicists themselves. Is there any evidence that working women—even M.B.A.s, even lawyers—see pregnancy this way? Who do the pundits think are mobbing infertility clinics and signing on for donated eggs? A couple needs two incomes just to pay the doctors.

Why is the primacy of genetics so attractive? At the moment, genetic determinism is having one of its periods of scientific fashion, fueling the fear that an adopted baby will never "really" be yours. At the same time, hardening class distinctions make the poor, who provide most adoptive babies, seem scary and doomed: What if junior took after his birth parents? It's not an accident that sperm donors and now egg donors are largely recruited among middle-class educated folk—they're not just white, they're successful and smart—and that the commercial aspects of the transaction ($50 for sperm, $1,500 for an egg) are disguised by calling it a "donation." You can buy a womb because wombs don't really matter, but if the all-important DNA must come from a third party, it should come as a gift between equals.

The main reason for our love affair with genes, though, is that men have them. We can't get all the way back to Aeschylus, with man as the seed sower and woman as flowerpot (although we acknowledge it in our language, when we call women "fertile" or "infertile," like farmland). Women, we now know, have seeds, too. But we can discount the aspects of procreation that women, and only women, perform. As the sociologist Barbara Katz Rothman has noted, Judge Parslow's decision follows the general pattern of our society, in which women's experiences are recognized to the extent that they are identical with men's, and devalued or ignored to the extent that they are different. Thus, Mary Beth Whitehead won back her parental rights because the New Jersey Supreme Court acknowledged her genetic contribution: Baby M was half hers. And the postmenopausally pregnant, egg-donated women achieve parental rights by being married to the babies' fathers, not through their own contributions.

Of the two practices—actually a single practice with two social constructions—gestational surrogacy is clearly the more repellent, but to see its real meaning it must be looked at with egg donation as its flip side. Taken together they bring pregnancy into line with other domestic tasks traditionally performed by women—housework, child care, sex. Performed within marriage, for no pay, these activities are slathered with sentimentality and declared beyond price, the cornerstone of female self-worth, family happiness and civilization itself. That is the world inhabited by prosperous married women now able to undergo pregnancy thanks to egg donation. That the egg is not their own is a detail; what counts is that they are able to have a profound and transforming life experience, to bond prenatally with their baby and to reproduce the genes of their husband. But look what happens when the checkbook and the marriage certificate are in the other hand: Now the egg is the central concern, pregnancy and childbirth merely a chore, prenatal bonding a myth. Like all domestic labor performed for pay—housecleaning, baby-sitting, prostitution—childbearing in the marketplace becomes disreputable work performed by suspect, marginal people. The priceless task turns out to have a price after all: about $1.50 an hour.

What should happen now? Some suggest that new methods of parenthood require a new legal principle: pre-conception intent. Instead of socio-bio-ethical headaches—Who is the mother? Who is the father? What's best for the child? What's best for society?—we could have a simple rule of thumb: Let the seller beware. But at what cost to economic fairness, to principles of bodily integrity, to the nonmarketplace values that shape intimate life? Why not let the buyer beware? We cannot settle thorny questions by simply refusing to ask them.

A doctrine of pre-conception intent could, moreover, turn ordinary family law into fruit salad. Most pregnancies in the United States, after all, are not intended by either partner. They occur for dozens of reasons: birth-control failure, passion, ignorance, mixed messages, fear. The law wisely overlooks these sorry facts. Instead, it says Here is a child, here are the parents, next case. Do we really want to threaten a philosophy aimed, however clumsily, at protecting children from pauperism and abandonment? If pre-conception intent caught on with the general public, no single mother would be able to win child support; no single father could win parental rights. A woman's right to abortion could be conditioned on her pre-conception intent as evidenced, for example, by her use or neglect of birth control. In fact, in several states, laws have already been proposed that would restrict abortion to women who could prove contraceptive failure (a near impossibility, if you think about it, which is probably the point).

Perhaps the biggest problem with pre-conception intent, however, is that it ignores almost everything about the actual experience of becoming a parent of either sex. Planning to have a baby is not the same as being pregnant and giving birth, any more than putting on sexy underwear is like making love. The long months of pregnancy and the intense struggle of childbirth are part of forming a relationship with the child-to-be, part of the social and emotional task of parenthood. Not the only part, or even a necessary part—I am not suggesting that adoptive parents do not "really" become mothers and fathers. But is there a woman who feels exactly the same about the baby in the ninth month, or during delivery or immediately afterward, as she did when she threw away her diaphragm? When friends and relatives assure ambivalent parents-to-be not to worry, they'll feel differently about the baby when they feel it kick, or go through Lamaze together, or first hold their newborn in their arms, are they only talking through their hats? Whether or not there is a purely biological maternal instinct, more mothers, and more fathers, fall in love with their babies than ever thought they would. Indeed, if they did not, most babies would die of neglect in their cribs. How can we respect this emotional and psychological process—indeed, rely on it—and at the same time forbid it to the Mary Beth Whiteheads and the Anna Johnsons? I don't think we can.

Pre-conception intent would wreak havoc on everyone—men, women and children—and for what? To give couples like the Calverts a risk-free shot at a genetically connected baby. It makes more sense to assimilate surrogacy to already existing values and legal principles. In my view, doing so would make payment illegal and prebirth contracts unenforceable. We don't let people sell their organs or work at slave wages; we don't hold new mothers to predelivery adoption arrangements; we don't permit the sale of children; we don't enforce contracts that violate human dignity and human rights. We respect the role of emotion and change and second thoughts in private life: We let people jilt their fiances, and we let them divorce their spouses. True, we uphold prenuptial agreements (a mistake, in my opinion), but they're about property. If someone signed a premarital agreement never to see his children again in the case of divorce, what judge would uphold it? Those children weren't even conceived when that contract was signed, the judge would point out—

and furthermore they have rights that cannot be waived by others, such as the right to contact with both parents after divorce. The children of surrogates—even nongenetic surrogates like Anna Johnson—have the right to know the women through whose body and through whose efforts they came into the world. We don't need any more disposable relationships in the world of children. They have quite enough of those already.

In order to benefit a very small number of people—prosperous womb-infertile couples who shun adoption—paid surrogacy does a great deal of harm to the rest of us. It degrades women by devaluing pregnancy and childbirth; it degrades children by commercializing their creation; it degrades the poor by offering them a devil's bargain at bargain prices. It creates a whole new class of emotionally injured children rarely mentioned in the debate: the ones the surrogate has already given birth to, who see their mother give away a newborn, or fight not to.

It is hard for Americans to see why they shouldn't have what they want if they can pay for it. We would much rather talk about individual freedoms and property rights, rational self-interest and the supposed sanctity of contracts, than about the common good or human dignity, or the depths below which no person should be allowed to sink. But even we have to call it quits somewhere. As we decided 130 years ago, the buying and selling of people is a very good place to draw the line.

Study/Discussion Questions

1. What does the author mean with the phrase "checkbook maternity"?
2. Who benefits from the various types of surrogate motherhood now available? Who is hurt by them, according to Pollitt?
3. Review the article and note the contradictions Pollitt points out in society's attitudes toward women as mothers. What makes a woman the mother of a particular baby?

The Mother

Gwendolyn Brooks

Abortions will not let you forget.
You remember the children you got that you did not get,
The damp small pulps with a little or with no hair.
The singers and workers that never handled the air.
You will never neglect or beat
Them, or silence or buy with a sweet.
You will never wind up the sucking-thumb
Or scuttle off ghosts that come.
You will never leave them, controlling your luscious sigh,
Return for a snack of them, with gobbling mother-eye.

I have heard in the voices of the wind the voices of my dim killed children.
I have contracted. I have eased
My dim dears at the breasts they could never suck.
I have said, Sweets, if I sinned, if I seized
Your luck
And your lives from your unfinished reach,
If I stole your births and your names,
Your straight baby tears and your games,
Your stilted or lovely loves, your tumults, your marriages, aches, and your
*   deaths,*
If I poisoned the beginnings of your breaths,
Believe that even in my deliberateness I was not deliberate.
Though why should I whine,
Whine that the crime was other than mine?—
Since anyhow you are dead.
Or rather, or instead
You were never made.

But that too, I am afraid,
Is faulty: oh, what shall I say, how is the truth to be said?
You were born, you had body, you died.
It is just that you never giggled or planned or cried.

Believe me, I loved you all.
Believe me, I knew you, though faintly, and I loved, I loved you
All.

THE POLITICS OF INCLUSION

Racism and Feminism:
The Issue of Accountability

bell hooks

By the early 1970s, despite many feminists' declarations of universal sisterhood, the women's liberation movement in the United States quaked with internal conflict over matters concerning race, class, and sexuality. Even among "sisters," many women complained, the incipient power and privilege structure of the wider society replicated itself. According to bell hooks, the racial discord that has pervaded American feminist organizations from the start of the second wave of feminism in the 1960s should come as no surprise. White women's rights activists, like the society they come from, have a long and ignoble history of racism. That modern feminists have compared their plight to that of African Americans does not make the analogy correct. Ultimately, hooks writes, "resolution of the conflict between black and white women cannot begin until all women acknowledge that a feminist movement which is both racist and classist is a mere sham, a cover-up for women's continued bondage to materialist patriarchal principles, and passive acceptance of the status quo."

American women of all races are socialized to think of racism solely in the context of race hatred. Specifically in the case of black and white people, the term racism is usually seen as synonymous with discrimination or prejudice against black people by white people. For most women, the first knowledge of racism as institutionalized oppression is engendered either by direct personal experience or through information gleaned from conversations, books, television, or movies. Consequently, the American woman's understanding of racism as a political tool of colonialism and imperialism is severely limited. To experience the pain of race hatred or to witness that pain is not to understand its origin, evolution, or impact on world history. The inability of American women to understand racism in the context of American politics is not due to any inherent deficiency in woman's psyche. It merely reflects the extent of our victimization.

No history books used in public schools informed us about racial imperialism. Instead

From *Ain't I a Woman: Black Women and Feminism*, © Gloria Watkins, Cambridge, Mass.: South End Press, 1981. Used by permission of South End Press.

we were given romantic notions of the "new world," the "American dream," America as the great melting pot where all races come together as one. We were taught that Columbus *discovered* America; that "Indians" were scalphunters, killers of innocent women and children; that black people were enslaved because of the biblical curse of Ham, that God "himself" had decreed they would be hewers of wood, tillers of the field, and bringers of water. No one talked of Africa as the cradle of civilization, of the African and Asian people who came to America before Columbus. No one mentioned mass murders of Native Americans as genocide, or the rape of Native American and African women as terrorism. No one discussed slavery as a foundation for the growth of capitalism. No one described the forced breeding of white wives to increase the white population as sexist oppression.

I am a black woman. I attended all-black public schools. I grew up in the south where all around me was the fact of racial discrimination, hatred, and forced segregation. Yet my education as to the politics of race in American society was not that different from that of white female students I met in integrated high schools, in college, or in various women's groups. The majority of us understood racism as a social evil perpetuated by prejudiced white people that could be overcome through bonding between blacks and liberal whites, through militant protest, changing of laws or racial integration. Higher educational institutions did nothing to increase our limited understanding of racism as a political ideology. Instead professors systematically denied us truth, teaching us to accept racial polarity in the form of white supremacy and sexual polarity in the form of male dominance.

American women have been socialized, even brainwashed, to accept a version of American history that was created to uphold and maintain racial imperialism in the form of white supremacy and sexual imperialism in

the form of patriarchy. One measure of the success of such indoctrination is that we perpetuate both consciously and unconsciously the very evils that oppress us. I am certain that the black female sixth grade teacher who taught us history, who taught us to identify with the American government, who loved those students who could best recite the pledge of allegiance to the American flag was not aware of the contradiction; that we should love this government that segregated us, that failed to send schools with all black students supplies that went to schools with only white pupils. Unknowingly she implanted in our psyches a seed of the racial imperialism that would keep us forever in bondage. For how does one overthrow, change, or even challenge a system that you have been taught to admire, to love, to believe in? Her innocence does not change the reality that she was teaching black children to embrace the very system that oppressed us, that she encouraged us to support it, to stand in awe of it, to die for it.

That American women, irrespective of their education, economic status, or racial identification, have undergone years of sexist and racist socialization that has taught us to blindly trust our knowledge of history and its effect on present reality, even though that knowledge has been formed and shaped by an oppressive system, is nowhere more evident than in the recent feminist movement. The group of college-educated white middle and upper class women who came together to organize a women's movement brought a new energy to the concept of women's rights in America. They were not merely advocating social equality with men. They demanded a transformation of society, a revolution, a change in the American social structure. Yet as they attempted to take feminism beyond the realm of radical rhetoric and into the realm of American life, they revealed that they had not changed, had not undone the sexist and racist brainwashing that had taught them to regard women unlike themselves as Others. Consequently, the Sisterhood they talked about has not become a reality, and the women's movement they envisioned would have a transformative effect on American culture has not emerged. Instead, the hierarchical pattern of race and sex relationships already established in American society merely took a different form under "feminism": the form of women being classed as an oppressed group under affirmative action programs further perpetuating the myth that the social status of all women in America is the same; the form of women's studies programs being established with all-white faculty teaching literature almost exclusively by white women about white women and frequently from racist perspectives; the form of white women writing books that purport to be about the experience of American women when in fact they concentrate solely on the experience of white women; and finally the form of endless argument and debate as to whether or not racism was a feminist issue.

If the white women who organized the contemporary movement toward feminism were at all remotely aware of racial politics in American history, they would have known that overcoming barriers that separate women from one another would entail confronting the reality of racism, and not just racism as a general evil in society but the race hatred they might harbor in their own psyches. Despite the predominance of patriarchal rule in American society, America was colonized on a racially imperialistic base and not on a sexually imperialistic base. No degree of patriarchal bonding between white male colonizers and Native American men overshadowed white racial imperialism. Racism took precedence over sexual alliances in both the white world's interaction with Native Americans and African Americans, just as racism overshadowed any bonding between black women and white women on the basis of sex. Tunisian writer Albert Memmi empha-

sizes in *The Colonizer and the Colonized* the impact of racism as a tool of imperialism:

> Racism appears . . . not as an incidental detail, but as a consubstantial part of colonialism. It is the highest expression of the colonial system and one of the most significant features of the colonialist. Not only does it establish a fundamental discrimination between colonizer and colonized, a sine qua non of colonial life, but it also lays the foundation for the immutability of this life.

While those feminists who argue that sexual imperialism is more endemic to all societies than racial imperialism are probably correct, American society is one in which racial imperialism supersedes sexual imperialism.

In America, the social status of black and white women has never been the same. In 19th and early 20th century America, few if any similarities could be found between the life experiences of the two female groups. Although they were both subject to sexist victimization, as victims of racism black women were subjected to oppressions no white woman was forced to endure. In fact, white racial imperialism granted all white women, however victimized by sexist oppression they might be, the right to assume the role of oppressor in relationship to black women and black men. From the onset of the contemporary move toward feminist revolution, white female organizers attempted to minimize their position in the racial caste hierarchy of American society. In their efforts to disassociate themselves from white men (to deny connections based on shared racial caste), white women involved in the move toward feminism have charged that racism is endemic to white male patriarchy and have argued that they cannot be held responsible for racist oppression. Commenting on the issue of white female accountability in her essay "'Disloyal to Civilization': Feminism, Racism, and Gynephobia," radical feminist Adrienne Rich contends:

If Black and White feminists are going to speak of female accountability, I believe the word racism must be seized, grasped in our bare hands, ripped out of the sterile or defensive consciousness in which it so often grows, and transplanted so that it can yield new insights for our lives and our movement. An analysis that places the guilt for active domination, physical and institutional violence, and the justifications embedded in myth and language, on white women not only compounds false consciousness; it allows us all to deny or neglect the charged connection among black and white women from the historical conditions of slavery on, and it impedes any real discussion of women's instrumentality in a system which oppresses all women and in which hatred of women is also embedded in myth, folklore, and language.

No reader of Rich's essay could doubt that she is concerned that women who are committed to feminism work to overcome barriers that separate black and white women. However, she fails to understand that from a black female perspective, if white women are denying the existence of black women, writing "feminist" scholarship as if black women are not a part of the collective group American women, or discriminating against black women, then it matters less that North America was colonized by white patriarchal men who institutionalized a racially imperialistic social order than that white women who purport to be feminists support and actively perpetuate antiblack racism.

To black women the issue is not whether white women are more or less racist than white men, but that they are racist. If women committed to feminist revolution, be they black or white, are to achieve any understanding of the "charged connections" between white women and black women, we must first be willing to examine woman's relationship to society, to

race, and to American culture as it is and not as we would ideally have it be. That means confronting the reality of white female racism. Sexist discrimination has prevented white women from assuming the dominant role in the perpetuation of white racial imperialism, but it has not prevented white women from absorbing, supporting, and advocating racist ideology or acting individually as racist oppressors in various spheres of American life.

Every women's movement in America from its earliest origin to the present day has been built on a racist foundation—a fact which in no way invalidates feminism as a political ideology. The racial apartheid social structure that characterized 19th and early 20th century American life was mirrored in the women's rights movement. The first white women's rights advocates were never seeking social equality for all women; they were seeking social equality for white women. Because many 19th century white women's rights advocates were also active in the abolitionist movement, it is often assumed they were anti-racist. Historiographers and especially recent feminist writing have created a version of American history in which white women's rights advocates are presented as champions of oppressed black people. This fierce romanticism has informed most studies of the abolitionist movement. In contemporary times there is a general tendency to equate abolitionism with a repudiation of racism. In actuality, most white abolitionists, male and female, though vehement in their antislavery protest, were totally opposed to granting social equality to black people. Joel Kovel, in his study *White Racism: A Psychohistory*, emphasizes that the "actual aim of the reform movement, so nobly and bravely begun, was not the liberation of the black, but the fortification of the white, conscience and all."

It is a commonly accepted belief that white female reformist empathy with the oppressed black slave, coupled with her recognition that she was powerless to end slavery, led to the development of a feminist consciousness and feminist revolt. Contemporary historiographers and in particular white female scholars accept the theory that the white women's rights advocates' feelings of solidarity with black slaves were an indication that they were anti-racist and were supportive of social equality of blacks. It is this glorification of the role white women played that leads Adrienne Rich to assert:

> . . . It is important for white feminists to remember that—despite lack of constitutional citizenship, educational deprivation, economic bondage to men, laws and customs forbidding women to speak in public or to disobey fathers, husbands, and brothers—our white foresisters have, in Lillian Smith's words, repeatedly been "disloyal to civilization" and have "smelled death in the word 'segregation'," often defying patriarchy for the first time, not on their own behalf but for the sake of black men, women, and children. We have a strong anti-racist female tradition despite all efforts by the white patriarchy to polarize its creatureobjects, creating dichotomies of privilege and caste, skin color, and age and condition of servitude.

There is little historical evidence to document Rich's assertion that white women as a collective group or white women's rights advocates are part of an anti-racist tradition. When white women reformers in the 1830s chose to work to free the slave, they were motivated by religious sentiment. They attacked slavery, not racism. The basis of their attack was moral reform. That they were not demanding social equality for black people is an indication that they remained committed to white racist supremacy despite their anti-slavery work. While they strongly advocated an end to slavery, they never advocated a change in the racial hierarchy that allowed their caste status to be higher than that of black women or men. In fact, they wanted that hierarchy to be maintained. Consequently, the white women's rights movement which had a lukewarm beginning in earlier reform activities emerged in full force in the wake of efforts to gain rights for black people precisely because white women wanted to see no change in the social status of blacks until they were assured that their demands for more rights were met.

White women's rights advocate and abolitionist Abby Kelly's comment, "We have good cause to be grateful to the slave for the benefit we have received to ourselves, in working for him. In striving to strike his irons off, we found most surely, that we were manacled ourselves," is often quoted by scholars as evidence that white women became conscious of their own limited rights as they worked to end slavery. Despite popular 19th century rhetoric, the notion that white women had to learn from their efforts to free the slave of their own limited rights is simply erroneous. No 19th century white woman could grow to maturity without an awareness of institutionalized sexism. White women did learn via their efforts to free the slave that white men were willing to advocate rights for blacks while denouncing rights for women. As a result of negative reaction to their reform activity and public effort to curtail and prevent their anti-slavery work, they were forced to acknowledge that without outspoken demands for equal rights with white men they might ultimately be lumped in the same social category with blacks—or even worse, black men might gain a higher social status than theirs.

It did not enhance the cause of oppressed black slaves for white women to make synonymous their plight and the plight of the slave. Despite Abby Kelly's dramatic statement, there was very little if any similarity between the day-to-day life experiences of white women and the day-to-day experiences of the black slave. Theoretically, the white woman's legal status under patriarchy may have been that of "property," but she was in no way subjected to the dehumanization and brutal oppression that was the lot of the slave. When white reformers made synonymous the impact of sexism on their lives, they were not revealing an awareness of or sensitivity to the slave's lot; they were simply appropriating the horror of the slave experience to enhance their own cause.

The fact that the majority of white women reformers did not feel political solidarity with black people was made evident in the conflict over the vote. When it appeared that white men might grant black men the right to vote while leaving white women disenfranchised, white suffragists did not respond as a group by demanding that all women and men deserved the right to vote. They simply expressed anger and outrage that white men were more committed to maintaining sexual hierarchies than racial hierarchies in the political arena. Ardent white women's rights advocates like Elizabeth Cady Stanton who had never before argued for women's rights on a racially imperialistic platform expressed outrage that inferior "niggers" should be granted the vote while "superior" white women remained disenfranchised. Stanton argued:

> If Saxon men have legislated thus for their own mothers, wives and daughters, what can we hope for at the hands of Chinese, Indians, and Africans?. . . . I protest against the enfranchisement of another man of any race or clime until the daughters of Jefferson, Hancock, and Adams are crowned with their rights.

White suffragists felt that white men were insulting white womanhood by refusing to grant them privileges that were to be granted black men. They admonished white men not for their sexism but for their willingness to allow sexism to overshadow racial alliances. Stanton, along with other white women's rights

supporters, did not want to see blacks enslaved, but neither did she wish to see the status of black people improved while the status of white women remained the same. At the beginning of the 20th century, white women suffragists were eager to advance their own cause at the expense of black people. In 1903 at the National American Woman's Suffrage Convention held in New Orleans, a southern suffragist urged the enfranchisement of white women on the grounds that it "would insure immediate and durable white supremacy." Historian Rosalyn Terborg-Penn discusses white female support of white supremacy in her essay "Discrimination Against Afro-American Women in the Woman's Movement 1830–1920":

> As early as the 1890's, Susan B. Anthony realized the potential to the woman suffrage cause in wooing southern white women. She chose expedience over loyalty and justice when she asked veteran feminist supporter Frederick Douglass not to attend the National American Woman Suffrage Association convention scheduled in Atlanta. . . .
>
> During the National American Woman Suffrage Association meeting of 1903 in New Orleans, the *Times Democrat* assailed the association because of its negative attitude on the question of black women and the suffrage for them. In a prepared statement signed by Susan B. Anthony, Carrie C. Catt, Anna Howard Shaw, Kate N. Gordon, Alice Stone Blackwell, Harriet Taylor Upton, Laura Clay, and Mary Coggeshall, the board of officers of the NAWSA endorsed the organization's states' rights position, which was tantamount to an endorsement of white supremacy in most states, particularly in the south.

Racism within the women's rights movement did not emerge simply as a response to the issue of suffrage; it was a dominant force in all reform groups with white female members. Terborg-Penn contends:

Discrimination against Afro-American women reformers was the rule rather than the exception within the woman's rights movement from the 1880's to 1920. Although white feminists Susan B. Anthony, Lucy Stone, and some others encouraged black women to join the struggle against sexism during the nineteenth century, antebellum reformers who were involved with women's abolitionist groups as well as women's rights organizations actively discriminated against black women.

In their efforts to prove that solidarity existed between 19th century black and white female reformers, contemporary women activists often cite the presence of Sojourner Truth at Women's Rights conventions to support their argument that white female suffragists were anti-racist. But on every occasion Sojourner Truth spoke, groups of white women protested. In *The Betrayal of the Negro*, Rayford Logan writes:

> When the General Federation of Women's Clubs was faced with the question of the color line at the turn of the century, Southern clubs threatened to secede. One of the first expressions of the adamant opposition to the admission of colored clubs was disclosed by the *Chicago Tribune* and the *Examiner* during the great festival of fraternization at the Atlanta Exposition, the Encampment of the GAR in Louisville, and the dedication of the Chickamauga battlefield. . . . The Georgia Women's Press Club felt so strongly on the subject that members were in favor of withdrawing from the Federation if colored women were admitted there. Miss Corinne Stocker, a member of the Managing Board of the Georgia Women's Press Club and one of the editors of the *Atlanta Journal*, stated on September 19: "In this matter the Southern women are not narrow-minded or bigoted, but they simply cannot recognize the colored

women socially. . . . At the same time we feel that the South is the colored woman's best friend."

Southern white women's club members were most vehement in their opposition to black women joining their ranks, but northern white women also supported racial segregation. The issue of whether black women would be able to participate in the women's club movement on an equal footing with white women came to a head in Milwaukee at the General Federation of Women's Clubs conference when the question was raised as to whether black feminist Mary Church Terrell, then president of the National Association of Colored Women, would be allowed to offer greetings, and whether Josephine Ruffin, who represented the black organization the New Era Club, would be recognized. In both cases white women's racism carried the day. In an interview in the *Chicago Tribune,* the president of the federation, Mrs. Lowe, was asked to comment on the refusal to acknowledge black female participants like Josephine Ruffin, and she responded: "Mrs. Ruffin belongs among her own people. Among them she would be a leader and could do much good, but among us she can create nothing but trouble." Rayford Logan comments on the fact that white women like Mrs. Lowe had no objection to black women trying to improve their lot; they simply felt that racial apartheid should be maintained. Writing of Mrs. Lowe's attitude toward black women, Logan comments:

> Mrs. Lowe had assisted in establishing kindergartens for colored children in the South, and the colored women in charge of them were all her good friends. She associated with them in a business way, but, of course they would not think of sitting beside her at a convention. Negroes were "a race by themselves, and among themselves they can accomplish much, assisted by us and by the

federation, which is ever ready to do all in its power to help them." If Mrs. Ruffin were the "cultured lady every one says she is, she should put her education and her talents to good uses as a colored wonman among colored women."

Anti-black feelings among white female club members were much stronger than anti-black sentiment among white male club members. One white male wrote a letter to the *Chicago Tribune* in which he stated:

> Here we have the spectacle of educated, refined, and Christian women who have been protesting and laboring for years against the unjust discrimination practiced against them by men, now getting together and the first shot out of their reticules is fired at one of their own because she is black, no other reason or pretence of reason.

Prejudices white women activists felt toward black women were far more intense than their prejudices toward black men. As Rosalyn Penn states in her essay, black men were more accepted in white reform circles than black women. Negative attitudes toward black women were the result of prevailing racist-sexist stereotypes that portrayed black women as morally impure. Many white women felt that their status as ladies would be undermined were they to associate with black women. No such moral stigma was attached to black men. Black male leaders like Frederick Douglass, James Forten, Henry Garnett and others were occasionally welcome in white social circles. White women activists who would not have considered dining in the company of black women welcomed individual black men to their family tables.

Given white fear of amalgamation between the races and the history of white male sexual lust for black females, we cannot rule out the possibility that white women were reluctant to acknowledge black women socially for fear of sexual competition. In general, white women did not wish to associate with black women because they did not want to be contaminated by morally impure creatures. White women saw black women as a direct threat to their social standing—for how could they be idealized as virtuous, goddess-like creatures if they associated with black women who were seen by the white public as licentious and immoral? In her speech to the 1895 delegates from black women's clubs, Josephine Ruffin told her audience that the reason white women club members did not want to join with black women was because of the supposed "black female immorality," and she urged them to protest the perpetuation of negative stereotypes about black womanhood:

> All over America there is to be found a large and growing class of earnest, intelligent, progressive colored women who, if not leading full, useful lives, are only waiting for the opportunity to do so, many of them still warped and cramped for lack of opportunity, not only to do more but to be more; and yet, if an estimate of the colored women of America is called for, the inevitable reply, glibly given, is: "For the most part, ignorant and immoral, some exceptions of course, but these don't count."
>   . . . Too long have we been silent under unjust and unholy charges. . . . Year after year southern women have protested against the admission of colored women into any national organization on the ground of the immorality of these women, and because all refutation has only been tried by individual work, the charge had never been crushed, as it could and should have been at first. . . . It is to break this silence, not by noisy protestation of what we are not, but by a dignified showing of what we are and hope to become, that we are impelled to take this step, to make of this gathering an object lesson to the world.

The racism white females felt toward black women was as apparent in the work arena as it was in the women's rights movement and in the women's club movement. During the years between 1880 and World War I, white women's rights activists focused their attention on obtaining for women the right to work in various occupations. They saw work for pay as the way for women like themselves to escape economic dependence on white men. Robert Smut, author of *Women and Work in America* (a work that would be more accurately titled *White Women and Work in America*), writes:

> If a woman could support herself in honor, she could refuse to marry or stay married, except on her own terms. Thus, work was seen by many feminists as an actual or potential alternative to marriage, and consequently, as an instrument for reforming the marriage relationship.

The efforts of white women activists to expand employment opportunities for women were focused exclusively on improving the lot of white women workers, who did not identify with black women workers. In fact, the black woman worker was seen as a threat to white female security; she represented more competition. Relationships between white and black women workers were characterized by conflict. That conflict became more intense when black women tried to enter the industrial labor force and were forced to confront racism. In 1919, a study of black women in industry in New York City was published called *A New Day for the Colored Woman Worker*. The study began by stating:

> For generations Colored women have been working in the fields of the south. They have been the domestic servants of both the south and the north, accepting the position of personal service open to them. Hard work and unpleasant work has been their lot, but they

have been almost entirely excluded from our shops and factories. Tradition and race prejudice have played the largest part in their exclusion. The tardy development of the south, and the failure of the Colored women to demand industrial opportunities have added further barriers. . . . For these reasons, the Colored women have not entered the ranks of the industrial army in the past.

> That they are doing so today cannot be disputed. War expediency, for a time at least, partially opened the door of industry to them. Factories which had lost men to the war and White women to the war industries, took on Colored women in their places. The demand for more skilled, semi-skilled and unskilled labor had to be met. The existing immigrant labor supply had already been tapped and the flow of immigration stopped, and semi-skilled White workers were being forced up into the really skilled positions by the labor shortage. Cheap labor had to be recruited from somewhere. For the first time employment bureaus and advertisements inserted the word "Colored" before the word "wanted." Colored women, untried as yet, were available in large numbers.

Black female workers who entered the industrial labor force worked in commercial laundries, food industries, and the less skilled branches of the needle trades, like the lamp shade industry which depended heavily on the labor of black women. Hostility between black and white female workers was the norm. White women did not want to compete with black women for jobs nor did they want to work alongside black women. To prevent white employers from hiring black females, white female workers threatened to cease work. Often white women workers would use complaints about black women workers as a way of discouraging an employer from hiring them.

White women employed by the federal government insisted that they be segregated from black women. In many work situations separate work rooms, washrooms, and showers were installed so that white women would not have to work or wash alongside black women. The same argument white women club members used to explain their exclusion of black women was presented by white women workers, who claimed black women were immoral, licentious, and insolent. They further argued that they needed the protection of segregation so that they would not catch "Negro" diseases. Some white women claimed to have seen black women with vaginal diseases. In one instance a white woman working in the office of the Recorder of Deeds, Maud B. Woodward, swore out an affidavit asserting:

That the same toilet is used by whites and blacks, and some of said blacks have been diseased evidence thereof being very apparent; that one negro woman Alexander has been for years afflicted with a private disease, and for dread of using the toilet after her some of the white girls are compelled to suffer mentally and physically.

Competition between black and white women workers for jobs was usually decided in favor of white women. Often black women were forced to accept jobs that were considered too arduous or taxing for white women. In candy factories black women not only wrapped and packed candy, they worked as bakers and in this capacity were constantly lifting heavy trays from table to machine and from machine to table. They were doing "loosening" in tobacco factories, a process formerly done solely by men. Investigators for the New York City Study reported:

Colored women were found on processes that White women refuse to perform. They were replacing boys at cleaning window shades, work which necessitates constant standing and reaching. They were taking

men's places in the dyeing of furs, highly objectionable and injurious work involving standing, reaching, the use of a weighted brush, and ill smelling dye. In a mattress factory they were found replacing men at "baling," working in pairs, wrapping five mattresses together and sewing them up ready for shipment. These women had to bend constantly and lift clumsy 160 pound bales.

In racially segregated work situations black women workers were usually paid a lower wage than white women workers. As there was little if any association between the two groups, black women did not always know of the disparity between their salaries and those of white women. Workers for the New York City study found that most employers refused to pay black women workers as much as white women for doing the same job.

Throughout the trades, differences in the wages of the Colored and White were unmistakable. While every other Colored woman was receiving less than $10.00 a week, of the White workers only one out of every six was so poorly paid. . . . A great many employers justified the payment of better wages to White women on the grounds of their greater speed. Foremen in the millinery factories, however, admitted that they paid the Colored workers less, even though they were more satisfactory than the White. . . .

This wage discrimination seems to have taken three forms. Employers have sometimes segregated the Colored workers, keeping the wage scale of the Colored departments lower than that of similar departments made up of White workers. . . . A second method has been to deny the Colored the opportunity of competing in piece work, as in the case of the Colored pressers in the needle trades who were paid $10.00 a week on a time rate basis, while the White pressers averaged $12.00 a week at piece work. The third form of discrimination has been the frank refusal of employers to pay a Colored woman as much as a White woman for a week's work.

As a group, white women workers wanted to maintain the racial hierarchy that granted them higher status in the labor force than black women. Those white women who supported employment of black women in unskilled trades felt they should be denied access to skilled process. Their active support of institutionalized racism caused constant hostility between them and black women workers. To avoid uprisings, many plants chose to hire either one race or the other. In plants where both groups were present, the conditions under which black women worked were much worse than those of white female workers. The refusal of white women to share dressing rooms, bathrooms, or lounge areas with black women often meant that black women were denied access to these comforts. In general black women workers were continually abused because of the racist attitudes of white women workers, and of the white working public as a whole. Researchers for the New York City study summed up their findings by making a plea that more consideration be given the black woman worker in industry:

> It has been apparent throughout this discussion that the coming of the Colored woman into our industries is not without its problems. She is doing work which the White woman is refusing to do, and at a wage which the White woman is refusing the accept. She replaced White women and men and Colored men at a lower wage and is performing tasks which may easily prove to be detrimental to her health. She is making no more mistakes than are common to a new and inexperienced industrial worker, yet she has the greatest of all handicaps to overcome.

What is the status of the Colored woman in industry with the coming of peace? At the time of greatest need for production and the greatest labor shortage in the history of this country Colored women were the last to be employed: they were not called into industry until there was no other available labor supply. They did the most uninteresting work, the most menial work and by far the most underpaid work. . . .

The American people will have to go very far in its treatment of the Colored industrial woman to square itself with that democratic ideal of which it made so much during the war.

Relationships between white and black women were charged by tensions and conflicts in the early part of the 20th century. The women's rights movement had not drawn black and white women close together. Instead, it exposed the fact that white women were not willing to relinquish their support of white supremacy to support the interests of all women. Racism in the women's rights movement and in the work arena was a constant reminder to black women of the distances that separated the two experiences, distances that white women did not want bridged. When the contemporary movement toward feminism began, white women organizers did not address the issue of conflict between black and white women. Their rhetoric of sisterhood and solidarity suggested that women in America were able to bond across both class and race boundaries— but no such coming together had actually occurred. The structure of the contemporary women's movement was no different from that of the earlier women's rights movement. Like their predecessors, the white women who initiated the women's movement launched their efforts in the wake of the 60s black liberation movement. As if history were repeating itself, they also began to make synonymous their social status and the social status of black people. And it was in the context of endless comparisons of the plight of "women" and "blacks" that they revealed their racism. In most cases, this racism was an unconscious, unacknowledged aspect of their thought, suppressed by their narcissism—a narcissism which so blinded them that they would not admit two obvious facts: one, that in a capitalist, racist, imperialist state there is no one social status women share as a collective group; and second, that the social status of white women in America has never been like that of black women or men.

When the women's movement began in the late 60s, it was evident that the white women who dominated the movement felt it was "their" movement, that is the medium through which a white woman would voice her grievances to society. Not only did white women act as if feminist ideology existed solely to serve their own interests because they were able to draw public attention to feminist concerns. They were unwilling to acknowledge that non-white women were part of the collective group women in American society. They urged black women to join "their" movement or in some cases the women's movement, but in dialogues and writings, their attitudes toward black women were both racist and sexist. Their racism did not assume the form of overt expressions of hatred; it was far more subtle. It took the form of simply ignoring the existence of black women or writing about them using common sexist and racist stereotypes. From Betty Friedan's *The Feminine Mystique* to Barbara Berg's *The Remembered Gate* and on to more recent publications like *Capitalist Patriarchy and the Case for Socialist Feminism,* edited by Zillah Eisenstein, most white female writers who considered themselves feminist revealed in their writing that they had been socialized to accept and perpetuate racist ideology.

In most of their writing, the white American woman's experience is made synonymous with the American woman's experience. While it is in no way racist for any author to write a book exclusively about white women, it is fundamentally racist for books to be published that focus solely on the American white woman's experience in which that experience is assumed to be the American woman's experience. For example, in the course of research for this book, I sought to find information about the life of free and slave black women in colonial America. I saw listed in a bibliography Julia Cherry Spruill's work *Women's Life and Work in the Southern Colonies,* which was first published in 1938 and then again in 1972. At the Sisterhood bookstore in Los Angeles I found the book and read a blurb on the back which had been written especially for the new edition:

> One of the classic works in American social history, *Women's Life and Work in the Southern Colonies* is the first comprehensive study of the daily life and status of women in southern colonial America. Julia Cherry Spruill researched colonial newspapers, court records, and manuscript material of every kind, drawing on archives and libraries from Boston to Savannah. The resulting book was, in the words of Arthur Schlesinger, Sr., "a model of research and exposition, an important contribution to American social history to which students will constantly turn."
>
> The topics include women's function in the settlement of the colonies; their homes, domestic occupation, and social life; the aims and methods of their education; their role in government and business affairs outside the home, and the manner in which they were regarded by the law and by society in general. Out of a wealth of documentation, and often from the words of colonial people themselves, a vivid and surprising picture—one that had never been seen before—emerges of the many different aspects of these women's lives.

I expected to find in Spruill's work information about various groups of women in American society. I found instead that it was another work solely about white women and that both the title and blurb were misleading. A more accurate title would have been *White Women's Life and Work in the Southern Colonies.* Certainly, if I or any author sent a manuscript to an American publisher that focused exclusively on the life and work of black women in the south, also called *Women's Life and Work in the Southern Colonies,* the title would be automatically deemed misleading and unacceptable. The force that allows white feminist authors to make no reference to racial identity in their books about "women" that are in actuality about white women is the same one that would compel any author writing exclusively on black women to refer explicitly to their racial identity. That force is racism. In a racially imperialist nation such as ours, it is the dominant race that reserves for itself the luxury of dismissing racial identity while the oppressed race is made daily aware of their racial identity. It is the dominance that can make it seem that their experience is representative.

In America, white racist ideology has always allowed white women to assume that the word woman is synonymous with white woman, for women of other races are always perceived as Others, as de-humanized beings who do not fall under the heading woman. White feminists who claimed to be politically astute showed themselves to be unconscious of the way their use of language suggested they did not recognize the existence of black women. They impressed upon the American public their sense that the word "woman" meant white woman by drawing endless analogies between "women" and "blacks." Examples of such analogies abound in almost every feminist work. In a collection of essays published in 1975 titled *Women: A Feminist Perspective,* an essay by Helen Hacker is included called "Women as a Minority Group" which is a good example of the way white women have used comparisons between "women" and "blacks" to exclude black women and to deflect atten-

tion away from their own racial caste status. Hacker writes:

> The relation between women and Negroes is historical, as well as analogical. In the seventeenth century the legal status of Negro servants was borrowed from that of women and children, who were under the patria potestas, and until the Civil War there was considerable cooperation between the Abolitionists and woman suffrage movement.

Clearly Hacker is referring solely to white women. An even more glaring example of the white feminist comparison between "blacks" and "women" occurs in Catherine Stimpson's essay "'Thy Neighbor's Wife, Thy Neighbor's Servants': Women's Liberation and Black Civil Rights." She writes:

> The development of an industrial economy, as Myrdal points out has not brought about the integration of women and blacks into the adult male culture. Women have not found a satisfactory way to bear children and to work. Blacks have not destroyed the hard doctrine of their unassimilability. What the economy gives both women and blacks are menial labor, low pay, and few promotions. White male workers hate both groups, for their competition threatens wages and their possible job equality, let alone superiority, threatens nothing less than the very nature of things. The tasks of women and blacks are usually grueling, repetitive, slogging, and dirty. . . .

Throughout Stimpson's essay she makes woman synonymous with white women and black synonymous with black men.

Historically, white patriarchs rarely referred to the racial identity of white women because they believed that the subject of race was political and therefore would contaminate the sanctified domain of "white" woman's reality.

By verbally denying white women racial identity, that is by simply referring to them as women when what they really meant was white women, their status was further reduced to that of non-person. In much of the literature written by white women on the "woman question" from the 19th century to the present day, authors will refer to "white men" but use the word "woman" when they really mean "white woman." Concurrently, the term "blacks" is often made synonymous with black men. In Hacker's article she draws a chart comparing the "castelike status of Women and Negroes." Under the heading "Rationalization of Status" she writes for blacks "Thought all right in his place." (?) Hacker's and Stimpson's assumption that they can use the word "woman" to refer to white women and "black" to refer to black men is not unique; most white people and even some black people make the same assumption. Racist and sexist patterns in the language Americans use to describe reality support the exclusion of black women. During the recent political uprisings in Iran, newspapers throughout the U.S. carried headlines that read "Khomeini Frees Women and Blacks." In fact, the American hostages freed from the Iranian Embassy were white women and black men.

White feminists did not challenge the racist-sexist tendency to use the word "woman" to refer solely to white women; they supported it. For them it served two purposes. First, it allowed them to proclaim white men world oppressors while making it appear linguistically that no alliance existed between white women and white men based on shared racial imperialism. Second, it made it possible for white women to act as if alliances did exist between themselves and non-white women in our society, and by so doing they could deflect attention away from their classism and racism. Had feminists chosen to make explicit comparisons between the status of white women and that of black people, or more specifically

the status of black women and white women, it would have been more than obvious that the two groups do not share an identical oppression. It would have been obvious that similarities between the status of women under patriarchy and that of any slave or colonized person do not necessarily exist in a society that is both racially and sexually imperialistic. In such a society, the woman who is seen as inferior because of her sex can also be seen as superior because of her race, even in relationship to men of another race. Because feminists tended to evoke an image of women as a collective group, their comparisons between "women" and "blacks" were accepted without question. This constant comparison of the plight of "women" and "blacks" deflected attention away from the fact that black women were extremely victimized by both racism and sexism—a fact which, had it been emphasized, might have diverted public attention away from the complaints of middle and upper class white feminists.

Just as 19th century white women's rights advocates' attempt to make synonymous their lot with that of the black slave was aimed at drawing attention away from the slave toward themselves, contemporary white feminists have used the same metaphor to attract attention to their concerns. Given that America is a hierarchical society in which white men are at the top and white women are second, it was to be expected that should white women complain about not having rights in the wake of a movement by black people to gain rights, their interests would overshadow those of groups lower on the hierarchy, in this case the interests of black people. No other group in America has used black people as metaphors as extensively as white women involved in the women's movement. Speaking about the purpose of a metaphor, Ortega Y Gasset comments:

> A strange thing, indeed, the existence in many of this mental activity which substitutes

one thing for another—from an urge not so much to get at the first as to get rid of the second. The metaphor disposes of an object by having it masquerade as something else. Such a procedure would make no sense if we did not discern beneath it an instinctive avoidance of certain realities.

When white women talked about "Women as Niggers," "The Third World of Women," "Woman as Slave," they evoked the sufferings and oppressions of non-white people to say "look at how bad our lot as white women is, why we are like niggers, like the Third World." Of course, if the situation of upper and middle class white women were in any way like that of the oppressed people in the world, such metaphors would not have been necessary. And if they had been poor and oppressed, or women concerned about the lot of oppressed women, they would not have been compelled to appropriate the black experience. It would have been sufficient to describe the oppression of woman's experience. A white woman who has suffered physical abuse and assault from a husband or lover, who also suffers poverty, need not compare her lot to that of a suffering black person to emphasize that she is in pain.

If white women in the women's movement needed to make use of a black experience to emphasize woman's oppression, it would seem only logical that they focus on the black female experience—but they did not. They chose to deny the existence of black women and to exclude them from the women's movement. When I use the word "exclude" I do not mean that they overtly discriminated against black women on the basis of race. There are other ways to exclude and alienate people. Many black women felt excluded from the movement whenever they heard white women draw analogies between "women" and "blacks." For by making such analogies white women were in effect saying to black women: "We don't acknowledge your presence as women in Ameri-

can society." Had white women desired to bond with black women on the basis of common oppression they could have done so by demonstrating any awareness or knowledge of the impact of sexism on the status of black women. Unfortunately, despite all the rhetoric about sisterhood and bonding, white women were not sincerely committed to bonding with black women and other groups of women to fight sexism. They were primarily interested in drawing attention to their lot as white upper and middle class women.

It was not in the opportunistic interests of white middle and upper class participants in the women's movement to draw attention to the plight of poor women, or the specific plight of black women. A white woman professor who wants the public to see her as victimized and oppressed because she is denied tenure is not about to evoke images of poor women working as domestics receiving less than the minimum wage struggling to raise a family single-handed. Instead it is far more likely she will receive attention and sympathy if she says, "I'm a nigger in the eyes of my white male colleagues." She evokes the image of innocent, virtuous white womanhood being placed on the same level as blacks and most importantly on the same level as black men. It is not simply a coincidental detail that white women in the women's movement chose to make their race-sex analogies by comparing their lot as white women to that of black men. In Catherine Stimpson's essay on women's liberation and black civil rights, in which she argues that "black liberation and women's liberation must go their separate ways," black civil rights is associated with black men and women's liberation with white women. When she writes of the 19th century women's rights movement, she quotes from the work of black male leaders even though black women were far more active in that movement than any black male leader.

Given the psychohistory of American racism, for white women to demand more rights from white men and stress that without such rights they would be placed in a social position like that of black men, not like that of black people, was to evoke in the minds of racist white men an image of white womanhood being degraded. It was a subtle appeal to white men to protect the white female's position on the race/sex hierarchy. Stimpson writes:

> White men, convinced of the holy primacy of sperm, yet guilty about using it, angry at the loss of the cozy sanctuary of the womb and the privilege of childhood, have made their sex a claim to power and then used their power to claim control of sex. In fact and fantasy, they have violently segregated black men and white women. The most notorious fantasy claims that the black man is sexually evil, low, subhuman; the white woman sexually pure elevated, superhuman. Together they dramatize the polarities of excrement and disembodied spirituality. Blacks and women have been sexual victims, often cruelly so: the black man castrated, the woman raped and often treated to a psychic clitoridectomy.

For Stimpson, black is black male and woman is white female, and though she is depicting the white male as racist, she conjures an image of white women and black men sharing oppression only to argue that they must go their separate ways, and in so doing she makes use of the sex/race analogy in such a way as to curry favor from racist white men. Ironically, she admonishes white women not to make analogies between blacks and themselves but she continues to do just that in her essay. By suggesting that without rights they are placed in the same category as black men, white women appeal to the antiblack-male racism of white patriarchal men. Their argument for "women's liberation" (which for them is synonymous with white women's liberation) thus becomes an appeal to white men to maintain the racial hierarchy that grants white women a higher social status than black men.

Whenever black women tried to express to white women their ideas about white female racism or their sense that the women who were at the forefront of the movement were not oppressed women they were told that "oppression cannot be measured." White female emphasis on "common oppression" in their appeals to black women to join the movement further alienated many black women. Because so many of the white women in the movement were employers of non-white and white domestics, their rhetoric of common oppression was experienced by black women as an assault, an expression of the bourgeois woman's insensitivity and lack of concern for the lower class woman's position in society.

Underlying the assertion of common oppression was a patronizing attitude toward black women. White women were assuming that all they had to do was express a desire for sisterhood, or a desire to have black women join their groups, and black women would be overjoyed. They saw themselves as acting in a generous, open, non-racist manner and were shocked that black women responded to their overtures with anger and outrage. They could not see that their generosity was directed at themselves, that it was self-centered and motivated by their own opportunistic desires.

Despite the reality that white upper and middle class women in America suffer from sexist discrimination and sexist abuse, they are not as a group as oppressed as poor white, or black, or yellow women. Their unwillingness to distinguish between various degrees of discrimination or oppression caused black women to see them as enemies. As many upper and middle class white feminists who suffer least from sexist oppression were attempting to focus all attention on themselves, it follows that they would not accept an analysis of woman's lot in America which argued that not all women are equally oppressed because some women are able to use their class, race, and educational privilege to effectively resist sexist oppression.

Initially, class privilege was not discussed by white women in the women's movement. They wanted to project an image of themselves as victims and that could not be done by drawing attention to their class. In fact, the contemporary women's movement was extremely class bound. As a group, white participants did not denounce capitalism. They chose to define liberation using the terms of white capitalist patriarchy, equating liberation with gaining economic status and money power. Like all good capitalists, they proclaimed work as the key to liberation. This emphasis on work was yet another indication of the extent to which the white female liberationists' perception of reality was totally narcissistic, classist, and racist. Implicit in the assertion that work was the key to women's liberation was a refusal to acknowledge the reality that, for masses of American working class women, working for pay neither liberated them from sexist oppression nor allowed them to gain any measure of economic independence. In *Liberating Feminism*, Benjamin Barber's critique of the women's movement, he comments on the white middle and upper class women's liberationist focus on work:

> Work clearly means something very different to women in search of an escape from leisure than it has to most of the human race for most of history. For a few lucky men, for far fewer women, work has occasionally been a source of meaning and creativity. But for most of the rest it remains even now forced drudgery in front of the ploughs, machines, words or numbers—pushing products, pushing switches, pushing papers to eke out the wherewithal of material existence.
>   . . . To be able to work and to have work are two different matters. I suspect, however, that few liberationist women are to be found working as menials and unskilled laborers

simply in order to occupy their time and identify with the power structure. For status and power are not conferred by work per se, but by certain kinds of work generally reserved to the middle and upper classes. . . . As Studs Terkel shows in *Working,* most workers find jobs dull, oppressive, frustrating and alienating—very much what women find housewifery.

When white women's liberationists emphasized work as a path to liberation, they did not concentrate their attention on those women who are most exploited in the American labor force. Had they emphasized the plight of working class women, attention would have shifted away from the college-educated suburban housewife who wanted entrance into the middle and upper class work force. Had attention been focused on women who were already working and who were exploited as cheap surplus labor in American society, it would have de-romanticized the middle class white woman's quest for "meaningful" employment. While it does not in any way diminish the importance of women resisting sexist oppression by entering the labor force, work has not been a liberating force for masses of American women. And for some time now, sexism has not prevented them from being in the work force. White middle and upper class women like those described in Betty Friedan's *The Feminine Mystique* were housewives not because sexism would have prevented them from being in the paid labor force, but because they had willingly embraced the notion that it was better to be a housewife than to be a worker. The racism and classism of white women's liberationists was most apparent whenever they discussed work as the liberating force for women. In such discussions it was always the middle class "housewife" who was depicted as the victim of sexist oppression and not the poor black and non-black women who are most exploited by American economics.

Throughout woman's history as a paid laborer, white women workers have been able to enter the work force much later than black women yet advance at a much more rapid pace. Even though all women were denied access to many jobs because of sexist discrimination, racism ensured that the lot of the white women would always be better than that of the black female worker. Pauli Murray compared the status of the two groups in her essay "The Liberation of Black Women" and noted:

> When we compare the position of the black woman to that of the white woman, we find that she remains single more often, bears more children, is in the labor market longer and in greater proportion, has less education, earns less, is widowed earlier, and carries a relatively heavier economic responsibility as family head than her white counterpart.

Often in discussions of woman's status in the labor force, white women liberationists choose to ignore or minimize the disparity between the economic status of black women and that of white women. White activist Jo Freeman addresses the issue in *The Politics of Women's Liberation* when she comments that black women have the "highest unemployment rates and lowest median income of any race/sex group." But she then minimizes the impact of this assertion in a sentence that follows: "Of all race/sex groups of full-time workers, nonwhite women have had the greatest percentage increase in their median income since 1939, and White women have had the lowest." Freeman does not inform readers that the wages black women received were not a reflection of an advancing economic status so much as they were an indication that the wages paid them, for so long considerably lower than those paid white women, were approaching the set norm.

Few, if any, white women liberationists are willing to acknowledge that the women's move-

ment was consciously and deliberately structured to exclude black and other non-white women and to serve primarily the interests of middle and upper class college-educated white women seeking social equality with middle and upper class white men. While they may agree that white women involved with women's liberationist groups are racist and classist they tend to feel that this in no way undermines the movement. But it is precisely the racism and classism of exponents of feminist ideology that has caused a large majority of black women to suspect their motives, and to reject active participation in any effort to organize a women's movement. Black woman activist Dorothy Bolden, who worked forty-two years as a maid in Atlanta, one of the founders of the National Domestic Workers, Inc., voiced her opinions of the movement in *Nobody Speaks for Me! Self Portraits of Working Class Women:*

> . . . I was very proud to see them stand up and speak up when it started. I'm glad to see any group do that when they're righteous and I know they have been denied something. But they're not talking about the masses of people. You've got different classes of people in all phases of life and all races, and these people have to be spoken up for too.
>
> . . . You can't talk about women's rights until we include all women. When you deny one woman of her rights, you deny all. I'm getting tired of going to those meetings, because there's none of us participating.
>
> They're still trying to put their amendment to the constitution, but they're not going to be able to do it until they include us. Some of these states know this, that you don't have all women up front supporting that amendment. They are talking about women's rights but which women?

It is often assumed that all black women are simply not interested in women's liberation. White women's liberationists have helped to perpetuate the belief that black women would rather remain in stereotypically female roles than have social equality with men. Yet a Louis Harris Virginia Slims poll conducted in 1972 revealed that sixty-two percent of black women supported efforts to change woman's status in society as compared to forty-five percent of white women, and that sixty-seven percent of black women were sympathetic to women's liberation groups compared with only thirty-five percent of white women. The findings of the Harris poll suggest it is not opposition to feminist ideology that has caused black women to reject involvement in the women's movement.

Feminism as a political ideology advocating social equality for all women was and is acceptable to many black women. They rejected the women's movement when it became apparent that middle and upper class college-educated white women who were its majority participants were determined to shape the movement so that it would serve their own opportunistic ends. While the established definition of feminism is the theory of the political, economic, and social equality of the sexes, white women liberationists used the power granted them by virtue of their being members of the dominant race in American society to interpret feminism in such a way that it was no longer relevant to all women. And it seemed incredible to black women that they were being asked to support a movement whose majority participants were eager to maintain race and class hierarchies between women.

Black women who participated in women's groups, lectures, and meetings initially trusted the sincerity of white female participants. Like 19th century black women's rights advocates, they assumed that any women's movement would address issues relevant to all women and that racism would be automatically cited as a force that had divided women, that would have to be reckoned with for true Sisterhood to emerge, and also that no radical revolutionary women's movement could take place until women as a group were joined in political solidarity. Although contemporary black women were mindful of the prevalence of white female racism, they believed it could be confronted and changed.

As they participated in the women's movement they found, in their dialogues with white women in women's groups, in women's studies classes, at conferences, that their trust was betrayed. They found that white women had appropriated feminism to advance their own cause, i.e., their desire to enter the mainstream of American capitalism. They were told that white women were in the majority and that they had the power to decide which issues would be considered "feminist" issues. White women liberationists decided that the way to confront racism was to speak out in consciousness-raising groups about their racist upbringings, to encourage black women to join their cause, to make sure they hired one non-white woman in "their" women's studies program, or to invite one non-white woman to speak on a discussion panel at "their" conference.

When black women involved with women's liberation attempted to discuss racism, many white women responded by angrily stating: "We won't be guilt-tripped." For them the dialogue ceased. Others seemed to relish admitting that they were racist but felt that admitting verbally to being racist was tantamount to changing their racist values. For the most part, white women refused to listen when black women explained that what they expected was not verbal admissions of guilt but conscious gestures and acts that would show that white women liberationists were anti-racist and attempting to overcome their racism. The issue of racism within the women's movement would never have been raised had white women shown in their writings and speeches that they were in fact "liberated" from racism.

As concerned black and white individuals tried to stress the importance to the women's movement of confronting and changing racist attitudes because such sentiments threatened to undermine the movement, they met with resistance from those white women who saw feminism solely as a vehicle to enhance their own individual, opportunistic ends. Conservative, reactionary white women, who increasingly represented a large majority of the participants, were outspoken in their pronouncements that the issue of racism should not be considered worthy of attention. They did not want the issue of racism raised because they did not want to deflect attention away from their projection of the white woman as "good," i.e., non-racist victim, and the white man as "bad," i.e., racist oppressor. For them to have acknowledged woman's active complicity in the perpetuation of imperialism, colonialism, racism, or sexism would have made the issue of women's liberation far more complex. To those who saw feminism solely as a way to demand entrance into the white male power structure, it simplified matters to make all men oppressors and all women victims.

Some black women who were interested in women's liberation responded to the racism of white female participants by forming separate "black feminist" groups. This response was reactionary. By creating segregated feminist groups, they both endorsed and perpetuated the very "racism" they were supposedly attacking. They did not provide a critical evaluation of the women's movement and offer to all women a feminist ideology uncorrupted by racism or the opportunistic desires of individual groups. Instead, as colonized people have done for centuries, they accepted the terms imposed upon them by the dominant group (in this instance white women liberationists) and structured their groups on a racist platform identical to that of the white-dominated groups they were reacting against. White women were actively excluded from black groups. In fact, the distinguishing characteristic of the black "feminist" group was its focus on issues relating spe-

cifically to black women. The emphasis on black women was made public in the writings of black participants. The Combahee River Collective published "A Black Feminist Statement" to explain their group's focus. In their opening paragraph they declared:

> We are a collective of black feminists who have been meeting together since 1974. During that time we have been involved in the process of defining and clarifying our politics, while at the same time doing political work within our own group and in coalition with other progressive organizations and movements. The most general statement of our politics at the present time would be that we are actively committed to struggling against racial, sexual, heterosexual, and class oppression and see as our particular task the development of integrated analysis and practice based upon the fact that the major systems of oppression are interlocking. The synthesis of these oppressions creates the conditions of our lives. As black women we see black feminism as the logical political movement to combat the manifold and simultaneous oppression that all women of color face.

The emergence of black feminist groups led to a greater polarization of black and white women's liberationists. Instead of bonding on the basis of shared understanding of woman's varied collective and individual plight in society, they acted as if the distance separating their experiences from one another could not be bridged by knowledge or understanding. Rather than black women attacking the white female attempt to present them as an Other, an unknown, unfathomable element, they acted as if they were an Other. Many black women found an affirmation and support of their concern with feminism in all-black groups that they had not experienced in women's groups dominated by white women; this has been one of the positive features of black women's groups. However, all women should experience in racially mixed groups affirmation and support. Racism is the barrier that prevents positive communication and it is not eliminated or challenged by separation. White women supported the formation of separate groups because it confirmed their preconceived racist-sexist notion that no connection existed between their experiences and those of black women. Separate groups meant they would not be asked to concern themselves with race or racism. While black women condemned the anti-black racism of white women, the mounting animosity between the two groups gave rise to overt expression of their anti-white racism. Many black women who had never participated in the women's movement saw the formation of separate black groups as confirmation of their belief that no alliance could ever take place between black and white women. To express their anger and rage at white women, they evoked the negative stereotypical image of the white woman as a passive, parasitic, privileged being living off the labor of others as a way to mock and ridicule the white women liberationists. Black woman Lorraine Bethel published a poem entitled "What Chou Mean We, White Girl? Or. The Cullud Lesbian Feminist Declaration of Independence" prefaced with the statement:

I bought a sweater at a yard sale from a white-skinned (as opposed to Anglo-Saxon) woman. When wearing it I am struck by the smell—it reeks of a soft, privileged life without stress, sweat, or struggle. When wearing it I often think to myself, this sweater smells of a comfort, a way of being in the world I have never known in my life, and never will. It's the same feeling I experience walking through Bonwit Teller's and seeing white-skinned women buying trinkets that cost enough to support the elderly Black Woman elevator operator, who stands on her feet all day taking them up and down, for the rest of her life. It is moments/infinities of conscious pain like these that make me want to cry/kill/roll my eyes suck my teeth hand on my hip scream at so-called radical white lesbians/feminists: "WHAT CHOU MEAN WE, WHITE GIRL?"

Animosity between black and white women's liberationists was not due solely to disagreement over racism within the women's movement; it was the end result of years of jealousy, envy, competition, and anger between the two groups. Conflict between black and white women did not begin with the 20th century women's movement. It began during slavery. The social status of white women in America has to a large extent been determined by white people's relationship to black people. It was the enslavement of African people in colonized America that marked the beginning of a change in the social status of white women. Prior to slavery, patriarchal law decreed white women were lowly inferior beings, the subordinate group in society. The subjugation of black people allowed them to vacate their despised position and assume the role of a superior.

Consequently, it can be easily argued that even though white men institutionalized slavery, white women were its most immediate beneficiaries. Slavery in no way altered the hierarchical social status of the white male but it created a new status for the white female. The only way that her new status could be maintained was through the constant assertion of her superiority over the black woman and man. All too often colonial white women, particularly those who were slave mistresses, chose to differentiate their status from the slave's by treating the slave in a brutal and cruel manner. It was in her relationship to the black female slave that the white woman could best assert her power. Individual black slave women were quick to learn that sex-role differentiation did not mean that the white mistress was not to be regarded as an authority figure. Because they had been socialized via patriarchy to respect male authority and resent female authority, black women were reluctant to acknowledge the "power" of the white mistress. When the enslaved black woman expressed contempt and disregard for white female authority, the white mistress often resorted to brutal punishment to assert her authority. But even brutal punishment could not change the fact that black women were not inclined to regard the white female with the awe and respect they showed to the white male.

By flaunting their sexual lust for the bodies of black women and their preference for them as sexual partners, white men successfully pitted white women and enslaved black women against one another. In most instances, the white mistress did not envy the black female slave her role as sexual object; she feared only that her newly acquired social status might be threatened by white male sexual interaction with black women. His sexual involvement with black women (even if that involvement was rape) in effect reminded the white female of her subordinate position in relationship to him. For he could exercise his power as racial imperialist and sexual imperialist to rape or seduce black women, while white women were not free to rape or seduce black men without fear of punishment. Though the white female might condemn the actions of a white male who chose to interact sexually with black female slaves, she was unable to dictate to him proper behavior. Nor could she retaliate by engaging in sexual relationships with enslaved or free black men. Not surprisingly, she directed her anger and rage at the enslaved black women. In those cases where emotional ties developed between white men and black female slaves, white mistresses would go to great lengths to punish the female. Severe beatings were the method most white women used to punish black female slaves. Often in a jealous rage a mistress might use disfigurement to pun-

ish a lusted-after black female slave. The mistress might cut off her breast, blind an eye, or cut off another body part. Such treatment naturally caused hostility between white women and enslaved black women. To the enslaved black woman, the white mistress living in relative comfort was the representative symbol of white womanhood. She was both envied and despised—envied for her material comfort, despised because she felt little concern or compassion for the slave woman's lot. Since the white woman's privileged social status could only exist if a group of women were present to assume the lowly position she had abdicated, it follows that black and white women would be at odds with one another. If the white woman struggled to change the lot of the black slave woman, her own social position on the race-sex hierarchy would be altered.

Manumission did not bring an end to conflicts between black and white women; it heightened them. To maintain the apartheid structure slavery had institutionalized, white colonizers, male and female, created a variety of myths and stereotypes to differentiate the status of black women from that of white women. White racists and even some black people who had absorbed the colonizer's mentality depicted the white woman as a symbol of perfect womanhood and encouraged black women to strive to attain such perfection by using the white female as her model. The jealousy and envy of white women that had erupted in the black woman's consciousness during slavery was deliberately encouraged by the dominant white culture. Advertisements, newspaper articles, books, etc., were constant reminders to black women of the difference between their social status and that of white women, and they bitterly resented it. Nowhere was this dichotomy as clearly demonstrated as in the materially privileged white household where the black female domestic worked as an employee of the white family. In these relationships, black women workers were exploited to enhance the social standing of white families. In the white community, employing domestic help was a sign of material privilege and the person who directly benefited from a servant's work was the white woman, since without the servant she would have performed domestic chores. Not surprisingly, the black female domestic tended to see the white female as her "boss," her oppressor, not the white male whose earnings usually paid her wage.

Throughout American history white men have deliberately promoted hostility and divisiveness between white and black women. The white patriarchal power structure pits the two groups against each other, preventing the growth of solidarity between women and ensuring that woman's status as a subordinate group under patriarchy remains intact. To this end, white men have supported changes in the white woman's social standing only if there exists another female group to assume that role. Consequently, the white patriarch undergoes no radical change in his sexist assumption that woman is inherently inferior. He neither relinquishes his dominant position nor alters the patriarchal structure of society. He is, however, able to convince many white women that fundamental changes in "woman's status" have occurred because he has successfully socialized her, via racism, to assume that no connection exists between her and black women.

Because women's liberation has been equated with gaining privileges within the white male power structure, white men—and not women, either white or black—have dictated the terms by which women are allowed entrance into the system. One of the terms male patriarchs have set is that one group of women is granted privileges that they obtain by actively supporting the oppression and exploitation of other groups of women. White and black women have been socialized to accept and honor these terms, hence the fierce competition between the two groups; a competition that has always been centered in the arena of sexual politics, with white and black women competing against one another for male favor. This competition is part of an overall battle between various groups of women to be the chosen female group.

The contemporary move toward feminist revolution was continually undermined by competition between various factions. In regards to race, the women's movement has become simply another arena in which white and black women compete to be the chosen female group. This power struggle has not been resolved by the formation of opposing interest groups. Such groups are symptomatic of the problem and are no solution. Black and white women have for so long allowed their idea of liberation to be formed by the existing status quo that they have not yet devised a strategy by which we can come together. They have had only a slave's idea of freedom. And to the slave, the master's way of life represents the ideal free lifestyle.

Women's liberationists, white and black, will always be at odds with one another as long as our idea of liberation is based on having the power white men have. For that power denies unity, denies common connections, and is inherently divisive. It is woman's acceptance of divisiveness as a natural order that has caused black and white women to cling religiously to the belief that bonding across racial boundaries is impossible, to passively accept the notion that the distances that separate women are immutable. Even though the most uninformed and naive women's liberationist knows that Sisterhood as political bonding between women is necessary for feminist revolution, women have not struggled long or hard enough to overcome the societal brainwashing that has impressed on our psyches the belief that no union between black and white women can ever be forged. The methods women have employed to reach one another across racial boundaries have been shallow, superficial, and destined to fail.

Resolution of the conflict between black and white women cannot begin until all women acknowledge that a feminist movement which is both racist and classist is a mere sham, a cover-up for women's continued bondage to materialist patriarchal principles, and passive acceptance of the status quo. The sisterhood that is necessary for the making of feminist revolution can be achieved only when all women disengage themselves from the hostility, jealousy, and competition with one another that has kept us vulnerable, weak, and unable to envision new realities. That sisterhood cannot be forged by the mere saying of words. It is the outcome of continued growth and change. It is a goal to be reached, a process of becoming. The process begins with action, with the individual woman's refusal to accept any set of myths, stereotypes, and false assumptions that deny the shared commonness of her human experience; that deny her capacity to experience the Unity of all life; that deny her capacity to bridge gaps created by racism, sexism, or classism; that deny her ability to change. The process begins with the individual woman's acceptance that American women, without exception, are socialized to be racist, classist, and sexist, in varying degrees, and that labeling ourselves feminists does not change the fact that we must consciously work to rid ourselves of the legacy of negative socialization.

If women want a feminist revolution—ours is a world that is crying out for feminist revolution—then we must assume responsibility for drawing women together in political solidarity. That means we must assume responsibility for eliminating all the forces that divide women. Racism is one such force. Women, all women, are accountable for racism continuing to divide us. Our willingness to assume responsibility for the elimination of racism need not be engendered by feelings of guilt, moral responsibility, victimization, or rage. It can spring from a heartfelt desire for sisterhood and the personal, intellectual realization that racism among women undermines the potential radicalism of feminism. It can spring from our knowledge that racism is an obstacle in our path that must be removed. More obstacles are created if we simply engage in endless debate as to who put it there.

Study/Discussion Questions

1. How has American feminism failed to address the problem of racism, in the author's view?
2. What privileges do white women have because they are white? Of which of these privileges are white women unaware, and why?
3. How have white women benefited from racism in the nineteenth and twentieth centuries?
4. Keep track of the attitudes and activities of white women that hooks defines as racist. How do they expand a "conventional" definition of racism?
5. What solutions does hooks see to the problems that divide black and white women?

The Feminist Movement: Where Are All the Asian American Women?

Esther Ngan-Ling Chow

Esther Ngan-Ling Chow, feminist sociologist and community activist, notes that Asian American women have been underrepresented in feminist movements in the United States since the 1960s. Chow cites numerous barriers to their participation, ranging from Asian women's internal conflict over racial versus gender identity to overt racism and classism within mostly-white women's organizations. In conclusion, she delineates five concrete strategies to increase Asian American women's feminist activism, an outcome that would benefit all. In particular, she asserts that Asian women must unite with other women of color who also experience "multiple oppression."

From its inception the feminist movement in the United States has been predominantly white and middle class. Like blacks, Hispanics, and other women of color, Asian American women have not joined white women and, thus far, have not made a great impact on the movement.[1] Since the late 1960s, Asian Americans have begun to organize themselves and build bonds with other women's groups to advocate for their civil rights as a racial minority and as women. Their relative lack of political activism stems from cultural, psychological, and social oppressions which historically discouraged them from organizing. This resulted in their apparent political invisibility and powerlessness.

POLITICAL ORGANIZING OF ASIAN AMERICAN WOMEN: AN OVERVIEW

Following the civil rights movement in the 1950s, and the feminist movement in the 1960s, Asian American women began to organize formally and informally to address various sources of discontent and social inequities, and to work towards improving conditions for themselves and the Asian American communities. However, political organizing among Asian American women has been slow and limited in many respects. Their political invisibility is related partly to their small numbers in the U.S. population, a result of past restrictive

U.S. immigration policies toward Asians. As of the 1980 census, Asian Americans comprise 1.6 percent (3.5 million) of the total U.S. population. Slightly over half of the Asian American population is female. In addition, ethnic diversity among Asian Americans and geographic dispersion make it difficult for them to organize and be perceived as a significant group with political force.

To some extent, political participation may be a class privilege for women who have the luxury of time, money, and energy. Slightly more than half of the Asian women in the United States are immigrants and they are generally preoccupied with balancing responsibilities at home, in the workplace, and in the community. Like their white counterparts, well-to-do or better-educated Asian American women formed the early women's groups, such as church organizations, social service centers, and women's professional societies.[2]

Few in number and with little institutionalized leadership, these groups have been traditional and conservative in nature, frequently serving as auxiliaries to male organizations that tend to support the male status quo. Only to a very limited extent have they functioned to advance the cause of women's liberation. While there have been efforts to organize Asian American women around specific issues and concerns (e.g., the unavailability or high cost of basic goods, preservation of history and poetry of the Angel Island Immigration Station, World War II internment camps), these attempts have generally lacked continuity and support, thus limiting the emergence of Asian American women as a formalized force.[3] However, these initial efforts of organizing served as a forum where women acquired leadership skills and political experience helpful in future organizing.

The civil rights and feminist movements guide Asian American women in many ways. They help them to become aware of their double disadvantaged positions as members of a racial minority and as females, to learn about the structural sources of their deprivation and social inequalities, and to acknowledge the need to resolve their unique problems.[4]

Following the lead of blacks, many Asian American organizations were created to combat racism and to work toward unity with other racial minorities. The women who joined these organizations are mostly middle-class, U.S.-born, college-educated, professional, and relatively established, and many are strong and active participants. Many others are aware they occupy subservient positions and are relegated to traditional women's functions. They know this prevents them from developing their potential or from holding leadership positions, but their ethnic pride and loyalty frequently keep them from revolt.[5]

More recently, Asian American women have recognized that some of these organizations have not been responsive to their particular needs and concerns. These members also protest that their intense involvement has not, and will not, result in equal participation and leadership development as long as the traditional sex-role relationship between Asian men and women remains unchanged. Despite their efforts at sensitizing Asian men about their attitudes towards, and treatment of, women, some Asian women have opted for a separate organization to deal with their specific issues and problems and to maximize their participation.[6]

Since the late 1960s, several Asian American women's groups have been established in local communities across the country. These include women's courses sponsored by college-level Asian American studies programs, community education programs, social service programs, women's unions, physical and mental health projects, and political interest groups. Many of these groups were short-lived because they lacked funding, leadership, grassroots support, membership, or strong networking. Susie Ling and Sucheta Mazumdar recently pointed out that a lack of momentum and direction also plagued many of the organizations.[7]

Contrary to the common belief about the passivity of Asian American women, they tend to be more actively involved in women's groups of their respective ethnic backgrounds and in Asian groups than in white feminist organizations. Many of them (e.g., National Organization of Pan Asian Women, Asian American Women United, Vietnamese Women's Association, Filipino American Women Network, and Cambodian Women for Progress, Inc.) are organized at the regional level and are in the process of expanding their influence and building networks from the grassroots level to a national one. For example, the Organization of Chinese American Women is nationally based, with over one thousand members throughout the United States. And the National Network of Asian and Pacific Women consists of many regional groups working to build a visible political force.

Like their white counterparts, the Asian women participants in the feminist movement are not homogeneous, but can be classified into two main types: the radical group and women's rights support group.[8] Many participants in the radical group joined the civil rights movement in the 1960s.[9] Subscribing to radical politics, some of these Asian women organized small study groups. They did research to analyze the circumstances and events causing the subordinate position of women, explored new ways of thinking to alter or revolutionize the social conditions of Asian American women, and sought collective action to end all forms of oppression, including sexism.[10]

The second group, the women's rights support group, consists of those who have gained confidence, leadership skills, and experience through women's groups within the Asian communities and have become active in various women's organizations of the larger society.[11] Some of its members witnessed or suffered from gender oppression within the Asian American communities and the society at large and then sought to organize women's groups with this and other specific women's concerns as their top priorities.

The radical group and women's rights support group differ more in their ideological positions than in their strategies and actions. The goals of the women's rights group are to combat sexism and racism, to achieve social equality and justice in society, and to increase the social participation of women at all levels. The goal of the radical group is to build a classless society, for its members believe that once the class struggle is over, sexism and racism will be resolved.[12] While the women's rights group subscribes to a reform ideology attempting to make more limited and gradual change within the social system, the radical group adheres to a radical ideology advocating large-scale revolutionary change that would eliminate structural barriers based on gender, race, class, and culture and lead to social equality and human liberation.

In other words, the women's rights group maintains a certain commitment to the basic structure of the system, viewing it as either essentially just or at least acceptable. Hence, their efforts are aimed at making specific improvements within the system. The radical group is, however, critical of the American system, which they see as never intending to include Asian Americans, nonwhites, or even the majority of working-class Americans.[13] Building a class movement and/or supporting the civil rights movement are primary concerns for some members of this group rather than actively joining the feminist movement in the larger society.

However, different as their political ideologies are, the two groups share many common tactics and strategies, such as consciousness raising, education and training, peaceful demonstration and rallies, establishment of counterinstitutions for women, active lobbying and negotiation for policy changes, and other program interventions.

BARRIERS TO POLITICAL ACTIVISM

In order to become and remain politically active, Asian American women must overcome many barriers at various levels: in individuals, in racial relations, in the cultural system, in the class structure, in gender role stratification, and in the legal-political system. These constitute the main sources of multiple oppression faced by this group of minority women and can be classified into two major types: internal and external barriers.

The former refers to those factors that are specifically inherent to Asian American women as a group, including psychological constraints, cultural restrictions, and patriarchy and structural impediments. The latter refers to those elements existing primarily in American society at large that have kept them from full involvement in the women's liberation movement, including legal-political barriers, racial insensitivity and unreceptivity, and class cleavage. External barriers are more invidious and harder for Asian American women to overcome than internal ones. These two types of barriers may be dialectical in nature, providing stability as well as contradiction in the life experience of many Asian American women.[14]

Internal Barriers

Psychological constraints. Because of their dual status, Asian American women derive their identification and self-esteem from both ethnicity and gender.[15] Although Asian American women may benefit from and contribute significantly to the feminist movement, joining such a movement seems to be a double bind for them because it pits ethnic identity against gender identity. It could also lead to absorption or cooptation into the larger society, resulting in an eventual loss of ethnic identity. In any case, Asian American women must deal with this identity crisis. The key issue here is how to balance one's ethnic and sexual or gender identification in order to develop a healthy self-concept.

Research has indicated that gender-role stereotypes are psychologically and socially detrimental to the personality and achievement of women.[16] And Asian American women suffer from racial stereotypes as well. All stereotypes, whether positive or negative, serve as self-fulfilling prophecies when contending with them gradually leads to internalizing them as part of an illusionary reality. Being perceived generally as subservient, obedient, passive, hard working, and exotic, Asian American women themselves become convinced that they should behave in accordance with these stereotyped expectations. But if they act accordingly, they are then criticized for doing so, becoming victims of the stereotypes imposed by others.[17] For Asian American women to develop their political potential, they must develop a positive self-concept and maintain psychological well-being.

Cultural restrictions. Although certain Asian values emphasizing education, achievement, and diligence account for the high level of aspiration and success of some Asian American women, other values hinder active political participation. Such cultural limitation is further compounded by the adjustment to American culture, which is often in conflict and contradiction with their ethnic one.

Four cultural dilemmas frequently face Asian American women: (1) obedience vs. independence; (2) collective (or familial) vs. individual interest; (3) fatalism vs. change; and (4) self-control vs. self-expression or spontaneity.[18] On the one hand, adherence to Asian values, that is, obedience, familial interest, fatalism, and self-control, tends to foster submissiveness, passivity, pessimism, timidness, inhibition, and adaptiveness, which are not necessarily conducive to political activism. On the other hand, acceptance of the American values of independence, individualism, mastery of one's environment through change, and self-expression generates self-interest, aggressiveness, initiative, and expressive spontaneity. All these traits tend to encourage political activism, but at the same time are incompatible with the family upbringing of most Asian American women. The key problem here is how to maintain a bicultural existence by selecting appropriate elements of both cultural worlds to make the best adaptation according to the demands of social circumstances.

Among Asian Americans, apathy and avoidance are common reactions to unpleasant and stressful situations, particularly when others are trying to involve them in political activity. Because one of the major reasons Asians immigrate to this country is to seek political refuge and escape the political purges and turmoils of their homelands,[19] this avoidance is not surprising. For example, generally and historically women in China have been socialized to be politically apathetic and now as immigrants are still discouraged from participating in organizations that challenge the status quo.

Unfamiliarity with the language is another factor that hinders the acculturation and political participation of Asian immigrant women. This barrier limits the extent to which Asian American women can express themselves, reduces their ability to make demands, restricts their access to many types of information, curtails the flow and scope of communication with others, and eventually limits the development of political efficacy in America. Although the English proficiency level of many Asian American women of foreign birth is generally adequate for functioning well in the workplace and in social circles, language remains a handicap for some. These women tend to prefer speaking in their native tongue, feel inhibited from engaging in open dialogue with others in English, and subsequently increase their political powerlessness and decrease their ability to influence others. The American-born are better able to overcome this communication

difficulty and thereby can participate readily in the larger society. However, their physical features still remind others of their foreign backgrounds, thus presumably limiting full acceptance by others in the larger society. The integration of Asian American women of diverse backgrounds and generations into both the Asian American communities and the larger feminist movement remains key for their future political activism.

Patriarchy and structural impediments. As long as patriarchy persists, the social institutions that encompass Asian American women will continue to perpetuate the devaluation and subjugation of women. School, family, workplace, and other social institutions within and outside the Asian communities all reinforce this gender-role conditioning. The education system has frequently failed to provide women with knowledge of their legal rights. The doctrine of three obediences for a Chinese woman to her father, husband, and son well illustrates her subservient roles. The male is still perceived as major breadwinner and the woman as homemaker. For many employed Asian American women, managing multiple roles is a significant problem. Those with young children are more likely than their white counterparts to stay at home.[20] Overburdened with family and work, and without much support and cooperation from their spouses and sometimes from other family members, Asian American women find political participation beyond their own ethnic group difficult, if not impossible.[21]

Although many Asian American women do engage in political organizing within ethnic communities, their activity in white feminist organizations is often perceived by their male partners and even their female peers as a move toward separatism. They are warned that the consequences of separation will threaten the male ego, damage working relationships between Asian men and women, and dilute efforts and resources for the Asian American cause. All these forces have impeded Asian American women from more active participation in the larger feminist movement.

External Barriers

Legal-political barriers. Historically, structural receptivity to Asian Americans, men and women alike, has been low in the United States. Legal and political barriers deeply rooted in the social system can be documented from the first immigration of Asians to this country. For example, fourteen pieces of legislation were written by state and federal governments to discriminate against the Chinese in America and to strip them of their rights as lawful members of society.[22] The economic exploitation and deprivation that frequently go hand in hand with legal exclusion under political dominance are strongly evident in the century-old history of Asian Americans.[23]

To prevent Asian Americans from forming a strong coalition and political force, U.S. immigration policies emphasized the importance of cheap labor and discouraged the formation of family unity by setting up restrictive quotas for women and children of Asian laborers. The virtual absence of Asian women until the 1950s and the enforcement of anti-miscegenation laws made it difficult for these laborers to find mates in this country. As a result, bachelor communities consisting mainly of single males became characteristic of many Asian ethnic groups.

Although many of these discriminatory laws have been revoked, the community still bears the long-term effects of cultural, socioeconomic, and political exploitation and oppression. Institutional discrimination and deprivation continue, but in new forms, such as the Immigration Reform and Control Act of 1986, which disproportionately affects people of color, including Asians, and exclusion elsewhere of Asian Americans as minorities entitled to special services and opportunities. As long as Asian Americans are not treated as full citizens of this country, their political participation and contribution will remain limited.

Racial insensitivity and unreceptivity. Along with other women of color, some Asian American women criticize the role that white women, in partnership with white men, play in defending and perpetuating racism.[24] The capitalist patriarchy has differential effects on white women and Asian American women. While white women experience sexism, Asian American women suffer from both racism and sexism. For example, sexual stereotypes compounded with racial stereotypes continue to degrade the self-image of Asian American women. White supremacy and male dominance, both individually and in combination, have detrimental effects on the political functioning of Asian American women. For this reason, white women are seen as partly responsible for perpetuating racial prejudice and discriminatory practices.

More specifically, Asian American women who are committed to fighting both sexism and racism feel that white feminists are not aware of or sympathetic to the differences in concerns and priorities of Asian American women. Although Asian American women share many common issues and concerns with white feminists, many tend to place a higher priority on eradicating racism than sexism. They prefer to join groups that advocate improved conditions for people of their own ethnic background rather than groups oriented toward women's issues only. They advocate for multiculturally sensitive programs, not ones just aimed at reforming gender inequality. For instance, they prefer multilingual childcare programs and counseling services that bridge communication gaps and promote cultural understanding.

Some white feminists may accept Asian American women and other women of color as an integral part of the movement in the abstract. But entrance into the predominantly white feminist organizations has not been extended to include them in actuality. The open-door policy allows Asian American women as members, but closed attitudes limit their efforts to work on issues and problems concerning Asian American women, to build coalitions, and to influence decision making. Without understanding the history and culture of Asian American women, some white feminists are impatient with the relatively low level of consciousness and apparent slow progress made by Asian American women in organizing. Their token presence indicates the superficial nature of the invitation to join. The same frustrations of voicelessness, namelessness, and powerlessness run parallel to the experience of white women trying to break into a male-dominated system, the "old-boy" network.[25] While white feminists belong to the center of the movement, Asian American women and women of color remain on its margin.[26]

Class cleavage. In addition to racial insensitivity, the typical middle- and upper-class composition of the feminist movement repels many Asian American women who feel more concern about working-class women.[27] The economic class structure has unfortunately created social barriers between working-class women and middle- or upper-class women. While affluent white women, because of their class entitlement, have more resources, extra time, and the personal energy for political organizing, working-class Asian American women struggle to survive and have little time to question the economic structure. They may not therefore fully understand how the class structure of America limits their aspirations and achievements. Furthermore, greater acceptance of traditional sex-typed ideology by Asian American women and their perception of the feminist movement as alien, radical, and irrelevant to their needs also account for their lack of participation. As a result, it is difficult for them to relate their own economic issues to other

women's concerns and place them in a larger sociopolitical context.

Class cleavage exists not only in the larger feminist movement, but also among Asian American women as well. While Asian American working-class women tend to see economic survival as a primary concern, those with high levels of education, social status, and income tend to be more concerned with job advancement, professional licensing requirements, and career development. Regardless of occupational levels, the immigrant status of Asian American women and their families does not enable them to adapt easily to current demands and requirements of the American labor market. Many experience tremendous status and financial losses as the result of immigration.

Ethnicity, however, cuts across all the class sectors, and provides a form of identification and social bonding among Asian American women from different classes. Limited efforts, such as providing tutoring, social, legal, and health services, women's shelters, counseling, job training programs, and outreach, are helping bridge the gap between class groups. Class barriers are thus much easier to overcome among Asian American women than between the white feminists and Asian American women from working-class backgrounds.

IMPLICATIONS AND CONCLUSION

Asian American women confront problems on multiple fronts. Thus no social movement that addresses only one of the problem areas can adequately resolve their multiple oppressions sexually, racially, legally, economically, and culturally. The feminist movement is not an exception to this, for the specific concerns of Asian American women are often not those of white feminists. Without recognizing these multiple oppressions, political participation in the larger movement will be incompatible with the definition, goals, and interests of the Asian American cause. In this case, the concept of feminism needs to be broadly defined to address the interconnectedness of sex, gender, race, class, and culture so that its defining character and meaning are grounded in the experience of various kinds of women, including Asian American women. Broadening feminism implies that sisterhood is inclusive regardless of one's race, class background, national origin, sexual preference, physical condition, and life-style. Then strategies of collective action are needed to address the specific needs of Asian American women, to overcome the barriers that block their political participation, and to strengthen their relationship with others in the feminist movement as well as human liberation as a whole.

If Asian American women participate in the larger feminist movement, they can benefit from as well as contribute to it. By and large, the movement has provided an impetus for the organizing and political activism of Asian American women. For some, working with white feminists has inspired critical examination of their subordinate status and limited role. They have been prompted to develop themselves fully as contributing members of the family, their ethnic community, and society, thus raising their level of consciousness. Through support from the movement, a number of Asian American women have established their own organizations and have gained skills in language, assertiveness, leadership, coalition building, and negotiation. Thus they are now able to communicate effectively with others and to build strong networks with groups of white women and women of color in the larger society.

In return, Asian American women can also contribute to the movement in unique ways. The presence of Asian American women and other women of color in feminist organizations and activities has sensitized white women to their ethnocentric views, broadened their con-

cerns, and challenged the existing social structure that has persistently defined and perpetuated sexist and racist values. As advocates for the civil rights, social equality, and human liberation of all people, Asian American women have shown support for feminist issues by participating in political activities (e.g., marches in support of the Equal Rights Amendment), forming coalitions with feminists on common issues (e.g., voter registration projects in the 1984 and 1988 elections), sharing resources for important causes, and providing leaders as representatives to women's meetings. They have also enlightened women in the larger movement concerning the uniqueness of their social and cultural backgrounds, the experience of the combined effects of sexism and racism, and the pressing needs of working-class women.

The increased involvement of Asian American women in the feminist movement will enhance the Asian American cause by broadening the perspective of their political struggle; by identifying more resources, channels, and opportunities existing in the larger society; and by gaining support through the formation of networks with diverse groups. Asian American women involved in both Asian American activism and the larger feminist movement have played an important role in decreasing sex and racial discrimination, in providing leadership and role models for others to emulate, and in paving the way for Asian American political visibility and efficacy in the society at large. As Rita Elway remarks, "Asian and Pacific women in elective office have, for the most part, introduced more community people to the political process; they have responded to a broader range of concerns both inside and outside of the community; they have advocated for civil rights on behalf of all ethnic minorities and women."[28]

Therefore, it is important that Asian American women should increase their political participation in the Asian American community as well as in society at large. Although some

Asian American women have been actively involved in their communities, their accomplishments are not less than those of white feminists in the larger society. Because the origins of many of the barriers encountered by Asian American women are beyond their control and are deeply embedded in the social structure, collective efforts are needed to solve these structural problems. Asian American women should join forces with others to increase their political clout and to work for lasting social change. Thus political activism is the first step toward becoming visible, eradicating the stereotype of passivity, and challenging the condition of namelessness. Political participation is also necessary to help overcome voicelessness as Asian American women, to gain power in making demands on their own behalf, and to address the pressing needs and problems of disadvantaged people. It is through political participation that Asian American women will be able to establish networks with other women's groups and to empower themselves in the struggle for equality, justice, and liberation for all people.

To effect their political course of action Asian American women must develop strategies and programs to overcome internal and external barriers. When developing appropriate courses of action, the differences in their historical pasts, the uniqueness of their subculture, and structural arrangements within the Asian American communities and in the larger society must be taken into account. What has successfully advanced the cause of other women's groups cannot be simply imposed on Asian American women.

Five major suggestions are outlined here. First, strategies targeted to overcome psychological barriers may include consciousness-raising techniques to deal directly with identity crises and conflicting loyalties resulting from the double status as women and as members of a racial minority group. Asian American women might develop a transcendent type of gender consciousness that encompasses concern for all forms of multiple oppression.[29] Education is one of the necessary ingredients for increasing political awareness and the power of Asian American women. The women need to develop leadership and organizational skills in order to become active in the political arena. They may identify outstanding women leaders as role models to emulate. Networking and coalition building would provide them mutual support and contact with other women's groups. Programs designed to overcome language difficulties and to improve communication skills and image management are also needed. The goal is to develop a healthy self-concept, positive in outlook, assertive in behavior, and androgynous in style.

Second, self-awareness and cultural programs aimed toward cultural pluralism may be designed to educate Asian American women. They can learn what past conditions and ineffectual activities have led to their current plight. These programs will assist them in seeking cultural resolutions by combining the parts of the Asian and American cultures that are compatible with one another and most appropriate given the demands of current social circumstances. By exposing Asian American women to a wide range of life options, they will learn to demand self-determination, to explore ways of self-expression, and to seek strategies for self-empowerment. They will realize that they can change the course of their life by their own actions.

Third, the role of males in the life struggle of Asian American women is a critical but unanswered question to be explored. As long as patriarchy persists, male dominance will exist inside and outside Asian American communities. While some Asian American women are willing to work with men in partnership for happiness and success, others may opt for independence from males politically and/or sexually. The issue here is that freedom of choice must be available to women if they are to be totally liberated.[30] Whatever choices Asian American women make, others, whoever they are, have to accept these women's definition of gender relationship and respect their choice of self-determination.

Fourth, white feminists and Asian American women should work to build a foundation for feminist solidarity and deal together with racism and classism. White feminists must first critically examine their attitudes and behavior toward women of color and different classes. They need to demonstrate consistency in attitudes and behavior when relating to Asian American women. They need to show sensitivity toward Asians and place the eradication of racism and classism as the top priority in the larger feminist movement. They should take responsibility for educating the general public about cultural and ethnic differences and join Asian American women in protesting and stopping actions that reinforce racism and classism.

Finally, Asian American women must unite with other women of color who, for the most part, share similar life circumstances, experience multiple oppression, and struggle for common goals. Unless the whole social structure is uprooted, many institutional barriers in law, housing, education, employment, economics, and politics that are deeply embedded in the system will remain unchanged. Only when different groups work effectively and strategically together as a political force will all women achieve a new political consciousness and gain collective strength, to supersede the race, gender, sexual, class, and cultural differences that now divide them.

NOTES

1. The term "Asian American" is used to refer to major Asian groups as well as Pacific Islanders. Because of the dearth and uneven information about different groups of Asians and Pacific Islanders, most of the discussion and observations are drawn primarily from the five largest Asian groups: Chinese, Japanese, Korean, Filipinos, and Vietnamese Americans.

2. Germaine Q. Wong, "Impediments to Asian-Pacific-American Women Organizing," in *Conference on the Educational and Occupational Needs of Asian-Pan-American Women* (Washington, D.C.: National Institute of Education, Department of Health, Education, and Welfare, 1980), 89–103.

3. Ibid.

4. Esther Ngan-Ling Chow, "The Development of Feminist Consciousness Among Asian American Women," *Gender and Society* 1, 284–299.

5. Wong, "Impediments to Organizing."

6. Black, Hispanic, and Asian American women alike seem to share some common experiences in conflicting loyalty and identity based on race and gender in the early stage of their respective movements. The Organization of Chinese American Women, which recently separated itself from the Organization of Chinese Americans, is a prime example of this gender struggle.

7. Susie Ling and Sucheta Mazumdar, "Editorial: Asian American Feminism," *Cross Currents* 6, 3–5.

8. Identification with these two major types is mainly for analytical purposes. It neither denies that other factions may exist among different groups of Asian American women nor that a mixed type of the two is possible. Two interviews with Asian American feminists, Sunni and Aurora, reflect these alternative viewpoints about the Asian American women's involvement in the feminist movement. See G. M. Lee, "One in Sisterhood," in *Asian Women*, ed. Editorial staff (Berkeley: University of California Press, 1971), 1, 19–21.

9. Wong, "Impediments to Organizing."

10. See Jeanne Quan, "Congresswoman Patsy Takemoto Mink," 116–118; Cindy Takemoto, "Pat Sumi: Off the Pedestal," 107–111; Grace

Lee Boggs, "The Future: Politics as End and as Means," 112–115; Yuriko Payton-Miyazaki, "Three Steps Behind and Three Steps Ahead," 116–118, all in *Asian Women.* See also Nellie Wong, Merle Woo, and Mitsuye Yamada, *Three Asian American Writers Speak Out on Feminism* (San Francisco: San Francisco Radical Women, 1979), and Wong, "Impediments to Organizing."

11. Juanita Lott and Canta Pian, *Beyond Stereotypes and Statistics: Emergence of Asian and Pacific American Women* (Washington, D.C.: Organization of Pan Asian American Women, 1979).

12. See Boggs, "The Future: Politics as Ends and Means," and Lucie Cheng, "Social Mobility of Asian American Women in America: A Critical Review," in *Conference of the Educational and Occupational Needs of Asian-Pacific-American Women,* 323–341.

13. Quan, "Patsy Takemoto Mink."

14. Patricia Madoo Lengermann and Jill Niebrugge-Brantley, "Contemporary Feminist Theory," in *Contemporary Sociological Theories,* ed. George Ritzer (New York: Alfred A. Knopf, 1988), 430–432.

15. Esther Ngan-Ling Chow, *Acculturation of Asian American Professional Women,* research monograph (Washington, D.C.: National Institute of Mental Health, Department of Health and Human Services, 1982); Chow, "Acculturation Experience of the Asian American Woman," in *Beyond Sex Roles,* ed. Alice Sargent (St. Paul: West, 1985), 238–251.

16. Inge K. Broverman, Susan Raymond Vogel, Donald M. Broverman et al., "Sex-Role Stereotypes: A Current Appraisal," *Journal of Social Issues* 28 (1972), 59–78, and Susan A. Basow, *Gender Stereotypes: Tradition and Alternatives,* 2d ed. (Monterey, Calif.: Brooks/Cole, 1986).

17. Esther Ngan-Ling Chow, "The Politics of Racial and Sexual Stereotypes at Work," paper presented at the annual meeting of the society for the Study of Social Problems, San Francisco, 1982.

18. Few significant variations were found among different subgroups in their adherence to Asian values and acceptance of American values in two survey samples of Asian American women on both the East and West Coasts. See Chow, *Acculturation of Professional Women.*

19. See Bok-Lim Kim and M. E. Condon, *A Study of Asian Americans in Chicago: Their Socio-Economic Characteristics, Problems and Service Needs* (Washington, D.C.: National Institute of Mental Health, Department of Health, Education, and Welfare, 1975); and Canta Pian, "Immigration of Asian Women and the Status of Recent Asian Women Immigrants," in *Conference on the Educational and Occupational Needs,* 181–210.

20. Pauline Fong and Amado Y. Cabezas, "Employment of Asian-Pacific American Women," in *Conference on the Educational and Occupational Needs,* 255–321.

21. Esther Ngan-Ling Chow, "Job Decision, Household Work and Gender Relations in Asian American Families," paper presented at the annual meeting of the American Sociological Association, Chicago, 1987.

22. Major legislation passed to ban and discriminate against Asians in America includes the 1850 Anti-Prostitution Law, the Naturalization Act of 1870, the Chinese Exclusion Act of 1882, the 1906 California Anti-Miscegenation Law, the California Alien Land Acts of 1913 and 1920, the Cabel Act of 1922, the Exclusion Act of 1924, and Executive Order 9066 in 1942–45, which put 112 ,000 Japanese Americans in concentration camps.

23. American history is filled with examples of such injustice, including anti-Chinese riots and massacres that forced the relocation of Chinese communities in many cities, mass internment and relocation of Japanese Americans during World War II, and land invasions and colonization in the Pacific Islands. See Judy Yung, *Chinese Women in America: A Pictorial History* (Seattle: University of Washington Press, 1986).

24. Chalso Loo and Paul Ong, "Slaying Demons with a Sewing Needle: Feminist Issues for Chinatown Women," *Berkeley Journal of Sociology* 27 (1982), 77–88; and Esther Ngan-Ling Chow, "Development of Feminist Consciousness."

25. Rosabeth Moss Kanter, *Men and Women of the Corporation* (New York: Basic Books, 1977).

26. Bell Hooks, *Feminist Theory: From Margin to Center* (Boston: South End Press, 1984) and *Ain't I a Woman: Black Women and Feminism* (Boston: South End Press, 1981).

27. Mitsuye Yamada, "Asian Pacific American Women and Feminism," in *This Bridge Called My Back: Writings by Radical Women of Color,* ed. C. Morage and G. Anzaldus (Watertown, Mass.: Persephone, 1981), 71–75; Loo and Ong, "Slaying Demons"; Chow, "Development of Feminist Consciousness"; and Cheng, "Social Mobility of Asian Women."

28. Rita Fujiki Elway, "Strategies for Political Participation of Asian/Pacific Women," in *Civil Rights Issues of Asian and Pacific Americans: Myths and Realities* (Washington, D.C.: U.S. Commission on Civil Rights, 1979), 133–139.

29. Chow, "Development of Feminist Consciousness."

30. See Alice Jardine and Paul Smith, eds., *Men in Feminism* (New York: Methuen, 1987).

Study/Discussion Questions

1. What psychological constraints make it less likely that Asian American women will join feminist organizations?
2. How are the "internal barriers" to feminist activism different for Asian American women than they are for white women?
3. How does Asian American culture discourage feminist activism?
4. How do race and class influence Asian American women's attitudes toward feminism?
5. What arguments does the author make in favor of Asian American women's feminist activism? How can Asian American women benefit from such activism, in the authors' view?

Homophobia: A Weapon of Sexism

Suzanne Pharr

As with any form of oppression, homophobia ostensibly offers a set of benefits to the oppressors and foists a set of penalties on the oppressed. Suzanne Pharr delineates each side of this win/lose equation in the case of homophobia. Among women, none of whom are fully empowered in this society, Pharr argues, homophobia serves to limit and control heterosexual women's lives as well as those of lesbians. It is not in any woman's interest, therefore, to buy into homophobic attitudes or behavior.

HOMOPHOBIA—the irrational fear and hatred of those who love and sexually desire those of the same sex. Though I intimately knew its meaning, the word homophobia was unknown to me until the late 1970s, and when I first heard it, I was struck by how difficult it is to say, what an ugly word it is, equally as ugly as its meaning. Like racism and anti-Semitism, it is a word that calls up images of loss of freedom, verbal and physical violence, death.

In my life I have experienced the effects of homophobia through rejection by friends, threats of loss of employment, and threats upon my life; and I have witnessed far worse things happening to other lesbian and gay people: loss of children, beatings, rape, death. Its power is great enough to keep ten to twenty percent of the population living lives of fear (if their sexual identity is hidden) or lives of danger (if their sexual identity is visible) or both. And its power is great enough to keep the remaining eighty to ninety percent of the population trapped in their own fears.

Long before I had a word to describe the behavior, I was engaged in a search to discover the source of its power, the power to damage and destroy lives. The most common explanations were that to love the same sex was either abnormal (sick) or immoral (sinful).

My exploration of the sickness theory led me to understand that homosexuality is simply a matter of sexual identity, which, along with heterosexual identity, is formed in ways that no one conclusively understands. The American Psychological Association has said that it is no more abnormal to be homosexual than to be left-handed. It is simply that a certain percentage of the population is. It is not healthier to be heterosexual or right-handed. What is unhealthy—and sometimes a source of stress and sickness so great it can lead to suicide—is homophobia, that societal disease that places such negative messages, condem-

From *Homophobia: A Weapon of Sexism* by Suzanne Pharr, Chardon Press, new expanded edition 1997, distributed by the Women's Project, 2224 Main St., Little Rock, AR 72206.

nation, and violence on gay men and lesbians that we have to struggle throughout our lives for self-esteem.

The sin theory is a particularly curious one because it is expressed so often and with such hateful emotion both from the pulpit and from laypeople who rely heavily upon the Bible for evidence. However, there is significant evidence that the approximately eight references to homosexuality in the Bible are frequently read incorrectly, according to Dr. Virginia Ramey Mollenkott in an essay in *Christianity and Crisis:*

> Much of the discrimination against homosexual persons is justified by a common misreading of the Bible. Many English translations of the Bible contain the word homosexual in extremely negative contexts. But the fact is that the word *homosexual* does not occur anywhere in the Bible. No extant text, no manuscript, neither Hebrew nor Greek, Syriac, nor Aramaic, contains the word. The terms *homosexual* and *heterosexual* were not developed in any language until the 1890's, when for the first time the awareness developed that there are people with a lifelong, constitutional orientation toward their own sex. Therefore the use of the word *homosexuality* by certain English Bible translators is an example of the extreme bias that endangers the human and civil rights of homosexual persons. (pp. 383–384, Nov. 9, 1987)

Dr. Mollenkott goes on to add that two words in I Corinthians 6:9 and one word in Timothy 1:10 have been used as evidence to damn homosexuals but that well into the 20th century the first of these was understood by everyone to mean masturbation, and the second was known to refer to male prostitutes who were available for hire by either women or men. There are six other Biblical references that are thought by some to refer to homosexuals but

each of these is disputed by contemporary scholars. For instance, the sin in the Sodom and Gommorah passage (Genesis 19:1–10) is less about homosexuality than it is about inhospitality and gang rape. The law of hospitality was universally accepted and Lot was struggling to uphold it against what we assume are heterosexual townsmen threatening gang rape to the two male angels in Lot's home. While people dwell on this passage as a condemnation of homosexuality, they bypass what I believe is the central issue or, if you will, sin: Lot's offering his two virgin daughters up to the men to be used as they desired for gang rape. Here is a perfectly clear example of devaluing and dehumanizing and violently brutalizing women.

The eight Biblical references (and not a single one by Jesus) to alleged homosexuality are very small indeed when compared to the several hundred references (and many by Jesus) to money and the necessity for justly distributing wealth. Yet few people go on a rampage about the issue of a just economic system, using the Bible as a base.

Finally, I came to understand that homosexuality, heterosexuality, bi-sexuality are morally neutral. A particular sexual identity is not an indication of either good or evil. What is important is not the gender of the two people in relationship with each other but the content of that relationship. Does that relationship contain violence, control of one person by the other? Is the relationship a growthful place for the people involved? It is clear that we must hold all relationships, whether opposite sex or same sex, to these standards.

The first workshops that I conducted were an effort to address these two issues, and I assumed that if consciousness could be raised about the invalidity of these two issues then people would stop feeling homophobic and would understand homophobia as a civil rights issue and work against it. The workshops took a high moral road, invoking participants' compassion, understanding, and outrage at injustice.

The eight-hour workshops raised consciousness and increased participants' commitment to work against homophobia as one more oppression in a growing list of recognized oppressions, but I still felt something was missing. I felt there was still too much unaccounted for power in homophobia even after we looked at the sick and sinful theories, at how it feels to be a lesbian in a homophobic world, at why lesbians choose invisibility, at how lesbian existence threatens male dominance. All of the pieces seemed available but we couldn't sew them together into a quilt.

As I conducted more workshops over the years I noticed several important themes that led to the final piecing together:

1. Women began to recognize that economics was a central issue connecting various oppressions;

2. Battered women began talking about how they had been called lesbians by their batterers;

3. Both heterosexual and lesbian women said they valued the workshops because in them they were given the rare opportunity to talk about their own sexuality and also about sexism in general.

Around the same time (1985–86), the National Coalition Against Domestic Violence (NCADV) entered into a traumatic relationship with the U.S. Department of Justice (DOJ), requesting a large two-year grant to provide domestic violence training and information nationally. At the time the grant was to be announced, NCADV was attacked by conservative groups such as the Heritage Foundation as a "pro-lesbian, pro-feminist, anti-family" organization. In response to these attacks, the DOJ decided not to award a grant; instead they formulated a "cooperative agreement" that allowed them to monitor and approve all work,

and they assured conservative organizations that the work would not be pro-lesbian and anti-family. The major issue between NCADV and the DOJ became whether NCADV would let an outside agency define and control its work, and finally, during never-ending concern from the DOJ about "radical" and "lesbian" issues, the agreement was terminated by NCADV at the end of the first year. Throughout that year, there were endless statements and innuendoes from the DOJ and some members of NCADV's membership about NCADV's lesbian leadership and its alleged concern for only lesbian issues. Many women were damaged by the crossfire, NCADV's work was stopped for a year, and the organization was split from within. It was lesbian baiting at its worst.

As one of NCADV's lesbian leadership during that onslaught of homophobic attacks, I was still giving homophobia workshops around the country, now able to give even more personal witness to the virulence of the hatred and fear of lesbians and gay men within both institutions and individuals. It was a time of pain and often anger for those of us committed to creating a world free of violence, and it was a time of deep distress for those of us under personal attack. However, my mother, like many mothers, had always said, "All things work for the good," and sure enough, it was out of the accumulation of these experiences that the pieces began coming together to make a quilt of our understanding.

On the day that I stopped reacting to attacks and gave my time instead to visioning, this simple germinal question came forth for the workshops: "What will the world be like without homophobia in it—for everyone, female and male, whatever sexual identity?" Simple though the question is, it was at first shocking because those of us who work in the anti-violence movement spend most of our time working with the damaging, negative results of violence and have little time to vision. It is sometimes difficult to create a vision of a world we have never experienced, but without such a vision, we cannot know clearly what we are working toward in our social change work.

From this question, answer led to answer until a whole appeared of our collective making, from one workshop to another.

Here are some of the answers women have given:

- Kids won't be called tomboys or sissies; they'll just be who they are, able to do what they wish.
- People will be able to love anyone, no matter what sex; the issue will simply be whether or not she/he is a good human being, compatible, and loving.
- Affection will be opened up between women and men, women and women, men and men, and it won't be centered on sex; people won't fear being called names if they show affection to someone who isn't a mate or potential mate.
- If affection is opened up, then isolation will be broken down for all of us, especially for those who generally experience little physical affection, such as unmarried old people.
- Women will be able to work whatever jobs we want, without being labeled masculine.
- There will be less violence if men do not feel they have to prove and assert their manhood. Their desire to dominate and control will not spill over from the personal to the level of national and international politics and the use of bigger and better weapons to control other countries.
- People will wear whatever clothes they wish, with the priority being comfort rather than the display of femininity or masculinity.
- There will be no gender roles.

It is at this point in the workshops—having imagined a world without homophobia—that the participants see the analysis begin to fall into place. Someone notes that all the things we have been talking about relate to sexual gender roles. It's rather like the beginning of a course in Sexism 101. The next question is "Imagine the world with no sex roles—sexual identity, which may be in flux, but no sexual gender roles." Further: imagine a world in which opportunity is not determined by gender or race. Just the imagining makes women alive with excitement because it is a vision of freedom, often just glimpsed but always known deep down as truth. Pure joy.

We talk about what it would be like to be born in a world in which there were no expectations or treatment based on gender but instead only the expectation that each child, no matter what race or sex, would be given as many options and possibilities as society could muster. Then we discuss what girls and boys would be like at puberty and beyond if sex role expectations didn't come crashing down on them with girls' achievement levels beginning to decline thereafter; what it would be for women to have the training and options for economic equity with men; what would happen to issues of power and control, and therefore violence, if there were real equality. To have no prescribed sex roles would open the possibility of equality. It is a discussion women find difficult to leave. Freedom calls.

Patriarchy—an enforced belief in male dominance and control—is the ideology and sexism the system that holds it in place. The catechism goes like this: Who do gender roles serve? Men and the women who seek power from them. Who suffers from gender roles? Women most completely and men in part. How are gender roles maintained? By the weapons of sexism: economics, violence, homophobia.

Why then don't we ardently pursue ways to eliminate gender roles and therefore sexism? It is my profound belief that all people have a spark in them that yearns for freedom, and the history of the world's atrocities—from the Nazi concentration camps to white dominance in

South Africa to the battering of women—is the story of attempts to snuff out that spark. When that spark doesn't move forward to full flame, it is because the weapons designed to control and destroy have wrought such intense damage over time that the spark has been all but extinguished.

Sexism, that system by which women are kept subordinate to men, is kept in place by three powerful weapons designed to cause or threaten women with pain and loss. As stated before, the three are economics, violence, and homophobia. The stories of women battered by men, victims of sexism at its worst, show these three forces converging again and again. When battered women tell why they stayed with a batterer or why they returned to a batterer, over and over they say it was because they could not support themselves and their children financially, they had no skills for jobs, they could not get housing, transportation, medical care for their children. And how were they kept controlled? Through violence and threats of violence, both physical and verbal, so that they feared for their lives and the lives of their children and doubted their own abilities and self-worth. And why were they beaten? Because they were not good enough, were not "real women," were dykes, or because they stood up to him as no "real woman" would. And the male batterer, with societal backing, felt justified, often righteous, in his behavior— for his part in keeping women in their place.

Economics must be looked at first because many feminists consider it to be the root cause of sexism. Certainly the United Nations study released at the final conference of the International Decade on Women, held in Nairobi, Kenya, in 1985, supports that belief: of the world's population, women do 75% of the work, receive 10% of the pay and own 1% of the property. In the United States it is also supported by the opposition of the government to the idea of comparable worth and pay eq-

uity, as expressed by Ronald Reagan who referred to pay equity as "a joke." Obviously, it is considered a dangerous idea. Men profit not only from women's unpaid work in the home but from our underpaid work within horizontal female segregation such as clerical workers or upwardly mobile tokenism in the workplace where a few affirmative action promotions are expected to take care of all women's economic equality needs. Moreover, they profit from women's bodies through pornography, prostitution, and international female sexual slavery. And white men profit from both the labor of women and of men of color. Forced economic dependency puts women under male control and severely limits women's options for self-determination and self-sufficiency.

This truth is borne out by the fact that according to the National Commission on Working Women, on average, women of all races working year round earn only 64 cents to every one dollar a man makes. Also, the U.S. Census Bureau reports that only 9 percent of working women make over $25,000 a year. There is fierce opposition to women gaining employment in the nontraditional job market, that is, those jobs that traditionally employ less than 25 percent women. After a woman has gained one of these higher paying jobs, she is often faced with sexual harassment, lesbian baiting, and violence. It is clear that in the workplace there is an all-out effort to keep women in traditional roles so that the only jobs we are "qualified" for are the low-paid ones.

Actually, we have to look at economics not only as the root cause of sexism but also as the underlying, driving force that keeps all the oppressions in place. In the United States, our economic system is shaped like a pyramid, with a few people at the top, primarily white males, being supported by large numbers of unpaid or low-paid workers at the bottom. When we look at this pyramid, we begin to understand the major connection between sexism and racism because those groups at the bottom of the pyramid are women and people of color. We then begin to understand why there is such a fervent effort to keep those oppressive systems (racism and sexism and all the ways they are manifested) in place to maintain the unpaid and low-paid labor.

Susan DeMarco and Jim Hightower, writing for *Mother Jones,* report that *Forbes* magazine indicated that "the 400 richest families in America last year had an average net worth of $550 million each. These and less than a million other families—roughly one percent of our population—are at the prosperous tip of our society. . . . In 1976, the wealthiest 1 percent of America's families owned 19.2 percent of the nation's total wealth. (This sum of wealth counts all of America's cash, real estate, stocks, bonds, factories, art, personal property, and anything else of financial value.) By 1983, those at this 1 percent tip of our economy owned 34.3 percent of our wealth. . . . *Today, the top 1 percent of Americans possesses more net wealth than the bottom 90 percent.*" (My italics.) (May 1988, pp. 32–33)

In order for this top-heavy system of economic inequity to maintain itself, the 90 percent on the bottom must keep supplying cheap labor. A very complex, intricate system of institutionalized oppressions is necessary to maintain the status quo so that the vast majority will not demand its fair share of wealth and resources and bring the system down. Every institution—schools, banks, churches, government, courts, media, etc.—as well as individuals must be enlisted in the campaign to maintain such a system of gross inequity.

What would happen if women gained the earning opportunities and power that men have? What would happen if these opportunities were distributed equitably, no matter what sex one was, no matter what race one was born into, and no matter where one lived? What if educational and training opportunities were equal? Would women spend most of our youth preparing for marriage? Would marriage be based on economic survival for women? What would happen to issues of power and control? Would women stay with our batterers? If a woman had economic independence in a society where women had equal opportunities, would she still be thought of as owned by her father or husband?

Economics is the great controller in both sexism and racism. If a person can't acquire food, shelter, and clothing and provide them for children, then that person can be forced to do many things in order to survive. The major tactic, worldwide, is to provide unrecompensed or inadequately recompensed labor for the benefit of those who control wealth. Hence, we see women performing unpaid labor in the home or filling low-paid jobs, and we see people of color in the lowest-paid jobs available.

The method is complex: limit educational and training opportunities for women and for people of color and then withhold adequate paying jobs with the excuse that people of color and women are incapable of filling them. Blame the economic victim and keep the victim's self-esteem low through invisibility and distortion within the media and education. Allow a few people of color and women to succeed among the profitmakers so that blaming those who don't "make it" can be intensified. Encourage those few who succeed in gaining power now to turn against those who remain behind rather than to use their resources to make change for all. Maintain the myth of scarcity—that there are not enough jobs, resources, etc., to go around—among the middle class so that they will not unite with laborers, immigrants, and the unemployed. The method keeps in place a system of control and profit by a few and a constant source of cheap labor to maintain it.

If anyone steps out of line, take her/his job away. Let homelessness and hunger do their work. The economic weapon works. And we end up saying, "I would do this or that—be openly who I am, speak out against injustice, work for civil rights, join a labor union, go to a political march, etc.—if I didn't have this job. I can't afford to lose it." We stay in an abusive situation because we see no other way to survive.

In the battered women's movement abusive relationships are said to be about power and control and the way out of them is through looking at the ways power and control work in our lives, developing support, improving self-esteem, and achieving control over our decisions and lives. We have yet to apply these methods successfully to our economic lives. Though requiring massive change, the way there also lies open for equality and wholeness. But the effort will require at least as much individual courage and risk and group support as it does for a battered woman to leave her batterer, and that requirement is very large indeed. Yet battered women find the courage to leave their batterers every day. They walk right into the unknown. To break away from economic domination and control will require a movement made up of individuals who possess this courage and ability to take risks.

Violence is the second means of keeping women in line, in a narrowly defined place and role. First, there is the physical violence of battering, rape, and incest. Often when battered women come to shelters and talk about their lives, they tell stories of being not only physically beaten but also raped and their children subjected to incest. Work in the women's anti-violence movement during almost two decades has provided significant evidence that each of these acts, including rape and incest, is an attempt to seek power over and control of another person. In each case, the victim is viewed as an object and is used to meet the abuser's needs. The violence is used to wreak punishment and to demand compliance or obedience.

Violence against women is directly related to the condition of women in a society that refuses us equal pay, equal access to resources, and equal status with males. From this condition comes men's confirmation of their sense of ownership of women, power over women, and assumed right to control women for their own means. Men physically and emotionally abuse women because they can, because they live in a world that gives them permission. Male violence is fed by their sense of their right to dominate and control, and their sense of superiority over a group of people who, because of gender, they consider inferior to them.

It is not just the violence but the threat of violence that controls our lives. Because the burden of responsibility has been placed so often on the potential victim, as women we have curtailed our freedom in order to protect ourselves from violence. Because of the threat of rapists, we stay on alert, being careful not to walk in isolated places, being careful where we park our cars, adding incredible security measures to our homes—massive locks, lights, alarms, if we can afford them—and we avoid places where we will appear vulnerable or unprotected while the abuser walks with freedom. Fear, often now so commonplace that it is unacknowledged, shapes our lives, reducing our freedom.

As Bernice Reagan of the musical group Sweet Honey in the Rock said at the 1982 National Coalition Against Domestic Violence conference, women seem to carry a genetic memory that women were once burned as witches when we stepped out of line. To this day, mothers pass on to their daughters word of the dangers they face and teach them the ways they must limit their lives in order to survive.

Part of the way sexism stays in place is the societal promise of survival, false and unfulfilled as it is, that women will not suffer violence if we attach ourselves to a man to protect us. A woman without a man is told she is vulnerable to external violence and, worse, that there is something wrong with her. When the male abuser calls a woman a lesbian, he is not so much labeling her a woman who loves women as he is warning her that by resisting him, she is choosing to be outside society's protection from male institutions and therefore from wide-ranging, unspecified, ever-present violence. When she seeks assistance from woman friends or a battered women's shelter, he recognizes the power in woman bonding and fears loss of her servitude and loyalty: the potential loss of his control. The concern is not affection or sexual identity: the concern is disloyalty and the threat is violence.

The threat of violence against women who step out of line or who are disloyal is made all the more powerful by the fact that women do not have to do anything—they may be paragons of virtue and subservience—to receive violence against our lives: the violence still comes. It comes because of the woman hating that exists throughout society. Chance plays a larger part than virtue in keeping women safe. Hence, with violence always a threat to us, women can never feel completely secure and confident. Our sense of safety is always fragile and tenuous.

Many women say that verbal violence causes more harm than physical violence because it damages self-esteem so deeply. Women have not wanted to hear battered women say that the verbal abuse was as hurtful as the physical abuse: to acknowledge that truth would be tantamount to acknowledging that virtually every woman is a battered woman. It is difficult to keep strong against accusations of being a bitch, stupid, inferior, etc., etc. It is especially difficult when these individual assaults are backed up by a society that shows women in textbooks, advertising, TV programs, movies, etc., as debased, silly, inferior, and sexually objectified, and a society that gives tacit approval to pornography. When we internalize these messages, we call the result "low self-esteem," a therapeutic individualized term. It seems to me we should use the more political expression: when we internalize these messages, we experience internalized sexism, and we ex-

perience it in common with all women living in a sexist world. The violence against us is supported by a society in which woman hating is deeply imbedded.

In "Eyes on the Prize," a 1987 Public Television documentary about the Civil Rights Movement, an older white woman says about her youth in the South that it was difficult to be anything different from what was around her when there was no vision for another way to be. Our society presents images of women that say it is appropriate to commit violence against us. Violence is committed against women because we are seen as inferior in status and in worth. It has been the work of the women's movement to present a vision of another way to be.

Every time a woman gains the strength to resist and leave her abuser, we are given a model of the importance of stepping out of line, of moving toward freedom. And we all gain strength when she says to violence, "Never again!" Thousands of women in the last fifteen years have resisted their abusers to come to this country's 1100 battered women's shelters. There they have sat down with other women to share their stories, to discover that their stories again and again are the same, to develop an analysis that shows that violence is a statement about power and control, and to understand how sexism creates the climate for male violence. Those brave women are now a part of a movement that gives hope for another way to live in equality and peace.

Homophobia works effectively as a weapon of sexism because it is joined with a powerful arm, heterosexism. Heterosexism creates the climate for homophobia with its assumption that the world is and must be heterosexual and its display of power and privilege as the norm. Heterosexism is the systemic display of homophobia in the institutions of society. Heterosexism and homophobia work together to enforce compulsory heterosexuality and that bastion of patriarchal power, the nuclear family. The central focus of the rightwing attack against women's liberation is that women's equality, women's self-determination, women's control of our own bodies and lives will damage what they see as the crucial societal institution, the nuclear family. The attack has been led by fundamentalist ministers across the country. The two areas they have focused on most consistently are abortion and homosexuality, and their passion has led them to bomb women's clinics and to recommend deprogramming for homosexuals and establishing camps to quarantine people with AIDS. To resist marriage and/or heterosexuality is to risk severe punishment and loss.

It is not by chance that when children approach puberty and increased sexual awareness they begin to taunt each other by calling these names: "queer," "faggot," "pervert." It is at puberty that the full force of society's pressure to conform to heterosexuality and prepare for marriage is brought to bear. Children know what we have taught them, and we have given clear messages that those who deviate from standard expectations are to be made to get back in line. The best controlling tactic at puberty is to be treated as an outsider, to be ostracized at a time when it feels most vital to be accepted. Those who are different must be made to suffer loss. It is also at puberty that misogyny begins to be more apparent, and girls are pressured to conform to societal norms that do not permit them to realize their full potential. It is at this time that their academic achievements begin to decrease as they are coerced into compulsory heterosexuality and trained for dependency upon a man, that is, for economic survival.

There was a time when the two most condemning accusations against a woman meant to ostracize and disempower her were "whore" and "lesbian." The sexual revolution and changing attitudes about heterosexual behavior may have led to some lessening of the power of the word *whore,* though it still has strength as a threat to sexual property and prostitutes are stigmatized and abused. However, the word *lesbian* is still fully charged and carries with it the full threat of loss of power and privilege, the threat of being cut asunder, abandoned, and left outside society's protection.

To be a lesbian is to be perceived as someone who has stepped out of line, who has moved out of sexual/economic dependence on a male, who is woman-identified. A lesbian is perceived as someone who can live without a man, and who is therefore (however illogically) against men. A lesbian is perceived as being outside the acceptable, routinized order of things. She is seen as someone who has no societal institutions to protect her and who is not privileged to the protection of individual males. Many heterosexual women see her as someone who stands in contradiction to the sacrifices they have made to conform to compulsory heterosexuality. A lesbian is perceived as a threat to the nuclear family, to male dominance and control, to the very heart of sexism.

Gay men are perceived also as a threat to male dominance and control, and the homophobia expressed against them has the same roots in sexism as does homophobia against lesbians. Visible gay men are the objects of extreme hatred and fear by heterosexual men because their breaking ranks with male heterosexual solidarity is seen as a damaging rent in the very fabric of sexism. They are seen as betrayers, as traitors who must be punished and eliminated. In the beating and killing of gay men we see clear evidence of this hatred. When we see the fierce homophobia expressed toward gay men, we can begin to understand the ways sexism also affects males through imposing rigid, dehumanizing gender roles on them. The two circumstances in which it is legitimate for men to be openly physically affectionate with one another are in competitive sports and in the crisis of war. For many men, these two experiences are the highlights of their lives, and they think of them again and again with nostalgia. War and sports offer a cover of all-male safety and dominance to keep away the notion of affectionate openness being identified with homosexuality. When gay men break ranks with male roles through bonding and affection outside the arenas of war and sports, they are perceived as not being "real men," that is, as being identified with women, the weaker sex that must be dominated and that over the centuries has been the object of male hatred and abuse. Misogyny gets transferred to gay men with a vengeance and is increased by the fear that their sexual identity and behavior will bring down the entire system of male dominance and compulsory heterosexuality.

If lesbians are established as threats to the status quo, as outcasts who must be punished, homophobia can wield its power over all women through lesbian baiting. Lesbian baiting is an attempt to control women by labeling us as lesbians because our behavior is not acceptable, that is, when we are being independent, going our own way, living whole lives, fighting for our rights, demanding equal pay, saying no to violence, being self-assertive, bonding with and loving the company of women, assuming the right to our bodies, insisting upon our own authority, making changes that include us in society's decision-making; lesbian baiting occurs when women are called lesbians because we resist male dominance and control. And it has little or nothing to do with one's sexual identity.

To be named as lesbian threatens all women, not just lesbians, with great loss. And any woman who steps out of role risks being called a lesbian. To understand how this is a threat to all women, one must understand that any woman can be called a lesbian and there is no real way she can defend herself: there is no way to credential one's sexuality. ("The Children's Hour," a Lillian Hellman play, makes this point when a student asserts two teachers are lesbians and they have no way to disprove it.) She

may be married or divorced, have children, dress in the most feminine manner, have sex with men, be celibate—but there are lesbians who do all those things. *Lesbians look like all women and all women look like lesbians.* There is no guaranteed method of identification, and as we all know, sexual identity can be kept hidden. (The same is true for men. There is no way to prove their sexual identity, though many go to extremes to prove heterosexuality.) Also, women are not necessarily born lesbian. Some seem to be, but others become lesbians later in life after having lived heterosexual lives. Lesbian baiting of heterosexual women would not work if there were a definitive way to identify lesbians (or heterosexuals).

We have yet to understand clearly how sexual identity develops. And this is disturbing to some people, especially those who are determined to discover how lesbian and gay identity is formed so that they will know where to start in eliminating it. (Isn't it odd that there is so little concern about discovering the causes of heterosexuality?) There are many theories: genetic makeup, hormones, socialization, environment, etc. But there is no conclusive evidence that indicates that heterosexuality comes from one process and homosexuality from another.

We do know, however, that sexual identity can be in flux, and we know that sexual identity means more than just the gender of people one is attracted to and has sex with. To be a lesbian has as many ramifications as for a woman to be heterosexual. It is more than sex, more than just the bedroom issue many would like to make it: it is a woman-centered life with all the social interconnections that entails. Some lesbians are in long-term relationships, some in short-term ones, some date, some are celibate, some are married to men, some remain as separate as possible from men, some have children by men, some by alternative insemination, some seem "feminine" by societal standards, some "masculine," some are doctors, lawyers and ministers, some laborers, housewives and writers:

what all share in common is a sexual/affectional identity that focuses on women in its attractions and social relationships.

If lesbians are simply women with a particular sexual identity who look and act like all women, then the major difference in living out a lesbian sexual identity as opposed to a heterosexual identity is that as lesbians we live in a homophobic world that threatens and imposes damaging loss on us for being who we are, for choosing to live whole lives. Homophobic people often assert that homosexuals have the choice of not being homosexual; that is, we don't have to act out our sexual identity. In that case, I want to hear heterosexuals talk about their willingness not to act out their sexual identity, including not just sexual activity but heterosexual social interconnections and heterosexual privilege. It is a question of wholeness. It is very difficult for one to be denied the life of a sexual being, whether expressed in sex or in physical affection, and to feel complete, whole. For our loving relationships with humans feed the life of the spirit and enable us to overcome our basic isolation and to be interconnected with humankind.

If, then, any woman can be named a lesbian and be threatened with terrible losses, what is it she fears? Are these fears real? Being vulnerable to a homophobic world can lead to these losses:

- *Employment.* The loss of job leads us right back to the economic connection to sexism. This fear of job loss exists for almost every lesbian except perhaps those who are self-employed or in a business that does not require societal approval. Consider how many businesses or organizations you know that will hire and protect people who are openly gay or lesbian.
- *Family.* Their approval, acceptance, love.
- *Children.* Many lesbians and gay men have children, but very, very few gain custody in court challenges, even if the other parent is a

known abuser. Other children may be kept away from us as though gays and lesbians are abusers. There are written and unwritten laws prohibiting lesbians and gays from being foster parents or from adopting children. There is an irrational fear that children in contact with lesbians and gays will become homosexual through influence or that they will be sexually abused. Despite our knowing that 95 percent of those who sexually abuse children are heterosexual men, there are no policies keeping heterosexual men from teaching or working with children, yet in almost every school system in America, visible gay men and lesbians are not hired through either written or unwritten law.

- *Heterosexual privilege and protection.* No institutions, other than those created by lesbians and gays—such as the Metropolitan Community Church, some counseling centers, political organizations such as the National Gay and Lesbian Task Force, the National Coalition of Black Lesbians and Gays, the Lambda Legal Defense and Education Fund, etc.—affirm homosexuality and offer protection. Affirmation and protection cannot be gained from the criminal justice system, mainline churches, educational institutions, the government.
- *Safety.* There is nowhere to turn for safety from physical and verbal attacks because the norm presently in this country is that it is acceptable to be overtly homophobic. Gay men are beaten on the streets; lesbians are kidnapped and "deprogrammed." The National Gay and Lesbian Task Force, in an extended study, has documented violence against lesbians and gay men and noted the inadequate response of the criminal justice system. One of the major differences between homophobia/heterosexism and racism and sexism is that because of the Civil Rights Movement and the women's movement racism and sexism are expressed more covertly (though with great harm); because there has

not been a major, visible lesbian and gay movement, it is permissible to be overtly homophobic in any institution or public forum. Churches spew forth homophobia in the same way they did racism prior to the Civil Rights Movement. Few laws are in place to protect lesbians and gay men, and the criminal justice system is wracked with homophobia.

- *Mental health.* An overtly homophobic world in which there is full permission to treat lesbians and gay men with cruelty makes it difficult for lesbians and gay men to maintain a strong sense of well-being and self-esteem. Many lesbians and gay men are beaten, raped, killed, subjected to aversion therapy, or put in mental institutions. The impact of such hatred and negativity can lead one to depression and, in some cases, to suicide. The toll on the gay and lesbian community is devastating.
- *Community.* There is rejection by those who live in homophobic fear, those who are afraid of association with lesbians and gay men. For many in the gay and lesbian community, there is a loss of public acceptance, a loss of allies, a loss of place and belonging.
- *Credibility.* This fear is large for many people: the fear that they will no longer be respected, listened to, honored, believed. They fear they will be social outcasts.

The list goes on and on. But any one of these essential components of a full life is large enough to make one deeply fear its loss. A black woman once said to me in a workshop, "When I fought for Civil Rights, I always had my family and community to fall back on even when they didn't fully understand or accept what I was doing. I don't know if I could have borne losing them. And you people don't have either with you. It takes my breath away."

What does a woman have to do to get called a lesbian? Almost anything, sometimes nothing at all, but certainly anything that threatens the status quo, anything that steps out of role, anything that asserts the rights of women, anything that doesn't indicate submission and subordination. Assertiveness, standing up for oneself, asking for more pay, better working conditions, training for and accepting a non-traditional (you mean a man's?) job, enjoying the company of women, being financially independent, being in control of one's life, depending first and foremost upon oneself, thinking that one can do whatever needs to be done, but above all, working for the rights and equality of women.

In the backlash to the gains of the women's liberation movement, there has been an increased effort to keep definitions man-centered. Therefore, to work on behalf of women must mean to work against men. To love women must mean that one hates men. A very effective attack has been made against the word *feminist* to make it a derogatory word. In current backlash usage, *feminist* equals *man-hater* which equals *lesbian.* This formula is created in the hope that women will be frightened away from their work on behalf of women. Consequently, we now have women who believe in the rights of women and work for those rights while from fear deny that they are feminists, or refuse to use the word because it is so "abrasive."

So what does one do in an effort to keep from being called a lesbian? She steps back into line, into the role that is demanded of her, tries to behave in such a way that doesn't threaten the status of men, and if she works for women's rights, she begins modifying that work. When women's organizations begin doing significant social change work, they inevitably are lesbian-baited; that is, funders or institutions or community members tell us that they can't work with us because of our "man-hating attitudes" or the presence of lesbians. We are called too strident, told we are making enemies, not doing good.

The battered women's movement has seen this kind of attack: the pressure has been to provide services only, without analysis of the causes of violence against women and strategies for ending it. To provide only services without political analysis or direct action is to be in an approved "helping" role; to analyze the causes of violence against women is to begin the work toward changing an entire system of power and control. It is when we do the latter that we are threatened with the label of man-hater or lesbian. For my politics, if a women's social change organization has not been labeled lesbian or communist, it is probably not doing significant work; it is only "making nice."

Women in many of these organizations, out of fear of all the losses we are threatened with, begin to modify our work to make it more acceptable and less threatening to the male-dominated society which we originally set out to change. The work can no longer be radical (going to the root cause of the problem) but instead must be reforming, working only on the symptoms and not the cause. Real change for women becomes thwarted and stopped. The word *lesbian* is instilled with the power to halt our work and control our lives. And we give it its power with our fear.

In my view, homophobia has been one of the major causes of the failure of the women's liberation movement to make deep and lasting change. (The other major block has been racism.) We were fierce when we set out but when threatened with the loss of heterosexual privilege, we began putting on brakes. Our best-known nationally distributed women's magazine was reluctant to print articles about lesbians, began putting a man on the cover several times a year, and writing articles about women who succeeded in a man's world. We worried about our image, our being all right, our being "real women" despite our work. Instead of talking about the elimination of sexual gender roles, we stepped back and talked about "sex role stereotyping" as the issue. Change around the edges for middle-class white women began to be talked about as successes. We accepted tokenism and integration, forgetting

that equality for all women, for all people—and not just equality of white middle-class women with white men—was the goal that we could never put behind us.

But despite backlash and retreats, change is growing from within. The women's liberation movement is beginning to gain strength again because there are women who are talking about liberation for all women. We are examining sexism, racism, homophobia, classism, anti-Semitism, ageism, ableism, and imperialism, and we see everything as connected. This change in point of view represents the third wave of the women's liberation movement, a new direction that does not get mass media coverage and recognition. It has been initiated by women of color and lesbians who were marginalized or rendered invisible by the white heterosexual leaders of earlier efforts. The first wave was the 19th and early 20th century campaign for the vote; the second, beginning in the 1960s, focused on the Equal Rights Amendment and abortion rights. Consisting of predominantly white middle-class women, both failed in recognizing issues of equality and empowerment for all women. The third wave of the movement, multi-racial and multi-issued, seeks the transformation of the world for us all. We know that we won't get there until everyone gets there; that we must move forward in a great strong line, hand in hand, not just a few at a time.

We know that the arguments about homophobia originating from mental health and Biblical/religious attitudes can be settled when we look at the sexism that permeates religious and psychiatric history. The women of the third wave of the women's liberation movement know that *without the existence of sexism, there would be no homophobia.*

Finally, we know that as long as the word lesbian can strike fear in any woman's heart, then work on behalf of women can be stopped; the only successful work against sexism must include work against homophobia.

Study/Discussion Questions

1. What do homosexuals lose because of homophobia in American society?
2. Who benefits from homophobia in our society?
3. Why are lesbians threatening to the status quo, according to the author?
4. How does homophobia influence the behavior of heterosexuals? In what ways do straight women order their lives and behavior so that they won't be seen as gay?
5. How do straight men do the same thing?

Politics of Aging:
I'm *Not* Your Mother

Barbara Macdonald

Barbara Macdonald's opposition to ageism among feminists has been groundbreaking and persistent. She talks here about the still uphill battle of raising feminist consciousness about old women's lives. Ignored, condescended to, or idolized superficially, old women have not yet been fully recognized by a movement that sprang from, and continues to respond to, young women's interests. Macdonald makes her demands perfectly clear when she says, "We are not your mothers, grandmothers, or aunts. We will never build a true women's movement until we can organize as equals, woman to woman, without the masks of these family roles."

Ageism permeates all our relationships. It affects the decisions made by every woman reading this: her decision whether or not to have a child, her relationship to her children, her parents and their parents, to older women she meets (or doesn't), what she wears, the products she buys. At a much deeper level, she is made to dread the last half of her life. Feminism has no choice but to examine ageism as a form of disempowerment of all women.

Has it never occurred to younger women activists organizing around "women's" issues that old women are raped, are battered, are poor, that old women perform unpaid work in and out of the home, that old women are exploited by male medical practitioners. that old women are in jail, are political prisoners, that old women

have to deal with racism, classism, homophobia, anti-Semitism? I read feminist publications and not once have come across any group of younger women enraged or marching or organizing legal support because of anything that happened to an old woman. I have to read the *Los Angeles Times* or *Ageing International* to find out what's happening to the women of my generation, and the news is not good. Worldwide, old women are the poorest of the poor; in this country old women are the largest adult poverty group; 40.2 percent of old African American women are poor. The conditions in public housing for the elderly—in which most of the residents are women—are scandalous. Though it is illegal, old women in nursing homes are still used as guinea pigs for experimental drugs, a practice eradicated years ago in prisons.

Activists are not alone in their ageism. Has it never occurred to those in women's studies, as they ignore the meaning and politics of women's lives beyond our reproductive years, that this is male thinking? Has it never occurred to feminist theorists that ageism is a central feminist issue? Read the books used in women's studies as an old woman reads them. They discuss the socialization of little girls from the moment of birth, the struggles of women through adulthood—and then it turns out that "adulthood" ends with menopause, or with some attention to the woman in her fifties who is a displaced homemaker. Well, try being an 85-year-old woman in a shantytown in L.A., just trying to cross the street, when a government economic index has valued your life at only $2,311 in the courts (in contrast to $717,630 for a 34-year-old man).

Meanwhile, as the numbers of old women rapidly increase, the young women students of five years ago are now in the helping professions as geriatricians and social workers, because that's where the jobs are. They may call themselves feminists, but lacking any analysis of women's aging, they define old women as needy, simpleminded, and helpless—definitions that correlate conveniently with the services and salaries they have in mind.

But it's worse than that. Professionals and academicians don't hesitate to exploit us. They come to us for "oral histories," for their own agendas, to learn their feminist or lesbian or working-class or ethnic histories, with not the slightest interest in our present struggles. They come to fill in much-needed data for a thesis, or to justify a grant for some "service" for old women that imitates the mainstream (and which they plan to direct), or they come to get material for biographies of our friends and lovers. But they come not as equals, not with any knowledge of what our issues may be. They come to old women who have been serving young women for a lifetime and ask to be served one more time, and then they cover up

their embarrassment as they depart by saying that they felt as though we were their grandmothers, or mothers, or aunts.

Let me say it clearly: we are not your mothers, grandmothers, or aunts. We will never build a true women's movement until we can organize as equals, woman to woman, without the masks of these family roles.

It should come as no surprise that ageism has its roots in the patriarchal family. But in the years it took to get the women's movement to address ageism, feminism has moved from a position in which we recognized that the family is a building block of patriarchy—the place where sexist hierarchical roles are learned, where the socialization of girls takes place, the unit by which women are colonized, manipulated, controlled, and punished for infractions—back to a position of reaffirming the family. Mainstream feminists are buying the notion that as long as a woman has " a career," family is a safe and wholesome place to be. Radical feminists affirm family as a cultural source—a way of understanding our strengths and oppression as African American, Hispanic American, Asian American, Native American, Jewish, or working-class women. This return to family is reflected in our writings, where the father is seen less and less as the oppressor and more as another family member, oppressed by white male imperialism. (And believe me, he is.)

It will be for future feminist historians to explain how it was that in our reaffirmation of the family we never questioned its contradictions to our earlier feminist theory. Nor can history fail to note that our return to family coincides with a reactionary administration's push back to "family values"—any more than it can ignore that our lesbian baby boom coincided with Reagan's baby boom to save the GNP.

Unfortunately, the challenge of ageism came late in this wave of U.S. feminism. It came at a time when professionalism was on the rise and co-opting the women's movement.

The "therapizing" of the personal at the cost of the political was devastating: there we were again, trying to change ourselves rather than working to change society. So obviously this was not a time when feminism could ingest and integrate a radical new analysis. Yet the personal is political, and if we are to understand ageism, we have no choice but to bring family again under the lens of a feminist politic. In the past we examined the father as oppressor, we examined the mother as oppressor of the daughters, but what has never come under the feminist lens is the daughters' oppression of the mother—that woman who by definition is older than we are.

The source of your ageism, the reason you see older women as there to serve you, comes from family. It was in the patriarchal family that you learned that mother is there to serve you, that serving you is her purpose in life. This is not woman's definition of motherhood. This is man's definition, a male myth enforced in family and which you still believe—to your peril and mine. It infantilizes you and it erases me.

This myth of motherhood is not just a Euro-American phenomenon. In *Black Feminist Criticism,* Barbara Christian shows us how this myth is uncovered by Alice Walker's fiction, and by Buchi Emecheta's novels about Ibuza life. In Emecheta's *The Joys of Motherhood,* the old mother comes to see that she does not have to give all to her children for the rest of her life. But it is too late; her daughter still expects her mother's sacrifice and can see her in no other light.

The old woman is at the other end of that motherhood myth. She must not fight for her own issues—if she fights at all it must be for "future generations." Her greatest joy is seen as giving all to her grandchildren. And to the extent that she no longer directly serves a man—produces his children or is sexually desirable to him—she is erased more completely than she was as mother.

I am often asked whether or not I see progress since I first addressed ageism. Sometimes when I read about feminists wanting to "honor their elders," extolling old "crones" for their "wisdom and experience" while offering them professional advice on how to grow old—and never soliciting our input, appointing us to their boards, or offering us any piece of the action—I can't stomach the sentimentality and hypocrisy. And then I'll get a letter or a phone call and I'll realize that some feminists have really heard me, and suddenly I'm filled with enthusiasm and hope again. Communities of women make changes slowly, but the individual woman's change is often rapid. It is that "click" of insight, and we are permanently changed, reexamining everything from a new perspective. (I have to admit—just in case anybody still thinks old women are full of wisdom—that I expected that the whole feminist community would simultaneously make a great political leap on this issue. I think they heard invisibility. They didn't hear equality.) On my best days I feel the larger hope—that feminism has begun to open up to all the diverse voices in this country and around the globe, and that we are changing in deep ways.

Reports on aging populations worldwide suggest that ageism is as widespread as the patriarchal family, and that it is about women. This division of generations is fostered by the multinational corporations for profit: something reportedly in excess of $50 million will be spent on the Pepsi Cola "New Generation" theme. Youth has been so empowered that a product need only be associated with the young, and a disempowered adult world will buy it, wear it, drive it, and (even if it kills them) eat it.

This glorification of youth is a false power. But as images from multinationals bombard us, they widen the division between women on the basis of age. No wonder that your power as a younger woman—even as you move into middle age—is measured by the distance you can keep between yourself and me.

Demonstrator at women's rights rally, New York, August 1980.

Yet it is terribly exciting to be growing old at this time. I belong to a generation of women who have never existed. Never in history have there been 30 million Americans over 65, 13 million of us over 75, and with every year that we grow older we find that our age group is made up more and more of women, women who are outside of family, and whom society would like to silence. In so many ways, growing old contradicts the stereotype of the woman hunched over. It is a time for raising your head and looking at the view from the top of the hill, a view of the whole scene never before perceived.

But when I talk about the exhilaration of growing old now, much of my feeling is sobered by what is becoming more and more apparent. Certainly the achievements in controlling epidemics, tuberculosis, syphilis, and pneumonia have changed our lives immeasur-

ably, and our longevity. But any woman of color has every right to ask, "What do you mean 'our' lives?" From 1984 to 1986, the average life expectancy of European Americans rose from 75.3 to 75.4, while it declined from 69.7 to 69.4 for African Americans. (A major cause of these deaths is said to be homicides—which is another way of blaming the victims.) Longevity has a lot to do with privilege, with how much society values your life, or how expendable you are.

Old women meet yet another obstacle in organizing to end our invisibility. For we too come from "family," where we too learned a dread of old women.

We have become the old women we dreaded to be, and every old woman knows how odd that experience is. We are the women we once saw as boring. We are the women we didn't want to look at. We are the women we expected should sit on the sidelines always loving and admiring us. And we are the women we were once told we must have "respect" for, this admonition to prevent our taunting, our jeers, our ignoring—to prevent our showing contempt for old women.

As long as we hold to this legacy of our own ageism into our 60s, 70s, and 80s, we oppress ourselves from within. But I believe that every one of us can most (or part) of the time separate ourselves from our internalized ageism, can know that we are seen as ugly, but know that we are not ugly, only old. We look at ourselves and watch our bodies change with a sense of wonder, and know we are in step with life. We see that young women expect us to give them unconditional love, to step aside and acknowledge that their lives are more important than our own. We hear a young woman speaking dismissively to us, and we know she would say she has respect for old women, and we know we will not settle for honor or respect. *We will not settle for less than equality.*

When confronted about their ageism, younger women frequently reply, "But we too experience ageism—at 50 and 40 and even 30." It is true that all women experience the stigma of age (as defined by men) from girlhood to very old age, but the degree of ageism a younger woman feels is always determined by her distance from that ultimate "old." Unless you eliminate that stigma at the extreme end of life where it derives, you permit the image makers to apply it to a greater or lesser degree throughout all of women's lives.

First, old women are devalued and marginalized. "Old" then moves from 60 down to 50, and then women begin to grow uneasy at 40 and 30, as the image makers begin to make 10- and 12-year-old girls into whores and madonnas. Now we are seeing a kind of "child worship," as politicians tell us that what's happening in our lives as adult women now isn't important: what's important is that "the children are our future." When this kind of belief in discarding the old for the new is pushed along the continuum to the ultimate, we have "fetus worship." And when the fetus is more important than the woman who carries it, feminism is in deep trouble.

Study/Discussion Questions

1. How are older women treated as unimportant and of no value in our society, according to Macdonald?
2. How should young women, particularly feminists, treat older women differently, in the author's view?
3. What does the author mean when she says "I'm not your mother"?
4. Who does she want to be in relation to younger women? Describe the relationship she would like.

The House Slave

Rita Dove

The first horn lifts its arm over the dew-lit grass
and in the slave quarters there is a rustling—
children are bundled into aprons, cornbread

and water gourds grabbed, a salt pork breakfast taken.
I watch them driven into the vague before-dawn
while their mistress sleeps like an ivory toothpick

and Massa dreams of asses, rum and slave-funk.
I cannot fall asleep again. At the second horn,
the whip curls across the backs of the laggards—

sometimes my sister's voice, unmistaken, among them.
"Oh! pray," she cries. "Oh! pray!" Those days
I lie on my cot, shivering in the early heat,

and as the fields unfold to whiteness,
and they spill like bees among the fat flowers,
I weep. It is not yet daylight.

From *The Yellow House on the Corner,* Carnegie-Mellon University Press, copyright © 1980 by Rita Dove; reprinted by permission of the author.

slave cabin, sotterly plantation, maryland, 1989

Lucille Clifton

in this little room
note carefully

aunt nanny's bench

three words that label
things
aunt
is my parent's sister
nanny
my grandmother
bench
the board at which
i stare
the soft curved polished
wood
that held her bottom
after the long days
without end
without beginning
when she   aunt nanny   sat
feet dead against the dirty floor
humming for herself   humming
her own sweet human name

The Weakness

Toi Derricotte

That time my grandmother dragged me
through the perfume aisles at Saks, she held me up
by my arm, hissing, "Stand up,"
through clenched teeth, her eyes
bright as a dog's
cornered in the light.
She said it over and over,
as if she were Jesus,
and I were dead. She had been
solid as a tree,
a fur around her neck, a
light-skinned matron whose car was parked, who walked on swirling
marble and passed through
brass openings—in 1945.
There was not even a black
elevator operator at Saks.
The saleswoman had brought velvet
leggings to lace me in, and cooed,
as if in the service of all grandmothers.
My grandmother had smiled, but not
hungrily, not like my mother
who hated them, but wanted to please,
and they had smiled back, as if
they were wearing wooden collars.
When my legs gave out, my grandmother
dragged me up and held me like God
holds saints by the
roots of the hair. I begged her
to believe I couldn't help it. Stumbling,
her face white

with sweat, she pushed me through the crowd, rushing
away from those eyes
that saw through
her clothes, under
her skin, all the way down
to the transparent
genes confessing.

VIOLENCE AGAINST WOMEN

Rape

Susan Griffin

In this selection from her book, Rape: The Power of Consciousness, *Susan Griffin makes the crucial point that rape is an act of violence, and not "simply" a sexual act. While myths of seductive victims and impulsive perpetrators abound, Griffin argues that rape in our society is in fact a much less haphazard occurrence than such fictions would suggest. Rape, she writes, "is a kind of terrorism which severely limits the freedom of women and makes women dependent on men."*

I

I have never been free of the fear of rape. From a very early age I, like most women, have thought of rape as part of my natural environment—something to be feared and prayed against like fire or lightning. I never asked why men raped; I simply thought it one of the many mysteries of human nature.

I was, however, curious enough about the violent side of humanity to read every crime magazine I was able to ferret away from my grandfather. Each issue featured at least one "sex crime," with pictures of a victim, usually in a pearl necklace, and of the ditch or the orchard where her body was found. I was never certain why the victims were always women, nor what the motives of the murderer were, but I did guess that the world was not a safe place for women. I observed that my grandmother was meticulous about locks, and quick to draw the shades before anyone removed so much as a shoe. I sensed that danger lurked outside.

At the age of eight, my suspicions were confirmed. My grandmother took me to the back of the house where the men wouldn't hear, and told me that strange men wanted to do harm to little girls. I learned not to walk on dark streets, not to talk to strangers, or get into strange cars, to lock doors, and to be modest. She never explained why a man would want to harm a little girl, and I never asked.

If I thought for a while that my grandmother's fears were imaginary, the illusion was brief. That year, on the way home from school, a schoolmate a few years older than I tried to rape me. Later, in an obscure aisle of the local library (while I was reading *Freddy the Pig*) I turned to discover a man exposing himself. Then, the friendly man around the corner was arrested for child molesting.

From *Rape: The Power of Consciousness,* San Francisco: Harper & Row, 1979, pp. 3–22. Copyright © Susan Griffin.

My initiation to sexuality was typical. Every woman has similar stories to tell—the first man who attacked her may have been a neighbor, a family friend, an uncle, her doctor, or perhaps her own father. And women who grow up in New York City always have tales about the subway.

But though rape and the fear of rape are a daily part of every woman's consciousness, the subject is so rarely discussed by that unofficial staff of male intellectuals (who write the books which study seemingly every other form of male activity) that one begins to suspect a conspiracy of silence. And indeed, the obscurity of rape in print exists in marked contrast to the frequency of rape in reality, for *forcible rape is the most frequently committed violent crime in America today.* The Federal Bureau of Investigation classes three crimes as violent: murder, aggravated assault, and forcible rape. In 1968, 31,060 rapes were reported. According to the FBI and independent criminologists, however, to approach accuracy this figure must be multiplied by at least a factor of ten to compensate for the fact that most rapes are not reported; when these compensatory mathematics are used, there are more rapes committed than aggravated assaults and homicides.

When I asked Berkeley, California's Police Inspector in charge of rape investigation if he knew why men rape women, he replied that he had not spoken with "these people and delved into what really makes them tick, because that really isn't my job. . . ." However, when I asked him how a woman might prevent being raped, he was not so reticent, "I wouldn't advise any female to go walking around alone at night . . . and she should lock her car at all times." The Inspector illustrated his warning with a grisly story about a man who lay in wait for women in the back seats of their cars, while they were shopping in a local supermarket. This man eventually murdered one of his rape victims. "Always lock your car," the Inspector repeated, and then added, without a hint of irony, "Of course, you don't have to be paranoid about this type of thing."

The Inspector wondered why I wanted to write about rape. Like most men he did not understand the urgency of the topic, for, after all, men are not raped. But like most women I had spent considerable time speculating on the true nature of the rapist. When I was very young, my image of the "sexual offender" was a nightmarish amalgamation of the bogey man and Captain Hook: he wore a black cape, and he cackled. As I matured, so did my image of the rapist. Born into the psychoanalytic age, I tried to "understand" the rapist. Rape, I came to believe, was only one of many unfortunate evils produced by sexual repression. Reasoning by tautology, I concluded that any man who would rape a woman must be out of his mind.

Yet, though the theory that rapists are insane is a popular one, this belief has no basis in fact. According to Professor Menachem Amir's study of 646 rape cases in Philadelphia, *Patterns in Forcible Rape,* men who rape are not abnormal. Amir writes, "Studies indicate that sex offenders do not constitute a unique or psychopathological type; nor are they as a group invariably more disturbed than the control groups to which they are compared." Alan Taylor, a parole officer who has worked with rapists in the prison facilities at San Luis Obispo, California, stated the question in plainer language, "Those men were the most normal men there. They had a lot of hangups, but they were the same hang-ups as men walking out on the street."

Another canon in the apologetics of rape is that, if it were not for learned social controls, all men would rape. Rape is held to be natural behavior, and not to rape must be learned. But in truth rape is not universal to the human species. Moreover, studies of rape in our culture reveal that, far from being impulsive behavior, most rape is planned. Professor Amir's study reveals that in cases of group rape (the "gangbang" of masculine slang) 90 percent of the rapes were planned; in pair rapes, 83 percent of the rapes were planned; and in single rapes, 58 percent were planned. These figures should significantly discredit the image of the rapist as a man who is suddenly overcome by sexual needs society does not allow him to fulfill.

Far from the social control of rape being learned, comparisons with other cultures lead one to suspect that, in our society, it is rape itself that is learned. (The fact that rape is against the law should not be considered proof that rape is not in fact encouraged as part of our culture.)

This culture's concept of rape as an illegal, but still understandable, form of behavior is not a universal one. In her study *Sex and Temperament,* Margaret Mead describes a society that does not share our views. The Arapesh do not " . . . have any conception of the male nature that might make rape understandable to them." Indeed our interpretation of rape is a product of our conception of the nature of male sexuality. A common retort to the question, why don't women rape men, is the myth that men have greater sexual needs, that their sexuality is more urgent than women's. And it is the nature of human beings to want to live up to what is expected of them.

And this same culture which expects aggression from the male expects passivity from the female. Conveniently, the companion myth about the nature of female sexuality is that all women secretly want to be raped. Lurking beneath her modest female exterior is a subconscious desire to be ravished. The following description of a stag movie, written by Brenda Starr in Los Angeles' underground paper, *Everywoman,* typifies this male fantasy. The movie "showed a woman in her underclothes reading on her bed. She is interrupted by a rap-

ist with a knife. He immediately wins her over with his charm and they get busy sucking and fucking." An advertisement in the *Berkeley Barb* reads, "Now as all women know from their daydreams, rape has a lot of advantages. Best of all it's so simple. No preparation necessary, no planning ahead of time, no wondering if you should or shouldn't; just whang! bang!" Thanks to Masters and Johnson even the scientific canon recognizes that for the female, "whang! bang!" can scarcely be described as pleasurable.

Still, the male psyche persists in believing that, protestations and struggles to the contrary, deep inside her mysterious feminine soul, the female victim has wished for her own fate. A young woman who was raped by the husband of a friend said that days after the incident the man returned to her home, pounded on the door and screamed to her, "Jane, Jane. You loved it. You know you loved it."

The theory that women like being raped extends itself by deduction into the proposition that most or much of rape is provoked by the victim. But this too is only myth. Though provocation, considered a mitigating factor in a court of law, may consist of only "a gesture," according to the Federal Commission on Crimes of Violence, only 4 percent of reported rapes involved any precipitative behavior by the woman.

The notion that rape is enjoyed by the victim is also convenient for the man who, though he would not commit forcible rape, enjoys the idea of its existence, as if rape confirms that enormous sexual potency which he secretly knows to be his own. It is for the pleasure of the armchair rapist that detailed accounts of violent rapes exist in the media. Indeed, many men appear to take sexual pleasure from nearly all forms of violence. Whatever the motivation, male sexuality and violence in our culture seem to be inseparable. James Bond alternately whips out his revolver and his cock, and though there is no known connection between the skills of gunfighting and love-making, pacifism seems suspiciously effeminate.

In a recent fictional treatment of the Manson case, Frank Conroy writes of his vicarious titillation when describing the murders to his wife:

> "Every single person there was killed." She didn't move.
> "It sounds like there was torture," I said. As the words left my mouth I knew there was no need to say them to frighten her into believing that she needed me for protection.

The pleasure he feels as his wife's protector is inextricably mixed with pleasure in the violence itself. Conroy writes, "I was excited by the killings, as one excited by catastrophe on a grand scale, as one is alert to pre-echoes of unknown changes, hints of unrevealed secrets, rumblings of chaos. . . ."

The attraction of the male in our culture to violence and death is a tradition Manson and his admirers are carrying on with tireless avidity (even presuming Manson's innocence, he dreams of the purification of fire and destruction). It was Malraux in his *Anti-Memoirs* who said that, for the male, facing death was the illuminating experience analogous to childbirth for the female. Certainly our culture does glorify war and shroud the agonies of the gunfighter in veils of mystery.

And in the spectrum of male behavior, rape, the perfect combination of sex and violence, is the penultimate act. Erotic pleasure cannot be separated from culture, and in our culture male eroticism is wedded to power. Not only should a man be taller and stronger than a female in the perfect love-match, but he must also demonstrate his superior strength in gestures of dominance which are perceived as amorous. Though the law attempts to make a clear division between rape and sexual intercourse, in fact the courts find it difficult to distinguish between a case where the decision to copulate was mutual and one where a man forced himself upon his partner.

The scenario is even further complicated by the expectation that, not only does a woman mean "yes" when she says "no," but that a really decent woman ought to begin by saying "no," and then be led down the primrose path to acquiescence. Ovid, the author of Western Civilization's most celebrated sex manual, makes this expectation perfectly clear:

> . . . and when I beg you to say "yes," say "no."
> Then let me lie outside your bolted door. . . .
> So Love grows strong. . . .

That the basic elements of rape are involved in all heterosexual relationships may explain why men often identify with the offender in this crime. But to regard the rapist as the victim, a man driven by his inherent sexual needs to take what will not be given him, reveals a basic ignorance of sexual politics. For in our culture heterosexual love finds an erotic expression through male dominance and female submission. A man who derives pleasure from raping a woman clearly must enjoy force and dominance as much or more than the simple pleasures of the flesh. Coitus cannot be experienced in isolation. The weather, the state of the nation, the level of sugar in the blood—all will affect a man's ability to achieve orgasm. If a man can achieve sexual pleasure after terrorizing and humiliating the object of his passion, and in fact while inflicting pain upon her, one must assume he derives pleasure directly from terrorizing, humiliating and harming a woman. According to Amir's study of forcible rape, on a statistical average the man who has been convicted of rape was found to have a normal sexual personality, tending to be different from the normal, well-adjusted male only in having a greater tendency to express violence and rage.

And if the professional rapist is to be separated from the average dominant heterosexual, it may be mainly a quantitative difference. For the existence of rape as an index to masculinity is not entirely metaphorical. Though this measure of masculinity seems to be more publicly exhibited among "bad boys" or aging bikers who practice sexual initiation through group rape, in fact, "good boys" engage in the same rites to prove their manhood. In Stockton, a small town in California which epitomizes silent-majority America, a bachelor party was given last summer for a young man about to be married. A woman was hired to dance "topless" for the amusement of the guests. At the high point of the evening the bridegroom-to-be dragged the woman into a bedroom. No move was made by any of his companions to stop what was clearly going to be an attempted rape. Far from it. As the woman described, "I tried to keep him away—told him of my Herpes Genitalis, et cetera, but he couldn't face the guys if he didn't screw me." After the bridegroom had finished raping the woman and returned with her to the party, far from chastising him, his friends heckled the woman and covered her with wine.

It was fortunate for the dancer that the bridegroom's friends did not follow him into the bedroom for, though one might suppose that in group rape, since the victim is outnumbered, less force would be inflicted on her, in fact, Amir's studies indicate, "the most excessive degrees of violence occurred in group rape." Far from discouraging violence, the presence of other men may in fact encourage sadism, and even cause the behavior. In an unpublished study of group rape by Gilbert Geis and Duncan Chappell, the authors refer to a study by W. H. Blanchard which relates,

> The leader of the male group . . . apparently precipitated and maintained the activity, despite misgivings, because of a need to fulfill the role that the other two men had assigned to him. "I was scared when it began to happen," he says. "I wanted to leave but I

didn't want to say it to the other guys—you know—that I was scared."

Thus it becomes clear that not only does our culture teach men the rudiments of rape, but society, or more specifically other men, encourage the practice of it.

II

Every man I meet wants to protect me. Can't figure out what from.
—*Mae West*

If a male society rewards aggressive, domineering sexual behavior, it contains within itself a sexual schizophrenia. For the masculine man is also expected to prove his mettle as a protector of women. To the naive eye, this dichotomy implies that men fall into one of two categories: those who rape and those who protect. In fact, life does not prove so simple. In a study euphemistically entitled "Sex Aggression by College Men," it was discovered that men who believe in a double standard of morality for men and women, who in fact believe most fervently in the ultimate value of virginity, are more liable to commit "this aggressive variety of sexual exploitation."

(At this point in our narrative it should come as no surprise that Sir Thomas Malory, creator of that classic tale of chivalry, *The Knights of the Round Table,* was himself arrested and found guilty for repeated incidents of rape.)

In the system of chivalry, men protect women against men. This is not unlike the protection relationship which the mafia established with small businesses in the early part of this century. Indeed, chivalry is an age-old protection racket which depends for its existence on rape.

According to the male mythology which defines and perpetuates rape, it is an animal instinct inherent in the male. The story goes that sometime in our pre-historical past, the male, more hirsute and burly than today's counterparts, roamed about an uncivilized landscape until he found a desirable female. (Oddly enough, this female is not pictured as more muscular than the modern woman.) Her mate does not bother with courtship. He simply grabs her by the hair and drags her to the closest cave. Presumably, one of the major advantages of modern civilization for the female has been the civilizing of the male. We call it chivalry.

But women do not get chivalry for free. According to the logic of sexual politics, we too have to civilize our behavior. (Enter chastity. Enter virginity. Enter monogamy.) For the female, civilized behavior means chastity before marriage and faithfulness within it. Chivalrous behavior in the male is supposed to protect that chastity from involuntary defilement. The fly in the ointment of this otherwise peaceful system is the fallen woman. She does not behave. And therefore she does not deserve protection. Or, to use another argument, a major tenet of the same value system: what has once been defiled cannot again be violated. One begins to suspect that it is the behavior of the fallen woman, and not that of the male, that civilization aims to control.

The assumption that a woman who does not respect the double standard deserves whatever she gets (or at the very least "asks for it") operates in the courts today. While in some states a man's previous rape convictions are not considered admissible evidence, the sexual reputation of the rape victim is considered a crucial element of the facts upon which the court must decide innocence or guilt.

The court's respect for the double standard manifested itself particularly clearly in the case of the People v. Jerry Plotkin. Mr. Plotkin, a 36-year-old jeweler, was tried for rape last spring in a San Francisco Superior Court. According to the woman who brought the charges, Plotkin, along with three other men, forced her at gunpoint to enter a car one night in October 1970. She was taken to Mr. Plotkin's fashionable apartment where he and the three other men first raped her and then, in the delicate language of the *S.F. Chronicle,* "subjected her to perverted sex acts." She was, she said, set free in the morning with the warning that she would be killed if she spoke to anyone about the event. She did report the incident to the police who then searched Plotkin's apartment and discovered a long list of names of women. Her name was on the list and had been crossed out.

In addition to the woman's account of her abduction and rape, the prosecution submitted four of Plotkin's address books containing the names of hundreds of women. Plotkin claimed he did not know all of the women since some of the names had been given to him by friends and he had not yet called on them. Several women, however, did testify in court that Plotkin had, to cite the *Chronicle,* "lured them up to his apartment under one pretext or another, and forced his sexual attentions on them."

Plotkin's defense rested on two premises. First, through his own testimony Plotkin established a reputation for himself as a sexual libertine who frequently picked up girls in bars and took them to his house where sexual relations often took place. He was the Playboy. He claimed that the accusation of rape, therefore, was false—this incident had simply been one of many casual sexual relationships, the victim one of many playmates. The second premise of the defense was that his accuser was also a sexual libertine. However, the picture created of the young woman (fully 13 years younger than Plotkin) was not akin to the lighthearted, gay-bachelor image projected by the defendant. On the contrary, the day after the defense cross-examined the woman, the *Chronicle* printed a story headlined, "Grueling Day For Rape Case Victim." (A leaflet passed out by women in front of the court-room was more succinct, "rape was committed by four men in a private apartment in October; on Thursday, it was done by a judge and a lawyer in a public courtroom.")

Through skillful questioning fraught with innuendo, Plotkin's defense attorney James Martin MacInnis portrayed the young woman as a licentious opportunist and unfit mother. MacInnis began by asking the young woman (then employed as a secretary) whether or not it was true that she was "familiar with liquor" and had worked as a "cocktail waitress." The young woman replied (the *Chronicle* wrote "admitted") that she had worked once or twice as a cocktail waitress. The attorney then asked if she had worked as a secretary in the financial district but had "left that employment after it was discovered that you had sexual intercourse on a couch in the office." The woman replied, "That is a lie. I left because I didn't like working in a one-girl office. It was too lonely." Then the defense asked if, while working as an attendant at a health club, "you were accused of having a sexual affair with a man?" Again the woman denied the story, "I was never accused of that."

Plotkin's attorney then sought to establish that his client's accuser was living with a married man. She responded that the man was separated from his wife. Finally he told the court that she had "spent the night" with another man who lived in the same building.

At this point in the testimony the woman asked Plotkin's defense attorney, "Am I on trial? . . . It is embarrassing and personal to admit these things to all these people. . . . I did not commit a crime. I am a human being." The lawyer, true to the chivalry of his class, apologized and immediately resumed questioning her, turning his attention to her children. (She is divorced, and the children at the time of the trial were in a foster home.) "Isn't it true that your two children have a sex game in which one gets on top of another and they—"That is

a lie!" the young woman interrupted him. She ended her testimony by explaining "They are wonderful children. They are not perverted."

The jury, divided in favor of acquittal ten to two, asked the court stenographer to read the woman's testimony back to them. After this reading, the Superior Court acquitted the defendant of both charges of rape and kidnapping.

According to the double standard a woman who has had sexual intercourse out of wedlock cannot be raped. Rape is not only a crime of aggression against the body; it is a transgression against chastity as defined by men. When a woman is forced into a sexual relationship, she has, according to the male ethos, been violated. But she is also defiled if she does not behave according to the double standard, by maintaining her chastity, or confining her sexual activities to a monogamous relationship.

One should not assume, however, that a woman can avoid the possibility of rape simply by behaving. Though myth would have it that mainly "bad girls" are raped, this theory has no basis in fact. Available statistics would lead one to believe that a safer course is promiscuity. In a study of rape done in the District of Columbia, it was found that 82 percent of the rape victims had a "good reputation." Even the Police Inspector's advice to stay off the streets is rather useless, for almost half of reported rapes occur in the home of the victim and are committed by a man she has never before seen. Like indiscriminate terrorism, rape can happen to any woman, and few women are ever without this knowledge.

But the courts and the police, both dominated by white males, continue to suspect the rape victim, *sui generis,* of provoking or asking for her own assault. According to Amir's study, the police tend to believe that a woman without a good reputation cannot be raped. The rape victim is usually submitted to countless questions about her own sexual mores and behavior by the police. This preoccupation is partially justified by the legal requirements for prosecution in a rape case. The rape victim must have been penetrated, and she must have made it clear to her assailant that she did not want penetration (unless of course she is unconscious). A refusal to accompany a man to some isolated place to allow him to touch her does not in the eyes of the court, constitute rape. She must have said "no" at the crucial genital moment. And the rape victim, to qualify as such, must also have put up a physical struggle—unless she can prove that to do so would have been to endanger her life.

But the zealous interest the police frequently exhibit in the physical details of a rape case is only partially explained by the requirements of the court. A woman who was raped in Berkeley was asked to tell the story of her rape four different times "right out in the street," while her assailant was escaping. She was then required to submit to a pelvic examination to prove that penetration had taken place. Later, she was taken to the police station where she was asked the same questions again: "Were you forced?" "Did he penetrate?" "Are you sure your life was in danger and you had no other choice?" This woman had been pulled off the street by a man who held a 10-inch knife at her throat and forcibly raped her. She was raped at midnight and was not able to return to her home until five in the morning. Police contacted her twice again in the next week, once by telephone at two in the morning and once at four in the morning. In her words, "The rape was probably the least traumatic incident of the whole evening. If I'm ever raped again, . . . I wouldn't report it to the police because of all the degradation. . . ."

If white women are subjected to unnecessary and often hostile questioning after having been raped, third world women are often not believed at all. According to the white male ethos (which is not only sexist but racist), third world women are defined from birth as "impure." Thus the white male is provided with a

pool of women who are fair game for sexual imperialism. Third world women frequently do not report rape and for good reason. When blues singer Billie Holliday was 10 years old, she was taken off to a local house by a neighbor and raped. Her mother brought the police to rescue her, and she was taken to the local police station crying and bleeding:

> When we got there, instead of treating me and Mom like somebody who called the cops for help, they treated me like I'd killed somebody. . . . I guess they had me figured for having enticed this old goat into the whorehouse. . . . All I know for sure is they threw me into a cell . . . a fat white matron . . . saw I was still bleeding, she felt sorry for me and gave me a couple glasses of milk. But nobody else did anything for me except give me filthy looks and snicker to themselves.
>
> After a couple of days in a cell they dragged me into a court. Mr. Dick got sentenced to five years. They sentenced me to a Catholic institution.

Clearly the white man's chivalry is aimed only to protect the chastity of "his" women.

As a final irony, that same system of sexual values from which chivalry is derived has also provided womankind with an unwritten code of behavior, called femininity, which makes a feminine woman the perfect victim of sexual aggression. If being chaste does not ward off the possibility of assault, being feminine certainly increases the chances that it will succeed. To be submissive is to defer to masculine strength; is to lack muscular development or any interest in defending oneself; is to let doors be opened, to have one's arm held when crossing the street. To be feminine is to wear shoes which make it difficult to run; skirts which inhibit one's stride; underclothes which inhibit the circulation. Is it not an intriguing observation that those very clothes which are thought to be flattering to the female and attractive to the male are those which make it impossible for a woman to defend herself against aggression?

Each girl as she grows into womanhood is taught fear. Fear is the form in which the female internalizes both chivalry and the double standard. Since, biologically speaking, women in fact have the same if not greater potential for sexual expression as do men, the woman who is taught that she must behave differently from a man must also learn to distrust her own carnality. She must deny her own feelings and learn not to act from them. She fears herself. This is the essence of passivity and, of course, a woman's passivity is not simply sexual but functions to cripple her from self-expression in every area of her life.

Passivity itself prevents a woman from ever considering her own potential for self-defense and forces her to look to men for protection. The woman is taught fear, but this time fear of the other; and yet her only relief from this fear is to seek out the other. Moreover, the passive woman is taught to regard herself as impotent, unable to act, unable even to perceive, in no way self-sufficient, and finally, as the object and not the subject of human behavior. It is in this sense that a woman is deprived of the status of a human being. She is not free to be.

III

Since Ibsen's Nora slammed the door on her patriarchical husband, woman's attempt to be free has been more or less fashionable. In this nineteenth-century portrait of a woman leaving her marriage, Nora tells her husband, "Our home has been nothing but a playroom. I have been your doll-wife just as at home I was papa's doll-child." And, at least on the stage, "The Doll's House" crumbled, leaving audiences with hope for the fate of the modern woman. And today, as in the past, womankind has not lacked examples of liberated women to emulate: Emma Goldman, Greta Garbo and Isadora Duncan all denounced marriage and the double standard, and believed their right to freedom included sexual independence; but still their example has not affected the lives of millions of women who continue to marry, divorce and remarry, living out their lives dependent on the status and economic power of men. Patriarchy still holds the average woman prisoner not because she lacks the courage of an Isadora Duncan, but because the material conditions of her life prevent her from being anything but an object.

In the *Elementary Structures of Kinship*, Claude Levi-Strauss gives to marriage this universal description, "It is always a system of exchange that we find at the origin of the rules of marriage." In this system of exchange, a woman is the "most precious possession." Levi-Strauss continues that the custom of including women as booty in the marketplace is still so general that "a whole volume would not be sufficient to enumerate instances of it." Levi-Strauss makes it clear that he does not exclude Western Civilization from his definition of "universal" and cites examples from modern wedding ceremonies. (The marriage ceremony is still one in which the husband and wife become one, and "that one is the husband.")

The legal proscription against rape reflects this possessory view of women. An article in the 1952–53 *Yale Law Journal* describes the legal rationale behind laws against rape:

> In our society sexual taboos, often enacted into law, buttress a system of monogamy based upon the law of "free bargaining" of the potential spouses. Within this process the woman's power to withhold or grant sexual access is an important bargaining weapon.

Presumably then, laws against rape are intended to protect the right of a woman, not for physical self-determination, but for physical "bargaining." The article goes on to explain explicitly why the preservation of the bodies of women is important to men:

> The consent standard in our society does more than protect a significant item of social currency for women; it fosters, and is in turn bolstered by, a masculine pride in the exclusive possession of a sexual object. The consent of a woman to sexual intercourse awards the man a privilege of bodily access, a personal "prize," whose value is enhanced by sole ownership. An additional reason for the man's condemnation of rape may be found in the threat to his status from a decrease in the "value" of his sexual possession which would result from forcible violation.

The passage concludes by making clear whose interest the law is designed to protect. "The man responds to this undercutting of his status as possessor of the girl with hostility toward the rapist; no other restitution device is available. The law of rape provides an orderly outlet for his vengeance." Presumably the female victim in any case will have been sufficiently socialized so as not to consciously feel any strong need for vengeance. If she does feel this need, society does not speak to it.

The laws against rape exist to protect rights of the male as possessor of the female body, and not the right of the female over her own body. Even without this enlightening passage from the *Yale Law Review*, the laws themselves are clear: In no state can a man be accused of raping his wife. How can any man steal what already belongs to him? It is in the sense of rape as theft of another man's property that Kate Millett writes, "Traditionally rape has been viewed as an offense one male commits against another—a matter of abusing his woman." In raping another man's woman, a man may aggrandize his own manhood and concurrently reduce that of another man.

Thus a man's honor is not subject directly to rape, but only indirectly, through "his" woman.

If the basic social unit is the family, in which the woman is a possession of her husband, the superstructure of society is a male hierarchy, in which men dominate other men (or patriarchal families dominate other patriarchal families). And it is no small irony that, while the very social fabric of our male-dominated culture denies women equal access to political, economic and legal power, the literature, myth and humor of our culture depict women not only as the power behind the throne, but the real source of the oppression of men. The religious version of this fairy tale blames Eve for both carnality and eating of the tree of knowledge, at the same time making her gullible to the obvious devices of a serpent. Adam, of course, is merely the trusting victim of love. Certainly this is a biased story. But no more biased than the one television audiences receive today from the latest slick comedians. Through a media which is owned by men, censored by a state dominated by men, all the evils of this social system which make a man's life unpleasant are blamed upon "the wife." The theory is: were it not for the female who waits and plots to "trap" the male into marriage, modern man would be able to achieve Olympian freedom. She is made the scapegoat for a system which is in fact run by men.

Nowhere is this more clear than in the white racist use of the concept of white womanhood. The white male's open rape of black women, coupled with his overweening concern for the chastity and protection of his wife and daughters, represents an extreme of sexist and racist hypocrisy. While on the one hand she was held up as the standard for purity and virtue, on the other the Southern white woman was never asked if she wanted to be on a pedestal, and in fact any deviance from the male-defined standards for white womanhood was treated severely. (It is a powerful commentary on American racism that the historical role of Blacks as slaves, and thus possessions without power, has robbed black women of legal and economic protection through marriage. Thus black women in Southern society and in the ghettoes of the North have long been easy game for white rapists.) The fear that black men would rape white women was classic paranoia. Quoting from Ann Breen's unpublished study of racism and sexism in the South, "The New South: White Man's Country," Frederick Douglass legitimately points out that, had the black man wished to rape white women, he had ample opportunity to do so during the Civil War when white women, the wives, sisters, daughters and mothers of the rebels, were left in the care of Blacks. But yet not a single act of rape was committed during this time. The Ku Klux Klan, who tarred and feathered black men and lynched them in the honor of the purity of white womanhood, also applied tar and feathers to a Southern white woman accused of bigamy, which leads one to suspect that Southern white men were not so much outraged at the violation of the woman as a person, in the few instances where rape was actually committed by black men, but at the violation of his property rights. In the situation where a black man was found to be having sexual relations with a white woman, the white woman could exercise skin-privilege, and claim that she had been raped in which case the black man was lynched. But if she did not claim rape, she herself was subject to lynching.

In constructing the myth of white womanhood so as to justify the lynching and oppression of black men and women, the white male has created a convenient symbol of his own power which has resulted in black hostility toward the white "bitch," accompanied by a fear on the part of many white women of the black rapist. Moreover, it is not surprising that after being told for two centuries that he wants to rape white women, black men have begun to actually commit that act. But it is crucial to note that the frequency of this practice is outrageously exaggerated in the white mythos. Ninety per-cent of reported rape is intra- not inter-racial.

In *Soul on Ice,* Eldridge Cleaver has described the mixing of a rage against white power with the internalized sexism of a black man raping a white woman.

> Somehow I arrived at the conclusion that, as a matter of principle, it was of paramount importance for me to have an antagonistic, ruthless attitude toward white women. . . . Rape was an insurrectionary act. It delighted me that I was defying and trampling upon the white man's law, upon his system of values and that I was defiling his women—and this point, I believe, was the most satisfying to me because I was very resentful over the historical fact of how the white man has used the black woman.

Thus a black man uses white women to take out his rage against white men. But, in fact, whenever a rape of a white woman by a black man does take place, it is again the white man who benefits. First, the act itself terrorizes the white woman and makes her more dependent on the white male for protection. Then, if the woman prosecutes her attacker, the white man is afforded legal opportunity to exercise overt racism. Of course, the knowledge of the rape helps to perpetuate two myths which are beneficial to white male rule—the bestiality of the black man and the desirability of white women. Finally, the white man surely benefits because he himself is not the object of attack—he has been allowed to stay in power.

Indeed, the existence of rape in any form is beneficial to the ruling class of white males. For rape is a kind of terrorism which severely limits the freedom of women and makes women dependent on men. Moreover, in the act of rape, the rage that one man may harbor toward another higher in the male hierarchy can be deflected toward a female scapegoat. For every man there is always someone lower on the social scale on whom he can take out his aggressions. And that is any woman alive.

This oppressive attitude towards women finds its institutionalization in the traditional family. For it is assumed that a man "wears the pants" in his family—he exercises the option of rule whenever he so chooses. Not that he makes all the decisions—clearly women make most of the important day-to-day decisions in a family. But when a conflict of interest arises, it is the man's interest which will prevail. His word, in itself, is more powerful. He lords it over his wife in the same way his boss lords it over him, so that the very process of exercising his power becomes as important an act as obtaining whatever it is his power can get for him. This notion of power is key to the male ego in this culture, for the two acceptable measures of masculinity are a man's power over women and his power over other men. A man may boast to his friends that "I have 20 men working for me." It is also aggrandizement of his ego if he has the financial power to clothe his wife in furs and jewels. And, if a man lacks the wherewithal to acquire such power, he can always express his rage through equally masculine activities—rape and theft. Since male society defines the female as a possession, it is not surprising that the felony most often committed together with rape is theft. As the following classic tale of rape points out, the elements of theft, violence and forced sexual relations merge into an indistinguishable whole.

The woman who told the following story was acquainted with the man who tried to rape her. When the man learned that she was going to be staying alone for the weekend, he began early in the day a polite campaign to get her to go out with him. When she continued to refuse his request, his chivalrous mask dropped away:

I had locked all the doors because I was afraid, and I don't know how he got in; it was probably through the screen door. When I woke up, he was shaking my leg. His eyes were red, and I knew he had been drinking or smoking. I thought l would try to talk my way out of it. He started by saying that he waned to sleep with me, and then he got angrier and angrier, until he started to say, "I want pussy," "I want pussy." Then, I got scared and tried to push him away. That's when he started to force himself on me. It was awful. It was the most humiliating, terrible feeling. He was forcing my legs apart and ripping my clothes off. And it was painful. I did fight him—he was slightly drunk and I was able to keep him away. I had taken judo a few years back, but I was afraid to throw a chop for fear that he'd kill me. I could see he was getting more and more violent. I was thinking wildly of some way to get out of this alive, and then I said to him, "Do you want money? I'll give you money." We had money but I was also thinking that if I got to the back room I could telephone the police—as if the police would have even helped. It was a stupid thing to think of because obviously he would follow me. And he did. When he saw me pick up the phone, he tried to tie the cord around my neck. I screamed at him that I did have the money in another room, that I was going to call the police because I was scared, but that I would never tell anybody what happened. It would be an absolute secret. He said, "okay," and I went to get the money. But when he got it, all of a sudden he got this crazy look in his eye and he said to me, "Now I'm going to kill you." Then I started saying my prayers. I knew there was nothing I could do. He started to hit me—I still wasn't sure if he wanted to rape me at this point—or just to kill me. He was hurting me, but hadn't yet gotten me into a stranglehold because he was still drunk and off balance. Somehow we pushed into the kitchen where I kept looking at this big knife. But I didn't pick it up. Somehow, no matter how much I hated him at that moment, I still couldn't imagine putting the knife in his flesh, and then I was afraid he would grab it and stick it into me. Then he was hitting me again and somehow we pushed through the back door of the kitchen and onto the porch steps. We fell down the steps and that's when he started to strangle me. He was on top of me. He just went on and on until finally I lost consciousness. I did scream, though my screams sounded like whispers to me. But what happened was that a cab driver happened by and frightened him away. The cab driver revived me—I was out only a minute at the most. And then I ran across the street and I grabbed the woman who was our neighbor and screamed at her, "Am I alive? Am I still alive?"

Rape is an act of aggression in which the victim is denied her self-determination. It is an act of violence which, if not actually followed by beatings or murder, nevertheless always carries with it the threat of death. And finally, rape is a form of mass terrorism, for the victims of rape are chosen indiscriminately, but the propagandists for male supremacy broadcast that it is women who cause rape by being unchaste or in the wrong place at the

wrong time—in essence, by behaving as though they were free.

The threat of rape is used to deny women employment. (In California, the Berkeley Public Library, until pushed by the Federal Employment Practices Commission, refused to hire female shelvers because of perverted men in the stacks.) The fear of rape keeps women off the streets at night. Keeps women at home. Keeps women passive and modest for fear that they be thought provocative.

It is part of human dignity to be able to defend oneself, and women are learning. Some women have learned karate; some to shoot guns. And yet we will not be free until the threat of rape and the atmosphere of violence is ended, and to end that the nature of male behavior must change.

But rape is not an isolated act that can be rooted out from patriarchy without ending patriarchy itself. The same men and power structure who victimize women are engaged in the act of raping Vietnam, raping Black people and the very earth we live upon. Rape is a classic act of domination where, in the words of Kate Millett, "the emotions of hatred, contempt, and the desire to break or violate personality," take place. This breaking of the personality characterizes modern life itself. No simple reforms can eliminate rape. As the symbolic expression of the white male hierarchy, rape is the quintessential act of our civilization, one which, Valerie Solanis warns, is in danger of "humping itself to death."

Study/Discussion Questions

1. According to Griffin, what kind of man rapes women?
2. What myths about women's desires and behavior make rape seem more acceptable?
3. In what ways is rape an "understandable" crime in our society? Do our ideas about masculinity make rape seem somehow logical?
4. How does rape serve the interests of all men, according to the author?
5. In what ways does the fear of rape dictate women's behavior? What freedoms can men enjoy because they do not fear rape?

Flash Exercise

Rape

Consider the impact the existence of rape has had on your life.
How often do you think about rape, and under what circumstances?
What messages have you learned about rapists?
What messages have you learned about women who get raped?
What might be different in your life if rape did not exist?

Acquaintance Rape: Revolution and Reaction

Paula Kamen

When then-Princeton graduate student Katie Roiphe published The Morning After: Sex, Fear, and Feminism on Campus *(Little, Brown) in 1993, she sparked a debate of great proportions among those concerned with violence against women. Arguing that radical feminists across the nation had exaggerated and distorted the danger young women face from rape, Roiphe asserted that feminists' heightened attention to danger on many campuses had made women more vulnerable in certain fundamental ways. In this article, Paula Kamen takes to task Roiphe and others who seem to be fighting for media time to denounce as apocryphal the current, and in her view, very real, "date rape" crisis. These denunciations, often drawing on false statistics, threaten to "push acquaintance rape back in the closet," according to Kamen. It would be better to spend our energies educating women and men, as a few innovative campus-based programs are doing, in rape prevention.*

Over the past decade, I have witnessed a startling new brand of sex talk—more disarming, uninhibited, and brazen than anything you would ever hear even on the most bold late-night 900-number party chat line or FCC-challenging radio talk show.

One particular conversation that comes to mind took place on an October evening among all males, not in the expected locker room, but in another distinct Old Spice-laced bastion: a fraternity house at the University of Wisconsin in Madison. The men addressed what had gone previously unspoken within their ivy-covered walls: the meaning of sex. Their mysterious, long-haired and heavy-set visitor, Joe Weinberg, was challenging them to think about any pressure they may feel to "score" and become part of the "boys' club." First, Weinberg explored some of the "universal" language men use. He then asked his group to come up with positive words to describe a sexually active female. There were none. Then the same to refer to a man. The list goes on: "Cassanova, stud, player . . ."

This type of discussion, which Weinberg has led with men on more than 150 campuses

From *"Bad Girls"/"Good Girls,"* edited by Nan Bauer Maglin and Donna Perry, Rutgers University Press, 1996, pp. 137–147. Copyright © 1996 by Paula Kamen.

throughout the country since 1986—and has recently expanded to include groups in high schools and prisons—takes rape prevention to new levels.

Here, at the University of Wisconsin, men are addressing men. And, Weinberg's recommendations go beyond the behavior modification steps of going out in groups and not drinking to extremes to actually look at how men perceive women. Not only does this new breed of educator address reducing the opportunity for assault, but they also challenge the types of attitudes that lead men to be motivated to rape. Instead of preaching or thought policing, as the words "peer educator" may imply, men like Weinberg often lead nonjudgmental discussions, where men are free to express their darkest and most un-PC thoughts and fears about women. Weinberg says he doesn't criticize men for what can be perceived as sexist or insensitive comments, which reflect what they personally and naturally have felt as males growing up in our culture.

This radical approach is part of a larger and evolving dialogue on the issue of acquaintance rape, which I have witnessed taking place over the last decade on college campuses and beyond. More men and women are questioning the roots of sexual violence and refining and focusing their critiques.

As testament to their success, young activists are provoking controversy—and a mighty backlash in the media. Critics attest that this activism has only been destructive, that action against acquaintance rape is just "sexual correctness" that is ruining sex and straitjacketing natural human activity with too many protective rules. But I have witnessed a different result of activism, a more liberating one than is most often lamented in the mainstream press. Activists now are assuming a challenge in talking about sex in new terms, with new candor, and demystifying it. They are encouraging women to take more control and men to understand and modify their behavior.

Weinberg, a former carpenter now in his early forties, got interested in this small but telling movement after joining Men Stopping Rape in Madison, one of 100 to 150 campus and community-based men's prevention groups operating in the early 1990s. Other men have become visible doing this work. At Brown University students sponsored a 1989 conference called Men Can Stop Rape Now. That same year, Ithaca Rape Crisis, Inc., surveyed 133 other community centers and found that 118 worked with male volunteers.[1]

Such workshops aren't a panacea to dismantle attitudes about aggression and domination; indeed, most men exposed to such antirape messages don't reach instant feminist epiphany, question fundamentals of their patriarchy-induced identity, and then devote their weekends to volunteering on the rape crisis lines. But, at least for a start, many young men are becoming more aware about sexual assault between acquaintances. For men my age and younger, in their teens and twenties, rape among people who know each other has at least become an issue, a legitimate topic in public debate—not simply dismissed as a night of bad sex or a private dare or joke as in the past.

Indeed, "acquaintance rape" is a bona fide term, now used regularly in mainstream society. It has been a heading in the *Reader's Guide to Periodical Literature* since 1992 ("date rape" since 1987), and a topic discussed at college orientations and even fraternity meetings nationwide for the past decade. In a recent *Chicago Tribune* report about one local student orientation, readers can see how date rape has become a standard issue in campus life.

In a residence hall lounge at Northwestern, a campus official read to about 60 students the university's definition of sexual assault.

The students also watched a campus-produced video on sexual assault, and afterward, the official led a discussion. Consent must be given clearly and unmistakably to avoid a charge of assault, she said. (James 1994: 2: 7)[2]

I have seen this movement to examine men's behavior evolve slowly. In 1985, when I was a freshman at the Big Ten giant, the University of Illinois in Urbana-Champaign, about the only rape prevention education offered throughout the country was directed exclusively toward women, warning them about strangers. But in the next few years I witnessed the university develop a model program for prevention and education that targets men. More and more university programs across the country have also evolved to look at acquaintance rape, and many schools are including a component to examine men's attitudes and responsibilities. This focus is radical because it takes the exclusive and historical burden of responsibility off women's shoulders. "It's acknowledging that men are the ones committing rape," said Barb Gilbert, an architect of my campus program, in a 1989 interview. "And the only role that women have is to the extent that we can prevent opportunity and prevent the effectiveness [protect ourselves]."

Men's antirape activism is part of a broad, hardly recognized, slowly developing sexual revolution of this generation. While the sexual revolution of the 1970s was largely about women saying yes (to really prove themselves liberated), a new movement is empowering them to also say no, along with when, where, and how. As a result, women are more closely examining what turns them off—and also what turns them on. They are daring to study and even critique what happens to them in bed. Young women are not content with the rules of the old 1970s sexual revolution, which have collapsed under the weight of their own rigidity—and stupidity. That movement, which was liberating mostly for men, has saddled women with too much old patriarchal baggage, including a continuing double standard for women, which discourages communication and hon-

esty from both sexes. Activists are striving for a new model and new freedoms that offer pleasure and freedom from absolute rules, as well as self-respect, autonomy, and responsibility. Their movement is parallel to others I have seen become increasingly visible on college campuses, including efforts to gain reproductive freedom, fight sexual harassment, and secure rights for gays and lesbians.

ANTIFEMINIST BACKLASH

Yet, in the past few years, I have also seen the antifeminist skeptics eclipse all others in the popular press and in slick upscale magazines. While feminists come in all ideological shapes and sizes, the most "wacky" ones have always made the best copy. Most magazine articles addressing acquaintance rape in 1993 and 1994 take the angle that date rape is mostly hype, and seriously question the extent and even the existence of the problem.[3]

A variety of critics, from lofty newspaper columnists to the writers of *Saturday Night Live,* have taken easy aim at "feminist antisex hysteria" by making fun of the extreme Antioch College guidelines, first widely publicized in 1993. The sexual offense policy from this small Ohio liberal arts college has come to represent feminists' supposedly overpowering rhetorical invasion of the minds of college students. The eight-page policy states that students must give and get verbal consent before "each new level of physical and/or sexual contact/conduct." "Sexual contact" includes the touching of thighs, genitals, buttocks, the pubic region, or the breast/chest area. The policy spells out six categories of offenses: rape, sexual assault, sexual imposition, insistent and/or persistent sexual harassment, nondisclosure of sexually transmitted diseases (STDs), and nondisclosure of positive HIV status. Complaints against violators can be brought before the campus judicial board.

Many conservative critics, including seemingly unlikely allies such as Camille Paglia and George Will,[4] employing every defense mechanism on a psychiatrist's diagnostic chart, reason that militant feminists have invented the problem of "acquaintance rape" and use this term at random to describe bad sex or an encounter that one regrets in the morning. Since the topic of date rape is no longer sexy because of its last few years of exposure in the press, this related topic—date-rape hysteria—has come in vogue. In 1993, "exposés" of date-rape hysteria have appeared as cover stories in *Newsweek* (in an article about "sexual correctness" [Crichton 1993]), *New York* magazine (Hellman 1993), and the *New York Times Magazine* (Roiphe 1993).[5] Christina Hoff Sommers reiterates many of these claims in *Who Stole Feminism?* (1994), boosted by three right-wing foundations that provided grants of at least $164,000 between 1991 and 1993 (Flanders 1994: 8).

A major leader of the date-rape hysteria charge was twenty-five-year-old Katie Roiphe, author of *The Morning After: Sex, Fear, and Feminism on Campus* (1993). She says such feminist discussion confuses young women into mislabeling a wide array of normal, often unpleasant, sexual experiences as rape. Her thesis is that the battle against date rape is a symptom of young women's general anxiety about sex. They allegedly displace their fear of sex onto a fear of rape. Roiphe reasons that since some cases are false, all claims of acquaintance rape are unfounded; if one is against rape, one must also be against sex. Those that speak out against rape are nothing but malleable dupes of feminists or hysterics, liars, or prudes.

A major gripe of Roiphe and others is that educators are putting an undue burden on men by advising them to obtain articulated mutual consent. "With their advice, their scenarios, their sample aggressive male, the message projects a clear comment on the nature of sexuality: women are often unwilling participants," Roiphe writes in her book (p. 61). Indeed, rape

educators do admit that women have been forced to have sex against their will by people they know. In contrast, Roiphe portrays an idealized, "post-feminist" reality that places men and women in a vacuum, untouched by social attitudes and pressures.

The greatest threat of Roiphe's distortions is that they push acquaintance rape back in the closet. Roiphe is characteristically narrow in her definition of what constitutes a "real" rape—incidents of violence that can never be confused with "bad sex." In her *New York Times Magazine* article, she gives as examples of rape brutal assaults by strangers, such as those of Bosnian girls and "a suburban teen-ager raped and beaten while walking home from a shopping mall" (p. 28). To back up her argument, Roiphe takes liberties with data. Her "findings" that discredit date-rape prevention work are often based on out-of-context second-hand false examples of radical feminist rhetoric and flimsy "evidence" that questions the validity of professionally scrutinized scientific studies.

A central target of Roiphe and others is a major influential 1985 survey by a University of Arizona Medical School professor Mary Koss sponsored by the Ms. Foundation and financed by the National Institute of Mental Health. One of the study's major findings was that 27.9 percent—or as most often quoted "one in four"—of the college women surveyed reported being the victim of a rape or attempted rape since the age of fourteen with a majority having known the assailants (Koss et al. 1987: 168; Warshaw 1988: 11).

Roiphe, Sommers and other critics cited here have condemned Koss's findings as invalid without ever contacting Koss to get her side of the story or further information. Roiphe repeats the most commonly waged criticism of Koss: "Seventy-three percent of the women categorized as rape victims did not initially define their experience as rape; it was Mary Koss, the psychologist conducting the study, who did." According to Roiphe "Today's definition has stretched beyond bruises and knives, threats of death or violence to include emotional pressure and the influence of alcohol."

However as all these critics failed to report, Koss makes clear that she used a standard legal definition of rape similar to that used in the majority of states (Koss et al. 1987: 166).[6] Also, contrary to Roiphe's allegations Koss did not make emotional pressure a variable in her 15.8 percent completed rape statistic. She does ask questions about "sexual coercion" but she does not include this group in the 27.9 percent statistic of rape or attempted rape (Koss et al. 1987: 166; Warshaw 1988: 207).

Koss explained to me that she included in her figures women who did not label their experiences as rape because of the prevailing public misconception that the law does not cover such cases of date rape. Also at the time of the 1985 survey public awareness about the possibility that an attack between acquaintances was legally rape was much lower than it is today.

Koss points out in her writings that the majority of her respondents who reported experiences legally defined as rape still indicated themselves that they felt victimized; she did not project this onto them. According to the study, as all these critics fail to mention, of respondents who reported an incident of forced sex (whether or not they called it rape) 30 percent considered suicide afterward, 31 percent sought psychotherapy, and 82 percent said the experience had changed them (Warshaw 1988: 66).

Another major attack on Koss's data is the inclusion of her question "Have you had sexual intercourse when you didn't want to because a man gave you alcohol or drugs?" Roiphe and Sommers exaggerate the importance of this in distorting her one-in-four statistic. Sommers actually goes on to conclude that "once you remove the positive responses to question eight the finding that one in four college women is a victim of rape or attempted rape drops to one in nine." But as Koss writes, without fac-

toring in this question the victims of rape or attempted rape actually fall from one in four to one in five (Flanders 1994: 6). Sommers took this error out of later printings of her book but still added that when this question is removed and you "subtract from the survey's results all the women who did not believe they were raped the incendiary 'One in Four' figure drops to between one in 22 and one in 33" (Sommers 1994: 215).[7]

Koss's one-in-four findings reflect those of almost every major peer-reviewed national and campus study even though Roiphe and Sommers completely dismiss the existence and validity of this vast body of research.[8] One of the most comprehensive of these studies is a nationwide federally funded 1992 survey by the National Victims Center. It reported that of the 2,008 respondents contacted randomly over the phone 14 percent reported a completed rape during their life excluding cases when they were passed out or otherwise unable to consent. This is comparable to Koss's 15.8 percent statistic of completed rapes.

But the most convincing evidence of the accuracy of Koss's study comes from the most accurate and comprehensive sex survey in America: the National Health and Social Life Survey (NHSLS) conducted by the National Opinion Research Center. In 1994 it was released in two books, one for a popular and another for an academic audience. The NHSLS found that since puberty 22 percent of women were forced by a man to do something sexually and 30 percent of them were forced by more than one man (Michael et al. 1994: 225; Laumann et al. 1994: 337). And even these numbers underestimate the true level of sexual violence in our society as the researchers point out: "Because forced sex is undoubtedly underreported in surveys because of the socially stigmatized nature of the event we believe that our estimates are probably conservative 'lower-bound' estimates of forced sex within the population" (Laumann et al. 1994: 322).

In more than three-quarters of the cases, the perpetrator was someone the woman knew well (22 percent), was in love with (46 percent), or married to (9 percent)—only 4 percent were attacked by a stranger. These forced sexual experiences had an impact on women's lives. Fifty-seven percent of the forced women (versus 42 percent of the rest) had emotional problems in the past year which interfered with sex, and 34 percent (versus 18 percent or those not forced) said sex in the past year was not pleasurable. Twenty percent (versus 12 percent of those not forced) generally said they were sometimes fairly unhappy or unhappy most of the time (Laumann et al. 1994: 226–227).[9]

The NHSLS data strongly confirm Koss's findings. It found that 25 percent of women eighteen to twenty-four had been forced to do something sexually (Laumann et al. 1994: 337). The survey also revealed that most of these attacks probably occurred when women were relatively young, since women eighteen to twenty-four had virtually identical rates of forced sex-about 25 percent. The slightly lower number of responses from older women can probably be accounted for by a greater reluctance to admit to being forced sexually and by a smaller number of sex partners.

These criticisms of Koss are not original or new. Roiphe and Sommers largely got their critiques of Koss's one-in-four figure secondhand, from Neil Gilbert, University of California, Berkeley, social welfare professor. Though Gilbert has never published anything about rape in a scholarly, peer-reviewed journal, he has written other critiques of Koss's research for the right-wing press. Gilbert's widely cited 1991 *Public Interest* article contains grave inaccuracies regarding Koss's data—falsely charging that Koss included "emotional coercion" as part of the definition of rape, for example. In Gilbert's 1991 and 1993 *Wall Street Journal* commentaries, his stated goal is to defeat the Violence against Women Act, which deals mainly with street crime and domestic violence

and was finally passed after years of debate in August 1994. A 1991 press release issued by the University of California, Berkeley, boasted that "partly as a result of Gilbert's research, Governor Deukmejian last year canceled all state funding for the school-based [child sex abuse] prevention programs."[10]

Despite Gilbert's partisan, nonacademic attacks on Koss's rigorously documented, peer-reviewed research, it is often Gilbert who is considered a scholar in press accounts and Koss who is treated as an ideologue. Even the *Chronicle of Higher Education* used this spin in a 1992 headline on the debate: "A Berkeley Scholar Clashes with Feminists over Validity of Their Research on Date Rape."

In exaggerating feminist "date-rape hysteria," reporters from the popular press have clearly taken the easiest and most superficial route in date-rape coverage. The media has failed to report routinely and in depth about acquaintance rape. Instead, the issue is covered in irregular waves when sensational cases come forth (for example, the Kennedy Smith case) or sexy controversy strikes (Roiphe's "exposé" of statistics). The press has barely broken ground in discussing the complexities, root causes, and influences of the crime of acquaintance rape—along with all issues involving violence against women.

When discussing feminism, as the Sommers and Roiphe coverage shows, reporters flock to cat fight angles. They pit an extreme antifeminist against an unwavering profeminist, giving the impression to the public that feminists all think and act alike and perceive the issues as clear-cut. Reporters too often take "scientific" criticism of feminists at face value, neglecting to investigate the supposedly refuted data.

Also missing in today's rape coverage is news about important efforts to curb violence against women. The press hardly mentioned the Senate Judiciary Committee's May 1993 report about the failure of the criminal justice system to recognize and prosecute rape, along with the status and content of the Violence Against Women Act. The media rarely investigates the criminal justice system's failure to recognize and prosecute acquaintance rapes. This covers the spectrum from police who label reports of rape among acquaintances as "unfounded" to jurors who dismiss a rape victim because she doesn't look "terrorized enough."

The press also needs to focus its lens beyond the comfortable and familiar middle-class university to the less beautifully and neatly landscaped outside world, populated by the vast majority of young women. Rape and activism do happen outside of college campuses. Gone unrecognized has been community feminist activism and education, which are often concentrated at rape crisis centers. (Indeed, the sensational reports of young nubile coeds from white and middle-class communities are more sexy to viewers and readers.)

However, the level of activism is still often most intense at four-year universities, enclaves that Roiphe, a Harvard graduate and Princeton graduate student, knows well. This is not because women there are brainwashed and trying to grab "very oppressed victim" status, as Roiphe describes; the reality is that they commonly have more time and opportunity to speak out on important issues. They are doing what others would—if given the resources. Instead of scorning the activists as privileged, as Roiphe does, I appreciate them for getting the message out the best way they can. Simply criticizing these feminists for causing the date-rape problem just pins all of the blame and all of the responsibility to stop rape on the same old group: women themselves.

But reporters are only part of the solution to more complex and effective dialogue about acquaintance rape. Those feminists and antifeminists debating these issues publicly have yet to discuss responsibly and realistically the subject of danger in sexual experiences. One side, starring Camille Paglia and Katie Roiphe, describes danger as a natural and unavoidable part of sexuality and says that women should just do the mature thing and accept it.[11] And feminists, usually the only ones in our society who dare to discuss how women are indeed victimized and advocate for them, too often singularly focus in public debate on the risks of sexual behavior and neglect to focus on the women's movement's historic goal to attain women's sexual freedom and autonomy.

We need to hear more arguments that go a step further: the reality is that danger exists, and women should be aware of the risks. But young people also have the right to expect safety. Fighting against date rape can also mean fighting for women's pleasure and sexual agency.

However, in the end, some "rape crisis" critics emerging in the early 1990s could have some positive effects. While Roiphe has egregious blind spots and fails to recognize the real danger and harm of acquaintance rape, she and others are inciting feminists to make definitions of abuse and assault clearer and not overly broad in writing and conversation. While she fails to discuss sexual pleasure, Roiphe may remind feminists to articulate and emphasize their goal for sexual agency. As she points out, the organized and vocal feminists that many young women see in the media and on campus often seem to concentrate solely on the victimization of women. With herself and her readers as examples, Roiphe also illustrates that young women—even we young feminists—aren't willing to blindly follow any party line. Instead of telling us what to think, feminists must encourage us to think critically.

When we hear more voices drawing more careful distinctions, discussing further complexities, and telling their stories, change will take place. But there is only so much women can do; action is still most crucially needed from men, who now comprise a relatively small chorus in the antirape movement. Only then, with both sexes involved in rape prevention, will we really know how it feels to experience a true sexual revolution.

NOTES

1. Parts of this profile of Weinberg are from my book, Kamen 1991: 328–333. For more information about male antirape activism, see Funk 1993.

2. Also see Celis 1992.

3. For example, an interview with Katie Roiphe in Stone 1993: 177 and views of Linda Fairstein and Katie Roiphe in Levine 1993.

4. These charges of "date-rape hype" first appeared in an article in *Playboy* by Stephanie Guttman (1990). Gilbert (1991) took up her critique, which was reiterated by Roiphe (1993). Also see Will 1993: 92 and Paglia 1991: 23.

5. Other publicity includes an excerpt of Roiphe's book in *Cosmopolitan,* "Date Rape: State of Siege" (January 1994): 148–151.

6. Koss describes her use of the specific Ohio state statute, as revised in 1980, to define rape as "vaginal intercourse between male and female, and anal intercourse, fellatio, and cunnilingus between persons regardless of sex. Penetration, however slight, is sufficient to complete vaginal or anal intercourse. . . . No person shall engage in sexual conduct with another person . . . when any of the following apply: (1) the offender purposely compels the other person to submit by force or threat of force, (2) for the purpose of preventing resistance the offender substantially impairs the other person's judgment or control by administering any drug or intoxicant to the other person." (Koss et al. 1987: 166).

7. Criticism made by Wilson (1994).

8. For an example from a single campus, see Marshall and Miller who report that more than one-fourth of the women (27 percent) and nearly one-sixth of the men (15 percent) surveyed had been involved in forced sexual intercourse while in a dating situation. (Marshall and Miller 1987: 46).

9. Criticism made by Wilson (1994).

10. Much of this criticism was originally published in my article in *EXTRA!* (Kamen 1993: 10–11).

11. Paglia writes, "Rape is one of the risk factors in getting involved with men. It's a risk factor. It's like driving a car. My attitude is, it's like gambling. If you go to Atlantic City—these girls are going to Atlantic City—and when they lose, it's like 'Oh, Mommy and Daddy, I lost.' My answer is stay home and do your nails, if that's the kind of person you are. My Sixties attitude is, yes, go for it, take the risk— if you get beat up in a dark alley in a street, it's okay. That was part of the risk of freedom, that's part of what we've demanded as women. Go with it" (Paglia 1992: 63).

REFERENCES

Celis, William III. 1992. "Growing Talk of Date Rape Separates Sex from Assault." *New York Times* (1 January): A1, B7.

Collison, Michele N-K. 1992. "A Berkeley Scholar Clashes with Feminists over Validity of Their Research on Date Rape." *Journal of Higher Education* (6 February): 35, 37.

Crichton, Sarah. 1993. "Sexual Correctness: Has It Gone Too Far?" *Newsweek* (25 October): 52–58.

Flanders, Laura. 1994. "The 'Stolen Feminism' Hoax." *EXTRA!* (September/October): 6–9.

Funk, Rus Ervin. 1993. *Stopping Rape: A Challenge for Men.* Philadelphia: New Society Publishers.

Gilbert, Neil. 1991a. "The Campus Rape Scare." *Wall Street Journal* (27 June): 10.

Gilbert, Neil 1991b. "The Phantom Epidemic." *Public Interest* 103: 54.

Gilbert, Neil. 1993. "The Wrong Response to Rape." *Wall Street Journal* (29 June): 19.

Guttman, Stephanie. 1990. "Date Rape: Does Anyone Really Know What It Is?" *Playboy* (October): 48–56.

Hellman, Peter. 1993. "Crying Rape: The Politics of Date Rape on Campus." *New York* (8 March): 33–37.

James, Frank. 1994. "Collegians Are Enrolled in Real Life." *Chicago Tribune* (16 September): section 2; 1, 7.

Kamen, Paula. 1989. "'No' Means 'No.'" *Chicago Tribune* (31 December): section 6; 8.

Kamen, Paula 1991. *Feminist Fatale: Voices from the Twentysomething Generation Explore the Future of the "Women's Movement."* New York: Donald I. Fine.

Kamen, Paula. 1993. "Erasing Rape: Media Hype an Attack on Sexual-Assault Research." *EXTRA!* 6 (November/December): 10, 11.

Koss, Mary, Christine A. Gidycz, and Nadine Wisniewski. 1987. "The Scope of Rape: Incidence and Prevalence of Sexual Aggression and Victimization in a National Sample of Higher Education Students." *Journal of Consulting and Clinical Psychology* 55: 162–170.

Koss, Mary, Lisa Goodman, Louise Fitzgerald, Nancy Russo, Gwendolyn Keita, and Angela Browne. 1994. *No Safe Haven.* Washington, DC: American Psychological Association.

Laumann, Edward O., John H. Gagnon, Robert T. Michael, and Stuart Michaels. 1994. *The Social Organization of Sexuality: Sexual Practices in the United States.* Chicago: University of Chicago Press.

Levine, Judith. 1993. "The Rape Debate." *Harper's Bazaar* (September): 236ff.

Marshall, Jon C., and Beverly Miller. 1987. "Coercive Sex on the University Campus." *Journal of College Student Personnel* (January): 38–42.

Michael, Robert T., John H. Gagnon, Edward O. Laumann, and Gina Kolata. 1994. *Sex in America: A Definitive Survey.* New York: Little, Brown.

National Victims Center and Crime Victims Research and Treatment Center. 1992. *Rape in America: A Report to the Nation* (23 April). Arlington, VA.

Paglia, Camille. 1992. *Sex, Art, and American Culture: Essays.* New York: Vintage.

Paglia, Camille. 1991. "Feminists Lead Women Astray on the Threat of Rape." *Philadelphia Inquirer* (15 February): 23.

Roiphe, Katie. 1993a. "Date Rape's Other Victim." *New York Times Magazine* (13 June): 26–30, 40, 68.

Roiphe, Katie. 1993b. *The Morning After: Sex, Fear, and Feminism on Campus.* Boston: Little, Brown.

Senate Judiciary Committee. 1993. *Violence Against Women: The Response to Rape: Detours on the Road to Equal Justice.*

Sommers, Christina Hoff. 1994. *Who Stole Feminism? How Women Have Betrayed Women.* New York: Simon & Schuster.

Stone, Judith. 1993. "Sex, Rape, and Second Thoughts." *Glamour* (October): 177.

Warshaw, Robin. 1988. *I Never Called It Rape.* New York: Harper & Row.

Will, George. 1993. "Sex Amidst Semi-Colons." *Newsweek* (4 October): 92.

Wilson, John. 1994a. "Sexless in America?" *The Prism* (28 October): 18, 19.

Wilson, John. 1994b. "Stolen Feminism." *Teachers for a Democratic Culture* (newsletter) (fall): 6–8.

Young, Cathy. 1992. "Women, Sex, and Rape: Have Some Feminists Exaggerated the Problem?" *Washington Post* (31 May): C1.

Study/Discussion Questions

1. What attitudes toward women and sex motivate men to commit acquaintance rape?
2. What evidence does Kamen present to support her contention that rape is relatively common?
3. Why does she think it is important to make this argument?
4. What criticisms does Kamen make of Katie Roiphe's arguments about acquaintance rape?
5. In what ways does Kamen think that these arguments are harmful to women?

Two or Three Things I Know for Sure

Dorothy Allison

Most violence in this country occurs between people who know each other well. Although the thought of rape by a stranger looms more terrifyingly for most women, this fact holds true for sexual violence against women and girls, as well. In this excerpt from Two Or Three Things I Know for Sure, *writer Dorothy Allison renders a searing account of her childhood. The violence she experienced continues to refract throughout her life. Yet with insistence, in this autobiographical account, she fights against the victim-blaming implicit in society's continued refusal to confront incest and other forms of child abuse fully.*

Let me tell you the mean story.

For years and years, I convinced myself that I was unbreakable, an animal with an animal strength or something not human at all. Me, I told people, I take damage like a wall, a brick wall that never falls down, never feels anything, never flinches or remembers. I am one woman but I carry in my body all the stories I have ever been told, women I have known, women who have taken damage until they tell themselves they can feel no pain at all.

That's the mean story. That's the lie I told myself for years, and not until I began to fashion stories on the page did I sort it all out, see where the lie ended and a broken life remained. But that is not how I am supposed to tell it. I'm only supposed to tell one story at a time, one story. Every writing course I ever heard of said the same thing. Take one story, follow it through, beginning, middle, end. I don't do that. I never do.

Behind the story I tell is the one I don't.

Behind the story you hear is the one I wish I could make you hear.

Behind my carefully buttoned collar is my nakedness, the struggle to find clean clothes, food, meaning, and money. Behind sex is rage, behind anger is love, behind this moment is silence, years of silence.

The man raped me. It's the truth. It's a fact.

I was five, and he was eight months married to my mother. That's how I always began to talk about it—when I finally did begin to talk about it.

I'd say, "It was rape, the rape of a child." Then I'd march the words out—all the old tearing awful words.

For years, every time I said it, said "rape" and "child" in the same terrible sentence, I would feel the muscles of my back and neck pull as taut as the string of a kite straining

Dorothy Allison as a little girl.

against the wind. That wind would blow and I would resist, then suddenly feel myself loosed to fall or flee. I started saying those words to get to that release, that feeling of letting go, of setting loose both the hatred and the fear. The need to tell my story was terrible and persistent, and I needed to say it bluntly and cruelly, to use all those words, those old awful tearing words.

I need to be a woman who can talk about rape plainly, without being hesitant or self-conscious, or vulnerable to what people might be saying this year.

I need to say that my mama didn't know what was going on, that I didn't tell her, that when I finally did tell someone it was not her. I need to say that when I told, only my mama believed me, only my mama did anything at all, that thirty years later one of my aunts could still say to me that she didn't really believe it, that he had been such a hardworking, good-looking man. Something else must have happened. Maybe it had been different.

How? I wanted to ask. How could it have been different for a five-year-old and a grown man? Instead I just looked at her, feeling fi-

nally strong enough to know she had chosen to believe what she needed more than what she knew.

Two or three things I know for sure, but none of them is why a man would rape a child, why a man would beat a child.

Why? I am asked. Why do you bring that up? Must you talk about that? I asked myself the same questions until finally I began to understand. This was a wall in my life, I say, a wall I had to climb over every day. It was always there for me, deflecting my rage toward people who knew nothing about what had happened to me or why I should be angry at them.

It took me years to get past that rage, to say the words with grief and insistence but to let go of the anger, to refuse to use the anger against people who knew nothing of the rape. I had to learn how to say it, to say "rape," say "child," say "unending," "awful" and "relentless," and say it the way I do—adamant, unafraid, unashamed, every time, all over again—to speak my words as a sacrament, a blessing, a prayer. Not a curse. Getting past the anger, getting to the release, I become someone else, and the story changes. I am no longer a grown-up outraged child but a woman letting go of her outrage, showing what I know: that evil is a man who imagines the damage he does is not damage, that evil is the act of pretending that some things do not happen or leave no mark if they do, that evil is not what remains when healing becomes possible.

All the things I can say about sexual abuse—about rape—none of them are reasons. The words do not explain. Explanations almost drove me crazy, other people's explanations and my own. Explanations, justifications, and theories. I've got my own theory. My theory is that rape goes on happening all the time. My theory is that everything said about that act is assumed to say something about me, as if that thing I never wanted to happen and did not know how to stop is the only thing that can be said about my life. My theory is that talking about it makes a difference—being a woman who can stand up anywhere and say, I was five and the man was big.

So let me say it.

He beat us, my stepfather, that short, mean-eyed truck driver with his tight-muscled shoulders and uneasy smile. He was a man who wasn't sure he liked women but was sure he didn't like smart, smart-mouthed tomboys, stubborn little girls who tried to pretend they were not afraid of him. Two or three things I know, but this is the one I am not supposed to talk about, how it comes together—sex and violence, love and hatred. I'm not ever supposed to put together the two halves of my life—the man who walked across my childhood and the life I have made for myself. I am not supposed to talk about hating that man when I grew up to be a lesbian, a dyke, stubborn, competitive, and perversely lustful.

"People might get confused," a woman once told me. She was a therapist and a socialist, but she worried about what people thought. "People might imagine that sexual abuse makes lesbians."

"Oh, I doubt it." I was too angry to be careful. "If it did, there would be so many more."

Her cheeks flushed pink and hot. She had told me once that she thought I didn't respect her—her oddly traditional life and commonplace desires, her husband of twelve years and female companion of five. Looking into her stern, uncompromising face brought back my aunts and their rueful certainty that nothing they did was ever quite right. Two or three things and none of them sure, that old voice whispered in my head while this woman looked at me out of eyes that had never squinted in regret.

"Tell me, though," I added, and shifted my shoulders like Aunt Dot leaning into a joke, "if people really believed that rape made lesbians, and brutal fathers made dykes, wouldn't they be more eager to do something about it? What's that old Marxist strategy—sharpen the contradiction until even the proletariat sees where the future lies? We could whack them with contradictions, use their bad instincts against their worse. Scare them into changing what they haven't even thought about before."

She opened her mouth like a fish caught on a razor-sharp line. For the first time in all the time I had known her I saw her genuinely enraged. She didn't think my suggestion was funny. But then, neither did I.

How *does* it come together, the sweaty power of violence, the sweet taste of desire held close? It rises in the simplest way, naturally and easily, when you're so young you don't know what's coming, before you know why you're not supposed to talk about it.

It came together for me when I was fifteen and that man came after me with a belt for perhaps the thousandth time and my little sister and I did not run. Instead we grabbed up butcher knives and backed him into a corner. And oh, the way that felt! For once we made him sweat with the threat of what we'd do if he touched us. And oh, the joy of it, the power to say, "No, you son of a bitch, this time, no!" His fear was sexual and marvelous—hateful and scary but wonderful, like orgasm, like waiting a whole lifetime and finally coming.

I know. I'm not supposed to talk about sex like that, not about weapons or hatred or violence, and never to put them in the context of sexual desire. Is it male? Is it mean? Did you get off on it? I'm not supposed to talk about how good anger can feel—righteous, justified, and completely satisfying. Even at seventeen, when I learned to shoot a rifle, I knew not to tell anyone what I saw and felt as I aimed that weapon. Every time I centered on the target it was his heart I saw, his squint-eyed, mean-hearted image.

I knew that the things I was not supposed to say were also the things I did not want to think about. I knew the first time I made love with a woman that I could cry but I must not say why. I cried because she smelled like him, the memory of him, sweaty and urgent, and she must not know it was not her touch that made me cry. Breathing her in prompted in me both desire and hatred, and of the two feelings what I dared not think about was the desire. Sex with her became a part of throwing him off me, making peace with the violence of my own desire.

I know. I'm not supposed to talk about how long it took me to wash him out of my body—how many targets I shot, how many women I slept with, how many times I sat up till dawn wondering if it would ever change, if I would ever change. If there would come a time in my life when desire did not resonate with fury.

Study/Discussion Questions

1. Why does Dorothy Allison tell this story?
2. What are the important parts of the story for her?
3. At whom is she angry in the story (in addition to her stepfather), and why?
4. What do you think would be different in the author's life if she had not been abused?
5. What does *she* think would have been different?

Too Sexy for My Shirt

By Debra Dickerson

The 1991 feature film Thelma and Louise *focused popular attention on the public sexual harassment of women, with its scenes of two women taking violent revenge against the everyday assaults—verbal and physical—women endure from men. Yet, as Debra Dickerson points out, nothing really changed as a result. In 1999, Dickerson still reports that a siege of unwanted remarks follows her down the street on a daily basis. Her analysis of this ubiquitous phenomenon of modern female existence in America (and far beyond, to be sure) canvasses a range of remedies to an underrecognized form of harassment.*

I am a spectacular beauty.

It's May now, and I walk the streets of the nation's capital free from my shrouding winter coat, making it impossible for male passersby to concentrate on their conversations. Cars slide to a precipitous halt at the mere sight of me, fishtailing as their brakes lock. Heads swivel on necks made suddenly rubbery by the merest glimpse of me. Eyes goggle. The glint of my ankle bracelet, the hint of a thigh as my skirt blows around—it's unfair, really, and I know I need to stop showing off "them fine legs." At least that's what the helpful truck driver yells after swooping to a stop in his deuce-and-a-half mere inches from me. My perfume, mingled with the inchoate sorcery that is moi, produces a fragrance so entrancing, so beguiling, it can only be called eau de Debra and it drives men to lunacy. How could they not sniff and snort with orgasmic plea-sure, lips loudly smacking, nostrils piggily flaring, lest I fail to notice their gyrations? What good are offerings made to a goddess who notices not?

So by all means, come a little closer. After all, I am woman and therefore a natural wonder. Like a waterfall or a pretty stand of trees. Feel free to waylay me. Block my path to inform me that you heartily approve of my "tight-ass" dress. Thank God that's settled. And don't forget to thrust your pelvis at me while you address my breasts. We beauties like it. Why else would we dress "that way"? Don't just scream at me from the far side of a four-lane road (across which I am apparently supposed to jog so that our destiny can be fulfilled at the bus stop named Federal Triangle). Come up from behind and whisper intimately, preferably Ebonically, in my ear. *Mais oui,* I'd love to "get witchou" *ce soir, cherie.* And you, Mr. Businessman. Come right on over and "accidentally" rub your penis against my "gorgeous ass," as you put it, as we wait at a light. Then look at me expectantly, waiting for the nooner which will no doubt now ensue. I can take a compliment.

And you, in the beat-up Pontiac: Should I cruelly refuse to answer your catcalls of love, by all means get out of your car and dog me for three blocks expressing your pain. I have now become a "fat, fucking skank," not a beauty, but I understand. You have every right to be angry. And don't worry. No one will intervene. But don't ask me for spare change while you're at it: Panhandling is strictly regulated and the cops will be all over you.

I am a vision. I must be.

God, I love spring.

"It was spring for me, too," chuckles Northwestern University law professor Cynthia Bowman. "That's when I got the idea for the article." Well, that and *Thelma & Louise.* It was 1991, two years before her controversial article ("Street Harassment and the Informal Ghetto-ization of Women") would appear in the *Harvard Law Review* and cause a national sensation. Already interested in the subject of sexual harassment, she saw that infamous movie and came away struck by the audience's approving blood lust when the movie stars blew up the pig truck driver's rig. An article was born when she ran afoul of her own pig truck driver shortly thereafter. She was captive at a red light with her windows rolled down to enjoy the beautiful weather when the two men in the next vehicle laid into Bowman with a stream of sex talk and ridicule that crushed her. The confluence of events made her realize that she'd been repressing a lifetime of such incidents. Canvassing her friends, she found that she was far from alone. Hooray for Hollywood; the professor decided to fight back.

In her article, Bowman labels street harassment a grueling, humiliating, and frightening fact of women's lives "that has not generally been viewed by academics, judges, or legislators as a problem requiring legal redress, either because these mostly male observers have not noticed the behavior or because they have considered it trivial and thus not within the proper scope of the law." It's certainly the case that many men haven't noticed it. When I discussed this article at our staff meeting, a male colleague asked, "Are you saying that when you leave this office, say to go to lunch, you'll be harassed?" He was shocked.

In her first-of-its-kind academic article, Bowman proposed an anti-harassment ordinance, featuring a $250 fine, "but, if I had it to do again," she said, "I might leave that out. It was an afterthought. Everyone fixated on the ordinance, but that's just the kind of thing you do in a law review article, you propose a remedy. I just wanted to stimulate discussion of how the law too often ignores women." Stimulate discussion she did. She was denounced from one corner of America to another as the epitome of political correctness and feminism run amok, then held aloft as an icon by legions of pissed-off women who wanted her to go even further. "I was astonished by the response," the rueful professor said this week, tired from grading end-of-year exams.

She wouldn't have been astonished if she lived here in D.C. "Women who've lived lots of places tell me it's worse here than anywhere else," says Denise Snyder, executive director of the D.C. Rape Crisis Center which offers training in dealing with street harassment. Quantifying an essentially untraceable phenomenon is extremely difficult, but it's certainly true that street harassment is a historically controversial topic here. In 1990, a summer series of three *Washington Post* articles on street harassment—one journalistic, one essayistic, and one op-ed—caused a firestorm.

But it wasn't until 1993, the year of Bowman's law review article, that war broke out, first locally, then nationally. *Washington Post* writer Phil McCombs wrote "StareMasters:

Every Day at Noon They Sit and Watch Their Dreams Go By," detailing a benign week of girl-watching at a construction site. The letters-to-the-editor pages and phone lines at the *Post* were so clogged with responses that the paper's ombudsman had to weigh in. D.C. Men Against Rape staged a protest at the construction site and national columnists took sides. ABC and CBS called. Maury Povich even wanted to fly McCombs and the construction workers to New York for a show. "Don't they have construction workers in New York?" he sensibly mused in a follow-up piece.

Filmmaker Maggie Hadleigh-West believes D.C.'s street harassment is among the worst. "My hard-on about street abuse formed when I lived in D.C.," she said. By the time she was living in New York, she had become so fed up she made a documentary about it, "War Zone," in which she confronts men who harass her. The original was shown in 1993 and caused the same kind of explosion that Bowman's article had. [A sequel came out in 1999.] Some of the men she confronts become quite abusive. "When we oppose street harassment and speak up, we make them suddenly self-conscious, we make them give up a privilege. They don't like it."

Indeed they do not. And on this issue, women's anger crosses ideological lines. Amy Holmes, a policy analyst with the conservative Independent Women's Forum and a widely featured political commentator, frequently fights back. Recently harassed by a small group of men as she left her office alone at 10 p.m., they cursed her when she ignored their "hey, baby's." "I was so mad, I whirled around and yelled, 'That's why I don't talk to guys like you!' I've even flipped some of these guys off, and I'm a polite, normal young woman. It's just gotten so bad." So bad in fact that TLC, a popular R&B trio of young women recently recorded a song, "No Scrubs," about the losers who hassle women on the streets.

Why do they do it? We're not talking about gallantry, or playful flirting or simple, unfrightened compliments. Why the abuse, the privacy invasion, the intimidation? Why do the construction workers on my block, for instance, make sudden loud noises with their machinery as I pass so they can laugh when I jump? I don't ask them. I'm afraid of escalation. When I lived in San Francisco, panhandling/drug addict/psychotic bums supported by asshole tourists congregated in my North Beach neighborhood and figured out my name and apartment. Remembering them tapping on my windows, I go to a different neighborhood and ask street harassers why they do it.

"Aw! There y'all go, there y'all go!" one man goes off. "Always complainin' when you should be happy. We like you, get it? We human men. We like your bodies. We like your . . . your . . . okay, I'll say it and it's your fault because I don't even talk like this—we like your titties! We like titties. We men. We like women, ain't no fags round here."

"Can't please a woman these days less you ready to go to jail," opined one man, fury twisting his features and making his nostrils flare.

"It's a compliment, all right, jeez," another said, eyes rolled heavenward in disgust. "Why is it so wrong to tell you that you're pretty? How much time you spend getting dressed this morning? How much makeup you got at home? Huh? It's for me, right? For men."

And if I don't care what random men think? "Maybe you're gay. Maybe that's all the problem, right there?"

His buddy, a quieter type who, alone among the five, had said nothing as I passed, added tentatively, "I'm a human being, too. All you have to do is say hi." And if we don't want to? He thought for a minute. "Why not just say it?" "It's a big miscommunication," Hadleigh-West says. "What they think they're sending is not what we're receiving. They say they're trying to tell us we're attractive, desirable, sexy. We feel assaulted." Says Snyder, "Men claim they do it to meet women. That's bullshit. There's a power dynamic at work with street harassment. It's at the base of any sexual harassment. They don't really think they'll get dates that way."

Adrian Davis, law professor at Washington College of Law at American University says street harassment has to be understood as on a continuum with sexual assault and stalking. "Women's impulse is to react. We want to respond when insulted but we fear assault. Sexual harassment in the workplace tells women they can't have an 'economic personality.' Sexual harassment on the streets prevents women from being able to fully enjoy the public sphere. If you leave home 'inappropriately,' i.e. to work or without a man, you are disciplined with sexual harassment."

As does Bowman in her article, Davis points out (rightly, in my experience) that women are much less likely to be harassed while with old people or children or, of course, a man. If I'm so devastatingly gorgeous, why is this never pointed out while I'm with my fiancé?

"Because they know it's wrong," says Snyder flatly.

Does it matter that this is most often pointed out to me (in graphic detail) by black men? Courtland Milloy, in one of those three 1990 *Washington Post* pieces, lamented the "black men who [make] the district a living hell for their sisters." Many of the female letter-writers made the same claim. Julianne

Malveaux as well has written about her own abuse from black males and the "contempt" some of them exhibit for black women. "We are at the low end of the food chain for them," she writes. So, yes, it matters if only because 95 percent of the harassment I receive comes from them. If that's group loyalty, I can live without it.

This summer [1999], the New York chapter of NOW's anti-violence committee is planning a campaign against street harassment. "A lot of street harassment comes from men working on the streets—movers, delivery men. If a woman can identity the company the harasser is working for, NOW will send them a letter describing the incident and asking them to take action," says Joanna Perlman of NOW.

Holmes disagrees with this tactic. "It's not a legal or employer problem. It's a social problem and that tattletale approach will only exacerbate the problem. We need to ask why these guys feel entitled to say these things, why men have forgotten to be civil and gentlemanly. The people who witness these incidents, men especially, need to speak up. We need social pressure. If the police or companies are the enforcers, people can tell themselves that harassers will be ticketed, it's not their responsibility."

I won't hold my breath until the people of America rise up and shame street harassers. I'll just keep hiding behind my sunglasses and Walkman until winter comes again and I can disappear into my big, shapeless coat.

Study/Discussion Questions

1. In the author's view, why do men make sexual comments to women on the street?
2. What makes street harassment unfair to women? How does it control women's behavior?
3. What do you think of the ordinance proposed in this article? Would it stop street harassment?
4. Should street harassment be treated the same way as panhandling (there is a law against asking for money on the street in many cities)? If not, why not?
5. Would this remedy be unfair to men? If you think so, what would make it unfair to men?

Battering: Who's Going to Stop It?

Ann Jones

Ann Jones, who has written widely about violence against women, provides a stark and succinct report on the current state of domestic violence in America. While the battered women's movement has done spectacular work sheltering women and pressing successfully for legal remedies to the plague of violence against women, more still needs to be done. Four or five women are murdered each day by current or former male partners. Twenty-seven percent of women ages eighteen to twenty-four have been attacked by a "romantic" partner in the past year. Yes, Jones says, women need to learn the difference between violence and love, but more urgently, men need to be forced to stop the violence.

He's fucking going nuts . . . ," Nicole Brown Simpson told a police dispatcher on October 25, 1993. Eight months later, after O. J. Simpson was arrested for the murder of his ex-wife and her friend Ronald Goldman, that 911-call was played and replayed on television and radio, plunging startled Americans into the midst of a typical terrifying incident of what we lamely call "domestic" violence. Previously, both O. J. Simpson and Jon Russo, vice president of the Hertz Corporation, which retained Simpson as its spokesman even after he pleaded no contest to assaulting Nicole in 1989, had described O.J.'s wife beating as a private "family matter" of no significance.

The press calls O.J. Simpson the most famous American ever charged with murder, but he's certainly not the first celebrity to be a batterer, or even to be implicated in homicide. In fact, the list of celebrity batterers from the sports world alone is a long one which includes boxer Sugar Ray Leonard, baseball star Darryl Strawberry, former University of Alabama basketball coach Wimp Sanderson, former heavyweight champ Mike Tyson (cited by then-wife Robin Givens and subsequently convicted of raping Miss Black Rhode Island), California Angels pitcher Donnie Moore (who shot and wounded his estranged wife, Tonya, before killing himself in 1989), and Philadelphia Eagles defensive lineman Blenda Gay (stabbed to death in 1976 by his battered wife, Roxanne, who said she acted in self-defense).

The list of entertainers named as batterers is also lengthy and star-studded. Tina Turner reported in her autobiography that husband Ike abused her for years. Ali MacGraw described the violent assaults of Steve McQueen. Sheila Ryan sued her then-husband James Caan in 1980, alleging that he'd beaten her. Madonna accused Sean Penn, and Daryl Hannah named Jackson Browne. Such incidents make titillating copy for scandal sheets and tabloid TV.

And such incidents continue to be commonplace—as all-American as football—precisely because so many people sill think of battering as, in O.J.'s words, "no big deal." But when America listened last June to that 911-tape, eavesdropping on the private, violent raging of the male publicly known as the cool, affable Juice, anyone could hear that what Nicole Brown was up against was a very big deal indeed. For the first time, Americans could hear for themselves the terror that millions of American women live with every day.

That terror begins with small, private, seemingly ordinary offenses. Take this list of complaints logged in a single week by the security office of one small institution. One woman harassed by "unwanted attention" from a man. One woman "annoyed" at finding "obscene photographs" in her desk. Two women "annoyed" by obscene phone calls from men. One woman sexually assaulted in her living quarters by a male acquaintance. One woman stalked by a man in violation of a restraining order.

Routine offenses? You bet. And they're increasingly common—not just because women are fed up with such behavior and reporting it more often, but because these days there's more and worse to report.

What makes this particular list of complaints noteworthy is that it comes from the security office at a small New England college—the sort of place where old stone buildings surround a quadrangle shaded by ancient trees. The sort of place where parents who can afford it send their daughters to be safe from the dangers of the "real" world, safe from violence and violent men. These days, however, there seems to be no safe haven. Not in exclu-

sive Brentwood. Not even on the picture-perfect college campus. Violence, which has always struck women of every social class and race, seems to be aimed increasingly at the young.

Last year, at Mount Holyoke College—the oldest women's college in the country—the student newspaper carried the front page headline "Domestic Violence on the Rise." Reported cases of "domestic" violence were increasing all across the country, according to student reporter Gretchen Hitchner—and on the Mount Holyoke campus as well. "There are five or six students on campus who have obtained stay-away orders," Hitchner reported.

Beyond the boundaries of the campus, the statistics grew worse. Statewide, in Massachusetts in 1991, a woman was murdered by a current or former husband or boyfriend every twenty days. By 1993, such a murder occurred once every eight days. Among the dead Tara Hartnett, a twenty-one-year-old senior psychology major at the nearby University of Massachusetts at Amherst. In February 1993, Tara Hartnett had obtained a restraining order against James Cyr, Jr, her former boyfriend and the father of her eleven-month-old daughter. In March, when Hartnett's roommates were away on spring break, Cyr broke in, stabbed Hartnett, set the house on fire, and left her to die of smoke inhalation.

"Incidents" like the murder of Tara Hartnett happen all the time. Every day, in fact, four or five women die in the United States at the hands of their current or former husbands or boyfriends. But recently feminists (like me) who call attention to these crimes have been taking a lot of heat for perpetuating the image of women as "victims." Critics charge that "victim feminists" exaggerate the dangers women face in male violence. Katie Roiphe, for example, suggests in her book *The Morning After* that most alleged cases of date rape involve nothing more than second thoughts by daylight after bad sex the night before. Battering, according to the critics, is nothing that any woman with moderate self-esteem and a bus token can't escape. What prevents women from exercising our full female power and strength, some say, is not male violence but the *fear* of violence induced by fuddy-duddy feminists who see all women as victims.

Could it be true that the apparent crime wave against women, on campus and off, is only a delusion of paranoid radical feminists? Is it real violence that keeps women down, or only feminists' hysterical perceptions that hamper us?

In Canada, where the same questions were raised, Statistics Canada attempted to find out by interviewing 12,300 women nationwide in the most comprehensive study of violence against women ever undertaken. The results were worse than expected. They showed violence against women to be far more common than earlier, smaller scale studies had indicated. They revealed that more than half of Canadian women (51 percent) have been physically or sexually assaulted at least once in their adult lives. And more than half of those women said they'd been attacked by dates, boyfriends, husbands, friends, family members, or other men familiar to them. One in ten Canadian women, or one million, had been attacked in the past year.

These figures apply only to Canada, but considering that the United States is a more violent culture all around, it's unlikely that women in the United States are any safer from attack. In fact, battering alone is now the single leading cause of injury to women in the United States. A million women every year visit physicians and hospital emergency rooms for treatment of battering injuries. The National Centers for Disease Control identify battering as a leading cause of the spread of HIV and AIDS, as countless batterers force "their" women into unprotected sex. The American Medical Association reports that 38 percent of obstetric patients are battered during pregnancy, and stud-

ies name battering during pregnancy a cause of birth defects and infant mortality.

Survivors confirm that a man often begins to batter during a woman's first pregnancy, when she is most vulnerable and least able to pack up and move. Marie's husband, a lawyer, beat her so severely during her seventh month that she went into labor. He then ripped out the phone, locked her in a second-floor bedroom, and left the house. She barely survived, and the little boy she bore that day has always been small and frail. Carol miscarried after her husband knocked her down and kicked her repeatedly in the belly. He threatened to kill her if she tried to leave. When she became pregnant again, he beat her again, saying, "I'm going to kill that baby and you, too." Instead, she killed him with his own gun and was sentenced to twenty years in prison, where she bore her child and gave it up for adoption. Jean left her husband after he repeatedly punched her in the belly while she was pregnant. Later, when a doctor told Jean that her daughter had epilepsy, he asked if Jean had suffered a fall or an "accident" of any kind during pregnancy. Now that her daughter is in college and still suffering seizures, Jean says, "I only lived with that man for a year, but he casts his shadow over every day of my life, and my daughter's, too."

Millions of women live with such consequences of male violence, but it's not surprising that many choose another way out. Battering is cited as a contributing factor in a quarter of all suicide attempts by women, and half of all suicide attempts by black women. At least 50 percent of homeless women and children in the United States are in flight from male violence. Only a few years ago the FBI reported that in the United States a man beat a woman every eighteen seconds. By 1989, the figure was fifteen seconds. Now it's twelve.

Some people take these facts and statistics at face value to mean that male violence is on the rise, while others argue that what's increasing is merely the *reporting* of violence. But no matter how you interpret the numbers, it's clear that male violence is not going *down.*

As crime statistics go, homicide figures are most likely to be accurate, for the simple reason that homicides produce corpses—hard to hide and easy to count. Homicide figures all across the country—like those in Massachusetts—indicate so clearly that violence against women is on the rise that some sociologists have coined a new term for a common crime: "femicide." The FBI estimates that every year men murder about three thousand wives and girlfriends. The conclusion is inescapable: male violence against women is *real.* And it is widespread.

Such violence was once thought of as the plague of married women, but battering, like date rape, affects young, single women as well. In its recent study, Statistics Canada found that a disproportionate number of women reporting physical or sexual assault were young. Women ages eighteen to twenty-four were more than twice as likely as older women to report violence in the year preceding the study; 27 percent of them had been attacked in the past year. In the United States, the first study of "premarital abuse," conducted in 1985, reported that one in five college students was the victim of "playful aggression," ranging from slapping and hitting to "more life threatening violence." When a guy who'd had too much to drink offered Sarah a ride home from a fraternity party, she turned him down and advised him not to drive. He waited for her outside and beat her up—to "teach the bitch a lesson," he said. Susan went home for her first break from college and told her hometown boyfriend that she wanted to date at school. In response, he deliberately pulled out clumps of her hair, broke her arm, and drove her car into a tree. After Bonnie broke up with a possessive guy she'd been dating at college, he sneaked into her home at night and smashed in her head with a hatchet. Typi-

cally, guys like this think they're *entitled* to get their way, by any means necessary. Resorting to violence seems justified to them. They think they've done nothing wrong—or at least no more than she *asked* for.

Even high school boys are acting out the macho myth. A study of white middle-class high school juniors and seniors found that roughly one in four had some experience of dating violence, either as victim or perpetrator. In another study one in three teenage girls reported being subjected to violence by a date. After reviewing many such studies of high school and college students, Barrie Levy, author of *In Love and in Danger: A Teen's Guide to Breaking Free of Abusive Relationships,* reports that "an average of twenty-eight percent of the students experienced violence in a dating relationship. That is more than one in every four students." Male counselors who work with wife beaters confirmed that many older batterers first began to use violence as teenagers, against their dates.

That doesn't mean that violence against young women is just "kid's stuff." According to the FBI, 20 percent of women murdered in the United States are between the ages of fifteen and twenty-four. Recently a high school boy in Texas shot his girlfriend for being "unfaithful," and for good measure he killed her best friend, too. Former police officer Barbara Arrighi, who has witnessed increased date rape, battering, and stalking among college students as assistant director for public safety at Mount Holyoke College, bluntly sums up the situation: "Anyone who doesn't believe America has a serious problem with violence against young women," she says, "is living in Lalaland."

Some who have studied dating violence say young women may be more vulnerable to male aggression because they believe so innocently in "true love." Schooled by romance novels and rock videos, which typically mingle sex and violence, they're more likely to mistake jealousy, possessiveness, control, and even physical or sexual assault for passion and commitment. In fact, in some surveys of college dating, about one-third of students interviewed reported that their relationships improve after violence—although most of the students who said so were men.

Consider the case of Kristin Lardner who was twenty-one in 1992 when her ex-boyfriend Michael Cartier gunned her down on a Boston street, then later shot himself: Kristin Lardner herself was scared to death of Michael Cartier, a man she had dated for only two months; and she did just what abused women are supposed to do. She stopped dating Cartier the first time he hit her; and when he followed her, knocked her down in the street, and kicked her unconscious, she got a restraining order against him. But even after she was murdered, Lardner's roommate and best friend still bought the "romantic" view of Michael Cartier's violence. She told reporters that Lardner had "cared" about Cartier, and "she was the only one who ever did. That's what pushed him over the edge when he lost her."

Young men, too, buy into this romantic scenario. One of Michael Cartier's male friends commented after the murder: "He loved her a lot and it was probably a crime of passion. He didn't do it because he's nuts," the friend said. "He was in love."

But Cartier's former girlfriend, Rose Ryan, also talked to reporters, and what she had to say put Michael Cartier's "love" in a new light. She had cared about Cartier, too, she said, and for months she had tried to make him happy with love and kindness and Christmas presents, even after he started to abuse her. It didn't work. Finally, after he attacked her with scissors, she brought assault charges against him and got him jailed for six months. Then, after Cartier murdered Kristin Lardner, Rose Ryan spoke about his "lovemaking." "After he hit me several times in the head," she said, "he started to cry." He would say, "I'm so sorry. I always hit

people I love." And the clincher: "My mother, she never loved me. You're the only one."

It's a familiar part of the batterer's control technique, that message. And it often works because it appeals at once to a woman's compassion and her power, snaring her in a web of "love" and "violence" as two contradictory concepts become inextricably entwined. It leads some women to reinterpret a boyfriend's violent behavior as passion. It leads some—like Rose Ryan for a while—to forgive and try to help a batterer to change. Attorney Lynne Gold-Birkin, founder of the American Bar Association's Committee on Domestic Violence and chair of the ABA's family law section, recently pointed out on ABC's *This Week with David Brinkley* that many married women subjected to abuse don't walk out at once "because they don't want the marriage to end; they want him to stop beating them." But in the end, as the story of Kristin Lardner shows, even a woman who tolerates no violence at all is not safe from it.

To find an explanation for the high rate of male violence against young women, we have to look to the source: to men. Many people still mistakenly believe that batterers are somehow different from ordinary men—that they are "crazy" men with short fuses who "lose control" of themselves and blow up, especially when under the influence of drink or drugs. But those who counsel batterers say that just the reverse is true: the battering man is perfectly in control of himself—and of the woman he batters. That, after all, is the purpose of battering. A man—of any age—threatens, intimidates, abuses, and batters a woman to make her do what he wants. It works. He gets his way, and as a bonus he gets a heady rush of experiencing his own power. As one reformed eighteen-year-old guy put it, "I enjoyed intimidating people." David Adams, director of Emerge, a Boston counseling program for batterers, points out that the same man who says he "loses control" of his temper with "his" woman will be perfectly calm when the police arrive. "Clearly he knows what he's doing," Adams says. "He's making rational choices about how to act with whom—on the basis of what he can get away with."

It's likely, then, that young women—even young women "in love"—get battered for the same reason older women get battered. Namely, they have minds of their own. They want to do what they want. Battered women are often mistakenly thought of as "passive" or "helpless" because some of them look that way after they've been beaten into submission and made hostage to terror. Their inability to escape is the result of battering, not its cause. According to one study, three out of four battering victims are actually single or separated women trying to get free of men who won't let them go. They are not merely victims; they are the resistance. But they are almost entirely on their own.

How can we help women get free of this violence? That's the question that survivors of battering and their advocates have been grappling with for twenty years. And they've done a phenomenal job. Never before in history has there been such an organization of crime victims united to rescue other victims and prevent further crimes. Although battered women's shelters are still so overburdened that they must turn away more women than they take in, they have provided safe haven over the years for millions of women and their children. Undoubtedly, they have saved thousands of lives.

In addition the battered women's movement has brought battering out of the private household and into the spotlight of public debate. There it has raised a much harder question: how can we make men stop their violence? To that end, the battered women's movement has pushed for—and achieved—big changes in legislation, public policy, and law enforcement.

The Violence Against Women Act, passed by Congress in 1994, is only one recent example. This bill correctly considers male violence against women as a violation of women's civil rights and provides a wide range of legal remedies for women.

But what's needed is a national campaign to go after the men at fault. Experts such as Susan Schechter, author of *Women and Male Violence,* say that men continue to use violence to get their way *because they can.* There's no reason for a man who uses violence to change his behavior unless he begins to suffer some real consequences, some punishment that drives home strong social and legal prohibitions against battering. In the short run, the most effective way to protect women and children, save lives, and cut down violence is to treat assault as the crime it is: to arrest batterers and send them to jail.

Usually, that's not what happens. Right now, most batterers suffer no social or legal consequences at all for their criminal behavior. Although police in most states and localities are now authorized to arrest batterers, many police departments still don't enforce the law. If police do make arrests, prosecutors commonly fail to prosecute. And if batterers are convicted, judges often release them—or worse, order them into marital counseling with the women they've assaulted. Many men are required to attend a few weekly sessions of a therapeutic support group where they shoot the breeze with other batterers, after which their crime is erased from the record hooks. (Counselors like David Adams who lead such groups are the first to say that the groups don't work.) One 1991 study found that among assaultive men arrested, prosecuted, convicted, and sentenced, less than 1 percent (0.9 percent) served any time in jail. The average batterer taken into custody by police is held less than two hours. He walks away laughing at his victim and at the police as well.

Even men convicted of near-fatal attacks upon their girlfriends or wives are likely to draw light sentences or be released on probation with plenty of opportunity to finish the job. The husband of Burnadette Barnes, for example, shot her in the head while she slept, served three months in prison for the crime, and was released to threatened her again. Desperate, Burnadette Barnes hired a man to kill her husband. She was convicted of murder and conspiracy to murder and sentenced to life in prison.

In Michigan, police officer Clarence Ratliff shot and killed his estranged wife, Carol Irons, who incidentally was the youngest woman ever appointed to the Michigan bench. (As a judge she was known to treat domestic violence cases seriously.) When the police tried to arrest Ratliff, he squeezed off a few wild shots before he surrendered. For killing his wife, Ratliff got ten to fifteen years; for shooting at the cops, two life terms plus some additional shorter terms for using a firearm.

Such cases make clear that in the scales of American justice men weigh more than women. Assaulting a male is a serious crime, but assaulting a woman or even killing her—well, that's not so bad.

We can do better. Thanks to the battered women's movement, we now know that any social, economic, or political development that counteracts sexism and promotes sex equality helps in the long run to eliminate violence by reducing the power men hold, individually and institutionally, over women. We now know that all the institutions to which battered women and children are likely to turn for help—hospitals, mental health facilities, social welfare services, child protective services, police departments, civil and criminal courts, schools, churches—must join a *concerted* effort to prevent violence before it occurs and stop it when it does. They must stand ready to defend the constitutional right that belongs to all women

(though no one ever speaks of it): the right to be free from bodily harm.

That's where college can set a good example for the rest of society. While public officials often seem to accept violence against women as an inevitable social problem, colleges can't afford to. They're obliged to keep their students safe. Mount Holyoke's Barbara Arrighi says,

> We've had to work at safety, but as a closed, self-contained system we have advantages over the big world. If one of our students is victimized, she finds a whole slew of helpers available right away—campus and city police, medical services, housing authorities, counselors, chaplains, academic deans. We'll ban offenders from the campus under trespass orders. We'll make arrests. We'll connect her to the county prosecutor's victim/witness assistance program. We'll go to court with her. We'll help her get a protective order or file a civil complaint. We take these things seriously. We don't try to pin the blame on her, and we don't fool around.

What Arrighi describes is the way the system ought to work in every community.

As things stand now, it's still up to women to make the system respond—and too often, on a case-by-case basis. It takes time, money, courage, and determination to get a result that looks like justice. Take the case of Stephanie Cain, for example. A college student, she had dated Elton "Tony" Ekstrom III for nine months. Then, during the course of one hour on the night of April 28, 1991, he beat her up. He punched and kicked her repeatedly, leaving her with a fractured nose and a face nearly unrecognizable to those who saw her immediately following the attack. Afterward, she said, she lost confidence and mistrusted people. She suffered seizures and had to drop out of college. Major surgery to reconstruct her nose permanently altered her appearance.

Ekstrom was arrested and charged with assault and battery with a dangerous weapon: his foot. But Stephanie Cain wasn't permitted to tell her story in court, for Ekstrom never went to trial. Instead he was allowed to plead guilty to a reduced charge of assault and battery. The judge gave him a two-year suspended sentence, and Ekstrom walked away—still thinking he'd done nothing wrong.

That result upset Stephanie Cain. Worried that Ekstrom might do the same thing to another woman, she decided to sue him for the damage he'd done. In December 1992, while she was back in college finishing her degree, she finally got her day in court. "The best part," she said, "was looking right at him, knowing I wasn't afraid of him anymore." After hearing her story, the jury awarded Cain and her parents $153,000 in damages for her injuries, medical expenses, and emotional distress. At last Ekstrom was to pay a price for his criminal act, as a civil court jury compensated Stephanie Cain for a crime the criminal court had failed to punish. "Every time I look in the mirror," Cain said, "I'm reminded of what happened. There's no reason he should just forget it."

The victory she won was a victory for all women. But it shouldn't have been that hard. And she shouldn't have had to fight for justice all by herself.

Study/Discussion Questions

1. What evidence does the author present to support her argument that battering is common?
2. What makes some men batter their wives and girlfriends (and other women)?
3. What makes it hard for women to leave battering husbands and boyfriends?
4. Why do men often get away with battering?
5. What needs to change in order to stop battering, according to the author? What changes in the law are necessary? What changes in social attitudes are necessary?

How Many Times

Marie Howe

No matter how many times I try I can't stop my father
from walking into my sister's room

and I can't see any better, leaning from here to look
in his eyes. It's dark in the hall

and everyone's sleeping. This is the part
where everything is perfect already and nothing changes,

where the water glass falls to the bathroom floor
and bounces once before breaking.

Nothing. Not the small sound my sister makes, turning
over, not the thump of the dog's tail

when he opens one eye to see him stumbling back to bed
still drunk, a little bewildered.

This is exactly as I knew it would be
And if I whisper her name, hissing a warning,

I've been doing that for years now, and still the dog
startles and growls until he sees

it's our father, and still the door opens, and she
makes that small oh turning over.

Children Must Have Manners

Belle Waring

Not morals. Manners. Grist for the guests.
They suck up the Scotch. Daddy
rattles my school report under their snouts.
See. I'm his prize piggie.
But soon as they exit,
he slaps my fat face
'cause I dropped a whole fifth.
Twelve years old.
The praise must have gone
to my head, Daddy says.

"Pig," he spits.
But when company's here,
pig's to smile till it splits.
One jangled day I'll forget
this face. Show up for breakfast
pig scraped to the bone.
Nights, alone with my face,
I peel it away, wring out the grin,
rinse it in pilfered rosewater.
While I sleep, let it work its roots.

From *Refuge* by Belle Waring © 1990. Reprinted by permission of University of Pittsburgh Press.

DEBATING SEX

The Fear That Feminism Will Free Men First

Deirdre English

Just as feminists have recognized bodily self-determination—and espe-cially the right to control their own sexuality and reproduction—as prerequisite to women's liberation, so too have antifeminist women seen connections between sexual liberation and women's vulnerability. Reject-ing the "sexual revolution" that began in the 1960s, and eschewing the legalization of abortion that followed, many right-wing women fear that men will shirk the obligation to marry and to provide for women they impregnate. But the answer to the economic and social precariousness of many women's lives, Deirdre English argues, is not antifeminism or sexual retrenchment.

For feminists, the most difficult aspect of the 1980s' backlash against women's abortion rights, and other emancipatory new rights and attitudes related to sex, is the fact that a large part of the anti-choice ("pro-life") movement is made up of women. What we have for the past ten years grown accus-tomed to calling the "women's movement" claimed to represent the collective good of all women: the opposition was expected to be male. But now we are faced with an oppos-ing women's movement, and one that also claims to stand for the best interests of all women. It is as confusing, as frustrating, as if at the height of the civil rights movement, a large percentage of blacks had suddenly orga-nized to say: "Wait a minute. We don't want

equal rights. We like things just the way they are."

The very existence of such a movement rep-resents a deep crisis in the community of women, and a profound challenge to the ana-lytical and synthetical powers of feminist theory. Before proceeding, an old feminist touchstone is a good reminder: though we may be in conflict with them, other women rarely prove to be our real enemies. Even in oppos-ing the politics of the anti-feminist woman, we must begin by recognizing and honoring her experiences, her prospects, her hopes and fears.

To do that, it is essential to separate the motivations of those men who organize against women's rights and the women who do so, even when they are found holding the same credo in the same organizations. For while men in the anti-abortion movement stand to increase the measure of male control over women, the women can gain nothing but greater sexual submission. Now that is a suspicious thing in itself, because any people asking only to give in to a more powerful group must be well convinced that their survival is at stake. After all, the anti-feminist woman is neither stupid nor incompetent, whatever she may wish her male leaders to believe. Legitimately enough, she has her own self-interest in mind, in a world in which she did not create the options.

THE OTHER WOMAN

Clearly, the anti-choice activist is not primarily concerned with refusing an abortion for herself; that she has the power to do no matter what the laws are. (By contrast, women in the pro-choice movement are almost invariably women who feel, at some level, a personal need for abortion rights.) But no one is taking away another person's right to bear children, no feminist is circumscribing individual ethical or religious beliefs that would prohibit abortion. What is solely at question to the anti-choice activist is the other woman's right to make this decision herself; her objective is to refuse social legitimation for abortion decisions that are not her own.

The anti-abortionists are, as they have been accused, seeking to impose their morality on society. But that is part of the very definition of moralism: a moralist is "one concerned with regulating the morals of others." The anti-abortion movement is a perfect example of a moralistic movement, and it demonstrates some interesting things about the limitations of moral systems.

In opposing the Right-to-Lifers, pro-choice advocates most frequently argue that a woman has an absolute right to control her own body.

The insistence on individual rights is at the foundation of the feminist position. A woman's right to control her own body encompasses endless new meanings in feminism: from the right to refuse sex (as in marital rape) to the right to a freely chosen sexuality; from the right to be protected from sexual violence to the right to plan one's own reproductivity. The complete realization of those rights alone would mark a new era for woman. For now, the recognition of woman's body as the *terra firma* of female liberation must be counted as one of the great political accomplishments of our day. But it is far from enough.

After all, this is a society: we are interdependent; individual actions have repercussions. The struggle is not and can never be only over the actual act of abortion. The struggle is necessarily over a larger sexual morality—and moral systems do have a bearing on virtually everybody's behavior. The anti-abortion people have tried to insist on single-issue politics, partly because it is much easier for them to attack the keystone of abortion than to defend the system of morality that is tied to compulsory motherhood. It falls to us to identify the moral system they are upholding and, at the same time, to define our own.

The anti-feminist woman is right about one crucial thing: the other woman's right to have an abortion does affect her. It does something very simple and, to many women, very upsetting: it takes away their ability not to choose. Where abortion is available, the birth of every baby becomes a willed choice, a purposeful act. And that new factor destroys the set of basic assumptions on which many traditional marriages have been based. It breaks the rules and wrecks the game.

THE SEX CONTRACT

Remember the rules of the old game? They began with this: men did not get to have sex with women (at least not women of their own class or higher) unless they married them. Then men were morally obligated to provide for the children they had helped to conceive. In other words, sex was supposed to incur a major responsibility for men—as it did for women. Only thirty years ago, the average marrying age in the United States was twenty for women and twenty-two for men, and hundreds of thousands of brides have been pregnant on their wedding day.

Men always complained about this sexual bargain. "Nature kidded us," said a young Irish Catholic father of two in a short story by Frank O'Connor. "We had our freedom and we didn't value it. Now our lives are run for us by women." But men's regrets, however deeply felt, were still the complaints of the relatively more powerful party. It was women who, for physical and financial reasons, really *needed* marriage.

In a society that effectively condoned widespread male sexual violence and severely restricted economic opportunities for women outside of marriage, the deck was heavily stacked. If men did not "value their freedom," women had little freedom to value. The one short-lived power women had was withholding sex; and even that was only good until marriage—possibly periodically thereafter, with the more tolerant husbands. But in general, women had to earn their keep not only with sex, but with submissiveness, and acceptance of the male not as an equal partner but as a superior. Seen in these terms, the marriage contract seems a little more like extortion under the threat of abandonment.

But to point this out is not the way to play the game. The essential thing about the system—like moral systems in general—is that everyone must play by the same rules. In the past, the community of women has often been hard on those who "give away" for free—or for money—what the rest trade for love and marriage. Then came birth control, the sexual revolution, and legalized abortion.

THE ESCAPE CLAUSE

It was the availability of relatively reliable contraception that provided the first escape clause to the old marital Russian roulette, both for men and women. The "99 percent effective" pill sparked the sexual revolution in the 1960s and 1970s and permitted women for the first time in history to decisively separate intercourse from reproduction. (Only after that historic schism could the modern woman's new fascination with discovering her own sexuality begin to emerge.)

For the most part, women of all classes and religions enthusiastically welcomed the advent of reliable contraception. True, it did have the effect of releasing men from some responsibility for their sexual acts, but the gains for women seemed much greater. Sexual liberation and birth control brought women new-found sexual pleasure, began to erode the double standard, allowed women to plan their pregnancies—and therefore participate in the work world on new terms—and in general seemed to tend to equalize the sexes. Other things, unfortunately, did not change so fast.

CATCH 22

Most women who want to have children still cannot make it, financially, without a man. In an era in which a increasingly larger number of people are spending significant parts of their lives outside of the marriage coupling, the socioeconomic differences between men and women become increasingly, painfully obvious. According to 1978 Bureau of Labor statistics, only some 7 percent of women make more than $15,000 per year, while more than 46 percent of men do. Marriage is still the major means of economic stability—even survival—for women.

In this sense, men have reaped more than their share of benefits from women's liberation. If women hold jobs, no matter how poorly paid, men may more easily renounce any responsibility for the economic support of women and children. Thus woman's meager new economic independence, and her greater sexual freedom outside the bounds of marriage, have allowed men to garner great new freedoms. Because there is no "trick of nature" to make the link between sex and fatherhood, and little social stigma on he who loves and leaves, a woman faces the abdication of any male responsibility for pregnancy—let alone for any ensuing children. If a woman gets pregnant, the man who twenty years ago might have married her may feel today that he is gallant if he splits the cost of an abortion. The man who might have remained in a dead-end marriage out of a sense of duty finds increasingly that he faces no great social disapproval if he walks out on his family, even while his kids are still in diapers.

Divorce leaves women putting a higher percentage of both their incomes and their time into child care. According to the U.S. Census the number of one-parent families headed by divorced women jumped almost 200 percent in one decade—from 956,000 in 1970 to 2.7 million in 1981. During the same period, the number of single-parent families headed by men actually declined. (Nationally, there are more youthful products of divorce cared for by relatives other than a parent than by their mothers alone.)

It is also worth noting the difference in the economic impact of divorce on fathers versus mothers. Roughly 40 percent of absent fathers contribute no money for child support after divorce, and the other 60 percent average a contribution of less than $2,000 per year. A recent study of 3,000 divorces showed, shockingly, that men improved their standard of living an average of 12 percent in the first year following divorce, while women with children saw their living standard decline by 73 percent. Under these circumstances, the fear has

risen that feminism will free men first—and might never get around to freeing women.

All this is not to imply that either men or women stay in loveless, unhappy marriages out of some sense of duty. Rather, both sexes need the right to change their circumstances. So far, our progress, like all progress, has been ragged: men, more independent to begin with, have been able to profit from women's new independence sometimes more fully than women themselves.

It seems revealing that the anti-feminist backlash, as well as the anti-sexual-liberation backlash, took so long to develop the momentum that it has today. It is the period of unremitting economic decline that has brought it on, the nightfall of economic prospects for women. It is as though the country reserved judgment during ten or fifteen years of experimentation with sexual politics, as long as economic conditions permitted it. In a climate of affluence, women had more hope of successfully freeing themselves from male-dominant relationships. But today, a greater number of working women are perceiving that the feminist revolution may not rapidly succeed in actually equalizing the material opportunities of the sexes. When working-class men no longer hold their own against unemployment, union-management rollbacks, or even inflation, what hope is there for women to close the economic gap between the male and female worker?

Giving up marriage and children for an interesting career may be one thing (although this is an either/or choice that men rarely face), but it may not be a decent trade for a dead-end job in the pink-collar ghetto. If men can no longer support families on a single paycheck, most women certainly cannot. The media presents us with the image of successful management-level women, but in fact even these women are almost always contained in middle-management positions, at under $20,000 a year. For the less-than-fervent feminist who is not prepared to pay any price at all for independence, the future looks bleak.

FEAR AND REACTION

It begins to seem clearer that the anti-feminist woman, like other women, is grappling with the terms of her survival. She is responding to social circumstances—a worsening economy, a lack of support and commitment from men—that feminists did not create and from which feminists also suffer the consequences. The conditions she faces face all women.

The differences lie in our strategies for dealing with all this. The anti-feminist woman's strategy is defensive: reactionary in the sense of reacting to change, with the desire to return to the supposedly simple solutions of the past. Like other patriotic or fundamentalist solutions, like going to war or being "born again," the longed-for return to the old feminine style seems to promise an end to complexity, compromise, and ambivalence. For many of the advocates of the anti-choice movement, the ideal is ready-made and well polished. It is the American family of the 1950s dad in the den with his pipe, mom in her sunny kitchen with cafe curtains, the girls dressed in pink and the boys in blue. It could be called nostalgic utopianism—the glorification of a lost past rather than an undiscovered future. What has not been accepted is that the route to that ideal is as impossible to find— and to many people, as little desired—as the road back to childhood.

To feminists, the only response to the dilemma of the present lies in pressing onward. We must continue to show how a complete feminist sexual and reproductive politics could lead to the transformation of all society, without curtailing the freedom of any individual. True reproductive freedom, for example, would inevitably require fair opportunities for financial equality, so that women could bear children without facing either dependency or impoverishment. There would be practical child care support for working parents of both sexes and an equal affirmation by men of their responsibility for parenthood. Yet, the individual's right to choose whether to bear a child would remain at the heart of the feminist position.

Today, the individual decision to have an abortion remains a sobering one; it puts a woman face-to-face with her dreams and her prospects and with the frequently startling fact that she is choosing not to be a passive victim, but rather an active shaper of her existence. The difficulties she will encounter as she continues to try to create her own destiny will repeatedly call for that same strength of will. In demonstrating it, she is already helping to bring about a new order of sexual equality, a world more worthy of the next generation. Few who have clearly seen the vision of that new world will want to turn back.

Study/Discussion Questions

1. According to English, why are many women afraid that feminism will "free men first"? What does she mean by this phrase?
2. What evidence does English present that this is already happening?
3. How does English think that women should try to fix the problem that feminism might liberate men more than women?

Pornography: Image and Reality

Sara Diamond

Political scientist Sara Diamond identifies a number of problems connected with pornography. In myriad ways, pornography serves to bolster an already existing system of inequality in our society, providing men in the process with more than mere titillation. The solution to the problems pornography poses, however, is not censorship, Diamond insists. Feminists need to pursue a range of alternative strategies instead.

It's not surprising that feminists have become fascinated with pornography. After all, it is the only visible, publicly accessible information about men's attitudes toward sexuality in general and women within sex in particular. For many women, the distorted images of pornography have become the symbol of men's hostility and violence against women. Women have expended tremendous effort to control the proliferation of pornography, seeking increased intervention by the police, courts, and various levels of government.

Surprisingly, however, feminism and porn have something in common. Both insist that women are sexual beings. Both have made sex an experience open to public examination and, now, debate. This difficult process of extricating sex from its once private domain cannot be abandoned in the fight against pornography. Feminist support for state censorship will lead us at a dead run into a dead end. We will find the exit blocked by highly organized conservative governments and male-dominated courts and police and the sexual freedom and control we require will be lost. Instead, we must work to repossess our sexuality, through sex education and the production of sex-positive imagery, and through changing the economic and social position of women and men—steps that will undermine the demand for sexist sexual imagery.

To explain these conclusions I plan to answer a series of questions. What is pornography? Who produces it? Who buys it and why? How does porn work as a set of images? What is the relationship of pornography to reality, fantasy, and behavior for men and women? What bearing does pornography have on sex? I want to suggest that pornography is complex and multilayered with a number of different—sometimes even contradictory—dimensions, which we oversimplify at our peril. I then want to suggest what feminists should do about pornography and what kind of alternative images we must develop.

YOU CAN TELL A MAGAZINE BY ITS CENTERFOLD

One of the greatest dangers we face when trying to understand pornography is confusing explicit sex with sexism. It is possible to create images of sexual experience that do not perpetuate the current imbalance of power between men and women. Other cultures have produced humorous, visually pleasurable or powerful images of lovemaking, free from degradation. Sexism enters the picture in the ways that the porn industry creates images and in the assumptions that people call upon when interpreting them.

In order to free sex from its armor of sexism, I want to talk about pornography in a different way from some feminists. In the 1983 Minneapolis ordinance they were instrumental in drafting, Andrea Dworkin and Catharine MacKinnon defined porn as "the sexually explicit subordination of woman graphically depicted, whether in pictures or in words." The legislation went on to outline in detail what specifically they considered to be oppressive. But this view of pornography is too simplistic, for it suggests that images of sex are the same as real sex, and that the images themselves are responsible for women's subordination.

In fact, pornography is many things: product made to be sold by a multimillion-dollar industry; a set of coded messages about sex, and male and female roles in this culture; and a specific form of sexual and cultural activity.

Pornography is produced by business interests for sale within an increasingly competitive market. To turn a profit, management must consider factors such as payment of models, camerapeople, and distributors and the cost of production equipment. These concerns influence both the quality of the product and the nature of the images that are produced. Much pornography is low budget and shoddy; little money is invested in script development. Some porn seems unrealistic, even ludicrous, unless the viewer is particularly interested in the activities shown.

Recently, increased competition in the industry has meant that porn producers have had to find new markets while keeping old customers satisfied. But while magazines such as *Playboy* may adapt to conform to changing standards of "sex appeal" or beauty, the central image in the vast majority of heterosexual pornography—that of a willing, sweet, young "girl"—remains the same. The constant nature of this ideal of womanhood provides reassurance and security for the consumers of pornography, who in buying a magazine or viewing a movie can possess in fantasy women (and their associated accoutrements) who would be unattainable in real life. In this sense, pornography is similar to advertising in that the consumer can buy the product but not the happiness or status that it promises. This unbridgeable gap between reality and fantasy encourages further purchases, whether of an advertised product or of pornography, which is a kind of advertising for—among other things—male power.

Pornography both directly exploits and indirectly exerts power over women. In the cutthroat and often coercive business they do not control, women are the critical raw material that is exchanged and molded. Not only do the images portray real women, but the finished product, which shows men symbolically controlling women during sex (either directly or through repeated scenarios of acquiescence and service), is then sold to men so that they can reassure themselves that they remain in positions of power socially and sexually. Heterosexual pornography expresses the industry's ideas about men's fantasies of sexual fulfillment and its own ideas of how men need to remain if they are to continue to buy pornography.

The industry's version of the male who reads pornography has a female corollary: the woman in pornography. Porn often pretends that women are malleable, obsessed with sex and willing to engage in any sexual act with any available partner. In violent pornography, men's supposed ability to control women is symbolized through degradation and destruction of the female body. Racist stereotypes are common; much pornography suggests that women of color are animal-like, insatiable. The plotlines or articles that accompany pictorials imply that gender identity and sexual behavior are "natural" and biologically determined. By portraying male aggression within sex as being perfectly natural, much pornography actually validates socially learned machismo.

Most pornography assumes an all-male audience. Porn movie houses and live theatres are environments where men find their response constantly reinforced by other men. Whatever doubts men may have about the accuracy of the images and the messages are repressed, for to acknowledge uncertainties would be to threaten the bonds of masculinity confirmed in these settings. Similarly, home video and magazines, which also rely heavily on the same stereotypes and conventions of action and narrative, also express an implied male agreement about sex, women, and by extension, men.

In daily life a woman's stance and facial expression communicate her sense of self, how she wants to be treated and what can be done to her. In pornography, the woman is often posed facing the viewer, her expression expectant or eager; or with her back to us, face turned over the shoulder to look at the viewer, waiting or even cowering submissively. When a man is shown, he is frequently positioned so that it is easy for the male viewer to imagine himself in the male model's place. The pleasure here is not about rejoicing in mutual seeing and touching, but about the clothed and invulnerable male observer watching and controlling the naked woman in the fantasy. (Female naked-

ness in this culture is most often interpreted as sexual availability, for it is in this way that the female nude has been presented and interpreted sine the advent of the oil painting tradition.)

The visual nature of porn images reinforces perceptions of male control over female bodies in another way as well. Because of the tendency in sexist culture to reduce women to functions rather than to cherish their individuality, feminists have rightly criticized the way pornography concentrates on fragments of the female form: a breast, foot, mouth. This allows the viewer to distance himself from the real person to whom the fragment belongs, avoiding the demands of relating to a whole, intelligent, emotional, and active woman. But it is also true that photography as a medium captures living, moving people and dynamic processes, immortalizing them outside of time and change. So while people may read images of fragments as frozen or deathlike, and hence when depicting women, as containing an added measure of misogynist feeling, this need not always be the case, nor is it inherent in visual fragmentation.

The immortalization effect of fragmentation also does something else: it gives the image another level of meaning, making it symbolic of memory or sentiment, seeming to express the "essence" of the complex process represented on the film. And, sexism aside, fragments are often more erotic than the whole image because they are associated with memories or dreams of pleasure for all of us. The prevalence of breasts, vaginas, women's mouths, and buttocks says as much about the power men have to fill social space with images of their dreams and desires as it does about the tendency of our sexist culture to fragment women. And given that power, it is not surprising that women's body parts have become symbols of heterosexual pleasure for both women and men.

On a different but related level, pornography also provides men with opportunities to indulge in "scopophilia"—the voyeuristic pleasure of simply looking without acting. This kind of sexual activity allows men to remain passive. They can be sexually unassertive as the images or narrative act to arouse them, without having to deal with potentially awkward or frightening social dynamics if they take the passive—the traditionally feminine—role in a sexual encounter. There are other aspects to voyeurism. We are inundated with visual imagery in North America, and I believe that the increased popularity of visual pornography can in part be attributed to this phenomenon. We have become used to experiencing pleasure and gathering information from visuals, so that while the voyeurism that pornography encourages is an ideological confirmation of men's power, it is also a contemporary way of fulfilling curiosity about sex in general, and about others' sexual activities.

All these aspects of pornography are in some sense easily visible, understandable, and evident. But there are other dimensions that do not immediately meet the eye and, almost paradoxically, seem to contradict pornography's more obvious aspects—at least those that claim that men are in complete control. Because I believe that in terms of *unconscious* messages, much pornography is ultimately about men's fears: of inadequacy, of being controlled by women emotionally and sexually through dependency, of losing power.

In recent years women have demanded sexual as well as social and economic equality. The fact that women can have clitoral orgasms independent of penetration has become widely known, as have many women's choices for lifestyles autonomous from men. Both these recent developments directly threaten culturally formed masculine sexual identities, and feminists have suggested that the recent boom in pornography may be part of the resultant anti-feminist backlash, for it reassures men that women are still under men's thumbs. There is no doubt in my mind that these recent devel-

opments are being felt at a deep level by many men. But they are not alone the cause of men's existing fears of women, fears that are old, deeply ingrained, and part of very traditional gender socialization.

Susan Lurie, writing from a neo-Freudian perspective, suggests the following process of psychological formation, one that could be described as "womb envy." According to Lurie, male babies and young boys identity with their mothers, who have nurtured them both physically and emotionally. But our society demands of young boys that they break the bond with the mother early in life. In this process, Lurie says, they learn that their penis—signaling their membership in the dominant group—is the source of their pleasure, individuality, and power in the world. They are forced to choose between identifying with their fathers or with their mothers—whom they love, but who have no penis and therefore no power. Given this training, boys fear being seen as women—without a penis, castrated—and thus losing their growing power in the world.

Lurie suggests that heterosexual intercourse simultaneously promises men self-fulfillment through pleasure and conquest and threatened loss of identity through contact with the vagina, the symbol of female sexuality. That a man experiences arousal from sexual contact with women is delightful, but also recalls his early childhood love for his mother, a love that he was forced to reject and fear. The heterosexual relationship becomes laden with conflict for men. The female sexual organs seem to represent the latent power of women, for unlike the exposed penis, women's genitals are self-contained and invulnerable. In intercourse the vagina acts upon the penis to change it, from erect, to orgasmic, to flaccid. In Lurie's view, "The vagina is like the imagination; not only does it take in and transform, it is internal." The woman's body appears to be what he has learned that only he as a male can be: active and transforming in the world. The womb, to which the vagina leads, has an even greater creative power; it can produce babies, again reminding the man of his former childhood dependency. For men, intercourse involves the contradiction of allowing an expression of individuality while threatening to destroy that sense of self by making them vulnerable.

The sexist messages within pornography offer comfort in the face of these fears. The exposure of women's sexual parts demonstrates both women's vulnerability and men's ability to control them. Violent images of sexual mutilation of women, by themselves and others, proves that women can be castrated instead of castrating. Sexist pornography provides a set of mythic ideas—feminists have said that mythic or not, they amount to lies—that serve to allay men's fear of losing power. They thus assuage deeply felt anxieties that, no doubt, are hard to live with for many men, even if the distress is unconscious. But these fears can only be deprived of their crippling effect on men if they are made explicit and analyzed, or defused through different erotic messages and surpassed (as suggested later)—not if they are constantly reinforced by the sexist symbolism inherent in most pornography. Other possibilities of identity and pleasure need to come alive in images and in life.

And this is not impossible. When a critical mixed setting exists—one in which men can allow themselves to identify and feel solidarity with women and resist the sexist masculine bonding encouraged by much pornography—the spell of porn can often be broken. A good illustration of this was the experience of Vancouver antipornography organizers when they showed three excerpts from Red Hot Video's particularly violent tapes in 1983. Those attending, including male reporters, were unanimously disturbed by the images. The usual porn theatre environment—the sense of an enclosed space controlled by men—was dispelled. By contrast, a women reporter later showed one of the tapes to colleagues in the newsroom. Here she was the only woman in a group of men. They ridiculed her and belittled her discomfort, telling her that the tape wasn't "real," just fantasy. In the first case, men's potential to identify with women was accentuated and produced positive results. In the second, men's fear of breaking masculine identification got the better of them.

IMAGE, REALITY AND BEHAVIOR: A COMPLEX INTERFACE

There is a prevalent belief in our culture that images represent reality in a literal way, when in fact they are the result of a whole series of manipulations. Camera angles (direct, from above or below); framing (close in to long shot); the composition of the picture (what comprises a scene and what in that scene is included in the final frame); the relationship of audio to video images (think of the difference between "No, no" and "Yes, yes" in a sex scene); editing styles (fast cuts versus real time, what is included and excluded); and sequence and implied plotline all intervene between the real experience and the image. These elements work together to provide a specific message, one constructed by the maker of the image, which is then interpreted by viewers who impose the conventions they have learned to use when "reading" visual symbols.

Just as images do not present a literal view of reality, so there is no direct relationship between what an image shows and what its viewer acts out. Feminist theorists such as Kathleen Barry and Laura Lederer espouse a version of behaviorist psychology, according to which the human male runs the treadmill of sexual violence for gratification in the same way a caged rat will run for cheese. Because some pornographic images suggest that sexual violence gives men more power and because the images result in orgasms (that is, this theory goes, positive reinforcement), pornography therefore conditions men to rape and abuse real women. While some men may be aroused by images of violence against women (including in nonsexually explicit contexts), few men will act on these images. The idea that every time women get a thrill from watching women TV cops Cagney and Lacey shoot a crime suspect we want to kill, or that scenes of destruction, bombing, or torture in which "our side" wins trigger our desire to hurt other human beings runs counter to most women's experience. The suggestion that consumers of pornographic material or other media products respond in zombie-like, imitative fashion to all powerful images is both false and frightening.

A similar misconception about the relation between image and experience is that the pornography viewer gets everything he needs—his whole sexual experience—from the image itself. In fact, there are other important contributing factors. In addition to the preconscious fantasies or memories pornography stimulates, its taboo nature combines with and accentuates the expectation of arousal virtually on its own. (I am watching porn, therefore I'm supposed to get turned on, therefore even if it's an image of a lettuce leaf I am going to get turned on.) Again the all-male, high-pressure environment in which a lot of porn is viewed may provide enough of a context for stimulation that the storyline or images don't really matter. In fact, men's responses are influenced by a wide range of elements, from the viewing context, to the specific images seen, to the relative absence of responsibility offered by the fantasy portrayed. While the porn industry (and some feminist theorists) may argue that men's attitudes toward sex are universal, there is actually an infinite variety of individual differences interwoven with their group similarities. There are men, for example, who enjoy being made love to, abandoning the role of aggressor/initiator; while others cannot relinquish their macho control. (Many men's experience and desire exist somewhere in be-

tween these poles.) It is quite possible that two such men would have very different emotional experiences when confronted with identical images.

Another aspect of the conditioning theory is the idea that men's response to pornography follows a continuum, that viewing soft-core porn inevitably leads men to seek out hard-core, violent material. Certainly both men's and women's definitions of what is "normal" in terms of sexual behavior changes over time, shifts that are related to social and economic trends. For example, the pressure from women for more sexual autonomy that began in the late '60s can be linked to such factors as the greater number of women entering the workforce, the availability of effective birth control and a general questioning of other social norms. But the notion that porn is addictive relies on the same faulty thinking that suggests that use of marijuana leads inevitably to heroin—patently untrue, as the experience of millions of North Americans proves. And the greater general visibility and acceptability of sexual imagery reflects not only the backlash against women but also real gains by the women's and gay movements in making sexuality an area of more open and explicit discussion and depiction.

In fact, one of the attractions of pornography is that it shows illicit acts that are safer, both legally and emotionally, when kept in the realm of fantasy. For some people not believing the fantasy psychologically allows arousal that the guilt of believing or doing would destroy. I am not saying, as the pornography industry often does, that pornography is a healthy release for violent men, but I do think there is a wide gulf between the fantasy, no matter how grotesque, and the reality. In trying to understand this fantasy/reality relationship it's useful for us as women to recall our own fantasy life: our imagination shifts and changes based on how much power we have in our lives and our relationships, as well as on the basis of our early patterns of sexual response. We, too, often engage in fantasies that we would not like to act out in our real lives. We may fantasize about sexual activity or people we have left behind; our fantasies are sometimes even the converse of our real lives.

Admittedly violent pornography and other violent media such as television do provide models for the minority of men who do act out sexual violence against women. But pornography influences reality in much the same way as the idea that "a woman's place is in the home" does, because both reinforce existing social structures. Our male-dominated legal system makes it easier for men to get away with violent behavior toward women; and pornography further pressures some—possibly many—women to do what is asked of them without complaint. (Check out the *Cosmo* sex advice columns too.) But these are problems with our values, our mass media, and our system of justice. Censorship won't make general ideas of violence against women go away; it won't make pornography disappear, just move underground. And even if porn were to miraculously disappear, violence against women would continue as long as other oppressive structures remained in place.

THIS IS WHO YOU WOULD BE AND COULD BE IF YOU WEREN'T YOU

The female viewer seldom sees her experience reflected in pornography or mainstream films or television. Consequently women have the difficult choice of either identifying with the man's point of view as expressed through script and image, or identifying with the screen woman and her experience, again created by men. The alternatives force women to choose between sustaining false expectations of women's behavior by objectifying other women or trying to live up to standards that usually defy experience.

For women, watching porn can draw us into a complex knot of pleasure and discomfort. While we may be aroused by the sexual activities depicted, most of us cannot avoid identification with the woman in the image, even if we occasionally and sometimes simultaneously identity with the man in the fantasy. Whatever pleasure we experience is often mixed with anxiety about our own sexuality being so different from that shown and anger at being forced into a role that does not represent who we are and what we need sexually. One Vancouver antipornography organizer studying violent pornography described the importance of understanding what aspects of the images she found pleasurable and the ways that these were immediately followed by images of pain. The structure of the video linked pleasure and pain again and again through fast editing, yet this bore no relationship to her own concept of enjoyable sex. She described her anger at having to constantly step backwards and remember that the images were constructed by real people to create a specific effect.

Women are taught to identity our own sexuality with an ideal of femininity. Many women describe a sense of being always watched, and of performing. Our culture equates women's sexuality with sexual availability; we learn from an early age to be coy, to flirt, to move seductively to make men respond to us. We learn to feel pleasure at the other's pleasure, to project sexuality in response to men's desire. This way we are continually told, we will be desired, loved, and taken care of. When we see images of other women being sexual with men, we project our identities onto the image, feeling the power relative to men. The depiction of sex can trigger memories or fantasies that are quite separate from that shown in the picture. The problem is that when we return to the actual image, we are usually confronted with a message that destroys our power and pleasure.

For many women sexual fantasy involves not only participation in a set of actions, but certain emotional settings and coordinates. Love magazines and mass-market romances are the equivalent of women's pornography. They often contain explicit details of love-making, but always in the framework of passion, "true love," and "tenderness." Invariably the stories include details of the setting, the heroine's wardrobe, the obstacles in her immediate situation. The descriptions of the dynamics in the relationship with the man (he is her boss, married to someone else, has denied her, is pursuing her, and so on) and the feelings before, during, and after intercourse are also always included. These and their placing in a larger narrative context are the things that differentiate women's from men's sexually explicit literature. But these "feelings" and descriptions are not necessarily benign or even positive frameworks for sexual experience. Indeed they are often vehicles that convey strong messages about the dangers of pre- and extramarital sex and many other types of behavior proscribed by traditional (that is, patriarchal) morality. In these, too, pleasure is often linked to issues of punishment and loss of power.

In fact, there is nowhere we as women can exist freely without being castigated for our sexuality. Part of many women's aversion to graphic sexual imagery may well stem from the literal or figurative kick in the teeth that comes with being a sexual woman. We are well-taught that to be treated properly we must keep our legs crossed at all times. Explicit sexual imagery makes us uncomfortable because it is public, and we have learned that to engage in public displays of sexuality is to be defined as a slut. Where boys learn that sex makes them powerful, we learn that it makes us powerless and bad.

Given the way that our sexuality is repressed and channeled in our childhood, it's no wonder that women often recoil from the idea of the depiction of sex. Thirty years ago, studies such as Kinsey's indicated that women responded less to visual stimuli than did men,

and women's greater sexual repression (relatively speaking) has often been cited to explain what they found. In part this explanation is probably valid. But there are other factors too: visual imagery is often inaccurate in representing what gives us pleasure; we may feel humiliated at the display of women in sexist poses; we may think that the men who are depicted in conventions which represent men's mistaken views of what turns us on look ridiculous.

The growing availability of pornography geared toward women and men and the increasing popularity of events such as male strip shows for women audiences indicate that women's lack of enthusiasm for sexually explicit visual stimulation may be changing as women become more skilled and assertive about seeking something for themselves within the current male-dominated sex culture—a concept that is backed up by recent studies. Still many factors will have to change—childhood and adult treatment of our sexuality, the representation of women and men within our visual culture—before we can evaluate with any objectivity if there is anything to the notion that women are less interested or moved by imagery per se.

One important example of the discrepancy between women's internal erotic experience and most pornographic depictions is the area of submission. There is a wide gap between the fantasies of submission that we construct for ourselves and those that porn fabricates for us. Most women seldom imagine being hurt by men in a sexual context, but many women do fantasize about being ravished. It is not surprising that women daydream about being uncontrollably desired in a culture in which our value as human beings is based on our attractiveness, and in which we are constantly prevented from acting out our desires. If we fantasize a partner taking complete control of a sexual encounter, then we are absolved from responsibility for our abandoned behavior. In this way we can mentally break sexual taboos that still remain in place in practice. We can also use fantasy to confront and explore what we are afraid of. But no matter how passive a woman is in her fantasy, she is still in control of it, she can end or change it as she desires. This is very different from the male variations on these fantasies created by the pornography industry. Needless to say, it is an entirely different situation from real rape and abuse.

Because pornography itself has so many levels and dimensions, it is my conclusion that strategies related to pornography must develop on a series of levels as well. However, it's important to begin by noting that fundamental changes in how sexual identities and behaviors are learned will not come about through suppressing images. No matter how insidious and antiwoman much pornography may be, it is not the primary cause of the repression of women's autonomous sexuality and the continued existence of male domination. Social and economic structures that create dependency on the sex market, reproduce the powerlessness of women, and perpetuate women's cultural objectification create misogynist culture, and it is against these we must take aim. Porn will exist either underground or in the mainstream, as it currently does, until the roots of sexism are uncovered and broken.

In fact, nothing short of the full feminist agenda outlined elsewhere in this book [*Women Against Censorship,* edited by Varda Burstyn, 1985] will resolve the problem of pornography. We need economic equality and to win the right to free sexual expression, and control of our bodies, so that women will no longer be forced to work in the sex industry or submit to sexual activity that they do not like. Sex education in the schools, birth control, day care, access to abortion, facilities for raped and battered women, rights for lesbians and gays, and education about sexual alternatives are necessary. But while there is no substitute for long-term political and economic change, in the short term feminists have an essential role

to play in developing an open and comprehensive discussion of sexuality and creating alternatives to the imagery offered by the porn industry.

We need to really talk about sex within the women's movement and within society in general. Narrowing such an exploration to porn inevitably leads to the idea that images cause the problems with sexuality in this culture, rather than simply portraying the problems. It reinforces in men's and women's minds the age-old notion that women are victims requiring protection rather than subjective sexual beings. Sexuality is a difficult and sometimes painful subject to discuss openly; we need a minimum of moralizing and a maximum of analysis.

Porn remains about the only source of explicit information on sex for young people. I can remember hours poring over my parents' blue novels or rifling secretively through *Playboy* at the corner drugstore. (And I wonder how many other feminists have emerged, critical perspectives intact, from an early flirtation with pornography.) Unless women provide alternative—and accessible—information and instruction about sexuality, porn's appeal as one of the few sources of information about sex, no matter how distorted, will remain.

This discussion can expand to include the ways that we are delighted and empowered by sexual experience. Men can challenge their response to pornography and engage male viewers in analysis and antiporn organizing. It is important for men to understand the ways that some components of their emotional and sexual selves are denied and others warped by pornography. Porn is in many ways less a women's issue than a men's issue, for the consumer is male and the product exists to assuage men's insecurities and fears.

Any tactics that we use that would directly affect the availability of porn should be chosen for their educational value: to show that this misrepresentation of women's bodies and identities makes us angry and to pose alternate ways of approaching sexuality in this culture. Community picket lines and sit-ins aimed at porn outlets can be effective, but only if we are careful about who we ally ourselves with and channel our anger, not calling for state censorship, but for consumers and communities to take responsibility for the images that they accept.

While images do not determine reality, they are unquestionably powerful. The women's movement is currently devoting vast economic and human resources to fighting existing pornography and other media imagery. It is my feeling that we would gain more by seeking resources to allow women to flood the market with feminist productions and to have access to the mass media in positions of real power and in large numbers. Imagine the impact that a woman-controlled television station could have. Widely distributed feminist imagery would be a provocative and active contradiction to the sexist imagery of all the current mass media.

While we are organizing for such access, a broad range of productions are needed. Documentary work needs to move beyond simply showing the content of pornography to examining the ways in which the meaning of porn images are created. One of the problems with existing educational material such as *Not a Love Story* and the slide show put together by the New York-based Women Against Pornography is that the format and camera positions force us to look over the shoulder of the viewer or through his eyes. If we are to look at pornography, we must recognize the way the images work so as not to feel victimized by its content or be unwitting collaborators in its voyeurism. We must also leave room in the discussion for our emotional and sexual responses to emerge.

An analysis of the relationship, historic and current, between the repression of sexuality and the appeal of pornography is needed and it could perhaps coincide with a feminist history of censorship. Cross-cultural work that exam-

ines alternative ways of representing sexuality could illustrate how our society isolates and contains sexuality in a limited and limiting framework. There is tremendous power in realizing that pornographic images are created by people and that we as women can construct imagery of equal or greater impact.

Many women would like to see their sexuality not as a separate part of their lives, but as an empowering aspect of who they are as individuals and in relation to others. We catch glimpses of this possibility when we experience our eroticism in creative work and play outside the sex act. Such feminist critics as Audre Lourde have argued that the power of pornography can be usurped by demonstrating the eroticism embedded in everyday experience and emotion; by framing sex within the context of other activities, rather than elevating it to a romanticized or lowering it to a "dirty" event; by showing women as multidimensional human beings. Work that indicates that men and women's experience of sexuality integrates intellectual, emotional, and physical processes is important in challenging porn's assumption that sex is naturally an uncontrollable, cathartic, and independent force.

But there must be, as well, a place for imagery that is totally concerned with sex. Our society is one in which sexuality is isolated and treated as a category unto itself. While expanding the definition of eroticism is valuable, we need to retain contact with sex in our creative work. Unless we directly address the issue of what gives us pleasure, we will again abandon that terrain to pornography. Some feminists have defined erotica as images about sexuality that show equal power relationships and exchanges between mutually loving and committed people. But who will define what constitutes "equality," "love," and "commitment"? And even if we agree on the meaning of these words, one woman's dream may be another's prison. This society has traditionally chained woman's sexuality to a love/monogamy ideal.

Let's not create new constraining ideas of what women's behavior should be, ideas that would rob us of our right to explore our desires on our own terms. We need to examine our feelings of lust, our desire for power, our objectification of others, how anger can be expressed within and through sexuality, our attraction to particular aspects of others' identities and images, and more, and not demand that our or others' fantasies conform to an abstract idea of politically correct sex.

At the same time as we examine erotic content, we need to look at visual stereotypes. In part, we can break the code through which images are read by contradiction, for reversing rules can force viewers to challenge their assumptions. We could put overalls onto women in lingerie; show men's fascination with their own image; challenge the stereotype of what a sexually active woman looks like; clothe women and leave men naked; interrupt standard porn scripts (for example, women breaking in on a rape scene and freeing the victim as they did in *Born in Flames,* or the victim resisting, defeating her rapist, and punishing, perhaps dismembering him.) As well, we can blur sexually explicit images, create an ambiance of desire, invest men with caring, sensitivity, and the desire to be made love to. Women can also exert control in the way that they compose images; through the placement of camera and those within its frame the ever present, invisible male voyeur can be banished.

Inevitably, given our individual differences and the vast, unexplored terrain of our sexuality, one woman's porn is another's erotic art. If we are honest about images and ideas that inspire our sexuality, I think we will find a combination of the old castoffs of our training in a patriarchal culture, the ignored and frustrated elements of our present sexuality and new glimpses of pleasure, freedom, and power. It is from the struggle with these conflicting feelings and impulses that really thoughtful and powerful imagery can emerge. It is impossible

to completely separate images from their historic contexts; even pleasant images of cabbages that unroll like labia or fields reminiscent of the folds and curves of women's bodies are rooted in a long-standing romantic ideal of feminine beauty, one created by men. We need to think through the images that we use and to understand what of our current sexuality we want to retain and develop.

In the last decade, women cultural producers have been creating all kinds of work that grapples with sexual themes. In the last three years several feminist-organized erotic art shows have been mounted in Vancouver, Toronto, and Montreal, featuring multimedia presentations. The 1981 Herotica erotic art show in Vancouver developed dynamic processes in choosing and making images for a show. Organizers first looked at porn and other "suggestive" images of women, then discussed the imagery that they found most appealing within the traditional ways of representing women and then consciously developed images that did not correspond to these categories. While the final visions were somewhat abstract and highly individual, the process of developing the show is a valuable model for work of its kind.

Entre Nous, directed by Diane Kurys, explored the deep friendship and erotic attraction that woman can feel for each other, and though it studiously avoids explicit imagery, it gives us a sense of erotic tension very different from most "malestream" films. Persimmon Blackbridge is a Vancouver artist who also conveys sexual energy in unusual, moving ways. In one of her sculptures two women hold hands, their bodies molded as though they were floating down a river, alive with the current pushed apart by the water's force but held together by their touch. The piece evokes a sense of orgasmic transcendence and individual integrity.

Feminist images often contain the impulse toward self-validation, of reassessing and enjoying our bodies. These examples also bespeak an alternative lesbian vision, and in doing so state that lesbianism exists as a positive form of sexuality. This is important in a culture in which heterosexuality is perceived and shown time and again to be "natural" and absolute. Concurrently, the development of alternate heterosexual imagery is very important, for it is heterosexual women's experience that is most often distorted by porn. Women can exert control over where and to whom we show our work. We can choose whether we want to show our fantasies (whether lesbian or heterosexual) to women alone or also use them to reeducate men. Showing erotic work in a context where it is discussed and analyzed helps to break down the traditional private space reserved for porn.

A number of feminist critics of pornography have resisted the idea of creating alternative imagery. They have said that such activity would only reinforce the male viewer's response to sexual images of women, and believe that even feminist erotica would support the market framework of pornography if it were produced to be sold within a capitalist culture market.

After examining the ways that pornographic images work, it is clear that there is no simple solution to the first issue. Male viewers of feminist-created erotica may well derive pleasure from the imagery, but surely feminists' objections are not to men's sexual pleasure per se, but to its current dependency on degrading images of women. Indeed, enjoying powerful images of women may break down men's fears of women by destroying the lies that porn tells

about women's passivity and desire to be dominated. There is an additional concern that some women express: Does the male viewer reinterpret even positive images of women through oppressive conventions by, for example, assuming that any naked woman is available? But there are two other factors whose importance overrides this. First, for most men skillful images that empower women are not easily assimilated into patriarchal and misogynist interpretations, so that the very notion of "availability" would dissolve if an image could signal that women were self-defining and in charge. Second, and most important, women must become less concerned about men's response to our images than with creating visual material that helps us define and fight for our own sexuality.

There is a great area of exploration that is in its infancy, despite important developments in video, film, visual and performing arts. Increased censorship and other forms of institutional control over our sexual experience are on the upswing. The organized right and the state want to silence our visions, for they understand their potential power, at the same time as they enforce their traditional vision of the family, suppress abortion, birth control, lesbian and gay sexuality, and sex education. Feminists can succumb to the pressures for censorship or we can aggressively present educational and artistic images that show the world as we view it and wish to see it, as part of a fight for a prowoman and sex-positive society.

Study/Discussion Questions

1. How does pornography reinforce sexual inequality in our society, in the author's view?
2. What does pornography give to men (in addition to sexual arousal)?
3. What messages about women's sexuality and desires are transmitted through pornography?
4. Why does Diamond think that censorship is the wrong response to pornography?
5. What alternatives to censorship does she believe that feminists should pursue?

Erotica and Pornography
A Clear and Present Difference

Gloria Steinem

Gloria Steinem weighed in early in the "sex debates" that divided feminists into opposing camps on the question of pornography. Published in Ms. *magazine in 1978, this essay attempts to distinguish between erotica and pornography. Though the terms are often confused in popular usage, Steinem claims that "a clear and present difference" separates the two. Erotica, rooted in eros, bears little resemblance to pornography, which stems etymologically and factually from violence, captivity, and disdain for women. Until these two concepts get untangled, Steinem insists, "there will be little murders in our beds—and very little love."*

Human beings are the only animals that experience the same sex drive at times when we can—and cannot—conceive.

Just as we developed uniquely human capacities for language, planning, memory, and invention along our evolutionary path, we also developed sexuality as a form of expression; a way of communicating that is separable from our need for sex as a way of perpetuating ourselves. For humans alone sexuality can be and often is primarily a way of bonding, of giving and receiving pleasure, bridging differentness, discovering sameness, and communicating emotion.

We developed this and other human gifts through our ability to change our environment, adapt physically, and in the long run, to affect our own evolution. But as an emotional result of this spiraling path away from other animals, we seem to alternate between periods of exploring our unique abilities to forge new boundaries, and feelings of loneliness in the unknown that we ourselves have created; a fear that sometimes sends us back to the comfort of the animal world by encouraging us to exaggerate our sameness.

The separation of "play" from "work," for instance, is a problem only in the human world. So is the difference between art and nature, or an intellectual accomplishment and a physical one. As a result, we celebrate play, art, and invention as leaps into the unknown; but any imbalance can send us back to nostalgia for our primate past and the conviction that the basics of work, nature, and physical labor are somehow more worthwhile or even moral.

In the same way, we have explored our sexuality as separable from conception: a pleasurable, empathetic bridge to strangers of the same species. We have even invented contraception—a skill that has probably existed in some form since our ancestors figured out the process of birth—in order to extend this uniquely human difference. Yet we also have times of atavistic suspicion that sex is not complete—or even legal or intended-by-god—if it cannot end in conception.

No wonder the concepts of "erotica" and "pornography" can be so crucially different, and yet so confused. Both assume that sexuality can be separated from conception, and therefore can be used to carry a personal message. That's a major reason why, even in our current culture, both may be called equally "shocking" or legally "obscene," a word whose Latin derivative means "dirty, containing filth." This gross condemnation of all sexuality that isn't harnessed to childbirth and marriage has been increased by the current backlash against women's progress. Out of fear that the whole patriarchal structure might be upset if women really had the autonomous power to decide our reproductive futures (that is, if we controlled the most basic means of production), rightwing groups are not only denouncing prochoice abortion literature as "pornographic," but are trying to stop the sending of all contraceptive information through the mails by invoking obscenity laws. In fact, Phyllis Schlafly recently denounced the entire Women's Movement as "obscene."

Not surprisingly, this religious, visceral backlash has a secular, intellectual counterpart that relies heavily on applying the "natural" behavior of the animal world to humans. That is questionable in itself, but these Lionel Tigerish studies make their political purpose even more clear in the particular animals they select and the habits they choose to emphasize. The message is that females should accept their "destiny" of being sexually dependent and devote themselves to bearing and rearing their young.

Defending against such reaction in turn leads to another temptation: to merely reverse the terms, and declare that all nonprocreative sex is good. In fact, however, this human activity can be as constructive or destructive, moral or immoral, as any other. Sex as communication can send messages as different as life and death; even the origins of "erotica" and

---

porn-, por'no-. From Greek *porne,* prostitute (prob. from *pernemi,* sell, as captives) . . . **por-nog'ra-phy,** *n.* **1.** Description of prostitutes and of prostitution . . . **2.** The expression or suggestion of the obscene in speaking, writing, etc.; licentious art or literature.

e-rot'ic, *a.* Of or pertaining to passionate love or sexual desire; suggested by or treating of love; amorous; amatory. . . . *n.* **1.** *Lit.* An amatory composition, especially in poetry. **2.** *sing. or pl.* A theory or science of love.

 —from *Funk & Wagnalls New Standard Dictionary of the English Language* "pornography" reflect that fact. After all, "erotica" is rooted in eros or passionate love, and thus in the idea of positive choice, free will, the yearning for a particular person. (Interestingly, the definition of erotica leaves open the question of gender.) "Pornography" begins with a root meaning "prostitution" or "female captives," thus letting us know that the subject is not mutual love, or love at all, but domination and violence against women. (Though, of course, homosexual pornography may imitate this violence by putting a man in the "feminine" role of victim.) It ends with a root meaning "writing about" or "description of" which puts still more distance between subject and object, and replaces a spontaneous yearning for closeness with objectification and a voyeur.

The difference is clear in the words. It becomes even more so by example.

Look at any photo or film of people making love, really making love. The images may be diverse, but there is usually a sensuality and touch and warmth, an acceptance of bodies and nerve endings. There is always a spontaneous sense of people who are there because they want to be, out of shared pleasure.

Now look at any depiction of sex in which there is clear force, or an unequal power that spells coercion. It may be very blatant, with weapons of torture or bondage, wounds and bruises, some clear humiliation, or an adult's sexual power being used over a child. It may be much more subtle: a physical attitude of conqueror and victim, the use of race or class difference to imply the same thing, perhaps a very unequal nudity, with one person exposed and vulnerable while the other is clothed. In either case, there is no sense of equal choice or equal power.

The first is erotic: a mutually pleasurable, sexual expression between people who have enough power to be there by positive choice. It may or may not strike a sense-memory in the viewer, or be creative enough to make the unknown seem real; but it doesn't require us to identify with a conqueror or a victim. It is truly sensuous, and may give us a contagion of pleasure.

The second is pornographic: its message is violence, dominance, and conquest. It is sex being used to reinforce some inequality, or to create one, or to tell us the lie that pain and humiliation (ours or someone else's) are really the same as pleasure. If we are to feel anything, we must identify with conqueror or victim. That means we can only experience pleasure through the adoption of some degree of sadism or masochism. It also means that we may feel diminished by the role of conqueror or enraged, humiliated, and vengeful by sharing identity with the victim.

Perhaps one could simply say that erotica is about sexuality, but pornography is about power and sex-as-weapon—in the same way we have come to understand that rape is about violence, and not really about sexuality at all.

Yes, it's true that there are women who have been forced by violent families and dominating men to confuse love with pain; so much so that they have become masochists. (A fact that in no way excuses those who administer such pain.) But the truth is that, for most women—and for men with enough humanity to imagine themselves into the predicament of women—true pornography could serve as aversion therapy for sex.

Of course, there will always be personal differences about what is and is not erotic, and there may be cultural differences for a long time to come. Many women feel that sex makes them vulnerable and therefore may continue to need more sense of personal connection and safety before allowing any erotic feelings. We now find competence and expertise erotic in men, but that may pass as we develop those qualities in ourselves. Men, on the other hand, may continue to feel less vulnerable, and therefore more open to such potential danger as sex with strangers. As some men replace the need for submission from childlike women with the pleasure of cooperation from equals, they may find a partner's competence to be erotic, too.

Such group changes plus individual differences will continue to be reflected in sexual love between people of the same gender, as well as between women and men. The point is not to dictate sameness, but to discover ourselves and each other through sexuality that is an exploring, pleasurable, empathetic part of our lives; a human sexuality that is unchained both from unwanted pregnancies and from violence.

But that is a hope, not a reality. At the moment, fear of change is increasing both the indiscriminate repression of all nonprocreative sex in the religious and "conservative" male world, and the pornographic vengeance against women's sexuality in the secular world of "liberal" or "radical" men. It's almost futuristic to debate what is and is not truly erotic, when many women are again being forced into compulsory motherhood, and the number of pornographic murders, tortures, and woman-hating images are on the increase in both popular culture and real life.

It's a familiar division: wife or whore, "good" woman who is constantly vulnerable to pregnancy or "bad" woman who is unprotected from violence. *Both* roles would be upset if we were to control our own sexuality. And that's exactly what we must do.

In spite of all our atavistic suspicions and training for the "natural" role of motherhood, we took up the complicated battle for reproductive freedom. Our bodies had borne the health burden of endless births and poor abortions, and we had a greater motive for separating sexuality and conception.

Now we have to take up the equally complex burden of explaining that all nonprocreative sex is *not* alike. We have a motive: our right to a uniquely human sexuality, and sometimes even to survival. As it is, our bodies have too rarely been enough our own to develop erotica in our own lives, much less in art and literature. And our bodies have too often been the objects of pornography and the woman-hating, violent practice that it preaches. Consider also our spirits that break a little each time we see ourselves in chains or full labial display for the conquering male viewer, bruised or on our knees, screaming a real or pretended pain to delight the sadist, pretending to enjoy what we don't enjoy, to be blind to the images of our sisters that really haunt us—humiliated often enough ourselves by the truly obscene idea that sex and the domination of women must be combined.

Sexuality is human, free, separate—and so are we.

But until we untangle the lethal confusion of sex with violence, there will be more pornography and less erotica. There will be little murders in our beds—and very little love.

Study/Discussion Questions

1. How does Steinem define erotica?
2. How does she define pornography?
3. Do you agree with her definitions? Do you think there is a clear difference between the two?
4. What makes erotica acceptable, in Steinem's view?
5. What makes pornography unacceptable, in her view?

Pornography, Oppression, and Freedom: A Closer Look

Helen Longino

Philosopher Helen E. Longino defines pornography as "verbal or pictorial material which represents or describes sexual behavior that is degrading or abusive to one or more of the participants in such a way as to endorse the degradation." The sexual content of the material alone is not the issue for feminists, she says; the combination of sex and degradation is. Because pornography defames and libels women, depriving them of their civil and human rights, it needs to be eliminated, Longino argues. Until that happens, we will not have a "cultural climate" that will tolerate women's liberation.

I. INTRODUCTION

The much-touted sexual revolution of the 1960s and 1970s not only freed various modes of sexual behavior from the constraints of social disapproval, but also made possible a flood of pornographic material. According to figures provided by WAVPM (Women Against Violence in Pornography and Media), the number of pornographic magazines available at newsstands has grown from zero in 1953 to forty in 1977, while sales of pornographic films in Los Angeles alone have grown from $15 million in 1969 to $85 million in 1976.[1]

Traditionally, pornography was condemned as immoral because it presented sexually explicit material in a manner designed to appeal to "prurient interests" or a "morbid" interest in nudity and sexuality, material which further-more lacked any redeeming social value and which exceeded "customary limits of candor." While these phrases, taken from a definition of "obscenity" proposed in the 1954 American Law Institute's *Model Penal Code,*[2] require some criteria of application to eliminate vagueness, it seems that what is objectionable is the explicit description or representation of bodily parts or sexual behavior for the purpose of inducing sexual stimulation or pleasure on the part of the reader or viewer. This kind of objection is part of a sexual ethic that subordinates sex to procreation and condemns all sexual interactions outside of legitimated marriage. It is this code which was the primary target of the sexual revolutionaries in the 1960s, and which has given way in many areas to more open standards of sexual behavior.

One of the beneficial results of the sexual revolution has been a growing acceptance of the distinction between questions of sexual mores and questions of morality. This distinction underlies the old slogan, "Make love, not war," and takes harm to others as the defining characteristic of immorality. What is immoral is behavior which causes injury to or violation of another person or people. Such injury may be physical or it may be psychological. To cause pain to another, to lie to another, to hinder another in the exercise of her or his rights, to exploit another, to degrade another, to misrepresent and slander another are instances of immoral behavior. Masturbation or engaging voluntarily in sexual intercourse with another consenting adult of the same or the other sex, as long as neither injury nor violation of either individual or another is involved, are not immoral. Some sexual behavior is morally objectionable, but not because of its sexual character. Thus, adultery is immoral not because it involves sexual intercourse with someone to whom one is not legally married, but because it involves breaking a promise (of sexual and emotional fidelity to one's spouse). Sadistic, abusive, or forced sex is immoral because it injures and violates another.

The detachment of sexual chastity from moral virtue implies that we cannot condemn forms of sexual behavior merely because they strike us as distasteful or subversive of the Protestant work ethic, or because they depart from standards of behavior we have individually adopted. It has thus seemed to imply that no matter how offensive we might find pornography, we must tolerate it in the name of freedom from illegitimate repression. I wish to argue that this is not so, that pornography is immoral because it is harmful to people.

II. WHAT IS PORNOGRAPHY?

I define pornography as *verbal or pictorial explicit representations of sexual behavior that,* in the words of the Commission on Obscenity and Pornography, *have as a distinguishing characteristic "the degrading and demeaning portrayal of the role and status of the human female . . . as a mere sexual object to be exploited and manipulated sexually."*[3] In pornographic books, magazines, and films, women are represented as passive and as slavishly dependent upon men. The role of female characters is limited to the provision of sexual services to men. To the extent that women's sexual pleasure is represented at all, it is subordinated to that of men and is never an end in itself as is the sexual pleasure of men. What pleases women is the use of their bodies to satisfy male desires. While the sexual objectification of women is common to all pornography, women are the recipients of even worse treatment in violent pornography, in which women characters are killed, tortured, gang-raped, mutilated, bound, and otherwise abused, as a means of providing sexual stimulation or pleasure to the male characters. It is this development which has attracted the attention of feminists and been the stimulus to an analysis of pornography in general.[4]

Not all sexually explicit material is pornography, nor is all material which contains representations of sexual abuse and degradation pornography.

A representation of a sexual encounter between adult persons which is characterized by mutual respect is, once we have disentangled sexuality and morality, not morally objectionable. Such a representation would be one in which the desires and experiences of each participant were regarded by the other participants as having a validity and a subjective importance equal to those of the individual's own desire and experiences. In such an encounter, each participant acknowledges the other participant's basic human dignity and personhood. Similarly, a representation of a nude human body (in whole or in part) in such a manner that the person shown maintains self-respect—e.g., is not portrayed in a degrading position—would not be morally objectionable. The educational films of the National Sex Forum, as well as a certain amount of erotic literature and art, fall into this category. While some erotic materials are beyond the standards of modesty held by some individuals, they are not for this reason immoral.

A representation of a sexual encounter which is not characterized by mutual respect, in which at least one of the parties is treated in a manner beneath her or his dignity as a human being, is no longer simple erotica. That a representation is of degrading behavior does not in itself, however, make it pornographic. Whether or not it is pornographic is a function of contextual features. Books and films may contain descriptions or representations of a rape in order to explore the consequences of such an assault upon its victim. What is being shown is abusive or degrading behavior which attempts to deny the humanity and dignity of the person assaulted, yet the context surrounding the representation, through its exploration of the consequences of the act, acknowledges and reaffirms her dignity. Such books and films, far from being pornographic, are (or can be) highly moral, and fall into the category of moral realism.

What makes a work a work of pornography, then, is not simply its representation of degrading and abusive sexual encounters, but its implicit, if not explicit, approval and recommendation of sexual behavior that is immoral, i.e., that physically or psychologically violates the personhood of one of the participants. Pornography, then, is verbal or pictorial material which represents or describes sexual behavior that is degrading or abusive to one or more of the participants *in such a way as to endorse the degradation.* The participants so treated in virtually all heterosexual pornography are women or children, so heterosexual pornography is, as a matter of fact, material which endorses sexual behavior that is degrading and/or abusive to women and children. As

I use the term "sexual behavior," this includes sexual encounters between persons, behavior which produces sexual stimulation or pleasure for one of the participants, and behavior which is preparatory to or invites sexual activity. Behavior that is degrading or abusive includes physical harm or abuse, and physical or psychological coercion. In addition, behavior which ignores or devalues the real interests, desires, and experiences of one or more participants in any way is degrading. Finally, that a person has chosen or consented to be harmed, abused, or subjected to coercion does not alter the degrading character of such behavior.

Pornography communicates its endorsement of the behavior it represents by various features of the pornographic context: the degradation of the female characters is represented as providing pleasure to the participant males and, even worse, to the participant females, and there is no suggestion that this sort of treatment of others is inappropriate to their status as human beings. These two features are together sufficient to constitute endorsement of the represented behavior. The contextual features which make material pornographic are intrinsic to the material. In addition to these, extrinsic features, such as the purpose for which the material is presented—i.e., the sexual arousal/pleasure/satisfaction of its (mostly) male consumers—or an accompanying text, may reinforce or make explicit the endorsement. Representations which in and of themselves do not show or endorse degrading behavior may be put into a pornographic context by juxtaposition with others that are degrading, or by a text which invites or recommends degrading behavior toward the subject represented. In such a case the whole complex—the series of representations or representations with text—is pornographic.

The distinction I have sketched is one that applies most clearly to sequential material—a verbal or pictorial (filmed) story—which represents an action and provides a temporal context for it. In showing the before and after, a narrator or film-maker has plenty of opportunity to acknowledge the dignity of the person violated or clearly to refuse to do so. It is somewhat more difficult to apply the distinction to single still representations. The contextual features cited above, however, are clearly present in still photographs or pictures that glamorize degradation and sexual violence. Phonograph album covers and advertisements offer some prime examples of such glamorization. Their representations of women in chains (the Ohio Players), or bound by ropes and black and blue (the Rolling Stones) are considered high-quality commercial "art" and glossily prettify the violence they represent. Since the standard function of prettification and glamorization is the communication of desirability, these albums and ads are communicating the desirability of violence against women. Representations of women bound or chained, particularly those of women bound in such a way as to make their breasts, or genital or anal areas vulnerable to any passerby, endorse the scene they represent by the absence of any indication that this treatment of women is in any way inappropriate.

To summarize: Pornography is not just the explicit representation or description of sexual behavior, nor even the explicit representation or description of sexual behavior which is degrading and/or abusive to women. Rather, it is material that explicitly represents or describes degrading and abusive sexual behavior so as to endorse and/or recommend the behavior as described. The contextual features, moreover, which communicate such endorsement are intrinsic to the material; that is, they are features whose removal or alteration would change the representation or description.

This account of pornography is underlined by the etymology and original meaning of the word "pornography." *The Oxford English Dictionary* defines pornography as "Description of the life, manners, etc. of prostitutes and their

patrons (from *porne* meaning "harlot" and *graphein* meaning "to write"); hence the expression or suggestion of obscene or unchaste subjects in literature or art."

Let us consider the first part of the definition for a moment. In the transactions between prostitutes and their clients, prostitutes are paid, directly or indirectly, for the use of their bodies by the client for sexual pleasure.[5] Traditionally males have obtained from female prostitutes what they could not or did not wish to get from their wives or women friends, who, because of the character of their relation to the male, must be accorded some measure of human respect. While there are limits to what treatment is seen as appropriate toward women as wives or women friends, the prostitute as prostitute exists to provide sexual pleasure to males. The female characters of contemporary pornography also exist to provide pleasure to males, but in the pornographic context no pretense is made to regard them as parties to a contractual arrangement. Rather, the anonymity of these characters makes each one Everywoman, thus suggesting not only that all women are appropriate subjects for the enactment of the most bizarre and demeaning male sexual fantasies, but also that this is their primary purpose. The recent escalation of violence in pornography—the presentation of scenes of bondage, rape, and torture of women for the sexual stimulation of the male characters or male viewers—while shocking in itself, is from this point of view merely a more vicious extension of a genre whose success depends on treating women in a manner beneath their dignity as human beings.

III. PORNOGRAPHY: LIES AND VIOLENCE AGAINST WOMEN

What is wrong with pornography, then, is its degrading and dehumanizing portrayal of women (and not its sexual content). Pornography, by its very nature, requires that women be subordinate to men and mere instruments for the fulfillment of male fantasies. To accomplish this, pornography must lie. Pornography lies when it says that our sexual life is or ought to be subordinate to the service of men, that our pleasure consists in pleasing men and not ourselves, that we are depraved, that we are fit subjects for rape, bondage, torture, and murder. Pornography lies explicitly about women's sexuality, and through such lies fosters more lies about our humanity, our dignity, and our personhood.

Moreover, since nothing is alleged to justify the treatment of the female characters of pornography save their womanhood, pornography depicts all women as fit objects of violence by virtue of their sex alone. Because it is simply being female that, in the pornographic vision, justifies being violated, the lies of pornography are lies about all women. Each work of pornography is on its own libelous and defamatory, yet gains power through being reinforced by every other pornographic work. The sheer number of pornographic productions expands the moral issue to include not only assessing the morality or immorality of individual works, but also the meaning and force of the mass production of pornography.

The pornographic view of women is thoroughly entrenched in a booming portion of the publishing, film, and recording industries, reaching and affecting not only all who look to such sources for sexual stimulation, but also those of us who are forced into an awareness of it as we peruse magazines at newsstands and record albums in record stores, as we check the entertainment sections of city newspapers, or even as we approach a counter to pay for groceries. It is not necessary to spend a great deal of time reading or viewing pornographic material to absorb its male-centered definition of women. No longer confined within plain brown wrappers, it jumps out from billboards that proclaim "Live X-rated Girls!" or "Angels in Pain" or "Hot and Wild," and from magazine covers displaying a woman's genital area being spread open to the viewer by her own fingers.[6] Thus, even men who do not frequent pornographic shops and movie houses are supported in the sexist objectification of women by their environment. Women, too, are crippled by internalizing as self-images those that are presented to us by pornographers. Isolated from one another and with no source of support for an alternative view of female sexuality, we may not always find the strength to resist a message that dominates the common cultural media.

The entrenchment of pornography in our culture also gives it a significance quite beyond its explicit sexual messages. To suggest, as pornography does, that the primary purpose of women is to provide sexual pleasure to men is to deny that women are independently human or have a status equal to that of men. It is, moreover, to deny our equality at one of the most intimate levels of human experience. This denial is especially powerful in a hierarchical, class society such as ours, in which individuals feel good about themselves by feeling superior to others. Men in our society have a vested interest in maintaining their belief in the inferiority of the female sex, so that no matter how oppressed and exploited by the society in which they live and work, they can feel that they are at least superior to someone or some category of individuals—a woman or women. Pornography, by presenting women as wanton, depraved, and made for the sexual use of men, caters directly to that interest.[7] The very intimate nature of sexuality which makes pornography so corrosive also protects it from explicit public discussion. The consequent lack of any explicit social disavowal of the pornographic image of women enables this image to continue fostering sexist attitudes even as the society publicly proclaims its (as yet timid) commitment to sexual equality.

In addition to finding a connection between the pornographic view of women and the denial to us of our full human rights, women are beginning to connect the consumption of pornography with committing rape and other acts of sexual violence against women. Contrary to the findings of the Commission on Obscenity and Pornography, a growing body of research is documenting (1) a correlation between exposure to representations of violence and the committing of violent acts generally, and (2) a correlation between exposure to pornographic materials and the committing of sexually abusive or violent acts against women.[8] While more study is needed to establish precisely what the causal relations are, clearly so-called hard-core pornography is not innocent.

From "snuff" films and miserable magazines in pornographic stores to *Hustler,* to phonograph album covers and advertisements, to *Vogue,* pornography has come to occupy its own niche in the communications and entertainment media and to acquire a quasi-institutional character (signaled by the use of diminutives such as "porn" or "porno" to refer to pornographic material, as though such familiar naming could take the hurt out). Its acceptance by the mass media, whatever the motivation, means a cultural endorsement of its message. As much as the materials themselves, the social tolerance of these degrading and distorted images of women in such quantities is harmful to us, since it indicates a general willingness to see women in ways incompatible with our fundamental human dignity and thus to justify treating us in those ways.[9] The tolerance of pornographic representations of the rape, bondage, and torture of women helps to create and maintain a climate more tolerant of the actual physical abuse of women.[10] The tendency on the part of the legal system to view the victim of a rape as responsible for the crime against her is but one manifestation of this.

In sum, pornography is injurious to women in at least three distinct ways:

1. Pornography, especially violent pornography, is implicated in the committing of crimes of violence against women.
2. Pornography is the vehicle for the dissemination of a deep and vicious lie about women. It is defamatory and libelous.
3. The diffusion of such a distorted view of women's nature in our society as it exists today supports sexist (i.e., male-centered) attitudes, and thus reinforces the oppression and exploitation of women.

Society's tolerance of pornography, especially pornography on the contemporary massive scale, reinforces each of these modes of injury: By not disavowing the lie, it supports the male-centered myth that women are inferior and subordinate creatures. Thus, it contributes to the maintenance of a climate tolerant of both psychological and physical violence against women.

IV. PORNOGRAPHY AND THE LAW

> Congress shall make no law respecting the establishment of religion, or prohibiting the free exercise thereof; or abridging the freedom of speech, or of the press; or the right of the people peaceably to assemble, and to petition the Government for a redress of grievances.
> —*First Amendment, Bill of Rights of the United States Constitution*

Pornography is clearly a threat to women. Each of the modes of injury cited above offers sufficient reason at least to consider proposals for the social and legal control of pornography. The almost universal response from progressives to such proposals is that constitutional guarantees of freedom of speech and privacy preclude recourse to law.[11] While I am concerned about the erosion of constitutional rights and also think for many reasons that great caution must be exercised before undertaking a legal campaign against pornography, I find objections to such a campaign that are based on appeals to the First Amendment or to a right to privacy ultimately unconvincing.

Much of the defense of the pornographer's right to publish seems to assume that, while pornography may be tasteless and vulgar, it is basically an entertainment that harms no one but its consumers, who may at worst suffer from the debasement of their taste; and that therefore those who argue for its control are demanding an unjustifiable abridgment of the rights to freedom of speech of those who make and distribute pornographic materials and of the rights to privacy of their customers. The account of pornography given above shows that the assumptions of this position are false. Nevertheless, even some who acknowledge its harmful character feel that it is granted immunity from social control by the First Amendment, or that the harm that would ensue from its control outweighs the harm prevented by its control.

There are three ways of arguing that control of pornography is incompatible with adherence to constitutional rights. The first argument claims that regulating pornography involves an unjustifiable interference in the private lives of individuals. The second argument takes the First Amendment as a basic principle constitutive of our form of government, and claims that the production and distribution of pornographic material, as a form of speech, is an activity protected by that amendment. The third argument claims not that the pornographer's rights are violated, but that others' rights will be if controls against pornography are instituted.

The privacy argument is the easiest to dispose of. Since the open commerce in pornographic materials is an activity carried out in the public sphere, the publication and distribution of such materials, unlike their use by individuals, is not protected by rights to privacy. The distinction between the private con-

sumption of pornographic material and the production and distribution of, or open commerce in, it is sometimes blurred by defenders of pornography. But I may entertain, in the privacy of my mind, defamatory opinions about another person, even though I may not broadcast them. So one might create without restraint—as long as no one were harmed in the course of preparing them—pornographic materials for one's personal use, but be restrained from reproducing and distributing them. In both cases what one is doing—in the privacy of one's mind or basement—may indeed be deplorable, but immune from legal proscription. Once the activity becomes public, however—i.e., once it involves others—it is no longer protected by the same rights that protect activities in the private sphere.[12]

In considering the second argument (that control of pornography, private or public, is wrong in principle), it seems important to determine whether we consider the right to freedom of speech to be absolute and unqualified. If it is, then obviously all speech, including pornography, is entitled to protection. But the right is, in the first place, not an unqualified right: There are several kinds of speech not protected by the First Amendment, including the incitement to violence in volatile circumstances, the solicitation of crimes, perjury and misrepresentation, slander, libel, and false advertising.[13] That there are forms of proscribed speech shows that we accept limitations on the right to freedom of speech if such speech, as do the forms listed, impinges on other rights. The manufacture and distribution of material which defames and threatens all members of a class by its recommendation of abusive and degrading behavior toward some members of that class simply in virtue of their membership in it seems a clear candidate for inclusion on the list. The right is therefore not an unqualified one.

Nor is it an absolute or fundamental right, underived from any other right: If it were there would not be exceptions or limitations. The first ten amendments were added to the Constitution as a way of guaranteeing the "blessings of liberty" mentioned in its preamble, to protect citizens against the unreasonable usurpation of power by the state. The specific rights mentioned in the First Amendment—those of religion, speech, assembly, press, petition—reflect the recent experiences of the makers of the Constitution under colonial government as well as a sense of what was and is required generally to secure liberty.

It may be objected that the right to freedom of speech is fundamental in that it is part of what we mean by liberty and not a right that is derivative from a right to liberty. In order to meet this objection, it is useful to consider a distinction explained by Ronald Dworkin in his book *Taking Rights Seriously*.[14] As Dworkin points out, the word "liberty" is used in two distinct, if related, senses: as "license," i.e., the freedom from legal constraints to do as one pleases, in some contexts; and as "independence," i.e., "the status of a person as independent and equal rather than subservient," in others. Failure to distinguish between these senses in discussions of rights and freedoms is fatal to clarity and understanding.

If the right to free speech is understood as a partial explanation of what is meant by liberty, then liberty is perceived as license: The right to do as one pleases includes a right to speak as one pleases. But license is surely not a condition the First Amendment is designed to protect. We not only tolerate but require legal constraints on liberty as license when we enact laws against rape, murder, assault, theft, etc. If everyone did exactly as she or he pleased at any given time, we would have chaos if not lives, as Hobbes put it, that are "nasty, brutish, and short." We accept government to escape, not to protect, this condition.

If, on the other hand, by liberty is meant independence, then freedom of speech is not necessarily a part of liberty; rather, it is a means

to it. The right to freedom of speech is not a fundamental, absolute right, but one derivative from, possessed in virtue of, the more basic right to independence. Taking this view of liberty requires providing arguments showing that the more specific rights we claim are necessary to guarantee our status as persons "independent and equal rather than subservient." In the context of government, we understand independence to be the freedom of each individual to participate as an equal among equals in the determination of how she or he is to be governed. Freedom of speech in this context means that an individual may not only entertain beliefs concerning government privately, but may express them publicly. We express our opinions about taxes, disarmament, wars, social-welfare programs, the function of the police, civil rights, and so on. Our right to freedom of speech includes the right to criticize the government and to protest against various forms of injustice and the abuse of power. What we wish to protect is the free expression of ideas even when they are unpopular. What we do not always remember is that speech has functions other than the expression of ideas.

Regarding the relationship between a right to freedom of speech and the publication and distribution of pornographic materials, there are two points to be made. In the first place, the latter activity is hardly an exercise of the right to the free expression of ideas as understood above. In the second place, to the degree that the tolerance of material degrading to women supports and reinforces the attitude that women are not fit to participate as equals among equals in the political life of their communities, and that the prevalence of such an attitude effectively prevents women from so participating, the absolute and fundamental right of women to liberty (political independence) is violated.

This second argument against the suppression of pornographic material, then, rests on a premise that must be rejected, namely, that the right to freedom of speech is a right to utter anything one wants. It thus fails to show that the production and distribution of such material is an activity protected by the First Amendment. Furthermore, an examination of the issues involved leads to the conclusion that tolerance of this activity violates the rights of women to political independence.

The third argument (which expresses concern that curbs on pornography are the first step toward political censorship) runs into the same ambiguity that besets the arguments based on principle. These arguments generally have as an underlying assumption that the maximization of freedom is a worthy social goal. Control of pornography diminishes freedom—directly the freedom of pornographers, indirectly that of all of us. But again, what is meant by "freedom"? It cannot be that what is to be maximized is license—as the goal of a social group whose members probably have at least some incompatible interests, such a goal would be internally inconsistent. If, on the other hand, the maximization of political independence is the goal, then that is in no way enhanced by, and may be endangered by, the tolerance of pornography. To argue that the control of pornography would create a precedent for suppressing political speech is thus to confuse license with political independence. In addition, it ignores a crucial basis for the control of pornography, i.e., its character as libelous speech. The prohibition of such speech is justified by the need for protection from the injury (psychological as well as physical or economic) that results from libel. A very different kind of argument would be required to justify curtailing the right to speak our minds about the institutions which govern us. As long as such distinctions are insisted upon, there is little danger of the government's using the control of pornography as precedent for curtailing political speech.

In summary, neither as a matter of principle nor in the interests of maximizing liberty can

it be supposed that there is an intrinsic right to manufacture and distribute pornographic material.

The only other conceivable source of protection for pornography would be a general right to do what we please as long as the rights of others are respected. Since the production and distribution of pornography violates the rights of women—to respect and to freedom from defamation, among others—this protection is not available.

V. CONCLUSION

I have defined pornography in such a way as to distinguish it from erotica and from moral realism, and have argued that it is defamatory and libelous toward women, that it condones crimes against women, and that it invites tolerance of the social, economic, and cultural oppression of women. The production and distribution of pornographic material is thus a social and moral wrong. Contrasting both the current volume of pornographic production and its growing infiltration of the communications media with the status of women in this culture makes clear the necessity for its control. Since the goal of controlling pornography does not conflict with constitutional rights, a common obstacle to action is removed.

Appeals for action against pornography are sometimes brushed aside with the claim that such action is a diversion from the primary task of feminists—the elimination of sexism and of sexual inequality. This approach focuses on the enjoyment rather than the manufacture of pornography, and sees it as merely a product of sexism which will disappear when the latter has been overcome and the sexes are socially and economically equal. Pornography cannot be separated from sexism in this way: Sexism is not just a set of attitudes regarding the inferiority of women but the behaviors and social and economic rules that manifest such attitudes. Both the manufacture and distribution of pornography and the enjoyment of it are instances of sexist behavior. The enjoyment of pornography on the part of individuals will presumably decline as such individuals begin to accord women their status as fully human. A cultural climate which tolerates the degrading representation of women is not a climate which facilitates the development of respect for women. Furthermore, the demand for pornography is stimulated not just by the sexism of individuals but by the pornography industry itself. Thus, both as a social phenomenon and in its effect on individuals, pornography, far from being a mere product, nourishes sexism. The campaign against it is an essential component of women's struggle for legal, economic, and social equality, one which requires the support of all feminists.[16]

NOTES

1. *Women Against Violence in Pornography and Media Newspage,* vol. II, no. 5 (June 1978); Judith Reisman in *Women Against Violence in Pornography and Media Proposal.*
2. American Law Institute *Model Penal Code,* sec. 251.4.
3. *Report of the Commission on Obscenity and Pornography* (New York: Bantam Books, 1979), p. 239. The Commission, of course, concluded that the demeaning content of pornography did not affect male attitudes toward women.
4. Among recent feminist discussions are Diana Russell, "Pornography: A Feminist Perspective" and Susan Griffin, "On Pornagraphy," *Chrysalis,* vol. I, no. 4 (1978), and Ann Garry, "Pornography and Respect for Women," *Social Theory and Practice,* vol. 4 (Spring 1978): 395–421.
5. In talking of prostitution here, I refer to the concept of, rather than the reality of, prostitution. The same is true of my remarks about

relationships between women and their husbands or men friends.

6. This was a full-color magazine cover seen in a rack at the check-out counter of a corner delicatessen.
7. Pornography thus becomes another tool of capitalism. One feature of some contemporary pornography—the use of black and Asian women in both still photographs and films—exploits the racism as well as the sexism of its white consumers. For a discussion of the interplay between racism and sexism under capitalism as it relates to violent crimes against women, see Angela Y. Davis, "Rape, Racism, and the Capitalist Setting," *The Black Scholar,* Vol. 9, No. 7, April 1978.
8. *The Oxford English Dictionary,* Compact Edition (London: Oxford University Press, 1971), p. 2242.
9. This tolerance has a linguistic parallel in the growing acceptance and use of nonhuman nouns such as "chick," "bird," "filly," "fox," "doll," "babe," "skirt," etc., to refer to women, and of verbs of harm such as "fuck," "screw," "bang" to refer to sexual intercourse. See Robert Baker and Frederick Elliston "'Pricks' and 'Chicks': A Plea for Persons." *Philosophy and Sex* (Buffalo, N.Y.: Prometheus Books, 1975).
10. This is supported by the fact that in Denmark the number of rapes committed has increased while the number of rapes reported to the authorities has decreased over the past twelve years. See *WAVPM Newspage,* Vol. II, No. 5, June, 1978, quoting M. Harry, "Denmark Today—The Causes and Effects of Sexual Liberty" (paper presented to The Responsible Society, London, England, 1976). See also Eysenck and Nias, *Sex, Violence and the Media* (New York: St. Martin's Press, 1978), pp. 120–124.
11. Urie Bronfenbrenner, *Two Worlds of Childhood* (New York: Russell Sage Foundation, 1970); H. J. Eysenck and D. K. B. Nias, *Sex, Violence, and the Media* (New York: St. Martin's Press, 1978); Michael Goldstein, Harold Kant, and

John Hartman, *Pornography and Sexual Deviance* (Berkeley: University of California Press, 1973); the papers of Diana Russell, Pauline Bart, and Irene Diamond in Laura Lederer, ed., *Take Back the Night* (New York: William Morrow, 1979).

12. Thus, the right to use such materials in the privacy of one's home, which has been upheld by the United States Supreme Court (*Stanley v. Georgia,* 394 U.S. 557), does not include the right to purchase them or to have them available in the commercial market. See also *Paris Adult Theater I v. Slaton,* 431 U.S. 49.

13. The Supreme Court has also traditionally included obscenity in this category. As not everyone agrees it should be included, since as defined by statutes, it is a highly vague concept, and since the grounds accepted by the Court for including it miss the point, I prefer to omit it from this list.

14. Cf. Marshall Cohen, "The Case Against Censorship," *The Public Interest,* no. 22 (Winter 1971), reprinted in John R. Burr and Milton Goldinger, *Philosophy and Contemporary Issues* (New York: Macmillan, 1976), and Justice William Brennan's dissenting opinion in *Paris Adult Theater I v. Slaton,* 431 U.S. 49.

15. Ronald Dworkin, *Taking Rights Seriously* (Cambridge: Harvard University Press, 1977), p. 262.

16. Many women helped me to develop and crystallize the ideas presented in this paper. I would especially like to thank Michele Farrell, Laura Lederer, Pamela Miller, and Dianne Romain for their comments in conversation and on the first written draft. Portions of this material were presented orally to members of the Society for Women in Philosophy and to participants in the workshops on "What Is Pornography?" at the Conference on Feminist Perspectives on Pornography, San Francisco, November 17, 18, and 19, 1978. Their discussion was invaluable in helping me to see problems and to clarify the ideas presented here.

Study/Discussion Questions

1. How does the author define pornography?
2. What makes pornography immoral, in the author's view?
3. In what ways does pornography harm women?
4. Describe the pornographic view of women.
5. How does this view lie about women, according to Longino?

First Sex
(for J.)

Sharon Olds

I knew little, and what I knew
I did not believe—they had lied to me
so many times, so I just took it as it
came, his naked body on the sheet,
the tiny hairs curling on his legs like
fine, gold shells, his sex
harder and harder under my palm
and yet not hard as a rock his face cocked
back as if in terror, the sweat
jumping out of his pores like sudden
trails from the tiny snails when his knees
locked with little clicks and under my
hand he gathered and shook and the actual
flood like milk came out of his body, I
saw it glow on his belly, all they had
said and more, I rubbed it into my
hands like lotion, I signed on for the duration.

The Slow Dance

Cherrie Moraga

Thinking of Elena, Susan —watching them dance together. The images return to me, hold me, stir me, prompt me to want something.

Elena moving Susan around the floor, so in control of the knowledge: how to handle this woman, while I fumbled around them. When Elena and I kissed, just once, I forgot and let too much want show, closing my eyes, all the eyes around me seeing me close my eyes. I am a girl wanting so much to kiss a woman. She sees this too, cutting the kiss short.

But not with Susan, Susan's arm around Elena's neck. Elena's body all leaning into the center of her pelvis. This is the way she enters a room, *leaning into the body of a woman.*

The two of them, like grown-ups, like women. The women I silently longed for. Still, I remember after years of wanting and getting and loving, still I remember the desire to be that in sync *with another woman's body.*

And I move women around the floor, too—women I think enamored with me. My mother's words rising up from inside me—"A real *man, when he dances with you, you'll know he's a* real *man by how he holds you in the back." I think,* yes, *someone who can guide you around a dance floor and so, I do. Moving these women kindly, surely, even superior. I can handle these women. They want this. And I do too.*

Thinking of my father, how so timidly he used to take my mother onto the small square of carpet we reserved for dancing, pulling back the chairs. She really leading the step, him learning to cooperate so it looked *like a male lead. I noticed his hand, how it lingered awkwardly about my mother's small back, his thin fingers never really getting a hold on her.*

From *Loving in the War Years: Lo que Nunca Paso por Sus Labios,* Cambridge, Mass.: The South End Press, 1983. Copyright © Cherrie Moraga.

I remember this as I take a woman in my arms, my hand moving up under her shoulder blade, speaking to her from there. It is from this *spot, the dance is directed. From* this *place. I tenderly, with each fingertip, move her.*

I am my mother's lover. The partner she's been waiting for. I can handle whatever you got hidden. I can provide for you.

But when I put this provider up against the likes of Elena, I am the one following/falling into her. Like Susan, taken up in the arms of this woman. I want this.

Catching the music shift; the beat softens, slows down. I search for Elena— the bodies, the faces. I am ready for you now. *I want age, knowledge.* Your body that still, after years, withholds and surrenders—keeps me there, waiting wishing. *I push through the bodies, looking for her. Willing. Willing to feel* this time *what disrupts in me. Girl. Woman. Child. Boy. Willing to embody what I will in the space of her arms. Looking for Elena. I'm willing, wanting.*

And I find you dancing with this other woman. My body both hers and yours in the flash of a glance.

I can handle this.

I am used to being an observer.

I am used to not getting what I want.

I am used to imagining what it must be like.

Bibliography/Filmography for Part II

REPRODUCTIVE RIGHTS

BOOKS

Arditti, Rita, Renate Duelli-Klein, and Shelley Minden, eds. *Test Tube Women: What Future for Motherhood?* Boston: Pandora Press, 1984.

Baehr, Ninia. *Abortion Without Apology: Radical History for the 1990s.* Boston: South End Press, 1990.

Bartlett, Jane. *Will You Be Mother?: Women Who Choose to Say No.* New York: New York University Press, 1995.

Daniels, Cynthia. *At Women's Expense: State Power and the Politics of Fetal Rights.* Cambridge: Harvard University Press, 1993.

Finger, Anne. *Past Due: A Story of Disability, Pregnancy, and Birth.* Seattle: Seal Press, 1990.

Gordon, Linda. *Woman's Body, Woman's Right: A Social History of Birth Control.* New York: Viking Press, 1976.

Luker, Kristin. *Abortion and the Politics of Motherhood.* Berkeley: University of California Press, 1984.

Petchesky, Rosalind Pollack. *Abortion and Women's Choice.* New York: Longman, 1984.

Raymond, Janice. *Women as Wombs: Reproductive Technologies and the Battle over Women's Freedom.* New York: HarperCollins, 1993.

Roberts, Dorothy. *Killing the Black Body: Race, Reproduction, and the Meaning of Liberty.* New York: Pantheon, 1997.

Simonds, Wendy. *Abortion at Work: Ideology and Practice in a Feminist Clinic.* New Brunswick, NJ: Rutgers University Press, 1996.

Solinger, Rickie. *Wake Up Little Susie: Single Pregnancy and Race Before* Roe v. Wade. New York: Routledge, 1992.

FILMS

Citizen Ruth (U.S., 1996). Alexander Payne.

The Handmaid's Tale (U.S., 1990). Volker Schlôndorff.

The Story of Women (France, 1988). Claude Chabrol.

THE POLITICS OF INCLUSION

BOOKS

Alexander, M. Jacqui, Lisa Albrecht, Sharon Day, Mab Segrest, and Norma Alarcon, eds. *The Third Wave: Feminist Perspectives on Racism.* New York: Kitchen Table-Women of Color Press, 1994.

Chow, Esther Ngan-ling, Doris Wilkinson, and Maxine Baca Zinn. *Race, Class, and Gender: Common Bonds, Different Voices.* Thousand Oaks, CA: Sage, 1996.

Cole, Johnetta, ed. *All American Women: Lines That Divide, Ties That Bind.* New York: Free Press, 1986.

Duberman, Martin, Martha Vicinus and George Chauncey, Jr., eds.. *Hidden from History:. Reclaiming the Gay and Lesbian Past.* New York: Meridian, 1990.

Echols, Alice. *Daring to Be Bad: Radical Feminism in America, 1967–1975.* Minneapolis: University of Minnesota Press, 1989.

hooks, bell. *Talking Back: Thinking Feminist, Thinking Black.* Boston: South End Press, 1989.

Kim, Elaine, ed. *Making More Waves: An Anthology of Writings by and About Asian American Women.* Boston: Beacon Press, 1997.

Macdonald, Barbara with Cynthia Rich. *Look Me In the Eye: Old Women, Aging and Ageism.* Minneapolis: Spinsters Ink, 1991.

McIntosh, Peggy. *White Privilege and Male Privilege: A Personal Account of Coming to See Correspondences Through Work in Women's Studies.* Working Paper No. 189, Wellesley College Center for Research on Women. Wellesley, MA 02181.

Rosen, Ruth. *The World Split Open: How the Modern Women's Movement Changed America.* New York: Viking, 2000.

Spelman, Elizabeth. *Inessential Woman: Problems of Exclusion in Feminist Thought.* Boston: Beacon Press, 1988.

Umansky, Lauri. *Motherhood Reconceived: Feminism and the Legacies of the Sixties.* New York: New York University Press, 1996.

Weisser, Susan and Jennifer Fleischner, eds. *Feminist Nightmares: Women at Odds: Feminism and the Problem of Sisterhood.* New York: New York University Press, 1994.

Zandy, Janet, ed. *Calling Home: Working Class Women's Writings: An Anthology.* New Brunswick, NJ: Rutgers University Press, 1990.

FILMS

Born in Flames (U.S., 1983). Lizzie Borden.
Stolen Moments (Canada, 1998). Margaret Wescott.

VIOLENCE AGAINST WOMEN

BOOKS

Armstrong, Louise. *Rocking the Cradle of Sexual Politics: What Happened When Women Said Incest.* Reading, MA: Addison-Wesley, 1994.

Bart, Pauline and Eileen Geil Moran. *Violence Against Women: The Bloody Footprints.* Thousand Oaks, CA: Sage, 1993.

Brownmiller, Susan. *Against Our Will: Men, Women, and Rape.* New York: Simon and Schuster, 1975.

Estrich, Susan. *Real Rape: How the Legal System Victimizes Women Who Say No.* Cambridge: Harvard University Press, 1987.

Jones, Ann. *Next Time She'll Be Dead: Battering and How to Stop It.* Boston: Beacon Press, 1994.

Morris, Celia. *Bearing Witness: Sexual Harassment and Beyond—Everywoman's Story.* Boston: Little Brown, 1994.

Morrison, Toni, ed. *Race-ing Justice, En-gendering Power: Essays on Anita Hill, Clarence Thomas, and the Construction of Reality.* New York: Pantheon, 1992.

Mykitiuk, Roxanne, Martha Albertson, and Martha A. Fineman, eds. *The Public Nature of Private Violence: The Discovery of Domestic Abuse.* New York: Routledge, 1994.

Randall, Margaret. *This Is About Incest.* Ithaca, NY: Firebrand Books, 1987.

Sanday, Peggy Reeves. *Fraternity Gang Rape: Sex, Brotherhood, and Privilege on Campus.* New York: New York University Press, 1990.

Sumrall, Amber and Dena Taylor, eds. *Sexual Harassment: Women Speak Out.* Freedom, CA: Crossing Press, 1992.

Walker, Alice. *The Color Purple.* New York: Washington Square Press, 1998.

White, Evelyn C. *Chain, Chain, Change: For Black Women Dealing with Physical and Emotional Abuse.* Seattle: Seal Press, 1985.

Wilson, Melba. *Crossing the Boundary: Black Women Survive Incest.* Seattle: Seal Press, 1994.

FILMS

The Accused (U.S., 1988). Jonathan Kaplan.

The Color Purple (U.S., 1985). Steven Spielberg.

Looking for Mr. Goodbar (U.S., 1977). Richard Brooks.

DEBATING SEX

BOOKS

Assiter, Alison and Carol Avedon, eds. *Bad Girls and Dirty Pictures: The Challenge to Reclaim Feminism.* London: Pluto Press, 1993.

Burstyn, Varda, ed. *Women Against Censorship.* Vancouver: Douglas and McIntyre, 1985.

Califia, Pat. *Public Sex: The Culture of Radical Sex.* Pittsburgh: Cleis Press, 1994.

Dworkin, Andrea. *Pornography.* New York: Dutton, 1981.

Jay, Karla, ed. *Lesbian Erotics.* New York: New York University Press, 1995.

MacKinnon, Catharine. *Only Words.* Cambridge: Harvard University Press, 1987.

Rothluebber, Francis B. *Nobody Owns Me: A Celibate Woman Discovers Her Sexual Power.* San Diego, Calif.: LuraMedia, 1994.

Showalter, Elaine. *Sexual Anarchy: Gender and Culture at the Fin de Siecle.* New York: Viking, 1990.

Snitow, Ann, Christine Stansell and Sharon Thompson, eds.. *Powers of Desire: The Politics of Sexuality.* New York: Monthly Review Press, 1983.

Suleiman, Susan Rubin, ed. *The Female Body in Western Culture: Contemporary Perspectives.* Cambridge, Mass.: Harvard University Press, 1986.

Vance, Carole, ed. *Pleasure and Danger: Exploring Female Sexuality.* Boston: Routledge and Kegan Paul, 1984.

Weeks, Jeffrey. *Sex, Politics and Society: The Regulation of Sexuality Since 1800.* New York:. Longman, 1981.

Weise, Elizabeth Reba, ed. *Closer to Home: Bisexuality and Feminism.* Seattle: Seal Press, 1992.

FILMS

Blue Velvet (U.S., 1986). David Lynch.

The Immaculate Collection (videos). Madonna.

Jeanne Dielman, #23 Quai du Commerce, 1080 Bruxelles (France, 1975). Chantal Ackerman.

The Last Seduction (U.S., 1994). John Dahl.

Not a Love Story (Canada, 1983). Bonnie Sherr Kline.

She's Gotta Have It (U.S., 1986). Spike Lee.

Female Perversions (U.S., 1997). Susan Streitfeld.

Something Wild (U.S., 1986). Jonathan Demme.

Working Girls (U.S., 1986). Lizzie Borden.

HOW THINGS SHOULD BE PART III

Uses of the Erotic:
The Erotic as Power

Audre Lorde

In this essay, Audre Lorde distinguishes between the "superficially erotic," which "has been encouraged as a sign of female inferiority," and the genuinely erotic, which is "a resource within each of us that lies in a deeply female and spiritual plane." Published during the height of the "sex wars" within feminism, this piece still defies easy categorization. At once condemning pornography and lauding sexuality, Lorde looks to the erotic as a source of strength for women and suggests that we infuse our lives with its charge.

There are many kinds of power, used and unused, acknowledged or otherwise. The erotic is a resource within each of us that lies in a deeply female and spiritual plane, firmly rooted in the power of our unexpressed or unrecognized feeling. In order to perpetuate itself, every oppression must corrupt or distort those various sources of power within the culture of the oppressed that can provide energy for change. For women, this has meant a suppression of the erotic as a considered source of power and information within our lives.

We have been taught to suspect this resource, vilified, abused, and devalued within western society. On the one hand, the superficially erotic has been encouraged as a sign of female inferiority; on the other hand, women have been made to suffer and to feel both contemptible and suspect by virtue of its existence.

It is a short step from there to the false belief that only by the suppression of the erotic within our lives and consciousness can women be truly strong. But that strength is illusory, for it is fashioned within the context of male models of power.

As women, we have come to distrust that power which rises from our deepest and nonrational knowledge. We have been warned against it all our lives by the male world, which values this depth of feeling enough to keep women around in order to exercise it in the service of men, but which fears this same depth too much to examine the possibilities of it within themselves. So women are maintained at a distant/inferior position to be psychically milked, much the same way ants maintain colonies of aphids to provide a life-giving substance for their masters.

Reprinted with permission from "Uses of the Erotic: The Erotic as Power" in *Sister Outsider: Essays and Speeches,* by Audre Lorde. © 1984. Published by The Crossing Press, Freedom, CA. Originally a paper delivered at the Fourth Berkshire Conference on the History of Women, Mount Holyoke College, August 25, 1978.

But the erotic offers a well of replenishing and provocative force to the woman who does not fear its revelation, nor succumb to the belief that sensation is enough.

The erotic has often been misnamed by men and used against women. It has been made into the confused, the trivial, the psychotic, the plasticized sensation. For this reason, we have often turned away from the exploration and consideration of the erotic as a source of power and information, confusing it with its opposite, the pornographic. But pornography is a direct denial of the power of the erotic, for it represents the suppression of true feeling. Pornography emphasizes sensation without feeling.

The erotic is a measure between the beginnings of our sense of self and the chaos of our strongest feelings. It is an internal sense of satisfaction to which, once we have experienced it, we know we can aspire. For having experienced the fullness of this depth of feeling and recognizing its power, in honor and self-respect we can require no less of ourselves.

It is never easy to demand the most from ourselves, from our lives, from our work. To encourage excellence is to go beyond the encouraged mediocrity of our society, is to encourage excellence. But giving in to the fear of feeling and working to capacity is a luxury only the unintentional can afford, and the unintentional are those who do not wish to guide their own destinies.

This internal requirement toward excellence which we learn from the erotic must not be misconstrued as demanding the impossible from ourselves nor from others. Such a demand incapacitates everyone in the process. For the erotic is not a question only of what we do; it is a question of how acutely and fully we can feel in the doing. Once we know the extent to which we are capable of feeling that sense of satisfaction and completion, we can then observe which of our various life endeavors bring us closest to that fullness.

The aim of each thing which we do is to make our lives and the lives of our children richer and more possible. Within the celebration of the erotic in all our endeavors, my work becomes a conscious decision—a longed-for bed which I enter gratefully and from which I rise up empowered.

Of course, women so empowered are dangerous. So we are taught to separate the erotic demand from most vital areas of our lives other than sex. And the lack of concern for the erotic root and satisfactions of our work is felt in our disaffection from so much of what we do. For instance, how often do we truly love our work even at its most difficult?

The principal horror of any system which defines the good in terms of profit rather than in terms of human need, or which defines human need to the exclusion of the psychic and emotional components of that need—the principal horror of such a system is that it robs our work of its erotic value, its erotic power and life appeal and fulfillment. Such a system reduces work to a travesty of necessities, a duty by which we earn bread or oblivion for ourselves and those we love. But this is tantamount to blinding a painter and then telling her to improve her work, and to enjoy the act of painting. It is not only next to impossible, it is also profoundly cruel.

As women, we need to examine the ways in which our world can be truly different. I am speaking here of the necessity for reassessing the quality of all the aspects of our lives and of our work, and of how we move toward and through them.

The very word *erotic* comes from the Greek word *eros,* the personification of love in all its aspects born of Chaos, and personifying creative power and harmony. When I speak of the erotic, then, I speak of it as an assertion of the lifeforce of women; of that creative energy empowered, the knowledge and use of which we are now reclaiming in our language, our history, our dancing, our loving, our work, our lives.

There are frequent attempts to equate pornography and eroticism, two diametrically opposed uses of the sexual. Because of these attempts, it has become fashionable to separate the spiritual (psychic and emotional) from the political, to see them as contradictory or antithetical. "What do you mean, a poetic revolutionary, a meditating gunrunner?" In the same way, we have attempted to separate the spiritual and the erotic, thereby reducing the spiritual to a world of flattened affect, a world of the ascetic who aspires to feel nothing. But nothing is farther from the truth. For the ascetic position is one of the highest fear, the gravest immobility. The severe abstinence of the ascetic becomes the ruling obsession. And it is one not of self-discipline but of self-abnegation.

The dichotomy between the spiritual and the political is also false, resulting from an incomplete attention to our erotic knowledge. For the bridge which connects them is formed by the erotic—the sensual—those physical, emotional, and psychic expressions of what is deepest and strongest and richest within each of us, being shared: the passions of love, in its deepest meanings.

Beyond the superficial, the considered phrase, "It feels right to me," acknowledges the strength of the erotic into a true knowledge, for what that means is the first and most powerful guiding light toward any understanding. And understanding is a handmaiden which can only wait upon, or clarify, that knowledge, deeply born. The erotic is the nurturer or nursemaid of all our deepest knowledge.

The erotic functions for me in several ways, and the first is in providing the power which comes from sharing deeply any pursuit with another person. The sharing of joy, whether physical, emotional, psychic, or intellectual, forms a bridge between the sharers which can be the basis for understanding much of what

is not shared between them, and lessens the threat of their difference.

Another important way in which the erotic connection functions is the open and fearless underlining of my capacity for joy. In the way my body stretches to music and opens into response, hearkening to its deepest rhythms, so every level upon which I sense also opens to the erotically satisfying experience, whether it is dancing, building a bookcase, writing a poem, examining an idea.

That self-connection shared is a measure of the joy which I know myself to be capable of feeling, a reminder of my capacity for feeling. And that deep and irreplaceable knowledge of my capacity for joy comes to demand from all of my life that it be lived within the knowledge that such satisfaction is possible, and does not have to be called *marriage,* nor *god,* nor an *afterlife.*

This is one reason why the erotic is so feared, and so often relegated to the bedroom alone, when it is recognized at all. For once we begin to feel deeply all the aspects of our lives, we begin to demand from ourselves and from our life-pursuits that they feel in accordance with that joy which we know ourselves to be capable of. Our erotic knowledge empowers us, becomes a lens through which we scrutinize all aspects of our existence, forcing us to evaluate those aspects honestly in terms of their relative meaning within our lives. And this is a grave responsibility, projected from within each of us, not to settle for the convenient, the shoddy, the conventionally expected, nor the merely safe.

During World War II, we bought sealed plastic packets of white, uncolored margarine, with a tiny, intense pellet of yellow coloring perched like a topaz just inside the clear skin of the bag. We would leave the margarine out for a while to soften, and then we would pinch the little pellet to break it inside the bag, releasing the rich yellowness into the soft pale mass of margarine. Then taking it carefully between our fingers, we would knead it gently back and forth, over and over, until the color had spread throughout the whole pound bag of margarine, thoroughly coloring it.

I find the erotic such a kernel within myself. When released from its intense and constrained pellet, it flows through and colors my life with a kind of energy that heightens and sensitizes and strengthens all my experience.

We have been raised to fear the yes within ourselves, our deepest cravings. But, once recognized, those which do not enhance our future lose their power and can be altered. The fear of our desires keeps them suspect and indiscriminately powerful, for to suppress any truth is to give it strength beyond endurance. The fear that we cannot grow beyond whatever distortions we may find within ourselves keeps us docile and loyal and obedient, externally defined, and leads us to accept many facets of our oppression as women.

When we live outside ourselves, and by that I mean on external directives only rather than from our internal knowledge and needs, when we live away from those erotic guides from within ourselves, then our lives are limited by external and alien forms, and we conform to the needs of a structure that is not based on human need, let alone an individual's. But when we begin to live from within outward, in touch with the power of the erotic within ourselves, and allowing that power to inform and illuminate our actions upon the world around us, then we begin to be responsible to ourselves in the deepest sense. For as we begin to recognize our deepest feelings, we begin to give up, of necessity, being satisfied with suffering and self-negation, and with the numbness which so often seems like their only alternative in our society. Our acts against oppression become integral with self, motivated and empowered from within.

In touch with the erotic, I become less willing to accept powerlessness, or those other supplied states of being which are not native to me, such as resignation, despair, self-effacement, depression, self-denial.

And yes, there is a hierarchy. There is a difference between painting a back fence and writing a poem, but only one of quantity. And there is, for me, no difference between writing a good poem and moving into sunlight against the body of a woman I love.

This brings me to the last consideration of the erotic. To share the power of each other's feelings is different from using another's feelings as we would use a Kleenex. When we look the other way from our experience, erotic or otherwise, we use rather than share the feelings of those others who participate in the experience with us. And use without consent of the used is abuse.

In order to be utilized, our erotic feelings must be recognized. The need for sharing deep feeling is a human need. But within the European-American tradition, this need is satisfied by certain proscribed erotic comings-together. These occasions are almost always characterized by a simultaneous looking away, a pretense of calling them something else, whether a religion, a fit, mob violence, or even playing doctor. And this misnaming of the need and the deed give rise to that distortion which results in pornography and obscenity—the abuse of feeling.

When we look away from the importance of the erotic in the development and sustenance of our power, or when we look away from ourselves as we satisfy our erotic needs in concert with others, we use each other as objects of satisfaction rather than share our joy in the satisfying, rather than make connection with our similarities and our differences. To refuse to be conscious of what we are feeling at any time, however comfortable that might seem, is to deny a large part of the experience, and to allow ourselves to be reduced to the pornographic, the abused, and the absurd.

The erotic cannot be felt secondhand. As a Black lesbian feminist, I have a particular feeling, knowledge, and understanding for those sisters with whom I have danced hard, played, or even fought. This deep participation has often been the forerunner for joint concerted actions not possible before.

But this erotic charge is not easily shared by women who continue to operate under an exclusively European-American male tradition. I know it was not available to me when I was trying to adapt my consciousness to this mode of living and sensation.

Only now, I find more and more women-identified women brave enough to risk sharing the erotic's electrical charge without having to look away, and without distorting the enormously powerful and creative nature of that exchange. Recognizing the power of the erotic within our lives can give us the energy to pursue genuine change within our world, rather than merely settling for a shift of characters in the same weary drama.

For not only do we touch our most profoundly creative source, but we do that which is female and self-affirming in the face of a racist, patriarchal, and anti-erotic society.

Study/Discussion Questions

1. What are the uses of the erotic, according to Audre Lorde?
2. What makes sexual feeling a good thing in her view?
3. How does her view of the erotic differ from the standard, "normal" American view today?

Living to Love

bel hooks

bell hooks's writings have been central to the development of African American feminism and to feminism in general. In this essay from her book Sisters of the Yam: Black Women and Self-Recovery, *hooks turns her attention to the need for love in black women's lives. With good reason, historically, black women and men learned to stifle their love for themselves and for one another, hooks argues. For black women, especially, to create lives of inner fulfillment, they need to give voice to what has been silenced. hooks says she envisions "a world where I can feel love, feel myself giving and receiving love, every time I walk outside my house . . ."*

Love heals. We recover ourselves in the act and art of loving. A favorite passage from the biblical Gospel of John that touches my spirit declares: "Anyone who does not love is still in death."

Many black women feel that we live lives in which there is little or no love. This is one of our private truths that is rarely a subject for public discussion. To name this reality evokes such intense pain that black women can rarely talk about it fully with one another. *The Black Women's Health Book* had no chapter focusing specifically on love. And the only time the word was evoked in a chapter heading, it was in a negative context. The subject was domestic violence, the title "Love Don't Always Make It Right." Already, this title distorts the meaning of genuine love—real love does make it right. One of the major tasks black women face as we work for emotional healing is to understand more fully what love is so that we do not imagine that love and abuse can be simultaneously present in our lives. Most abuse is life-threatening, whether it wounds our bodies or our psyches. Understanding love as a life-force that urges us to move against death enables us to see clearly that, where love is, there can no disenabling, disempowering, or life-destroying abuse.

Because many black women make care synonymous with love, we confuse the issue. Care can take place in, for example, a familial context where there is also abuse, but this does not mean that love is present. In this essay, I would like to offer ways to think about love that deepen our understanding of its meaning and practice. I want to shed light on the way our specific historical experience as black people living in a racist society has made it difficult and at times downright impossible for

From *Sisters of the Yam: Black Women and Self-Recovery,* Boston: South End Press, 1993, pp. 129–147.

us to practice the act and art of loving in any sustained way.

It has not been simple for black people living in this culture to know love. Defining love in *The Road Less Traveled* as "the will to extend one's self for the purpose of nurturing one's own or another's personal growth," M. Scott Peck shares the prophetic insight that love is both an "intention and an action." We show love via the union of feeling and action. Using this definition of love, and applying it to black experience, it is easy to see how many black folks historically could only experience themselves as frustrated lovers, since the conditions of slavery and racial apartheid made it extremely difficult to nurture one's own or another's spiritual growth. Notice that I say difficult, not impossible. Yet, it does need to be acknowledged that oppression and exploitation pervert, distort, and impede our ability to love.

Given the politics of black life in this white-supremacist society, it makes sense that internalized racism and self-hate stand in the way of love. Systems of domination exploit folks best when they deprive us of our capacity to experience our own agency and alter our ability to care and to love ourselves and others. Black folks have been deeply and profoundly "hurt," as we used to say down home, "hurt to our hearts," and the deep psychological pain we have endured and still endure affects our capacity to feel and therefore our capacity to love. We are a wounded people. Wounded in that part of ourselves that would know love, that would be loving. The choice to love has always been a gesture of resistance for African-Americans. And many of us have made that choice only to find ourselves unable to give or receive love.

Our collective difficulties with the art and act of loving began in the context of slavery. It should not shock us that a people who were forced to witness their young being sold away; their loved ones, companions, and comrades beaten beyond all recognition; a people who

knew unrelenting poverty, deprivation, loss, unending grief, and the forced separation of family and kin; would emerge from the context of slavery wary of this thing called love. Yet, some slaves must have dreamed that they would one day be able to fully develop their capacity to love. They knew first-hand that the conditions of slavery distorted and perverted the possibility that they would know love or be able to sustain such knowing.

Though black folks may have emerged from slavery eager to experience intimacy, commitment, and passion outside the realm of bondage, they must also have been in many ways psychologically unprepared to practice fully the art of loving. No wonder then that many black folks established domestic households that mirrored the brutal arrangements they had known in slavery. Using a hierarchical model of family life, they created domestic spaces where there were tensions around power, tensions that often led black men to severely whip black women, to punish them for perceived wrongdoing, that led adults to beat children to assert domination and control. In both cases, black people were using the same harsh and brutal methods against one another that had been used by white slave owners against them when they were enslaved. We know that life was not easy for the newly manumitted black slaves. We know that slavery's end did not mean that black people who were suddenly free to love now knew the way to love one another well.

Slave narratives often emphasize time and time again that black people's survival was often determined by their capacity to repress feelings. In his 1845 narrative, Frederick Douglass recalled that he had been unable to experience grief when hearing of his mother's death since they had been denied sustained contact. Slavery socialized black people to contain and repress a range of emotions. Witnessing one another being daily subjected to all manner of physical abuse, the pain of overwork, the pain of brutal punishment, the pain of near-starvation, enslaved black people could rarely show sympathy or solidarity with one another just at that moment when sympathy and solace was most needed. They rightly feared reprisal. It was only in carefully cultivated spaces of social resistance, that slaves could give vent to repressed feelings. Hence, they learned to check the impulse to give care when it was most needed and learned to wait for a "safe" moment when feelings could be expressed. What form could love take in such a context, in a world where black folks never knew how long they might be together? Practicing love in the slave context could make one vulnerable to unbearable emotional pain. It was often easier for slaves to care for one another while being very mindful of the transitory nature of their intimacies. The social world of slavery encouraged black people to develop notions of intimacy connected to expedient practical reality. A slave who could not repress and contain emotion might not survive.

The practice of repressing feelings as a survival strategy continued to be an aspect of black life long after slavery ended. Since white supremacy and racism did not end with the Emancipation Proclamation, black folks felt it was still necessary to keep certain emotional barriers intact. And, in the worldview of many black people, it became a positive attribute to be able to contain feelings.

Over time, the ability to mask, hide, and contain feelings came to be viewed by many black people as a sign of strong character. To show one's emotions was seen as foolish. Traditionally in southern black homes, children were often taught at an early age that it was important to repress feelings. Often, when children were severely whipped, we were told not to cry. Showing one's emotions could lead to further punishment. Parents would say in the midst of painful punishments: "Don't even let me see a tear." Or if one dared to cry, they threatened further punishment by saying: "If

you don't stop that crying, I'll give you something to cry about."

How was this behavior any different from that of the slave owner whipping the slave but denying access to comfort and consolation, denying even a space to express pain? And if many black folks were taught at an early age not only to repress emotions but to see giving expressions to feeling as a sign of weakness, then how would they learn to be fully open to love? Many black folks have passed down from generation to generation the assumption that to let one's self go, to fully surrender emotionally, endangers survival. They feel that to love weakens one's capacity to develop a stoic and strong character.

When I was growing up, it was apparent to me that outside the context of religion and romance, love was viewed by grown-ups as a luxury. Struggling to survive, to make ends meet, was more important than loving. In that context, the folks who seemed most devoted to the art and act of loving were the old ones, our grandmothers and great grandmothers, our granddaddys and great granddaddys, the Papas and Big Mamas. They gave us acceptance, unconditional care, attention, and, most importantly, they affirmed our need to experience pleasure and joy. They were affectionate. They were physically demonstrative. Our parents and their struggling-to-get-ahead generation often behaved as though love was a waste of time, a feeling or an action that got in the way of them dealing with the more meaningful issues of life.

When teaching Toni Morrison's novel *Sula,* I am never surprised to see black female students nodding their heads in recognition when reading a passage where Hannah, a grown black woman, asks her mother, Eva: "Did you ever love us?" Eva responds with hostility and says: "You settin' here with your healthy-ass self and ax me did I love you? Them big old eyes in your head would a been two holes full of maggots if I hadn't." Hannah is not satisfied with this answer for she knows that Eva has responded fully to her children's material needs. She wants to know if there was another level of affection, of feeling and action. She says to Eva: "Did you ever, you know, play with us?" And again Eva responds by acting as though this is a completely ridiculous question:

> Play? Wasn't nobody playin' in 1895. Just 'cause you got it good now you think it was always this good? 1895 was a killer girl. Things was bad. Niggers was dying like flies . . . What would I look like leapin' 'round that little old room playin' with youngins with three beets to my name?

Eva's responses suggest that finding the means for material survival was not only the most important gesture of care, but that it precluded all other gestures. This is a way of thinking that many black people share. It makes care for material well-being synonymous with the practice of loving. The reality is, of course, that even in a context of material privilege, love may be absent. Concurrently, within the context of poverty, where one must struggle to make ends meet, one might keep a spirit of love alive by making a space for playful engagement, the expression of creativity, for individuals to receive care and attention in relation to their emotional well-being, a kind of care that attends to hearts and minds as well as stomachs. As contemporary black people commit ourselves to collective recovery, we must recognize that attending to our emotional well-being is just as important as taking care of our material needs.

It seems appropriate that this dialogue on love in *Sula* takes place between two black women, between mother and daughter, for their interchange symbolizes a legacy that will be passed on through the generations. In fact, Eva does not nurture Hannah's spiritual growth, and Hannah does not nurture the spiritual growth of her daughter, Sula. Yet, Eva does embody a certain model of "strong" black womanhood that is practically deified in black life. It is precisely her capacity to repress emotions and do whatever is needed for the continuation of material life that is depicted as the source of her strength. It is a kind of "instrumental" way of thinking about human needs, one that is echoed in the contemporary song Tina Turner sings—"What's love got to do with it?"

Living in a capitalist economy clearly informs the way black people think about love. In his essay, "Love and Need: Is Love a Package or a Message?" the Catholic monk Thomas Merton explains the way we are taught, via a market economy and the mass media that promotes it, to think of ourselves and of love as a commodity. His comments are worth quoting at length:

> Love is regarded as a deal. The deal presupposes that we all have needs which have to be fulfilled by means of exchange. In order to make a deal you have to appear in the market with a worthwhile product, or if the product is worthless, you can get by if you dress it up in a good-looking package. We unconsciously think of ourselves as objects for sale on the market. . . . In doing this we come to consider ourselves and others not as *persons* but as *products*—as "goods," or in other words, as packages. We appraise one another commercially. We size each other up and make deals with a view to our own profit. We do not give ourselves in love, we make a deal that will enhance our own product, and therefore no deal is final.

Since so much of black life experience has been about the struggle to gain access to material goods, it makes sense that many of us not only over-value materiality but that we are also more vulnerable to the kind of thinking that commodifies feelings and makes it appear that they are only another kind of "material" need that can be satisfied within the same system of exchange used with other goods. The combined forces of racist and sexist thinking have had a particularly negative influence on black women's attitudes about our relation to material goods. Not only have we been socialized to think of our bodies as a "product" to be exchanged, we are also made to feel that it is our responsibility to deliver needed products to others. Given that so many black women are the sole providers in black households, as Eva is in *Sula,* it is not surprising that we are often obsessed with material comfort, with finding the means to provide material well-being for ourselves and others. And, in this role, black women may be most unwilling to cultivate the practice of loving. We may be quite dedicated to caring for the needs of others, particularly material needs. Our need to love and be loved may be fundamentally denied, however. After all, it is ultimately "easier to worry about how you gonna' get a dollar to buy the latest product than it is to worry about whether there will be love in your house."

Love needs to be present in every black female's life, in all of our houses. It is the absence of love that has made it so difficult for us to stay alive or, if alive, to live fully. When we love ourselves we want to live fully. Whenever people talk about black women's lives, the emphasis is rarely on transforming society so that we can live fully, it is almost always about applauding how well we have "survived" despite harsh circumstances or how we can survive in the future. When we love ourselves, we know that we must do more than survive. We must have the means to live fully. To live fully, black women can no longer deny our need to know love.

If we would know love, we must first learn how to respond to inner emotional needs. This may mean undoing years of socialization where we have been taught that such needs are unimportant. Let me give an example. In her recently published book, *The Habit of Surviving: Black Women's Strategies for Life,* Kesho Scott opens the book sharing an incident from her life that she feels taught her important survival skills:

> Thirteen years tall, I stood in the living room doorway. My clothes were wet. My hair was mangled. I was in tears, in shock, and in need of my mother's warm arms. Slowly, she looked me up and down, stood up from the couch and walked towards me, her body clenched in criticism. Putting her hands on her hips and planting herself, her shadow falling over my face, she asked in a voice of barely suppressed rage, "What happened?" I flinched as if struck by the unexpected anger and answered, "They put my head in the toilet. They say I can't swim with them." "They" were eight white girls at my high school. I reached out to hold her, but she roughly brushed my hands aside and said, "Like hell! Get your coat. Let's go."

Straight-away it should be evident that Kesho was not learning that her emotional needs should be addressed at this moment. In her next sentences she asserts: "My mother taught me a powerful and enduring lesson that day. She taught me that I would have to fight back against racial and sexual injustice." Obviously, this is an important survival strategy for black women. But Kesho was also learning an unhealthy message at the same time. She was made to feel that she did not deserve comfort after a traumatic painful experience, that indeed she was "out-of-line" to even be seeking emotional solace, and that her individual needs were not as important as the collective struggle to resist racism and sexism. Imagine how different this story would read if we were told that as soon as Kesho walked into the room, obviously suffering distress, her mother had comforted her, helped repair the damage to her appearance, and then shared with her the necessity of confronting (maybe not just then, it would depend on her psychological state whether she could emotionally handle a confrontation) the racist white student who had assaulted her. Then Kesho would have known, at age thirteen, that her emotional well-being was just as important as the collective struggle to end racism and sexism—that indeed these two experiences are linked.

Many black females have learned to deny our inner needs while we develop our capacity to cope and confront in public life. This is why we can often appear to be functioning well on jobs but be utterly dysfunctional in private. You know what I am talking about. Undoubtedly you know a black woman who looks together, in control on the job, and when you drop by her house unexpectedly for a visit, aside from the living room, every other space looks like a tornado hit it, everything dirty and in disarray. I see this chaos and disorder as a reflection of the inner psyche, of the absence of well-being. Yet until black females believe, and hopefully learn when we are little girls, that our emotional well-being matters, we cannot attend to our needs. Often we replace recognition of inner emotional needs with the longing to control. When we deny our real needs, we tend to feel fragile, vulnerable, emotionally unstable, and untogether. Black females often work hard to cover up these conditions. And we cover up by controlling, by seeking to oversee or dominate everyone around us. The message we tell ourselves is, "I can't be falling apart because I have all this power over others."

Let us return to the mother in Kesho's story. What if the sight of her wounded and hurt daughter called to mind the mother's deep unaddressed inner wounds? What if she was critical, harsh, or just downright mean, because she did not want to break down, cry, and stop being the "strong black woman"? And yet, if she had cried, her daughter might have felt her pain was shared, that it was fine to name that you are in pain, that we do not have to keep the hurt bottled up inside us. What the mother did was what many of us have witnessed our mothers doing in similar circumstances—she

took control. She was domineering, even her physical posture dominated. Clearly, this mother wanted her black female presence to have more "power" than that of the white girls.

A fictional model of black mothering that shows us a mother able to respond fully to her daughters when they are in pain is depicted in Ntozake Shange's novel *Sassafrass, Cypress and Indigo.* Throughout this novel, Shange's black female characters are strengthened in their capacity to self-actualize by a loving mother. Even though she does not always agree with their choices she respects them and offers them solace. Here is part of a letter she writes to Sassafrass who is "in trouble" and wants to come home. The letter begins with the exclamation: "Of course you can come home! What do you think you could do to yourself that I wouldn't love my girl?" First giving love and acceptance, Hilda later chastises, then expresses love again:

> You and Cypress like to drive me crazy with all this experimental living. You girls need to stop chasing the coon by his tail. And I know you know what I'm talking about. . . . Mark my words. You just come on home and we'll straighten out whatever it is that's crooked in your thinking. There's lots to do to keep busy. And nobody around to talk foolish talk or experiment with. Something can't happen every day. You get up. You eat, go to work, come back, eat again, enjoy some leisure, and go back to bed. Now, that's plenty for most folks. I keep asking myself where did I go wrong? Yet I know in my heart I'm not wrong. I'm right. The world's going crazy and trying to take my children with it. Okay. Now I'm through with all that. I love you very much. But you're getting to be a grown woman and I know that too. You come back to Charleston and find the rest of yourself. Love, Mama

It troubled me that it was difficult to find autobiographical narratives where black daughters describe loving interactions with black mothers. Overall, in fiction and autobiography, black mothers are more likely to be depicted as controlling, manipulative, and dominating, withholding love to maintain power over. If, as Jessica Benjamin suggests in *The Bonds of Love,* it is "mutual recognition" that disrupts the possibility of domination, then it is possible to speculate that black women who suffer a lack of recognition often feel the need to control others as a way to be noticed, to be seen as important. In Kesho's story the mother refuses to see her daughter's pain. By erasing her pain, she also erases that part of herself that hurts. And the message she gives is you can deny pain by the experience of power, in this case the power to return to a setting where you have been hurt and demand retribution. If black women were more loved and loving, the need to dominate others, particularly in the role of mother, would not be so intense. It is healing for black women who are obsessed with the need to control, to be "right," to practice letting go.

The great black civil rights activist Septima Clarke names that her personal growth was enhanced by letting go the need to be in control. For her this meant unlearning dependency on hierarchical models that suggest the person in power is always right. At one time she believed that whites always knew better than blacks what was good for our well-being. In *Ready from Within,* she declares:

> Because I had a very strong disciplined mother, who felt that whatever she had in her mind was right, I felt that whatever I had in my mind was right, too. I found out that I needed to change my way of thinking, and in changing my way of thinking I had to let people understand that their way of thinking was not the only way.

The art and practice of loving begins with our capacity to recognize and affirm ourselves. That is why so many self-help books encour-

age us to look at ourselves in the mirror and talk to the image we see there. Recently, I noticed that what I do with the image that I see in the mirror is very unloving. I inspect it. From the moment I get out of bed and look at myself in the mirror, I am evaluating. The point of the evaluation is not to provide self-affirmation but to critique. Now this was a common practice in our household. When the six of us girls made our way downstairs to the world inhabited by father, mother, and brother, we entered the world of "critique." We were looked over and told all that was wrong. Rarely did one hear a positive evaluation.

Replacing negative critique with positive recognition has made me feel more empowered as I go about my day. Affirming ourselves is the first step in the direction of cultivating the practice of being inwardly loving. I choose to use the phrase "inwardly loving" over self-love, because the very notion of "self" is so inextricably bound up with how we are seen by and in relation to others. Within a racist/sexist society, the larger culture will not socialize black women to know and acknowledge that our inner lives are important. Decolonized black women must name that reality in accord with others among us who understand as well that it is vital to nurture the inner life. As we examine our inner life, we get in touch with the world of emotions and feelings. Allowing ourselves to feel, we affirm our right in be inwardly loving. Once I know what I feel, I can also get in touch with those needs I can satisfy or name those needs that can only be satisfied in communion or contact with others.

Where is the love when a black woman looks at herself and says: "I see inside me somebody who is ugly, too dark, too fat, too afraid—somebody nobody would love, 'cause I don't even like what I see"; or maybe: "I see inside me somebody who is so hurt, who is just like a ball of pain and I don't want to look at her 'cause I can't do nothing about that pain." The love is absent. To make it present, the individual has to first choose to see herself, to just look at that inner self without blame or censure. And once she names what she sees, she might think about whether that inner self deserves or needs love.

I have never heard a black woman suggest during confessional moments in a support group that she does not need love. She may be in denial about that need but it doesn't take much self-interrogation to break through this denial. If you ask most black women straight-up if they need love—the answer is likely to be yes. To give love to our inner selves we must first give attention, recognition, and acceptance. Having let ourselves know that we will not be punished for acknowledging who we are or what we feel we can name the problems we see. I find it helpful to interview myself, and I encourage my sisters to do the same. Sometimes its hard for me to get immediately in touch with what I feel, but if I ask myself a question, an answer usually emerges.

Sometimes when we look at ourselves, and see our inner turmoil and pain, we do not know how to address it. That's when we need to seek help. I call loved ones sometimes and say, "I have these feelings that I don't understand or know how to address, can you help me?" There are many black females who cannot imagine asking for help, who see this as a sign of weakness. This is another negative debilitating worldview we should unlearn. It is a sign of personal power to be able to ask for help when you need it. And we find that asking for what we need when we need it is an experience that enhances rather than diminishes personal power. Try it and see. Often we wait until a crisis situation has happened when we are compelled by circumstance to seek the help of others. Yet, crisis can often be avoided if we seek help when we recognize that we are no longer able to function well in a given situation. For black women who are addicted to being controlling, asking for help can be a loving practice of surrender, reminding us that we do not

always have to be in charge. Practicing being inwardly loving, we learn not only what our souls need but we begin to understand better the needs of everyone around us as well.

Black women who are *choosing* for the first time (note the emphasis on choosing) to practice the art and act of loving should devote time and energy showing love to other black people, both people we know and strangers. Within white-supremacist capitalist patriarchy, black people do not get enough love. And it's always exciting for those of us who are undergoing a process of decolonization to see other black people in our midst respond to loving care. Just the other day T., whom I mention in another chapter [of *Sisters of the Yam*], told me that she makes a point of going into a local store and saying warm greetings to an older black man who works there. Recently, he wanted to know her name and then thanked her for the care that she gives to him. A few years ago when she was mired in self-hate, she would not have had the "will" to give him care. Now, she extends to him the level of care that she longs to receive from other black people when she is out in the world.

When I was growing up, I received "unconditional love" from black women who showed me by their actions that love did not have to be earned. They let me know that I deserved love; their care nurtured my spiritual growth. Black theologian and mystic Howard Thurman teaches us that we need to love one another without judging. Explaining this in an essay on Thurman's work, Walter Fluker writes:

> According to Thurman, there is within each individual a basic need to be cared for and understood in a relationship with another at a point that is beyond all that is good and evil. In religious experience, this inner necessity for love is fulfilled in encounter with God and in relation to other, the person is affirmed and become aware of being dealt with totally.

Many black people, and black women in particular, have become so accustomed to not being loved that we protect ourselves from having to acknowledge the pain such deprivation brings by acting like only white folks or other silly people sit around wanting to be loved. When I told a group of black women that I wanted there to be a world where I can feel love, feel myself giving and receiving love, every time I walk outside my house, they laughed. For such a world to exist, racism and all other forms of domination would need to change. To the extent that I commit my life to working to end domination, I help transform the world so that it is that loving place that I want it to be.

Nikki Giovanni's "Woman Poem" has always meant a lot to me because it was one of the first pieces of writing that called out black women's self-hatred. Published in the anthology, *The Black Woman,* edited by Toni Bambara, this poem ends with the lines: "face me whose whole life is tied up to unhappiness cause it's the only for real thing I know." Giovanni not only names in this poem that black women are socialized to be caretakers, to deny our inner needs, she also names the extent to which self-hate can make us turn against those who are caring toward us. The black female narrator says: "how dare you care about me you ain't got no good sense—cause I ain't shit you must be lower than that to care." This poem was written in 1968. Here we are, more than twenty years later, and black women are still struggling to break through denial to name the hurt in our lives and find ways to heal. Learning how to love is a way to heal. That learning cannot take place if we do not know what love is. Remember Stevie Wonder singing with tears in his eyes on national television: "I want to know what love is. I want you to show me."

I am empowered by the idea of love as the will to extend oneself to nurture one's own or another's spiritual growth because it affirms that love is an action, that it is akin to work. For black people it's an important definition because the focus is not on material well-being. And while we know that material needs must be met, collectively we need to focus our attention on emotional needs as well. There is that lovely biblical passage in "Proverbs" that reminds us: "Better a dinner of herbs, where love is, than a stalled ox and hatred therewith."

When we as black women experience fully the transformative power of love in our lives, we will bear witness publicly in a way that will fundamentally challenge existing social structures. We will be more fully empowered to address the genocide that daily takes the lives of black people—men, women, and children. When we know what love is, when we love, we are able to search our memories and see the past with new eyes; we are able to transform the present and dream the future. Such is love's power. Love heals.

BIBLIOGRAPHY

Bambara, Toni Cade, ed. *The Black Woman.* New York: New American Library, 1970.

Benjamin, Jessica. *Bonds of Love: Psychoanalysis, Feminism and the Problem of Domination.* New York: Pantheon, 1988.

Clark, Septima Poinsette. *Ready from Within: Septima Clark and the Civil Rights Movement.* Navarro, CA: Wild Trees Press, 1986.

Merton, Thomas. *Loving and Living.* New York: Harcourt Brace Jovanovich, 1979.

Morrison, Toni. *Sula.* New York: New American Library, 1973.

Peck, M. Scott. *The Road Less Traveled.* New York: Simon & Schuster, 1978.

Scott, Kesho Yvonne. *The Habit of Surviving: Black Women's Strategies for Life.* New Brunswick, NJ: Rutgers University Press, 1991.

Shange, Ntozake. *Sassafras, Cypress and Indigo.* New York: St. Martin's Press, 1982.

White, Evelyn. *The Black Women's Health Book: Speaking for Ourselves.* Seattle, WA: Seal Press, 1990.

Study/Discussion Questions

1. How did slavery constrain African Americans emotionally, according to hooks?
2. What is the difference between "living to love" and "material care"?
3. What can black women do to make their own lives more fully loving?
4. Do you think that hooks' ideas about love apply outside of the African American community?
5. How can poverty make it hard to love in the way she describes?
6. What advantages do white people have in living to love?

Bearded Ladies:
Women in Comedy

Molly Haskell

In this selection from her book Holding My Own in No Man's Land:
Women and Men, Film and Feminists, *film critic Molly Haskell shows
that it is possible to embrace both popular culture and feminism. On
television, of all places, she finds heartening examples of strong, funny
women who are tearing down worn stereotypes of what women can and
should be. "Through our comic surrogates," she writes, "women can now
see themselves as works of art in a funhouse mirror, beauties and beasts
along a spectrum of roles that defy political correctness with a vengeance."*

Because they live in a world in which
serious-minded folks can still get points
for claiming never to watch television,
Respected Culture Arbiters, when they come
out of the closet with their secret addictions,
do so with a certain elegantly tortured defen-
siveness to placate the highbrows. Just so,
television's superior serial dramas—crime
shows (*N.Y.P.D. Blue* and *Homicide*) and the
hospital shows (*E.R.* and *Chicago Hope*)—have
recently been getting some well-placed attention from the literati. These long-running series, with their ethnically varied casts, superior women's roles, and feeling for complex
characters evolving over time, deserve all the
accolades they get. But these shows aren't the
only ones that are beating Hollywood at its
own narrative game. I'd suggest that it's in the
field of comedy, including that much despised

genre the sit-com, that television is exploding
all over the place. Both within the precincts
of network television and in the outer reaches
of cable, there are uncommonly raunchy, innovative, sophisticated shows, many of them
women-driven, that are tackling male-female
conflict and sexual taboo and the undercur-
rent of women's rage, subjects that mainstream
movies won't touch with a ten-foot pole.
Hollywood's only concession to the "transgres-
sive" is that reassuring staple, a big male star
in fright-wig drag.

What movies rarely give us is the other side
of the coin, the funny and terrifying spectacle
of a woman taking on the coloring and aggression of the male. The tacit assumption was that,
unlike the female impersonator, the male impersonator, the strident female comic, just
wasn't funny. A little tough-guy bravado, a little

blatant penis envy here and there was okay, even flattering, as long as the bounds of femininity remained in place. Well, I'm here to tell you that there's a new breed of women comics who are crossing the lines and testing boundaries, not just of what's taboo and what isn't, but—more dangerously—what's funny and what isn't.

In a recent profile on the television star Roseanne, a fellow comedian recalled a riotous bit she'd performed at a Denver club where the two were both doing stand-up and waiting tables. According to the admirer, now a writer on her show, she had gone onstage to do a routine about bikers when she looked and saw the place filled with them—fifty black-clad bruisers and their girlfriends. Hesitating a minute, but urged on by her backstage buddies, she went through with it. "I really hate bikers," she said. "You know, they all got tobacco juice in their beards. They piss on the side of the road. And the men are even worse!"

The audience fell out of their chairs. This little outrage from the early Roseanne (she was making a dollar and a half an hour, plus tips) was a foretaste of the uproariously rude down-and-dirty comedian to come: the special twist on sexual machismo, the need to blow things up from the inside and substitute "uterus power" for "penis power."

Just as I was pondering the humor of ladies with facial hair, Brett Butler came along with a similar routine. She's talking, in her southern drawl, about New York being a Bigots' Buffet. Rednecks from her native Dixie have come to visit, and they're in the Bronx when they are startled to behold "mustachioed Sicilians . . . and their boyfriends."

What was going on with hirsute women? Even Woody Allen had a hairy unisex gag: "I [was] hitchhiking west and being picked up by two native Californians," he recalls in a monologue in his collection, *Side Effects,* "a charismatic young man with a beard like Rasputin's and a charismatic young woman with a beard like Svengali's."

These jokes obviously tap into our confusion about sex roles in the age of androgyny: that moment when, walking along a sidewalk, we see two people ahead of us, arm in arm, both with pony tails, and we wonder which, if either, is the woman. Remember the Bearded Lady at the circus? She was a freak of nature, supposedly, but also a cautionary figure. As we stood there, transfixed and giggling with adolescent anxiety, she seemed to be saying: This is what could happen to you if you don't give up your tomboyish ways and become All Female.

Women with male hormones, women with male secondary sex characteristics, might be a metaphor for these new women comics, the bearded ladies who are crossing gender boundaries and breaking the rules of humor. They are an aggressive bunch and they would have to be: comedy, particularly the stand-up variety, is an act of aggression, a violent ripping apart of the conventions and clichés by which we live. We watch with equal parts discomfort and glee as someone else's beliefs, color, eccentricities are ridiculed and our fears—mostly of embarrassment, of exposure—are vicariously exorcised. Without overindulging in the romantic fantasy of the wounded artist, it seems logical to assume that this kind of savagery comes out of pain cauterized, or transmuted, into comic revenge. There have been far fewer women comics over the years for obvious reasons: Women are on earth to mend, not rend, the social fabric. We are the healers, the civilizers; we nurture, mediate, sympathize, tame, and domesticate.

Or so goes the myth, now being given a run for its money by one woman comic after another. Why indeed should men have all the fun and the fury? Giving vent to the rage and disillusionment that was previously papered over by the will to please or channeled into political activism, women comics and women in comedy series are letting it all hang out in ways that once might have provoked retaliation by censors. Roseanne mocks and ridicules the sacred cows of mainstream America, those very institutions whose products her show is pushing. Murphy Brown's pregnancy without benefit of husband caused a high-level snit and still pinches nerves in the body politic.

In the past, women comedians might exaggerate, even tumble, but there was a clear division between the clowns (Bea Lillie, Martha Raye) and the ladies. Well, Mae West was no lady and would be insulted to be so labeled, but her act was more femme than butch, even if it bordered on female impersonation. There was a kind of either/or governing comedy and women: comedy was the last resort of the homely woman. You were either favored by fortune: pretty therefore popular, therefore normal, Daddy's little darling; or you were a plain Jane, therefore a misfit who needed to develop wit and personality to claim the attention and love denied you.

There were a few anomalies: Carole Lombard, being both gorgeous and goofy, was an exception that proved the rule.

The screwball tradition, in which women like Lombard, Katharine Hepburn, Claudette Colbert, Rosalind Russell could be brainy, nutty, and beautiful, was unique. For the most part, movies didn't know what to do with women who combined such powerhouse qualities. The most successful gambit for a smart funny "looker" was to play dumb: Judy Holliday was an adorably shrewd fluff, while Lucille Ball, of gorgeous gams and model good looks, turned into the screwball Lucy, blithe savager of Ricky's best-laid plans. They slyly put the torch to all sorts of conventional expectations but had to do it by pretending to be dopier than they were. Like Carol Burnett, they put on their comic personae like clown suits: Burnett could never have gotten away with some of her more acid numbers—the

corrosive Mama-and-Eunice feature, for example—if she hadn't been so high-spirited and congenial as partygiver-hostess for the Carol Burnett show.

The seventies were self-consciously serious, an era of political activism: we marched, signed petitions, stormed the barricades to win reproductive rights and equal pay. We were too focused on the business at hand to laugh at ourselves. Even that decade's queen of comedy, Mary Tyler Moore, was notable more for the emotional intensity and guiding conscience she brought to the workplace than for her own intrinsic funniness. Her seriousness was a foil, her anxiety that of the single woman not yet comfortable in her singleness, still waiting for Mr. Right to make his entrance. Now two decades later, we've come far enough to be able to jeer at our own romantic illusions, to take a rueful view of the idea of "having it all," and to acknowledge that the results of the so-called sexual revolution have been ambiguous at best.

Okay, so we've emerged from the repressions of Victorianism wherein sex was unmentionable, contraception barely existed, pregnancy out of wedlock was a social tragedy, and women weren't thought to have libidos at all. But how free are we? That is, are women who like sex or have multiple lovers really exempt from the taint of being thought "loose," promiscuous, even tarts? And are women who *don't* want to have sex really free to say No? From the evidence of series like *Grace Under Fire* and *Cybill*, surely men had even more to be grateful for: there being (theoretically) no onus attached to the pursuit of sexual pleasure, they could now get all they wanted without having to get married or even say I love you. They could play the field forever and if suddenly seized by an urge to settle down, they could lie down till it went away; or they could marry and then, when the urge wore off, get a quicky no-fault divorce. And women might find themselves "free" once again, but this time with a couple of kids and a drop in income, scratching out a survival existence and harassing her ex for child support.

Is *this* what equality means? asks one harried woman after another. To be saddled like Grace with three children, a factory job, and little faith in marriage or men? Or like Cybill, with two children, one grandchild, and two ex-husbands in one's twilight years! And still feeling sexy. To be friend, employer, denmother, and unpaid shrink to a group of egomaniacal me-decade drop-ins running a barely profitable bookstore-coffee bar (*Ellen*). To be raising a child or children alone (*Murphy Brown, Absolutely Fabulous*). To be trying to have a child without sacrificing a high-powered career (*Mad About You*).

Classic comedy came from the head-on collision of men refusing to grow up and women insisting that they do. The gags of Chaplin and Keaton, or W. C. Fields or the Marx Brothers, radiated from the basic premise of turning order into chaos, busting up the living room furniture, and fleeing the terrifying stultifying rule of The Wife. Even *The Simpsons,* that durably funny cartoon series by MTM and *Rhoda* guru James Brooks, is a kind of smirky triumph of dumb-male entropy over what, in the gender dynamics of the show, is seen as the earnestly civilizing influence of women. Such sacred cows as upward mobility, self-improvement, and the importance of education, along with the smarts of Lisa and the sweetness of Marge, hold little weight against the boorish cunning of the male side of the family, as Bart follows Homer's slackerish footsteps into a downscale spiral of screw-up, goof-off, loserdom.

If women are fighting back, it's partly against having been cast in the role of nag and relationship-bore. As women in power roles become more common, and men as helpmeets and supporters become less taboo, we can exorcise our nervousness through gags and storylines that play on these very reversals and fears.

Women's comedy is the continuation of consciousness-raising by other means, with all the issues that once formed the agenda of group therapy and editorials now incorporated into the ongoing drama of frustration and comic release. The continuing imbalance of power, the refusal of men to commit, form an ongoing leitmotif: "A friend of mine asked me how I get rid of a guy I don't want," said Rita Rudner. "I just tell him I love you, I want you to be the father of my children. He leaves skid marks."

Or Brett Butler's rueful line: "You know Bill Clinton, you've met guys like him at a bar. You know that every word out of his mouth is a lie, but you just don't want to go home alone."

The humor is directed at men, but it is also directed at ourselves, at "smart women who make foolish choices," at the conflicts that just won't go away. A "Guerrilla Girls" cartoon says: "Don't agonize over whether to work or stay home with your kids—you'll feel guilty either way." And suddenly, hearing that truth, realizing the absurdity and *universality* of our predicament, we feel better. With humor, we share emotional burdens together.

In one show, Roseanne, wanting space to "create," isolates herself in a basement office in an attempt to write. By emphasizing the truly limited condition of the working-class woman, she shows in extremis the harrowing truth of most women's existence: The desire to express oneself, to be independent, is one that can be fulfilled only intermittently or in rare circumstances. We are bound, if not by biology, then by those very forces of *wanting* to care for the young, for others, that fuel the ire, or comic inspiration, of male comedians. What the retrogressive, still-yearning princess in us would deny, comedy forces us to look at, over and over again. We can no longer depend on the kindness and staying power of husbands; besides, in a society that values remunerated work, it feels good to bring home a paycheck. The paradoxes of women's position, the contradictions within ourselves, are brought into the open, and in the catharsis of laughter we feel a momentary release from pressure and relief at the realization that others are in the same boat.

Old myths and expectations die hard, and ancient impulses lie in wait to ambush us like phantom limbs. On one episode of *Ellen,* she decides to entertain in grand style—a Martha Stewart fall dinner, complete with an autumn foliage centerpiece and Martha Stewart herself as honored guest. Only it's California, so they have to use palm fronds instead of autumn foliage, and her oven has a breakdown, so instead of Cornish hens, they send out for pizza. Martha, sharing the joke of which she is also the butt, smiles benignly and unflappably as Ellen chokes and sputters, unable to execute this newest version of society's ideal woman. Setting a gorgeous table with crystal and iron-only linen—just like the one Mom did or didn't—is a fantasy we all entertain from time to time, but let's admit it's beyond the grasp of most of us, so why not leave it in the realm of fantasy.

Comedy writing, most people in the business will say, comes out of anguish, of being dissed or dysfunctional, a misfit in school or abused at home. Even such apparently nice girl–nice guy types as Mary Tyler Moore and Kelsey Grammar have written autobiographies of childhood torment, substance abuse, loneliness.

At a panel on comedy at Columbia University's School of the Arts, Fred Wolf of *Saturday Night Live* claimed, "They're all dysfunctional. I've known a lot of them, and every comedy writer I've ever known is seriously dysfunctional."

Roseanne maintained that if she hadn't become a comedian, she would have become a serial killer—perhaps not realizing that a serial killer, in a different form, is just what she *has* become. This is a woman who revels in firing employees of her show, who rakes her abusive family over the coals at every opportunity, who beheads and castrates like a mythic monster . . . or a ruthless CEO or a blood-

thirsty tyrant! Revenge in the form of a scorched earth policy, taking no prisoners—isn't this a form of homicide? The tip-off is the language comedy uses to describe itself. "We murdered them," "They died laughing," "We almost croaked," that joke "killed" them.

There's a spectrum of women comedians, ranging from the Nice Girls (Ellen De Generes, Helen Hunt, Cybill Shepherd) to the Furies, with various forms of survivors in between. When they lapse, when they find themselves waiting by the phone or tippling over into masochism, they're the first ones to realize it and make a joke about it. In fact, you might say that each character is really two characters: yesterday's woman who self-destructs, sabotages herself, and clings, and her emerging self—probably wrung through the wheel of psychotherapy—who sees and jeers and resolves to do better next week.

Even the women who play second bananas—Roz on *Frazier,* Elaine in *Seinfeld*—refuse to get stuck in some subordinate, spear-carrying role. Roz is not a lead, but she has her scars and her smarts. She's like the Eve Arden sardonic-foil, but less sexually marginal than those comic women of the forties who played the heroine's best friend. Even the English cutie who is dad John Mahoney's aide is a peppery antidote to the father-son and brother-brother hugfest. Elaine on *Seinfeld* is both pal to the guys and balloon-puncturer of some of their more fatuous flights of self-congratulatory fancy. It's true that their wise-ass mystique usually triumphs over alternate versions of reality—what's one dame to a bunch of perpetually adolescent guys?— but she strikes a blow for common sense. Murphy Brown with her slow burns and delicious sarcasm, her shameless egocentricity, dominates her show, but Corky has evolved from cupcake to serious reporter.

At the other end of the spectrum are the Furies, women like Roseanne, Brett Butler, and Jennifer Saunders's Edina on the British series *Absolutely Fabulous.* They give vent to a kind of free-floating rage at everything: husbands, ex-husbands, lovers, children, neighbors, parents, the System, the politically correct.

For these women anger is mother's milk; their style represents a major defection from the femininity program. Once it was the better part of valor, where "ladies" were concerned, to control your temper. It would have been no more seemly to display your anger in public than to go to a party with a bra strap showing. Now women ("ladies" no longer) are expected to sound off regularly, whack an offending male, and keep a good pot of bile on the perpetual boil. "Rage," as Brett Butler says, "is not born overnight. You have to coax it with rusty forceps from a womb of malcontent." We go into therapy to cultivate our anger, as if it were a rare plant in need of careful nurturing.

On one show, Roseanne and family are visiting Disneyland, when a brief altercation with an unctuously smiling official occurs. Roseanne, imitating the professional grin and niceness of the guard, the behavioral equivalent of the squeaky-clean, ultra-sanitary theme park atmosphere, resolves the problem. "This polite stuff really works," she says. Pause. "But I feel so dirty."

The "womb of malcontent" proves endlessly fecund on that wildest and funniest of comedy series, *Absolutely Fabulous*. Edina, the fortyish mom played by writer-star Jennifer Saunders, ignores her ultra-straight teenage daughter (Julia Sawalha as the marvelous Saffron) when she is not actively ridiculing her.

Eddy is flamboyantly and relentlessly narcissistic. Boundless is her appetite for shopping, eating, drinking, drug-taking, traveling, abusing all and sundry—indeed almost any activity in preference to the glum prospect of spending a caring moment with her daughter, or one of fleeting filial devotion with her tiresomely sweet mother.

On the night of the Super Bowl, Comedy Central offered re-runs of *Ab Fab* billed as "Not the Super Bowl." Refugees from the Pitts-

burgh-Dallas grunt-off and its attendant hype found relief in berserk matriarchal mayhem as Eddy and longtime pal Pat (Joanna Lumley) wreaked havoc on Eddy's mother and the vengefully sane and unflappable Saffron. This was presumably as far from the Super Bowl as you could get. But was it? As Eddy pushes Pat away from the breakfast table and throws her things on the floor; as Pat, with Eddy and Saffron in Morocco, prances around with an old British dipsomaniac who has just jumped Saffron; as Eddy, on her fortieth birthday, takes an aerosol can to her candle-bedecked cake and blow-sprays the candles and the cake to kingdom come; as one of her ex-husbands, in a rage, fills her bed with cigarette ashes; I thought: and they call *football* violent!

Ab Fab, like *The Simpsons,* sometimes makes me uncomfortable, since it quite deliberately and audaciously throws out the baby of responsibility with the bathwater of social pieties. Eddy and her buddy Pat send up women's obsession with weight, with style, with hunky younger men, with the miracles of cosmetic surgery, even as they celebrate flagrant derelictions of duty in the form of falling-down-drunkenness, slovenliness, smoking, and not using recycled paper—all on more or less the same level. But that's what makes it so exhilaratingly cutting-edge. For one thing, no matter how remiss we feel in our own lives, we have to be doing a better job of it than Eddy! That, and the enormously vital bond the two women share, a kind of updated post-sixties flipped-out version of Lucy and Ethel.

This glorious sisterhood, as well as the specter of fortyish women, ripely sexual but anxious about aging, marks its American counterpart, the softer but often enchanting *Cybill.* Christine Baranski's Maryann, like Lumley's Pat, is tall, stylish, sardonic, her slender body made to hold a champagne glass in one hand, a cigarette in the other, political correctness be damned. Maryann plays the embittered divorcee and mischief-maker to Cybill's no-nonsense very contemporary Earth Mother, an out-of-work actress who is trying to hold the split ends of her life together. The show closely parallels the real Cybill's own life, and its trump card is Cybill's refreshingly un-*angst*-ridden reaction to aging. However ambivalent we may be about blond beauty queens, the spectacle of an aging "looker" touches female nerves and brings discomfort. Not relying on the gallows humor of many age-obsessed comediennes, Cybill seems glad to be where she is. Her thigh-slapping sense of fun, and our feeling that she is having a grand time and has really come into her own as a *performer,* invigoratingly redeems the hollow old cliché about aging with grace!

The subject and tone of comedy differs significantly according to the age group (and gender): the twenty-somethings are still dreaming about romance and having it all (see *Friends*); the over-thirties are wrestling with lost illusions; and the over-forties, with lost illusions and lost youth. These, as you might expect, are the angriest and the funniest. On one *Ab Fab* show, Eddy and Pat imagine themselves twenty-five years down the road: hunched over, shrewish, thrashing the air with their canes, cackling like witches. Together, they have turned the holy terrors of aging outward, unleashed their combined womanpower upon the world.

If stand-up, at its most ferocious, is still more men's terrain than women's, it may be that something in its aggressiveness is still anathema to women. I know that at one time, a man of my acquaintance would watch Comedy Central for hours on end, whereas after the first two or three solos, I would feel pinned to the sofa, gasping for air. It brought back that terrifying childhood feeling of being tickled against your will. It was as if the comedian hadn't succeeded unless he had his hand around your throat, while you begged for mercy. The determination to "slay" you, to pile on one gag after another until you scream "Stop! Stop!," becomes a kind of assault: war

The TV show *Cybill* humorously tackled female aging.

by other means. And that kind of all-out aggression seems to have been testosterone-driven . . . and best appreciated by that half of the human species who are hormonally attuned to cutthroat combat.

There's a connection here, whether you want to call it women's innate need to hold things together, their Darwinian strategy for passing their genes along, or simply a habit that dies hard. When a woman comic loses her empathy through an obsession with her own hurts—as in the case of Roseanne—then the womb of malcontent turns sour, uterus power becomes an excuse for megalomania, and there's a danger of failing to connect with the vulnerabilities of the audience. Roseanne's extremism becomes a form of blackmail: "If you're not as angry as I am," she seems to be saying, "then you're a sellout." Taking herself too seriously as a one-woman revolution, she's in danger of losing that sense of humor about herself which is the essence of comedy—and is the all-important ingredient in the surge of women into the field. Where once melodrama (the "weeper") was the form best adapted to the emotional needs of women and their restricted status in the world, now the resources of comedy and its cerebral approach to opportunity and failure signal a transcendence over experience, a triumph over victimhood. Holding a stage alone, making jokes, carving out a persona that says "take me as I am"—women are throwing down the gauntlet not just to men but to the little girl inside, raised on the age-old command, best said by the French: "Sois belle et tais-toi" (Be beautiful and be quiet).

You might say women for the first time have the luxury of contemplating themselves as human beings as well as women: instead of just reacting to men's initiatives, or sharing in men's reflected glory, they are acting on their own. Constance Rourke, in her wonderful 1931 book *American Humor,* quotes Henri Bergson to show how the Yankee as a comic figure entered the national stage: "'The comic comes into being just when society and the individual, freed from the worry of self-preservation, begin to regard themselves as works of art.'" Rourke dates the emergence of "embellished self-portraiture which nations as well as individuals may undertake" at 1815: America was coming into its own as a country, and with sufficient detachment to examine just what it was. The comics were, of course, male. It is only now that the American female is sufficiently disengaged from her biological destiny and domestic vocation—her mandate to live through and for others—that she can stand back and wonder who she is and where she is going.

The "deconstruction" of traditional roles that academics engage in—the perception that women are not born but made (Simone de Beauvoir) or, in the current parlance, "constructed"—is merely a fancy-talk way of describing the taking-apart that women comics do every night. Ellen both displays and mocks women's excess of empathy when, after watching and commenting on the monotonous to-and-fro of her pet goldfish, she suddenly leaps (figuratively) into the bowl and *becomes* that pet goldfish, now watching Ellen's lumbering maneuvers with goggle-eyed tolerance. Cybill is so attuned to daughter Zoe's rage that when the fiery adolescent treats her mother too sweetly, Cybill becomes suspicious and sends her off to school with the words: "You better come home with some abuse for your mother!" Eddy makes fun of collagen lips and liposuction by having a fantasy in which she grotesquely sucks and morphs into a woman who is all lips and microscopic body.

Through our comic surrogates, women can now see themselves as works of art in a funhouse mirror, beauties and beasts along a spectrum of roles that defy political correctness *with a vengeance.*

Study/Discussion Questions

1. Are women comedians unfeminine? Is it unwomanly to be funny at all, or are there certain ways of being funny that are off-limits to women?
2. In the examples Haskell gives, what are women comedians making fun of today?
3. Why does Haskell see their work as a sign of progress for women?
4. Which jokes (retold in this essay) did you think were funny?
5. If you watch TV, keep a journal of what you find funny on TV for a week. When you watch women being funny, what makes you laugh? What makes you uncomfortable?

What About the Boys?

Ellen Goodman

In 1993, the Ms. Foundation inaugurated an annual "Take Our Daughters to Work Day." The idea was to give girls, ages nine to fifteen, a positive glimpse of the world of work. Soon after its creation, however, syndicated columnist Ellen Goodman remarks, the event seemed to turn into a backlash-driven "What About the Boys Day." In this short and to-the-point commentary, Goodman reminds the aggrieved that there are 364 other days a year!

Where was I when "Take Our Daughters to Work" Day got turned into "What About the Boys?" Day? How did an event created to give girls a turn in the spotlight end up with so much attention on boys? And why does this sound familiar?

In 1992, an enterprising group of women came up with an idea to counteract the incredible shrinking aspirations of adolescent girls.

They'd read the dismal news that somewhere after fourth grade, girls' horizons collapsed along with their self-esteem. Their confident voices were replaced by awkward silences or "I don't knows."

The women at the Ms. Foundation hoped that even a one-day workplace special would give girls a positive look at the future. "We said, girls are important," recalls the president, Marie Wilson.

"They ought to be visible, valuable, and heard."

The idea of taking daughters to work took off. For one day in 1993 and another in 1994, the conversation and attention in thousands of workplaces across the country focused on girls.

But almost from the beginning, there was a choir of boys and others in the background chanting "It isn't fair." Now, as the third annual "Take Our Daughters to Work" Day approaches on April 27, Wilson says, the calls she has had from the media have become variations on the theme of "What About the Boys?"

This could easily be dismissed as an example of the media's perennial search for a new angle. But this year many companies are feeling pressured to change the emphasis and the name to "Take A *Child* to Work" Day.

In some ways, this controversy has become an ironic reflection of the very problem the daughters' day founders set out to counter.

In fact, it's a reflection of the research about what goes on in the classroom itself. In room after room, the boys' hands shoot up first, demanding and getting the lion's share of the teacher's attention.

The same thing is happening everywhere. These days, every time Black History Month rolls around, someone is sure to say, "What about White History Month?" Every affirmative action—and I use the words literally—designed to make up for past discrimination is reviled as present discrimination.

Talk about unfairness to men and you'll get a sympathetic nod. Talk about unfairness to women and you will—take my word for it—get accused of male-bashing.

There is more attention to instances and anecdotes of preferential treatment than to the patterns of prejudicial treatment. In this case, we are urged to worry about being fair to boys' aspirations.

Meanwhile a full 95 percent of the senior managers in the country are men.

I wonder if the current attention focused on every male protest is an automatic response to power. Last fall, when the GOP victory was attributed to angry white men, a panoply of Democrats, including women, sounded like battered wives asking themselves, "What did I do to make him mad?"

Is that what's going on here? A nervous response to angry males, junior division?

I know that every boy does not become a CEO. As Marie Wilson says, "Who in their right mind would say that boys don't need exposure to work?"

Work and family are so segregated now that few children actually know what their parents do all day. There are sons, especially in poverty, with as great a need for mentoring, for seeing and being seen in the workplace, as daughters.

But this event was never intended to be a Career Day. It was meant specifically to focus on girls between 9 and 15, to offer an alternative message to the one that most still get from society at this critical time in life. Indeed, when a number of companies invited boys last year, some reported that the boys took over and the girls were pushed again to the periphery of this work playground.

So, what about the boys? Those who want a sons' day at work can surely find a men's organization to do what the Ms. Foundation did.

There are 364 other days in the year.

But if we are talking about a day in which both boys as well as girls will get to hear messages that society rarely offers, well, I am reminded of what Justice Ruth Ginsberg once said, "If I had an affirmative action program to design, it would be to give men every incentive to be concerned about the rearing of children." What about a day devoted to fathering, to caretaking? If that doesn't seem as glamorous as work, as prestigious as a job, well, that's the problem, isn't it?

Last year, more than 30 million adults and girls became a part of "Take Our Daughters to Work" Day. This year we can expect more.

It isn't broke. It doesn't need fixing. In fact, it's part of the fixing.

Study/Discussion Questions

1. What do girls have to gain from being taken to work by their mothers?
2. Why is being taken to work a different experience for boys than for girls?
3. What happens to "Take Our Daughters to Work" Day when both boys and girls are taken to work?
4. What does Goodman think that boys would gain from staying home with their fathers?

Body Image: Third Wave Feminism's Issue?

Amelia Richards

Talking back to the nay-sayers who proclaim feminism dead, a "third wave" of feminists, made up of women now in their twenties or teens, has emerged in the 1990s. What concerns the women of the "third wave"? Perhaps more than anything else, says Amelia Richards, young feminists care about "body image." For many, "our bodies have become the canvasses upon which our struggles paint themselves." In an era in which identity politics and popular culture mingle and permeate the personal and public lives of young people, "body image" might be the best rallying call to feminism, says Richards. "Even young women who don't identify as feminists offer heartfelt and complex emotions on the topic."

In the United States, each wave of feminism has fought its own battles with body image. The suffragists of the late nineteenth and early twentieth centuries rebelled against corsets and fought the characterization of women's-righters as unfeminine, homely, and pretentious "blue-stockings." In the 1960s and '70s, the second wave of feminists fought stereotyping that pegged them as humorless, ugly, and anti-sex. Women struggled to be taken seriously, to be more than just pretty faces and pin-up girls. They wanted to be defined by their minds rather than their bodies.

In the late 1990s, among the rising third wave of feminists, image and body are at the center of feminist analysis. For many women, our bodies have become the canvasses upon which our struggles paint themselves. Body image, in fact, may be the pivotal third wave issue—the common struggle that mobilizes the current feminist generation.

The first two waves of feminism were organized movements, with clearly defined goals. The first wave fought to establish women's right to be citizens—to vote, own property, divorce and inherit money. The second wave's agenda was to elevate women's status to that of men.

In the third wave, we've expanded the fight for equal status. We are aware of the need to express our various identities—racial, ethnic, sexual, political, religious, and class—as well as our feminist identity. This individuality is necessary, but it also poses a challenge. Because we now have many different paths to—and definitions of—empowerment, it's become difficult to organize a unified movement. In this wave of feminism, you're as likely to run into women who defend, enjoy, and create pornography as you are to come across feminists who see pornography as the ultimate oppressor. You are also likely to find women who are tired of the pressure to act and look "perfect." Others pack their feminist toolkits with lipstick and nail polish, forgetting that while lipstick and nail polish aren't feminist concerns, the right to choose—or not choose—them is.

It's also difficult to unite everyone under an umbrella term like feminism when the third wave feminist vocabulary has been co-opted by the media. For example, "girl power" has been transformed from an expression of individuality and empowerment to a slick marketing slogan. And many women have taken the bait, assuming that the "girl power" label comes complete with feminist securities such as reproductive freedom, freedom from violence, and other issues played out on women's bodies.

To unite today's young women, we need to focus on a particular issue and then bring together the diverse feminist opinions on the matter to create a rich, complex dialogue. Better to disagree than to be silent, to fill out feminism rather than trim it down.

Second wave feminists named our struggles—domestic violence, sexual harassment, equal pay for work of equal value, which had lain silenced until then—and lobbied for laws that would protect us. Now, our generation has turned the focus inward. Tellingly, our relationships with our bodies often signal how far we still have to go. It is evident not only in how we treat them, but in how their role continues to permeate our existence and dictate our lives.

So where do we begin? Although "body image" won't make it into Congress, related issues will—for instance, sports, reproductive

rights, and affirmative action. As young feminists, we can point out how these individual and personal issues are linked to a larger political agenda.

Body image is significant as a rallying focus because it speaks not only to the converted but also to the "I'm not a feminist, but . . . I'm tired of measuring myself against an impossible-to-achieve beauty standard" contingent. It can catalyze our dormant or displaced activism, primarily because it's both a cultural and a political issue—and we are a pop culture–driven generation. Mention teen magazines, for example, and many young women react viscerally, offering stories of how fat/ugly/ethnic/misfitting/self-hating the magazines made them feel. Even young women who don't identify as feminists offer heartfelt and complex emotions on the topic.

Perhaps that's why much of third wave feminism has centered on pop culture, rather than legal and political strategies. Our activism is directed at our most visible "oppressors"—the media and entertainment industries. Rather than holding marches or rallies, many young women create zines, websites, music, films, and videos that counter images we deem insulting or dangerous.

In the visual world of the late twentieth century, however, the outside counts as well as the inside. We use our appearance—bodies, clothing, style—to express our inner convictions, our pride, our affiliations, our identities, our insecurities and our weaknesses. In a generation focused on identity issues—and unafraid to show them to the public—our bodies, and how we adorn them, can express who we are.

But, as young women redesign feminism, we run the risk of being misinterpreted as all image, no substance—as having no collective agenda. Too often, image becomes a convenient cover-up for issues we haven't resolved, just as eating disorders often manifest more deeply rooted problems such as childhood abuse.

We have to be careful not to fall into the trap of only having our bodies and our images speak for who we are—what we think, what we feel, what we do. Images and slogans are too easily co-opted and robbed of the substance they have the potential to convey. Instead, we must take this opportunity to seize control of our bodies and the forces that manipulate them—mostly the advertising and entertainment industries.

A feminist world is often where women find themselves when they get fed up with the representation of women in the media. It's a place to express all the rage, realization, and healing that follow—and to find a support community of people who have had similar experiences. Once feminists reach a point of understanding that we are not these images—that we don't have to look like Claudia Schiffer to be beautiful—then what? The silence, at that point, is deafening. We're supposed to go out and educate other women about loving their bodies, to save them from eating disorders. But if, as leaders, we dare to expose our own unresolved body image issues, we have to worry about tarnishing our feminist credibility. We're not supposed to have those problems anymore.

But we do. I do. As a feminist, I feel helpless at times, caught in a double standard. At "Ask Amy," my online feminist advice column, I confront painfully honest letters from young women who are dealing with their own eating disorders or body issues. What do I tell them? I could ignore the fact that the women we see thriving are those who fall under the rubric of athletic, attractive, slim, good-looking, fit, healthy. I could forget that, statistically, thin women have a greater chance of being accepted to elite colleges than heavier women do even if their credentials are identical; and that it isn't poverty that causes obesity, but obesity that causes poverty. But I see it as my responsibility to be honest with my correspondents. Body image issues, like most any other painful life experience, become less difficult once an open dialogue begins. So my advice usually includes my own experience. I tell them how I struggled with bulimia and how I eventually realized that developing my own identity is more important than pleasing other people.

The road to a solution is certainly a feminist one. It includes women creating our own beauty standards rather than following those dictated by corporations. It includes pointing out that this problem affects men, too. (Men are only slightly less likely to be concerned about their body image than women are, and a reported 10 percent of those suffering from eating disorders are men.) It means better sex education and more forums to talk about body image. But we can't stop there. We must create a dialogue that extends beyond these forums and into our daily lives, a dialogue that leads us to less shame, less denial, and more room for individuality. It's up to the third wave of feminism to make sure this conversation continues and that a support network exists.

Study/Discussion Questions

1. What feminist issues does Richards see as part of the larger issue of body image?
2. Why does she think that young feminists should focus on body image? Do you agree with her?
3. How do the media and entertainment industries oppress women? What do you think? What does the author think?
4. Pick a fashion magazine (ideally one that you yourself read) and examine the pictures and text. According to the magazine, what should women look like, and how can they achieve that look? What looks/behavior/attitudes does the magazine prescribe for its readers?

Flash Exercise

Create a Utopia

Write a 6-8 page paper in which you present a utopia for women. What would the ideal society for women be like? What type of government, economy, family arrangements, educational system, criminal justice system, medical care, reproductive techniques, religious values, cultural values, and so on would that society have? And most important, why? You don't need to cover every angle imaginable. Rather, try to present a coherent plan for your utopia and explain exactly why the society you present would be good for women. Use your imagination! The society can be realistic or fantastical; it can be in the past, present, or future.

One way to think about this paper is to go over the various problems facing women—today and in the past —in the United States. Decide which of these problems you wish to correct in your utopia. Then, give some thought to the conditions that produce the problems you are focusing on. What, in your view, causes the unequal treatment of women in our society? Is there an overarching cause or does each instance of inequality or violence need to be viewed separately? Are the causes the same in different historical periods? If so, why? If not, what particular circumstances lead to particular results, and why? In other words, come up with a guiding theory or analysis to help put your thoughts in order. Finally, think of ways to solve the problems you list. These solutions form the structure of your utopia.

Bibliography for Part III

BOOKS

Baker, Christina Looper and Christina Baker Kline. *The Conversation Begins: Mothers and Daughters Talk About Living Feminism.* New York: Bantam Books, 1997.

Bookman, Ann and Sandra Morgan. *Women and the Politics of Empowerment.* Philadelphia: Temple University Press, 1988.

Findlen, Barbara, ed. *Listen Up: Voices from the Next Feminist Generation.* Seattle: Seal Press, 1995.

Gilman, Charlotte Perkins. *Herland* (1915). New York: Pantheon, 1979.

Green, Karen and Tristan Taormino, eds. *A Girl's Guide to Taking Over the World: Writings from the Girl Zine Revolution.* New York: St. Martin's Press, 1997.

Hanlon, Gail, ed. *Voicing Power: Conversations with Visionary Women.* Boulder, CO: Westview Press, 1997.

Hutner, Frances C. *Our Vision and Values: Women Shaping the 21st Century.* Westport, Conn.: Praeger, 1994.

Kamen, Paula. *Feminist Fatale: Voices from the "Twentysomething" Generation Explore the Future of the "Women's Movement."* New York: Donald I. Fine, 1991.

Walker, Rebecca, ed. *To Be Real: Telling the Truth and Changing the Face of Feminism.* New York: Anchor Books, 1995.

INDEX

A

Abele v. Markle, 239
abolitionist movement, 391–392
abortion
    funding for, 361
    infertility and, 373
abortion politics, 134, 491, 494
    chronology of, 334–349
abortion practitioners, 335–336, 338, 346
abortion rights, 351–353
    disability and, 355–362
abortion trials, 336–338
Absolutely Fabulous, 548, 549–550, 551, 552
acquaintance rape, 462–468
Adams, David, 483–484
Addams, Jane, 132
adolescence
    concerns in, 31–38
    early, 25–30
    friendship in, 84–88
    Marisa Navarro on, 49–53
    in nineteenth century, 67–70, 71–72
    menstruation in, 31–38
    motherhood in, 40–48
Adolescent Family Life (AFL) program, 47
adoption, 146
    by gay parents, 171–172
    motherhood and, 142–146
    surrogacy and, 382
adoption rate, 346
adoption reform, 145

adultery, 512
Aeschylus, 382
affirmative action, 209, 390
African Americans, 536
    feminism and, 388–411
    matriarchal family of, 134
    See also black women
African women, 14
ageism, 317–320, 438
Ageism in the Lesbian Community (Copper), 320
agency vs. communion, 103, 104, 114
aggression. *See* violence
aging, 313
    politics of, 438–442
Aid to Families with Dependent Children (AFDC), 45, 132, 134, 136, 203–204, 205
AIDS, 481
    women with, 276–286
Ainsworth, Mary, 134
Alan Guttmacher Institute, 282
Albelda, Randy, 203–206
Allen, Woody, 546
Allison, Dorothy, 471–474
allocentric vs. autocentric, 103, 104
Aman, Carolyn J., 208–216
American Asian Worldwide Service, 180, 182
American Bar Association, 483
American Center for Law and Justice, 146
American Foundation for AIDS Research (AmFAR), 279
American Humor (Rourke), 552
American Magazine, 368

American Medical Association, 335
American Society for the Study of Sterility, 364
Amir, Menachem, 449, 452
Anastos, Kathryn, 277
androgyny, 307, 546
anorexia, 127
Anthony, Susan B., 393
anti-intellectualism, 20
Antioch College, 464
antirape activism, 464
appearance, physical, 313, 317–320, 555–557
Are You There, God? It's Me, Margaret (Blume), 32, 37
Ariès, Philippe, 102
Arrighi, Barbara, 482, 485
art
    Alice Walker on, 227–231
    erotic, 505
    feminist, 505–506
artificial insemination, 172, 381
artists, women, 233–238, 239–246
Asch, Adrienne, 360
Asian American women
    barriers to activism among, 415–418
    feminist movement and, 412–421
    political organizing among, 412–414, 419–420
Asian Americans, 116–123, 421
Asian women, as mail-order brides, 179–183
"Ask Amy," 557
Atjehnese families, 107, 108
attachment, in children, 134

attractiveness, aging and, 313, 317–320
autocentric milieu, 114
AZT, 278

B

Baby M, 134–135, 380, 382
Bacon, M. K., 103
"bad girls," rape and, 454
Baird, Zoe, 135
Bakan, David, 103, 113, 114
Balint, Alice, 114
Ball, Lucille, 547
Bambara, Toni Cade, 189, 543
Baranski, Christine, 550–551
Barber, Benjamin, 404
Barnard College, 159
Barnes, Burnadette, 485
Barren in the Promised Land (May), 363
Barry, Herbert, 103
Barry, Kathleen, 499
bathroom, teenage girls and, 36
battered women, 426, 428, 479–486
battered women's movement, 430, 435–436, 484
batterers, characteristics of, 483–484
beauty, 53
    aging and, 317–320
    standards of, 556
Bell Curve, The (Murray & Hernnstein), 136
Bell, Becky, 344
Benjamin, Jessica, 541
Berg, Barbara, 399
Bergmann, Barbara, 11
Bergson, Henri, 552
Berkeley Public Library, 460
Bethel, Lorraine, 408
Betrayal of the Negro (Logan), 394
Bettelheim, Bruno, 114
Bible, homosexuality and, 425
Bibring, Grete, 109
birth control, 45, 370, 492
birthrate, U.S., 152
Black Feminist Criticism (Christian), 440
black feminist groups, 407–408

black liberation movement, 398–399
black people, as metaphors, 401–402
black women
    creativity of, 226–232
    discrimination against, 393–395
    economic status of, 405
    feminism and, 388–411
    hair and, 54–57
    HIV and, 276, 278
    in labor force, 396–398
    love needs of, 535–543
    as mothers, 130, 540–541
    negative stereotypes of, 395–396
    prejudice against, 395
    reproductive rights and, 344–345
    single, 187
    in slavery, 130, 228–229
    sterilization of, 353
Black Women's Health Book, The, 535
Blackbridge, Persimmon, 505
Blanchard, W. H., 452
Blumberg, Lisa, 359–360
Blume, Judy, 37
bodily functions, embarrassment of, 35–37
body, 491
    aging and, 441
    in pornography, 497
body image, 52–53, 54–57
    aging and, 318
    as feminist issue, 555–557
body language, 53
Bolden, Dorothy, 405
bondage, 514
Bonds of Love, The (Benjamin), 541
Boston Women's Health Book Collective, 252–257
boundary confusion, 105
Bowen v. Kendrick, 343
Bowlby, John, 134
Bowman, Cynthia, 476
Boyle, Kay, 322
boys
    gender-role training of, 102–103
    play activities of, 197
    relation to mother, 99–100
breast cancer, 259–275
breastfeeding, 128

Breen, Ann, 458
brides, mail-order, 179–183
Brooks, Gwendolyn, 385–386
Broussard, John, 179–180, 182
Brown, Louise, 369
Brown University, 463
Buck, Carrie, 132
Buck v. Bell, 132
Burleigh, Margaret, 72
Burnett, Carol, 547
Butler, Brett, 546, 548, 550
Butler, Parke Lewis, 65

C

Caan, James, 480
Cain, Stephanie, 485–486
Calderone, Mary S., 335
California, no-fault divorce law in, 13
California School Employees Association, 211
Callender, Eunice, 71, 72
Calvert, Crispina, 379, 381
Canada
    comparable worth legislation in, 213
    violence against women in, 481
    women's work week in, 196
cancer, 259–275, 279
capitalism, 18, 404
Capitalist Patriarchy and the Case for Socialist Feminism (Eisenstein), 399
career. *See* work
Carlson, Rae, 103–104
Cartier, Michael, 483
Cassatt, Mary, 233–235
celebrities, as batterers, 479–480
censorship, 495, 504, 519
Center for Research on Women (Memphis State University), 12
Center for Women Policy Studies, 280, 282
Centers for Disease Control (CDC), 277, 281
cervical cancer, 279
Chamberlain, Mary, 253, 254, 255, 256, 257

Chambers, Veronica, 54–57

Chappell, Duncan, 452

chastity, 453

Chicago, Judy, 239–246

Child, I. L., 103

Child, Lydia Maria, 129

child development, 96

child sex abuse, 42, 46
    infertility and, 374–375

child support, 205

childbearing, surrogate, 379–384

childbearing rights, 351–353

Childbearing Rights Information
    Project, 351–353

childbirth, 383
    in nineteenth century, 70–71

childcare, 46, 109, 205–206, 493
    in Britain, 200–201

childhood, changing concept of, 102

childlessness, 366, 368, 369

childrearing experts, 128, 131

children
    abused, 126
    of gay parents, 434

Children's Hour, The (Hellman), 433

Chinese, discrimination against, 417

Chinese Americans, 116–123, 414,
    416

chivalry, 452–453

Chodorow, Nancy, 13, 95–111

Choosing Children Network, 171

Chow, Esther Ngon-Ling, 412–421

Christian, Barbara, 440

Christian Coalition, 145

Christianity and Crisis (Mollenkott),
    425

Chu, Susan, 281

Citizens for Humane Abortion Laws,
    335

citizenship, 8

civil rights movement, 414

Clarke, Septima, 320, 541

class privilege, 404

class structure, 418

class struggle, 414

classism, 405, 421

Cleaver, Eldridge, 458

Cliett, Valerie, 353

Clifton, Lucille, 444

coalitions, political, 419, 420

cognitive style, analytic vs. relational,
    104

Cohen, Mardge, 277, 280

Cohen, Rosalie, 104, 114

Coleman, Diane, 356, 357–358

collective bargaining, 199

college, Women's Studies courses in,
    3–9, 10–15, 17–21

college men, sexual aggression in, 452

college music curriculum, 8

college orientations, 463–464

college students, battering of, 482,
    483

colleges
    acquaintance rape at, 463–464
    student safety at, 485
    women's, 12

Colonizer and the Colonized, The
    (Memmi), 390

Combahee River Collective, 407

comedy, 545–552

Commission on Obscenity and
    Pornography, 512, 516

common law, English, 129

communication patterns, gender
    differences in, 218–221

communion vs. agency, 114

comparable worth, 208–216

comparison other, 210, 211

compensable factors, 212

conditioning theory, pornography
    and, 499–500

condoms, HIV and, 282

Congressional Caucus for Women's
    Issues, 279, 282

Conroy, Frank, 451

consciousness-raising groups, 406

constitutional rights, pornography
    and, 517

contraception, 334, 370, 492

contract motherhood, 380

control, 430

conversations, workplace, 218–221

Cooper, Anna Julia, 188

Copper, Baba, 320

Coronet magazine, 367–368

Cottle, Tom, 185

Cotton, Deborah, 279

Couper, Mary Black, 72

courtship rituals, 69

Craig, Polly, 380

creative energy, 531–532

creativity, women's, 224–225, 226–
    232

crime, 449, 484
    against women, 479–486

critical thinking, 8

cultural devaluation, 110

cultural values, homosexuality and,
    73–74

culture, male aggression and, 450

custody battles, 175, 434

custody law, 129, 134–135

Cybill, 547, 550–551, 552

Cyr, James, Jr., 480

D

Daniels, Cynthia, 135

Darwinism, 131

date rape, 462, 465

dating, violence in, 482, 483

Davis, Adrian, 478

day care, 134, 135

de Beauvoir, Simone, 11, 37–38, 153,
    552

Degas, Edgar, 233, 234

degradation, in pornography, 497,
    513, 514

DeMarco, Susan, 429

Denver, 211

dependency, 96, 97
    of females, 108, 109

Derricotte, Toi, 148, 445–446

Deutsch, Helena, 73, 97, 101, 105

devaluation, cultural, 110

Devitt, Neal, 256

diaries, nineteenth-century, 69–70

Diamond, Sara, 495–506

Dickerson, Debra, 475–478

diethylstilbestrol (DES), 375

differentiation, 105, 108

dimorphism, 11

disabiliphobia, 358

disability, abortion rights and, 355–362

Disability Rag & Resource, 359

discrimination, 403

  against black women, 393–395, 405

  against Chinese, 417

  job, 11, 200, 209

division of labor, between sexes, 195–196

divorce, 13, 493

Dixon, Dazon, 278

doctors, on hospital abortion boards, 338–344

doctrine of tender years, 129

Doe v. Bolton, 1972

Doll's House, The (Ibsen), 456

domestic routine, 160

domestic violence, 7, 426, 480

double standard, 452, 453

  aging and, 318

Douglass, Frederick, 393, 458, 536

Dove, Rita, 443

dreadlocks, 54–57

Dubroff, Jessica, 127

Duke University, 3, 9

Duncan, Isadora, 456

DuPont, Eleuthera, 68, 69

DuPont, Sophie, 69, 71, 72

Durkheim, Emile, 114

Dworkin, Andrea, 496

Dworkin, Ronald, 518

E

earned income tax credits (EITC), 206

economic inequality, 429, 503

economics, sexism and, 428–429

education, pay and, 210

egg donation, 381, 383

ego boundaries, 96, 98, 103, 104–106, 113

ego strength, 114

Ehrenreich, Barbara, 253, 255, 256, 257

Eisenstein, Zillah, 399

Ekstrom, Elton, III, 485–486

El-Sadr, Wafaa, 277–278

elderly, rights of, 438–442

Elementary Structures of Kinship (Levi-Strauss), 456

Ellen, 548, 549, 552

Elway, Rita, 419

embeddedness, 104, 105, 108

Emechera, Buchi, 440

Emerge, 483–484

Emerson, Mary, 72

Emlen, Peggy, 71

emotions, repressing, 537

employment, sex discrimination in, 11, 200, 209

empowerment, 556

energy, creative, 531–532

England, Paula, 208–216

England, in middle ages, 253, 254

English, Deirdre, 253, 255, 256, 257, 490–494

English common law, 129

Entre Nous, 505

Epstein, Cynthia Fuchs, 12, 13

Equal Opportunities Commission, 200

Equal Pay Act, 209, 214

equal rights, 392

erotic, as power, 530–534

erotica, 507–510, 513

eroticism, 451, 504–505

Erstad, Corinne, 127

ethnic identity, of Asian American women, 415

ethnocentrism, 419

Europe, in middle ages, 253, 254

evolutionary theory, 130–131

excellence, striving for, 531

Executive Order 11246 (affirmative action), 209

F

Faludi, Susan, 369

family, 457

  as building block of patriarchy, 439

  girls' and boys' differential experience of, 104

  lesbian-headed, 169–177

  reaffirmation of, 439

  single-parent, 135–136, 203–206, 214, 493

  slave, 536

  study of, 13

  work and, 493, 554

family structure, feminine personality and, 95–111

family values, 19, 45–46, 439

fantasies, 500–501

  men's, 496

  women's, 501–502

Farnham, Marynia, 133

father

  as role model, 110

  role of, 99, 440

  See also family

fatigue, "housewife," 160

Fauci, Anthony, 279

fear

  of change, 494

  of desires, 533

  of feminism, 17–21

  of political commitment, 20

  of rape, 448–449, 456

  of violence, 481

feeblemindedness, 132

femicide, 482

feminine fulfillment, mystique of, 153

feminine identity, 96

Feminine Mystique, The (Friedan), 151–162, 399, 404

feminine personality, family structure and, 95–111

femininity, 12

  ideal of, 501

  loss of, 158

  motherhood and, 335

  stereotype of, 455–456

feminism

  aging and, 438–442

  Asian American women and, 412–421

  backlash against, 17–18, 435, 464–465, 490, 493

feminism (*continued*)

broadening, 419

challenges of, 21

disability concerns and, 361

fear of, 17–21

maternalism movement and, 132

motherhood and, 133

negative effects of, 490–494

as political ideology, 8, 391

pornography and, 495, 503

pro-choice movement and, 360

racism and, 52, 388–411

second-wave, 134

third-wave, 555–557

white women and, 406, 417, 418

feminist consciousness, 18

feminist ideology, 399, 405, 406

feminist revolution, 410–411

fertilization, 365

in vitro, 369, 380

fetal rights, 135, 360

fetus

"defective," 357–358

subordination of pregnant woman

to, 343–344

fetus worship, 442

field dependence, 104

Filipino women, as mail-order brides,

180, 181

Finkbine, Sherri, 335

First Amendment rights, 516, 517,

518

Fliess, Robert, 98

Florence, Louis, 180, 182

Fluker, Walter, 542

Forster, Margaret, 311–316

Fox, Bertha and Feroline, 90

fragmentation, in pornography, 497

France, women's work week in, 196

Frazier, 549

free market, wages and, 214

freedom of speech, 517, 518

Freeman, Jo, 405

Freud, Sigmund, 59–60, 74, 100,

101, 114

Friedan, Betty, 151–162, 399, 404

friendships

in adolescence, 84–88

women's, 59–74

G

Gay Men's Health Crisis (GMHC),

280

gay community, 170

Geertz, Hildred, 107

Geis, Gilbert, 452

gender, distinguished from sex, 11

gender consciousness, 18

gender differences

in communication patterns, 218–

221

in personality, 95–96

gender identity, 13, 52–53, 95, 96

of Asian American women, 415

formation of, 99–102

gender-role identification, 99–102

gender-role learning, 102–103

gender-role stereotypes, 415

gender roles, 427–428

among Asian Americans, 413

changing, 11

in nineteenth century, 63–64

post–World War II, 339

General Federation of Women's

Clubs, 394

genetic determinism, 382

genetic screening, 359

Georgia Women's Press Club, 394

Germain, Adrienne, 12

gestational surrogacy, 379–384

Gibson, Elizabeth Bordley, 68, 69,

70–71, 72

Gilbert, Barb, 464

Gilbert, Neil, 467

Gilligan, Carol, 14

Gingrich, Newt, 136

Ginsberg, Ruth, 554

girl power, 556

girl watching, 475–478

girlhood, 25–30

girls

gender-role training of, 102–103

menstruation and, 31–38

play activities of, 197

Giovanni, Nikki, 543

Gold-Birkin, Lynne, 483

Goodman, Ellen, 380, 553–554

Gordon, Mary, 233–238

government programs, for teenage

mothers, 45, 47

government regulation, of wages,

214, 215

Grace Under Fire, 547

Greer, Germaine, 195–201, 313

Grew, Mary, 72

Griffin, Susan, 448–460

Griswold v. Connecticut, 338

Guerrilla Girls, 548

guilt, 84, 105

Guntrip, Harry, 102, 108

Gutmann, David, 103, 113, 114

Guttmacher, Alan, 341

gynecological infections, 277

H

*Habit of Surviving, The: Black

Women's Strategies for Life*

(Scott), 539

Hacker, Helen, 400, 401

hair care, black women and, 54–57

Hampton, Fanny, 65

Hamrol, Lloyd, 241, 244, 245, 246

harassment, street, 475–478

Harper's Bazaar, 156

Harris v. McRae, 342

Harrison, Michelle, 381

Hartman, Mary, 14

Hartnett, Tara, 480

Haskell, Molly, 545–552

healing, women and, 252–257

health care, 206

for pregnant teens, 47

health care reform, 358

health insurance, abortion and, 348

Heilbrun, Carolyn, 9

Hellman, Lillian, 433

Heritage Foundation, 426

Herotica art show, 505

Herrnstein, Richard, 136

Hershey, Laura, 355–362

heterosexism, 20, 431–433

high school, 27–28

all-women's, 186–187

battering in, 482

socialization in, 49–52

higher education, differential pay in, 198
Hightower, Jim, 429
Hill, Paul, 348
Hillingdon Hospital, 199
hiring, discrimination in, 209
history, 333
    of abortion politics, 334–349
    American, 389, 390
    of women as healers, 252–257
    women's, 59–74
Hitchner, Gretchen, 480
HIV, 276–286, 481
Hodgson, Jane, 239
Hodgson v. Minnesota, 345
Hogeland, Lisa Marie, 17–21
Holding My Own in No Man's Land:
    Women and Men, Film and
    Feminists (Haskell), 545
Holiday, Billie, 455
Holliday, Judy, 547
Holmes, Amy, 477, 478
homelessness, 481
homicides, 482
homophobia, 19, 424–436
homosexuality, 424
    Freud on, 74
    "latent," 73
    mother's role in, 127
homosexuals, perceptions of, 432
hooks, bell, 388–411, 535–543
hospital abortion boards, 338–344, 346
Hoth, Daniel, 277
Houppert, Karen, 31–38
housewifery, 67, 153–161, 404
housework
    cross-cultural studies of, 196
    gender differences in, 198
    politics of, 163–167
How I Learned to Drive (Vogel), 38
Howe, Fanny, 222
Howe, Florence, 9
Howe, Marie, 487
HRT (hormone replacement therapy), 312, 315
Human Genome Project, 359

human papillomavirus (HPV), 278–279
Hurston, Zora, 228
Hyde Amendment, 347, 353

I

identification, 109, 110–111
    gender role, 99–100
    with mother, 97
    positional vs. personal, 113
illegitimacy, 344–345
illness, dealing with, 259–275
images, reality and, 499
immigrants, Asian, 413, 417
Immigration Reform and Control Act, 417
imperialism, 401
    racial, 388–389, 390
    sexual, 389, 390
In Love and In Danger: A Teen's Guide
    to Breaking Free of Abusive
    Relationships (Levy), 482
In Search of Gay America (Miller), 169–177
In Search of Our Mothers' Gardens (Walker), 226–232
in vitro fertilization (IVF), 369, 380
incest, 127, 374–375, 430
independent living movement, 358
India, mothers in, 98
individual rights, 491
individuation, 96, 97–98, 105–106
Indonesia, 107
Indonesian women, as mail-order brides, 182
industrialization, gender roles and, 129
infant mortality, 127, 131
infants, attachment of, 97
infertility, 363–376
Inskeep, Maria, 65
International Decade on Women, 428
intimacy, between women, 60
intrauterine device (IUD), 375
Ireland, Jennifer, 135
Irons, Carol, 485
Izquierdo, Elisa, 136

J

James, Norma, 353
Japanese American Citizens League, 179, 180, 182, 183
Java, 103, 107, 108
Jay, Robert R., 103, 107
Jedlicka, Davor, 179, 181
Jefferis, Martha, 65, 66
Jen, Gish, 116–123
Jewish mother, 133
job discrimination, 11, 200, 209
    against black women, 397–398, 405
job evaluation, 199
job evaluation studies, 212, 213
job satisfaction, 198
Johnson, Anna, 379, 381, 384
Jones, Ann, 479–486
Journal of the American Medical Association, 366
joy, 532
Joys of Motherhood, The (Emechera), 440
Jue, Sally, 282
justice, 210

K

Kamen, Paula, 462–468
Keane, Noel, 380
Kelly, Abby, 392
Kelly, Joan, 10
Kenyon, Jane, 299–302
Kessler-Harris, Alice, 12
Kim, Bok Lim, 182
kin relations, culture and, 107–108
kin ties, 65
Kirjavainen, Leena, 197
Kirkpatrick, Jeane J., 12
Kirstein, Kurt, 180
kitchen, as center of women's lives, 152–153
Klepfisz, Irena, 192
Koss, Mary, 465–466, 467
Kovel, Joel, 391
Kramer, Larry, 166
Krim, Mathilde, 279, 282
Kroger, W. S., 367

Ku Klux Klan, 458
Kumin, Maxine, 93
Kurys, Diane, 505

L

labor force
    black women in, 396–398
    women's status in, 127, 199, 405
labor markets, 214–215
Ladd-Taylor, Molly, 125–137
Lardner, Kristin, 483
Larsen, Nella, 228
Latina women
    HIV and, 278
    sterilization of, 353
laws
    abortion, 334–349
    against rape, 456–457
    comparable worth, 214
    discriminatory, 417
Le Repos (Manet), 236
Leach, Penelope, 128
Lederer, Laura, 499
leisure, as masculine privilege, 196–
    197
lesbian baiting, 433
lesbian identity, 52–53
lesbian scholars, 14
lesbians, 505–506
    aging and, 320
    discrimination against, 424
    with HIV, 281
    as parents, 169–177
    perception of, 432
letter writing, in nineteenth century,
    60–74
Levi-Strauss, Claude, 456
LeVine, Robert, 113
Levy, Barrie, 482
Lewis, Eleanor Curtis, 68
Lewis, Nelly Parke Custis, 69, 70, 72
liberal arts, Women's Studies in, 3–9
Liberating Feminism (Barber), 404
liberty, 518
libidinal theory, Freud's, 59–60
life expectancy, 441
Life magazine, 152

Lifton, Betty Jean, 142–146
Ling, Susie, 413–414
Logan, Rayford, 394
Logan, Sally, 71
Lombard, Carole, 547
London, mothers and daughters in,
    107, 108
longevity, 441
Longino, Helen, 511–520
Look magazine, 157
Lorde, Audre, 248–250, 259–275,
    504, 530–534
Los Angeles, growing up in, 49–52
love
    female, 63
    need for, 535–543
Luker, Kristin, 134
Lumley, Joanna, 550
Lundberg, Ferdinand, 133
Lurie, Susan, 498

M

Macdonald, Barbara, 318, 438–442
MacGraw, Ali, 479–480
MacInnes, James Martin, 454
MacKinnon, Catherine, 496
Mademoiselle, 36–37
magazines
    teen, 33–35
    women's, 152
Maginnis, Pat, 335
mail-order brides, 179–183
Mainardi, Pat, 163–167
Malaysian women, as mail-order
    brides, 182
male hierarchy, 457
male supremacy, abortion politics
    and, 346
Malleus Maleficarum, 254
Malory, Sir Thomas, 452
Malraux, 451
Malveaux, Julianne, 478
mammy stereotype, 130
Manet, Edouard, 236
Manigault, Harriet, 69, 70
Mannarino, Melanie, 33
Manning, Martha, 84–88
Manson, Charles, 451

manumission, 409
marriage
    career and, 152, 493
    in nineteenth century, 70–71
    as system of exchange, 456
    Victorian, 73
    women's age at, 152
marriage contract, 492
Martin, Emily, 36, 365
masculine gender identification, 99–
    100
masculine identity, 96
masculine personality, 95
masculinity, 12, 13, 307, 452, 459
mass media
    body image and, 556
    pornography and, 516
    representation of women in, 557
mastectomy, 264–266
materiality, 538–539
maternal instinct, 363
maternalism, 132
matrifocal societies, 106–109
maturity, independence and, 108
May, Elaine Tyler, 363–376
Mazumdar, Sucheta, 413–414
McCombs, Phil, 476–477
McGovern, Theresa, 280
McQueen, Steve, 480
Mead, Margaret, 113, 450
Medea, 128
media. *See* mass media
Medicaid, 361
medical practitioners, abortion and,
    334–336, 338–344, 346
medical textbooks, 365
medicine, female practitioners of,
    252–257
Meehan, Maude, 323
Memmi, Albert, 390
Memphis State University, 12
men's studies, 13
menarche, 37
menopause, 304–310, 311–316
menstruation, 31–38, 305
mental illness
    role of mothers in, 127
    Steinem essay on, 287–298

Mernissi, Fatima, 115
Merton, Thomas, 538
metaphor, 401–402
Mexican Americans, 49–53
middle age, 313
middle ages, 253, 254
middle-class, kinship relations in, 109
middle school, 25–27
midwifery, 256
Mildred Pierce, 133
Mill, John Stuart, 163
Miller, Neil, 169–177
Millett, Kate., 457, 460
Millman, Marcia, 113
Milloy, Courtland, 478
Millsaps, Susanne, 359
minimalist vs. maximalist debate, 13–14
minorities
    discrimination against, 417
    feminism and, 412–421
minority group, women as, 400–401
minority studies, 12
miscarriage, 365, 372
misogyny, 432, 433
misunderstandings, communication, 218–219
Mitscherlich, Alexander, 99
Mizz, 197–198
Modern Woman: The Lost Sex (Farnham & Lundberg), 133
Mollenkott, Virginia Ramey, 425
momism, 133
Moore, Donnie, 479
Moore, Mary Tyler, 547
Moraga, Cherrie, 523–524
Morales, Rosalie, 320
moralism, 491
morality, pornography and, 512
Morella, Constance, 282
Morisot, Berthe, 235–238
Morning After, The: Sex, Fear, and Feminism on Campus, 462, 465, 480
Morrison, Toni, 537
mother blaming, 125–137
mother-daughter relationship(s), 238
    adult, 123–124

    black, 540–541
    culture and, 106–110
    ego boundaries and, 104–106
    in nineteenth century, 66–67
    personality and, 95–96
mother role, 96, 97, 110
motherhood
    avoidance of, 366
    compulsory, 491
    contract, 380
    as defining trait of womanhood, 335
    myth of, 440
    scientific, 130
    teen, 40–48
    as unifying factor among women, 132
    Victorian ideal of, 129
mothers
    adoptive vs. birth, 142–146
    black, 536, 537–538, 539, 540
    psychotic, 98
    single, 135–136, 203–204, 214, 493
    working, 135, 200–201
mothers' pensions, 132
Moulton, Nancy, 361
movies, screwball, 547
Moynihan, Daniel Patrick, 134
Ms. Foundation, 553
mujer, la, 49–53
Muller v. Oregon, 135
multiple regression analysis, 212
Munchausen's Syndrome by Proxy, 127
murder, of women, 480, 482
Murphy Brown, 548
Murray, Charles, 136
Murray, Pauli, 405
Musgrove, Jeannie Field, 61

N

nakedness, 497
Nalder, Marjorie and Lawrence, 220–221
NARAL, 338, 339, 340, 347, 359, 360

National Abortion Rights Action League (NARAL), 340, 347, 359, 360
National American Woman's Suffrage Convention, 393
National Association for Repeal of Abortion Laws, 338
National Association of Colored Women, 394
National Black Women's Health Project, 278
National Cancer Institute, 277
National Coalition Against Domestic Violence, 426, 430
National Council for Adoption, 145
National Domestic Workers, 405
National Gallery, 235
National Gay and Lesbian Task Force, 434
National Health and Social Life Survey, 466, 467
National Institute of Allergy and Infectious Diseases (NIAID), 277, 279
National Institutes of Health (NIH), 279
National Network of Asian and Pacific Women, 414
National Opinion Research Center, 466
National Organization for Women (NOW), 360, 478
National Sex Forum, 513
National Victims Center, 466
Native American women, sterilization of, 353
Native Americans, racism against, 390
nature vs. nurture, 14
Navarro, Marisa, 49–53
needs
    emotional, 540
    material, 538–539
negotiating, gender differences in, 219–220
Negro Family: The Case for National Action, The (Moynihan), 134
neuroses, "female," 160
New Day for the Colored Woman Worker, A, 396

New Era Club, 394

New Right, 134

New Woman, 131

New York Times, 155, 156, 157

Newsweek, 156–157

Noble, Vicki, 307

Nobody Speaks for Me! Self-Portraits of Working-Class Women, 405

NOW, 360, 478

nuclear family, 13, 107, 432

nudes, 497, 512

nurses, employment of, 215

O

O'Barr, Jean Fox, 3–9

object-relations theories, 113

obscenity, 508, 511

obstetrics and gynecology, 364

occupations, women's, 199, 209–210, 211

oedipal crisis, 99, 101

Oedipus conflict, 113–114

Office of Adolescent Pregnancy, 47

O'Keefe, Georgia, 236–237, 320

Olds, Sharon, 92, 522

oppression
    of black women, 390
    degrees of, 403
    psychology of, 166
    racial, 14
    of women, 110, 402, 426, 458–459

Oregon State University, 11

Organization of Chinese American Women 414, 421

Ortega Y Gasset, 401–402

Our Bodies, Ourselves, 252–257

outworkers, 200

Ovid, 451

P

Paglia, Camille, 465, 468, 469

paintings, by female artists, 233–238, 239–246

parental rights, 383

parenting
    advice on, 128, 131
    egalitarian, 14
    lesbians and, 169–177

Parslow, Richard, 379, 380

passivity, of rape victims, 456

patriarchal societies, 98

patriarchy, 389, 393, 427, 439, 456, 460
    in Asian American communities, 416–417
    white supremacist capitalist, 18–19

pay
    gender gap in, 198, 204, 206, 208–216, 493
    of working women, 428

pay equity, 209

pay equity plans, 213

pay levels, 212

p'Bitek, Okot, 228

Peck, M. Scott, 536

pediatrics, 131

pelvic inflammatory disease, 369

penis envy, 101, 114

Penn, Rosalyn Terborg, 393–394, 395

pensions, mothers', 132

People v. Jerry Plotkin, 453

Perkins, William, 254

Perlman, Joanna, 478

permissiveness, of mothers, 128

personal as political, 19, 20

Personal Responsibility Act, 126

personality
    feminine, 95–111
    male, 103

physical appearance, 313, 317–320, 555–557

personality development, 96–102

Planned Parenthood v. Casey, 346

play, gender differences in, 197

Pleck, Joseph H., 196

Plotkin, Jerry, 453–454

poetry
    Audre Lorde on, 248–250
    Phillis Wheatley's, 228–230

point factor system, 212

political participation
    of Asian American women, 412–414, 419–420
    of women, 8–9

politics, feminism and, 8, 19–20

Politics of Women's Liberation, The (Freeman), 405

Pollitt, Katha, 379–384

Pomeroy, Kelly, 179–180

pop culture, 556
    sexuality and, 42

pornography, 495–506, 511–520
    defined, 508, 512, 514
    erotica and, 507–510
    law and, 516–519
    violence and, 431
    violence in, 497, 499, 514, 515

poverty
    emotions and, 538
    sterilization and, 353
    women and, 203–206

power
    erotic, 530–534
    hidden sources of, 248
    male, 410, 430, 458–459
    pornography and, 496, 509

pre-conception intent, 383–384

pregnancy
    battering during, 481
    contraindications to, 239
    definition of, 343–344
    drug use during, 135
    HIV and, 278
    out-of-wedlock, 344–345
    psychological aspects of, 382
    surrogate, 134–135, 379–384
    teen, 40–48

prejudice, against black women, 393–396

prenatal screening, 358, 359

privacy, right to, 517

pro-choice movement, 355, 360, 491

pro-life movement, 355, 490, 491

problem-solving approach, in women's studies, 8

pronatalism, 363, 369–372

proportional justice, 210–211

prostitution, 42, 514

psychoanalytic theory, of infertility, 366–367
Psychological Care of Infants and Children (Watson), 131
psychological anthropology, 96
puberty, 37–38, 50
Puerto Rico, sterilization abuse in, 352, 353

Q

Quayle, Dan, 136
quilts, as art form, 6, 230
Quindlen, Anna, 123–124, 380

R

race, abortion politics and, 344
racism
    against Asian Americans, 417–418
    dealing with, 539–540
    economics and, 429
    feminism and, 388–411
    as political ideology, 389
    in pornography, 497
    white female, 391
radical movements, 20
Rainbow Ridge Consultants, 179–180
Rainey, "Ma," 230
rape, 430, 448–460
    acquaintance, 462
    of children, 471–474
    definition of, 466
    fear of, 448–449, 456
    as natural behavior, 449–450
    race and, 458
rape laws, 456–457
rape prevention, 464, 468
Ratiliff, Clarence, 485
Ready from Within (Clarke), 541
Reagan, Bernice, 430
Redbook, 155, 157
Redstockings, 163, 338
Reiskin, Julie, 356–357
Remembered Gate, The (Berg), 399
Renoir, Jean, 235
repression, of sexuality, 503, 504
reproductive choice, infertility and, 370

reproductive rights, 491, 494
    disability and, 355–362
    history of, 333–347
reproductive technologies, 379–384
Republican Motherhood, 129
Rich, Adrienne, 14, 390–391, 392
Rich, Cynthia, 317–320
Richard, Amelia, 555–557
right to work, women's, 396
rights of women, 519
Ripley, Sarah Alden, 67, 69, 70, 71, 72
Road Less Traveled, The (Peck), 526
Robinson, Robin A., 40–48
Roe v. Wade, 338, 339, 340, 346
Roiphe, Katie, 462, 465, 466, 468, 480
romance novels, 502
romantic relationships, feminism and, 19
Room of One's Own, A (Woolf), 224–225, 228, 230
Roosevelt, Theodore, 131
Rorke, Robert, 33
Roseanne, 546, 547, 548, 549, 550, 551
Rosie the Riveter, 12
Ross, Betsy, 6
Rossi, Alice, 14
Rothman, Barbara Katz, 382
Rourke, Constance, 552
Rubin, Gayle, 10–11
Rudner, Rita, 548
Ruffin, Josephine, 394, 395
Russo, Jon, 479
Rust v. Sullivan, 345
Ryan, Rose, 483

S

salary, negotiation of, 220–221
Salk, Lee, 380
San Jose, 211
Sandler, Bernice, 8
Sanger, Carol, 135
Sassafrass, Cypress and Indigo (Shange), 540

Saunders, Jennifer, 549–550
Sawalha, Julie, 550
scarcity, myth of, 429
Schechter, Susan, 484
schizophrenia, 127
Schlafly, Phyllis, 508
school, gender role training in, 102–103
scientific motherhood, 130
scopophilia, 498
Scott, Kesho, 539
screwball comedy, 547
sculpture, 241
Second Sex, The (de Beauvoir), 11, 37–38, 153
segregation, 394
    of black female workers, 396–397
sex, 110
Seinfeld, 549
self-defense, 456
self-esteem
    of Asian American women, 415
    verbal violence and, 431
    of women, 108, 110
sensuality, 53, 532
Serena, Norma Jean, 353
Seventeen magazine, 33–34, 36
sewing, home, 152–153
sex, 512, 513
    as communication, 508–509
    attitudes toward, 500
    distinguished from gender, 11
Sex and Temperament (Mead), 450
sex contract, traditional, 491–492
sex differences, in personality, 95–96
sex discrimination, in employment, 200, 209
sex offenders, 449
sex roles, expectations about, 95
sex segregation, 110
sexism, 7, 427, 519–520
    documentation of, 11
    economics and, 428–429
    gender roles and, 427–428
    labor force and, 404
    pornography and, 496
    racism and, 393
    in South, 458

sexual abuse, of children, 127, 471–474

sexual difference, study of, 12, 13–14

sexual harassment, 476

sexual identity, 424, 425, 503
    development of, 433–434

sexual imagery, explicitly, 502

sexual liberation, 492

sexual morality, 491

sexual objectification of women, 512

sexual organs, 498

sexual politics, 451–452

sexual problems, 159

sexual revolution, 511-512

sexual violence, 462–468, 499, 516

sexuality
    culture and, 50–51
    as form of expression, 507
    men's attitudes toward, 495
    popular culture and, 42
    repression of, 503, 504
    study of, 6–7
    Victorian, 73
    women's, 501

Shakespeare, William, 224

Shakti Woman (Noble), 307

Shange, Ntozake, 540

Shepard, Cybill, 550–551

Sheppard, Anne Jefferis, 66–67, 68, 70

Sheppard-Towner Maternity and Infancy Act, 132

Showalter, Elaine, 12

Shriver, Maria, 369

Shuman, Paula, 280

Siegel, James T., 107

similarity principle, 211

Simpson, Mona, 89–91

Simpson, Nicole Brown, 479, 480

Simpson, O. J., 479, 480

Simpsons, The, 548

single mothers, 135–136, 214, 493
    poverty and, 203–204

single women, 185–191
    battering of, 482

sisterhood, 410
    rhetoric about, 402, 403

SISTERLOVE, 278

sisters, 89–91
    in nineteenth century, 65

Sisters of the Yam: Black Women and Self-Recovery, 535

sit-coms, 545–552

Sittenfeld, Curtis, 25–30

Slater, Philip E., 98, 105, 113

slavery, 458, 536–537
    feminism and, 392
    white women as beneficiaries of, 408–409

slaves, female, 130, 228–229

Smith, Bessie, 230

Smith, Clementine, 72

Smith, Elizabeth McKie, 68

Smith, Lillian, 392

Smith, Susan, 126, 136

Smith-Rosenberg, Carroll, 59–74

Smithsonian institution, 230

Smut, Robert, 396

Snyder, Denise, 476, 477–478

social policies, 13

social protection, 46–47

social structure, mother-daughter relationship and, 106–110

social workers, 132

socialization, 96
    of personality, 103
    racist, 389

socioeconomic gap, between men and women, 492

Solanis, Valerie, 460

Solinger, Rickie, 333–347

Sommers, Christine Hoff, 465, 466

Sontag, Susan, 318

Sorkow, Harvey, 135

Soul on Ice (Cleaver), 458

Spain, women's work week in, 196

speaking, gender differences in, 2189

speech, freedom of, 517, 518

spending patterns, gender differences in, 197

spermicides, 282

spinsterhood, 188

spiritual growth, 542

spirituality, 532

Spock, Dr., 128

Spruill, Julia Cherry, 399–400

stand-up comedy, 546, 551

Stanton, Elizabeth Cady, 314, 393

Starr, Brenda, 450

Steiglitz, Alfred, 236–237

Steinem, Gloria, 287–298, 507–510

stereotypes
    Asian American, 415
    of Asian women, 182
    in pornography, 497

sterilization, 132
    abortion and, 341–342
    abuse of, 351–353

Stewart, Martha, 549

Stewart, Porter, 137

Stiehm, Judith, 12

Stimpson, Catharine R., 10–15, 400, 402–403

Stocker, Corinne, 394

Stone, Abraham, 363

Stone, Elizabeth, 190

Stone, Merlin, 253

street harassment, 475–478

stress, infertility and, 364, 365–366

submissiveness, 455–456
    depiction of, 502–503

suburban housewife, 153–161

Sudden Infant Death Syndrome (SIDS), 127

suffragists, 393

suicide, 114

suicide attempts, by battered women, 481

Sula (Morrison), 537–538

Supreme Court
    abortion decisions of, 338, 339, 340, 342, 343, 344, 345, 346
    sterilization ruling of, 132
    working mothers and, 135

surrogate pregnancy, 134–135, 379–384

survivors, of men's violence, 19–20

Sward, Susan, 370

Symons, Gladys L., 179

Szasz, Thomas, 255

T

Take Our Daughters to Work Day, 553–554

Taking Rights Seriously (Dworkin), 518

Talking from 9 to 5 (Tannen), 218

Tampax ads, 35–36

Tannen, Deborah, 218–221

Tax, Meredith, 105

taxes, 206

Taylor, Alan, 449

Teen magazine, 33–34, 35

teen motherhood, 40–48

television, sit-coms on, 545–552

tender years, doctrine of, 129

Tennessee, adoption laws in, 145

Terrell, Mary Church, 394

Terry, Randall, 334, 343

thalidomide, 356

Thelma & Louise, 476

Third Life of Grange Copeland (Walker), 231

Thomas, Herman H., 364

Thompson, Clara, 73, 114

Tilly, Chris, 203–206

Time magazine, 155

TLC, 477

Tom Cottle Show, 185

Toomer, Jean, 226–232

Towers Perrin, 198

Truth, Sojourner, 394

Turner, Tina, 479

Tyson, Mike, 479

U

Umansky, Lauri, 125–137

U.N. Human Development Report, 196

unemployment, male, 200

unions, 199, 213–214

universities
  acquaintance rape at, 463–464
  student safety at, 485

Universities and Colleges Employment Association, 198

University of Colorado–Colorado Springs, 11

University of Massachusetts–Amherst, 12

University of Wisconsin–Madison, 462–463

unwed mothers, 40–48, 344–345

U.S. Department of Justice, 426

Utah, abortion politics in, 359

V

vagina, 498

Valen, Margaret, 364

verbal violence, 431

Vermund, Sten, 278–279

victims
  of battering, 479–480
  crime, 484
  rape, 450, 453–455
  women as, 11–12

Victorian sexual ethos, 73–74

Villanueva, Alma Luz, 304–310

Villapando, Venny, 179–183

violence
  dating, 482
  fear of, 481
  as means of keeping women in line, 430
  threat of, 431

violence against women, 18, 19–20, 430–431, 479–486, 501

Violence Against Women Act, 467, 468, 484

violent pornography, 497, 499, 512, 514, 515

virginity, 452

visiting, tradition of, 64, 70, 107

Vogel, Paula, 38

vote, right to, 393

voyeurism, 498

W

wages
  of black women workers, 397–398, 405
  free market and, 214–215
  gender gap in, 198, 204, 206, 208–216

Wake Up Little Susie: Single Pregnancy and Race Before Roe v. Wade (Solinger), 344

Walker, Alice, 226–232, 440

Walker, Bree, 358–359

Waring, Belle, 488

Washington, Mary Helen, 185–191

Watson, John, 131

Waxman, Barbara Faye, 359

wealth, 429

Webster v. Reproductive Health Services, 344

weddings, 70, 456

weekends, for working women, 197

Weinberg, Joe, 462–463

Weitzman, Lenore J., 13

welfare benefits, 136

welfare policy, 41

welfare programs, 132, 203–206
  black women and, 345
  sterilization and, 352, 353

welfare reform, 45, 205

Wellesley, Jane, 198

Wellesley College Center for Research on Women, 14–15, 37

West, Mae, 452, 547

West, Maggie Hadleigh, 477

Wharton, Katherine, 71

Wheatley, Phillis, 228–229

White, Paulette Childress, 191

White Racism: A Psychohistory (Kovel), 391

white supremacy, 389, 393–394, 417

white womanhood, 457–458

Whitehead, Mary Beth, 134–135, 380, 382

Whiting, John W. M., 98

Who Stole Feminism? (Sommers), 465

Whole Woman, The (Greer), 195–201

wife beating, 479

Wilder, Marcy, 360

Will, George, 465

Williams, Lenore, 34

Willmott, Peter, 107

Wilson, Marie, 553, 554

Wilson, Michelle, 281

Winnicott, Donald, 143

Wister, Sarah Butler, 61

witches, female healers as, 253, 254–255

Wizard of Id, 318

Wolf, Fred, 549

Wolfe, Leslie, 280

Wolfe, Maxine, 279

Woman in the Body, The (Martin), 36

"Woman Poem" (Giovanni), 543

woman's sphere, 129–130

womanhood
    equated with motherhood, 363
    ideal of, 496
    white, 457–458

womb envy, 498

Women: A Feminist Perspective
    (Hacker), 400

Women Against Violence in
    Pornography and Media, 511

Women and Work in America (Smut),
    396

Women, Infants, and Children
    (WIC), 45

Women's Caucus of AIDS Coalition
    to Unleash Power (ACT UP),
    279

women's club movement, 394–395

women's colleges, 12

women's culture, 18

women's groups, Asian American,
    413–414

Women's Health Equity Act, 282

women's liberation
    black civil rights and, 400, 402–
    403
    housework and, 163

women's (liberation) movement, 388–
    411, 490
    backlash against, 435
    black women's rejection of, 406
    effect of homophobia on, 436
    pornography and, 504
    third wave of, 436
    white women's domination of,
    398–399

*Women's Life and Work in the Southern
    Colonies* (Spruill), 399–400

Women's Studies
    fear of feminism and, 17–21
    goals of, 5
    heterosexual bias in, 14
    issues and approaches in, 10–15
    men in, 7–8
    necessity for, 3–9
    perspective of, 6–7
    scholarship in, 11–12
    what it does for students, 7–9

Women's Studies movement, origins
    of, 5

Woodward, Maud B., 397

Woolf, Virginia, 224–225, 228, 230,
    237

work
    as path to liberation, 404
    stress and, 364
    unpaid, 196, 198, 204, 429
    women and, 195–201

work week, women's, 196

workfare, 46

workforce. *See* labor force

working-class women, 404

workplace, communication patterns
    in, 218–221

World's Women 1995, The (United
    Nations), 196

Worth, Dooley, 282

writers, female, 228

Wylie, Philip, 133

Y

Yale Law Review, 456–457

Yamamoto, Joe, 183

Young, Mary A., 281

Young, Michael, 107

youth, glorification of, 440